The New Authoritarianism

Vol 3: A Risk Analysis of the Corporate/Radical-Right Axis

Edited by Alan Waring

GW00725390

THE NEW AUTHORITARIANISM

Vol 3: A Risk Analysis of the Corporate/Radical-Right Axis

Edited by Alan Waring

Bibliografische Information der Deutschen Nationalbibliothek
Die Deutsche Nationalbibliothek verzeichnet diese Publikation in der Deutschen Nationalbibliografie; detaillierte bibliografische Daten sind im Internet über http://dnb.d-nb.de abrufbar.

Bibliographic information published by the Deutsche Nationalbibliothek
Die Deutsche Nationalbibliothek lists this publication in the Deutsche Nationalbibliografie; detailed bibliographic data are available in the Internet at http://dnb.d-nb.de.

Cover picture: ID 110722616 © Antwon Mcmullen | Dreamstime.com

ISBN-13: 978-3-8382-1493-1
© *ibidem*-Verlag, Stuttgart 2021
Alle Rechte vorbehalten

Printed in the EU

Dedications

The editor dedicates this volume to three different parties:

All those who have ever been victims of authoritarianism, of any description and from any source.

All those who are engaged in the study of and combatting authoritarianism, especially but not exclusively radical-right authoritarianism. This includes the editor's colleagues at CARR (Centre for Analysis of the Radical Right).

'Brother Les', a champion of good against evil, of personal liberty, and the dignity of 'The Person' that 'The State' challenges within a necessary framework of governance, law, order, national security and world order. His encyclopaedic breadth and depth of knowledge of modern history, religious history, the origins of power for extremist ideologies, politico-corporate abuses, and the consequences of all of these, applied in counselling organs of the state, was both an inspiration and an eye-opener. His penetrating and provocative challenges to the editor's assertions and opinions during numerous debates helped mould Volume 3. Thank you Brother, and *halilya*!

Contents

List of Figures and Tables

List of Cases

List of Personal Profiles

List of Abbreviations and Acronyms

ADL	Anti-Defamation League (US)
AfD	Alternative für Deutschland (Alternative for Germany, political party)
AML	Anti-Money Laundering
BAME	Black, Asian, and Minority Ethnic
Big 5	Personality theory comprising five components
BLM	Black Lives Matter movement
BNP	British National Party
BP	British Petroleum
Brexit	Exit of Britain from the European Union
BRT	Business Round Table (US)
CARR	Centre for Analysis of the Radical Right
CDC	Centers for Disease Control (US government)
CEO	Chief Executive Officer
CMA	Competition and Markets Authority (UK)
Covid-19	A coronavirus of the SARS family
CPNI	Centre for the Protection of National Infrastructure (UK)
CPS	Crown Prosecution Service (UK)
DCMS	Department for Digital, Culture, Media and Sport (UK)
DEFRA	Department of Environment, Food and Rural Affairs (UK)
EC	European Commission
ECB	European Central Bank
ECHR	European Court of Human Rights; alternatively European Convention on Human Rights
ECJ	European Court of Justice
EDL	English Defence League
EEC	European Economic Community
EHRC	Equality and Human Rights Commission (UK)
EHS	Environment, Health, and Safety
ENISA	European Agency for Network and Information Security
EP	European Parliament
EPA	Environmental Protection Agency (US)
EU	European Union
FBI	Federal Bureau of Investigation

FDA	Federal Drug Administration
Five Star	Italian radical centre-right political party, also known as MSP
FN	Front National (France)
FPÖ	Freiheitliche Partei Österreichs (Austrian Freedom Party)
FR	Face Recognition
FTC	Federal Trade Commission (US)
FTSE	Financial Times Stock Exchange (Index)
GARM	Global Alliance for Responsible Media
GDP	Gross Domestic Product
GFC	Global Financial Crisis
GOP	Grand Old Party (synonym for the US Republican Party)
HMRC	Her Majesty's Revenue and Customs (UK taxation authority)
HOC	House of Commons (UK Parliament)
IMF	International Monetary Fund
IS	Islamic State
ISIS	Islamic State in Iraq and Syria
IT	Information technology
JCPOA	Joint Comprehensive Plan of Action
KKK	Ku Klux Klan (US)
KP	Kyoto Protocol
MEP	Member of European Parliament
MMR	Measles, Mumps, and Rubella
MP	Member of Parliament
MSP	See Five Star
NATO	North Atlantic Treaty Organisation
Neo-con	Neo-conservative (US)
NHS	National Health Service
NIC	National Intelligence Council (US)
NPI	National Policy Institute (US)
NSA	National Security Agency (US)
NS131	A UK far-right extremist group
Obamacare	Patient Protection and Affordable Care Act 2010 (US)
OECD	Organization for Economic Cooperation and Development
ONS	Office for National Statistics (UK)
OSH	occupational safety & health

ÖVP	Österreichische Volkspartei (Austrian People's Party)
PCA	Paris Climate Accord
PEGIDA	Patriotische Europäer gegen die Islamisierung des Abendlandes (Germany)
PR	public relations
PT	Prospect Theory
QAnon	A US-founded radical-right online group disseminating conspiracy theories
QRA	Quantified Risk Assessment
RWA	Right Wing Authoritarianism
SAR	Suspicious Activity Report
SARS	Severe Acute Respiratory Syndrome
SDO	Social Dominance Orientation
SIOA	Stop Islamization of America (US)
S&P	Standard & Poor's (US-based stock market index)
SPLC	Southern Poverty Law Centre
UHC	Universal Health Care
UK	United Kingdom (of Great Britain and Northern Ireland)
UKIP	United Kingdom Independence Party
UN	United Nations
UNCAC	United Nations Convention Against Corruption
US	United States (of America)
USDC	US District Court
USDoJ	US Department of Justice
WASP	White Anglo-Saxon Protestant
WFA	World Federation of Advertisers
WHO	World Health Organisation
WWI	World War One
WWII	World War Two
YAF	Young America's Foundation (US radical-right body)

Foreword

While becoming something of a cliché to remark that we are living in dangerous times, repeated reminders of this fact remain important. Respected and impartial international organisations have independently reported sound evidence that, in the early decades of the 21st century, democracy is in retreat across the globe, most spectacularly in the United States, and to a greater or lesser degree in many other countries with established democratic traditions. Fuelled by increasingly powerful computerised electronic surveillance systems, overwhelming media controls, and endemic corruption, as well as creating dystopian repressive conditions for their own populaces, authoritarian regimes also seek to substantially influence democratic processes outside their borders. At the other end of the political spectrum, democracies—all of which have been severely tested by the coronavirus pandemic, have placed much faith in the goodwill and trust of their citizens to conform to sometimes draconian 'lockdown' conditions. Existential risks—including a potential post-pandemic economic meltdown, multi-faceted threats posed by climate change, and an ever-present danger of nuclear war, reinforce the notion that the third decade of the 21st century will almost certainly be the most dangerous since the one that witnessed World War Two.

That war was imposed on an already troubled world by three right-wing authoritarian regimes which have their contemporary equivalents in countries that fervently stoke nationalistic pride, allude to perceived historical injustices, and that have the capacity to inflict massive casualties on those they deem to be their enemies. It is said that democracies rarely go to war with other democracies. While there may be rare exceptions to this dictum, it is probably largely correct. However, what happens when democracies pass the threshold at which their democratic processes—most critically, media freedom, rule of law, free and fair elections—come under serious threat? As they move rightwards along the political spectrum, at what point do they effectively become authoritarian regimes? It is key potential threats from radical-right elements into which this important book, along with its two companion volumes, provides numerous insights.

Despite humans all being one species, our evolutionarily rapid widespread dispersions have rendered us prey to divisions based on superficial physical appearances, powerful belief systems, and nationalistic fervour based on borders that are historically derived and often arbitrarily-defined. Economic inequalities of hitherto unparalleled orders of magnitude have assisted in increasing political polarization and fermenting social discontent. To this social maelstrom has been added fear, often stoked by mass migrations triggered, *inter alia*, by political and/or ethno-religious persecution, economic repression, hunger, or despair, which has helped to drive an upsurge in radical-right ideological movements.

As with the previous two volumes in the series, editor Alan Waring has assembled an impressive array of highly knowledgeable contributors whose respective expertise addresses growing threats posed by radical-right political groups, corporations, and agencies based in contemporary democratic societies. Driven by conspiratorial agendas that repudiate scientific facts, repeatedly reinforced by silos of social media platform material, like internally generated firestorms driven by climate-fuelled drought and bushfires, radical-right elements create and spread their own passionately crazy versions of reality. The frightening speed at which technology has facilitated the spread of such dystopian ideas and calls to action has barely been tempered by a few countries' fragile attempts to curb the influence of the poisonous messaging via global media organisations.

This volume delves more deeply into a pivotal component of the phenomenon—the fusion of mutual interests between the corporate world and radical-right politics. Case studies, conspiratorial agendas, promulgation of misinformation, and money flows—including corruption—are among the evidence provided for similarities between corporate and radical-right authoritarianism, and their symbiotic threats to representative democracy. The final chapter reviews how mutual interests of radical-right politics and corporate interests threaten democratic order, processes, and institutions—notably the role of radical-right 'deep state' conspiracy theories.

By way of balancing the threats posed by radical-right movements, promising developments for potentially curbing the corporate/radical-right axis are discussed. Like the first two, this volume ends on a call for 'muscular moderation' to combat radical-right threats, a difficult albeit compelling challenge. Despite its rather gloomy overall analysis, the book's more optimistic view in the short-to-medium term emanates from positive leadership, an anti-authoritarian 'new model corporation', and instances in which major corporations have overtly rejected radical-right world-views within their own organisations, and when relating to others.

The coming decade presents the world's agencies and citizens with a stark choice between, on the one hand, an increasingly deliberate global distribution of disinformation designed to spread fear and chaos and, on the other hand, reinforcing those democratic values and institutions that, with proper care and maintenance, have the capacity to steadily erode radical threats to the world's people, and their socio-cultural environments, as well as to its natural environment and diverse non-human species. Widespread scientific education is critical in all these endeavours. Like the previous volumes, the risk management framework adopted carefully analyses the nature of threats posed by radical-right elements in democratic and quasi-democratic societies. This logical evidence-based approach provides an exemplar of what can bring hope to a troubled world. It is one important element in what must be constant endeavours for truth and natural justice sought by freedom-loving people everywhere.

Dr A. Ian Glendon[1]
Associate Professor (rtd.)
School of Applied Psychology, Griffith University, Queensland, Australia

---

[1]   See contributor affiliations and biography, pages 525-526.

Acknowledgements

In addition to the authors themselves, the editor would like to thank the following for their support and various contributions to this book. For encouraging the creation of this book from its earliest inception:

- Professor George Boustras, Professor in Risk Assessment and Director of the Centre for Risk and Decision Sciences (CERIDES), European University Cyprus.
- Emeritus Professor Matthew Feldman, Director of the Centre for Analysis of the Radical Right (CARR), UK.
- Dr Ian Glendon, Formerly Associate Professor, School of Applied Psychology, Griffith University, Gold Coast Campus, Queensland, Australia, and for contributing the Foreword as well as reviewing chapters.
- 'Brother Les', on the consequences for the individual, society, national security, and world order, of sustaining extremist ideologies and tacitly endorsing politico-corporate abuses.

For advising on the book's development and/or reviewing drafts of various chapters:

- Dr William Allchorn, Associate Director of the Centre for Analysis of the Radical Right (CARR), UK, for authorising inclusion of passages from the editor's CARR *Insight* blogs.
- Dr Nicolas Bichay, Assistant Professor at Michigan State University, Department of Political Science, and CARR Fellow (Centre for Analysis of the Radical Right), UK.
- Dr Nathan Brooks, Senior Lecturer in Forensic Psychology, Central Queensland University, Australia.
- Richard Brooks, Nick Wallis and *Private Eye* magazine in relation to their campaigning articles on, and reviewing the case study on, the UK Post Office's treatment of sub-postmasters.
- Professor Mickey Huff, Director of Project Censored, Diablo Valley College, California USA.
- Professor Alan Irwin, Department of Organization, Copenhagen Business School, for reviewing a draft for Professor Fischbacher-Smith.

- Dr Michael Walton, Chartered Psychologist and former Fellow Director at the Centre for Leadership, Exeter University, now visting Professor, Department of Managerial Psychology and Sociology, Prague University of Economics and Business; Visiting Senior Lecturer, Thammasat University Business School, Bangkok.
- Friends and relevant observers for 'sanity checks': John Broadway, retired naval officer and programme manager in capital network projects and social services; James Hardy, MA in terrorism and security studies; Gavin Jones, author, columnist, and political and social commentator.

Dr Anton Shekhovstov, Valerie Lange and colleagues at Ibidem Verlag for their support, guidance, professionalism, and efficiency throughout the lengthy publishing process.

Last, but by no means least, my wife Mehri, who (once again) put up with numerous periods of my detachment from family life during the creation of this book.

Introduction: Corporate Authoritarianism, the Radical Right, and Risk

By Alan Waring[1]

Overview

This book is a companion to its earlier volumes from Ibidem:

> *The New Authoritarianism Vol 1: A Risk Analysis of the US Alt-Right Phenomenon* (2018).
> *The New Authoritarianism Vol 2: A Risk Analysis of the European Alt-Right Phenomenon* (2019).

Volume 3 provides a more detailed examination of mutually beneficial interactions and support between, on the one hand, powerful corporate leaders, executives, and wealthy oligarchs and, on the other, radical-right political leaders, parties and intermediary organisations promoting radical-right causes. This volume also examines the character and role of corporate authoritarianism in advancing radical-right ideas and its egregious impact on employees, customers and vulnerable other parties. Risks analysed include exposures of differing parties, and risks to representative democracy. Promising developments to potentially curb the corporate/radical-right axis are discussed.

Target Readership

Readers of Volume 3 may align with a broad spectrum of academic and professional groups that share a common need to unravel and consider impacts of resurgent nationalism and ultra-conservative agendas on risk issues affecting corporations, businesses, governments, institutions, the judiciary, the media, individual citizens and others. That shared need extends to understanding how corporate sympathisers and their agents encourage and boost the radical right politically, whether by financial donations, media manipulation, or undue influence on policy and action. Volume 3's content recognizes

---

[1]   See contributor affiliations and biography, page 525.

that gaining understanding of such threats is also likely to engender a need to consider protective strategies.

In addition to a wide range of scholars and academics, such readers could include risk analysts and risk managers, corporate governance specialists, politicians and political analysts, intelligence officers, corporate security specialists, corporate ethics and integrity managers, anti-corruption specialists, consumer affairs specialists, economists, investment analysts, criminologists, lawyers, journalists, psychologists and other behavioural scientists.

Students on Master's and other post-graduate courses, in such subjects as business administration, risk management, security and counter-terrorism, corporate ethics, government administration, political science, and international relations, are also likely to find the book of value.

The Book's Rationale

Volumes 1 and 2 covered the Alt-Right (Alternative Right) phenomenon respectively in the US and Europe. The term 'Alt-Right' is attributed to the radical-right academic Paul Gottfried (2008), later promulgated by the far-right propagandist Richard Spencer. In those volumes, the editor's definition of Alt-Right was: (1) as an ideology, the spectrum of right-wing world-views outside traditional conservatism, which begins with a dissatisfaction with the mainstream political process and character and frustration by perceived impotence of traditional conservatism, and runs through populist, far-right, and extreme-right ideology, and (2) as an identifiable group, those having such world-views (Waring 2018, 48, 461; 2019, 53-54, 413). In this volume, the label radical-right has been used in preference to Alt-Right, since the former has become the more prevalent usage globally.

It is important to emphasize that the radical-right phenomenon presents a spectrum or continuum of harmfulness. At one end of the spectrum, there are the least harmful populist entities (e.g. UKIP) that fall just beyond the boundary of the ultra-conservative wings of mainstream conservative parties (e.g. UK Conservative Party). Further to the right are increasingly far-right entities that actively disseminate hate messages and tolerate, and often encourage, violence as a political instrument (e.g. BNP, EDL and Britain First)—see Davidson and Berezin (2018). Further right still are extremist entities that not only actively disseminate hate messages and neo-Nazi propaganda but also openly engage in violence and terrorism as political weapons (e.g. National Action and other proscribed far-right terrorist groups). The editor's definition for radical right is the same as his definition of Alt-Right, while recognizing that others may have their own definitions. For example, some writers refer to UKIP as a far-right party and to BNP, EDL and Britain First as extreme-right. The CARR Report "'*Faces' of the Radical Right*" (Henderson 2020) expressed a preference for the 'radical right' term to be used only for officially non-violent elements seeking to secure radical-right ideological advances via the electoral process, while reserving the term 'extreme right' for elements seeking political advance by revolutionary overthrow, including violence, followed by a palingenetic rebirth of an ethnically, religiously and ideologically purified population. The radical-right ideology (encompassing both extreme and non-extreme adherents) is characterized by an authoritarian belief in nationalism, nativism, racial (usually white) superiority, religious (usually nominally Christian) superiority and prejudicial emphases on creating and maintaining inequalities between alleged deserving groups (winners/predators) and undeserving groups (losers/victims) classified as such by virtue of ethnicity, religion, employment status, poverty, migrant status, political beliefs, and other potential distinctions.

In addition to Volumes 1 and 2, the evolving scope of the radical right is amply covered by such websites as Hope Not Hate (www.hopenothate.org), and the Centre for Analysis of the Radical Right (CARR) and its *Insight Blog* (www.radicalrightanalysis.com), as well as reviews of the contemporary UK radical right such as Allchorn (2017), Carvalho (2015), Copsey (2010), Davison and Berezin (2018), Feldman (2019a,b), Feldman and Pollard (2016), Goodwin (2011), Henderson (2020), Jackson (2016), Lee (2019), Macklin (2019), Mondon and Winter (2020), and Pilkington (2016). The US far right is covered by e.g. Lyons (2017a, b) and Michael (2003; 2006; 2008; 2014; 2016; 2017), as well as by the Southern Poverty Law Center (www.splccenter.org), the Anti-Defamation League (www.adl.org), and such observers as Neiwert (2017), Posner (2019) and Smith (2019). European populist and far-right coverage is exemplified by authors in Bevelander and Wodak (2019), Wodak (2015; 2018), Wodak and Rheindorf (2019), and other authors in Waring (2019a).

Proceeding from the detailed but broad-spectrum baseline analysis presented in the first two volumes, Volume 3 delves more deeply into an aspect of the radical-right phenomenon they touched on, namely the fusion of mutual interests between the radical-right political world and the corporate world. Mayer (2016; 2017) refers to it as, in part, the application of "dark money". The mutual interests and synergies between these two entities reveal how the vast wealth of particular oligarchs, the corporations they own or control, and the charitable status of the right-wing foundations they establish, continue to support and encourage the political and societal objectives of radical-right ideology and its leaders. These two worlds feed off, enable and strengthen each other, as Bloom and Rhodes (2016; 2018) observe in their analysis of corporate authoritarianism and the threat to US democracy. The authoritarian style and excesses of some corporate chiefs are often remarkably similar to those of certain radical-right political leaders, President Trump (2016-2021) being a notable example. See e.g. Bakan (2004), Brulle (2014), Michaels (2020), and Oklobdzija (2019).

In addition to radical-right political authoritarianism, some corporate organisations also demonstrate analogous traits in their abuses of consumers, employees, and others. Chapters in this volume provide graphic examples. For example, the recent Covid-19 pandemic has revealed very publicly those organisations that responded to multi-dimensional threats (e.g. to public and employee health, continuing employment, and customer contracts), in a high integrity, public spirited demonstration of corporate social responsibility, and those organisations that did the opposite and adopted an authoritarian 'winners/predators' stance akin to the Trumpian radical-right model of governance. In some cases, corporate leaders are also unequivocally radical-right supporters. Of course, not all examples of bad corporate attitudes and conduct reflect a conscious and wilful political commitment and support for radical-right ideology. Nevertheless, there is abundant evidence that the general tone and character of corporate authoritarianism is often remarkably similar to that of radical-right authoritarianism.

Risk and the Corporate/Radical-Right Context

In contrast to other books on the radical right and authoritarianism, this book is not just a philosophical, sociological, political, or economic examination of the phenomenon but is also explicitly a risk analysis. The risk concept itself is, of course, not without controversy and the risk analysis and assessment discipline encompasses the spectrum of both pure and opportunity/speculative risks (ISO 2018; Waring 2013; Waring & Glendon 1998). Assessment techniques appropriate to pure risk areas such as engineering, fire, safety, white collar crime and credit control may not be appropriate to speculative risk areas such as political risk, investment, HR strategy, IT strategy, foreign policy, and international relations, where more qualitative and heuristic assessment methods come to the fore (Glendon & Clarke 2016; Shrader-Frechette 1991). As has been noted elsewhere (Waring & Glendon 1998), corporate executives frequently confuse and conflate these two different risk types, for example typically in applying speculative/opportunity risk trade-offs to risks that actually demand a pure risk approach (e.g. Covid-19, climate change): see Sales (2019). For example, in March-June 2020, Trump and his radical-right supporters at all levels clamoured for removal of Covid-19 lockdown restrictions in the US on the basis that it was more important to save the economy than people's lives. Such trade-off criteria, i.e. that an increase in deaths would be 'acceptable' (but to whom?), demonstrate the lack of moral imperative redolent of speculative/opportunity risk evaluation misapplied to such pure risk matters. This book adopts a primarily qualitative and heuristic approach to the corporate/radical-right risk narrative, using a risk assessment technique applied systematically in chapter 10.

In pursuing a risk analysis, this book recognizes that there should be no *a priori* assumptions about what risk exposures exist within particular contexts or who is 'at risk' from them. Certainly, it may be convenient to assume that the radical right, on the one hand, and corporate interests, on the other, each represents a source of threat(s) to various parties who thereby may be subject to a variety of risk exposures. However, such a uni-directional model is unrealistic and, indeed, a cogent analysis must also consider what risk exposures affect imputed risk sources. For example, although many may regard the radical right as a threat to democracy, and be alarmed at the perceived threat posed by electoral successes by populist and hard right-wing parties in recent years (e.g. in Germany, Hungary, Italy, Poland, US), the speed with which their voting successes may go into sharp reverse reveals a major risk exposure for such parties. For example, by May 2017 the number of UK Independence Party elected officials at both national and local levels had all but disappeared in less than a year, and in local government elections a year later only three UKIP candidates were elected. Political oblivion beckoned (Waring 2019, 112), as indeed followed for both UKIP and its derivative Brexit Party in the 2019 General Election. Similarly, both the far-right Party for Freedom of Geert Wilders in Holland (van der Valk 2019) and the Front National (now Rassemblement National) of Marine Le Pen in France (Goodliffe 2019) following years of growing success, fared badly in the 2017 general elections. In Austria, the far-right FPÖ managed to persuade the ruling centre-right ÖVP to enter into coalition, thereby enabling the introduction of far-right policies wrapped in the ÖVP mantle (Wodak & Rheindorf 2019). However, the coalition collapsed in 2019 over the scandal of the FPÖ leader Heinz-Christian Strache (the Austrian Vice-Chancellor) caught on video seemingly inducing Russian business interests to pay bribes for contracts. Dubious credibility, relentless unpleasant rhetoric from such parties, propaganda based on fear and faked facts, as well as unpopular policy failures and personal scandals, are all likely to eventually combine to motivate rejection at the ballot box. The risk of hubris and no longer being acceptable or taken seriously by an electorate is a political risk faced by any radical-right (or indeed any) party but, of course, electoral demise eliminates neither its ideology nor its core supporters, including powerful corporate interests and donors.

As for corporations, there exists in the 'new model corporation' model (British Academy 2018) a potential for organisations to steer away from an egregious authoritarian character that Bakan's polemic (2004) and others so graphically allege and chapters here further exemplify. Somewhat surprisingly, there is recent evidence (chapter 12) that at least some major and global corporations are publicly rejecting toxic quasi-radical-right beliefs and assertions in favour of an ethos founded on 'the new model' and positive leadership (chapter 4).

The Book's Style, Content, Authors and Structure

This book follows academic discipline and seeks to provide evidence and references to support statements made or at least clarify any necessary distinctions between facts, assertions, arguments and opinions. However, with such a controversial subject, and potential evocation of strong emotions (whether for or against particular ideologies or exponents of them), there is a temptation for authors to slip into polemical expression in their narratives. Indeed, there is currently an unresolved debate among academics about whether traditional scholarly neutrality must be maintained or whether authors could legitimately take a strong for/against position and use polemic in support of it. The editor takes the view that the traditional approach should prevail as far as possible, but recognizes that sometimes polemic can be very effective in communicating key issues. Should any instances of polemic occur, he takes full responsibility for any criticism that may arise.

The potential scope for the content of a book such as this is huge and, if fully comprehensive, its size would be prohibitive. Moreover, with the inherently fast-moving nature of current affairs and developments, it is not possible to capture all relevant events and to be up-to-date, which in any event is more the task of journalists and news media. From systems science, a holistic approach only requires inclusion of the perseverant essence of the whole and not every ephemeral component of the whole (Checkland 1999; von Bertalanffy 1972). Therefore, in deciding on content, the editor has taken a selective approach to a number of areas in an attempt to provide a reasonably representative coverage of key issues.

The book is fortunate to benefit from contributions from an eclectic group of six authors with backgrounds variously in psychology, sociology, history, political science, international relations, organisational analysis and risk analysis, who have specialised in studies of the populist and far right in the United States, UK, mainland Europe and elsewhere. Details of the authors' affiliations are presented in the section About the Editor and Authors.

The book is in three parts. Part 1 on the Nature of the Corporate/Radical-Right Axis comprises four chapters. Chapter 1 considers the fusion of mutual interests that characterize corporate and radical-right authoritarianism. Chapters 2 and 3 on 'Zombieland Revisited' are a two-part examination of the psychopathology of authoritarianism in the politico-corporate domain, as an aid to understanding the thinking and behaviour of respective protagonists and potentially predicting future actions. Chapter 4 reviews the phenomenon of toxic leadership in organisations, whether corporate entities, political parties, political groups, or governing administrations, and what positive leadership alternatives may be available.

Part 2 comprises five chapters that examine aspects of the corporate/radical-right axis, either in relation to particular authoritarian beliefs and perceptions about real-world risk exposures (e.g. climate change, Covid-19, globalization, 'dark money', conspiracy theories), and/or in relation to authoritarian power dynamics, toxic leadership, populism, and abuses and victims of political ideology and in relation to particular economic sectors (e.g. airlines, energy, health care, telephony/internet/social media).

Part 3 Conclusion comprises three chapters that synthesise the various analyses from Parts 1 and 2. Chapter 10 provides systematically a common risk analysis and assessment framework to all the risk exposures identified in Part 2. The penultimate chapter provides an evaluation of the risk analysis and makes a prognosis for how the corporate/radical-right axis might develop and how far it is likely to increase its influence. The final chapter reviews how the fusion of mutual interests between radical-right politics and corporate interests threatens democratic order, processes and institutions. Potential strategies to limit the threat, in so far as it may exist, are identified.

References

Allchorn, W. 2017. "The Evolving Face of the Contemporary UK Far Right". Paper presented at the Political Studies Association Annual Conference Session 10, University of Strathclyde, Glasgow, April 12, 2017.

Bakan, J. 2004. *The Corporation: The Pathological Pursuit of Profit and Power.* Toronto: Free Press (Simon & Schuster).

Bevelander, P. and Wodak, R. (eds). 2019. *Europe at the Crossroads: Confronting Populist, Nationalist and Global Challenges.* Lund, Sweden: Nordic Academic Press.

Bloom, P. and Rhodes, C. 2016. "Corporate Authoritarianism and the New American Anti-democracy". *Common Dreams.* October 23, 2016.

Bloom, P. and Rhodes, C. 2018. *CEO Society: The Corporate Takeover of Everyday Life.* London: Zed Books.

British Academy. 2018. *Reforming Business for the 21st Century—A Framework for the Future of the Corporation.* November 2018. London: The British Academy.

Brulle, R.J. 2014. "Institutionalizing Delay: Foundation Funding and the Creation of U.S. Climate Change Counter-movement Organizations". *Climatic Change*, Vol 122, 681-694.

Carvalho, J. 2015. "The End of the Strategic Opening? The BNP's Window of Opportunity in the 2000s and its Closure in the 2010s". *Patterns of Prejudice*, 49(3), 271-293.

Checkland, P. 1999. *Systems Thinking, Systems Practice: Includes a 30-year Retrospective.* Chichester UK: John Wiley & Sons.

Copsey, N. 2010. *The EDL: Challenging Our Country and Our Values of Social Inclusion, Fairness and Equality.* November 2010. Faith Matters Report. www.faith-matters.org.

Davidson, T. and Berezin, M. 2018. "Britain First and the UK Independence Party: Social Media and Movement-party Dynamics". *Mobilization: An International Quarterly*, 23(4), 485-510. DOI 10.17 813/1086-671X-23-4-485.

Feldman, M. 2019a. "Evolution of the Radical Right: an Interview with Matthew Feldman". *CARR Insight Blog*, March 6, 2019. London: Centre for Analysis of the Radical Right. https://www.radicalrig htanalysis.com/2019/03/06/the-evolution-of-the-radical-right -an-interview-with-matthew-feldman/.

Feldman, M. 2019b. "The Radical Right in Britain". *CARR Insight Blog.* June 21, 2019. London: Centre for Analysis of the Radical Right. https://www.radicalrightanalysis.com/2019/06/21/the-radica l-right-in-britain/.

Feldman, M. and Pollard, J. 2016. "The Ideologies and Ideologues of the Radical Right: an Introduction". *Patterns of Prejudice*, Vol 50, issue 4-5, 327-336.

Glendon, A.I. and Clarke, S.G. 2016. *Human Safety and Risk Management: a Psychological Perspective.* 3rd edition. Boca Raton, Florida: CRC Press/Taylor & Francis.

Goodliffe, G. 2019. "Marine Le Pen and the Front National in France: Between Populisms in the 2017 Elections and Beyond". In *The New Authoritarianism Vol 2: A Risk Analysis of the European Alt-Right Phenomenon,* edited by Alan Waring, 227-249. Stuttgart: Ibidem Verlag.

Goodwin, M. 2011. *New British Fascism: Rise of the British National Party.* London: Routledge.

Gottfried, P. 2008. "The Decline and Rise of the Alternative Right". Address to H.L. Mencken Club AGM. November 23, 2008. Reproduced December 1, 2008 in *Taki's Magazine.* www.tkimag.com.

Henderson, A. 2020. *"Faces" of the Radical Right. A Report.* Edited by Matthew Feldman. August 2, 2020. London: Centre for the Analysis of the Radical Right. https://www.radicalrightanalysis.com/wp-content/uploads/2020/08/CARR-report-oD.pdf. [accessed September 30, 2020].

ISO. 2018. *ISO 31000 Risk Management—Principles and Guidelines.* International Organization for Standardization. Geneva, Switzerland: ISO.

Jackson, P. 2016. *Colin Jordan and Britain's neo-Nazi Movement: Hitler's Echo.* London: Bloomsbury.

Lee, B. 2019. *Overview of the Far-Right.* Paper commissioned by the Commission for Countering Extremism and funded by the Centre for Research and Evidence on Security Threats. July 19, 2019. Lancaster University: CREST.

Lyons, M.N. 2017a. *Ctrl-Alt-Delete: The Origins and Ideology of the Alternative Right.* Somerville, MA: Political Research Associates.

Lyons, M.N. 2017b. *Insurgent Supremacists: The US Far Right's Challenge to State and Empire.* Oakland, Ca: PM Press.

Macklin, G. 2019. *Failed Fuhrers: A History of Britain's Extreme Right.* Abingdon, Oxon: Routledge.

Mayer, J. 2016. *Dark Money: The Hidden History of the Billionaires Behind the Rise of the Radical Right.* New York: Penguin Books.

Mayer, J. 2017. "The Reclusive Hedge-fund Tycoon Behind the Trump Presidency". *The New Yorker.* March 17, 2017. https://www.newyorker.com/magazine/2017/03/27/the-reclusive-hedge-fund-tycoon-behind-the-trump-presidency.

Michael, G. 2003. *Confronting Right-Wing Extremism and Terrorism in the USA.* Abingdon, Oxon UK: Routledge.

Michael, G. 2006. *The Enemy of My Enemy: The Alarming Convergence of Militant Islam and the Extreme Right.* Lawrence KA: University Press of Kansas.

Michael, G. 2008. *The American Far Right.* Gainesville, FL: University of Florida.

Michael, G. (ed). 2014. *Extremism in America.* Gainesville, FL: University of Florida.

Michael, G. 2016. "The Seeds of the Alt-Right, America's Emergent Right-wing Populist Movement". *The Conversation*, November 23, 2016. http://theconversation.com.

Michael, G. 2017. "The Rise of the Alt-Right and the Politics of Polarization in America". *Skeptic Magazine*, February 1, 2017. Altadena, Ca: The Skeptics Society.

Michaels, D. 2020. *The Triumph of Doubt—Dark Money and the Science of Deception.* Oxford UK: Oxford University Press.

Mondon, A. and Winter, A. 2020. *Reactionary Democracy—How Racism and the Populist Far Right Became Mainstream.* London: Verso Books.

Neiwert, D. 2017. *Alt-America: The Rise of the Radical Right in the Age of Trump.* London: Verso.

Oklobdzija, S. 2019. "Public Positions, Private Giving: Dark Money and Political Donors in the Digital Age". *Research & Politics.* February 25, 2019. https://doi.org/1011777/2053168019832475. [accessed May 21, 2020].

Pilkington, H. 2016. *Loud and Proud: Passion and Politics in the English Defence League.* Manchester: Manchester University Press.

Posner, S. 2019. "Right Makes Might". *The New Republic.* March 25, 2019. https://newrepublic.com/article/153276/republicans-congress-courted-nativist-authoritarian-leaders.

Sales, P.J. 2019. Directors' Duties and Climate Change: Keeping Pace with Environmental Challenges. Lecture to Anglo-Australian Law Society, Sydney, August 27, 2019. Lord Justice Sales. London: UK Supreme Court. https://www.supremecourt.uk/docs/speech-190827.pdf. [accessed September 5, 2020].

Shrader-Frechette, K.S. 1991. *Risk and Rationality: Philosophical Foundations for Populist Reforms.* Berkeley: University of California Press.

Smith, D. 2019. "Betsy DeVos: the Billionaire Republican Destroying Public Education". *The Guardian.* December 27, 2019. https://www.theguardian.com/us-news/2019/dec/27/betsy-devos-trump-republicans-education-secretary.

van der Valk, I. 2019. "Wilders' Party for Freedom and the Dutch Alt-Right". In *The New Authoritarianism Vol 2: A Risk Analysis of the European Alt-Right Phenomenon,* edited by Alan Waring, 251-272 (263-264). Stuttgart: Ibidem Verlag.

von Bertalanffy, L. 1972. "The History and Status of General Systems Theory". *Academy of Management Journal*, 15(4), 407-426.

Waring, A. 2013. *Corporate Risk and Governance: an End to Mismanagement, Tunnel Vision and Quackery.* Farnham, UK: Gower/Taylor & Francis.

Waring, A. 2018. "The Alt-Right, Human Rights, and the Law". In *The New Authoritarianism Vol 1: A Risk Analysis of the US Alt-Right Phenomenon,* edited by Alan Waring, 303-335 (308). Stuttgart: Ibidem Verlag.

Waring, A. 2019a. *The New Authoritarianism Vol 2: A Risk Analysis of the European Alt-Right Phenomenon,* edited by Alan Waring. Stuttgart: Ibidem Verlag.

Waring, A. 2019b. "Brexit and the Alt-Right Agenda in the UK". In *The New Authoritarianism Vol 2: A Risk Analysis of the European Alt-Right Phenomenon,* edited by Alan Waring, 95-120. Stuttgart: Ibidem Verlag.

Waring, A. and Glendon, A.I. 1998. *Managing Risk: Critical Issues for Survival and Success into the 21st Century.* Andover, UK: Cengage/Thomson.

Wodak, R. 2015. *The Politics of Fear: What Right-wing Populist Discourses Mean.* London: Sage.

Wodak, R. 2018. "The Radical Right and Anti-Semitism". In *The Oxford Handbook of the Radical Right*, edited by Jens Rydgren. DOI: 10.1093/oxfordhb/9780190274559.013.4.

Wodak, R. and Rheindorf, M. 2019. "The Austrian Freedom Party". In *The New Authoritarianism Vol 2: A Risk Analysis of the European Alt-Right Phenomenon,* edited by Alan Waring, 171-197 (177-190). Stuttgart: Ibidem Verlag.

Part 1:

The Authoritarian Nature of the Corporate/Radical-Right Axis

Chapter 1:
Corporate and Radical-Right Authoritarianism: A Fusion of Mutual Interests and Dark Money

By Alan Waring[1]

Abstract

This chapter first summarises the evolution of radical-right authoritarianism in the 21st century and its dissimulating character, seeking to align with larger established mainstream/centrist political parties and even to attempts to persuade them to enter into formal coalition. Such backdoor empowerment tactics have achieved modest success in Austria and Italy and are likely to be a continuing feature of radical-right politics generally. These tactics and overall ideological thrust are then examined in the light of growing synergies between the corporate and radical-right political worlds. Profiles are presented of wealthy corporate leaders, foundations and other committed inter-mediaries who have donated vast sums of money to radical-right causes, and many of whom have also been more actively involved in advancing radical-right ideology. The potential for harm to democracy and to society by the application of such 'dark money' is addressed. The impact of authoritarian reductionism on a number of risks and related matters is analysed.

Key words: authoritarianism, radical-right, corporate, leaders, reductionism, abuses, risks.

Authoritarianism

Is bossiness in an individual necessarily a mark of authoritarianism? Directing others to get something done in a particular way or at a particular speed may suggest simply a tendency to dominate and control to ensure good functionality and efficiency, and may not be harmful. On a virtual continuum linked to personality, beliefs, needs and motives, authoritarianism is deeper and more perseverant than mere bossiness and, depending on the individual, ranges from relatively

---

[1]   See contributor affiliations and biography, page 525.

harmless manifestation through an increasingly pathological character to an extreme expression typical of neo-Nazis. Waring and Paxton (2018, 55-58; 2019, 63-66) review salient psychological factors and links to political preferences, highlighting the 'Big 5' model (McCrae & Costa 2003) on personality, right-wing authoritarianism (Altemeyer 1996;1998; Duckitt & Sibley 2010), social dominance orientation (Caprara & Vecchione 2013; Duckitt & Sibley 2010; Sibley & Duckitt 2008; Sidanius & Pratto 1999), narcissism (Post 2015), and the 'dark triad' (Furnham et al 2013; Jones & Paulhus 2011). Brooks et al (2020) and Fritzon et al (2016) provide in-depth analysis and results of recent studies on corporate psychopathy, and also highlight differences between anti-social personality disorder and psychopathy as well as the paradox of some psychopaths exhibiting both negative and positive characteristics. See also Simon (2018) on elite deviance.

In this volume, authoritarianism is defined as: (1) A belief in or support for strict obedience to the authority of a particular orthodoxy, dogma, individual, or group, at the expense of personal freedom, (2) The overbearing and intimidating tactics frequently displayed by authoritarians, (see Waring 2018a, 461; 2019, 413).

The Neo-Radical Right

The old fascist authoritarianism of Western far-right regimes over the first half of the 20th century was replaced in the second half by a gradual evolution of different forms of authoritarianism among the far right, a process that quickened in the first two decades of the 21st century. Since 2000, the remnants and late 20th century descendants of earlier neo-Nazi and similar extreme-right political parties and groups have largely declined in membership numbers and popular support, for example in the UK, the National Front (Jackson 2016; Macklin 2019) and British National Party (Carvalho 2015; Goodwin 2011). They have been eclipsed by newer groups and parties of a less totalitarian bent (some more extreme than others), but nonetheless sharing with their predecessors similar nationalist and nativist beliefs, ethno-religious and other discriminatory agendas, and an authoritarian style (Allchorn 2017; Copsey 2010; Davidson & Berezin 2018; Feldman 2019a, b; Feldman & Pollard 2016; Lee 2019; Pilkington 2016; Turner-Graham 2019; Waring 2019a).

The evolution of the far right in the US is documented by e.g. Michael (2003; 2006; 2008; 2014; 2016; 2017) and Lyons (2017a, b), while Paxton (2018a) analyses the contemporary radical-right example of the former Trump administration and a pliant Republican Party which enthusiastically supports many traits of far-right ideology. On the extreme fringes of the radical-right spectrum, neo-Nazi and similar groups such as Atomwaffen and The Base still flourish in the US, some of which have been classified as domestic terrorist groups (e.g. National Alliance, Aryan Nations) (see also *Intelligence Report* online magazine and *Hate Watch Blog* from the Southern Poverty Law Center), and, in the UK, National Action, Scottish Dawn, NS131, Atomwaffen and System Resistance Network (Allen 2017; Turner-Graham 2019). For further discussion of the contemporary radical right in the US and Europe, readers should refer to chapter 8 by Professor George Michael in this volume, and to volumes 1 and 2 of this series, and also to Allchorn (2017), Feldman (2019a, b), Lee (2019), and Nagle (2017).

The lesson from earlier far-right failures to achieve political breakthroughs learned by the newer radical-right entities of the 21st century in different countries is that, for them to be taken seriously and to survive, they needed to be perceived differently in society compared to their predecessors. In particular, they needed to be adaptive and constantly to reformulate their messages and delivery (Richardson 2017). This would enable them to engage with a worried populace in a rapidly changing world, with their contemporary fears and anxieties, their thirst for easy 'quick-fix salvation' solutions, their short attention span, and their love affair with the Internet and social media.

The chameleon-like surface presentation and dissimulation by the newer far right, rather than by changes to their core platforms (see Adams et al 2006; Adams & Somer-Topcu 2009), reveal themselves in three distinct but related ways. First, by offering narratives that are variously and/or in any combination subtle, brutal, emollient, frightening, seductive, ambiguous, indirect and direct, they often make it difficult for observers to be sure exactly what their true positions and messages are, and their narratives may have to be deconstructed in order to reveal the hidden far-right authoritarian intent. In their analysis of the far-right FPÖ in Austria, Wodak and Rheindorf (2019) provide graphic examples of the FPÖ double-face (i.e. frontstage to the public; backstage to far-right sympathisers) and its wide-ranging spectrum of discursive artfulness seeking to beguile a weary and fearful population into believing its assertion that Austria was on the edge of disaster that only FPÖ policies and strategies could effectively prevent. FPÖ propaganda has included, on the one hand, unsubstantiated blunt allegations that Austria was being overrun by Muslim hordes intent on destroying its national identity, culture and Christian heritage and, on the other, coded anti-Semitic language and allusions about alleged Jewish conspiracies. Similar propaganda and rhetoric about alleged immigrant and ethno-religious threats to their own country have been issued by the ruling far-right Fidesz Party of Viktor Orbán in Hungary, the far-right AfD in Germany (Özvatan & Forchtner 2019), the far-right Lega Party in Italy, some Polish far-right parties, a number of British radical-right parties and groups (e.g. UKIP, English Defence League, Britain First) (Davidson & Berezin 2018; Masters 2018; Turner-Graham 2019; Waring 2019b), and far-right activists and sympathisers in the US including President Trump and the Alt-Right caucus among Congress members within the Republican Party (e.g. Neiwert 2017; Posner 2019; Weigel 2016).

The second dissimulation appears when smaller far-right political parties repackage their ideas so as to appear aligned with larger 'normal' mainstream/centrist parties (Mondon & Winter 2018; 2020), thereby encouraging centrist political parties to adopt/absorb their ideas into their policies i.e. so-called "poldering" (Bruning 2016; van der Valk 2019, 263-264) and, simultaneously, making their own image more appealing to a wider public. For example, the FPÖ did this successfully by influencing the policies of the ruling ÖVP (Austrian People's Party) so as to shift the latter's centre of political gravity further to the right (Wodak & Rheindorf 2019, 176-178). Similarly, it has been argued (Waring 2019b; c) that since 2016 the ruling British Conservative Party has become much more authoritarian owing to the influence of the populist far-right Brexit Party and UKIP, as well as from far-right 'fellow travellers' who form the European Research Group of Conservative MPs. Posner (2019) argued similarly about the growing influence of the Alt-Right caucus within the US Republican Party and the Trump administration. This radical-right caucus includes Senators Ted Cruz, Ron Johnson, Mike Lee and Rand Paul, and Representatives Michelle Bachmann, Andy Biggs, Louie Gohmert, Paul Gosar, Marjorie Taylor Greene, Steve King, Ron Paul, Scott Perry, Robert Pittenger, and

Corey Stewart. Records also show that many among this caucus have close engagement with the far right in Europe.

Third, radical-right political parties seek to gain actual political power via a backdoor route by persuading mainstream/centrist parties to enter into formal coalition with them. The most prominent example thus far has been how readily in Austria the populist conservative ÖVP under Sebastian Kurz seized the opportunity to strengthen its ruling administration by power sharing with the FPÖ. In return for their voting bloc in favour of ÖVP, Kurz gave cabinet and ministerial posts to FPÖ far-right stalwarts and accepted an influx of distinctly far-right authoritarian policies that FPÖ insisted on, especially immigration curbs, ethno-religious discrimination, and curbs on press freedom. See Wodak and Rheindorf (2019, 176-178). In Italy, the coalition between the far-right Lega and the radical populist 5 Star (MSP) party enabled them to form a ruling bloc which had nationalist/nativist policies and a far-right agenda.

Synergies Between the Corporate World and Radical-Right Political World

A crucial feature of the penetration, success, and normalization of radical-right ideology in the political arena is that of the synergies between political and corporate worlds. The two worlds feed off, enable and strengthen each other (e.g. Birch 2007; Bloom & Rhodes 2016; 2018; Crouch 2014). This is not to suggest that all corporate chiefs and business owners are enamoured by or enthusiastic about radical-right ideology and agendas. Many senior executives, especially those of publicly listed companies, distance themselves from radical or extreme politics, either out of conviction and/or in order to maintain corporate governance standards and to avoid unnecessary legal liabilities and damage to corporate reputation. Indeed, in principle, it may be acceptable and non-controversial for corporate interests to lobby politicians and for politicians to seek financial support from big business for their political campaigns. Nevertheless, there is an obvious risk of undue influence or, worse, bribery and/or corruption, all of which runs counter to the public interest. A glaring example of how such relationships can go badly wrong is provided by the so-called 'Ibiza video scandal' in 2019 in which the Austrian far-right FPÖ leader Heinz-Christian Strache, who in the coalition with Sebastian

Kurz's ÖVP was Austria's Vice-Chancellor, was caught on video at a dinner party in Ibiza offering to fix government contracts to a woman posing as the niece of a Russian oligarch. Strache was forced to resign (Groendahl 2020) and came under police investigation for fraud. The FPÖ-ÖVP coalition collapsed and the ÖVP formed a new coalition with the Green Party.

Apart from the potential for fraud and corruption relating to greed and personal financial enlargement, there is also the potential for unhealthy promulgation of political agendas that suit both political and corporate interests. On the one hand, far-right politicians and parties may obtain financing from corporate donors for their media and advertising campaigns and for targeted social media promotions. In extreme cases, such financing may facilitate unlawful abuses on behalf of political clients as happened, for example, with the Cambridge Analytica abuses of millions of *Facebook* users leading up to national elections in 2016 leading up to the presidential election in the US and the Brexit referendum in the UK (see below and Paxton 2018b, 353-354). On the other hand, corporate donors with radical-right sympathies may feel encouraged and emboldened by the strengthening of their political protégés to conduct their own businesses in an authoritarian and regressive manner, and possibly to the harm and detriment of employees, other categories and society at large.

An example of how corporate leaders have allied themselves to radical-right causes is provided by the arrest and charge of the CEO of Cogensia, a Chicago-based marketing technology company, for his participation in the far-right mob attack on the Capitol building on January 6, 2021 (Charter 2021; Egan 2021; Zeffman 2021).

The relationship between radical-right political policies and programmes that benefit corporate interests and vice-versa has been the subject of analysis by Bloom and Rhodes (2016; 2018) on corporate authoritarianism and the threat to US democracy. The authoritarian style and excesses of some corporate chiefs and CEOs is often strikingly similar to that of radical-right political leaders. As they note in relation to President Trump as a high-profile example, and also unusually as both a radical-right political leader and a corporation owner:

> "The appeal of the populist demagogue is the same as that of the all-powerful CEO. Both celebrate authoritarian and anti-democratic notion of leadership. This is a culture where winning at all costs and vanquishing opponents is prized while deliberation and shared power is scoffed at as weak and girlish.

The goal is the domination of others for one's own pleasure and profit."
(Bloom & Rhodes 2016)

Wealthy Donors

Wealthy US individuals, mainly owners or CEOs of large corporations or business empires, who are known radical-right supporters, include Robert Mercer, William Regnery II, the two Koch brothers [one, David Koch, died in August 2019], members of the DeVos family, the Lynne and Harry Bradley Foundation, and the Coors brewing family. The right-wing American Enterprise Institute, for example, reportedly receives most of its funding from the Donors Capital Fund to which the Koch, De Vos and Bradley families are major contributors, as well as directly from them (Kotch 2017). According to Neiwert (2017, 114), the right-wing think tank Americans for Prosperity is funded by David Koch, while the Independence Institute is funded by the Castle Rock Foundation set up by the Coors family. Hackett (2016) lists nine billionaires, some of whom are right-wing activists, who, in addition to Mercer, contributed to Donald Trump's political campaign e.g. T. Boone Pickens, Stanley Hubbard. Steve Mnuchin, the billionaire former hedge fund manager, is cited in Hackett's list as Trump's chief fundraiser and became Treasury Secretary in President Trump's cabinet. See also Coles (2019; 2020) and Halliday et al (2018) on billionaire backers of the radical right.

Although the Koch brothers had a long history of giving financial support to radical-right political causes, including the Tea Party faction of the Republican Party, and had built up connections with Trump over some years, they declined to contribute to his 2016 presidential election campaign. They appear to have been more focussed on neoliberal economics and a libertarian reduction of government 'interference' in citizens' lives, and not on the more draconian and ugly manifestations of radical-right authoritarianism that Trump represents. Other financial supporters, such as Mercer and Regnery, were less squeamish and more enthusiastic about the far right.

Profile 1.1: Robert Mercer

According to Mayer (2016; 2017), Robert Mercer is the co-CEO of Renaissance Technologies, a highly profitable US-based hedge fund, and the head of the Mercer Family Foundation, which finances primarily right-wing causes and the campaigns of right-wing politicians. David Magerman, a former long-term close associate of Mercer in his hedge fund company, described him as "an extreme example of modern entrepreneurial philanthropy" (Di Stefano 2017). Mercer's ideological and strategic adviser was Steve Bannon (profiled in Waring 2018a, 146-151), who had been Trump's presidential campaign director in the latter stages of his 2016 election campaign and his first Chief Strategist on entering the White House up to Bannon's dismissal in August 2017. While not in the same wealth bracket as Mercer, Bannon too had previously made a respectable fortune in the banking sector.

Over several years up to the 2016 election success, Bannon had been a key protagonist in several radical-right promoting organisations and projects, many of them inter-related and funded by Robert Mercer. As noted above, for years Mercer invested heavily in Bannon as a radical-right political activist and in *Breitbart News*, into which he invested US$10 million. Bannon became *Breitbart's* controlling editor in 2012 and then its executive chairman. As the de facto political adviser to the Mercers (Robert and daughter Rebekah), Bannon was also the common link between them and many of their beneficiaries, whether Trump or useful facilitators and instruments such as *Breitbart News* and Cambridge Analytica.

Bannon persuaded Mercer to invest US$5 million in Cambridge Analytica, which Bannon set up and in which he was also a board director and vice-president, even after entering The White House as Trump's Chief Strategist. In 2018, a huge international scandal erupted surrounding Cambridge Analytica's misuse of personal data 'harvested' from millions of *Facebook* account holders in the US and UK, without their knowledge or agreement, during national elections in the US and UK and the 2016 Brexit Referendum in the UK, as well as allegations of electoral interference and misuse of donated finance (Cadwalladr 2018; Cadwalladr & Graham-Harrison 2018a, b; Paxton 2018b, 353-354). As a result, Cambridge Analytica ceased operations and went into receivership in 2018. However, reverberations from the scandal continued. For example, the UK parliamentary committee interim report on disinformation and fake news (HoC 2018) calling for greater regulatory control of the internet, social media and artificial intelligence (AI) abuses (such as perpetrated by Cambridge Analytica using *Facebook* personal data), was followed in April 2019 by the Online Harms White Paper (DCMS 2019) (revised July 2019). The government is considering the recommendations favourably and intends to appoint the existing Communications Regulator (Ofcom) as the new Online Harms Regulator (DCMS 2020). Heavy fines and penalties for transgressors, both companies and individuals, are mooted but whether these will be at the levels suggested by Waring and Paxton (2019, 387-389) i.e. commensurate with annual corporate revenues, typically in the US$70bn to US$135bn range for *Facebook* and *Google*, and jail sentences for the most serious offenders, remains to be seen.

Profile 1.2: William Regnery II

According to the Southern Poverty Law Center:

> "William H. Regnery II is the most reclusive member of the Regnery family, a right-wing publishing dynasty that wields tremendous influence among mainstream conservatives and far-right extremists......Regnery has become a major figure in the white nationalist movement, having founded the National Policy Institute, a white supremacist 'think tank', and the Charles Martel Society, which publishes *The Occidental Quarterly*, a racist, anti-Semitic and pseudo-scholarly 'journal'." (SPLC website 2020).

Well-known far-right activists who have been associated with Regnery e.g. as editorial board members of the Charles Martel Society's *The Occidental Quarterly*, include Kevin MacDonald, a director of the far-right white supremacist American Freedom Party (see e.g. MacDonald 2002; 2004), Virginia Abernethy, a former vice-presidential candidate for the American Third Position (later renamed the American Freedom Party), and Jared Taylor, founder of the white nationalist New Century Foundation (see e.g. Taylor 1993).

To broaden his range of influence and create a more substantial campaigning image, in 2005 Regnery, along with Charles Martel Society colleagues Samuel T. Francis and Louis R. Andrews, established the National Policy Institute (NPI) as a research and advocacy organisation for promoting "the American majority's unique historical, cultural and biological inheritance." Some initial funding came from the Pioneer Fund, a long-established major fund for racist studies and propaganda, especially in the area of scientific racism and eugenics. In 2011, Richard Spencer joined the NPI as President and Creative Director, where he runs the NPI publishing house *Washington Summit Publishers*, which publishes journals under the *Radix* imprint. Initially, NPI staff comprised individuals from the Charles Martel Society, such as MacDonald, Francis and Taylor, who became authors in *Radix* publications with Spencer as editor (e.g. Spencer 2012).

Regnery is reportedly still active behind the scenes in NPI, but since 2012 has kept a low profile, although SPLC (2020) reported an incident in 2014 when he was arrested in Hungary trying to evade an immigration ban relating to his intention to attend a far-right conference in Budapest. For all practical purposes, Richard Spencer is now the public face and leader of NPI.

Profile 1.3: Richard Spencer

Spencer, an unapologetic far-right champion, came to the NPI with a background in the early days of the Alternative Right (Alt-Right) movement when he wrote supportive articles about it in *The American Conservative* and *Taki's Magazine*. He founded and edited an on-line blog *Alternative Right* (now AltRight.com) and implies on the NPI website (NPI 2020) that he invented the term Alternative Right in 2010, a view widely accepted. Certainly, Spencer did much to publicize and promulgate the term 'Alt-Right'. However, according to Michael (2017), the term was first used in 2008 when Paul Gottfried, a conservative academic, while addressing the H.L. Mencken Club on "The Decline and Rise of the Alternative Right", implied that the 'alternative right' was a dissident far-right ideology that rejected mainstream conservatism. As the author wrote in regard to Gottfried (2008):

> "The so-called intellectual basis for the Alt-Right appears to be little more than an attempt to gain falsely some measure of credibility, respectability and social acceptability for what was, and is, a set of prejudiced beliefs in the primacy of inequality and the fostering of racial discrimination and white supremacy." Waring (2018a, 42)

In 2017, Spencer attracted much criticism and opprobrium to himself and the NPI for his videoed rants and defiant support for a provocative far-right march through Charlottesville, Virginia, on October 5, 2017, less than two months after the notorious 'Charlottesville massacre' (Eggert 2017). On August 8, 2017, during a 'Unite the Right' far-right march through the centre of Charlottesville by white supremacists, some armed with clubs and firearms, a young white supremacist drove his car at speed into peaceful counter-protesters, killing one person and injuring 19 others. Despite the almost universal and rapid condemnation of the August incident (Trump being an exception in taking several days before reluctantly acknowledging the crime), Spencer not only supported it but also decided to hold yet another similar march in Charlottesville on October 5 (Svrluga 2017).

Swinn (2019) provides a relationship diagram[2] purporting to depict connections and relationships between various radical-right donors, intermediaries and radical-right activists, in the US and beyond. The diagram links wealthy oligarch donors Robert Shillman (CEO of Cognex), Robert Mercer, and Nina Rosenwald (the Sears, Roebuck & Co heiress), with funding and facilitation of radical-right foundations, intermediaries and activists. The cited foundations include several of those listed in Table 1.1 (Appendix 1.1) plus some others. Cited radical-right intermediaries include the David Horowitz Freedom Center, *Breitbart News*, Stop Islamization of America (SIOA) e.g. activists Pamella Geller and Robert Spencer, and the far-right *Infowars* website. The British far-right activist Tommy Robinson holds the distinction of a Shillman Fellowship and is also linked to *Infowars*. See Coles (2019; 2020), Halliday et al (2018) and Keatinge et al (2019) on far-right funding links.

---

[2]   Caution advised as this diagram has not been validated and may involve confirmation bias.

Profile 1.4: Arron Banks

Arron Fraser Andrew Banks was a controversial right-wing protagonist throughout the second decade of the 21st century, both as a corporate leader and as an active participant in populist radical-right politics in Britain. A colourful, flamboyant character, Banks demonstrated his ideological credentials in various ways. For example, April 23, 2017, during an interview by Andrew Neil on *BBC 1 Sunday Politics*, he stated clearly that he strongly advocated a 10-year ban on immigrants, with a primary focus on Muslims (*YouTube* 2017). On July 16, 2017, he issued a *Twitter* diatribe reiterating his call for a ban on Muslim immigration into the UK and added a demand for "levelling all Saudi/Qatari funded mosques" (Cork 2017).

Moreover, Banks has been a heavy donor of financial support to radical-right causes, notably the United Kingdom Independence Party (UKIP) while it was led by Nigel Farage, and the Leave.EU campaign for Britain to quit the European Union (so-called Brexit). Over several years, he pledged a series of donations to UKIP, notably £1 million in 2014 alone. In late October 2017, he was estimated to have made political contributions totalling to that date nearly £10 million (Sloan & Campbell 2017). In addition to donations to UKIP, he injected large sums into organisations dedicated to securing Brexit, which was a *cause célèbre* for the radical right. These donations included large sums to the Leave.EU campaign, an organisation he co-founded with Richard Tice in July 2015. Despite his rhetoric against 'big city elites', like Banks and many other wealthy individuals of the radical right, Tice is a prime example of the genre they all apparently despise. He is a multi-millionaire Chief Executive of Quidnet Capital Partners, an asset management company based in London's exclusive Mayfair district, as well as being a major shareholder of Sunley Family Limited (Hope Not Hate 2019). Banks revelled in being labelled as one of the "bad boys of Brexit", a group that included Tice.

Over the period 2014 to 2017, Banks, Tice, and Farage were embroiled individually or severally in a series of controversies and scandals that epitomised the 'bad boy' image they sought to project. At one level, all three at various times made public statements or comments judged by many to be inflammatory opinion and incitement to hatred based on ethno-religious prejudice (Hope Not Hate 2019). At another level, the organisations they ran (UKIP and Leave.EU) engaged in disseminating inflammatory and fear-inducing propaganda, for example anti-immigrant and anti-Muslim advertisements designed to panic scared voters into backing Brexit in the 2016 Referendum. These advertisements bore a striking resemblance in content and tone to some of those used by the far-right FPÖ in Austria in the 2008-2018 period (depicted in Wodak & Rheindorf 2019) and the far-right AfD in Germany in its 2016 and 2017 election campaigns (depicted in Özvatan & Forchtner 2019).

Two separate *Channel 4 News* investigations also cited evidence that Leave.EU had engaged in scandalous conduct during its Brexit campaigning. First, it alleged (*C4* 2019a) that Leave.EU had sponsored the creation of a propaganda video based on faked footage of supposed 'migrants' entering Britain illegally in a small boat across the Channel, which it published on *Facebook* just before the 2016 Referendum. The programme further alleged that a series of fake photos were shot for the Leave.EU campaign, purporting to show two British women being assaulted by migrants, although a planned press release centred on these photos by Leave.EU never went ahead. In its second investigation, *C4* (2019b) alleged that Leave.EU had targeted advertisements to appeal not only to the general public and its own UKIP supporters (i.e. the populist far-right) but also to those of more extreme far-right parties and groups. While such adverts would no doubt have been in keeping with the far-right message and tone of those of its general adverts cited above (eight examples of which are depicted in Hope Not Hate 2019), no hard evidence of a deliberate targeting of the more extreme-right within the radical-right spectrum has been forthcoming.

Banks' financial donations and his business and personal finances are as controversial as his political beliefs and commitments. While Sloan and Campbell (2017) had estimated his total political contributions to be some £10 million, other investigators (Pegg & Campbell 2018) were quoting a figure of £12.4 million being paid by Banks' company Better for the Country Limited to Leave.EU Group Limited (also controlled by Banks) for "administrative services", details of which remain opaque other than being described by Leave.EU's chief executive as "campaign management services". This figure is on top of his contributions to UKIP totalling several million pounds. See also Cadwalladr et al (2018).

Controversies about Banks' political donations centre not on the amounts per se, or his right to make such donations, but rather on the source of his funds and their legitimacy, on whether Leave.EU kept within statutory limits on its campaign spending, and on whether he had fully paid any taxes due. Ultimately, the Electoral Commission (2018) found that Leave.EU had under-reported loans from Banks in relation to the Referendum and that Leave.EU's duty holder under electoral law ('the responsible person') had committed an offence under pre-poll transaction reporting requirements, which contributed to a further offence in respect of its referendum campaign spending return. Further, although Banks was reported by Leave.EU to be the sole provider of its loan funds, in fact the two companies that he controlled and which acted as conduits for the transfers, Rock Services Limited and Better for the Country Limited (BFTCL), should also have been reported as part of the providing arrangements. Leave.EU was found to have failed to include £77,380 in its referendum spending return, which related to fees paid to BFTCL as its campaign organiser. Leave.EU should also have reported non-staff spending of £644,672 and staff spending of £125,802. Invoices for 97 payments totalling £80,224 were also not provided.

Other controversial donations allegedly made by Banks included 'grace and favour' funding of Nigel Farage's living costs and overseas political engagements over the year after the Brexit referendum in 2016, which totalled some £450,000 as detailed in Walker (2019) and *BBC* (2019). Investigations by the *BBC* (Rana & Clegg 2018) resulted in more damaging allegations that Banks had made corrupt payments to a Lesotho government minister in return for facilitating his application for a prospecting licence for his Senqu River mining operations in Lesotho. The sum of £65,000 was cited as being transferred by Banks in 2013 into the personal account of Mr Thesele Maseribane, government minister and leader of the Basotho National Party. Further, Banks was alleged to have covered the costs of the leader's campaign rallies to the tune of

£350,000, and paid for his living expenses while in exile following a coup in 2014.

Further allegations arose that Banks had sought suspect Russian money to bail out his three South African diamond mines owned by his company Diamond Rocks, which had been performing poorly and required either capital injection or outright sale (Cadwalladr & Jukes 2018; *C4* 2018). The close and favourable contacts between Banks, Farage, the Leave.EU team and Donald Trump and his campaign team heightened concern in view of known Russian interference in the US Presidential election (NIC 2017; USDoJ 2018a, b).

Both Sloan and Campbell (2017) and *C4* (2018) suggested that Banks' own stated finances did not tally remotely with his known level of spending. The *C4* report quoted Damian Collins MP, chair of the UK parliamentary DCMS Select Committee investigating foreign interference in the 2016 referendum and UK national elections in general, directly questioning three times why Banks would need to hunt for Russian investment if he were so rich and when he had spent so lavishly on Brexit.

Committed Intermediaries and Enablers

In addition to the individual radical-right politicians and corporate leaders themselves, numerous intermediaries have radical-right commitments, such as ideological 'think tanks', right-wing research groups, right-wing philanthropic foundations, public and media relations consultants, lobbying groups, and other influencers promoting the supposed common cause of big business and radical-right politicians. While the Regnery organisations (the Charles Martel Society and the National Policy Institute) are prime examples, there are many more. Posner (2019) cites in the US the radical-right Freedom Caucus, Paul Manafort, the Heritage Foundation, and *Breitbart*, to which may be added many others as in Table 1.1. (see Appendix 1.1) and in Swinn (2019)—e.g. John M. Olin Foundation, Allegheny Foundation, Fairbrook Foundation, The Carthage Foundation, The Randolph Foundation, and wealthy corporate heirs such as Julie Jenkins Fancelli, an heir to the Publix founder (Ramachandran et al 2021), and Nina Rosenwald, heir to the Sears, Roebuck & Co fortune.

While all of those in Table 1.1 are representative of radical-right thinking, not all are linked to extremists. Some clearly are, such as advocating or participating in violence (e.g. Richard Spencer/NPI and the Charlottesville incidents). Others limit themselves to disseminating ethno-religious prejudice and hatred and white nationalist/nativist ideology, either directly, or via invited speakers, protégés, sponsored individuals, or sponsored 'research'. For example, the white nationalist and eugenics promoter Charles Murray has been frequently sponsored since the 1990s as a speaker by the AEI. Similarly, the Young America's Foundation (YAF) has on its speaker list such far-right protagonists as Ann Coulter, Ted Nugent, David Horowitz, Robert Spencer, and Matt Walsh. Senior members of the YAF organisation itself are also cited by Kotch (2017) as being directly linked to far-right causes by donations to the Charles Martel Society and to the political campaign funds of Republican Representative Steve King, a well-known white nationalist. Further, YAF board member James B. Taylor is also a former president of the National Policy Institute (NPI), the far-right 'think tank' founded in 2005 and run by Richard Spencer since 2011. As noted above, Spencer's far-right ideology promulgates white supremacist philosophy and agendas via publications under the NPI's *Radix* imprint. See also Coles (2019; 2020) and Halliday et al (2018).

The David Horowitz Freedom Center has been cited as a speaking sponsor of the British-born Milo Yiannopoulos, the former *Breibart News* staffer notorious as a radical-right self-publicist for his controversial views on such topics as homosexuality and under-age sex (see ADL 2018; Neiwert 2017; Yiannopoulos 2017). New Century Foundation, National Policy Institute, VDare, and the Charles Martel Society are cited by Kunzelman (2016) as examples of white nationalist groups who raise millions of dollars by claiming tax-exempt charitable status. Many of those listed in Table 1.1 are closely linked and frequently collaborate. For example, the anti-Muslim SIOA protagonists Pamella Geller and Robert Spencer are associated with the Mercer and Shillman Foundations. Geller was employed at *Breitbart News* and works closely with Rebel Media funded by Mercer. Spencer collaborates with the David Horowitz Foundation, which is funded by the Rosenwald Foundation and others and backed by Shillman. Project Veritas, also funded by Shillman, runs the far-right *Infowars*.

Profile 1.5: Paul Manafort

Of all the examples in Table 1.1, Paul Manafort stands out as different in that he is neither a significant donor nor a committed radical-right ideologue. Instead, although associated with several radical-right protagonists, he has been a very well-connected lobbyist, especially in Washington, for foreign authoritarian leaders, regimes and business interests. Clients variously cited are Viktor Yanukovych, the former Ukrainian President, some wealthy Ukrainian and Russian oligarchs, as well as Ferdinand Marcos, a former Philippines President. In addition, he was a campaign manager for a succession of US Republican presidential candidates, the most recent being Donald Trump for the period before Steve Bannon assumed that role. His connections with high-level individuals in the US administration, such as Trump, strengthened his attractiveness to foreign clients. However, in 2017 and 2018, he came under two US criminal investigations which resulted in his being charged and tried on serious offences. First, in Virginia, he was convicted on six out of eight counts of tax evasion totalling some US$6 million, knowingly filing false tax returns, bank fraud totalling some US$6 million, and failing to report foreign bank accounts. For these convictions, he was sentenced in March 2019 to 47 months in prison (Sullum 2019). A week later in a Washington court, having pleaded guilty to witness tampering, a tax fraud conspiracy against the US government, money laundering, failure to report foreign bank accounts, failure to register as a foreign agent, and lying to the Department of Justice, he was sentenced to a further three-and-a-half-years in prison to run consecutively with the earlier penalty (Smith 2019; Sullum 2019).

As to motives, while Manafort clearly had a strongly conservative world-view and was in broad agreement with the various authoritarian causes he facilitated, as Judge Jackson in the Washington court observed, it would appear that personal greed was the prime motivator for his criminal conduct. At his peak, Manafort's net personal worth had been put at US$70 million (CNW 2019), falling to US$50 million in 2018 (NWP 2019), and then to some US$1 to 2 million in 2019 (CNW 2019; WP 2020) as hubris took its toll. On December 27, 2020, he was pardoned by President Trump.

In many ways, Manafort came to epitomise the egregious character of the axis formed by radical-right political and business interests and the latter's arrogant expectation that vast wealth entitled them, with impunity, to corruptly buy political influence and personal advantage. Manafort's connection with Trump added to the latter's image as someone who pledged to clean up the sleazy corruption of the 'Washington swamp' but who did little or nothing in that regard.

As Lawrence et al (2019) noted, many US-based radical-right policy and opinion-forming institutions and their financial backers also support similar bodies in other countries, particularly Britain, through the Atlas Network, which is a US-headquartered global coalition of more than 450 right-wing promoting bodies. For example, in Britain, the European Research Group, the Centre for Policy Studies, the Institute for Economic Affairs, the Economists for Free Trade, the Legatum Institute, and others, enjoy a close relationship with Atlas associates in the US. In Canada, similar right-wing bodies include the Justice Centre for Constitutional Freedoms, the Aurea Foundation, the Lotte and John Hecht Foundation, the Donner Canadian Foundation, the Fraser Institute, and the Montreal Economic Institute, of which a number are part of the Atlas Network.

Profile 1.6: Dominic Cummings

Among ultra-conservative policy and opinion-formers in the UK, since the 1990s Dominic Cummings has been especially prominent and arguably the most controversial. The profile by Parker (2020) plots his career path from the 1990s up to his role as strategy adviser/director to Prime Minister Boris Johnson. He was highly thought of by many on the right wing of the Conservative Party and he injected an intellectual rigour that many thought lacking in neo-conservatism. Despite his undoubted intellectual skills, however, his inter-personal skills were less well received. He presented as a hyper-authoritarian, driven, fixated, intellectual narcissist, and visually he typically dressed casually and appeared unkempt. He is reportedly a great believer in himself, his ideas and his self-certified superior intelligence and is very disparaging of those he considers intellectual weaklings or who might attenuate or interfere with his mission.

There has been speculation in political and media circles that he may be a high functioning sociopath. Indeed, the former Conservative Prime Minister David Cameron was reported to have described him as "a career psychopath" (Mason 2014). However, Klitzman (2016), Post (2015), Singer (2017) and Waring and Paxton (2018, 74; 2019, 82) invoke the 'Goldwater Rule' and specifically caution against 'armchair diagnoses' of this kind, in relation to Donald Trump, Cummings or, indeed, any other person. Nevertheless, for the sake of this discussion, it is defensible to summarize the defining characteristics of sociopathic and psychopathic personalities. See also more detailed analysis by Antony Vass in chapter 3.

According to APA (2013), Hirstein (2013) and Kiehl and Buckholtz (2010), such personalities are characterized by a combination of (a) perpetration of harm to others with either no self-recognition of their own harmfulness or not caring about it, (b) no empathy for those harmed (although empathy may be feigned), (c) no conscience, remorse or guilt, (d) a ruthless end-justifies-the-means and 'what-can-I get-away-with?' attitude and behaviour, (e) (for psychopaths) inability to form normal emotional or social bonds (although these may be feigned), (f) (for sociopaths) limited ability to form normal emotional or social bonds e.g. family and close friends but not more widely (although these may be feigned). Whereas psychopathy has a combined genetic and learned/acquired origin, sociopathy is regarded as an acquired disorder.

Hare (2003; 2016) produced a 20-item list of such characteristics. Prominent among these are: (a) showing a glib and superficial charm, (b) shallow and insincere emotions, (c) confidence trickery and manipulation, (d) propensity for pathological lying, (e) grandiose self-worth and narcissism, (f) scapegoating and blaming others for own failings, (g) reacting badly to rejection. More general discussion on so-called "snakes in suits" is provided by Babiak and Hare (2007) and Hare (1999). More recent in-depth studies are provided by Brooks (2020), Brooks et al (2020) and Fritzon et al (2016). With growing awareness of the negative and potentially damaging effects of disordered personalities, the question arises as to whether any government or organisation dare take a risk that a forthright, assertive and determined 'wunderkind' in their midst is not, in fact, masking an underlying pathological personality

(Brooks et al 2020, 333). See also Walton (2007a; b; 2010; 2020a; b; c), and Vass in chapter 3 and Smallman in chapter 4 of this volume.

Cummings reportedly has a pugnacious, irritable, and angry personality, with a bullying tendency. In 2020, allegations were made by a former senior official of the Confederation of British Industry that Cummings tried to push him down stairs, and then grabbed him by the tie and threatened him with a clenched fist, after they had clashed during a joint radio interview in 1999 (*BBC* 2020; Moore 2020). Before this allegation surfaced, he had already gained notoriety for the summary sacking of a civil servant adviser to the Chancellor of the Exchequer and eviction from her office under armed police escort, as well as threats to other civil servants to do as he demanded 'or else'. Cummings himself was a high-level contract consultant and not a government employee, and therefore his peremptory sacking of a proper civil servant not even reporting to him but to Chancellor Sajid Javid caused much consternation and anger, both in the Civil Service and political and media circles. When Cummings went further and got the Prime Minister to authorize and sanction his selective sackings more generally of ministerial advisers and civil servants without consultation and replace them with his radical-right placemen, Javid reportedly resigned in disgust. Other centrist ministers were then sacked in short order and replaced by others loyal to the radical-right cause. It appeared that Cummings had carried out political subversion of cabinet government and the civil service and, by any other name, a bloodless putsch by radical-right interests. This coup had a striking similarity to that orchestrated by Steve Bannon in getting the Alt-Right Republican renegade Donald Trump elected as President in 2016 (see Waring (2018a, 147). To many observers, Cummings too acted like the political officer of a radical-right politburo, constantly badgering Prime Minister Johnson to stick to his (i.e. Cummings') radical-right plan, while bullying recalcitrant ministers and key civil servants into doing the same or else face his wrath.

However, perhaps the most striking example of Cummings' personality and modus operandi came in May 2020 when a major scandal erupted over his reported violations of the national Covid-19 public health rules. On March 23, the Prime Minister announced the health protection lockdown rules, which included every person being expected to self-isolate as much as possible by staying at home, and especially if a household member showed signs and symptoms of Covid-19 infection. Dominic Cummings, as the Prime Minister's Personal Adviser, was a party to the Cabinet's lockdown rules formulation. It emerged that in late March 2020, after both he and his wife developed covid-19 symptoms, they drove their two children from the family home in London some 250 miles north to his parents' home in County Durham (see e.g. Ford & Hamilton 2020; Swinford 2020). This action alone was widely interpreted as a flagrant breach of the rules that Cummings himself had helped draw up. Cummings was in fact diagnosed as having the Covid-19 infection. It further emerged that, while staying at his parents' home, he took his wife and one child for a trip out by car to the tourist attraction of Barnard Castle, according to eyewitnesses, and thereby constituting another Covid-19 rule violation.

These are the bare undisputed facts. However, a huge political furore erupted, which was inflamed by Cummings not only refusing to publicly apologize but, on the contrary, also to brazenly deny that he had broken the rules. This denial sought to show that, in fact, he had been fully compliant and indeed had only done what any parent would do to ensure that the grandparents could provide childcare while Cummings and his wife were still affected by the Covid-19 virus (Ford & Hamilton 2020; Swinford 2020). He had, he asserted, conducted himself correctly and reasonably. His trip to Barnard Castle had been, he asserted, to test that his vision would be alright for his forthcoming drive back to London. The Prime Minister publicly backed Cummings and stated on 24 May that he should neither resign nor be sacked since he had done nothing wrong.

Rather than killing the scandal, the Prime Minister's intervention worsened the public outcry (Elliott et al 2020a; Kenber 2020). Allegations of hypocrisy, arrogance, mendacity, and abuse of position flowed thick and fast, not only from the media e.g. Foges (2020) and opposition political parties but also surprisingly from right-wing Conservative politicians, who ordinarily would have supported Cummings. MPs across the political spectrum were reporting heavy postbags and e-mails with angry complaints from constituents about Cummings' conduct and attitude and the Prime

Minister's support. One junior minister resigned in protest, while other ministers and MPs issued highly critical public statements and social media comments. At least 60 Conservative MPs, including a then current minister, eleven former ministers, and a former Prime Minister, demanded Cummings' resignation or sacking, while polls indicated that both Johnson and the Conservative Party had suffered a huge slump in popularity (Elliott et al 2020b; Fisher & Grylls, 2020). As Rifkind (2020) and many other commentators observed, by "treating the rest of us like idiots" Cummings had eroded public support for the Covid-19 lockdown at a particularly critical juncture when such continuing support was vital so as to prevent a resurgence of infection across the country. Moreover, in appearing to defend the indefensible, the Prime Minister projected himself as weak, psychologically dependent, and compromised by his aide Cummings, as if their roles were reversed and in reality Cummings was in charge of policy while Johnson was his compliant servant (Martin 2020). The moral authority of the government and the Prime Minister had been badly damaged (Kelly 2020) and accountability had been casually discarded (Rachman 2020).

Cummings' explanations for his conduct, culminating in an unprecedented public statement and press conference by him on May 25, appeared to many observers to be artful sophistry. Uncharacteristically, at this press event he presented a calm, almost humble, demeanour, while steadfastly denying that he had done anything wrong or even questionable. Cummings' sophistry and defiant performance in this scandal was encapsulated in his comment when confronted by journalists demanding answers to how he felt about allegedly violating the Covid-19 rules that everyone else had to follow. His reply, captured on video, was simply "I don't care". Whatever the strengths of his intellect and potential contribution to administrative reforms, such as his radical restructuring plans for the Cabinet Office and the Civil Service, these became overshadowed, if not eclipsed, by his unappealing, antagonistic personality.

As noted above, Cummings is in a very similar mould to his US counterpart Steve Bannon. Like Bannon, Cummings is a radical-right 'revolutionary', a disrupter who thirsts for a palingenetic rebirth of society, governance and institutions in which the old alleged liberal decay is swept aside and replaced by a radical-right

'New Order'. Bannon, Cummings and their acolytes share two salient characteristics: (1) a ruthless determination to secure a permanent radical-right stamp on the governance of their respective
country (and other countries), and (2) a 'by any and all means necessary' methodology to achieve this objective, including manipulation, distortion, disruption and subversion of democratic institutions, processes and standards (see Cadwalladr 2019). Cummings
was forced to resign his position, along with other hard-line Brex-
iteer advisers to the Johnson government, in November 2020, following a reported revolt by moderates, many Conservative MPs,
and the Prime Minister's own dissatisfaction with Cabinet Office
disharmony blamed on Cummings (Swinford & Wright 2020).

Potential for Harm to Democracy and Society

While there is no suggestion that relationships per se between corporations, oligarchs, influencers, and politicians are necessarily unlawful, the question arises as to whether such relationships are liable to
corrupt temptations that are likely to lead to promulgation of political
interests and agendas that may harm a democratic society or vulnerable sections of it. Michaels (2020) and Oklobdzija (2019) are critical
of 'dark money' manipulation of political emphases and outcomes in
democratic societies. Bloom and Rhodes (2018) note that overall the
mutual influences hold troubling implications for the future of democracy, a point also made by Mondon and Winter (2020) especially in
relation to malign influence by such agents as radical-right leaning
journalists and media organs. For example, does such manipulation
risk the distortion and undermining of democracy and the hijacking of
governance to unduly favour the wealthy and the powerful at the expense of the rest of society? Does it become a self-affirming process
that encourages some of those with wealth to believe that they can,
and are entitled to, buy political outcomes? It is a question of whether
amoral calculation and unsavoury, if not harmful, methods will come
to be normalized in the pursuit of egregious radical-right political motives and/or personal greed. The money (whether clean and transpar-
ent or 'dark' and surreptitious) is, perhaps, less of a threat in itself [af-
ter all, parties of all ideologies are funded by wealthy donors and interest groups] than the weak relationship these particular corporations and radical-right organisations have with liberal democracy.

Authoritarianism and illiberal democracy, if not elective radical-right dictatorship, are far more likely where power and advantages to both corporate and radical-right mutual interests over disfavoured others are conferred as a result of 'dark money' funding motivated by ideology and greed.

The mutual admiration and synergy between corporate and radical-right leaders masks two paradoxes. First, in the US one of the populist radical right's biggest rhetorical enemies is globalisation of trade, the selfish corporate interests that accompany it, and the undue manipulation, deals and trade-offs between corporate interests and politicians in Washington at the expense of ordinary citizens. One of President Trump's boasts was that as President he would clean up this 'Washington swamp', a theme he returned to in May 2020: "One of the things I said, we have to expose the deep state, you know, drain the swamp... I had no idea the swamp was like this....and there are still plenty of others in there. But we are draining the swamp like nobody's ever drained the swamp" (Charter 2020). In 2016, he promised he would clear out the liberal elites and protect the 'little man'. In reality, Trump's radical-right administration strengthened its ties with big corporations and wealthy oligarchs and made no discernible attempt to sanitize the politico-corporatism in Washington. He merely replaced the liberal sleaze with his illiberal sleaze, the liberal elites with his illiberal elites. For example, he appointed to his cabinet the radical-right billionaire Steve Mnuchin as Secretary of the Treasury, as well as Betsy DeVos, billionaire member of the DeVos family foundation noted for its radical-right funding, as Education Secretary. Regarded widely as a staunch radical-right ideologue, and having no substantive expertise in education, Betsy DeVos proved to be a highly divisive and controversial figure. The US education world railed against her lack of competence, impartiality and integrity, including allegations that, overall, her attitude and actions while Secretary amounted to a concerted programme to destroy public education in favour of the private sector (Litvinov 2019). Other allegations included her decision to remove existing protections for college students alleging sexual harassment and sexual assault, which led to her being accused of being a defender of rapists (Smith 2019). In the midst of the Covid-19 crisis, she claimed (July 16, 2020) in a radio interview that children should go back to school as they did not catch the disease and were "stoppers" of Covid-19 transmission (Kessler 2020). According to the *Wall Street Journal* (Ramachandran et al 2021), Julie Jenkins Fancelli, the heiress to the Publix supermarket chain, donated some US$300,000 to fund Trump's January 6 rally at the Washington Ellipse from which many proceeded to participate in the mob attack on the Capitol. As a further example of Trump's radical-right elite protégés, when the wealthy politico-corporate intermediary and Trump's former campaign manager, Paul Manafort, was convicted and jailed in 2019 (see profile above) for multiple counts of bank fraud, tax evasion, money laundering and other related crimes, Trump publicly dismissed it as a "fake witch-hunt". He later pardoned Manafort, further implying that Manafort should never have been prosecuted.

The second paradox concerns the radical right's much-vaunted claim to ensure 'freedom' for the population—from government regulation and interference in their lives, from gun controls, from socialized or universal health care, from obligations to protect vulnerable citizens, juxtaposed by the neo-liberal freedom for business to operate with few restrictions or controls. Trump indeed took steps to achieve such policy objectives. Yet, the radical right's notion of freedom appears quite different to the normal universally accepted human freedoms (as per Universal Declaration of Human Rights UN 1948) and, in particular, entitlement to life, proper health care, absence of discrimination or ill-treatment based on ethnicity, religion, nationality, political beliefs, or sexual orientation. The radical right's idealized notion of freedom is one that seeks to advance their own particular freedoms, and the benefits and advantages they gain from them, while denying basic human rights freedoms to an underclass of vulnerable sectors of society—the poor, the unemployed, the chronically ill, immigrants, ethno-religious and other minorities. In essence, the radical right seek their own freedoms at the expense of other people's freedoms, based on maintaining, and even increasing, fundamental injustices and inequalities between the deserving (i.e. themselves and their supporters) and the undeserving (i.e. the vulnerable underclass and those who reject radical-right values). On radical-right supporters in the US, Neiwert (2017) referred to the populist Alt-Right 'producerist' view of themselves as hard-working patriots compared to the worthless, non-contributing 'others' below them who should be 'eliminated'. Nevertheless, some populist radical-right parties have supported such socialist policies and programmes as welfare, benefit systems, and unemployment support, but more motivated by vote-winning than by ideological conviction e.g. in Italy, the far-right Lega party when power sharing with the MSP/5 Star Party.

Risk and Authoritarian Reductionism—a Neglected Perspective

As Waring (2019e; 2020a; b) observed, the radical right in every re-spect is characterized by reductionist thinking and by its products e.g. policies, propaganda, and strategies based on falsification of data and deliberate over-simplification of cause-effect relationships, with the aim of scapegoating political rivals, ethno-religious minorities, and other vulnerable groups for all manner of alleged societal ills. How-ever, this characteristic is often taken-for-granted by observers and academic analysts and overlooked as a crucial factor that renders rad-ical-right ideology particularly dangerous to society and to democ-racy. A major reason why radical-right ideology is so harmful *is* its over-arching reductionism and mendacity.

As an example, in radical-right terms, MMR (measles, mumps, rubella) is reduced to a set of allegedly relatively minor health threats whereas [quoting discredited quack science from a struck-off physi-cian Andrew Wakefield (Deer 2020)] MMR vaccine is falsely cited as a major cause of autism in children. The underlying justification ap-pears to emanate from the radical right's fear of removal of the free-dom of parental choice, coupled with a belief that scientists who sup-port vaccination (i.e. the vast majority, the CDC, WHO, etc) are part of a left-wing conspiracy to undermine conservative governance and the economy. Radical-right supporters are heavily represented among anti-vax supporters, who include Trump[3] in the US as well as far-right parties in France, Italy and elsewhere, whose undue influence on the public has resulted in decreased vaccination leading to measles epi-demics, mumps outbreaks, and some fatalities. In February 2020, Trump also contradicted the CDC and WHO on the seriousness of the coronavirus threat, dismissing the scale of the threat as a "hoax" and

---

[3]   Paradoxically, despite supporting the anti-vax movement, in November 2020 Trump sought falsely to claim credit for the US programme to develop anti-covid vaccines and praised their anticipated public health success.

claiming that his media enemies were using false coronavirus stories as a weapon to undermine him politically. Within three weeks (March 16), his so-called "hoax" had become a global pandemic with every country seriously impacted, including the US. Nevertheless, on March 24, Trump was still expressing his belief—and urging the population to believe—that the epidemic in the US would be nearly over "by Easter" i.e. in less than three weeks, regardless of the WHO's and CDC's predictions of many months and despite his proposed financial rescue package for the nation of some US$2 trillion which Congress passed on March 25. This very positive measure notwithstanding, it is difficult not to deduce that Trump imagined that somehow the Covid-19 pandemic was just some trivial, pesky nuisance that could be defeated rapidly, and to order, by wishful thinking, money and decree.

By 28 March, with the number of infections rising rapidly, the mayors of major US cities and hospital doctors were pleading for tens of thousands of extra ventilation units, whereas Trump was expressly criticising such demands as being grossly exaggerated (Pavia 2020). By mid-April (i.e. after Easter), with US Covid-19 cases at over 285,000 and deaths at over 25,000, and still rising, Trump was still trying to minimize the perceived scale of the crisis and falsely announce its imminent end, while blaming China, the WHO and the media for causing the crisis. By mid-May, he was forcefully arguing against CDC and WHO warnings that nevertheless state governors should relax the protective restrictions on their populations so they could return to work and reactivate the economy. A large number of Republican governors duly complied, thereby implicitly applying a speculative/opportunity risk trade-off that the economy was more important than people's lives and public health, and that the highly likely resulting increase in infections and deaths was 'acceptable' (at least to radical-right supporters). It appeared that Trump regarded his re-election as of such paramount importance that the economy must be in a better state during campaigning, and that this would therefore require a mass return to work i.e. lifting the Covid-19 lockdown regardless of the public health consequences. Gambling with thousands of lives in this way not only demonstrated amoral calculation but also ran a huge political risk for Trump and the Republican Party if the pandemic flared up again as a consequence of their actions. By September 1, 2020, the number of Covid-19 cases in the US had exceeded 6 million and Covid-19 deaths had exceeded 185,000 (CDC 2020a), with new infections still over 40,000 per day. By late-November, US infections were over 13 million, with deaths over 265,000, and 165,000 new cases daily, and deaths forecast to exceed 300,000 by Christmas (CDC 2020b). Nevertheless, despite the uncontrolled spread of the virus, Trump was still insisting that lockdown restrictions should be fully lifted, against the advice of the government's own medical and scientific experts. By the first week of January 2021, US infections had risen to 20 Million, with 350,000 deaths (CDC 2021a). On Trump's final day in office, January 19, 2021 the numbers had risen to 23,839,868 infections and some 400,000 deaths (CDC 2021b). The short-term catastrophic effects of Trump's repeated dismissal of Covid-19 as a "hoax", his repeated rejection of the need for rigorous public health routines, and his encouragement of citizens and businesses to ignore pandemic controls in favour of economic activity and personal freedom, were laid bare.

In contrasting numerous graphic examples of Trump being in denial towards the Covid-19 crisis with the "enduring goodness" of the American people, Bryant (2020) commented on March 24, 2020:

> "Trump, in common with all populists and demagogues, favours simple solutions to complex problems…..but the tricks of an illusionist, or the marketing skills of the sloganeer, do not work here. This is a national emergency….that can't be tweeted, nicknamed or hyped away. The facts are inescapable: the soaring numbers of the dead."

As another example, from before his 2016 election and since then, Trump not only consistently denied the existence of climate change but also denied its anthropogenic cause, especially an industrial one, or that its effects will be unduly damaging or that bad environmental events cannot be addressed by normal emergency measures. Ross and Bevensee (2020) addressed the rise of eco-fascism and noted how characteristic radical-right reductionist tendencies, and focus on "The Other", blaming an array of enemies, and disseminating conspiracy theories, had rendered the radical right bereft of any credible methodology for understanding and action on the systemic complexities of climate change. For example:

> "Part of the reality of climate scepticism is due to the fact that climate change is a vastly complex and non-linear set of interconnected problem spaces, and authoritarianism can understand little else than centralized flows and

> direction of inquiries through a single channel, creating perverse incentives up and down the hierarchy." Ross and Bevensee (2020, 27)

Also of note is that while the radical right artificially deflate some risks (e.g. Covid-19, climate change), they inflate others. For example, Trump persistently inflated the incidence and risk of violent criminality among immigrants (whether legal or illegal) from or via Mexico, contrary to known facts. He has also similarly falsely inflated the risk of terrorism from Muslim immigrants and visitors to the US (Verney 2018).

Another example of reductionism is provided by the current vogue for algorithms in political life and policy making. The term algorithm is a fancy term for any well-defined set of instructions or route map for solving a class of problem, typically presented as 'logic diagrams' e.g. decision sequence diagrams, fault trees, event trees. Algorithms are particularly useful for subject matter that relates to technical, engineering and scientific domains, and lie at the design core of all computer systems and other technical systems. Applied to such inanimate topics, algorithms may be very accurate and reliable for prediction and control of such systems. Unfortunately, the more that systems involve human beings engaging in consideration, evaluation, judgement, decision, and action, the more that algorithms are inaccurate and unreliable for prediction and control. Human beings are complex and fallible and the outputs of their cognition are variable, unpredictable, and often wickedly contrary, thereby weakening any system that relies on their input (Checkland 1999; Vickers 1983a, b; Waring 1996). This weakness increases the more complex the system and the larger the numbers of people within it or interacting with it. However, such caveats frequently go unrecognized or ignored by zealous radical-right salvationists, especially those in senior government roles as policy advisers, strategists, and technocrats, who detest the inconvenience of caveats. For example, Dominic Cummings (see profile earlier) is reportedly an almost fanatical believer in using algorithms to 'solve' major policy problems. Excessive reliance on reductionist algorithms was probably involved in such UK government policy failures as roll-out of Covid-19 'track-and-trace' and 'mass testing' in 2020, and the 2020 national GCSE results determined by computer instead of by written examination. The fallacies of misapplied reductionist algorithms and sure-fire programmatic change have been recognized since at least the 1970s e.g. the evidential failures of the 'corporate excellence' formula advocated by Peters and Waterman (1982) and the warnings of Beer et al (1990) and Mintzberg (1994a, b).

A recent study by Zmigrod et al (2021) suggests that ideological attitudes such as authoritarian, reductionist and dogmatic thinking have a cognitive biological basis whereby exponents have an inability to tackle complex cognitive tasks. For them, reductionism is a predisposition for reducing uncertainty and feeling in control, correlating with dogmatic and authoritarian attitudes and statements.

As Waring (2020a, b) noted, the apparent motives for why the radical right engages in reductionist manipulation and fakery centre on four processes, which they believe will bring their cause political and populist benefits: (1) authoritarian revisionism, (2) manipulation of risk perceptions, (3) confirmation bias in propaganda, and (4) mendacity combined with amoral calculation. Radical-right reductionism has played well to a populist audience looking for salvation from perceived problems and threats. The radical right has been skilful in weaving into its narrative an artful rhetoric and imagery concerning problems and threats that are in some cases real but also conflated with far more that are exaggerated or invented. Playing on populist fears, the radical right then proposes itself and its policies as their only salvation. Corporate supporters of this authoritarian ideology have promoted the reductionist mantra, both actively and behind the scenes. The resulting populist support, based on psychological dependence, may work for a time if the promise of salvation seems plausible and realistic. However, ultimately, populist support is likely to wane as enacted radical-right policies fail in the face of real-world complexity.

Authoritarian Revisionism

In their revisionist processes, radical-right exponents indulge in the erasure from their narrative of inconvenient or unwelcome facts from the accepted knowledge base of history and science. See, for example, Michaels (2020) and Valencia Garcia (2020). For example, in direct denial of systemic complexity theory (Checkland 1999; von Bertalanffy 1972; Waring 1996; Wilson & van Haperen 2015), protagonists pretend that the vast body of knowledge on the complexity of problems and issues relating to society, science, economics, health, social reforms, human rights, foreign relations, and governance in general, as developed over the past half century, is irrelevant, or is fake science, or never even existed. The radical-right policies, narratives and actions of the Trump administration provide stark *in extremis* examples of such revisionism on many fronts and in various forms.

The radical right seek to regress to the 'simple truths and values' of an imaginary past world of the 1960s and earlier, when relatively simple mechanistic, biological or economic 'explanations' provided a comforting illusion of order, certainty, neatly stacked 'problems-and-solutions', and simplistic salvation models and 'programmes' for correcting deviations from their dogma and their assertions of what constituted the correct normative order. Examples of radical-right salvation cure-alls range from Trump's Mexican Wall and Orbán's anti-Muslim border controls, to the palingenetic ultranationalist ethno-religious and political cleansing demanded by the more extreme end of the radical-right spectrum, to radical-right advocacy of or sympathy with discredited eugenics theories of inferiority of certain races.

Complexity theory regards real-world problems and issues as 'messes' i.e. systems of problems that defy resolution simply by picking off component problems one-by-one or even in groups, because in doing so the 'mess' simply adapts itself and survives in a modified and unresolved form (Ackoff 1974; Horn & Weber 2007; Waring 1996). Messes require the systemic whole to be tackled i.e. holistically. Despite an overwhelming trend over the past 45 years among governments, policy research groups, and academia towards adopting holistic approaches, the radical right have persisted with their reductionist and revisionist world-view. For example, as discussed in Waring (2019e; 2020a) and chapter 5 in this volume, some of the radical right (e.g. economist George Reisman) seriously argue for reintroduction of minimalist social, employment and environmental policies similar to those of Victorian times, and the wholesale removal of protective legislation for work people. Nevertheless, because radical-right propaganda overall offers a seductive 'salvation' model, as the 21st century has progressed, radical-right salvation ideas have gained widespread populist support among weary and fearful societies demanding 'solutions'.

Manipulation of Risk and Crisis Perceptions

US President Trump attempted persistently throughout 2020 to downplay the Covid-19 risk, against all official advice and statements from the CDC, WHO and other health experts. His various bizarre public statements included such assertions as: the whole phenomenon was a hoax conjured up by his political and media opponents to damage him politically; Covid-19 was no more dangerous than influenza; his administration had vanquished the pandemic in the US, a claim repeated several times over 2-3 months as the incidence and death rates were actually rising; drinking sodium hypochlorite solution, a disinfectant oxidizing agent not intended for administration to humans and dangerous by mouth, would protect people; other treatments not approved by the FDA should be allowed e.g. hydroxychloroquine and oleandrin (Zeffman 2020); exposing people to strong UV radiation would kill the virus; Covid-19 had been biologically engineered in a laboratory in China and either deliberately or negligently released, with the net effect of weakening US global supremacy. None of these assertions or recommendations had any credible factual basis.

Trump's official policy was also to deny that climate change exists or, if it did, then it was neither human-created nor a major threat to the world (see above and e.g. Waring 2018a). That policy implies a belief that there is no systemic cause-effect relationship between human activity, global warming/climate change, and extreme weather events, that therefore no special preventative measures or contingency planning is required, and that existing emergency response provisions are adequate since extreme weather events would remain rare, unpredictable and non-catastrophic (see e.g. Brulle 2014; Carmichael and Brulle 2017). In radical-right terms, the 'problem' and its risks are thereby reduced to zero, as they do not exist. The motive behind Trump's extraordinary 'wishful thinking' position appeared to be linked to his desire not to upset some industries (e.g. coal) whose activities might incur unwelcome extra environmental controls if climate change were accepted as a real phenomenon. It should be noted that whereas some companies in the US energy sector (e.g. some coal mining corporations) were delighted by Trump's radical-right policy position on global climate change, others disagreed with it and a number, including BP, Shell, Exxon Mobil and Chevron and two large coal companies, Cloud Peak Energy and Peabody Energy, openly criticised it (Waring 2018b, 294). Thus, it should not be inferred or assumed that all corporate leaders are unswerving supporters of radical-right beliefs and policies. Denial, inversion and subversion of scientific facts, plus outlandish assertions and allegations having a very flimsy scientific basis, appear to be used by Trump and fellow radical-right protagonists as a means to minimize the public's perceptions of the various risks, so as to receive public and electoral support in meeting their political objectives and agenda.

Confirmation Bias in Propaganda

The radical right exhibit a strong preference for any evidence, opinion or assertion that they believe strengthens their position. While not unique in seeking to present their best case (in common with most people), the radical right stand out in the relentless and aggressive way that they disseminate their propaganda by all forms of media, especially online and social media. Radical-right leaders, politicians, ideologues, opinion formers, commentators, corporate supporters and supportive journalists selectively include in their narratives only those items and assertions that tend to confirm and support radical-right objectives and, conversely, exclude any material that contradicts or challenges radical-right ideology or that casts the radical right in a poor light [on confirmation bias, see Dror & Fraser-Mackenzie 2008; Kahan et al 2017; Shermer 2018].

For example, as Waring (2020a, b) noted, the recent sudden increases in MMR cases (including deaths) officially attributed to anti-vax campaigns supported by the radical right will be ignored, while stories of populist support for the anti-vax position will receive favourable publicity. Stories of heroism of fire-fighters and emergency services workers in the conflagrations in California and Australia will dominate the narratives of radical-right administrations and their supporters, while climate change (if mentioned at all) will be vehemently denied as a primary causal factor in the fires. Viktor Orbán will boast of a huge success in his 'Hungary for Hungarians only' policy in the way his massive border fencing and strict controls have stopped the alleged Muslim takeover of the country, while ignoring the fact that historically Hungary has only ever had a miniscule Muslim population—a classic false proposition to evoke fear in the native population followed by their relief when the (non-existent) threat is neutralized. If the non-existent Muslim hordes have not entered the country, then populists believe that clearly Orbán's policy was correct and effective. Trump, his populist radical-right supporters and compliant journalists will play up the economic imperatives of relaxing, if not totally removing, the Covid-19 protections while playing down the consequential harm to public health, including deaths.

Mendacity and Amoral Calculation

As Waring (2020a, b) further observed, radical-right leaders and supporters persistently lie in order to advance their political ideology, persuade the public of their righteousness, and to cover up their own bad conduct. For example, according to *The Washington Post* on October 14, 2019, President Trump had made 13,435 false or misleading statements since taking office. By August 27, 2020, that number had risen to 22,247 (Kessler et al 2020). While it may be anticipated that all politicians 'stretch the truth' to their advantage, and some brazenly lie from time to time, the scale of Trump's mendacity is exceptional and unprecedented. Trump, his administration and the radical-right establishment turned amoral calculation, lying and dissemination of false facts and fake news into a central plank of official policy rather than just something to be used as an ad hoc convenience. Their stance towards the Covid-19 pandemic, for example, speaks for itself. In addition, as outlined above, corporate authoritarianism also typically involves mendacity and amoral calculation as an instrument in the ruthless attainment of personal and/or corporate objectives by any and all means necessary, regardless of harm to others.

Conclusion

The penetration, success and normalisation of radical-right ideology in the political arena reflect synergies between political and corporate interests. The two domains feed off, enable and strengthen each other. While in principle it may be acceptable for corporate interests to lobby politicians and for politicians to seek financial support from big business for their political campaigns, nevertheless there is an obvious risk of 'dark money' fostering undue influence or, worse, bribery and/or corruption, all of which is against the public interest and which, in the worst case, threatens democracy. This is all the more so in relation to radical-right political interests and sympathetic corporate world-views and interests that merge for their mutual benefit at the expense of disfavoured and often powerless groups who become victims.

Fusion of mutual interests between the radical right and particular corporate interests is evidenced by shared authoritarian world-views, attitudes, opinions, judgements and conduct—especially involving amoral thinking and calculation. Further, they may be encouraged to drift into unlimited areas and modes of opportunity, eventually crossing the dividing line between merely amoral conduct and into illegal and potentially major criminal activity, whether this involves egregious conduct towards employees, customers or other parties, or wilful undermining of democratic order, processes and institutions.

Appendix 1.1.

Table 1.1:   Examples of Intermediaries Promoting or Funding Radical-Right Policies in the US

Intermediaries Having Radical-Right Orientation	Focus	Estimated Financial Worth/Annual Budget (indicative values only)	Owners/Controllers/Principal Funders
American Enterprise Institute (AEI)	Research and advocacy of radical-right causes.	Annual revenue US$61.7m+ (2018).	Donors Capital Fund (Donors Trust); CEO Arthur Brooks.
Americans for Prosperity	Radical-right advocacy and lobbying on libertarian, free market, minimalist government, and climate change denial.	Annual revenue US$57m (2017).	Koch; Donors Capital Fund; Donors Trust; Scaife Foundation; Claude R. Lambe Foundation; DeVos family; Bradley family; COO, Tim Phillips.
Breitbart	Media disseminating radical-right opinion and propaganda e.g. *Breitbart News*.	US$10m investment from Robert Mercer; US$3.8m donations from Lynne & Harry Bradley Foundation over 2001-2010.	Robert Mercer; Steve Bannon former editor-in-chief.
Castle Rock Foundation (Adolph Coors Foundation) *[NB no connection with either the Castle Rock TV horror*	Funding radical-right causes; promoting freedom and minimalist government.	Annual revenue US$9.8m (2014). Subsequent data unavailable.	Coors family

series, or with Castle Rock Entertainment film company]		
Cato Institute	Scholarly research into libertarian conservatism, free market, minimalist government; climate change denial.	Annual revenue US$36.7m (2017).	Koch; Lynne & Harry Bradley Foundation; President and CEO, Peter N. Goettler.
Charles Martel Society	White nationalism; genetic theories of white racial superiority.	Raised US$568,526 in donations 2007-2014; Annual revenue US$100,000 (2019).	William Regnery II.
David Horowitz Freedom Center	Ultra-conservative and radical-right propaganda; Islamophobic messaging.	Annual revenue US$6.9m (2018).	Lynne & Harry Bradley Foundation; Scaife Foundation; founder and CEO David Horowitz.
Donors Capital Fund	Funding radical-right charitable-status causes.	Annual revenue US$113m (2017). Fund value US$49m (2017).	Koch family; DeVos family; Lynne & Harry Bradley Foundation; Lawson R. Bader, president and CEO.
Freedom Caucus	Radical-right group of Republican congressmen.	Not available.	Rotational chair, Representative Andy Biggs, October 1, 2019.
Government Accountability Institute	Countering liberal ideology and Democrat politicians, especially the Clintons.	Annual revenue US$2.6m (2018).	Steve Bannon; Peter Schweizer.

Heritage Foundation	Funding radical-right causes.	Current assets US$16m including US$5.5m from donors (2019); Long-term assets US$350m (2019).	Coors family; Scaife Foundation; Koch (Lambe Foundation); Donors Capital Fund.
Independence Institute	Radical-right research and campaigning body promoting individual freedom, free market, minimalist government, and gun rights.	Annual revenue US$2.7m (2019)	Castle Rock Foundation; Coors family; Lynne & Harry Bradley Foundation; President, John Caldera.
John Templeton Foundation	Philanthropic research funding on religious/spiritual issues relating to health, happiness and prosperity; on philosophical 'big questions' of science; on individual freedom and free markets.	Annual revenue US$113m (2019); fund worth US$2.81bn (2018).	President, Heather Templeton Dill.
Media Research Center	Distributor of radical-right propaganda, countering liberal bias, denial of climate change.	Annual revenue US$13.5m (2018).	Lynne & Harry Bradley Foundation; Scaife Foundation; Castle Rock Foundation; Founder and president, L. Brent Bozell III.
Mercatus Center	Radical conservative policy research, promoting free market and change.	Annual revenue US$28.9m (2018).	George Mason University; Director, Tyler Cowen.

National Policy Institute	White supremacist; neo-Nazi views.	Raised US$442,482 in donations (2007-2014).	William Regnery II; Richard Spencer.
New Century Foundation	Funding far-right projects e.g. *American Renaissance* journal and genetic racial theories.	Total revenue US$425,306 (2017).	Pioneer Fund (1994-1999).
Paul Manafort	Right-wing lobbyist and political consultant to authoritarian foreign leaders and their agents; former campaign manager to five US presidential Republican candidates including Donald Trump.	Reportedly paid US$60m fees by Ukrainian oligarchs alone, including US$12m undeclared; Jailed 2019 for tax evasion, bank fraud, and money laundering. Pardoned by Trump in December 2020.	Wealthy authoritarian political clients in e.g. Ukraine, Africa, Philippines, Pakistan.
Pioneer Fund	Research on genetic racial theories; advocacy of anti-immigration and eugenics.	US$200k (2003) from sole donor Walter P. Kistler. Subsequent data unavailable.	Walter P. Kistler; Chairman, Richard Lynn.
Sarah Scaife Foundation	Radical-right public policy research; anti-immigrant and anti-Muslim advocacy.	Total revenue US$50m (2018); Investment assets book value US$600m (2018).	Richard Mellon Scaife.
VDare Foundation	Far-right anti-immigrant, nationalist/nativist advocacy.	Raised US$4.8m in donations 2007-2015. Subsequent data unavailable.	Peter Brimelow; Happy Penguins LLC; Fidelity Investments Charitable Gift Fund.

Young America's Foundation (YAF)	Radical-right promotion and promulgation of freedom, free market, minimalist government.	Annual revenue US$33m (2019); Total assets US$81m (2019).	Koch; DeVos; President, Ron Robinson.

Source: compiled from intermediaries' own websites, IRS published data, Charity Navigator, Dun & Bradstreet, FactCheck, Influence Watch, SourceWatch, Southern Poverty Law Center.

References

Ackoff, R. 1974. *Redesigning the Future: A Systems Approach to Societal Problems.* Chichester, UK: John Wiley & Sons.

Adams, J., Clark, M., Ezgrow, L. and Glasgow, G. 2006. "Are Niche Parties Fundamentally Different from Mainstream Parties? The Causes and the Electoral Consequences of Western European Parties' Policy Shifts 1976-1998". *American Journal of Political Science*, 50(3), 513-529.

Adams, J. and Somer-Topcu, Z. 2009. "Policy Adjustments by Parties in Response to Rival Parties' Policy Shifts: Spatial Theory and the Dynamics of Party Competition in Twenty-five Post-war Democracies". *British Journal of Political Science*, 39(04), 825-846.

ADL. 2018. *From Alt-Right to Alt-Lite: Naming the Hate.* Anti-Defamation League. New York: ADL. https://www.adl.org/. [accessed January 31, 2018].

Allchorn, W. 2017. "The Evolving Face of the Contemporary UK Far Right". Paper presented at the Political Studies Association Annual Conference Session 10, University of Strathclyde, Glasgow, April 12, 2017.

Altemeyer, R.A. 1996. *The Authoritarian Specter.* Cambridge, MA: Harvard University Press.

Altemeyer, R.A. 1998. "The Other 'Authoritarian Personality'". In *Advances in Experimental Social Psychology,* edited by M.P. Zanna. Vol. 30, 47-91. New York: Academic Press.

APA. 2013. *Diagnostic and Statistical Manual of Mental Disorders,* 5th edition. Arlington, VA: American Psychiatric Association.

Babiak, P. and Hare, R.D. 2007. *Snakes in Suits: When Psychopaths Go to Work.* London: Harper Collins.

BBC. 2018. "Vote Leave Chief Dominic Cummings Denies Cambridge Analytica Links". *BBC News.* March 23, 2018. https://www.bbc.co.uk/news/uk-politics-43518628. [accessed March 21, 2020].

BBC. 2019. "Leave.EU Founder Confirms he Funded Nigel Farage in Year After Referendum". *BBC News.* May 17, 2019. https://www.bbc.co.uk/news/uk-politics-48315552.

BBC. 2020. "Taking Control: the Dominic Cummings Story". *BBC Two.* March 19, 2020. https://www.bbc.co.uk/programmes/m000ggnm.

Beer, M., Eisenstat, R.A., and Spector, B. 1990. "Why Change Programs Don't Produce Change". *Harvard Business Review*, 68(6), 158-166. https://hbr.org/1990/11/why-change-programs-dont-produce-change.

Birch, K. 2007. "The Totalitarian Corporation?" *Totalitarian Movements and Political Religions*, Vol 8 No 1, 153-161, March 2007.

Bloom, P. and Rhodes, C. 2016. "Corporate Authoritarianism and the New American Anti-democracy". *Common Dreams*. October 23, 2016.

Bloom, P. and Rhodes. C. 2018. *CEO Society: The Corporate Takeover of Everyday Life*. London: Zed Books.

Brooks, N. 2020. "The Tangled Web: Psychopathic Personality, Vulnerability and Victim Selection". In *Corporate Psychopathy: Investigating Destructive Personalities in the Workplace*, edited by K. Fritzon, N. Brooks, and S. Croom. 295-325. Cham, Switzerland: Palgrave Macmillan.

Brooks, N., Fritzon, K. and Croom, S. 2020. "Corporate Psychopathy: Entering the Paradox and Emerging Unscathed". In *Corporate Psychopathy: Investigating Destructive Personalities in the Workplace*, edited by K. Fritzon, N. Brooks, and S. Croom. 327-365. Cham, Switzerland: Palgrave Macmillan.

Brulle, R.J. 2014. "Institutionalizing Delay: Foundation Funding and the Creation of U.S. Climate Change Counter-movement Organizations". *Climatic Change*, Vol 122, 681-694.

Bruning, H. 2016. "Polder and Politics". *Open Democracy*. February 25, 2016. https://www.opendemocracy.net/.

Bryant, N. 2020. "Coronavirus: What this Crisis Reveals about US—and its President". *BBC News*. March 24, 2020. https://www.bbc.co.uk/news/world-us-canada-52012049.

C4. 2018. "Exclusive: Court Documents Claim New Arron Banks Links with Russia". *Channel 4 News*. July 20, 2018. https://www.channel4.com/news/exclusive-court-documents-claim-new-arron-banks-links-with-russia.

C4. 2019a. "Revealed: How Leave.UK Faked Migrant Footage". *Channel 4 News*. April 16, 2019. https://www.channel4.com/news/revealed-how-leave-eu-faked-migrant-footage.

C4. 2019b. "Revealed: Brexit Group Covered Up its Targeting of Right-wing Extremists". *Channel 4 News*. April 17, 2019. https://www.

channel4.com/news/revealed-brexit-group-covered-up-its-targeting-of-right-wing-extremists.

Cadwalladr, C. 2018. "I Made Steve Bannon 'Psychological Warfare Tool': Meet the Data War Whistleblower". *The Guardian*. March 18, 2018.

Cadwalladr, C. 2019. "The Real Reason We Should Fear the Work of Dominic Cummings". *The Guardian*. September 7, 2019. https://theguardian.com/politics/2019/sep/07/smash-and-grab-dominic-cummings-democracy. [accessed March 18, 2020].

Cadwalladr, C. and Graham-Harrison, E. 2018a. "Revealed: 50m Facebook Files Taken in Record Data Breach". *The Observer*. March 18, 2018.

Cadwalladr, C. and Graham-Harrison, F. 2018b. "Cambridge Analytica and Facebook Accused of Misleading MPs over Data Breach". *The Guardian*. March 18, 2018.

Cadwalladr, C. and Jukes, P. 2018. "Arron Banks 'Met Russian Officials Multiple Times Before Brexit Vote'". *The Guardian*. June 9, 2018. https://www.theguardian.com/politics/208/jun/09/arron-banks-russia-brexit-meeting.

Cadwalladr, C., Graham-Harrison, E. and Townsend, M. 2018. "Revealed: Brexit Insider Claims Vote Leave Team May have Breached Spending Limits". *The Guardian*. March 24, 2018. https://theguardian.com/politics/2018/mar/24/brexit-whistleblower-cambridge-analytica-beleave-vote-leave-shamir-sanni. [accessed March 18, 2020].

Caprara, G.V. and Vecchione, M. 2013. "Personality Approaches to Political Behaviour". In *The Oxford Handbook of Political Psychology*. 2nd edition, edited by L. Huddy, D.O. Sears and J.S. Leavy. Oxford: Oxford University Press.

Carmichael, J.T. and Brulle, R.J. 2017. "Elite Cues, Media Coverage, and Public Concern: an Integrated Path Analysis of Public Opinion on Climate Change'. *Journal of Environmental Politics*, Vol 26, 232-252.

Carvalho, J. 2015. "The End of the Strategic Opening? The BNP's Window of Opportunity in the 2000s and its Closure in the 2010s". *Patterns of Prejudice*, 49(3), 271-293.

CDC. 2020a. Covid-19 Infections and Deaths in the US as at September 1, 2020. US Centers for Disease Control. https://www.cdc.gov/covid-data-tracker/index.html#cases.

CDC. 2020b. Covid-19 Infections and Deaths in the US as at November 30, 2020. US Centers for Disease Control. https://www.cdc.gov/covid-data-tracker/index.html#cases.

CDC. 2021a. Covid-19 Infections and Deaths in the US as at January 4, 2021. US Centers for Disease Control. https://www.cdc.gov/covid-data-tracker/index.html#cases.

CDC. 2021b. Covid-19 Infections and Deaths in the US as at January 19, 2021. US Centers for Disease Control. https://www.cdc.gov/covid-data-tracker/index.html#cases.

Charter, D. 2020. "Draining the Swamp is Back". *The Times.* May 9, 2020. Page 38.

Charter, D. 2021. "US Capitol Under Siege". *The Times.* January 7, 2021. Page 1.

Checkland, P. 1999. *Systems Thinking, Systems Practice: Includes a 30-year Retrospective.* Chichester UK: John Wiley & Sons.

CNW. 2019. "Paul Manafort Net Worth". *Celebrity Net Worth.* https://www.cebritynetworth.com/richest-businessmen/lawyers/paul-manafort-net-worth/.

Coles, T.J. 2019. "The Billionaires Behind the Far-right". *Counterpunch.* May 3, 2019. https://www.counterpunch.org/2019/05/03/the-billionaires-behind-the-far-right/. [accessed July 19, 2020].

Coles, T.J. 2020. "How Britain's Ultra-nationalists are being Bankrolled by Ultra-rich Foreigners". *The London Economic.* June 18, 2020. https://www.thelondoneconomic.com/politics/how-britains-ultra-nationalists-are-being-bankrolled-by-ultra-rich-foreigners/18/06/. [accessed July 19, 2020].

Copsey, N. 2010. *The EDL: Challenging Our Country and Our Values of Social Inclusion, Fairness and Equality.* November 2010. Faith Matters Report. www.faith-matters.org.

Cork, T. 2017. "UKIP Donor Likened to National Front after Calling for Muslim Immigration Ban and 'Levelling of Mosques'". *Bristol Post.* July 16, 2017. www.bristolpost.co.uk.

Crouch, C. 2014. "Dealing with Corporate Political Power". *Open Democracy.* February 3, 2014. https://www.opendemocracy.net/en/opendemocracyuk/dealing-with-corporate-political-power/. [accessed April 4, 2020].

Davidson, T. and Berezin, M. 2018. "Britain First and the UK Independence Party: Social Media and Movement-party Dynamics".

Mobilization: An International Quarterly, 23(4), 485-510. DOI 10.17813/1086-671X-23-4-485.

DCMS. 2019. *The Online Harms White Paper: Government Response to the Committee's Twelfth Report.* Received July 23, 2019. Published September 9, 2019. Commons Select Committee. London: UK Parliament. https://www.gov.uk/government/organisations/department-for-digital-culture-media-sport.

DCMS. 2020. "Government Minded to Appoint Ofcom as Online Harms Regulator". Department for Digital, Culture, Media and Sport. February 12, 2020. London: DCMS. https://www.gov.uk/government/organisations/department-for-digital-culture-media-sport.

Deer, B. 2020. *The Doctor Who Fooled the World: Andrew Wakefield's War on Vaccines.* London: Scribe.

Di Stefano, J.N. 2017. "When a Hedge Fund Billionaire 'Buys' Democracy: Magerman on Mercer". *Philadelphia Inquirer.* March 1, 2017. https://www.inquirer.com/philly/blogs/inq-phillydeals/Billionaires_and_Democracy_Magerman_Mercer_Renaissance_Trump_Bannon_Conway.html.

Dror, I.E. and Fraser-Mackenzie, P.A.F. 2008. "Cognitive Biases in Human Perception, Judgement, and Decision Making: Bridging Theory and Real World". In *Criminal Investigative Failures*, edited by Kim Rossmo, 53-67. Abingdon, Oxon UK: Taylor & Francis.

Duckitt, J and Sibley, C.G. 2010. "Differential Effects of Right Wing Authoritarianism and Social Dominance Orientation on Outgroup Attitudes and their Mediation by Threat from and Competitiveness to Outgroups". *Personality and Social Psychology Bulletin*, 32, 1-13.

Egan, M. 2021. "CEO Arrested For Breaching the US Capitol During Trump-Fueled Insurrection". *CNN Business.* January 9, 2021. https://edition.cnn.com/2021/01/09/business/capitol-hill-ceo-arrested-trump/index.html.

Eggert, N. 2017. "Charlottesville: What Made Trump Remarks so Offensive?" *BBC News.* August 16, 2017. https://www.bbc.co.uk/news/world-us-canada-40948812.

Electoral Commission. 2018. *Report on an Investigation In Respect of the Leave.EU Group Limited.* May 11, 2018. London: The Electoral Commission.

Elliott, F., Fisher, L., Swinford, S., and Kenber, B. 2020a. "Cummings: I did not Break Lockdown Rules'. *The Times*. May 26, 2020. Pages 1-2.

Elliott, F., Swinford, S., Hamilton, F. and Courea, E. 2020b. "PM Suffers Poll Slump as Cummings Revolt Grows". *The Times*. May 27, 2020. Pages 1 and 6.

Feldman, M. 2019a. "Evolution of the Radical Right: an Interview with Matthew Feldman". *CARR Insight Blog*, March 6, 2019. London: Centre for Analysis of the Radical Right. https://www.radical rightanalysis.com/2019/03/06/the-evolution-of-the-radical-ri ght-an-interview-with-matthew-feldman/.

Feldman, M. 2019b. "The Radical Right in Britain". *CARR Insight Blog*, June 21, 2019. London: Centre for Analysis of the Radical Right. https://www.radicalrightanalysis.com/2019/06/21/the-radica l-right-in-britain/.

Feldman, M. and Pollard, J. 2016. "The Ideologies and Ideologues of the Radical Right: an Introduction". *Patterms of Prejudice*, Vol 50, issue 4-5, 327-336.

Fisher, L. and Grylls, G. 2020. "Hunt Leads Backbench Revolt as he Rails at 'Clear Breach of Rules'". *The Times*. May 27, 2020. Pages 6-7.

Foges, C. 2020. "Cummings Makes a Mockery of his Own Policy". *The Times*. May 25, 2020. Page 19.

Ford, R. and Hamilton, F. 2020. "Feverish Days and PM's Closest Adviser is not Out of the Woods". *The Times*. May 25, 2020. Pages 4-5.

Fritzon, K., Bailey, C., Croom, S. and Brooks, N. 2016. "Problem Personalities in the Workplace: Development of the Corporate Personality Inventory". In *Psychology and Law in Europe: When West Meets East*. Edited by P.A. Granhag, R. Bull, A. Shaboltas, and E. Dozortseva, 139-166. Boca Raton, FL: CRC/Taylor & Francis.

Furnham, A., Richards, S.C. and Paulhus, D.L. 2013. "The Dark Triad of Personality: a 10 Review". *Social and Personality Psychology Compass*, 7(3), 199-216.

Goodwin, M. 2011. *New British Fascism: Rise of the British National Party*. London: Routledge.

Gottfried, P. 2008. "The Decline and Rise of the Alternative Right". Address to H.L. Mencken Club AGM. November 23, 2008. Reproduced December 1, 2008 in *Taki's Magazine*. www.tkimag.com.

Groendahl, B. 2019. "Austria's Nationalist Vice Chancellor Quits Over Video Scandal". *Bloomberg*. May 18, 2019. https://www.bloom

berg.com/news/articles/2019-05-18/austria-s-fpoe-offers-to-r
eplace-strache-with-hofer-apa-reportsJuly 12. [accessed July 12,
2020].

Hackett, R. 2016. "Here are the Billionaires Backing Trump". *Fortune.*
August 3, 2016. https://www.fortune.com/2016/08/03/trump
-billioanire-backers-list/.

Halliday, J., Beckett, L. and Barr, C. 2018. "Tommy Robinson: from Local Loud Mouth to International Far-right Poster Boy". *The
Guardian.* December 7, 2018. https://www.theguardian.com/uk
-news/2018/dec/07/tommy-robinson-the-us-money-behind-t
he-far-right-mouthpiece. [accessed July 19, 2020].

Hare, R.D. 1999. *Without Conscience: The Disturbing World of the Psychopaths Among Us.* First published 1993. New York: Guilford
Press.

Hare, R.D. 2003. *Manual for the Revised Psychopathy Checklist*, 2nd edition. Toronto, Canada: Multi-Health Systems.

Hare, R.D. 2016. "Psychopathy, the PCL-R, and Criminal Justice: Some
New Findings and Current Issues". *Canadian Psychology*, Vol
57(1), Feb 2016, 21-34.

Hirstein, W. 2013. "What is a Psychopath?". *Psychology Today* blog col-
umn. January 30, 2013.

HoC. 2018. *Disinformation and 'Fake News': Interim Report.* Digital,
Culture, Media and Sports Committee. Report HC 363. July 29,
2018. London: House of Commons.

Horn, R.E. and Weber, R.P. 2007. *New Tools for Resolving Wicked Problems: Mess Mapping and Resolution Mapping Processes.* Water-
town, MA: Strategy Kinetics LLC. https://www.strategykinetics.
com/New_Tools_For_Resolving_Wicked_Problems.pdf. [accessed
August 5, 2020].

Jackson, P. 2016. *Colin Jordan and Britain's neo-Nazi Movement: Hitler's Echo.* London: Bloomsbury.

Jones, D.N. and Paulhus, D.L. 2011. "Differentiating the Dark Triad
with the Interpersonal Circumplex". In *Handbook of Interpersonal Psychology: Theory, Research, Assessment and Therapeutic
Intervention*, edited by L.M. Horowitz and S. Strack. Hoboken,
New Jersey: Wiley.

Kahan, D.M., Jamieson, K.H., Landrum, A.R. et al. 2017. "Culturally Antagonistic Memes and the Zika Virus: an Experimental Test". *Journal of Risk Research*, 20(1), 1-40.

Keatinge, T., Keen, F. and Izenman, K. 2019. "Fundraising for Rightwing Extremist Movements: How they Raise Funds and How to Counter it". *RUSI Journal*, Vol 164 No. 2. May 31, 2019. Royal United Services Institute, Centre for Financial Crime and Security Studies. London: RUSI.

Kelly, B. 2020. "Cummings Affair Vindicates Johnson's Critics and Destroys the Government's Moral Authority'. *Reaction Life.* May 26, 2020. https://www.reaction.life. [accessed May 26, 2020]

Kenber, B. 2020. "'I Tried to do the Right Thing but Reasonable People May Disagree'". *The Times.* May 26, 2020. Pages 4-5.

Kessler, G. 2020. "DeVos's Claim that Children are 'Stoppers' of Covid-19'. *The Washington Post.* July 23, 2020. https://www.washingtonpost.com/politics/2020/07/23/devoss-claim-that-children-are-stoppers-covid-19/. [accessed August 3, 2020].

Kessler, G., Rizzo, S. and Kelly, M. 2020. "Trump is Averaging More Than 50 False or Misleading Claims a Day". *The Washington Post.* October 22, 2020. https://www.washingtonpost.com/politics/2020/10/22/president-trump-is-averaging-more-than-50-false-or-misleading-claims-day/. [accessed November 11, 2020].

Kiehl, K.A. and Buchholtz, J.W. 2010. "Inside the Mind of a Psychopath". *Scientific American Mind,* Sept/Oct, 22-29.

Klitzman, R. 2016. "Trump and Questions about Sociopathy and Narcissism". *Psychology Today.* October 30, 2016. https://www.psychologytoday.com/intl/blog/am-i-my-genes/201610/trump-questions-about-sociopathy-and-narcissism.

Kotch, A. 2017. "How the Right-wing Koch and DeVos Families are Funding Hate Speech on College Campuses Across the U.S.". *AlterNet.* April 18, 2017. https://alternet.org/2017/04/rightwing-billionaires-are-intentionally-funding-hate-speech-college-campuses/. [accessed March 20, 2020].

Kunzelman, M. 2016. "White Nationalist Groups Raise Millions with Tax-exempt Charities". *Associated Press.* December 22, 2016. https://www.apnews.com/ae1c8163ac574bb3bd1f3facfca5fb83.

Lawrence, F., Evans, R., Pegg, D. et al. 2019. "How the Right's Radical Thinktanks Reshaped the Conservative Party". *The Guardian.*

November 29, 2017. https://www.theguardian.com/politics/20 19/nov/29/how-the-rights-radical-thinktanks-reshaped-the-co nservative-party. [accessed March 18, 2020].

Lee, B. 2019. *Overview of the Far-Right.* Paper commissioned by the Commission for Countering Extremism and funded by the Centre for Research and Evidence on Security Threats. July 19, 2019. Lancaster University: CREST.

Litvinov, A. 2019. "DeVos Swipes at Public School Educators as She Defends Privatization Agenda to Media". *Education Votes.* May 8, 2019. Washington DC: National Education Association. https://educationvotes.nea.org/2019/05/08/devos-swipes-at-public-school-educators-as-she-defends-privatization-agenda-to-media/. [accessed August 3, 2020].

Lyons, M.N. 2017a. *Ctrl-Alt-Delete: The Origins and Ideology of the Alternative Right.* Somerville, MA: Political Research Associates.

Lyons, M.N. 2017b. *Insurgent Supremacists: The US Far Right's Challenge to State and Empire.* Oakland, Ca: PM Press.

MacDonald, K.B. 2002. *Culture of Critique: An Evolutionary Analysis of Jewish Involvement in Twentieth Century Intellectual Movements.* 2nd edition. Bloomington IN: Author House.

MacDonald, K.B. 2004. "Understanding Jewish Influences: a Study in Ethnic Activism". *Occidental Quarterly,* November 2004. The Charles Martel Society.

Macklin, G. 2019. *Failed Fuhrers: A History of Britain's Extreme Right.* Abingdon, Oxon: Routledge.

Martin, I. 2020. "PM has Proved his Dependence on Aide". *The Times.* May 26, 2020. Page 5.

Mason, R. 2014. "PM Backs Michael Gove but Suggests Former Aide was a 'Career Psychopath". *The Guardian.* June 18, 2014. https://theguardian.com/politics/2014/jun/18/david-cameron-dominic-cummings-career-psychopath. (accessed March 21, 2020).

Masters, J. 2018. "Anti-Islam Activist Tommy Robinson Appointed as UKIP Adviser". November 23, 2018. *CNN.* https://edition.cnn.com/2018/11/23/uk/tommy-robinson-ukip-gbr-intl/index.html.

Mayer, J. 2016. *Dark Money: The Hidden History of the Billionaires Behind the Rise of the Radical Right.* New York: Penguin Books.

Mayer, J. 2017. "The Reclusive Hedge-fund Tycoon Behind the Trump Presidency", *The New Yorker*, March 17, 2017. https://www.new yorker.com/magazine/2017/03/27/the-reclusive-hedge-fund-tycoon-behind-the-trump-presidency.

McCrae, R.R. and Costa, P.T. 2003. *Personality in Adulthood: A Five Factor Theory Perspective.* 2nd edition. New York: Guilford Press.

Michael, G. 2003. *Confronting Right-Wing Extremism and Terrorism in the USA.* Abingdon, Oxon UK: Routledge.

Michael, G. 2006. *The Enemy of My Enemy: The Alarming Convergence of Militant Islam and the Extreme Right.* Lawrence KA: University Press of Kansas.

Michael, G. 2008. *The American Far Right.* Gainesville, FL: University of Florida.

Michael, G. (ed). 2014. *Extremism in America.* Gainesville, FL: University of Florida.

Michael, G. 2016. "The Seeds of the Alt-Right, America's Emergent Right-wing Populist Movement". *The Conversation*, November 23, 2016. http://theconversation.com.

Michael, G. 2017. "The Rise of the Alt-Right and the Politics of Polarization in America". *Skeptic Magazine*, February 1, 2017. Altadena, Ca: The Skeptics Society.

Michaels, D. 2020. *The Triumph of Doubt—Dark Money and the Science of Deception.* Oxford UK: Oxford University Press.

Mintzberg, H. 1994a. *The Rise and Fall of Strategic Planning: Reconceiving Roles for Planning, Plans, Planners.* New York: Free Press. https://mintzberg.org/books/rise-and-fall-strategic-planning.

Mintzberg, H. 1994b. "Rethinking Strategic Planning, Part 1: Pitfalls and Fallacies". *Long Range Planning,* 27(3), 12-21. https://mintzberg.org/articles/rethinking-strategic-planning.

Mondon, A. and Winter, A. 2018. "Understanding the Mainstreaming of the Far Right". August 26, 2018. *openDemocracy.* https://www.opendemocracy.net/en/can-europe-make-it/understanding-mainstreaming-of-far-right/.

Mondon, A. and Winter, A. 2020. *Reactionary Democracy—How Racism and the Populist Far Right Became Mainstream.* London: Verso.

Moore, M. 2020. "Cummings Tried to Push Me Down the Stairs, Businessman Tells BBC". *The Times.* March 19, 2020. Page 23.

Nagle, A. 2017. *Kill All Normies: Online Culture Wars from 4Chan and Tumblr to Trump and the Alt-Right.* Arlesford, Hants UK: Zero Books.

Neiwert, D. 2017. *Alt-America: The Rise of the Radical Right in the Age of Trump.* London: Verso.

NIC. 2017. *Background to "Assessing Russian Activities and Intentions in Recent US Elections": The Analytic Process and Cyber Incident Attribution.* Intelligence Community Assessment Report ICA 2017-01D. 6 January 2017. Office of the Director of National Intelligence. National Intelligence Council. Washington DC.

NWP. 2019. "Paul Manafort Net Worth". *Net Worth Post.* September 29, 2019. https://www.networthpost.org/paul-manafort-net-worth.

Oklobdzija, S. 2019. "Public Positions, Private Giving: Dark Money and Political Donors in the Digital Age". *Research & Politics.* February 25, 2019. https://doi.org/10.11777/2053168019832475. [accessed May 21, 2020].

Özvatan, Ö. And Forchtner, B. 2019. "The Far-right Alternative für Deutschland in Germany: Towards a Happy Ending?". In *The New Authoritarianism Vol 2: A Risk Analysis of the European Alt-Right Phenomenon,* edited by Alan Waring, 199-225. Stuttgart: Ibidem Verlag.

Parker, G. 2020. "Dominic Cummings Has 'Done' Brexit. Now He Plans to Reinvent Politics". *Financial Times Magazine,* Life and Arts. January 16, 2020. https://www.ft.com/content/0bf8a910-372e-11ea-a6d3-9a26f8c3cba4. [accessed March 19, 2020].

Pavia, W. 2020. "New York's Overwhelmed Doctors Complain of 'Wartime Conditions'". *The Times.* March 28, 2020. Pages 16-17.

Paxton, R. 2018a. "The Alt-Right and Resurgent US Nationalism". In *The New Authoritarianism Vol 1: A Risk Analysis of the US Alt-Right Phenomenon,* edited by Alan Waring, 85-103. Stuttgart: Ibidem Verlag.

Paxton, R. 2018b. "The Alt-Right, Post-truth, Fake News, and the Media". In *The New Authoritarianism Vol 1: A Risk Analysis of the US Alt-Right Phenomenon,* edited by Alan Waring, 337-361. Stuttgart: Ibidem Verlag.

Pegg, D. and Campbell, I. 2018. "Arron Banks Company Provided £12m of Services to Leave.EU". *The Guardian.* May, 9, 2018. https://

www.theguardian.com/politics/2018/may/09/arron-banks-company-provided-12m-of-services-to-leaveeu.

Peters, T and Waterman, R.H. 1982. *In Search of Excellence: Lessons Learned from America's Best-Run Companies.* London: Harper & Row.

Pilkington, H. 2016. *Loud and Proud: Passion and Politics in the English Defence League.* Manchester: Manchester University Press.

Posner, S. 2019. "Right Makes Might". *The New Republic.* March 25, 2019. https://newrepublic.com/article/153276/republicans-congress-courted-nativist-authoritarian-leaders.

Post, J.M. 2015. *Narcissism and Politics: Dreams of Glory.* Cambridge: Cambridge University Press.

Rachman, J. 2020. "Take Back Control? Cummings Scandal Reveals Crisis of Accountability". *Reaction Life.* May 26, 2020. https://www.reaction.life. [accessed May 26, 2020].

Rahman, K. 2018. "Arron Banks is Ordered to Pay £163,000 Tax Bill on £1m Ukip Donation'. *Mail Online.* November 6, 2018.

Ramachandran, S., Berzon, A. and Ballhaus, R. 2021. "Jan. 6 Rally Funded by Top Trump Donor, Helped by Alex Jones, Organizers Say". *Wall Street Journal.* January 30, 2021. https://www.wsj.com/articles/jan-6-rally-funded-by-top-trump-donor-helped-by-alex-jones-organizers-say-11612012063?st=yckxwlyitkb0ozr&reflink=share_mobilewebshare. [accessed February 1, 2021].

Rana, M. and Clegg, R. 2018. "Arron Banks: Brexit Donor Paid Thousands to Lesotho Government Minister". *BBC News.* July 24, 2018. https://www.bbc.co.uk/news/uk-44939665.

Richardson, J. 2017. *British Fascism: A Discourse-Historical Analysis.* Stuttgart: Ibidem Verlag.

Rifkind, H. 2020. "Can't Cummings See the Damage He's Done?". *The Times.* May 26, 2020. Page 23.

Ross, A.R. and Bevensee, E. 2020. "Confronting the Rise of Eco-fascism Means Grappling with Complex Systems". *CARR Research Insight Series*, 2020.3. July 2020. London: Centre for Analysis of the Radical Right. https://www.radicalrightanalysis.com/2020/07/07/carr-research-insight-series-confronting-the-rise-of-eco-fascism-means-grappling-with-complex-systems/. [accessed August 5, 2020].

Shermer, M. 2018. "For the Love of Science—Combating Science Denial with Science Pleasure". *Skeptic.* January 2018, page 73. www.scientificamerican.com.

Sibley, C.G. and Duckitt, J. 2008. "Personality and Prejudice: a Meta-analysis and Theoretical Review". *Personality and Social Psychology Review*, 12, 248-279.

Sidanius, J. and Pratto, F. 1999. *Social Dominance: An Intergroup Theory of Social Hierarchy and Oppression.* Cambridge: Cambridge University Press.

Simon, D.R. 2018. *Elite Deviance,* 11th edition. Abingdon, Oxon: Routledge/Taylor & Francis.

Singer, T. 2017. "Trump and the American Selfie: Archetypal Defences of the Group Spirit". In *A Clear and Present Danger: Narcissism in the Era of President Trump*, edited by L. Cruz and S. Buser, 17-48. Asheville NC: Chiron Publications.

Sloan, A. and Campbell, I. 2017. "How did Arron Banks Afford Brexit?". *Open Democracy.* October 19, 2017. https://www.opendemocra cy.net/en/dark-money-investigations/how-did-arron-banks-af ford-brexit/.

Smith, D. 2019. "Paul Manafort Given Seven-year Prison Term and Severe Rebuke from Judge". *The Guardian.* March 13, 2019. https://www.theguardian.com/us-news/2019/mar/13/paul-manafort-second-sentencing-hearing-donald-trump.

Spencer, R. (ed). 2012. *The Great Erasure: The Reconstruction of White Identity.* Edited by R. Spencer. Radix Vol 1. National Policy Institute. Arlington, VA: Washington Summit Publishers.

SPLC. 2020. "William H. Regnery II. Profile". Southern Poverty Law Center. https://www.splcenter.org/fighting-hate/extremist-file s/individual/william-h-regnery-ii. [accessed March 23, 2020].

Sullum, J. 2019. "Here is What Paul Manafort was Convicted of Doing". *Reason.* March 11, 2019. https://www.reason.com/2019/03/11 /here-is-what-paul-manafort-was-convicted/.

Svrluga, S. 2017. "'We Will Keep Coming Back': Richard Spencer Leads Another Torchlight March in Charlottesville". *Washington Post.* October 9, 2017. https://www.washingtonpost.com/news/grad e-point/wp/2017/10/07/richard-spencer-leads-another-torch light-march-in-charlottesville/.

Swinford, S. 2020. "Cummings Acted Like any Father, Insists PM". *The Times*. May 25, 2020. Pages 1-2.

Swinford, S. and Wright, O. 2020. "Cummings Forced Out in Purge of Brexiteers". *The Times*. November 14, 2020. Pages 1 and 2.

Swinn, J. 2019. "Shillman/Mercer/Rosenwald Alt-media Network". Alternative Media Infographic. Jon Swinn blogspot. March 8, 2019. https://theworldneedsthisman.blogspot.com/2019/03/bob-shillman-robert-mercer-nina.html. [accessed July 3, 2020].

Taylor, J. 1993. *Paved with Good Intention: the Failure of Race Relations in Contemporary America*. New York: Carroll and Graf Publishers.

Turner-Graham, E. 2019. "The Politics of Cultural Despair: Britain's Extreme Right". In *The New Authoritarianism Vol 2: A Risk Analysis of the European Alt-Right Phenomenon*, edited by Alan Waring, 121-147. Stuttgart: Ibidem Verlag.

UN. 1948. *Universal Declaration of Human Rights*. General Assembly Resolution 217A. December 10, 1948. Paris: United Nations General Assembly.

USDoJ. 2018a. *Indictment: US v. Internet Research Agency LLC et al.* Case 1:18-cr-00032-DLF. 16 February 2018. US Department of Justice. District of Columbia. Washington DC: USDoJ.

USDoJ. 2018b. "Grand Jury Indicts 12 Russian Intelligence Officers for Hacking Offenses Related to the 2016 Election". *Justice News*. July 13, 2018. Office of Public Affairs. US Department of Justice. District of Columbia. Washington DC: USDoJ.

van der Valk, I. 2019. "Wilders' Party for Freedom and the Dutch Alt-Right". In *The New Authoritarianism Vol 2: A Risk Analysis of the European Alt-Right Phenomenon*, edited by Alan Waring, 251-272 (263-264). Stuttgart: Ibidem Verlag.

Verney, K. 2018. "The Alt-Right, Immigration, Mass Migration and Refugees". In *The New Authoritarianism Vol 1: A Risk Analysis of the US Alt-Right Phenomenon*, edited by A. Waring. 247-271. Stuttgart: Ibidem Verlag.

Vickers, G. 1983a. *Human Systems are Different*. London: Harper & Row.

Vickers, G. 1983b. *The Art of Judgement: A Study of Policy Making*. London: Harper & Row.

von Bertalanffy, L. 1972. "The History and Status of General Systems Theory". *Academy of Management Journal*, 15(4), 407-426.

Walker, P. 2019. "Arron Banks Gave "£450,000 Funding to Nigel Farage After Brexit Vote"'. *The Guardian.* May 17, 2019. https://www.theguardian.com/politics/2019/may/16/arron-banks-allegedly-gave-450000-funding-to-nigel-farage-after-brexit-vote.

Walton, M. 2007a. "Leadership Toxicity—an Inevitable Affliction of Organizations?". *Organizations and People,* 14(1), 19-27.

Walton, M. 2007b. "Toxic Leadership". In *Leadership: The Key Concepts,* edited by J. Gosling and A. Marturano. Oxford: Routledge.

Walton, M. 2010. "Senior Executives: Behavioural Dynamics". *HRM Review,* August, 10-18.

Walton, M. 2020a. "Leadership Toxicity: Our Own Corporate 'Covid-Tox' Pandemic". *Effective Executive.* IUP Publications, Vol XXIII, (2), 7-11.

Walton, M. 2020b. "Tackling Leadership Toxicity: An HRM Priority". *HRM Review.* IUP Publications, Vol XVI (3), June, 25-34.

Walton, M. 2020c. "Identify, Track and Trace Disruptive Workplace Behaviour: Towards Enhancing Organisational Performance". *HRM Review.* IUP Publications, Vol XVI (4), December, 1-7.

Waring, A. 1996. *Practical Systems Thinking.* Aldershot UK: Thomson/Cengage.

Waring, A. (ed). 2018a. *The New Authoritarianism Vol 1: A Risk Analysis of the US Alt-Right Phenomenon,* edited by A. Waring. Stuttgart: Ibidem Verlag.

Waring, A. 2018b. "The Alt-Right, Environmental Issues, and Global Warming". In *The New Authoritarianism Vol 1: A Risk Analysis of the US Alt-Right Phenomenon,* edited by A. Waring, 273-301. Stuttgart: Ibidem Verlag.

Waring, A. (ed). 2019a. *The New Authoritarianism Vol 2: A Risk Analysis of the European Alt-Right Phenomenon,* edited by A. Waring. Stuttgart: Ibidem Verlag.

Waring, A. 2019b. "Jekyll-and-Hyde: What Creates a Far-right Supporter?". Part 1 December 12, 2019, Part 2 December 13, 2019. *CARR Insight* blog. London: Centre for Analysis of the Radical Right. https://www.radicalrightanalysis.com/2019/12/12/jekyll-and-hyde-what-creates-a-far-right-supporter-part-1/; https://www.radicalrightanalysis.com/2019/12/13/jekyll-and-hyde-what-creates-a-far-right-supporter-part-2/.

Waring, A. 2019c. "Brexit and the Alt-Right Agenda in the UK". In *The New Authoritarianism Vol 2: A Risk Analysis of the European Alt-Right Phenomenon,* edited by Alan Waring, 95-120. Stuttgart: Ibidem Verlag.

Waring, A. 2019d. "The New Authoritarianism and the Glorification of Amoral Calculation". *CARR Insight Blog.* October 1, 2019. London: Centre for Analysis of the Radical Right. https://www.radic alrightanalysis.com/2019/10/01/the-new-authoritarianism-an d-the-glorification-of-amoral-calculation/.

Waring, A. 2019e. "The Five Pillars of Occupational Safety and Health in a Context of Authoritarian Socio-Political Climates". *Safety Science,* 117, 152-163.

Waring, A. 2020a. "Can the Radical Right's Reductionist Narrative Withstand Real World Complexity?" *Fair Observer.* April 24, 2020. https://www.fairobserver.com/region/north_america/ alan-waring-radical-right-reductionism-narratives-donald-tru mp-politics-news-14311/.

Waring, A. 2020b. "Can the Radical Right's Reductionist Narrative Withstand Real World Complexity?" *CARR Insight Blog,* July 3, 2020. London: Centre for Analysis of the Radical Right.

Waring, A. and Paxton, R. 2018. "Psychological Aspects of the Alt-Right Phenomenon". In *The New Authoritarianism Vol 1: A Risk Analysis of the US Alt-Right Phenomenon,* edited by Alan Waring, 53-82. Stuttgart: Ibidem Verlag.

Waring, A. and Paxton, R. 2019. "Potential Strategies to Limit the Alt-Right Threat". In *The New Authoritarianism Vol 2: A Risk Analysis of the European Alt-Right Phenomenon,* edited by Alan Waring, 375-411 (387-389). Stuttgart: Ibidem Verlag.

Weigel, D. 2016. "The 'Alt Right' Finds a Home Inside the Republican Party". *The Washington Post.* July 21, 2016.

Wilson, B. and van Haperen, K. 2015. *Soft Systems Thinking, Methodology and the Management of Change.* London: Palgrave Macmillan.

Wodak, R. and Rheindorf, M. 2019. "The Austrian Freedom Party". In *The New Authoritarianism Vol 2: A Risk Analysis of the European Alt-Right Phenomenon,* edited by Alan Waring, 171-197 (177-190). Stuttgart: Ibidem Verlag.

Wolff, M. 2018. *Fire and Fury—Inside the Trump White House.* London: Little Brown.

WP. 2020. "Paul Manafort Net Worth". *Wealthy Persons.* https://www.
wealthypersons.com/paul-manafort-net-worth-2020-2021/.

Yiannopoulos, M. 2017. *Dangerous.* Self-published. New York: Dangerous Books.

YouTube. 2017. "Don't Ban the Burka, Ban Muslims Instead". *BBC 1.*
Andrew Neil's Sunday Politics. April 23, 2017. https://www.you
tube.com/watch?v=t01XtLvJxU.

Zeffman, H. 2020. "Trump Backs 'Untested' Plant Extract as Treatment". *The Times.* August 18, 2020. Page 15.

Zeffman, H. 2021. "Smashing Glass and Gunfire as Mob Shames US Democracy". *The Times.* January 7, 2012. Pages 2-3.

Zmigrod, L., Eisenberg, I.W., Bissett, P.G. et al. 2021. "The Cognitive
and Perceptual Correlates of Ideological Attitudes: a Data-Driven
Approach". *Philosophical Transactions of the Royal Society B*, Vol
376, Issue 1822. April 12, 2021. Published online February 22,
2021. doi.org/10.1098/rstb.2020.0424

Chapter 2:
Zombieland Revisited Part 1: Genesis of Social and Psychological Aspects of the Absurd, State and Corporate Authoritarianism

By Antony A. Vass[1]

Abstract

This chapter, considered in tandem with chapter 3, is part of a whole that examines the authoritarian mindset, which in an almost religious fundamentalist manner becomes intrusive, abusive and repressive and places democratic values and the democratic experience under serious threat. This mindset finds expression in interpersonal relationships, corporate business, political ideology and processes, media communications, and state policy. The discussion is a critique of both authoritarian values and democracy's failures to deal with its broader structural and institutional characteristics, which provide a fertile ground for despotic relationships to grow and prosper. A variety of interdependent social and psychological settings are critically examined and evaluated. These settings destabilise personal, social, economic, and political relationships; facilitate unequal and oppressive power relationships; put democracy to shame; and help explain why the authoritarian juggernaut is gathering momentum. Wealthy corporations, oligarchs, Establishment figures, politicians and governments collaborate among themselves and with radical-right figures to pursue mutual goals and interests at the expense of large sectors of the population and to the detriment of democracy. Maintaining and widening inequalities and cultivating an authoritarian milieu are part of their strategy. This is despite their frequent assertions that they are empowering people, providing unfettered freedoms, and protecting their democratic interests and human rights. This chapter critically considers these inequalities which define the structural, institutional and social relations that act as a springboard for despotism. A

---

[1]   See contributor affiliations and biography, pages 527-528.

conceptual strategy for more equity is offered, which can help create a more viable and inclusive democracy.

Key words: mindset, democracy, authoritarianism, oppression, normalisation, inequality

The Authoritarian Mindset

This and the next chapter are not about 'zombies', fictional post-apocalyptic zombie films, or other similar depictions of a world taken over by moronic beings. 'Zombieland' is a metaphor for the emerging authoritarian values and practices in Western democracies (Gessen 2020; Waring 2018a; 2019) which are transforming democratic institutions into authoritarian ones that risk creating singular masters and obedient servants.

Authoritarian values are dominated by arrogance and a blind belief by those who subscribe to them that they are the centre of the universe. Anything different or antithetical to that perspective is heretical and must be either converted or eliminated. It is a mindset full of self-indulgence, self-praise and self-righteousness. It expresses hostility to alternative beliefs or opinions (Herriot & Scott-Jackson 2002) and cultivates resistance to anything that deviates from its values, norms, scriptures, dogmas or ideologies. This mindset preaches suspicion and opposition to diversity and inclusivity. It engenders racial animosity, prejudice and bigotry. It promotes acceptance of the belief that it is not only right to dominate others but also right to be submissive and obedient to higher authority. It requires commitment, conformity and loyalty. It represents a radical, almost cult-like culture not so dissimilar to religious fundamentalism.

This mindset exhibits an aversion to evidence, argument or reasoning. It builds on falsehoods, conspiracies and an alternative reality. It admires and plays on toughness and jingoism. It incorporates highly rigid and compartmentalised thinking. It communicates in simple one-dimensional exchanges and rhetoric. It supports a relentless expansion of strict policing and rides high on a law-and-order ticket. It loves tax cuts for high earners and considers inequalities as a natural, if not divine, process that promotes and bestows rights and duties about hard work and achievement. It divides individuals and groups into the deserving and the undeserving, Achievement, recognition, status, privilege and material success are assumed as justified entitlements by the deserving. It creates a dichotomy between "winners/predators" and "losers/victims" (Waring 2018b, 308). Engaging with this mindset is like "arguing with zombies" (Krugman 2020; see also Kaiser 2020; Mallaby 2020).

In the broader political landscape, this mindset has a precise modus vivandi that taps the worst personal fears of an audience and promotes its authoritarian make-up with a torrent of patriotic slogans and a nationalist agenda to win over the popular vote. It builds on the claim that chaos and disorder are caused by an incorrigible lot of liberals, anarchists, leftists, communists and broader criminal elements—often lumped together and branded 'socialists'. So, a strong and uncompromising leader with a devoted base of believers is presented as a basic requirement for the protection, preservation, maintenance or restoration of order, tradition and greatness. The leader, who rises to the occasion and speaks the language of this mindset, expects to draw applause, achieve an idol-like cult status, and become a role-model for others to follow. The leader demands compliance and the unconditional support and loyalty of a strong base. Ardent believers offer such devotion because their leader is perceived as the embodiment of truth and inspiration.

Consider, for example, the following statements:

> "As long as there are peoples on this earth, there will be nations against nations and they will be forced to protect their vital rights in the same way as the individual is forced to protect his rights. One is either the hammer or the anvil...It is our purpose to prepare...for the role of the hammer. ..We will take every step ...which increases the strength of our people. We...will dash anyone to pieces who should dare hinder us in this undertaking..." (1)

> "Nothing is possible unless one will commands, a will which has to be obeyed by others, beginning at the top and ending only at the very bottom...I will likewise be obeyed when I must take command." (2).

> "...And...as we meet here tonight, there is a growing danger that threatens every blessing our ancestors fought so hard for, struggled, they bled to secure. Our nation is witnessing a merciless campaign to wipe out our history, defame our heroes, erase our values, and indoctrinate our children...One of their weapons is cancel culture...We will not be silenced...It is time to plant our flag...This country will be everything...that our enemies fear...My fellow citizens, [our] destiny is in our sights." (3)

> "If our opponents prevail no one will be safe in our country, and no one will be spared...I'm the only thing standing between the American Dream and

total anarchy, madness, and chaos...it sounds so egotistical...But there was no other way to say it...I'm the one..." (4)

The speeches come from two distinct and unrelated individuals in different historical periods, but they are united in their core message by the language of authoritarianism. The state must grow stronger and must dominate. It can only happen with a strong leader at the helm who must command obedience.

When one considers the sources of those speeches, the discomfort grows. The first two extracts (1) and (2) come from Adolf Hitler's speeches in Munich, March 15, 1929 and Nuremberg, September 14, 1935 respectively. The third (3) and fourth (4) are extracts from Donald Trump's speeches at Mount Rushmore July 4, 2020 and the Council for National Policy Meeting, August 21, 2020 respectively.

Of course, it is not suggested that Adolf Hitler and Donald Trump share much in common other than the language of authoritarianism. The first passionately espoused the merits of authoritarianism and succeeded in building such a state. He then moved on in deed to drag the world to the Holocaust. The other exploited passion and nationalism to promote a particular world-view about selfishness, strong leadership and domination to pursue his personal, albeit authoritarian, agenda. He succeeded in creating a divided, polarised and violent country with many neighbourhoods becoming "battle spaces" (Mullen 2020). Simultaneously, he managed to increase his executive powers by chipping away at the constitution (Goldberg 2020).

What is of specific relevance here is the type of language used to justify the deeds undertaken and the deeds which may follow. The two cases share a steadfast view of the world that challenges difference and diversity, criticism, and non-compliance. The dominant fundamentalist value conveyed in a simple, common-sense statement is that a strong nation led by strong leadership is the only way to fend off domestic and external threats. A tough monopolistic type of leadership is presented as the avatar of the people's mind and soul, their anger and frustrations, their needs and solutions to them.

Language—in a spoken, written or non-verbal manner—communicates and defines social reality. As W.I. Thomas, a forefather of the theoretical perspective of symbolic interactionism (cf. Blumer 1969) observed, "If [people] define situations as real, they are real in their consequences". Words and symbols matter. As part of communication, they confirm and reinforce meanings that are attached to our understanding of our social world. They determine how we act and react in social encounters and how we interpret our social experiences. However, language is not just about communication. Language is also a filter of our perceptions and thoughts about the world around us. Simultaneously, as we engage in the process of filtration and communication, language becomes a constructor, enhancer and modifier of those perceptions and thoughts (Benitez-Burraco 2017).

Therefore, the language which inspires the insidious spread of autocracy is a craft and an all-embracing process. It involves a combination of nostalgia for the great past and tradition; the rejection of liberalism and modernity as corrupt and corrupting; the rejection of science, intellectualism and reasoning and their replacement with absurd simplicity and irrationalism; an obsession with selective populism that berates diversity, difference and multiculturalism; the skilful use and manipulation of the media, social media and other channels of communication to create fear, suspicion, confusion, disorder and distraction through misinformation, disinformation and conspiracy theories; the castigation of the liberal press as an instrument of political subversion and the enemy of the people; the constant undermining of an independent judiciary; a challenge to the legitimacy of the electoral process and the existence of competing political parties; the formation of domestic and external coalitions with similarly-minded political leaders, groups and interests—from powerful corporations, political parties, media and pressure groups to other existing or emerging authoritarian leaders. Moreover, as these authoritarian values take root, despotic leaders—whether openly or insidiously— claim 'legitimacy' for an extension of their powers and term in office. The post-US 2020 election debacle of challenges to the legitimacy of the results (Hemmer 2020) is but an example of the drift towards this despotic mentality which claims a monopolistic entitlement to govern and rule by unconditional obedience.

This authoritarian mindset with its choice and deployment of a particular form of language and vocabulary, in combination with other well-rehearsed tactics which create, spread and consolidate its base, may be usefully summarised by utilising Inglis' (2019) "10-point checklist" for autocrats, albeit in an adapted and modified form:

(1) The extension and gradual dominance of executive power over other institutions that leads to the destabilisation and reduction of checks and balances.

(2) A gradual repression of dissent and the erosion of accountability.

(3) An expansion and retention of oligarchical corporate elites, radical-right groups and political parties which form coalitions that support authoritarian leaders.

(4) The enhancement and use of populism and nationalism.

(5) The control and manipulation of information by distorting facts and craftily blending propaganda with misinformation and disinformation.

(6) The definition of the opposition as enemies of the state and consequently rendering them as the enemies of the people.

(7) The manipulation and the covert sabotaging of free expression and free elections.

(8) The manufacture and amplification of internal and external threats to galvanise popular support for the extension of the leader's powers and the enactment of more stringent and oppressive measures.

(9) The formation of coalitions of similarly minded rulers whether from the radical left or the radical right as long as the authoritarian mindset is spread and shared from continent to continent. Such coalitions do not arise merely out of membership by the authoritarian rulers to their own exclusive despotic club but also through disciples who vigorously advocate and defend the shift to autocratic rule. These are either individuals or corporations.

(10) The skilful dissemination, exchange and sharing of propaganda and information by autocratic rulers and states assisted by exploiting the very democratic value of free speech, scholarly works, international and intergovernmental information exchange platforms.

What follows is a detailed look at this mindset as it is expressed in a variety of personal and social contexts. These contexts and their relationships put democracy to shame and explain why as an open political system it is on the run whilst a menacing authoritarian juggernaut is gathering speed. In this chapter, they include inequality and its destabilising personal and social consequences. In the next chapter, the analysis continues with an examination of corruption and crimes of the powerful; the rise of technology, the militarisation of the police, the expansion of surveillance and the broader means of social control; the rise of despotic leaders, their strong base of followers, personality traits and personality disorders; and emerging new forms of oppression which undermine democracy and allow authoritarianism to take root. The dangers that lie ahead are discussed, and throughout suggestions are offered as to how democracy might survive. As is emphasised, these critically assessed social and psychological contexts and their emerging relationships, while covered on an individual basis, are all interconnected and interdependent.

The discussion is unapologetically and unreservedly a critique of the rise of despotic values, authoritarian relationships, and a state-and-corporate fundamentalist culture which is aided and abetted by radical-right politics. It focuses on, and draws its arguments from, the socio-economic and political scene in the US and UK.

Before critical discussion, a number of background concepts and topics require attention. First, setting the record straight about the type of democracy that is defended, and noting that democracy is not a perfect system. Second, that democracy's strengths can also be its weaknesses that succeed in creating unequal and oppressive relationships, which are then accommodated and allowed to exist. Here, issue is taken with the concept of 'the tyranny of the majority'. Third, that democracy has a capacity to 'normalise' and make undesirable issues appear acceptable and normal. Fourth, that authoritarianism is not an unchallengeable monolith. There is resistance to it and dissent.

Finally, the bigger and broader contemporary picture must be acknowledged. The discussion takes place at a time when 'normality' is in tatters and in its place a new 'normal' is emerging. The world is experiencing trauma and is threatened by a drift to social, economic and political disorder due to a 'natural disorder'—a pandemic—which could push democracies further still towards an authoritarian nightmare. The social disaster of Covid-19 is yet another illustration of how (a) the human propensity to work together to form and preserve civil society creates friction, social divisions, social control, and inequalities in the pursuance of more personal, social, economic and political power; and how (b) this leads people to a situation whereby the desire for freedom is simultaneously manipulated and capped by a desire to dominate and be dominated. From corporate boardrooms to democratic and despotic government, the experience is one of exploitation of disasters (whether natural or human-made) to promote the well-being of some people at the expense of others. This insatiable appetite to dominate and exploit others (even when it is done for altruistic motives, e.g. philanthropy, public health protection) leads to Western democratic states becoming and presenting more like private corporate enterprises than publically accountable entities. As an entity, and in collaboration with corporate business, typically the state is busy broadening its reach by enacting new powers to observe and euphemistically 'protect' citizens. In the process, it captures in its net more and more aspects of individuals' personal characteristics, belief systems, emotions, and expressed behaviour for the purposes of a more centralised and oppressive state with unlimited powers.

Democracy as an Ideal Type

In the real world of diverse social and political systems, there is no such thing as an *'Ideal type'* of democracy in the Weberian sense (Weber 1949; see also, Aron 2018; Svedberg & Agevall 2016; Waters & Waters 2015). The perfect democracy exists only as a hypothetical possibility. Rather, what exists in practice is an adulterated and blurred construction that tries to resemble what a democracy ought to look like.

In its purest Ideal type, a democratic state would be one having the following characteristics: (1) political parties represent diverse interests and compete on an equal basis for power; (2) representative government is elected through uninterrupted and free elections for a defined period until new and fresh elections take place; (3) citizens have the right and freedom without hindrance or objection to participate in elections to elect their chosen government and leaders; (4) there is a free and independent media, freedom of speech, expression and assembly; (5) there is a political culture which encourages and promotes these freedoms; (6) there is an independent judiciary; (7) the rule of law and the principle of social justice apply equally and stand above any citizen or privilege; (8) there is the right to equal opportunities including health care provision and access to health care for all; (9) there is transparency and accountability and legitimate checks and balances in operation to ensure that there is no misuse or abuse of power; (10) citizens have the right to challenge, resist and remove elected leaders if those leaders are found to misuse or abuse their powers.

In the real world, democracy is a more loosely defined entity. As a type of society and governance, it falls short of the above Ideal type. It is, in fact, a nebulous term that can mean different things to different people, which is often exploited even by authoritarian regimes for public consumption. For instance, one may have a less than positive view of Brazilian democracy or Turkish democracy but their presidents Jair Bolsonaro and Recep Tayyip Erdogan respectively swear to the opposite: the openness, transparency, accountability, elections and freedoms that are present in their countries. Indeed, more often than not, such leaders have attacked Western democracies, particularly European, for being undemocratic, xenophobic and insular.

Moreover, it is not just about the fact that those who govern in democratic states are most of the time detached from their own people. For example, the 'We the People' that defines the American constitution could not be further from the truth in reality. Governance is not so plural but skewed toward an oligarchic representation of interests and privilege. It is also about social injustice, severe and growing socio-economic, educational and health inequalities, greed and avarice, misinformation and disinformation, corruption and exploitation by the few for the few. In our turbulent times, the term 'democracy' is being borrowed and stamped as a convenient label on almost every activity which needs to be seen as legitimate, open and fair. Even though many governments are despotic states that resist and repress freedom of speech, expression and assembly, breach human rights and use "a variety of subterfuges to manage or undermine the electoral process" (Roth 2009), they still manage to label their corrupt regimes 'democratic'.

The abuse of democracy is commonplace because there is not a universally acceptable and tight definition against which countries and their governments can be meticulously judged and approved or not. Further, when they are judged, the judgement is a political one. Political violence, electoral manipulation and fraud, press censorship, repression of civil society, use of coercion including military rule and more have all been used to subjugate populations in the name of democracy (Roth 2009). Social, ideological, commercial, strategic, (and as examined in detail in the following chapter) personal characteristics and psychological factors mesmerise and push established democracies to often 'close their eyes' to such abuses thus "making it easier for sham democrats to pass themselves off as the real thing" (Roth 2009, 141).

Parallel to socio-political and other structures which undermine and adulterate democracy, there is also the disconcerting part played by authoritarian leaders, who exploit the social cracks and weaknesses of democracy and who camouflage and wrap themselves in the colours of democracy, to promote and propagate their own agendas. By skillfully exploiting the cracks created by partisan politics and the support offered by nominally democratic institutions (e.g. corporate and party political interests) which broaden the basis of support, despotic rulers' tenure lengthens (Gandhi & Przeworski 2007). They succeed in shifting and pushing governance and social institutions in general into becoming less democratic and more authoritarian. This then assists them to consolidate their grip on power. Through the corrosion of the judiciary, an onslaught on the media and the electoral process, the centralisation of power, contempt for debate, reasoning and expert knowledge, and the shifting of social and cultural norms, democracies are thus being dismantled and transformed into autocracies (cf. Gessen 2020; *Washington Post* 2020).

The Tyranny of the Majority

Democracy may be desirable but its strengths are also its worst enemy. In other words, it is the enemy within, and less the enemy from outside, which threatens its base. One such flaw is its undefined scope to perpetuate inequalities. This process exhibits what Alexis de Tocqueville in his *Democracy in America* termed "the tyranny of the majority", meaning an indifference of the majority to the needs of minorities. This creates, de Tocqueville argued, social divisions, exploitation, oppression and inequality within and between groups, which leaves an unsettling effect on democracy. It puts it in jeopardy.

The concept of 'the tyranny of the majority' is not about the oppression of minority groups only. Nor does it restrict itself to the legal anomalies and oppression which may arise in the corporate world of boardrooms and their decision-making policies if minority shareholders' rights cannot be protected well enough. In a democracy, the concept may also apply to the actual workings of the political system itself which includes elections, political representation and policy-making. In this case, it arises out of democracy's own contradictions: winning an election but still expecting the political party in government to work in a bipartisan manner for plural interests rather than those of the few.

In democracies, there is always a sense of achievement when a political party wins an election with a big, or what is called a 'healthy', majority. This is often celebrated as a triumph for democracy because 'the people have spoken', and therefore governance can now take place without hindrance or obstruction. However, in fact this is a fundamental risk to consensual politics. For instance, there may be a clash between a majority vote that allows a political party to form a government but another political party to form a majority vote in a legislative branch of government (e.g. the case of a US Democratic Party president versus a Senate Republican majority amply illustrates the point). Conversely, where the same political party is represented at the executive level and with a majority in the legislative branch of government (e.g. as in Trump's administration with a Senate Republican majority) the same one-sided undemocratic process takes effect. Similarly, in the context of a parliamentary democracy as in the UK, a big Conservative Party majority in parliament means that there is little chance of establishing political consensus, coalitions and bipartisan politics. They render democratic opposition ineffective in providing a true challenge to the ruling party. Policy becomes selective to favour individual or party political interests. It disfavours broader, more plural interests and adds to the risk of corruption as there is little in the way of checks and balances. Unchecked ruling political party majorities are, effectively, akin to the monolithic single-party ideology that characterises authoritarian states, whether on the right or left of the political spectrum. Through the pretence of practising legitimate democratic rights, they may introduce authoritarian rule and policies which favour the few but certainly not the common good. It is both a backdoor introduction of oppressive practices and a front door opening for ushering in undemocratic principles and practices.

The Normalisation of Oppression, Absurdity and the Creation of 'Cheerful Robots'

As oppressive practices take hold, in the longer term a normalisation process sets in that begins to legitimise them. In sociological and psychological terms, the absurdity and simplicity of language and symbols used, years of political oppression, violence and social conflict in general, religious and ethnic cleansing, and persecution have the unanticipated consequence of saturating the collective conscience. This happens despite a parallel open or underground resistance to such language, values and repressive practices. In due course, after continuous exposure, there develops a particular type of a psychological state of mind, a fatigue, which accepts such matters as a normal response to an abnormal social environment. In other words, there develops a belief that 'the world is what it is, so why bother about it'. C. Wright Mills referred to this passivity as the "danger of malaise" which creates "cheerful robots", whereby there is tacit acceptance of what is given and taken for granted as normal. This tacit acceptance is about unequal and depressingly manipulative relationships (Mills 1959; Jones 2018). This is not exactly apathy, though that is part of it. It is a mental withdrawal from extreme and challenging social and moral events. It succeeds in neutralising human sensitivities to what on previous occasions and times might have be seen as unacceptable and reprehensible. Individuals, and in a broader sense society, become socially inoculated and immune to cruelty, oppression and repression of freedoms. It is a process which, once it has become deeply engrained in the social structure, is deemed normal. This capacity to accept the world as it is perceived to be and be inclined to get on with life and, in Robert K. Merton's terms, ritualistically "play the game" (Merton 1957), becomes a general, standard response. Hitherto intolerable acts and deeds begin to be seen and defined as tolerable and inconsequential (Stanley 2018).

It is in that context that the language, values and culture which are shared by corporatism and authoritarianism can be understood. In the most part, these involve restrictive practices, elimination of the opposition, often obscene remuneration for members, and concentration of resources and power in the hands of a selected few at the exclusion of outsiders. Basking in the glory of nepotism, cronyism and broader corruption, and grabbing personal profits and benefits of all sorts to the detriment and exclusion of broader sections of the population, are shared characteristics. Both corporatism and authoritarianism draw a defined and almost impenetrable boundary between the few who govern and their inner circle, and all those others who sit outside that circle. It sets them up as a unique social class which exists above and apart from the vast majority of common others. Privilege, money, and power remain highly protected and guarded commodities by the few for the few.

Within that context, a corporate culture in hand with a parallel state culture creates a set of authoritarian norms which promote and propagate a value orientation of the superiority of privately run strong corporations. This, its proponents argue, enables the creation of a work ethic that produces wealth. As wealth is produced based on the principle of a free market, it assists in the enrichment of the democratic process (Klein 2007; 2017). Such narrative is equated with individual freedom and choice, healthy competition, transparency and in-built checks and balances which guard against corruption. It promotes the belief that such structures, if left free of external controls and market manipulation, enhance the attainment of the lofty goals of personal achievement and attainment, and provide for all the people the desire to do better and aim higher.

Corporate fundamentalist culture (Perry 2017) creates, therefore, what one may call a *corporate rationality*. This rationality is on the increase, not because individuals fail to use reason to realise that they do not share much with such rationality but because they are driven to believe that such rationality is linked to their personal freedom, democratic structures, organisational efficiency, and promotion of opportunity in achieving and attaining a desirable goal (e.g. the 'American Dream').

However, this corporate rationality's normative formulations are found to be lacking in an empirical sense. The above value-laden qualities give lie to the claim that all are equal under the law and that success comes with hard work. A perpetual myth about meritocracy is created which camouflages the unequal distribution of opportunity. It claims to provide for solutions to domestic and global issues, if only one tries hard enough to go up the ladder. It is all, therefore, about effort and fair competition. However, success is not attained and measured by how much education, intelligence or aspirations one has, though important as they are in themselves. Rather, as so many sociological studies in the 1960s and 1970s consistently showed, success and achievement are a function of social class, the home, the school, education in prestigious universities—particularly the Oxbridge or Ivy League educational establishments—and overall the privileges, affluence, wealth and opportunities which one is fortunate enough to receive and command (Sandel 2020).

Resistance to Oppression

The shift to authoritarianism is not a monolithic and inevitable process. There are dissenting voices, from within and outside both democratic and authoritarian states, which resist oppression. The US 2020 election results show that although the authoritarian mindset may remain very strong (e.g. over 74 million of the electorate voted for Trump), people have the power to reject and eject leaders for something different. They find ways to challenge the suppression of their rights by open defiance or underground movements or both. Even in a situation whereby a political party shifts towards the radical right, there are dissenting voices. In the course of Trump's presidency and his excesses, his abuse of power and his efforts to undermine the outcome of the 2020 election, the Republican Party (GOP) remained tight-lipped throughout. This deafening silence said much about the GOP and its shift to radical-right politics. In fact, one could argue, the GOP found expression of its own radical-right political agenda through Donald Trump (Stevens 2020). However, against that grain, several prominent Republicans publicly denounced president Trump's divisive and despotic policies. These included former president George W. Bush, Senator Mitt Romney, James Mattis former US secretary of defence, Mike Mullen former chairman of the joint chiefs of staff, and Chris Christie former governor of New Jersey and an avowed supporter of Trump (see e.g. Goldberg 2020; Mullen 2019; 2020).

Societies are not just blindly led into the authoritarian (or democratic) camp without opposition. In that sense, neither democracy nor despotic regimes should be taken for granted as static and permanent forces and not subject to social change. So, although there is currently a gradual shift to a more autocratic rule, it does not necessarily mean that it is a closed process. There is resistance, open or underground, and often social change comes about when it is least expected and initiated by the least expected social groups which for many years have been marginalised and denied their democratic rights. As Herbert Marcuse juxtaposed, it is usually these kinds of social movement, which flare up spontaneously as localised, disjointed and limited outcries about bigotry, exploitation and oppression, that often grow into more organised serious forces of social change (Marcuse 1955; 1964).

The Rise of Authoritarianism

The *Democratic Index* compiled by the Economist Intelligence Unit (EIU), which looks at 167 countries (166 sovereign states of which 164 are UN members), shows a depressing picture of a world sliding into authoritarianism. Despite obvious difficulties and flaws in any attempt to categorise countries according to their political systems and characteristics, there appears to be, nonetheless, a downward trend in democracy and an upward trend in authoritarianism.

The global score for democracy has fallen dramatically to the worst average score registered since the EIU first produced the index in 2006. The most notable downgrading refers to the US. It now ranks 25 down the scale and falls into the definition of a 'flawed democracy'. Although the UK remains in the 'full democracies' category, it is ranked lower down the scale to number 14 (EIU 2020).

Overall, according to the index 55 countries (32.9%) are "authoritarian" (e.g. China, Iran, Belarus, Saudi Arabia, North Korea, Russia, UAE); 37 (22.1%) are "hybrid democracies" and fast moving into authoritarianism (e.g. Turkey, Pakistan, Lebanon); 53 (31.7%) are "flawed democracies" (e.g. Singapore, Mexico, Shri Lanka, Thailand, Serbia, Romania, Poland, Bulgaria, Israel, US). It must be pointed out here that since the publication of the index, some of these countries (for instance, Poland, Bulgaria, Hungary, Turkey and Israel) have seen a further downward drift to authoritarianism. Finally, in terms of "full democracies" only 23 (13.2%) of the countries looked at are classified as such (e.g. Norway, Sweden, Denmark, New Zealand, Finland, Canada and UK). The index notes that the UK has been falling further down the democratic index since 2016 and the Brexit Referendum (EIU 2020).

Another index which measures a specific characteristic of an open (democratic) or closed (authoritarian) society is the world press freedom index compiled by Reporters Without Borders (RSF). The index assesses the "level of pluralism, media independence, the environment for the media and self-censorship, the legal framework, transparency, and the quality of infrastructure that supports the production of news and information" (RSF 2020).

RSF reports that since 2013 the global situation has deteriorated by 13%. The index warns that the next decade will be crucial for the sustainment or loss of a free, independent and reliable press. It finds that ownership of media outlets is concentrated in the hands of a few wealthy and powerful individuals and corporations which pose conflicts of interest and a threat to media pluralism and independence. The suppression of media freedom—assisted by the Covid-19 pandemic which has given governments a unique chance to censor both major outbreaks and suppression of media freedom—has expanded. Although European states, particularly Scandinavian countries, continue to fare relatively well, there is, nonetheless, a growing hostility "even hatred towards journalists and this crisis has now worsened."

Another international study by the Varieties of Democracy Institute at the University of Gothenburg in Sweden adds further credence to the conclusion that democracies are being eroded by ruling parties which push their countries to authoritarian rule. In particular the study is scathing about the GOP in that it has evolved into an autocratic party not dissimilar to the ruling parties in authoritarian societies. The research notes a significant shift in the GOP since 2000, but especially since the emergence of Donald Trump in 2016, to oppressive politics and the adoption of tactics comparable to ruling nationalist parties as those in Turkey, Hungary, Poland and India. They find that the GOP is almost synonymous with violence against opponents and collusion with radical-right groups which pursue an authoritarian agenda (Luhrmann et al 2020; Pemstein et al 2020).

In summary, the curtailment of pluralism at various levels has brought democratic and authoritarian states closer together. This convergence sees the first falling under the spell of authoritarianism whilst the latter appear to be expanding and improving their despotic grip on a geopolitical scale.

Inequality: A Springboard for the Authoritarian Relationship

Income and Wealth
According to global data, more than 70% of the world's adults own less than US$10,000 in total wealth. Their wealth covers just three per

cent of all global wealth (Inequality Organisation 2018a). In contrast, the world's wealthiest people, who constitute just over 8% of the global population, own 86% of global wealth. The share of income commanded by just one per cent of the population has increased in 59 out of 100 countries between 1990 and 2015 (United Nations 2020). Inequalities and disparities in income and wealth, health, chronic health conditions, mental health and mortality are a function of access to opportunity, age, gender and sexual orientation, disability, race and ethnicity, religion, economic and social status. The more unequal societies are, the less successful they are in reducing inequality of opportunity and their citizens fail to receive equitable treatment. Inequalities transmit and concentrate political influence amongst those who are better off (United Nations 2020).

With nearly 80% of multimillionaires residing in the US and Europe, Western democracies dominate the world's share of wealth which is in the hands of a few. In the first quarter of 2020, 10% of Americans owned 80% of the stock market. According to *Forbes* (2020), just 10 of the richest billionaires owned over $975 billion in combined wealth in 2020, and altogether America's 400 richest are worth a record US$3.2 trillion (Dolan et al 2020). This vast sum exceeds many countries' Gross National Product (GNP). Some examples may help to understand the scope of this huge disparity and put it in perspective: in 2019, the GNPs in US$ were for US 21.6 trillion; Germany 4.5 trillion; UK 2.8 trillion; France 2.8 trillion; Australia 1.4 trillion; Norway 441 billion; Denmark 368 billion; Malta 13.7 billion (Macro Trends 2020).

At a time when the Covid-19 pandemic is hitting hard the pockets of most people and indeed the financial fortunes of countries across the globe, these super-rich individuals' wealth is accelerating at an obscene speed. While millions of people are losing their jobs, and there may not be any jobs available after the pandemic especially for those who are not highly educated and skilled or able to work online, the power, status and economic position of some corporate giants is increasing relentlessly (Richter 2020). By May 2020, the fortunes of Amazon shot up by 26%; Apple by nearly two per cent; Alphabet by over 13%; Microsoft by 15%; and *Facebook* by over 18% compared to their pre-Covid positions.

The chief executive officers (CEOs) of US and European corporations do not just enjoy high remunerations. They also benefit from massive handouts and retirement benefits (lump-sums and pensions amongst them). For example, it is estimated that in 2015 the retirement benefits and savings of 100 top CEOs in the US totalled nearly five billion dollars which was equivalent to the entire benefits received by over 50 million (40%) of all American families put together (Inequality Organisation 2018b).

Market fluctuations, accumulated savings and assets, stocks and shares, mutual funds, investments of large amounts of equity in special schemes and businesses, stocks and other assets all combine to provide the wealthy with disproportionate benefits and open opportunities which see their wealth skyrocketing. On current trends, the world's richest one per cent will accrue US$305 trillion and control as much as 64% of the world's wealth by 2030. Although one can argue about these figures and suggest that some of the poor have benefited and moved up the economic ladder, the fact remains that the rich are fast becoming preposterously richer (Matthews 2019).

Even in such countries as Denmark, despite the public presentation of Scandinavian countries as a model of 'happiness' and content, egalitarian democracy, tolerance, openness, transparency and by-and-large an accommodating welfare state, inequality not only exists but is also on the rise. Danes are experiencing a social drift into xenophobia and sharper inequalities in employment, income, housing and quality of housing and, generally, they perceive the gap between rich and poor to be expanding (Ortiz 2020).

The trend toward extreme income and wealth also concentrates political power in the hands of an oligarchy of predominantly white males. Meanwhile others, particularly white working class families, women, people of colour and other minority groups, continue to remain under-represented in highly-paid jobs, other benefits and representation in government and business's executive boards. For instance, in the UK, parliamentary democracy has always been in the hands of an elite and the prerogative of a few selected and most privileged individuals who constitute just six per cent of the general population. Many politicians in government are multimillionaires who have vast wealth coming from inheritance, property portfolios, and interests in industry and commerce.

Gender and Ethnicity

In terms of women's representation in the UK parliament, although women constitute 51% of the general population, about 34% of MPs are women. It follows that when the composition of the Cabinet is examined, ministerial posts are by far a men's club: 73% versus 23% of women (Watson et al 2020). Ministerial posts are the preserve of a selected minority of privately educated individuals of whom nearly 50% are Oxbridge graduates. Three-quarters of the 55 British Prime Ministers in all periods have been Oxbridge educated. This may not appear significant until this figure is contrasted with the one per cent of the general population who make it to these esteemed academic institutions.

In terms of ethnicity, there has been a gradual increase in representation that is positive. Ethnic minority groups constitute 14% of the UK general population. In the current 2020 parliament, just over 12% per cent of MPs are from ethnic minority groups. Three members (14%) out of 21 of Cabinet ministers are from an ethnic minority background.

Moving to business corporations, according to the Financial Reporting Council (FRC), over 52% of FTSE 250 companies and most of the FTSE 350 in the UK do not even attempt to mention ethnicity in their policy and do not have targets for a more diverse composition and representation. Nearly 60% (150 out of 256 companies looked into), did not have at least one director of colour on their boards (FRC 2020).

In the US, the Harvard Law School Forum on Corporate Governance (2019) reports that although some movement has been made to increase women and ethnic minorities in board representation, this change is slow to come by. For the Fortune 500, over 80% of new executives appointed were white of which nearly 60% were white men. For the Fortune 100 board seats of new executives, 77% were white of which 51% were white men. The report's conclusion is that "Overall, this year's census provides powerful metrics on the slow change of diversity in the boardroom" (see also Deloitte 2019). This is more noticeable in such technology giant corporations as Amazon, *Facebook, Google*, Intel, and Microsoft. People of colour make up less than four per cent of the workforce and less than three per cent of the senior management at *Facebook*. As of May 2018, of all ten executives on

Amazon's Board of directors three were women but none was from people of colour. Women make only 20% of public company directors in the US and only 22% globally. In general, company boards are constituted by individuals who share similar socio-economic, gender and ethnic characteristics (Schindlinger 2020; Kerber et al 2020).

Health, Health Care Provision, and Related Metrics

Whether economies experience cycles of austerity or economic growth or severe retraction, the wealthiest always benefit. They remain untouched and continue to accumulate wealth at the expense of the rest of the population, irrespective of economic downturns. The disproportionate accumulation of capital accentuates inequality not just in income and wealth, employment and education but also in other spheres such as health, infant mortality, life chances, and life expectancy. The worst excesses in terms of infection and mortality rates, underlying serious medical conditions, social isolation, and mental ill-health, are borne by poorer communities, particularly people of colour and indigenous populations (Abedi et al 2020; *Lancet* 2020; Myers 2020).

As inequality of opportunity to do better worsens from generation to generation, inequality between the poor and the rich gets worse (Dias 2009). In consequence, life expectancy, drug and substance abuse related mortality, and suicide rates amongst the poor take a direct hit (Carson et al 2020; Public Health UK 2018). When social characteristics are added to the equation, including ethnicity and those who identify as lesbian, gay, bisexual or transgender (LGBT), such groups do worse and experience higher rates of poor mental health (Williams et al 2020).

When a multiplicity of social factors are measured (e.g. income, jobs and job security, education, skills and training, disability, crime and justice, housing and quality of housing, and provision of services) to determine the quality of life in terms of health care and access to health care services, it is consistently found that "people living in the most deprived areas of England experience a worse quality of care than people in the least deprived areas" (Scobie & Morris 2020).

In the US, inequalities and disparities in the treatment of different groups by income and wealth, education, gender and sexual orientation, disability, job security, housing and eviction, life opportunities, mortality, mental health, chronic medical conditions and ill-health, and access to health care provision, are stark and persistent owing to a systemic and entrenched inequality rather than "individual or group behavior" (Baciu et al 2017; Carratala & Maxwell 2020; Desmond 2018). It is generally found that poverty and ethnicity are directly associated with higher rates of HIV/AIDS-related illness, Covid-19 infections and generally with poor health. Significantly, when income and wealth inequality are controlled, the most influential factor associated with these inequalities of infection and ill-health is race and ethnicity. It means that African Americans and other ethnic groups (especially indigenous populations and people from a Hispanic origin) bear the brunt of deaths, infection and general ill-health (Baciu et al 2017; Brown & Ravallion 2020).

Treatment under the Law

Similarly, race and ethnicity, social class, gender, education, income and wealth have all been associated with disparities in law enforcement and sentencing practices of courts. The growing public outcry in the US and European countries since 2018 concerning police treatment of people of colour and other minorities is a case in point. At another level, ethnic minorities appear to be over-represented in custodial institutions. This cannot be explained by merely taking into account the type of crime committed. In general, this question of inequitable treatment under the law has received canonical status in the field of criminology and social justice. It led to an explosion of studies in the 1980s through to the 1990s and the debates continue unabated to the present day (see for example, Spohn and Cederblom 1991; Engen et al 2003; Mitchell 2005; Vass 1990; Wingerden et al 2016).

Clearly, the typical Establishment narrative i.e. that law enforcement agencies and the judiciary apply the law on an equal basis because they are void of social and personal influences in making decisions, is simply suspect. Law enforcement and court sentencing are susceptible to influences that cannot be separated from social, moral and political considerations. Decisions, in the course of social encounters with the police, other law enforcement agencies and the judiciary are not just based on perception and interpretation of the presented or alleged facts. They also involve the personal characteristics and the perceived demeanour of participants. These perceptions and interpretations are themselves affected by the values and the world-view of the interpreters and the social context within which those interpretations are reached. As such, it begs the question whether in any given instance the law can be equally and consistently applied (cf. a speech by Lord Mance 2011).

Justice Amy Coney Barrett's claim in the course of the Senate Judiciary Committee proceedings for her appointment as Justice to the US Supreme Court in the month of October 2020 is a case in point. Justice Barrett asserted that she would remain apolitical if appointed. Referring to the US constitution and answering questions about her known stance on matters of abortion, gun control and the Patient Protection and Affordable Care Act (commonly known as 'Obamacare'), she retorted:

> "...meaning doesn't change over time and it's not for me to update it or infuse my own policy views into it".

If that were true, the world around her would have been in deep freeze for over 230 years. It would be a very odd occasion if her judgement on court cases in 2020 were based on the views, norms, values and expectations or cultural depictions inscribed in the constitution which dates from over two centuries earlier. Changes in the way in which society functions can only be understood, measured, assessed, and interpreted in the course of social relationships which exist in a particular context and at a particular time. Definitions and meanings of acceptability and normality, laws, what constitutes infractions of laws, rules and regulations, norms and values change over time as society changes. It is both absurd and dangerous for anyone to claim that their interpretation of the rule of law, and the meaning attached to that instrument and the rights it bestows on its citizens, would be applied in a religiously observed manner as an accurate reflection of what was meant, intended and proposed by the original thinkers. It is a narrative which both takes the form of 'one size fits all' and asserts an android impartiality for judges which, in reality, is impossible for any human to deliver no matter how hard they try to ignore their unavoidable predispositions, world-view and prejudices.

Studies on the behaviour of people in everyday interaction, organisational relationships, work relationships, the enforcement of laws, rules and regulations, sentencing practices of lower and higher courts, have shown conclusively that flexibility and discretion are applied. Social life would not be possible without a flexible interpretation and application of such rules, norms and expectations which guide social encounters. However, it is that same elasticity which also creates inequity of treatment. Discretion can also mean unwarranted disparities, discrepancies, discrimination and inconsistency in the way individuals are treated by the police and the courts and the law in general (Engel 2004). For instance, the same or different police officers in different locations are found to react differently to different individuals, despite the latter's commission of exactly the same offences. Similarly, courts are found to treat offenders of diverse social and ethnic backgrounds differently in different parts of the country. The narrative that decisions are not judgemental gives a false impression that the rule of law and the personal rights afforded by it fit equally well all citizens and consequently that social justice is equally served.

Covid-19 Related Inequalities

The onset of Covid-19 has starkly highlighted inequalities which exist in society at all levels discussed here. However, the pandemic is also redefining and exemplifying the divisions between age groups. It is becoming the funnel through which the corporate rationality of productive and unproductive labour is again allowed to flow freely to influence policy. This rationality puts an economic value on the means of production and thus a value on contribution. Productive labour is perceived to be desirable. In contrast, unproductive labour is seen as undesirable and a disposable class. Ageism, therefore, has been brought to the fore once more and is undergoing a social process of transformation to fit into the needs of a new and emerging normalcy of a disrupted economic and social order.

People aged 65 and over are more susceptible to the serious medical complications of Covid-19 and are afflicted with excess mortality rates (Aron 2020; Aron & Muellbauer 2020). This means that in comparison to younger groups, a disproportionately higher level of social and health care provision is required for that group. Ageism therefore is gripping through and taking a new meaning. A growing political message is slowly being advocated that it is alright for the elderly to be confined for their own good; and to allow the provision of scarce health care resources to be made available to the younger generations who are active and productive in the economy.

A perception of worth-and-productivity, that socially stigmatises and discriminates against those who are not considered useful or economically productive, is not new. However, the pandemic may be gradually exaggerating this stigmatisation process. As lockdowns become a common and universal approach to the containment of social interaction to limit infection, they also create pressure on the economy. It is, therefore, easy and tempting in such cases for governments and corporations to justify protection of the economy by targeting certain vulnerable populations and applying policies which curtail their social relationships. Through a policy of exclusion of the elderly, by what has been euphemistically called "focussed protection" (Kulldorff et al 2020), the active labour force in the economy—the younger generation—is allowed to escape confinement and lockdowns so as to keep the economy going (Sample 2020).

Although denials have been issued that so-called 'focussed protection' or other similar euphemisms such as 'cocooning' the vulnerable to allow others to build up a 'herd immunity' are about confinement and neglect (cf. Janaskie & Gartz 2020), it is hard not to see the connection between 'protection', 'confinement' and 'neglect'. In fact, this shift toward opening up the economy to create 'herd immunity', while 'protecting', or 'cocooning' or 'restricting' the elderly and other vulnerable groups with underlying medical conditions, has received sharp condemnation. For instance, Dr Anthony Fauci, US Director of the Institute of Allergy and Infectious Diseases, has called the idea of 'focussed protection' sheer "nonsense" and "ridiculous" (Thomas 2020).

The existence of such a policy of confinement and neglect has also been denied by some European states, particularly German and Danish authorities, as they claim to afford equal treatment to all age groups. Nonetheless, in Sweden neglect of elders led to care home residents to account for almost 50% of deaths linked to Covid-19 in the country. It has been alleged that "an institutional reluctance to admit [ill residents] to hospital is costing lives" and that elders and others in residential homes are expendable (Savage 2020; Paterlini 2020; Howard 2020).

Similar high infection and mortality rates were observed in residential establishments during the first wave of infection in the UK. Charges of neglect and dereliction of duty were levied against the government by social and health care critics. Residential workers claimed that they were instructed to ignore the needs of elderly residents to protect the needs of other age groups and allow the National Health Service (NHS) to cope with the crisis.

Notwithstanding the question about social exclusion on grounds of active or inactive participation in the economy, or saving limited health care resources, there is also in this debate the promotion of falsehoods and distortion of facts. It is implied in the message that young people either do not contract the novel coronavirus or, even if they do, they remain asymptomatic. The fact is they do get infected and can transmit the infection, despite being asymptomatic. Current research findings are in agreement that infection leaves serious after-effects on health: it harbours long-term and lingering damage including chronic fatigue, cardiovascular, neurological and muscular complications and hearing loss which may affect both symptomatic and asymptomatic individuals (Couzin-Frankel 2020; Kilic et al. 2020; Mayo Clinic 2020; Quan-Xin et al 2020;).

There is also the sheer number of people in the 65 plus age group, a fact which poses serious theoretical and practical questions regarding their management. For example, in the US, 49 million people (15% of the US population) are over 65 years of age (ACL 2018). In the UK, 12 million people are aged 65 and over. This constitutes 18% of the UK population (Age UK 2019). These facts show the magnitude and scale of the control and surveillance net that advocates of 'focussed protection' may be promoting inadvertently. Such advocacy is theoretically and empirically suspect and morally dubious. The idea of 'shielding' the elderly and the vulnerable to release others to work and function normally is manifestly absurd and suggests amoral calculation.

The real concern about a policy of 'confinement' and exclusion from 'welfare and health care provision' according to age and other characteristics is that once such policy is in full swing, it may not stop there. Once policy has been allowed to erode moral boundaries, it becomes a sliding scale: there is little to stop society from shifting its attention to other social groups and ceremoniously pass them through similar corridors of control, segregation, exclusion and confinement. The next step would be to turn attention to people who are known to be more susceptible to illness and higher mortality rates. Once again the focus of discrimination, if not repression, will be the poor, ethnic minorities, individuals with disabilities, the unemployed and the unskilled, who are all shown to suffer from chronic social and health issues and are more susceptible to infection. For example, Trump's four years as US President provided an unabashed exposé of his personal/ideological separation of society into, on the one hand, deserving winners/predators like himself and his "producerist" supporters (Neiwert 2017, 4) who believe they are entitled to grab every benefit and privilege, and on the other, an undeserving loser/victim underclass of worthless 'others' who are cast as entitled to nothing, including health care and other inalienable human rights (Waring 2018b, 313-315).

Discriminatory Sets and Authoritarian Justifications

The more a society's approach and response to social problems are based on an evaluation of who is useful and who is not in the economy, or who will be given more preference over others, the more it runs the risk of normalising prejudice and discrimination on the basis of age, gender, sexual orientation, disability, and ethnicity. The more a society slides down that moral scale, the more it becomes tolerant of discriminatory and oppressive practices. Already, this downward drift in moral responsibility is emerging in unexpected places. The Swiss Society for Intensive Care is promoting a policy that the 'imperilled', i.e. those with such medical conditions as diabetes or heart problems, and those aged 60 and over, should sign a declaration stating their wish to forego treatment or care, in order to allow hospital space and scarce medical resources to accommodate the needs of other groups.

Therefore, overall, the question becomes why democracies continue to accommodate, and in fact encourage, the existence of inequality despite the repression it creates. Reasons are varied. In broad terms, in its general form and particularly economic terms, inequality can be conceptualised as a direct result of the exploitation of capital for surplus value and wealthy individuals' attempts to safeguard their fortunes (Mather 2015). The wealthy are averse to progressive redistribution. They want to remain wealthy and protect their assets. They utilise their capital to maximise their gains and typically conceal their profits in tax havens or through other means, including inventive accounting processes. Wealthy individuals, financial institutions, banks, insurance corporations, hedge funds, and giant transnational corporations, shift and recycle wealth in such a manner that most of it remains hidden and preserved. For example, on the declaration of the policy intention to introduce tax reforms and higher taxes on the rich by president-elect Joe Biden, wealthy Americans and corporations scrambled to make amendments to their financial arrangements to preserve and protect their assets; and to ensure that their ability to transfer wealth (e.g. tax-free up to nearly US$12 million introduced by the Trump administration in 2017) was not jeopardised. In effect, income and wealth are carefully and systematically re-routed for better accumulation and greater surpluses. The power of capital bestows on its owners the ability to influence market, social and political forces. They control the movement of labour and influence policy which promotes and increases social controls, challenges immigration and applies stiffer border controls. Economic inequality is thus both a systemic consequence of the social relations of capital which define social divisions in society, and the cause of the state's own duplicity and participation in the sustainment of these divisions and unequal relationships.

The impact of (a) structural changes in the economy (e.g. automation), (b) the role of big corporations (for example the pharmaceutical industry) which perpetuate the quest for profit at the cost of public health (as in the opioid epidemic in the US), and (c) the disappearing blue-collar jobs which managed in the past to support working class families in some manner or other, all conspire to create low pay and transitional jobs, which increase social and economic insecurity and inequality further. In turn, they increase ill-health and serious medical conditions (Case & Deaton 2020).

Expanding social, economic, health, and other inequalities, all conspire to sharply amplify power relationships and the social divisions between the haves and the have-nots. Growing economic insecurity and social exclusion experienced by the less fortunate give vent to popular anger and resentment and may lead to an anti-establishment and xenophobic fervour.

This anger and resentment is managed and diffused by an intrinsic socialisation process that acts as a diversionary measure. It conditions oppressed groups to believe that their problems are not systemic but personal. Democracies are good at espousing a state and corporate rationality, which asserts that the free-market system offers equality of opportunity. This deception is based on the classic argument that cultivates and propagates a convenient myth that transferring wealth to the wealthy generates investment, jobs and financial security for all (Krugman 2020). The myth also asserts that the accumulation of income and wealth is earned through personal effort, and that it has nothing to do with exploitation or lack of policies of progressive redistribution. Besides, this mindset argues, such policies are an affront to personal freedoms. So, any discrepancies or inequalities which arise are simply a personal matter due to the fact that, for those who do well, it is because they try harder than others. Through this selective fantasy, the systemic existence of inequality is allowed to continue unabated because "people are groomed and socialized" to accept inequalities, and a "radical redistribution that would level differences" is not seen as democratic (Page & Jacobs 2009; Sandel 2020).

However, at the same time, this grooming process is careful enough to inject a glimmer of expectation and hope that everyone ought to have equal opportunity in making it to the top. So "working hard and getting a good education is the secret to success" (Page & Jacobs 2009, 36). Nevertheless, good education is relative because in absolute terms it is also a function of income and opportunity. It is also riddled with and dictated by social stratification and university leagues according to standing and prestige. Inevitably, this justifies and allows corporate bosses and the privileged to master incomes "more than twenty times the estimates for unskilled workers and sales clerks…and the CEOs of S&P 500 companies reaped [in 2007] US$14,000,000 per year: seven hundred times more than the average factory worker and 540 times more than [a] sales clerk" (Page & Jacobs 2009, 37).

So, the usual solutions to inequality through the "rhetoric of rising" to the top (Sandel 2020), according to each person's efforts, skills or talents, have mesmerised social relationships in democratic capitalism by making people believe in their system of government. The reality is, however, that social mobility has remained a lost cause while social stratification continues and prospers. In general terms, those who are born to poor parents tend to remain poor: inequality, absolute and relative, is an endemic and perpetual beast. Although people are socialised to see failure as part of their own make-up and blame themselves for their predicament, they are, nonetheless, still experiencing grief and envy thus sharing, as a group, an in-built resentment against the ruling elite and excessively remunerated CEOs. When someone like Donald Trump comes along by presenting himself as an embodiment of anti-elitism, and presents as being everything that everyone should aspire to be—successful and rich—the popular resentment experienced by such groups against a privileged elite crystallises into becoming a political mass. This mass finds unity and common expression by the prospect of a rising despotic leader who becomes their voice of discontent. They call for policy and action to stop the rot and return the country to the good old-fashioned parameters of rule and order, the cult of tradition and the good old way of life (Sandel 2020). It all adds up to a populist and nationalist fervour which gives rise to social division and tribalism, but successfully hides the real cause of those hardships and divisions.

In turn, these social divisions play into the hands of rulers and the wealthy. They deliberately encourage and promote populism and nationalism by instilling fear (e.g. immigration, lost ideals, feminism, anarchism, and extremism) to create yet more Trojan horses to act as diversionary tactics to make citizens believe that their political, traditional and personal values are being threatened. As citizens become preoccupied with these values, they lose sight of deep-rooted economic and social inequality and fail to do something about it (Solt 2011).

Married to this exploitation of inequality for political and economic ends and the rise of populism and nationalism is the emergence of a "cultural backlash" against "progressive cultural change" (Inglehart & Norris 2019). It is a resentful counter-revolutionary 'retro backlash', especially evident amongst poorly educated white men, and religious and ethnic majorities. It is a psychological state of mind that is rich in inventing scapegoats and is guided by anti-immigrant attitudes, a suspicion of globalisation and the liberal establishment. It encourages the expansion and proliferation of radical (particularly radical-right) groups for which flags, guns, God and country become unified as a defence against lost values, mores and liberty. These groups consider that these traditional values and mores have been eroded and are being replaced by unacceptable and alien progressive values (e.g. multiculturalism, immigration, abortion, same-sex marriage, women's rights, and broader gender and sexual orientation issues). As a state of mind, this 'cultural backlash' is characterised by a strong support for authoritarian values and tough-talking demagogic politicians who promise to reverse the decline, offer jobs and economic security, deal with immigration, close borders, withdraw citizenships, restore the traditional values of the family and marriage, and give back the people their lost identity.

The rise of populist and nationalist rhetoric, and despotic language and expression, becomes more pronounced as societies become more unequal. The personal and social consequences of inequality— lack of opportunities, job insecurity, poor education, poor health, inadequate health care provision, the daily struggle to meet absolute and relative needs, exclusion, discrimination, fear and intimidation— all conspire to create a psychological vortex of frustration, despondency, bigotry, and anger. This vortex is then channelled and expressed through a vocabulary that is rich in derogatory terms about opponents but remains highly complimentary about despotic and dominant leadership.

The populist and nationalist fervour that emerges is essentially regressive: it increases conflict across the horizontal base of the inequality triangle, where diverse majority and minority social groups are competing for scarce resources and opportunities. Populism and nationalism are not interested, nor are they remotely effective, in challenging vertical inequality between the well-off social groups and the worst-off social groups lower down the ladder. This may be explained by the fact that the wealthy elites succeed in remaining distant from the base of the social triangle where most of the turbulence occurs. They stay out of reach while social groups, which are struggling and competing for symbiotic existence and survival further down the base of the social ladder, end up resenting, blaming and reacting against each other. Populist and nationalist politics is about the exploitation of inequalities by creating dissent. It sets the poor and needy of diverse social and ethnic backgrounds at each other's throat while the wealthy and the less visible or accessible are left to siphon off the desired economic, political and social benefits.

Towards a Strategy for Tackling Inequality

The current pandemic has not only exposed these social facts of inequality but has also exaggerated them. The social and economic context of inequality can be theoretically conceived in the shape of a 'K'. Democracy is represented by the vertical axis which holds the upper and lower arms. The upper arm represents the socially and economically privileged classes. The lower arm represents the most vulnerable social groups which experience discrimination, poverty, unemployment, poor education, destitution, ill-health and lack of health care provision. The centre point which joins the two groups is the so-called fast disappearing middle-class. Unless something is done to redress the imbalance to close the gap between the two, the upper arm will keep going north while the lower arm will keep going south thus exacerbating social divisions further still.

The pandemic's economic and social consequences are such that governments are borrowing on a grand scale in order to keep economies going. The Institute of International Finance (IIF) estimates that by 2021 global debt will reach US$277 trillion as a result (IIF 2020). Responsible governments will need to find ways to bridge the financial deficit between over-borrowing and over-spending. Personal and corporate taxation and other measures will have to be considered to raise multimillions to manage the huge national debt which threatens the very social stability of the domestic and international economy. One of the pandemic's unanticipated economic and social consequences may be that it has opened a window of opportunity for democratic societies to reassess their priorities and apply fair and equal treatment for all.

In essence, it can be argued that governments have an opportunity and a social obligation to act through social policy and progressive taxation to share wealth and, with it, social and political power and justice. They can do so by retarding and lowering the upper arm of the 'K' thus limiting the wealth and resources enjoyed by the very rich. Simultaneously, by diverting wealth, resources and opportunities to the poor, the lower arm of the 'K relationship is gradually helped to move upwards. As this happens, such policy raises these groups out of extreme poverty and poor health and assists them to gain access to a good standard of health care provision and experience better life-chances. In a more egalitarian democratic society, the two arms ought to range somewhere close to the middle. At that level, differences and variations between groups may thus still exist on an undulating horizontal axis that allows social mobility and guards against excesses: extreme wealth and extreme poverty. It may also limit the stigmatisation process of the 'them' and 'us' mentality which divides people into deserving and undeserving classes. In other words, such a position still allows diversity and difference in a socially responsible manner and, close to the middle point, permits a middle ground to exist that reflects and accommodates the middle classes.

Simultaneously, the shift of the two arms toward a middle ground and a balanced approach serves to protect against social extremes that can often lead to unsustainable cracks in a democracy. At a time of extreme absolute and relative need, such radical but socially responsible policy will not only protect the most vulnerable groups from disproportionate taxation but also help lift living standards for most people. It may provide an exit from the dilemma how to raise much needed revenue to avoid serious social and political dislocations that may result from impoverished global economies. As social policy goes, it may set the scene for a more inclusive society and a more inclusive type of democracy.

Of course, this advocacy for risk management of the economy and inequality on a broader basis is anathema to the mindset which has dominated state and corporate rationality for far too long. Unfortunately, this persistent mindset is at work again. In the US, the GOP is rediscovering the 'blessings' of tight monetary policies and reduction of taxes for the rich by espousing the usual falsehoods that such policy leads to jobs and freedom of choice. It is a matter of time before president-elect Biden's proposed policy of progressive taxation is put to rest by Congress and powerful lobbyist interests. In the UK, the current Chancellor of the Exchequer on November 22, 2020 expressed the usual parallel advocacy, namely that there is an urgency for public expenditure to be checked, and that public employees' wages (including nurses, social care workers, ambulance crews and generally the low-paid—the very people who have been in the forefront of the fight against Covid-19) will have to be frozen. Nothing appears to be on the cards to make the very wealthy to play their long overdue part in contributing their fair share to the economic and social reconstruction of the country and, as it stands, that of a democracy.

Conclusion

The authoritarian mindset encompasses a steadfast contrarian worldview that cannot tolerate equality or any form of equity in the economy and its social relations. This flies in the face of claims that liberal democracies care for their diverse populations. Instead of offering equitable treatment by opening up opportunities and access to equal life-chances for all their populations [whether in employment, income, wealth, political participation and representation or health irrespective of social class, age, gender, sexual orientation, race and ethnicity] they are found to accept and in fact deliberately exacerbate such inequalities that lead to widespread social, economic and political exploitation and repression.

The persistent and relentless rise of inequality is a major contributor to the concomitant rise of authoritarianism, in which wealthy corporations, corporate leaders, oligarchs, Establishment figures, politicians and governments collaborate to pursue mutual goals and interests at the expense of large sectors of the population and to the detriment of democracy. Inequality and authoritarianism feed off each other. This is despite the frequent assertions of such parties that they are empowering people, providing unfettered freedoms, and protecting their democratic interests and human rights. This persistent overarching environment leads inevitably to the normalisation process where inequalities are allowed to exist whether in corporate business or in broader society for the benefit of the few at the expense of the 'others'. The exhibited characteristic of obstinacy, refusal and ferocious opposition to accept change and a fairer society that afflicts this authoritarian mindset in a pathological manner is such that any attempt to engage constructively with this mindset becomes an almost impossible , unachievable and stressful task.

As discussed further in the following chapter, these inequalities take a more sinister character when considered within broader social and psychological perspectives and contexts. A combination of personal, interpersonal and institutional factors and circumstances [corruption, white-collar crime and the subversion of the rule of law by the powerful, policing, the abuse of technology, surveillance, repressive leaders and repressive corporate business regimes] create stressful, manipulative and often disastrous social relationships within the workplace, broader economy and political landscape. Working in tandem, these personal, interpersonal, social and psychological forces generate an authoritarian rationality that is busy constructing the case for powerless, passive and obedient subjects who follow the leader, the signal and the command.

References

Abedi, V., Olulana, O. and Avula, V. et al. 2020. "Racial, Economic, and Health Inequality and Covid-19". *J. Racial and Ethnic Disparities*. https://link.springer.com/article/10.1007/s40615-020-00833-4.

ACL. 2018. *Profile of Older Americans*. Administration for Community Living (ACL). April 2018. US Department of Health and Human Services. Washington DC: ACL. https://acl.gov/sites/default/fil es/Aging%20and%20Disability%20in%20America/2018Older AmericansProfile.pdf.

Age UK. 2019. *Later Life in the United Kingdom 2019*. May 2019. London: Age UK. https://www.ageuk.org.uk/globalassets/age-uk/docum ents/reports-and-publications/later_life_uk_factsheet.pdf.

Aron, J. 2020. "Transatlantic Excess Mortality Comparisons in the Pandemic". August 20, 2020. *OurWorldindata.org*. https://ourworl dindata.org/uploads/2020/08/Aron-and-Muellbauer-Transat lantic-excess-mortality-comparison.pdf.

Aron, J. and Muellbauer, J. 2020. "Measuring Excess Mortality: England is the European Outlier in the Covid-19 Pandemic". May 18, 2020. *Vox EU Organisation*. https://voxeu.org/article/us-excess -mortality-rate-covid-19-substantially-worse-europe-s.

Aron, R. 2018. *Main Currents in Sociological Thought: Durkheim, Pareto, Weber*. Vol II. Bosa Roca, US: CRC Press Inc., imprint Taylor & Francis Inc.

Baciu, A., Negussie, Y., Geller, A. et al. (eds). 2017. *Communities in Action: Pathways to Health Equity: The State of Health Disparities in the United States*. National Library of Medicine. National Center for Biotechnology Information. January 11, 2017. Washington DC: National Academies Press. https://pubmed.ncbi.nlm.nih.gov /28418632/

Benitez-Burraco, A. 2017. "How the Language We Speak Affects the Way We Think". *Psychology Today*. February 2, 2017.

Blumer, H. 1969. *Symbolic Interactionism: Perspectives and Method*. Englewood Cliffs, NJ: Prentice-Hall.

Brown, C.S. and Ravallion, M. 2020. *Inequality and the Coronavirus: Socioeconomic Covariates of Behavioral Responses and Viral Outcomes Across US Counties*. Working Paper 27549. National Bureau of Economic Research, Cambridge, MA: NBER. https://www.nber.orga/paper/w27549

Carratala, S. and Maxwell, C. 2020. *Health Disparities by Race and Ethnicity: Fact Sheet*. May 7, 2020. Washington, DC: Center for American Progress. https://www.americanprogress.org/issues/race/reports/2020/05/07/484742/health-disparities-race-ethnicity/

Carson, P., Blackey, H., Dunbar, S. et al. 2020. *Health Inequalities: Annual Report 2020*. Dept. of Health Northern Ireland. Belfast, UK: DoH. https://www.health-ni.gov.uk/news/health-inequalities-annual-report-2020.

Case, A. and Deaton, A. 2020. *Deaths of Despair and the Future of Capitalism*. Princeton, NJ: Princeton University Press.

Couzin-Frankel, J. 2020. "From 'Brain Fog' to Heart Damage, Covid-19's Lingering Problems Alarm Scientists". *Science*. July 31, 2020. Health, Coronavirus: doi:10.1126/science.abe1147. https://www.sciencemag.org/news/2020/07/brain-fog-heart-damage-covid-19-s-lingering-problems-alarm-scientists.

Deloitte. 2019. "Women and Minorities on Fortune 500 Boards: More Room to Grow". *WSJ Risk and Compliance Journal*. December 3, 2020. First reported in *WSJ Deloitte CFO Insights and Analysis*. March 3, 2019. https://deloitte.wsj.com/cfo/2019/03/21/women-and-minorities-on-fortune-500-boards-more-room-to-grow/.

Desmond, M. 2018. *Evicted: Poverty and Profit in the American City*. New York: Broadway Books.

De Tocqueville, A. 1961. *Democracy in America*. New York: Schocken Books. First published in two volumes 1835-1840.

Dias, P.R. 2009. "Inequality of Opportunity in Health: Evidence from a UK Cohort Study". *Health Economics*, 18, 1057-1074. July 30, 2009.

Dolan, K.A., Peterson-Withorn, C. and Wang, J. (eds.). 2020. *The Forbes 400 2020: The Definitive Ranking of the Wealthiest Americans in 2020.* September 8, 2020. https://www.forbes.com/forbes-400/.

EIU. 2020. *Democracy Index 2019: World Democracy Report.* The Economic Intelligence Unit (EIU). https://www.eiu.com/topic/democracy-index.[accessed August 3, 2020].

Engel, C. 2004. *Inconsistency in the Law: In Search of a Balanced Norm.* Reprint of report number 20004/16. Max Planck Institute of Research on Collective Goods, Bonn. http://www.hdl.handle.net/10419/19898.

Engen, R.L. Gainey, R.R., Crutchfield, R.D. et al. 2003. "Discretion and Disparity Under Sentencing Guidelines: The Role of Departures and Structured Sentencing Alternatives". *Criminology*, 41(1), 99-130.

Forbes. 2020. "Forbes Releases 39th Annual Forbes 400 Ranking of the Richest Americans". *Forbes Press Release.* September 8, 2020. https://www.forbes.com/sites/forbespr/2020/09/08/forbes-releases-39th-annual-forbes-400-ranking-of-the-richest-americans/?sh=7ee9d79b335b.

FRC. 2020. "Most UK Companies' Approach to Board Ethnic Diversity is Unsatisfactory". Financial Reporting Council (FRC). February 5, 2020. www.frc.org.uk/news/february-2020-(1)/.

Gandhi, J. and Przeworski. A. 2007. "Authoritarian Institutions and the Survival of Autocrats". *Comparative Political Studies*, 40(1), 1279-1301.

Gessen, M. 2020. *Surviving Autocracy.* New York: Riverhead Books.

Goldberg, J. 2020. "James Mattis Denounces President Trump, Describes Him as a Threat to Constitution". *The Atlantic.* June 3, 2020. https://www.theatlantic.com/politics/archive/2020/06//james-mattis-denounces-trump-protests-militarization/612640/.

Harvard Law School. 2019. *Missing Pieces Report: The 2018 Board Diversity Consensus of Women and Minorities on Fortune 500 Boards.* Harvard Law School Forum on Corporate Governance. February 5, 2019. https://corpgov.law.harvard.edu/2019/02/05/missing-pieces-report-the-2018-board-diversity-census-of-women-and-minorities-on-fortune-500-boards/.

Hemmer, N. 2020. "Democracy Didn't Win. It Survived". *CNN Opinion.* November 10, 2020. https://edition.cnn.com/2020/11/10/opi nions/democracy-didnt-win-it-survived-hemmer/index.html.

Herriot, P. and Scott-Jackson, W. 2002. "Globalization, Social Identities and Employment". *Brit. J. Management* 13(3), 249-257.

Howard, J. 2020. "A Herd Immunity Strategy to Fight the Pandemic Can Be 'Dangerous', Experts Say. Here's Why". *CNN.* September 1, 2020. Updated October 17, 2020. https://edition.cnn.com/20 20/09/01/health/herd-immunity-coronavirus-pandemic-expla iner-wellness/index.html.

IIF. 2020. *Global Debt Monitor: Attack of the Debt Tsunami.* Institute of International Finance (IIF). November 18, 2020. Washington, DC: IIF.

Inequality Organisation. 2018a: "Global Inequality". Inequality Organ- isation. Washington, DC: Institute for Policy Studies. https://in equality.org/facts/global-inequality/.

Inequality Organisation. 2018b. "Inequality and Health". Inequality Organisation, Washington, DC: Institute for Policy Studies. https://inequality.org/facts/inequality-and-health/.

Inglehart, R. and Norris, P. 2019. *Cultural Backlash: Trump, Brexit, and Authoritarian Populism.* Cambridge: Cambridge University Press.

Inglis, S. 2019. "So You Want to be an Autocrat? Here's the 10-Point Checklist". *The Conversation.* November 19, 2019. https://the conversation.com/so-you-want-to-be-an-autocrat-heres-the- 10-point-checklist-125908.

Janaskie, A. and Gartz, M. 2020. "The Great Barrington Declaration is Not Saying 'Lock Up Grandma'". American Institute for Economic Research (AIER). October 8, 2020. Great Barrington, MA: AIER. https://www.aier.org/article/the-great-barrington-declaration -is-not-saying-lock-up-grandma/.

Jones, R. 2018. "Engineering Cheerful Robots: An Ethical Considera- tion". *Information*, 2018, 9, 152, 1-11. (Switzerland). Research Gate. June, 2018. doi:10.3390/info9070152. https://www.resea rchgate.net/publication/325967373_Engineering_Cheerful_Ro bots_An_Ethical_Consideration.

Kaiser, C. 2020. "Arguing with Zombies Review: Paul Krugman Trumps the Republicans". *The Guardian.* May 3, 2020. https://

www.theguardian.com/books/2020/may/03/arguing-with-zo
mbies-review-paul-krugman-trump-republicans.

Kerber, R., Coster, H. and McLymore, A. 2020. "US Companies Vow to Fight Racism but Face Critics on Diversity". *Reuters.* June 10, 2020. https://www.reuters.com/article/us-minneapolis-police-companies-insight-idUSKBN23H1KW.

Kilic, O., Kalcioglu, M.T., Cag, Y. et al. 2020. "Could Sudden Sensorineu-ral Hearing Loss be the Sole Manifestation of Covid-19? An In-vestigation into SARS-Cov-2 in the Etiology of Sudden Sensori-neural Hearing Loss". *Int. J. Infectious Diseases,* 97, 208-211.

Klein, N. 2007. *The Shock Doctrine: The Rise of Disaster Capitalism.* New York: Knopf.

Klein, N. 2017. *No is Not Enough: Resisting Trump's Shock Politics and Winning the World We Need.* Chicago, Ill: Haymarket Books.

Krugman, P. 2020. *Arguing with Zombies: Economics, Politics, and the Fight for a Better Future.* London: W.W. Norton.

Kulldorff, M., Gupta, S. Bhattacharya, J. et al. 2020. "The Great Barring-ton Declaration". October 4, 2020. American Institute for Eco-nomic Research (AIER). Great Barrington, MA: AIER. https://www.globalresearch.ca/the-great-barrington-declaration/572 6289.

Lancet, The. 2020. "World Report". *The Lancet,* 395(10232), 1243-1244. April 18, 2020.

Lord Mance. 2011. "Should the Law be Certain?". The Oxford Shrieval Lecture given in the University Church of St Mary The Virgin, Ox-ford: Oxford University. October 11, 2011.

Luhrmann, A. Dupont, N. Masaaki, H. et al. 2020. "Varieties of Party Identity and Organization V-Party Dataset VII". Varieties of De-mocracy. V-Dem Project". doi.org/10.23696/vpartydsv1.

Macro Trends.2020. "U.S. GNP 1962-2020". *Macrotrends.net.* https://www.macrotrends.net/countries/USA/united-states/gnp-gross -national-product.

Mallaby, S. 2020. "Cool It, Krugman...The Self-Sabotaging Rage of the New York Times Columnist". *The Atlantic.* February 14, 2020. https://www.theatlantic.com/magazine/archive/2020/01/re view-paul-krugman-arguing-with-zombies/603052/.

Marcuse, H. 1955. *Eros and Civilization: A Philosophical Inquiry into Freud.* Boston: Beacon Press.

Marcuse, H. 1964. *One Dimensional Man*. Boston: Beacon Press.

Mather, Y. 2015. "Poverty, Inequality and Economic Nationalism: the Problem of Capitalism". *Redline World Press*. October 23, 2015.

Matthews, D. 2019. "Are 26 Billionaires Worth More Than Half of the Planet? The Debate Explained". *Vox*. January 22, 2019. https://www.vox.com/future-perfect/2019/1/22/18192774/oxfam-inequality-report-2019-davos-wealth.

Mayo Clinic. 2020. "Covid-19 (Coronavirus): Long-Term Effects". *Mayo Clinic*. October 7, 2020. https://www.mayoclinic.org/diseases-conditions/coronavirus/in-depth/coronavirus-long-term-effects/art-20490351.

Merton, R.K. 1957. *Social Theory and Social Structure*, revised edn. New York: Free Press.

Mills, C.W. 1959. *The Sociological Imagination*. New York: Oxford University Press.

Mitchell, O. 2005. "A Meta-Analysis of Race and Sentencing Research: Explaining the Inconsistencies". *J. Quantitative Criminology*, 21(4), 439-466.

Mullen, M. 2019. "Stop the Slaughter of Our Children with These Weapons of War". *The Atlantic*. August 9, 2019. https://www.theatlantic.com/ideas/archive/2019/08/michael-mullen-stop-slaughter-our-children/595807/.

Mullen, M. 2020. "I Cannot Remain Silent: Our Fellow Citizens are Not the Enemy, and Must Never Become So". *The Atlantic*. June 2, 2020. https://www.theatlantic.com/ideas/archive/2020/06/american-cities-are-not-battlespaces/612553/.

Myers, J. 2020. "5 Things Covid-19 has Taught Us About Inequality". *World Economic Forum*. August 18, 2020. https://www.weforum.org/agenda/2020/08/5-things-covid-19-has-taught-us-about-inequality/.

Neiwert, D. 2017. *Alt-America: The Rise of the Radical Right in the Age of Trump*. London:Verso.

Ortiz, J. 2020. *Poverty in Denmark and the Welfare State*. The Borgen Project. Denmark. October 2, 2020. https://borgenproject.org/poverty-in-denmark/.

Page, B.I. and Jacobs, L.R. 2009. *Class War? What Americans Really Think About Economic Equality*. Chicago: University of Chicago Press.

Paterlini, M. 2020. "Closing Borders is Ridiculous: the Epidemiologist Behind Sweden's Controversial Coronavirus Strategy". *Nature,* 580, p.574. April 21, 2020.

Pemstein, D., Daniel, K.L., Marquardt, E.T., et al. 2020. *The V-Dem Measurement Model: Latent Variable Analysis for Cross-National and Cross-Temporal Expert-Coded Data.* V-Dem Working Paper No. 21, 5th ed. Varieties of Democracy Institute, University of Gothenburg. Gothenburg, Sweden: V-dem.

Perry, E. 2017. "ABC's Corporate Fundamentalist Culture—An Analysis of its Sustainability". Cherwell HR Team, Observational Research Management Report. December 10, 2017. *Academia.* https://www.academia.edu/35452212/ABC_s_Corporate_Fun damentalist_Culture_An_Analysis_of_its_Sustainability.

Public Health England. 2018. "Research and Analysis: Inequalities in Health". Ch. 5 in *Public Health Profile for England.* UK Government. https://www.gov.uk/government/publications/health-p rofile-for-england-2018/chapter-5-inequalities-in-health.

Quan-Xin, L., Xiao-Jun, T., Qiu-lin, S., et al. 2020. "Clinical and Immunological Assessment of Asymptomatic SARS-COV-2 Infections". *Nature Medicine*, 26, 1200-1204, August 2020.

Richter, F. 2020. "Tech Giants Shrug Off Covid-19 Crisis". *Statista.* October 30, 2020. https://www.statista.com/chart/21584/gafam-revenue-growth/.

Roth, K. 2009. "Despots Masquerading as Democrats". *J. Human Rights Practice*, 1(1), 140-155.

RSF. 2020. *2020 World Press Freedom Index: Entering a Decisive Decade for Journalism, Exacerbated by Coronavirus.* Reporters Without Borders (RSF). Paris: RSF. https://rsf.org/en/2020-world-press-freedom-index-entering-decisive-decade-journalism-ex acerbated-coronavirus.

Sample, I. 2020. "The Costs are Too High: the Scientist Who Wants Lockdown Lifted Faster". *The Guardian.* June 5, 2020. https:// www.theguardian.com/world/2020/jun/05/the-costs-are-too-high-the-scientist-who-wants-lockdown-lifted-faster-sunetra-gupta.

Sandel, M.J. 2020. *The Tyranny of Merit: What's Become of the Common Good?* London: Penguin.

Savage, M. 2020. "What's Going Wrong in Sweden's Care Homes?" *BBC News*. Stockholm. May 19, 2020. https://www.bbc.com/news/amp/world-europe-52704836.

Schmidt, M.S. 2020. *Donald Trump v. The United States: Inside the Struggle to Stop a President*. New York: Penguin Random House.

Schindlinger, D. 2020. "Want Gender Balance in Boardrooms? Here are 3 Alternatives to Quotas". *Fortune*. April 25, 2020. https://fortune.com/author/dottie-schindlinger/.

Scobie, S. and Morris, J. 2020. *Quality and Inequality: Digging Deeper.* Quality Health Watch Briefing. Nuffield Trust. https://www.nuffieldtrust.org.uk/resource/quality-and-inequality-digging-deeper.

Solt, F. 2011. "Diversionary Nationalism: Economic Inequality and the Formation of National Pride". *J. Politics*, 73(3), 821-830.

Spohn, C. and Cederblom, J. 1991. "Race Disparities in Sentencing: A Test of the Liberalism Hypothesis". *Justice Quarterly*, 8(3), 305-327.

Stamper, N. 2006. *Breaking Rank: A Top Cop's Expose of the Dark Side of American Policing*. New York: Hachette Book Group.

Stanley, J. 2018. *How Fascism Works: The Politics of Us and Them*. New York: Random House.

Stevens, S. 2020. *It Was All A Lie: How The Republican Party Became Donald Trump*. New York: Knopf.

Svedberg, R. and Agevall, O. 2016. *The Max Weber Dictionary: Key Words and Central Concepts*, 2nd ed. Stanford, CA: Stanford University Press.

Thomas, N. 2020. "Fauci Slams Idea of Herd Immunity: Letting 'Things Rip' Without Protection is 'Ridiculous'". *CNN*. October 15, 2020. https://www.edition.cnn.com/world/live-news/coronavirus-pandemic-10-15-20-int/.

United Nations. 2020. *Inequality in a Rapidly Changing World: World Social Report 2020*. Department of Economic and Social Affairs. UN. https://www.un.org/development/desa/dspd/wp-content/uploads/sites/22/2020/01/World-Social-Report-2020-FullReport.pdf.

Vass, A.A. 1990. *Alternatives to Prison: Punishment, Custody and the Community*. London: Sage Publications.

Waring, A. (ed). 2018a. *The New Authoritarianism Vol 1: A Risk Analysis of the US Alt-Right Phenomenon.* Stuttgart: Ibidem-Verlag.

Waring, A. 2018b. "The Alt-Right, Human Rights, and the Law". In *The New Authoritarianism Vol. 1: A Risk Analysis of the US Alt-Right Phenomenon*, edited by A. Waring , 303-335. Stuttgart: Ibidem-Verlag.

Waring, A. (ed). 2019. *The New Authoritarianism Vol 2: A Risk Analysis of the European Alt-Right Phenomenon.* Stuttgart: Ibidem-Verlag.

Washington Post. 2020. "Global Freedom Would Suffer Grievous Harm in a Second Trump Term". Editorial Board Opinion. *The Washington Post.* August 28, 2020. https://www.washingtonpost.com /opinions/2020/08/28/global-freedom-would-suffer-grievous -harm-second-trump-term/?arc404=true.

Waters, T. and Waters, D. 2015. *Weber's Rationalism and Modern Society: New Translations on Politics, Bureaucracy, and Social Stratification.* London: Palgrave Macmillan.

Watson, C., Uberoi, E. and Kirk-Wade, E. 2020. *Women in Parliament and Government.* Research Briefing. UK Parliament. February 25, 2020. London: House of Commons Library. https://commonsli brary.parliament.uk/research-briefings/sn01250/.

Weber, M. 1949. *The Methodology of the Social Sciences.* Edited and translated by E.A. Shils and H.A. Finch. Glencoe, Ill: Free Press.

Williams, E., Buck, D. and Babalola, G. 2020. *What are Health Inequalities?* February 18, 2020. London: The King's Fund. https://www. kingsfund.org.uk/publications/what-are-health-inequalities.

Wingerden van, S. Wilsem van, J. and Johnson, B.D. 2016. "Offenders' Personal Circumstances and Punishment: Toward a More Refined Model for the Separation of Sentencing Disparities". *Justice Quarterly*, 33(1), 100-133.

Chapter 3:
Zombieland Revisited Part 2:
Pathological Corruption of Democracy

By Antony A. Vass[1]

Abstract

This chapter completes Zombieland Revisited by further examining crucial aspects of the authoritarian psychopathology that contaminates liberal democracy. Such contamination typically entails fraud and other crimes of powerful individuals and entities (corporate, institutional and political) and all-too-frequent government collusion. Key topics analysed include licit and illicit economies enabled by corruption and crime, Trump's financial dealings and use of executive power, corporate cronyism and political sleaze, subversion of criminal justice and the rule of law, and iniquities of the arms trade. The rise of technology, its uses and abuses, the militarisation of policing, the expansion of state and corporate surveillance and social control (e.g. electronic and cyber surveillance, face recognition) are examined in detail. The personal characteristics of 'democratic' despotic leadership in corporate business and politics and those of ardent followers are laid bare, including recent research on related personality types, traits and associated psychopathologies. The refinement of new forms of social control which play on freedom of speech and expression is discussed. Particular emphasis is given to the language of communication that gives rise to what the author labels as 'linguistic anarchy' which acts as a powerful means of subjugation.

Key words: corruption, Trump, policing, social control, personality traits, language

Corruption and Crimes of the Powerful: "Wherever Law Ends, Tyranny Begins"

In Chapter 2, it was argued that the failure of liberal democracy to curtail inequalities impacts on vast numbers of people in personal,

---

[1]   See contributor affiliations and biography, pages 527-528.

interpersonal, structural, and institutional contexts and helps to entrench the spread of authoritarianism. The issues of inequality bring into sharp focus the realisation that state and corporate rationality about market relations, profit, love for austerity measures and regressive tax cuts, and the perpetuation of bigotry and discrimination, cannot survive without a mentality of deep-seated greed, corruption and sleaze.

Greed is an insatiable appetite for more money, wealth and power but it extends to all relationships. In Erich Fromm's understanding, greed is a 'bottomless pit' which sees no end to people's desire to fulfill their inordinate quest for social status, vanity, personal gratification and self-promotion (Fromm 1942). In contemporary terms and in the world of corporate business, greed is presented as a natural necessity. It oils the wheels of business, corporate finance and success. The words of the main character of Gordon Gekko in Oliver Stone's film *Wall Street* capture its essence: "Greed...is good. Greed is right, greed works". However, as the story of Gekko unfolds, the protagonist's greed is ultimately revealed to be intertwined with market manipulation, fraud and corruption on a big scale.

Democracies are often seen as doing better than authoritarian states at controlling corruption due to their alleged free institutions, open competition and structural procedures that provide checks and balances which guard against corruption and abuse of power. It is claimed that autocracies manage to control petty and bureaucratic corruption but simultaneously engineer corruptive practices which allow their rulers to accrue vast amounts of financial and other benefits. So, autocracies need something like a "selectorate" group to act as a checking mechanism in the absence of regularised elections (Besley & Kudamatsu 2007) or broader strategic prescriptions for institutional controls (Kukutschka 2018).

However, the difference between corruption in democracies and in autocracies is relative and subject to normative interpretations rather than empirical facts. Empirical data are not particularly complimentary to democracies (Kukutschka 2018). Corruption and crimes of the powerful are found in abundance in Western democracies and act as another push down into the pit of autocratic rule. Institutional corruption is rife. Despite systemic attempts to regulate and stamp out corruption in the UK and US, it remains an intrinsic aspect of the corporate fundamentalist culture of exclusivity, privilege, restrictive practices, and moral tenets about the benefit of a free market without regulation and unchecked profit maximisation at any cost (Chayes 2020; Chiu 2019).

Corporate Fraud, Corruption, and Government Collusion

At the personal and corporate level, manipulation and fraud are now reaching epidemic proportions. Worldwide more than €16 billion (US$19 billion) was lost to various types of money fraud particularly forex (foreign exchange) market transactions in 2016. The UK Financial Conduct Authority (FCA) reported that in 2018, out of nearly 6,000 investment scams, 5,000 (83%) related to share, bond, forex and cryptocurrencies fraud. This is easy to understand. Daily forex transactions account for billions, even trillions, in combined currencies. There are, therefore, rich pickings to be had by fraudulent activities.

The extent to which formal institutions (from governments to banks and public and private corporations) are involved in subterranean, clandestine, corrupt, illicit, and criminal activity, such as fraud and money-laundering, is immense. For example, from leaked documents known as the FinCEN files as recently as September 2020, over 2,000 suspicious activity reports (SARs) for the period 2000 to 2017 suggest that an estimated two trillion US dollars was laundered "through some of the world's biggest banks and how criminals used anonymous British companies to hide their money" (*BBC Panorama* 2020).

It is not the first time leaks have implicated formal and regulated institutions involved in widespread clandestine operations for profit. In 2014, what came to be known as LuxLeaks, showed how rich corporations used tax deals in Luxembourg to reduce or minimise their tax liabilities. In 2015, leaked documents known as SwissLeaks, showed how HSBC Swiss Private Bank helped rich clients in tax avoidance schemes. In 2016, the Panama Papers revealed how wealthy people use offshore tax heavens to avoid taxes. In 2017, leaked papers known as the Paradise Papers revealed offshore accounts of politicians and business leaders in their attempt to keep their wealth under wraps.

The 2020 leaked FinCEN documents implicate corporate America and corporate Europe, and more specifically the corporate world of financial institutions in the UK, Germany and US, (which include financial corporation giants such as Barclays, Deutsche Bank, HSBC, JP Morgan, and Standard Chartered). These institutions appear to act as the epicentres of SARs and are deeply and extensively involved in transactions that relate to the fraudulent administration and dispersal of 'dirty' money (including the fortunes made by Chinese and Russian oligarchs and cartels) around the globe. Such corporate structures, according to the leaked FinCEN files, silently facilitate illicit transactions instead of applying and enforcing laws and moral expectations about money-laundering or related suspicious activity.

The 2007-2008 global financial meltdown was caused by greedy banks and the pathological Machiavellian culture of CEOs. Through excessive risk-taking, they created a ripple effect so severe that it resulted in a global recession. It led to hitherto unseen levels of unemployment, the collapse of the housing market, millions losing their homes and becoming homeless and destitute. It led to the bankruptcy of Lehman Brothers bank and the domino effect crumbled the global banking sector. In just the US and Europe alone, the losses incurred were estimated to be in the order of over one trillion dollars in the form of toxic assets. It led to democratic states in Europe (e.g. Greece, Italy, Spain and Cyprus) falling into an unmanageable national debt, while it forced Iceland into bankruptcy. Poverty rose globally as governments and central banks struggled to maintain some order by spending trillions of dollars of tax payers' money to bail out banks. Despite this, many CEOs left their positions with golden handshakes, multimillion handouts in pension rights and a myriad of other benefits. Hardly any of those responsible, from banks to CEOs to financial associates and politicians, were brought to justice. In the US, only one such person was sentenced to a few months in prison, none was prosecuted in the UK or, as far as records go, in Europe. Only Iceland pursued twenty such individuals who were subsequently convicted and imprisoned (cf. Merle 2018; Wikipedia 2020).

In another recent case, Germany, the perceived bastion and powerhouse of democratic Europe, was shaken by the biggest post-war corporate fraud committed by Wirecard which was regarded as 'Germany's PayPal'. Wirecard was exposed for its extensive (global) fraudulent and sophisticated accounting practices and phantom ac-counts. Its executives ran a criminal racket which defrauded creditors of billions of euros. Its fraudulent operations went beyond corrupt company CEOs. They engulfed German regulatory authorities, banks, the press, investors, and ordinary people. It collapsed, with a loss of €3.3 billion (US$3.9 billion) in debts and €1.9 billion (US$2.3 billion) missing from its accounts (Storbeck 2020). The scale of fraud commit-ted was such that investigations into Wirecard's activities continue and appear to have no end.

At another level, the scandal regarding the 'Citizenship by In-vestment Programme' (CIP), whereby the state colludes with the rich to provide the latter with citizenship and a passport which allows res-idence and free access to European Union states, has been recently brought to the fore by investigative journalism (e.g. *Al Jazeera* 2020a, 2020b). The CIP scheme is run by a number of EU countries (e.g. Por-tugal, Malta, Cyprus, Austria and Bulgaria, though in 2020 Cyprus claimed closure of the scheme). It is also evident in a more structured way in the UK (Arton Capital 2020; UK Government 2020). Such coun-tries as Austria, France, and Greece may not publicly participate in such a scheme, but nonetheless are found to provide passports to wealthy individuals of choice based on favour and patronage.

The scheme discriminates against ordinary applicants, favours the rich and privileged, and adds to inequality of opportunity. It is also open to widespread corruption. Criminals, fraudsters, money-laun-derers, oligarchs, and people with dubious backgrounds are found to be accommodated. Rich applicants from such dubious backgrounds receive favourable treatment by a network of immovable property de-velopers, estate agents, civil servants, lawyers, politicians, and senior government officials and members of parliament.

This global 'kleptomania' culture (Bergis 2020), which is often accompanied by violence, extortion and other corrupt practices, af-flicts both despotic and democratic states. It succeeds in enriching and sustaining dictatorships and maintaining skewed democracies. As money buys power, at the heart of this interconnected and globalised organisation of thieving is the acquisition and monopolisation of power. It concentrates wealth and power in the hands of the few and often anonymous interests, while it maintains poverty and inequality and social divisions in general (Bergis 2020). The global economy is riddled with rigged trade deals, tax evasion, theft, and the exploitation of the natural environment, all of which benefit rich individuals and rich countries at the cost of the poor and poor countries. This harms not only the livelihoods and the welfare of millions of people but also the stability of democracy on a global scale (Hickel 2017).

Unregulated and deeply engrained in corporate culture, such greed and manipulation work against the democratic ethos of openness and transparency and equal treatment for all. It exacerbates the unequal distribution of wealth and adds to social and economic inequalities. Perversely, when things go wrong (as in the 2007-2008 economic crisis and the 2020-2021 economic meltdown), corporations which normally sing the financial merits of democratic capitalism and free market relations by decrying state interference and regulation, are first in the queue to beg and receive billions of dollars in state aid or state cheap loans. Their insatiable appetite for financial benefit and profit is such that when the occasion arises they quickly transform themselves into cheerful converts and recipients of massive amounts of public funds, only to use such funds to invest elsewhere for more financial benefit or to sustain expensive executive salaries. Ethical considerations do not seem to play well with business. By grabbing massive amounts of state aid or loans, they succeed in haemorrhaging the public purse and destabilising social relations in the economy. Their actions assist in the maintenance of an asymmetrical and inequitable system of social relations and the loss of public trust in democratic leadership and government.

In the US, for example, many rich companies 'with substantial market value', and the ability to raise their own capital through markets, received and accepted money under the Paycheck Protection Program (PPP) when the money was meant for keeping smaller businesses afloat. Although some of these corporations promised to return the money, others resisted or refused, claiming that they were entitled to the loans (Whalen et al 2020). According to data compiled by the *Washington Post*, rich and influential publicly traded companies received "more than one billion in funds" which were meant for small businesses to retain staff in employment. In fact, a number of these corporations continued to pay their executives on average well over two million dollars in annual salaries at a time when millions of workers were being put on furlough or made redundant. In some cases, chief executives' remuneration and other benefits equalled the value of the loans received by those companies. Moreover, as Congress and the Trump administration permitted companies with multiple subsidiaries to apply and receive such assistance separately, the policy favoured big corporations and their Republican donors (O'Connell et al 2020).

In the UK it is a similar story. The blunders of the Conservative government in failing to face the facts of a galloping infectious novel coronavirus that wreaked havoc in the economy and social relations are many. These failures also include the fact that Boris Johnson's government allocated billions of pounds worth of contracts to companies of choice and preference for the provision of personal protective equipment (PPE) to the NHS. At least two contracts costing multimillions to the public purse were found to have been paid to dormant companies. Contracts went to "unusual companies, without open competition or transparency and some of these companies are closely linked to the government" (Monbiot 2020). Government officials, including MPs, were found to procure deals where they had direct interests. Some £18 billion (US$24 billion) was spent without transparent accountability and £10.5 billion (US$14 billion) appears to have vanished from accounts (National Audit Office 2020).

Corporate Cronyism and Political Sleaze

Furthermore, matters of cronyism and irregular links between the government and rich billionaire property developers have been alleged (Woodstock 2020). Conservative party donors, who supported the withdrawal of the UK from the European Union (Brexit), influenced policy and publicly supported post-Brexit trade reforms that would bring them financial savings and tax benefits (Savage 2020).

The broader concern about sleaze and suspect dealings—which are normally attempted and carried out in the dark corridors of power away from the public eye—is that policy determination and policy making are engineered and executed by often anonymous, unelected and unaccountable appointees who remain hidden away or are appointed as 'advisers' by presidents, prime ministers, ministers, senators, members of parliament and so on who constitute the echelons of government. Their influence on policy and the way they wield power over democratically elected governments remains a point of contention. In the UK, for instance, Johnson's Conservative government appears to be unduly guided by a small inner circle of confidants and advisers whose personal or ideological preferences are often bolstered and legitimised by the Conservative Party majority in parliament. In the words of an observer "the guiding principle seems to be brazen cronyism, coupled with the arrogance of those who believe they are untouchable and that rules are for little people" (Freedland 2020).

However, corruption is not restricted to financial relations. The Trump administration's stranglehold on democracy was bolstered by a relentless push toward partisan politics and a radical-right ideology. Throughout, even after the 2020 election and in the transitional period before relinquishing power to a new administration, such behaviour included the purge of high ranking and other officials regarded or perceived as disfavouring the president. The purge was not just local. It spread throughout the period 2016 to 2020 across all democratic institutions. It included the dismantling of watchdog bodies; the introduction of policies favouring party colours, personal gain and populist agendas; the appointment of a US Attorney General who, instead of being impartial and representative of all Americans by upholding the constitution, chose to act as a personal attorney general to the president. His actions included the firing of a US federal prosecutor—Geoffrey Berman, US attorney for the Southern District of New York—whose office happened to be investigating corruption claims against the president's personal lawyer Rudolph Giuliani. These anti-democratic activities were largely condoned by the GOP[2] and its higher echelons and the leaders of the Senate Republican majority. Added to this was the interwoven aspect of corporate interests which were expressed through direct donations in return for favours or through a strong and influential body of lobbyists on behalf of big corporations and their wealthy executives.

Trump's Personal and Political Finance Activities

On a more individual and personal level, it is worth focussing on Donald Trump to get a glimpse of what happens at the top. The president has always boasted about being the most successful businessman on

---

[2]   GOP—Grand Old Party i.e. US Republican Party

the planet but was found, according to *Washington Post's* fact check, to have lied about his financial empire. Between 1990 and 2009, he filed six times for bankruptcy protection of his financial empire in order to wipe out billions of dollars in debts and leave others to pick up the tab and bear the fallout.

The self-proclaimed richest president in American history boasted, at the time of his announcement to bid for the presidency of the United States in 2016, that he would self-fund his campaign and that he was independent of lobbyists, individual and corporate donors. "I'm really rich", he declared. In short, that he was free of any interests and that his only aim was to fight the rotten elite establishment and "make America great again". Although he followed that promise for some time in his campaign for the Republican Party nomination to the presidency (April 2015 to June 2016), on securing the nomination he accepted outside donations worth US$234 million while he put up US$16 million. It is claimed that, on taking office, he shifted US$1.3 million donors' contributions into his business by charging his own re-election campaign for rent, food, lodging and other expenses. In other words, "$1.3 million of donor money has turned into $1.3 million of Trump money" (Alexander 2019).

Another investigation of Trump's financial empire and relationship to Deutsche Bank reveals that, as deregulation of markets was the call of the day in Western democracies and obscene profits for big corporations marked the experience of the day, Deutsche Bank in 1995 embarked on an expansion of its financial activities by taking high-profile investment risks. As profits sky-rocketed, greed called for more risks and the bank's portfolio of acquisitions grew. One of its more controversial activities was its alleged involvement in dubious and criminal dealings e.g. laundering billions of Russian roubles and converting them into US dollars (Enrich 2020). In this game of high risk activity for profit, the bank entered in a financial relationship with Donald Trump. It is said that the bank failed to check Trump's usual exaggerated claims about his net worth or his use of flattery and self-praise, smooth talk, and persuasion about his financial wizardry. Loans started flowing into Trump's accounts for buildings, casinos and resorts. As loan repayments failed to materialise, the bank called in the massive US$48 million debt that had accrued. Trump refused to pay on the basis of *force majeure* and counterclaimed for damages (Enrich 2020).

More recently, the *New York Times,* having had access to Trump's tax records extending over more than two decades, revealed a person struggling financially and being in "hundreds of millions in debt coming due" (Buettner et al 2020). He paid US$750 dollars in tax in 2016 and nothing for the previous ten years of reported losses. According to the *New York Times,* his financial challenges and pressures "...put him in potential and often direct conflict of interest with his job as president...His properties have become bazaars for collecting money directly from lobbyists, foreign officials and others seeking face time, access or favor" (Buettner et al 2020). Despite his personal attacks on China; his claims that Democrats were China's pawns; the trade war he had instigated against China, and his labelling of the novel coronavirus as the 'Chinese virus', his tax files also revealed that he had a 'cosy' relationship with the Chinese. He kept a secret Chinese bank account; he showed profits of nearly six million dollars from sale of property to a Chinese investor; he became the owner of several trademarks in China; his daughter Ivanka Trump, an adviser to the president, received export subsidies in China for her name brand handbags; and attempts were made by his family to attract Chinese real estate investment for exchange of favours (McIntire et al 2020). All along, these dealings and Trump's overall approach to governance were guided by self-interest and an appetite for personal gain (Bolton 2020), and a sustained belief that he was the brightest, wisest and shrewdest wizard of wealth, governance and opportunity (Woodward 2020). See also Pettypiece (2020), Santucci (2020), and Tindera (2020), and on 'dark money' Montellaro (2020).

Subversion of Criminal Justice

It is not that this sleazy world of politics just helps politicians and corporate business in their quest for financial, social and political benefits. Abuse of authority is often converted into coercion. It translates into raw power and dereliction of duty. Corrupt relationships undermine social justice and the proper workings of the rule of law in all social spheres, but especially in the area of criminal justice.

Crimes of the powerful, or what Edwin Sutherland originally called "white-collar crime" (Sutherland and Cressey 1996), creates a situation of 'them' and 'us'. Through interference in the justice process, either by direct intervention to influence both the process and outcomes or by turning a blind eye to the commission of illicit acts committed by the powerful, there is what one may describe as a law for the lion and a law for the ox. It blatantly discriminates in the treatment of crimes of the ruling classes and crimes of the poor. It becomes a major challenge to the social stability and maintenance of democracy that preaches equal treatment under the law. Although the powerful conveniently regard financial crimes as crimes-without-victims, nevertheless, as noted above, such crimes leave behind a devastating impact on economies and people's lives. The criminal code defines such crimes as serious criminal offences which often attract lengthy prison sentences.

In the period January 2017 to November 2020, President Trump used his executive clemency powers (without resort to the Justices' Office of the Pardon Attorney) to pardon twenty-nine individuals who were closely linked to him or his administration, or who were avowed supporters of his and the GOP. He used his clemency powers on the basis that he, being the president and chief law enforcement officer in the country, had unlimited executive powers and was well within his 'total' jurisdiction to do so.

Within the same period, he pardoned or commuted the prison sentences of no less than nineteen convicted individuals. The felonies committed by such high ranking or 'favoured' individuals included tax fraud and making false statements; receiving money for favours and having connections with the criminal fraternity; financial scandals and embezzlement; soliciting bribes for the appointment of seats in the Senate; hacking of competitors' computers; obstruction of justice; actively involved in receiving, selling and generally dealing in stolen property; money-laundering and hiding proceeds; money-laundering and conspiracy to commit health care fraud; conspiracy to distribute illicit drugs; false statements to the FBI, witness tampering and perjury (*Associated Press* 2020; Behrmann 2020; Brandus 2020). On 25 November 2020, Trump's pardon of Michael Flynn, his first national security adviser who was convicted of false statements to the FBI, raised speculation that Trump would deliver more pardons and commutations before leaving office. In fact, in the aftermath of the 2020 US election results, in one of his raging tweets, Trump repeated his intent (as he had alluded to in the course of his impeachment proceedings) that he would exercise his executive power to pardon himself of any charges or attempts to convict him of any crime or wrongdoing. Later reports suggest that he would also pardon his children and son-in-law as well as others in the face of adversity and because they were "treated badly", although he did not do so, apparently on legal advice.

This world of wheeling-and-dealing, unethical, criminal, and other misdeeds carried out in the name of democracy promotes practices which are akin to those only expected or experienced in authoritarian regimes. Abandoning or undermining the rule of law, bending or subverting the rules for profit and personal gain, attacking the core values of transparency, accountability, fair and equitable treatment of all citizens can only be an attack on the sustainment and viability of democracy. Moreover, it opens a Pandora's Box by encouraging other rulers and governments who instead of aspiring to model themselves on the democratic ideal learn to justify their own activities on these very flaws, practices and down-right excesses of democracy.

In the European Union (EU), there is a growing concern about the despotic direction that member states—Poland, Hungary and Bulgaria in particular—are heading to. Their hardening of attitudes on social issues, abuses of the rule of law, corruption, and curtailment of media freedom has led one EU Commissioner, Vera Jourova, to observe that democratic institutions are being transformed into an "illiberal democracy". Added to those concerns, the EU is expressly rattled by another 'silent' but increasing undercurrent in the perceived breakdown of the rule of law: the black market stockpile and supply of weapons.

The Iniquitous Arms Trade

The EU Commission does not have direct authority over the sale of arms by member states. Such countries as France, Germany and Italy, and Britain newly independent of the EU, have a morally questionable arms trade that covers the globe and in many instances supplies advanced weapons to some of the roughest and toughest authoritarian regimes currently in existence. However, this trade in arms which member states are fully engaging in through so-called 'export licences' is also supplemented by corrupt practices, as for example the diversion of weapons from licenced exports to terrorist organisations or armed militias in some of the most volatile spots on the planet. Corruption in arms sales is of particular importance. It not only creates another route to the accumulation and distribution of dirty money, but also compromises democratic governance and threatens social relations, peace and civil rights within countries and between countries and contributes to the humanitarian crisis afflicting the world.

Other than the steady rise of a tightening grip on the free press, the judiciary, free assembly and movement, there is also the increasing involvement of Balkan and Central European states (Bulgaria, Croatia, Czech Republic, Hungary, Romania, Slovakia) in clandestine arms operations. According to the London based Tactics Institute of Security and Counter Terrorism, clandestine operations together with licenced operations in the arms trade are out of control. The Tactics Institute claims that weapons find their way to extreme groups and non-governmental militias in conflict zones (e.g. Eritrea, Iraq, Libya, Syria, and Yemen) before being redirected and "reused-recycled" to organised criminal groups and terrorist groups operating in Europe. It warns that the arms market not only inflames violence and conflict, but also generates huge amounts of illicit earnings. These are then channelled into other vices for more profit, political favours, and widespread corruption among government officials, a rise in organised crime, the radicalisation of social groups and the rise of extremism (Tactics Institute 2020). Recently, the Austrian and German authorities uncovered an illegal arms trade and supply of recycled weapons distributed to Austrian and German militant radical-right groups.

Licit and Illicit Economies Blurred by Sanctioned Corruption and Crime

These clandestine operations require corrupt providers and corrupt receivers. In any organised form, the transactional process between corrupt sellers and corrupt buyers takes place and is policed in the context of what Paul Rock (1973) called "popular unawareness". In other words, they are mostly discreet and hidden from the public eye. This allows officials and rogue traders to strike bargains between them for mutual benefits. Of course, such corrupt relationships do not happen outside the workings of organised legitimate settings. On the contrary, they exist and take place within the legitimacy of a state and corporate organisational brief that the ends justify the means.

When corruption and crimes of the powerful in all their forms are put in a theoretical context of social relationships and social organisation, democratic capitalism is found to breed and accommodate illegality. As Ruggiero and Vass (1992) have argued, there is an uneasy symbiotic and existential relationship between "the formal (licit) and informal (illicit) economy". In essence, although this corrupt relationship of coexistence between legality and illegality may appear to contradict, bedevil and adulterate democratic core values, it also offers essential but unequal economic and social benefits at one and the same time (see also Gounev & Ruggiero 2014).

In other words, as the huge amounts of dirty and corrupt money from diverse illegal activities are transacted, circulated, invested, and filter down, they succeed in becoming an intrinsic aspect of the formal, licit economy. Such money takes the form of savings, security deposits, shares, and investments in real estate in the commercial, private and public sector and in other guises. As such, the formal economy and informal economy are found to be intertwined, blurred and negotiable. Any attempt made to distinguish between the two as separate entities becomes, by definition, a false dichotomy. As in authoritarian states, the interconnection and interdependence of the formal and informal economy is now so deeply engrained in the workings of a democracy, from Europe to the US and beyond, that any notion of stamping out the informal economy and its clandestine values can only leave Western democratic states and the global economy in tatters. As the illicit economy feeds off the formal economy and the licit economy profits and survives by accommodating the illicit economy, a structural dependence is established that keeps lubricating and maintaining the wheels of economic, social and political power relationships. It creates a set of socio-economic and political relationships which, if tampered with, may have a profound effect on both the stability of the economy as a whole and the stability of government.

By the same token, the symbiotic existence of the licit and illicit economies produces structural fissures, irregularities and inequities which impact on social relations: it encourages and maintains social divisions in society, perpetuates a cycle of corruption, inequality, political favours, privilege and patronage. Democracy's accommodation of corrupt practices makes it hostage to economic and political pressure. Its capacity to be open and accountable is largely compromised.

It leads to an endemic loss of trust in those who govern and allows despondency and cynicism to emerge.

In summary, once corruption is allowed to become engrained in the fabric of society it makes a stain on it. As that stain is absorbed, it becomes an integral part of the fabric. At one and the same time, the stain *is* the fabric and what also *blemishes* it. Corruption and crimes of the powerful are another way of acting above the rule of law and another means to exploitative and repressive relationships. Although one may not justifiably agree with various aspects of John Locke's (1632-1704) philosophy, his observation in chapter 18 of his *Two Treatises of Government, Book II*, that "wherever law ends, tyranny begins" gives food for thought (see also, Stanford Encyclopaedia of Philosophy 2020). Once the rule of law is not applied fairly and equitably but is, instead, used and abused by authority to favour particular individuals, to engage in clandestine activities, or turn a blind eye to corrupt practices, it can only be to the detriment of the people. Such abuse is concomitant with a tyrannical government (Packer 2020). Remarkably, Locke goes further than that observation: namely, that as democratic government exists by consent, it follows that when such leaders are found to abuse their powers, the people have every legitimate right to fight for their rights, resist and replace those corrupt rulers by any means available to them.

Technology, the Militarisation of the Police and Expansion of Surveillance

In Durkheimian terms (Durkheim 1951, 1984; Aron 2018) the transition from traditionalism to modernity means that old methods of keeping individuals under surveillance and control shift from informal means (e.g. the neighbourhood, the family, the community) to formal means administered by the state and its apparatus (e.g. laws, police, courts). Although the shift to modernity poses serious challenges to maintaining order, the loss of traditionalism is replaced and compensated by individualism. Whilst individualism requires control, it affords nonetheless a sense of liberation from the tyranny of the community collective. Modernity offers individuals now living in a society of 'strangers' a sense of freedom.

In the course of time and profound social change, surveillance and control become more centralised and the state, together with big private corporations, exercises a monopoly of coercion. In the process of a never-ending struggle to deal with internal and external threats (real or imaginary), order and security, the state shields itself with a panoply of social control 'weapons'. It constantly invents new methods of surveillance or upgrades and refines existing ones. This is done either alone or in close collaboration or links with private corporations and agencies. They are united in their value of monopolising the means of policing populations and exercising power while propagating new sources of profit at one and the same time.

Technology and Social Control

Technology has contributed to improvements in just about every walk of life and the overall human experience. Advances in mobility, medicine and health care in general, food production and distribution, communications and education are just a few examples.

Technological advances, particularly in artificial intelligence (AI), have helped to boost and improve health-care facilities and provision for patients. They have provided much needed support to people with special needs by offering them the ability and opportunity to engage in cognitive expression, communication and thus social interaction. Technology has, in many respects, liberated some individuals from a life of dependency, excessive solitude, isolation and social stigma. Simultaneously, it has helped to break down prejudice and discrimination in the workplace, the home, the school, and generally in any socially defined space. Also, technology has managed to broaden peoples' communication channels to such a level that it has opened up opportunities for social contact between individuals that could not have been possible otherwise. Indeed, in the age of Covid-19, in the absence of technological innovation there would have been a disastrous breakdown in social interaction and the human need to keep in touch with others. In this state of affairs and in the absence of technology, there would have been far more serious personal troubles (e.g. mental health) and social consequences (e.g. the economy and a disengagement of people from other people and social institutions). Such a state of affairs could have posed an imminent threat to social organisation and societal stability.

However, against the positive side of technology there are also limitations, social negatives and serious concerns. Science and technology are not neutral and free of human values. In fact, they are laden with normative statements and often hide repressive social experiences. They contain internal contradictions with a potential for more liberation and more oppression at the same time (Feenberg 1999; 2002; Habermas 2003; Kellner & Best 2001; Marcuse 1955, 1964). They contribute to the positive experience of more freedoms but equally serve to increase and broaden the power of particular elite groups over others.

These elites' control, use and promotion of advances in technology empowers them to systematically and sophisticatedly rule over those whose labour is no longer required as a result of fragmentation, elimination and automation of work tasks. Many people lower down the socio-economic ladder become, through changes promoted by technology, redundant labour, lose their jobs and become an unemployable class. On a broader historical social scale, technology has been linked to more centralisation or a gradual dispersal of centralisation to accommodate the broader higher echelons of private corporate interests, less openness, more secrecy, less transparency, less accountability, more controls, and thus an expansion of authoritarian values and the emergence of despotic states where control of their populations now derives from distant and often unknown or anonymous structures.

The push for technology by emphasising its benefits to society is done through an efficient cultural socialisation process that manages to persuade people that technology is good for them and their existential survival. As people accept that cultural version of the benefits of technology, they become the object of study, manipulation and control while falsely believing that they are given more freedom and entertainment. Whilst technology promotes new ways of moving societies forward and assists some individuals to sustain a 'happier' life, at the same time the relationship between individuals and their rulers is transformed into one which is more remote and impersonal. Authority is both more centralised and more diffused. Social relationships which define social divisions remain, become more complex and obscure. A new social order is managed by an encroachment on people's personal space and liberties. As the new order is gradually accepted and normalised, more controls appear necessary to manage the new context. The new order is also an unequal experience. It creates a sharper and more pronounced division between those who are the subject of surveillance and control, those who become the instrument of enforcement, and those who create and define the new social reality.

Militarisation of Policing

A particular aspect of this relationship between social order and its maintenance is the expansion of social control by means which, in the past, could only be seen as an intrinsic feature of strict authoritarian states. One specific example of this symbolic and actual change is the transformation of the police. Symbolically, in combating crime and social unrest, the police now present more like menacing warriors covered from head-to-toe in dark helmets, suits and boots and armed with an impressive collection of weaponry akin to the antagonist Darth Vader from the *Star Wars* franchise. They present far more like images from tough despotic states than open democratic societies.

In action, the contrast with the old friendly community 'cop' could not be starker. Western democracies have for long been engaged in the gradual militarisation of police forces. These forces are now characterised by the deployment of a highly advanced arsenal of technological means to control individuals and crowds. This militarisation of police forces and the "dark side of police culture" (Stamper 2006) leads to the enforcement of state and intrinsically corporate power by often very brutal and unaccountable means. It is a reflection of democracies evolving, and whose policing institutions are gradually being shaped, into an occupying army of 'righteous warriors'. This adds to concerns about the rise of alien and despotic powers which are far removed from their communities and which escape public inspection of their legitimacies.

The push to technologise and weaponise the formal means of social control to fight a war against perceived thuggery and broader social disorganisation has developed into a sophisticated industry of suppressing expression and stifling calls for social justice. Other than the real effects of violence and brutality which arise from such a transformation of policing, there is also the less understood and hidden fact that this development broadens the social distance between the state and its people by precipitating tensions, social conflict and disorder. The police have become more alienated from the people they are supposed to serve and the people have become more hostile to the former and their demeanour, thus creating loss of trust and raising questions about the state's own legitimacy (see e.g. Balko 2014; Stamper 2006, 2016; Stott & Pearson 2006, 2007; Tsoukala et al 2016; Whitehead 2015).

The militarisation and weaponisation of almost every available social space is reaching epidemic proportions. Private and hitherto out of bounds spaces are now open to scrutiny. The use of drones is a point in case. Other than their broader use, current experimentation with small 'independently thinking' weaponised drones (and the gradual miniaturisation of robotics) to tackle urban social unrest and warfare is fast taking shape (Atherton 2020). This new technology currently in development allegedly enables such drones to enter, snoop, scoop and monitor and, if required, attack any perceived threat within confined spaces including difficult-to-access places inside private and public buildings.

As social control becomes even more sophisticated and weaponised and broadens its net, such evolution is repeatedly and steadfastly justified and explained in terms of a desperate effort to preserve democracy and its values. However, the fact is that when that happens, and authorities apply legal and policing sanctions by aiming to be more efficient in weeding out 'troublesome' groups by resort to advances in technological surveillance, formal social control networks expand by taking in their net not just specifically targeted social groups but broader society. The result of this expansion and weaponisation of social order means restriction of personal freedoms, human and civil rights.

Surveillance and advances in technology, therefore, other than increasing inequalities by creating a new underclass of people who are left behind and are excluded from market relations due to their 'technological illiteracy' or their inability to afford access to technology, also transform and broaden the net of surveillance and social control to include private and public places. This expansion puts individuals under the watchful eye of neighbours, technology corporate structures, and the state, which centralises all such information to build huge banks of data on each one of its citizens. As technology accelerates in development, it creates its own momentum. It becomes a force of its own and, as it expands beyond the confines of restriction and regulation, it leaves individuals unaware or ignorant of the fact that their freedoms are coming under threat. Such developments expand without affording citizens equivalent protections, transparency, clear and enforceable rights, checks and balances to safeguard their privacy, human and civil rights. As the means of oppressive surveillance increase to capture whole new populations, the more such technological advances affect the human existence through the curtailment and loss of freedoms both in an objective and subjective way.

Electronic and Cyber Surveillance: Social Interaction Redefined

A particular worrying development which has followed very closely the availability and expansion of the internet is cybercrime and cyberattacks. Individuals' private emails are hacked and fed with disinformation to alter or reinforce their opinions on particular personal and political issues. On a broader level, democratic states are coming under severe pressure from authoritarian state cyberattacks (allegedly Russia, China, North Korea and Iran amongst others) which put social and political institutions at risk. It has to be said, that democratic states are not so innocent in that regard either. They do exactly the same. There is what one may call a cyberwarfare going on. The point is that malicious state cyberattacks create a fertile ground to sow the seeds of social division and conflict within domestic politics. They are a weapon that has the capability to target and disrupt democratic institutions as for example by influencing and adulterating the results of elections, inciting social conflict and ripping apart any notion of social consensus.

Inevitably, technological change is not only about overt policing. It is also about covert activity and an array of less obvious electronic surveillance. This includes computers, the internet, smartphones, smart devices like speakers and listening devices which scan surroundings and wait for instructions, displays, streaming devices, remote security devices for home security, smoke detectors, home assistant devices, cameras, social networks, biometrics, drones and other aerial devices, digital technology, data profiling, corporate and state shared intelligence data, autonomous vehicles, satellite imagery, radio frequency identification, tagging, global positioning systems, microchip implants and, more recently, the development of 'track and trace' apps.

The development of track and trace apps which monitor and identify infected individuals' locations and whereabouts though helpful in promoting public health and limit contagion, are an open invitation for the proliferation of a wider net of surveillance which goes beyond public health. The European Court of Justice (ECJ) ruled on October 6, 2020 that the mass use of apps and generally unrestrained mass surveillance of telephones and internet data is unlawful. This has given a legal boost to privacy rights advocates and may thwart the unwarranted and dangerous expansion of the social control net. It may stop some governments from ramping up their means of surveillance by exploiting public health concerns. However, attempts to control technology giants like *Twitter*, Alphabet's *Google* and *Facebook*, their powers and monopolies (as the US Senate Commerce Committee and the EU Commission have been attempting to do) are by and large inconsequential given that the genie is already out of the bottle.

The new breed of track and trace apps have another dark side. They may be the prelude to a number of other worrying trends. In due course, other than adding to surveillance, they may also alter the very core norms which guide human social interaction. Theoretically, when a red alert is sent out warning individuals that someone in the vicinity or close proximity is infected, the recipients of the warning will naturally try to avoid the risk of contagion. By avoiding the risk it will mean *distancing* themselves from anyone close by disrupting engagement in social interaction. In such a scenario, a *widening* of social distance (i.e. withdrawal and avoidance) will be sought in order to disengage from contact. But social interaction works on the principle of *narrowing* social distance between participants to engender communication and social organisation. In time, repeated interruptions in social contact and encounters will lead to a state of interactional anomie where the rules of social interaction begin to break down (Goffman 1959, 1983, 1995; see also, Romania 2020). It may mean that a new form of social malaise may be in the making. Instead of people seeking interaction to form social organisational relationships, they will learn to disengage through what may be termed a process of social '*dis*'interaction: replacing close, face-to-face encounters with distant, remote and mechanical as opposed to active relationships. The new order of doing things from afar will be defined, guided and controlled by technology which will act as the central creator, enabler and promoter of the emerging new working consensus about the rules and norms of social relationships.

Face Recognition Technology

Currently the emphasis is on FR expansion. Briefly, FR biometric scans record the geometry of the face by concentrating on distinctive features known as the 'golden triangle'—from the eyes, cheeks, nose and mouth to the chin—to create a face print. Once a face print is achieved it is compared to all available face prints stored in the database of the system to see if a match exists to identify individuals. It requires stationed (as in streets or shopping centres) or mobile (as in police vans) camera systems in both private and public domains to capture and process individuals' face. Given its infinite possibilities of scanning people without interruption, FR allows easy and quick access to a vast database of individuals for surveillance, law enforcement, health matters and national security considerations.

FR has been widely used in everyday consumer goods and gadgets like smartphones (for unlocking them and allowing access to data or running and accessing bank accounts). At an institutional level FR has taken a completely different meaning. It has been extensively deployed by despotic states on grounds of national security, terror and control of Covid-19 contagion. In China for example, an advance system is in operation that is connected to a network of CCTV cameras with the consequence that FR can scan up to two billion faces within a few seconds. It is directly used for the surveillance and control of China's populations. Russia is following suit with a massive expansion of FR in its cities to monitor the identities of its citizens. Anecdotal reports suggest that the system other than surveilling its citizens it also leads to corruption. Lawsuits by affected individuals whose identities and personal data are put up for sale by corrupt police are being pursued.

In what appears to be the first country to roll out FR as a national identity document (ID) scheme, Singapore has recently established a direct link between FR surveillance technologies and track and trace apps. The Singapore authorities have adopted FR technology known as 'Sing-Pass' as an ID to monitor contagion, citizens' movements and to act as a means to establishing a broader surveillance network. This will affect more than four million of its residents. 'Sing-Pass' is now applied at airports, the local economy and access to private and public services.

In the aftermath of the coronavirus pandemic therefore, intrusions in privacy and expansion of controls have gained ground worldwide. Despite ECJ judgements and broader civil rights concerns about the risks, European states and the UK promote FR technology as an invaluable tool in identifying individuals and fighting crime and social unrest. In the US, although some states have banned the technology until further consideration of its legal status and thus possible misuse and violation of civil liberties, civil rights campaigners claim that state agencies and private organisations—particularly in the wake of social unrest following George Floyd's murder—are widely using FR openly and covertly.

FR technology is currently unreliable and discriminatory. Algorithms designed to identify 'suspects' and detect 'suspicious movement' are loaded against people of colour and other minorities as facial structural characteristics and skin colour appear to elude a reliable assessment. However, its popularity and attraction in creating a rich database for the recognition of individuals means that its wider, universal deployment in every social space for the surveillance of vast numbers of people at little cost is but a matter of time. In fact as lockdowns are becoming a regular aspect of the present normalcy, their use is expanding in hitherto 'free environments' as for instance in education. Online exam proctoring software monitors authencity of identity through FR and embarks on an unaccountable and invasive collection of mass personal and private data from candidates who remain oblivious to the fact that they are being monitored.

From Cheerful Robots to Human Automatons

States' never ending pursuit of social order and national security together with corporate business' never ending pursuance of profit maximisation and market dominance through technological innovation and development are transforming what are now managed and inverted democracies into something more sinister. They cultivate and establish the moral, economic, political, social and cultural rules which allow the establishment of a sophisticated surveillance based on a network of technological devices which are beginning to determine and control every aspect of their citizens' private and public lives. In this context C. Wright Mills' (Mills 1959; see also, Jones 2018) 'cheerful robots' (when exploitation and repression are accepted and legitimated by the willful participation of the people) ceases to be much of relevance. Rather, under the advance and expansion of technology married to advances in neuroscience which can successfully tap into human neurons and makes manipulation of the brain and behaviour possible (e.g. currently used for positive medical purposes) societies may be in the process of creating a pool of *human automatons* instead. Meaningful social engagement with each other, communication and expression will be of a utilitarian character and a matter of instruction, programming and manipulation. Moreover, when individuals do engage emotionally, it may not be without their every thought, move and skin reaction being monitored and guided from a far-removed and often anonymous tyrannical elite.

In traditional communities, citizens were under the tyranny of the village fraternity, the watchful eye of a neighbour and the oppression of close familiarity. In modernity, citizens are fast coming under the 'cult of the utilitarian individual' and the watchful eye of a new tyrannical collective—the state and private corporations. In an age of rising technology that brings new forms of inequality and corruption and a growing new order of mass surveillance, mass manipulation, the alienation and dissociation from ones' self and from others, the recognisable boundaries that differentiate open from closed societies are fast disappearing.

Tough Leaders, the Herd Mentality, Personality Traits and Linguistic Anarchy

Big-Talking Autocrats

At the helm of social forces which are driving Western democracies into the ambit of authoritarianism sits a new breed of autocratic leaders, closely followed by a fanatical and committed base of followers. In his attempts to supersede decisions made by US state governors in their efforts to control the pandemic, on April 13, 2020 Donald Trump claimed unlimited executive powers:

> "When somebody's President of the United States, the authority is total. And that's the way it's got to be. It's total. It's total."

President Trump's 2020 election rallies in the aftermath of his Covid-19 infection and recovery were a continuation of the same presentations: boastful claims about his power and rare personal qualities. His hallmark of being amoral, divisive, offensive and dangerous took precedence. In addition to the disinformation, name-calling, sarcasm and scaremongering, he also revved up his base by repeating his 'Lock them up!' line—as he did against Hillary Clinton in the 2016 election. On October 16, 2020, at his pre-election rally in Macon, Georgia, and within 16.29 minutes of his speech, he told his followers:

> "Sleepy Joe Biden is the living embodiment of the corrupt political class...The Biden family is a corrupt enterprise...It makes crooked Hilary Clinton look like an amateur...I'll tell you something. Lock them up. You should lock them up. Lock up the Bidens. Lock up Hillary. Lock them up." (*REV* 2020a)

On October 17, 2020, in his rally in Muskegon, Michigan, and just two weeks after the FBI and state authorities had foiled an alleged radical-right militia plot to kidnap Michigan governor Gretchen Whitmer and put her on 'trial' for 'treason', he attacked the Michigan governor for being oppressive. Within 6.37 minutes he fomented his base's passions by charging:

> "We are all Patriots...The Democrat party... [is] now the party of socialists, Marxists and left-wing extremists...The people of Michigan must stop these anti-American radicals..."

In seconds, his followers chanted: "Lock them up! Lock them up! Lock them up!" to which Trump responded, "Lock them all up!" (*REV* 2020b).

The bravado and masculinity of tough leaders is also epidomised by Boris Johnson, the UK prime minister who plays on those qualities to distinguish himself from more mortal folk. In addressing the Conservative Party Conference on October 6, 2020, he acknowledged that when he had caught Covid-19 he was "too fat" but still "in the peak of health". Then he lashed out at his critics by expressing his tough masculinity and tough leadership:

> "I have read a lot of nonsense recently, about how my own bout of Covid has somehow robbed me of my mojo. And of course this is self-evident drivel, the kind of seditious propaganda that you would expect from people who don't want this government to succeed, who wanted to stop us delivering Brexit

and all our other manifesto pledges—and I can tell you that no power on earth was and is going to do that—and I could refute these critics of my athletic abilities in any way they want: arm-wrestle, leg-wrestle, Cumberland wrestle, sprint-off, you name it."

Authoritarian Leadership—The Trump Syndrome

Leadership, whether in corporate business or government or broader political systems, matters. The type of leader elected or appointed can, and does, make a difference to relations, how a country or company are run, and for what purpose. In that sense, the personality attributes of a leader, and how those attributes relate to followers' attributes and the broader social scene, are vital in understanding social relations and whether those relations prove productive or disruptive.

In this instance, the following concentrates on Donald Trump as a good example that provides a rich tapestry of information about personality traits, the authoritarian mindset and the authoritarian relationship. Trump's attributes make quite a long list. It consists of a complex web of intriguing characteristics which appear to go far beyond a straight-forward diagnosis of a single personality type. Rather, the plethora of characterisations, which appear to constitute traits of his personality, may represent, accommodate and reflect a variety of types of personality and personality disorders. Such is the abundance and garden variety of his traits that it can make more sense to refer to them in terms of a syndrome: the *Trump Syndrome.*

This syndrome is dominated by an expression of pseudo-masculinity, a tough guy, a 'macho' man and a patriot image presentation. This macho man takes on the world single-handedly with the support of a loyal and ardent base. This relationship between the mindset and personality of an autocratic leader and a base of followers is built on the notion that the leader commands and the base obeys and follows. It is a special type of relationship between ruler and subject which requires a particular type of mentality about dominance and obedience to make it work.

Illustratively, in the course of an interview with George Stephanopoulos (*ABC News' Town Hall* 2020) Trump was asked about the coronavirus which was out of control and how to stop it. An angry Trump retorted that the solution was simple: the nation needed to build a *"herd mentality"*, when of course he meant 'herd immunity'. This slip of the tongue aptly captured what the despotic mindset is all about. Such a mentality requires a dominant leader (the shepherd) and a base of followers (the flock) who are submissive and easily prone to manipulation. In the hands of a skilful, sinister and manipulative leader, a sleepy, 'grazing' herd can turn into an army of aggressive, untowardly fanatical believers. The storming of the US Capitol by Trump die-hard followers on January 6, 2021, was not a spontaneous combustive, isolated incident. It was testimony to that herd culture, its historical antecedents (the rise of the radical right) and Trump's relationship with his 'flock'. Once such a herd culture has been established, believers are capable and willing to commit seditious or other ruckus acts to defend their leader, his commands, sermons and demeanour.

The exhaustive list of characterisations which define Trump's mindset and demeanour are summarised below:

> Arrogance, extreme sensitivity to criticism and fear of rejection or abandonment; a calculative, untruthful and manipulative approach to relationships on a profit or loss basis; lack of emotional and social attachment; an inability to relax and deal with the perpetual stress-induced cycle of personal, political and other events; denial and a fear of facing reality and the world-at-large by hiding behind an unreal and scripted world; denial of wrongdoing and a compulsive need to use scapegoats by blaming others for one's misfortunes; a narcotic and obsessive dependency on social media as a medium of communication and a megaphone to spread the 'word' about allegiance to the leader in language which is a rich admixture of self-praise, sermons, an explosive torrent of abuse against opponents, name-calling, repressed emotions, conspiracies, misinformation and disinformation; denial of science and knowledge-based information and a fear of complex arguments and scientific reasoning; denial of any association with particular events, individuals or situations if they are perceived as a personal threat or counterproductive; and if association is proven, it is quickly neutralised by invoking ignorance and innocence; a neurotic, incoherent and incongruent thought process which is exposed through a simplistic and repetitive vocabulary; an unusually mixed-up, intense, often vitriolic verbal, written and non-verbal form of expression; difficulty in keeping emotions in check; an almost obsessive wish to be over-consumed with trivialities; an impulsiveness and compulsiveness to lie; a big, fragile ego and behaviour characterised by egocentrism and narcissism; megalomania and acting like an imperial monarch with an expressed need for others to follow with single-minded obedience; a self-impression of being exceptionally gifted and unique like no other; an intolerance to alternative views and difference; susceptible to tantrums and a child-like desperation for constant love, praise and recognition; an ambivalence about personal identity, values and morals; a loner and inward looking; riddled with suspicion and mistrust of others; vindictive to anyone who is perceived disloyal and disobedient; an exaggerated, if not delusional, belief that everyone

is out to get him or harm him; an uncontrollable need to manipulate others; a love for recklessness, disruption and social chaos to serve personal interests without regard to moral boundaries, social consequences or the feelings and wellbeing of others; unreliable and predictably unpredictable; and possessed by an 'either you are with me, or against me' world-view.

The Trump Syndrome is thus a complex set of attributes that, if clinically sorted and applied, could well open the floodgates of what is often defined as a severe form of antisocial personality disorder that includes common features which make a psychopath, or a sociopath, or both.

It is unsurprising, therefore, that President Trump has been variously referred to as a psychopathic or sociopathic autocrat who calls protesters or anyone who may object to him or disagrees with his opinions as un-American, un-patriotic and "terrorists" (Dewan 2020; Trump 2020). The formation of these personality traits is explained as a result of inconsistent and unstable parenting which is associated with psychopathology (Dwairy 2008). More specifically, that it is related to the lack of parental affection, an oppressive, emotionally charged and deprived home experience characterised by a remote mother and a "high-functioning sociopath" father who is a bully, xenophobic, racist and sexist (Trump 2020).

Boris Johnson, like Trump, has also been variously described by opinion columnists and armchair theorists, as a narcissist and a sociopath. Specifically, such commentary asserts that: he is a serial and compulsive liar, deceitful, self-centred, egocentric, a bully, impulsive and irresponsible; he puts his self-interest before others; he exhibits a false sense of security when in fact he is often out of his depth; he compensates his weaknesses with arrogance and single-mindedness; he sees himself as a new Winston Churchill (see, for instance, his marvel of the "great statesman", Johnson 2014) who works hard to be the bastion of democracy but who is instead acting like a spoiled and unruly child; he is surrounded and managed by an inner circle of arrogant, almost despotic, ideologues of unelected policy-makers; and he has a big, fragile ego and is intolerant of any criticism (e.g. Crace 2019, 2020; Hattenstone 2020; Toynbee 2007). For instance:

'The thin-skinned, unprepared opportunist... cannot tolerate a word of scrutiny or criticism. It is like dealing with a toddler...The prime minister's ability to misjudge...is borderline sociopathic...People are losing their jobs. People are terrified about the future. And yet to Boris it all feels like a big game where the only thing at stake is his fragile ego...In terms of emotional development, Boris is barely out of nappies." (Crace 2020)

In order to put these characterisations in perspective, some clarifications are needed. Psychopaths are, by-and-large, believed to be genetically predisposed, whilst sociopaths are seen as the consequence of an adverse social environment (e.g. parenting). Neuroscience claims that the two ought to be kept as separate entities and thus treated as distinct personality traits because they appear to share distinct differences in brain functioning and imaging (Pemment 2013).

Psychopaths are seen as more calculative and manipulative, more willing to breach laws and moral standards, have no remorse and hardly any regard for others' experiences or feelings as long as they get what they want. They conduct their affairs with such tenacity and determination that they make every effort to remain protected and unscathed: they deny knowledge of any deviant act. They invent every plausible or implausible excuse to prove their innocence whilst blaming others around them for being the culprits. Basically, they work under the notion that there are a lot of people out there who are 'suckers' and easy prey who can be exploited and manipulated. In other words, in the mind of psychopaths, there is out there a herd mentality that allows unscrupulous persons or leaders to extract loyalty and submission by leading the 'herd' to the direction they desire and, if need be, even to the sacrificial altar just in order to extract whatever benefits they desire. In realising this execution of power by exercising dominance over others, psychopaths derive pleasure and a sense of fulfilment but rarely with any hint of guilt.

Sociopaths tend to be more erratic, impulsive and temperamental. They can be reckless and oblivious to the consequences of their behaviour. They are deep-down loners (though they may camouflage that when in a group by presenting as 'extraverts') and have difficulty in forming emotional and social attachments. They are good at recognising others who appear to share similar characteristics and, for that matter, they are frequently found mingling with like-minded people.

The traits exhibited by the Trump Syndrome, present a much more complex picture of personality that not only exhibits traits of psychopathy and sociopathy but goes well beyond that to accommodate broader classifications that may hide a mixed and varied personality type and disorder. While despotic leaders may well be readily assigned in general terms under the diagnostic nomenclature of an authoritarian personality and other related types, such a classification may hide traits of a far more complicated structure of a multi-dimensional authoritarian personality at work.

In broad terms, Trump's traits appear to fulfill the requirements of an authoritarian personality (Adorno et al 1950; Christie & Jahoda 1954; Stewart & Hoult 1959; Stenner 2005). Nevertheless, particular and distinctive aspects of that repertoire of personal characteristics [such as manipulation, unemotional coldness, detachment and indifference, lack of morality, recklessness, selfishness and the idea that goals justify the means] give an impression of an even more involved picture of authoritarianism. Furthermore, the manipulative aspects of despotic leadership are not restricted to directly observable exploitative behaviour. They include other means which go under the radar to penetrate the most ardent defence mechanisms of an audience. Other than non-verbal means and symbols, these include a particular type of verbal communication. The language of this communication has a distinct structure and syntax which cajoles followers to submission. Thus, Trump's language is short, simplistic, repetitive and rhetorical and at an educational level characteristic of nine-to-eleven year olds (Kayam 2018). The elementary use of language and its simplicity has a purpose. It limits critical reasoning and accordingly neutralises critical thought by making everything appear as clear as crystal. It makes the despotic leader feel capable and important. It galvanises the leader's audience by arousing emotions, populism, nationalism and anti-intellectualism. This adds to the despot's popularity and creates a grassroots niche for those who believe they share with their leader the same world-view. These particular and distinct characteristics, together with the language of communication, though broadly authoritarian are more reminiscent of common features which characterise the psychological traits of fascism (Eco 1995) and Machiavellianism.

In the exhibits of Trump's Syndrome, therefore, there is an interface between facets of authoritarianism in its broader conception; fascism (Berry 2016; Stanley 2018); and aspects of the 'dark triad' personality namely Machiavellianism, narcissism and psychopathy (Paulhus & Williams 2002). However, as if to convolute matters further, there is in those exhibits a diverse abundance of characteristics (signs and symptoms) which not only act as indicators of a personality disorder of the psychopathic or sociopathic or narcissistic type but also as indicators of a broader constellation of traits which run along a continuum of nosologies. Illustratively, if reference is made to the DSM-5 classification (American Psychiatric Association 2013), the Trump Syndrome has components of traits which cut across the whole spectrum of pathology. They may well indicate Cluster A personality disorder (e.g. paranoid, schizoid); Cluster B personality disorder (e.g. antisocial, borderline, histrionic, narcissistic); and Cluster C personality disorder (e.g. avoidant, obsessive-compulsive) at one and the same time.

Additionally, there are two aspects of the Trump Syndrome which give further food for thought. The first is denial of reality. In terms of grief and bereavement, denial is a normal response to loss. However, authoritarian leaders' denial is pathological. It is delusional. Delusion is a core element of their make-up. They create their own alternative virtual reality fantasy whereby their avatar is a pumped-up Herculean figure taking the form of an unbeatable hero who is out there to fight aliens of all sorts and always, after many personal sacrifices, rises to the occasion to claim his trophy. In this fantasy, authoritarians become the symbol of good leadership that does not allow for failure or defeat. Defeat is not an option. It is for losers. This fantasy may provide a uniquely colourful spectacle to the main protagonist, but in real life it succeeds in creating serious adverse personal and social consequences for everyone else who is within the leader's influence and far beyond.

The creation of an alternative reality of delusion and an intolerance of failure is linked to another aspect of the mindset and behaviour of despotic leadership: rigidity and the inability to accept defeat even in the face of defeat. In contradictory terms, therefore, they hate losers but are themselves bad losers. They cling onto their panoramic fantasy and do everything to hold on to power. They are willing to use every manipulative manoeuvre to quash the opposition and, if they fail, they resort to the deployment of the state apparatus to suppress rebellion and any calls for them to step down. They use all kinds of tricks and demonic fireworks to stop the voice of the people from being heard. Rather, they hear their own voice, and that is good enough for them because their voice is (they believe) the voice of the people. They challenge elections on the grounds of thuggery, external interference or irregularities, electoral fraud and generally accuse the opposition of attempts to fabricate the results. They surround themselves with an inner circle of devotees who masquerade as matter-of-fact experts who run around spreading the leaders' gospel, launching investigations and a plethora of legal activity to sow the seeds of suspicion and doubt and invariably stall the transfer of power. In the process, the aim is to stoke social unrest and disobedience or even create an international crisis as excuses to legitimise more state brutality against citizens and engineer the fervour of populism and nationalism to see off these manufactured threats. In all, they use every imaginable machination to buy them time to continue holding on to office and prolonging their grip on power. Trump demonstrated all these tactics throughout his presidency.

The above observations may suggest that an understanding of the various facets and components of despotic leadership and how they impact on behaviour and relations in diverse contexts require a more flexible and dimensional approach to categorisations of traits and diagnoses of psychopathology than distinct, rigid and categorical clinical entities are able to offer (Board & Fritzon 2003).

Trump's example may well imply that when traits are considered in the light of their profound breadth and interwoven simplicity with complexity, there is the hypothetical likelihood that despotic leaders' diverse and intricate personal characteristics can hide a much more encompassing active and reactive functional and simultaneously dysfunctional, disruptive, deceptive and chaotic type of personality than has been recognised. Furthermore, it may also suggest that this often toxic multifactorial psychological mixture of interacting constellations may be of such magnitude that it makes these leaders highly unresponsive and less amenable to influence or change. They may be so *systemically* entrapped by their deeply engrained multitude of conflicting and intermingling traits and types of deviant behaviour that they are beyond redemption. If so, it makes their position and role as leaders even more problematic and controversial.

Research Findings on Authoritarian Leaders

Although there is still much to speculate, learn and understand about leadership and despotic leaders in particular, research in the area offers invaluable insights into the mindset of such leaders, their relationships with associates and followers and their social milieu.

By and large, whichever way one looks at personality traits and psychopathology, whatever the confusion and often inconsistencies (Slattery 2009), and whatever conceptual formulations are presented or theoretical strands applied to a variety of contexts—interpersonal relationships, the workplace and governance—the same relatively consistent conclusion is reached: that the psychology of authoritarian leaders spells trouble (Altemeyer 1996; Ashforth 1994; Benson & Hogan 2008; Higgs 2009; Kets De Vries 1993; Kets De Vries & Miller 1985; Maccoby 2004).

According to research findings, authoritarian traits in general (and specifically Machiavellianism, narcissism, psychopathic or sociopathic attributes, psychoticism, cognitive rigidity, intolerance, dogmatism, prejudice and ideological bias) are prevalent in Western democratic states. They appear to affect both liberally and conservatively minded individuals. However, on the whole, individuals on the right of the political spectrum exhibit such tendencies far more than those on the left (Ditto et al 2019; Wetherill et al 2013). Liberals score higher in cognitive reflection, 'integrative complexity', reasoning and tolerance, while conservatives score higher on matters of social order, strict social institutions, a closed-mind, anti-ambiguity, cognitive and perceptual rigidity, dogmatism and intolerance (Baron & Jost 2019). Moreover, conservatives are more likely than liberals to spread "'fake news', political misinformation, and conspiracy theories throughout their online social networks" (Baron & Jost 2019, 293). On the issue of flexibility of mind or rigidity of mind (i.e. open or closed to changes in attitudes and beliefs), it is found that people who believe that opinions should change according to the evidence are more likely to accept scientific argument and reasoning and are more liberal regarding ideological and partisan affiliations and moral values (Pennycook et al 2020).

The psychological make-up of authoritarian leaders and the psychological make-up of their base (as in the case of President Trump and his followers), which determine the relationship between the two, reinforces findings and juxtapositions that the authoritarian relationship is indeed characterised by personality types which are expressly of a social dominance orientation (SDO) and right wing authoritarianism (RWA) categories (Dean & Altemeyer 2020; see also Altemeyer 1996; 1998; Duckitt 2001; Feather 1998; Lippa & Arad 1999; Pratto et al 1994; 1997: Sidanius & Pratto 1999: Son Hing et al 2007). These followers are ethnocentric and strongly believe in inequality between social groups, supremacy, and person-to-person or group dominance over others, and a blind acceptance of authority and control. They also demonstrate submissiveness, fear of change and difference, and a blind allegiance to a strong and tough authoritarian leader. They blame societal ills on others and express a strong sense of self-righteousness. When personality types expressly of the SDO and RWA type are put together, they do indeed collude to create a volatile relationship (Dean & Altemeyer 2020). Prejudice, discrimination and negativity appear to be core elements which cement the union between SDO and RWA subjects. About 12% of these followers score high on SDO and RWA scales. Although not all are prepared to go to the extreme in support of their leader, they aspire to Trump's power of "a wannabe dictator conspicuously displaying his inchoate authoritarian rule" (Dean & Altemeyer 2020, 24).

The puzzle, therefore, of why so many Americans voted for Trump in the 2020 election (over 74 million, the highest number ever received by a presidential loser in US history), and why he continues to have such an avowed base of followers, is somewhat demystified by these psychological findings. In particular, Dean and Altemeyer's estimate of 50 million followers appears an underestimate given the actual election results. More revealing and even explosive is that these findings confirm the strong fusion between leader and base and raise the spectre of an upsurge in violence, or more generally social protests and conflict, even in the absence of Trump because his legacy has permeated social institutions. A *CNBC*/Change Research Poll in the aftermath of the 2020 election found that well over 73% of Trump voters did believe his message that there was massive fraud and that Trump did win the election and ought to be the legitimate president-elect (Bramuk 2020). If the election results, therefore, are taken as an indicator of the fervour and volatility of this authoritarian relationship and Dean and Altemeyer's estimate that approximately 12% of hardcore Trump followers are both high in SDO and RWA is accepted, it suggests that there are nine million of them in the US. Even though some may not subscribe to extreme measures, it begs the question how many out of that mass may be prepared to use force and intimidation to support their 'wannabe dictator' or anyone else who may replace him.

Practical Implications for Leadership Selection

The above findings, other than leading to theoretical concerns about personality traits and their influence in giving rise to an authoritarian relationship, also raise practical concerns about the selection of leaders in democracies and in corporate business.

In terms of corporate business, the combination of SDO and RWA characteristics and the exertion of dominance and influence over others create questionable practices. As a result, it is argued, the selection of the type of leader should be a major consideration for organisations. As Son Hing et al (2007, 80) suggest:

> "Organizations should be cautious about selecting people high in SDO for leadership positions when contextual factors (e.g. reward systems) encourage unethical decision making...We believe that within hierarchical organizations, well established, powerful individuals are likely to be high in SDO. To avoid the situation in which they influence protégés to behave in an unethical fashion, one might be wise to pair mentors high in SDO with protégés lower in RWA or SDO... [W]e recommend that organizations strive to create workplace cultures that emphasize not profiteering or exploitation but the importance of ethics and the judicious questioning of authority."

Similar claims that many corporate business executives exhibit higher SDO, particularly psychopathic traits, than the normal distribution found in the general population are also made by others (Board & Fritzon 2003; Brooks & Fritzon 2016). They consider that while one per cent of people[3] in the community can show psychopathic traits, these traits are more common in the corporate world with a prevalence of between 3% and 21%. These 'successful psychopaths' who are deemed 'high-flyers' are characterised by lack of empathy or guilt, they are egocentric and superficial, willing to engage in illicit and unethical practices, and have a "toxic impact on their employees". Such leaders create chaos and tend to "play people off against each other" (Brooks & Fritzon 2016).

Therefore, it is argued that corporate business ought to test a candidate's character traits first and then consider their skills (Brooks

---

[3]   This may vary. Others put it at 2-3%, e.g. Gawda & Czubak 2017.

et al 2020; Fritzon et al 2016). Specifically, at the core of the display of authoritarian relationships in the workplace, are the dark triad traits of narcissism, Machiavellianism and psychopathy. These lead, according to these authors, to "manipulation, callous behaviour, and self-centeredness". They manifest themselves in various forms of destructive behaviour including harassment, bullying, aggression, occupational stress, and fraud. In their pursuit of maintaining power and personal benefits, they engage in "harsh management tactics" and "manipulative behaviours". These benefits are extracted from the "collective" and thus such leaders act in predatory and "counterproductive work behaviour" which results in the victimisation of others (Brooks et al 2020; see also, Kessler et al 2010).

Dilemmas and Caveats

The relevance of personality traits in corporate business and the broader political scene is undoubtedly a question that needs to be addressed, particularly if one agrees with the notion that selection of corporate business leaders (Brooks et al 2020) and state leaders (Bennett 2020) should be undertaken on grounds of 'fitness' based on character traits, physical and mental health. Ethical or practical issues notwithstanding, selecting leaders in corporate business without also considering selection of the workforce begs the question how useful that process is. As discussed earlier, it takes two to tango. Authoritarianism is a relationship. So, if research findings are to be taken seriously, it is a high-risk situation to blend people together who are high in SDO and RWA attributes, as that fusion can create risky and exploitative relationships. Without also screening personality traits among the workforce, focussing on the selection of leaders alone leaves an incomplete process. Whether indeed such risk management is practically plausible or acceptable on ethical grounds is yet to be considered. Even if considered, conclusions will fall short of any consensus. They will be marred by the values and the normative characteristics of the observers.

These dilemmas become more eminent in the context of political leaders. Shifting from organisations to broader relationships in society, the research problem of how leaders are selected (and then freely elected), and whether it is proper in a democracy to have personality profiles of citizens, and how those profiles are used, by whom and for what purpose, boggles the mind. Other than ethical considerations, in view of the discussion earlier on surveillance and control, such measures if applied (even under the belief that they serve a positive purpose) run the risk of opening new chapters on issues of inequality, manipulation, exclusion, and social control. The implications of such a psychological screening process are simply disconcerting. There is a real and almost inevitable possibility that such practices may be put to abuse (wittingly or unwittingly) for the discrimination of particular individuals and social groups, as for instance in terms of social class, gender, sexual orientation, race and ethnicity. Furthermore, even if these concerns are dispelled, such a practice assumes that tests and scales are accurate measurements and apply on a universal, cross-cultural context: they may well not.

Returning to the cautionary tale about weaknesses in depicting traits and attributing personality types and disorder, one must not lose sight of the fact that such depictions are controversial and constantly evolving (Waring & Paxton 2018, 53-82). They are perceptions based on normative contextual, cultural and ethnic definitions of how individuals present and behave (cf. Camilleri 2018; Gawda & Czubak 2017). As such, they are often found to be an admixture of unclear definitions and evaluations whose nosologies are constantly being changed and modified as the history of definitions and scales show. Thus they are hardly of any practicable value or scope in varied instances and in cross-cultural contexts. For example, despite the fact that psychopathy may be a useful term in understanding behaviour which significantly diverges from what is expected of moral standards in society, the notion of a psychopathic personality, its use, applicability, or usefulness remains a contentious concept (Blackburn 1988). As a consequence, it is not often included within standardised psychiatric diagnostic systems (Abdalla-Filho & Völlm 2020; Robitz 2018). Similarly, 'narcissism' which is also deemed to be a clinical manifestation of instability can be part of everyday normality (Lunbeck 2014; Walsh 2015). In fact, it has been suggested that all individuals should expect to experience a variety of changing and shifting psychological states and psychological challenges over their lifetime (Dolan 2020, 10).

Building personality traits and personality disorder definitions, scales and measurements are useful attempts to systematise and enable the interpretation and diagnosis of diverse personal and interpersonal, but often intermingling, characteristics. These tools allow researchers and practitioners to synthesise those characteristics which appear to be common and similar and those which appear different. From that, frameworks and standards may be constructed for making sense of the social world. They are evaluations and judgements of what an individual's psychological make-up is and how that compares with what is deemed desirable or undesirable, acceptable or unacceptable. In that sense, as Taylor et al (1973) argued a long time ago, much of what goes into a scale to define and measure a personality type and, significantly, what goes in to draw profiles of personality disorders is socially defined and thus social in character. They are expressions of society but, at the same time, expressions of power relationships, and how these power relationships allow particular individuals or groups to codify, evaluate and judge personal, interpersonal and broader social relationships as normal, abnormal, desirable or undesirable. The history of psychology and psychiatry in democratic but also, in particular, authoritarian states, is often littered with examples of abuses. They have been used as weapons to obfuscate and silence dissent. 'Gulag' did not just happen in the Soviet Union; nor did Uighur camps in modern China. Democracies have created through the centuries their own 'Gulags' and 'Uighur camps' in many forms and shapes.

It is important to dispel any misunderstanding which may arise here. It is not argued that personality traits and disorders do not exist and they are a myth. On the contrary, not only do they exist but they also define both the strength and the vulnerability of the human experience. What is presented here is that although personality types, psychopathology and measurements provide considerable insight and understanding of authoritarian leaders and the authoritarian relationship, and without them any explanations of risk and risk management would be inconceivable, *we should also guard against their possible limitations and the risks they pose if misused and abused.* On the one hand, they have the power to inform and educate about individuals and relationships and, on the other, they have the power to distort our judgements and guide us in the opposite direction. They can allow and give impetus to discrimination, exclusion, rejection and ejection. In other words, classifications of personalities and personality disorders have the power to inform and direct our actions to minimise and manage risk but, at the same time, they can encourage the emergence of labels and stigmas which adversely affect the kind of perception, opinion and beliefs people have about each other and relationships in general.

Language, Linguistic Anarchy and Freedom of Speech

Closely related to the above risks from categorisations which have intended or unintended consequences are, as constantly alluded to throughout, matters of language. Authoritarianism, authoritarian traits and relationships; inequalities; surveillance and control; the rise of a corporate fundamentalist culture and relations in the workplace (Perry 2017); the sustainment of that culture and the lack of corporate social responsibility, despite efforts to make corporations more responsible and less corrupt (Chiu 2019), cannot be divorced from the influence of language in shaping and giving impetus to those relations. The language of the authoritarian mindset is an essential part of the process of creating and espousing an authoritarian culture and establishing the authoritarian relationship between leader and subjects.

More specifically, embedded in the complex web of personality traits, power relationships and outcomes there is a growing and emerging socially developed language that threatens to deconstruct the sacrosanct democratic ideal of freedom of speech and expression. This social development is what can be termed as *linguistic anarchy*. This is a state of linguistic normlessness. It is a state of collapsing moral boundaries which allow offensive and oppressive language to become an acceptable norm in social encounters. Linguistic anarchy is fast becoming part of the repertoire of tools which are used as a means to determining righteousness, monopoly of power, and the submission of others under one's sphere of influence and dominance.

The language of authoritarianism and the authoritarian relationship are amplified, given impetus, guidance, and legitimacy by the megaphone of a powerful oligarchical, indeed in some instances monopolistically run, right-wing press. Social media then process this language and its message, twists it further and, to use president Barack Obama's word in an interview with historian David Olusaga (*BBC* 2020), powerfully "turbocharges" it to reach huge and broader populations. Through obscene and degrading language, camouflaged as typically acceptable and normal, the authoritarian, discriminatory and offensive message translates into a linguistic weapon which is fired at anyone who is set up as a target of attack, with the intended purpose of discrediting and bringing the targeted subject into submission.

Currently, linguistic anarchy is increasing exponentially and appears unstoppable. This is partly because of the very nature of the authoritarian relationship, which stokes dysfunctional relationships by utilising depressingly arrogant and offensive language as an expression of its mindset and its zeal for raw power; and partly because there is a serious lack of knowledge of how to regulate it. For example, despite the fact that European states, particularly Germany, have some of the toughest laws in existence to control hateful posts, hate speech, defamation, incitement to commit crimes and violence, their law enforcement agency Europol is almost at loss as to how to regulate such offensive and arrogant language.

Freedom of speech and expression is an unequal relationship. What is funny and humorous for one person may be serious and demeaning to another. There is a value attached to our verbal and non-verbal encounters. Freedom of speech and expression is a power relationship. For one person, the use of abusive or discriminatory language may be regarded as the exercise of a basic fundamental civil right. For another, such language may be received as loss of that right and viewed as insulting, offensive, and a serious breach of respect and acceptable codes of conduct. This relationship therefore raises issues about tolerance. Democracy survives on tolerance. However, once tolerance becomes regressive and repressive (depending on which side one is), democracy ought to put the brakes on and become "intolerant" (Wolff et al 1969). In Marcuse's argument, in an unequal democratic society exercising "tolerance" is a misconception because it "fortifies the conservation of the status quo" (Marcuse 1969). Tolerance may work well for those who can apply their linguistic domination, as long as the subjects of subjugation cheerfully accept their prescribed inferior status and refrain from responding in similar terms. For those on the receiving end, tolerance, especially when linguistic anarchy is conjured up in disguise as being an innocent 'joke', adds insult to injury. At that level, abuse of the freedom of speech and expression becomes a coercive but effective social weapon that is utilised to exercise control over others. It generates patronage and thus rights of privilege, favouritism, corruption, and vindictiveness. In the hands of oppressive people, linguistic anarchy becomes a tyrannical tool. In order to fend off the tyranny, tolerance must be turned into 'intolerance' which rejects abuse, manipulation, exploitation, and subordination.

Inevitably, serious philosophical and practical questions arise from the above conceptualisation of linguistic anarchy, tolerance and intolerance. In particular, in view of the very relative nature of the concept of tolerance, it is almost impossible to draw the line where tolerance stops and intolerance begins or what happens once intolerance has set in. However, that is exactly where the problem lies. Linguistic anarchy and its tolerance say far more about structural and institutionalised forms of discrimination and subordination than just differences of expression in interpersonal relationships. Standing up to linguistic anarchy therefore requires intolerance beyond the personal and the interpersonal. It requires broader institutional responses to it on the basis that in a democracy non-offensive, accommodating, and inclusive language matters for the stability of freedom of speech and expression and the maintenance of orderly social encounters. Conversely, by not doing anything to disable or neutralise linguistic anarchy, tolerance adds to the tyranny of authoritarianism.

Unfortunately, the Internet and social media in particular allow and facilitate the following: transmission and amplification of speech and expression on a largely uninterrupted and uncontrollable scale; the radicalisation of white and ethnic groups through often conspiratorial plots, e.g. QAnon; the rise of authoritarian leaders and followers; the rise of radical-right militias, white supremacists and other extremist groups; and the general social and political climate of the present times. This facilitation has contributed to the expansion and weaponisation of language as another means to keeping certain individuals or groups marginalised and excluded from full and equal participation in social relationships. Linguistic anarchy has added to the normalisation, and worryingly enough to the legitimation, of abusive and divisive language, and to the confusion about where the democratic moral standards and boundaries of freedom of speech and expression are drawn before they become indecently offensive, authoritarian and intolerable.

Unregulated codes of oppressive speech and expression are fast becoming the new and revamped designer tool of subjugation and control in democratic authoritarianism. However, there is more to this linguistic anarchy. In unleashing this linguistic normlessness, other than serving an ulterior sinister motive (as in Trump's case), there appears to be a fundamental misconception about freedom of speech and expression. Freedom of speech and expression has never meant to be all things to all people, where anyone and everyone are free to say or do whatever they choose. There are, in freedom of speech and expression, defined moral boundaries which ought to act as checks and balances on our private and public behaviour. Freedom is not about being free to be abusive, offensive and indecent to others and act so with impunity. For instance the statement "A mask is a mask. It is not a political statement" attempts to entice personal and social responsibility to avert a public health hazard. In response, a reactionary statement is flung: "My face, my freedom, my choice". If so, why not extend the reactionary argument to theft? "I fancy your property, I take it"; or driving speeds, "My car, my choice, my speed"; or rape, "My desire, my need, my gratification"; or offending and criminal behaviour in general, "My freedom to do as I please"; or anything at all where rules and expectations apply? Moral issues and social responsibility are not about what we do for ourselves, but what we also do for others.

If by being 'free' means engaging in linguistic anarchy, running a reign of terror with words and other expressions or acts against people we do not agree with, that is not democracy: it is once more a state of anomie that adds to the authoritarian relationship. It is a state of relativism where everything goes and everything is possible and where acceptable social norms and moral imperatives regarding respect for others collapse. Such a state of linguistic normlessness puts the very concept of freedom in disrepute. It turns the idea of fraternity and coexistence, and the rules which are expected to guide behaviour, on their head. In the absence of those ethical and moral boundaries that allow every person the right to be treated with dignity and respect, the human experience of freedom becomes an experience of oppression and suppression, prejudice and bigotry. It is an experience where the privileged, the strong and loudest, the most verbally and physically abusive, the most dangerous who are often insulated behind anonymous social media accounts or the barrel of a gun, a knife or an axe, and generally those capable of exercising coercion over others because of their beliefs or ethnic, gender or social status, have a free and uninterrupted reign. The decent, the weak, the 'different' and the principled become, in that context, the social casualties of this globally emerging and spreading democratic inequality.

A Synthesis of the Parts and a Cautionary Tale

In chapter 2 and the present chapter, the 'Zombieland' metaphor was deployed to capture the radical fundamentalist mindset of repressive values, attitudes and practices which evoke a sustained assault on Western liberal democracies and help to entrench the spread of authoritarianism. The corrosive aspects of this mindset were examined in a multitude of social contexts at both the micro and macro levels. It presents as a cult-like rigid and reactionary mentality that thrives on arrogance, exploitation, strong and abusive language, immorality and hostility to anything which is different and does not perfectly fit its cognitive and behavioural schemas. It survives and finds refuge in an alternative reality, absurdity, conspiracies, discrimination and prejudice. This mindset is so entrenched in its own self-indulgence and existential purpose that challenging it is almost like 'arguing with zombies' (Krugman 2020).

The US experience demonstrates what is at stake. Trump may have lost the 2020 election for the presidency but his mindset, machinations and legacy as a despotic, manipulative, abusive and corrosive irritant have succeeded in setting up a parallel despotic shadow state ready and willing to take over. The Trump Tower of Autocracy is halfway up in construction. It may still be in its incipient stages but its completion may only be a matter of time. It may not have to house the owner once it has been fully erected. On completion it would be open for residence to anyone of his many aspiring self-serving radical-right GOP disciples or other apostles eager enough to pick up the sceptre and trumpet the merits of despotic discipline.

Trump's persona demonstrates that beyond the structural and institutional forces which are unleashed and go to work to inflict serious damage to democracy, the distinct role played by the personal attributes of despotic leaders ought to be of concern to those worried about the loss of freedoms. Specifically, careful attention should be paid to these leaders' cold-bloodedness, callousness and amoral behaviour. Trump was consistent about his intentions throughout his reign: to change the system from within and do away with ethical and moral codes of conduct that characterise a democratic culture. He hit hard at that culture. His skilful use and adaptation of language to promote an alternative radically despotic culture proved effective. Trump's open and encrypted messages and often repulsive language acted as the elixir of the authoritarian relationship. His supporters were oxygenated and mesmerised by the seductiveness of that relationship. They enriched that relationship by their own sinister display of unequivocal support culminating in social unrest, disobedience and insurrection. Tyranny is not about ethics, mores and feelings. In the mind of despots, polite language, behaviour and feelings stand in the way of achieving greatness. Characteristically, even in the direst moments facing the country, Trump the 'wannabe dictator' expressed no regrets or remorse whatsoever.

The shift toward a despotic culture under Trump's presidency, the storming of the US Capitol and what followed thereafter shattered the false belief that democratic institutions are safe and infallible. It needed a leader in the stature of Donald J. Trump to prove the point that democratic leaders (everywhere) can command raw power and act with impunity if they are willing and prepared to go that far. For instance, as was pointed out in chapter 2, there is nothing much to stop a determined UK prime minister and the cabinet from abusing their power if they command a strong parliamentary party majority that renders the opposition almost irrelevant. The same legitimacy that gives authority to democratic relationships, values and decisions simultaneously offers opportunities for corruption and the exercise of despotic power. There is, simply, a thin line to tread between democracy and autocracy.

In recognition of these fallibilities and fragilities, one wonders whether there is any will left in those who still believe in democracy to deconstruct the authoritarian monstrosity that is gradually taking shape. Timothy Snyder's (2017) twenty lessons on tyranny which come down to a single but basic principle, the need to speak out and be heard, may have passed its due date. The prescription may be a case of too little, too late. Attempts to emancipate lost democratic systems and institutions, restore, reform or adjust them to a standard close enough to resemble a true democracy appear to be waning. So what does one do to even attempt to keep democracy alive, and hopefully make it safer and better?

Maybe, part of the answer can be found somewhere in the midst of the issues and their remedies which have been covered here. What the other part maybe is hard to pin down. It may have more to do with the power of ideas, cultural and moral imperatives than measurable social facts.

Keeping democracy safe and alive by revamping and reconstructing its constituent parts with built-in defence mechanisms to detect, fight and protect against the occasional megalomaniacs or cabals who emerge from time to time to assume all power for themselves is a must. However, doing so is a long and onerous road to follow. This road is not another Herculean feat the kind of which it was found in the alternative reality of the Trump Syndrome. The road to democracy is more like an *Odyssey* where Ulysses embarks on a long and hazardous journey "to strive, to seek, to find, and not yield".[4] The journey is perpetual and its outcomes can never be foretold or ascertained. Even if the road to democracy is possible, all obstacles are overcome, and its lost institutions and relationships can be slowly re-assembled and restored, the qualities of civility and fairness (which include an intolerance of inequalities, exploitation, linguistic anarchy or any sort of oppression and repression) are required to keep democratic leadership and relationships stable and viable. It is about *decency*. Decency is a personal and moral quality. It refers to character and humility, flexibility and openness, trust and accountability, and an enduring willingness to behave and act better towards others. It affords those others who are close to us or afar the benefit of respect, dignity and inclusivity irrespective of creed, culture, age, ability, gender, sex, sexual orientation, race or ethnicity.

References

ABC News' Town Hall. 2020. "President Donald Trump: An Interview with George Stephanopoulos". *ABC News*. September 16, 2020. https://abcnews.go.com/politics/trumps-abc-news-town-hall-full-transcript/story?id=73035489.

---

[4]   The quoted words are from Alfred, Lord Tennyson's poem *"Ulysses"*, 1833.

Abdalla-Filho, E. and Völlm, B. 2020. "Does Every Psychopath Have an Antisocial Personality Disorder?" *Brazilian J. Psychiatry*, 42 (3), 241-242. doi: 10.1590/1516-4446-2019-0762.

Adorno, T.W., Frenkel-Brunswik, E., Levinson, D.J. and Sanford, R.N. 1950. *The Authoritarian Personality*. New York: Harper and Row.

Alexander, D. 2019. "Trump Has Shifted $1.3 Million of Campaign-donor Money Into his Business". *Forbes*. March 20, 2019. https://www.forbes.com/sites/danalexander/2019/03/20/trump-has-now-shifted-13m-of-campaign-donor-money-into-his-business/?sh=198e400e7aaf.

Al Jazeera. 2020a. "The Cyprus Papers". *Al Jazeera*. August 23, 2020. www.aljazeera.com.

Al Jazeera. 2020b. "Cyprus Officials Implicated in Plan to Sell Passport to Criminals". *Al Jazeera*. October 12, 2020. www.aljazeera.com.

Altemeyer, B. 1996. *The Authoritarian Specter*. Cambridge, MA: Harvard University Press.

Altemeyer, B. 1998. "The Other 'Authoritarian Personality'". In *Advances in Experimental Social Psychology*, edited by M.P. Zanna. 30, 47-92, San Diego, CA: Academic Press.

American Psychiatric Association. 2013. *Diagnostic and Statistical Manual of Mental Disorders (DSM-5)*. Arlington, VA: APA.

Aron, R. 2018. *Main Currents in Sociological Thought: Durkehim, Pareto, Weber*. Vol. II. Basa Roca, US: CRC Press Incl. (Taylor & Francis Incl. imprint).

Arton Capital 2020. "United Kingdom: Residency & Citizenship by Investment". Arton Capital. https://www.artoncapital.com.

Associated Press. 2020. "Here's Everyone that Trump Granted Clemency to on Tuesday". *Associated Press Market Watch*. February 18, 2020.

Ashforth, B. 1994. "Petty Tyranny in Organisations". *Human Relations*, 47(7), 755-778.

Atherton, K.D. 2020. "UK Mounts Shotguns on Drone for Urban Battles". *Forbes*. September 30, 2020. https://www.forbes.com/sites/kelseyatherton/2020/09/30/uk-mounts-shotguns-on-drone-for-urban-battles/?sh=11448fcb11dc.\

Balko, R. 2014. *Rise of the Warrior Cop: The Militarization of America's Police Forces*. New York: Public Affairs (Perseus Books).

Baron, J. and Jost, J.T. 2019. "False Equivalences: Are Liberals and Conservatives in the United States Equally Biased?". *Perspectives on Psychological Science*, 14(2), 292-303.

BBC. 2020. "Barack Obama Talks to David Olusaga". Interview. November 13, 2020. *BBC One.* https://www.bbc.co.uk/mediacentre/latestnews/2020/barack-obama-david-olusoga.

BBC Panorama. 2020. "FinCEN Files: HSBC Moved Ponzi Scheme Millions Despite Warning". *BBC Panorama.* September 20, 2020. https://www.bbc.co.uk/news/uk-54225572.

Behrmann, S. 2020. "'Abandoned the Rule of Law': Lawmakers React to Trump Granting Clemency to Roger Stone". *USA Today.* July 11, 2020.

Bennett, C. 2020. "For the Health of the Nation, Shouldn't Johnson's Medical Fitness for Office be Scrutinized?" *The Guardian.* October 21, 2020.

Benson, M. and Hogan, R. 2008. "How Dark Side Leadership Personality Destroys Trust and Degrades Organisational Effectiveness". *Organisations & People*, 15(3), 10-18.

Bergis, T. 2020. *Kleptomania: How Dirty Money is Conquering the World.* New York: Harper Collins.

Berry, L. 2016. "Umberto Eco on Donald Trump: 14 Ways of Looking at a Fascist: The Leading Republican Presidential Candidate is More Mussolini than Hitler". *Literary Hub.* February 29, 2016.

Besley, T. and Kudamatsu, M. 2007. *Making Autocracy Work.* May 2007. The Suntory Centre. London: London School of Economics. http://eprints.lse.ac.uk/3764/1/Making_Autocracy_Work.pdf.

Blackburn, R. 1988. "On Moral Judgements and Personality Disorders: The Myth of Psychopathic Personality Revisited". *Brit. J. Psychiatry*, 153, 505-512.

Board, B.J. and Fritzon, K. 2003. "Disordered Personalities at Work". *Psychology, Crime & Law*, 11(1), 17-22. doi:10.1080/106883160310001634304.

Bolton, J. 2020. *The Room Where it Happened: A White House Memoir.* New York: Simon & Schuster.

Bramuk, J. 2020. "Almost No Trump Voters Consider Biden the Legitimate 2020 Election Winner". *CNBC.* November 23, 2020. www.cnbc.com.

Brandus, P. 2020. "Trump Pardons Demonstrate His Belief that White-collar Crime Isn't Real Crime". *Associated Press*. February 19, 2020.

Brooks, N. and Fritzon, K. 2016. "Corporate Psychopaths are Common and Can Wreak Havoc in Business". Conference Paper. *Australian Psychological Society (APS) Congress.* Melbourne. September 13-16, 2016.

Brooks, N., Fritzon, K. and Croom, S. 2020. "Corporate Psychopathy: Entering the Paradox and Emerging Unscathed". Chapter 10 in *Corporate Psychopathy: Investigating Destructive Personalities in the Workplace,* edited by N. Brooks, K. Fritzon and S. Croom, 327-365. Cham, Switzerland: Palgrave Macmillan.

Buettner, R., Craig, S. and McIntire, M. 2020. "Long-concealed Records Show Trump's Chronic Losses and Years of Tax Avoidance". *The New York Times*. September 27, 2020.

Camilleri, R. 2018. "Personality Disorders". Sage Journals. *InnoVait*, 11 (7), 357-361. (https://doi.org/10.1177/1755738018769685.

Canter, L. 2020. "Coronavirus: Employers to be Given 30 Days to Admit to Furlough Fraud". *Yahoo Finance UK*. June 13, 2020.

Chayes, S. 2020. *Everybody Knows: Corruption in America*. London: C. Hurst & Co. Publishers.

Chiu, I.H-Y. 2019. "An Institutional Theory of Corporate Regulation". *Northwestern J. of International Law & Business,* 39(2), 85-170.

Christie, R. and Jahoda, M. (eds). 1954. *Studies in the Scope and Method of "The Authoritarian Personality"*. Glencoe, Ill: Free Press.

Crace, J. 2019. "Boris Johnson Tries to Unhappen Saturday with Sociopathic Unreasoning". *The Guardian*. October 21, 2019. https://www.theguardian.com/politics/2019/oct/21/boris-johnson-tries-to-unhappen-saturday-with-sociopathic-unreasoning.

Crace, J. 2020. "Like a Borderline Sociopath, Johnson Again Misjudges the Mood of the Chamber". *The Guardian*. July 15, 2020. https://www.theguardian.com/politics/2020/jul/15/borderline-sociopath-boris-johnson-misjudges-mood-chamber-pmqs.

Dean, J.W. and Altemeyer, B. 2020. *Authoritarian Nightmare: Trump and His Followers*. New York: Melville House Publishing.

Dewan, A. 2020. "Trump is Calling Protesters who Disagree with Him Terrorists: That Puts Him in the Company of the World's Autocrats". *CNN*. July 27, 2020. https://edition.cnn.com/2020/07/25/politics/us-protests-trump-terrorists-intl/index.html.

Ditto, P.H., Liu, B.S., Clark, C.J., et al. 2019. "At Least Bias is Bipartisan: a Meta-Analytic Comparison of Partisan Bias in Liberals and Conservatives". *Perspectives on Psychological Science*, 14(2), 273-291.

Dolan, E.W. 2020. "New Psychology Study Finds People Typically Experience Shifting Mental Disorders Over their Lifespan". *JAMA New Work Open,* 3(4), 21 April, doi:10.1001/jamanewworkopen .2020.3221.

Duckitt, J. 2001. "A Dual-Process Cognitive-Motivational Theory of Ideology and Prejudice". In *Advances in Experimental Social Psychology*, edited by M.P. Zanna. 33, 41-113. San Diego, CA: Academic Press.

Durkheim, E. 1951. *Suicide: A Study in Sociology*. Transl. J.A. Spaulding and G. Simpson. Glencoe Ill.: The Free Press of Glencoe. First published 1897.

Durkheim, E. 1984, *The Division of Labour in Society*. Transl. W.D. Halls. New York. The Free Press. First published 1895.

Dwairy, M.A. 2008. "Parental Inconsistency Versus Parental Authoritarianism: Associations with Symptoms of Psychological Disorders". *J. Youth Adolescence*, 37, 616-626.

Eco, U. 1995. "Ur-Fascism". N*ew York Review of Books*. June 22, 1995. https://www.nybooks.com/articles/1995/06/22/ur-fascism/.

Enrich, D. 2020. *Dark Towers: Deutsche Bank, Donald Trump and an Epic Trail of Destruction*. New York: Custom House.

Feather, N.T. 1998. "Reaction to Penalties for Offenses Committed by the Police and Public Citizens: Testing a Social-Cognitive Process Model of Retributive Justice". *J. Personality and Social Psychology*, 75, 528-544.

Feenberg, A. 1999. *Questioning Technololgy*. New York: Routledge.

Feenberg, A. 2002. *Transforming Technology*. New York: Oxford University Press.

Foucault, M. 1971. *Madness and Civilization*. London: Tavistock.

Freedland, J. 2020. "It's Taken Just 12 Months for Boris Johnson to Create a Government of Sleaze". *The Guardian*. August 7, 2020. https://www.theguardian.com/commentisfree/2020/aug/07/ its-taken-just-12-months-for-boris-johnson-to-create-a-government-of-sleaze.

Fritzon, K., Bailey, C., Croom, S. et al. 2016. "Problem Personalities in the Workplace: Developments of the Corporate Personality

Inventory". In *Psychology and Law in Europe: When the West Meets East*. Edited by P.A. Granhag, R. Bull, A. Shaboltas, and E. Dozortseva, 139-166. Boca Raton, Fl: CRC/Taylor & Francis. doi:10.1201/9781315317045.

Fromm, E. 1942. *The Fear of Freedom*. London: Routledge & Kegan Paul. Originally published in the US under the title *Escape from Freedom*. Farrar & Rinehart, 1941.

Gawda, B. and Czubak, K. 2017. "Prevalence of Personality Disorders in General Population Among Men and Women". *Psychological Reports*, 120(3), 503-519. Doi:10.1177/0033294117692807

Goffman, E. 1959. *The Presentation of the Self in Everyday Life*. New York. Doubleday.

Goffman, E. 1983. "The Interaction Order". *American Sociological Review*, 48(1), 1-17. https://doi.org/10.2307/2095141.

Goffman, E. 1995. "On Face-Work: An Analysis of Ritual Elements in Social Interaction". *Psychiatry*, 15(4), 451-463.

Gounev, P. and Ruggiero, V. 2014. *Corruption and Organized Crime in Europe: Illegal Partnerships*. London: Routledge.

Habermas, J. 2003. *The Future of Human Nature*. Cambridge: Polity Press.

Hattenstone, S. 2020. "In Boris Johnson's Long History of Lies, the Marcus Rashford One is the Strangest". *The Guardian*. June 21, 2020. https://www.theguardian.com/commentisfree/2020/jun/21/boris-johnson-lies-marcus-rashford-prime-minister.

Hickel, J. 2017. *The Divide: A Brief Guide to Global Inequality and its Solutions*. London: Penguin Random House.

Higgs, M. 2009. "The Good, the Bad and the Ugly: Leadership and Narcissism". *J. Change Management*, 9(2), 165-178.

Johnson, B. 2014. *The Churchill Factor: How One Man Made History*. London: Hodder & Stoughton.

Jones, R. 2018, "Engineering Cheerful Robots: An Ethical Consideration". *Information(Switzerland) MDPI*, published online, June 4. DOI: 10.3390/info9070152.

Kayam, O. 2018. "The Readability and Simplicity of Donald Trump's Language". *Political Studies Review*, 16(1), 73-88.

Kellner, D. and Best, S. 2001. *The Postmodern Adventure: Science, Technology and Cultural Studies at the Third Millennium*. New York: Guildford Press.

Kessler, S.R., Bandelli, A.C. Spector, P. et al. 2010. "Re-examining Machiavelli: A Three-Dimensional Model of Machiavellianism in the Workplace". *J. Applied Social Psychology*, 40(8), 1868-1896.

Kets De Vries, M.F.R. 1993. *Leaders, Fools, and Impostors: Essays in the Psychology of Leadership*. San Francisco: Jossey-Bass.

Kets De Vries, M.F.R. and Miller, D. 1985. "Narcissism and Leadership: An Object Relations Perspective". *Human Relations*, 38(6), 583-601.

Kinderman, P. 2015. "Imagine There's No Diagnosis, it's Easy if You Try". *Psychological Review*, 2(1), 154-161.

Kinderman, P.A. 2019. *A Manifesto for Mental Health: Why We Need a Revolution in Client and Health Care*. Cham, Switzerland: Springer Nature.

Kinderman, P., Read, J., Moncrieff, J. et al. 2012. "Drop the Language of Disorder". *Evidence Based Mental Health*, 16(1), doi: 10.1136/eb-2012-100987.

Krugman, P. 2020. *Arguing with Zombies: Economics, Politics and the Fight for a Better Future*. London: W.W. Norton.

Kukutschka, R.M.B. 2018. "Anti-Corruption Strategies for Authoritarian States". Transparency International. May 20, 2018. Berlin: Transparency International U4 Anti-Corruption Centre.

Laing, R.D. 1990. *The Politics of Experience and the Bird of Paradise*. London: Penguin.

Lippa, R. and Arad, S. 1999. "Gender, Personality, and Prejudice: The Display of Authoritarianism and Social Dominance in Interviews with College Men and Women. *Journal of Research in Personality*, 33, 463-493.

Lunbeck, E. 2014. *The Americanization of Narcissm*. Cambridge, MA.: Harvard University Press.

Maccoby, M. 2004. "Narcissistic Leaders: The Incredible Pros, the Inevitable Cons". *Harvard Business Review*, 82(1), 92-101.

Marcuse, H. 1955. *Eros and Civilization: A Philosophical Inquiry into Freud*. Boston: Beacon Press.

Marcuse, H. 1964. *One Dimensional Man*. Boston: Beacon Press.

Marcuse, H. 1969. "Repressive Tolerance" in R.P. Wolff, M. Barrington Jr. and H. Marcuse, *A Critique of Pure Tolerance*. Boston: Beacon Press, *95-137*, updated version.. First published 1965.

McIntire, M., Buettner, R. and Craig, S. 2020. "Trump on Records Shed New Light on Chinese Business Pursuits". *The New York Times.* October 20, 2020. https://www.nytimes.com/2020/10/20/us/trump-taxes-china.html.

Merle, R. 2018. "A Guide to the Financial Crisis—10 Years Later". *The Washington Post.* September 10, 2018.

Mills, C.W. 1959. *The Sociological Imagination.* New York: Oxford University Press.

Monbiot, G. 2020. "If You Think the UK Isn't Corrupt, You Haven't Looked Hard Enough". *The Guardian.* September 10, 2020. https://www.theguardian.com/commentisfree/2020/sep/10/uk-corrupt-nation-earth-brexit-money-laundering.

Moncrieff, J. 2008. *The Myth of the Chemical Cure: A Critique of Psychiatric Drug Treatment.* Basingstoke, UK: Palgrave Macmillan.

Moncrieff, J. 2013. *The Bitterest Pills: The Troubling Story of Antipsychotropic Drugs.* London: Palgrave Macmillan.

Montellaro, Z. 2020. "A Looming Milestone: $1B in Dark Money Spending". *Politico.* September 14, 2020. https://www.politico.com/newsletters/weekly-score/2020/09/14/a-looming-milestone-1b-in-dark-money-spending-790383.

National Audit Office. 2020. *Investigating into Government Procurement During the Covid-19 Pandemic.* National Audit Office (NAO) Report. November 18, 2020. London: NAO. https://www.nao.org.uk/report/government-procurement-during-the-covid-19-pandemic/.

O'Connell, J., Rich, S. and Whoriskey, P. 2020. "Public Companies Receive $1billion in Stimulus Funds Meant for Small Business". *The Washington Post.* May 1, 2020.

Packer, G. 2020. "The Inside Story of the Mueller Probe's Mistakes". Review of Andrew Weissmann, 2020, "Where Law Ends: Inside the Mueller Investigation". *The Atlantic.* September 21, 2020.

Paulhus, D.L. and Williams, K.M. 2002. "The Dark Triad of Personality: Narcissism, Machiavellianism and Psychopathy". *J. Research in Personality*, 36(6), 556-563.

Pemment, J. 2013. "Psychopathy Versus Sociopathy: Why the Distinction has Become Crucial". *Aggression and Violent Behavior.* dx.doi.org./10.1016/j.arb.2013.07.001.

Pennycook, G., Cheyne, J.A., Koehler, D.J. et al. 2020. "On the Belief that Beliefs Should Change According to Evidence: Implications for Conspiratorial, Moral, Paranormal, Political, Religious and Science Beliefs". *Judgment and Decision Making*, 15(4), 476-498.

Perry, E. 2017. "ABC's Corporate Fundamentalist Culture—An Analysis of its Sustainability". Cherwell HR Team, Observational Research Management Report. December 10, 2017. *Academia*. https://www.academia.edu/35452212/ABC_s_Corporate_Fundamentalist_Culture_An_Analysis_of_its_Sustainability.

Pettypiece, S. 2020. "Trump Pardons Former 49ers Owner Eddie De-Bartolo Jr." *NBC News*. February 18, 2020. https://www.nbcnews.com/politics/white-house/trump-grants-clemency-former-49ers-owner-eddie-debartolo-jr-n1138041.

Pratto, F., Sidanius, J., Stallworth, L.M. et al. 1994. "Social Dominance Orientation: A Personality Variable Predicting Social and Political Attitudes". *J. Personality and Social Psychology*, 67, 741-763.

Pratto, F., Stallworth, L.M., Sidanius, J. et al. 1997. "The Gender Gap in Occupational Role Attainment: A Social Dominance Approach". *J. Personality and Social Psychology*, 72, 37-53.

REV. 2020a. "Donald Trump, Macon, Georgia Rally Speech Transcript". *REV*. October 16, 2020. https://www.rev.com/blog/transcripts/donald-trump-macon-georgia-rally-speech-transcript-october-16.

REV. 2020b. "Donald Trump Michigan Rally Speech Transcript". *REV*. October 17, 2020. https://www.rev.com/blog/transcripts/donald-trump-michigan-rally-speech-transcript-october-17.

Robitz, R. 2018. "What are Personality Disorders?" November 2018. *American Psychiatric Association*. Washington DC: APA. https://www.psychiatry.org/patients-families/personality-disorders/what-are-personality-disorders.

Rock, P. 1973. *Making People Pay*. London: Routledge & Kegan Paul.

Romania, V. 2020. "Interactional Anomie? Imaging Social Distance after Covid-19: A Goffmanian Perspective". *Sociologica*, 14(1). https://sociologica.unibo.it/article/view/10836/10961

Roth, M. and Kroll, J. 1986. *The Reality of Mental Illness*. Cambridge: Cambridge University Press.

Ruggiero, V. and Vass, A.A. 1992. "Heroin Use and the Formal Economy: Illicit Drugs and Licit Economy". *Brit. J. Criminology*, 32(3), 273-291.

Santucci, J. 2020. "Donor to Pro-Trump Group Sues to Get his Money Back After Dropped Election Lawsuits". *USA Today*. November 27, 2020.

Savage, Michael. 2020. "Brexit Backers Tate & Lyle Set to Gain £73m End of EU Trade Tariffs". *The Guardian*. August 8, 2020. https://www.theguardian.com/business/2020/aug/08/brexit-backers-tate-lyle-set-to-gain-73m-from-end-of-eu-trade-tariffs.

Scheff, T. 1996. *Being Mentally Ill*. Chicago, Ill: Aldine.

Sidanius, J. and Pratto, F. 1999. *Social Dominance: An Intergroup Theory of Social Hierarchy and Oppression*. Cambridge: Cambridge University Press.

Slattery, C. 2009. *The Dark Side of Leadership: Troubling Times at the Top*. Sydney: Semann & Slattery.

Snyder, T. 2017. *On Tyranny: Twenty Lessons from the Twentieth Century*. New York: Tim Duggan Books (Penguin Macmillan House imprint).

Son Hing, L.S. Bobocel, D.R., Zanna, M.P. et al. 2007. "Authoritarian Dynamics and Unethical Decision Making: High Social Dominance Orientation Leaders and High Right-Wing Authoritarianism Followers". *J. Personality and Social Psychology*, 93(1), 67-81.

Stamper, N. 2006. *Breaking Rank: A Top Cop's Expose of the Dark Side of American Policing*. Hachette Book Group.

Stamper, N. 2016. *To Protect and Serve: How to Fix America's Police*. New York: Nation Books.

Stanford Encyclopedia of Philosophy. 2020. "Locke's Political Economy", particularly section 4, "Consent, Political Obligation and the Ends of Government". *Stanford Encyclopedia of Philosophy*, first published November 9, 2005; revised October 6, 2020. Stanford, CA: Stanford University.

Stanley, J. 2018. *How Fascism Works: The Politics of Us and Them*. New York: Random House.

Stenner, K. 2005. *The Authoritarian Dynamic*. Cambridge: Cambridge University Press.

Stewart, D. and Hoult, T. 1959. "A Social Psychological Theory of the Authoritarian Personality". *American J. Sociology*, 65(3), 274-279.

Storbeck, O. 2020. "Wirecard: The Frantic Final Months of a Fraudulent Operation". *Financial Times*. August 25, 2020. https://www.ft.com/content/6a660a5f-4e8c-41d5-b129-ad5bf9782256.

Stott, C. and Pearson, G. 2006. "Football Banning Orders, Proportionality, and the Public Order Policing". *Howard J. Crime and Justice*, 45(3), 241-254.

Stott, C. and Pearson, G. 2007. *Football "Hooliganism", Policing and the War on the "English Disease"*. London: Pennant Books.

Sutherland, E.H. and Cressey, D.R. 1996. *Principles of Criminology*. 7th ed. Philadelphia, PA: J.P. Lippincott.

Szasz, T.S. 1991. "The Anti-Psychiatry Movement". In *150 Years of British Psychiatry, 1841-1991*, edited by G.E. Berrios and H. Freeman. London: Gaskell.

Tactics Institute. 2020. *UAE/KSA Opportunism, Captive States & the Arms Trade in South-Eastern Europe*. London: Tactics Institute for Security and Counter Terrorism.

Taylor, I., Walton, P. and Young, J. 1973. *The New Criminology*. London: Routledge & Kegan Paul.

Tindera, M. 2020. "Here Are The Billionaires Backing Donald Trump's Campaign". *Forbes*. April 24, 2020. https://www.forbes.com/sites/michelatindera/2020/04/17/here-are-the-billionaires-backing-donald-trumps-campaign/?sh=450551d37989.

Toynbee, P. 2007. "Boris the Jester, Toff, Serial Liar and Sociopath for Mayor". *The Guardian*. July 17, 2007. https://www.theguardian.com/commentisfree/2007/jul/17/comment.pressandpublishing.

Trump, M. 2020. *Too Much and Never Enough: How My Family Created the World's Most Dangerous Man*. New York: Simon & Schuster.

Tsoukala, A., Pearson, G. and Coenen, P.T.M. eds. 2016. *Legal Responses to Football Hooliganism in Europe*. 1st edition. The Hague, NL: T.M.C. Asser Press (Springer).

UK Government. 2020. "Investor Visas ('Tier 1'). https://www.gov.uk/tier-1-investor.

Walsh, J. 2015. *Narcissism and its Discontents*. Basingstoke: Palgrave Macmillan.

Waring, A. and Paxton, R. 2018. "Psychological Aspects of the Alt-Right Phenomenon". In *The New Authoritarianism Vol 1: A Risk Analysis of the US Alt-Right Phenomenon,* edited by Alan Waring, 53-82. Stuttgart: Ibidem Verlag.

Wetherill, G.A., Brandt, MJ. and Reyna, C. 2013. "Discrimination Across the Ideological Divide: The Role of Value Violations and Abstract Values in Discrimination by Liberals and Conservatives". *Social Psychological and Personality Science*, 4(6), 658-667.

Whalen, J., Gregg, A. and Ye Hee Lee, M. 2020. "Some Businesses Won't Return Funds Despite Pressure from Trump Administration". *The Washington* Post. April 28, 2020.

Whitehead, J.W. 2015. *Battlefield America: The War on the American People.* New York: Select Books.

Wikipedia. 2020. "Financial Crisis of 2007-2008". *Wikipedia.* October 14, 2020.

Wolff, R.P., Barrington, M. Jr., and Marcuse, H. 1969. *A Critique of Pure Tolerance.* 1st published 1965. Boston: Beacon Press.

Woodstock, A. 2020. "No 10 Refuses to Say whether Boris Johnson Had Contact with Richard Desmond while Prime Minister". *The Independent*, June 17. https://www.independent/co.uk/news/uk/politics/boris-johnson-richard-desmond-property-develop r-robert-jenrick-a9571026.html.

Woodward, B. 2020. *Rage.* New York: Simon & Schuster.

Chapter 4:
Positive versus Toxic Leadership in the Corporate and Political Spheres

By Clive Smallman[1]

Abstract

Over 2020-2021, corporate and political leaders worldwide were placed under immense stress. A minority of leaders stepped up as exemplars of what leaders should be: positive, authentic and progressive. Others have distinguished themselves only by their buffoonery, narcissism and glaring psychopathy. This chapter explores why leadership matters to the stability, good governance, and prosperity of society and any organisation, looking first at the sad phenomenon that is toxic leadership. The chapter then widens the discussion through an exploration of an authoritative typology of leadership, before addressing positive leadership, its meaning, effects and development. The discussion is grounded in examples from business and politics. It further draws on a range of disciplinary literature.

Key words: leadership, corporate, political, typology, positive, toxic

Leadership Matters

At the time of writing (early 2021), looking back over the past 50 years or so, it is difficult to recall a more fractious or worrisome time in global politics and business. A 90-year-old relative went further; she could not recall a darker time in the world since 1939. Deeper introspection and wider exploration suggest that widespread current anxiety is not solely attributable to the occurrence and dreadful social and economic impacts of the severe acute respiratory syndrome coronavirus 2 (SARS-CoV-2, also known as Covid-19) pandemic of 2020-2021.

It would be absurdly easy (and understandable) to attribute much of the world's present predicament to the rise of Donald Trump and other populist politicians worldwide (e.g. Jair Bolsonaro, Rodrigo

---

[1]   See contributor affiliations and biography, pages 526-527.

Duterte, Recep Tayyip Erdoğan, Boris Johnson, Viktor Orbán). Para-doxically, they and their followers commonly attribute the world's problems to 'socialism' and Marxism. They frequently point to countries that practise state capitalism or left-leaning populism (e.g. Nicolas Maduro) as proof of the ills of so-called 'left-wing politics' and a lack of faith in the market mechanism. Equally, progressives and anarchists worldwide delight in shaming the leaders of technology giants for their 'absurd' wealth as much as right-wing conspiracy theorists blame mythical global, 'liberal' elites, for just about anything with which the 'neo-cons' disagree. Furthermore, let us not go into the quicksand that is religious fundamentalism (basically an alternate form of populism).

For some, the new US President in 2021, coupled to the advent of Covid-19 vaccines, signalled a 'new normal'. For many more, including the author, it feels decidedly abnormal. The global malaise that developed over the early 2000s, accelerated through Trump's Presidency and the Covid-19 pandemic will resist easy resolution, since it has more in-depth and broader origins, but with one common theme: *toxic leadership*.

Toxic Leadership Defined

'Toxic' leadership has almost certainly existed for as long as *homo sapiens*. Toxic leaders are "maladjusted, malcontent and often malevolent, even malicious" (Whicker 1996, p. 11). They engage in destructive, counterproductive behaviours and exhibit dysfunctional personality characteristics, both to the extent that they inflict lasting and severe harm to their followers, organisations, society, or the natural environment (Cohen 2016; Kellerman 2004; Lipman-Blumen 2004).

Toxic leaders' success comes through destroying others and their works. Their mission is to suppress followers, while simultaneously holding them in thrall. They seek to control, relishing conflict and protectionism (Davis 2016). In short, they induce disorderly entropy in individuals (Csíkszentmihályi 2008, pp. 36-38), organisations (Anheier & Moulton 1999, pp. 274-279) and politics (Anheier & Moulton 1999, pp. 279-282). They promote the vices of ignorance, fear, inhumanity, injustice, impulsiveness and subservience (Jarvis 2004; Peterson & Seligman 2004). They fail to provide coherent direction or structure, leading to disabling (if often sub-conscious) self-doubt in their followers. They undermine followers and opponents alike through offering opaque or perverse feedback on actions taken at their behest (whether they work or not), further 'de-structuring' rationality. Most have clinically undiagnosed but readily observable personality disorders (American Psychiatric Association 2013). At best, they are self-absorbed narcissists, and at worst they are murderous psychopaths (Boddy 2015b; Fennimore & Sementelli 2016; Michalak & Ashkanasy 2018; Nai 2018; Neo et al 2016)[2].

In the corporate world, toxic leadership ultimately creates decreased performance, productivity and output at best. Nevertheless, where such 'leaders' are allowed free rein, while they might superficially generate significant returns for investors, more often than not they are purely self-interested "natural born opportunists" (Fennimore 2017). All too frequently, any supernormal returns they generate are often short-lived (Laguda 2020; Lipman-Blumen 2004; Whicker 1996). As Cameron (2012, p. 9) notes, organisations managed by toxic 'leaders' are prone to be unprofitable, ineffective, inefficient, error-prone, and unethical, built on internal and external relationships that are 'harmful'. When under external or internal stress, they struggle to adapt owing to rigid adherence to the toxic leader's vision of how things should be. Individuals within such organisations are commonly prone to a higher incidence of physiological and psychological illness. At worst, such organisations may impact society more generally (Kulik et al 2020).

In politics, toxic leaders frequently and deliberately damage democracy itself (e g. Economist (2021); Smith (2020)). When in their pomp, these poisonous politicians often and readily 'pull the wool' over the eyes of the very voters who put them into power. Such 'leaders' commonly eviscerate economic common sense, prostitute political power, sour social order and besmirch science that does not fit with their warped world view (Ashcroft 2016; Lipman-Blumen 2004; Nai 2018; Whicker 1996).

---

[2]   Editor's note: Other psychological studies variously covering toxic leadership in the political and/or corporate spheres include Babiak and Hare (2007), Brooks et al (2020), Fritzon et al (2016), Furnham at al (2013), Hare (2003; 2016), Kets de Vries (1993), Post (2015) and Walton (2007a; b; 2020a; b; c), as addressed in chapters 1, 3, 5 and 7.

Short-term, they often improve the fickle stock-exchanges of the world, always on the lookout for the 'quick buck' that goes with the social sector cuts and lurch to market fundamentalism that inevitably follows the election of right-wing toxic leaders. Longer-term, their economic programmes rarely produce any meaningful growth (usually slowing it over the long-term), based on the myth that is 'trickle-down economics' (Picketty 2014). Should they be superficially 'socialist', negative social impact too frequently follows. It is common to see increasingly abject poverty as the new socialist 'leader' and their cronies rapaciously liberate resources for their benefit. They 'over-promise' and 'under-deliver', while they and their closest family and allies accrue vast benefits.

The Rise of Toxic Leadership in the Corporate and Political Spheres

Examples of appalling individuals who took advantage of and manipulated their followers for their own ends litter history: Caligula; Pope John XII; King John (of Robin Hood fame); 'Ivan the Terrible'; Henry XIII; Adolf Hitler and his homicidal entourage. More recently, there have been Joseph Stalin, Pol Pot, Saddam Hussein, Robert Mugabe, Hugo Chávez, and Vladimir Putin. Also, Margaret Thatcher, Ronald Reagan, George W. Bush and, in the latter stages of their careers, Tony Blair and Bill Clinton, all stand accused of questionable behaviour at best and war crimes at worst.

The current era has its share of toxic leaders in politics and business. Donald Trump is a frequently cited example (Ashcroft 2016), who is frequently referred to in this chapter. In reading one highly regarded definition of toxic leadership (Whicker 1996), Trump meets every single criterion (Ashcroft 2016). Nevertheless, as indicated earlier, Trump is not alone, albeit he is the toxic leader *du temps*.

Jeff Bezos of Amazon has many customers, but few friends amongst his employees, progressive politicians and trade unionists. Travis Kalanick, the founder of Uber, has a less than stellar reputation for good behaviour outside the boardroom and occasionally in one of his rides. Elon Musk has an interesting relationship with his board and shareholders. Mark Zuckerberg, *Facebook's* founder, is under substantial political pressure.

Not all toxic leaders enjoy a public profile. Many such 'leaders' hide in plain sight and the background in politics. Corporate sociopaths (as well as the occasional psychopath) stalk the offices and production lines of enterprises of all sizes (Boddy & Taplin 2017; Boddy 2015a, 2015b; Cohen 2016; Fennimore 2017; Fennimore & Sementelli 2016; Neo et al 2016). The more fortunate of us never encounter one of these challenging people. Sadly, a substantial minority of humankind, including the author, have had one or more close encounters.

The Impact of Toxic Leadership

Political Impacts

At worst, the political impact of toxic leadership is *war*. Setting aside the psychotic initiation of war to execute an extreme political or religious agenda, the cynical among us would point to the prosecution of wars as a means of saving leaders or asserting political leadership. Margaret Thatcher's arguably unnecessary, costly invasion of the Falkland Islands is a case in point. Supported by Tony Blair, George W. Bush's Iraq invasion did not have an evidentiary basis. War at whatever scale has human and economic costs.

Outside of war, toxic leadership's impacts are apparent in *corruption* or the *marginalisation* of minorities, opponents or dissidents.

Corruption is the use of powers by politicians or government officials or their network contacts for illegitimate private gain. In some jurisdictions (e.g. Hong Kong), wider corporate or even private abuses of a similar nature are also considered to be examples of corruption that are unlawful. It takes many forms, including bribery, embezzlement, extortion, graft, influence-peddling, parochialism, patronage, nepotism, and cronyism. Essentially it is about a perverse marketplace where there is an exchange of money or 'favours' between parties to ensure gain for one or the other, often at the expense of broader society or the natural environment. Where money does not change hands, the implicit arrangement is that favours are reciprocal. In extreme circumstances, political corruption links to criminality, including human trafficking, money laundering, drug trafficking, and tax evasion.

For example, it is hard to go past the endemic corruption that was readily apparent in the final days of Trump's Presidency, when he issued widespread pardons not just to political supporters but to convicted war criminals and child murderers too (*Economist* 2020a). He further asked Georgia's Secretary of State to 'find' enough votes to overturn the election result (Blackhall 2021). That noted, it is important to be clear that corruption cares not one bit for political beliefs; left-wing and right-wing share equally in its occurrence.

Corruption is an individual choice, not a consequence of political alignment. Just as 'trickle-down' economics is an appealing right-of-centre theory that fails because of avarice, so too, socialism while a good theory, often fails because of corrupt politicians. Venezuela is a commonly cited example of the 'ills' of socialism. However, it is the choices of individual toxic leaders (Hugo Chávez and now Nicolás Maduro) in that country that have led it down a ruinous path. Widespread corruption layered over an oil price crash is what broke the economy, indeed not free health care. It is common for right-wing commentators to point out the ills of 'socialism', or worse still 'communism', in some countries. However, in practice, many nations so identified practice a corruption-laden form of 'state capitalism' rather than the Marx-inspired political system that their 'leaders' espouse (e.g. Russia, China).

The marginalisation of minorities, opponents or dissidents is parochialism, a form of corruption. It is mentioned here because of its everyday use by toxic political leaders. Marginalisation cynically deepens the commitment of followers to a supposedly common cause. Its use by authoritarian states emphasises the 'ultimate power' they have over their populace, by demonising or dehumanising defined groups. Unfortunately, history records rather too many cases of murderous parochialism, which are often denied by latter-day toxic political leaders.

The ongoing attempts of Trump and the Republican Party in America to suppress voting rights of minorities in the USA are parochialism at its nadir. The build-up to and events following the 2020 Presidential election saw various means deployed to prevent people from voting or to prove their votes were invalid (*Economist* 2020b). The extraordinary events in Washington, DC on January 6, 2021 were no less than sedition.

In the United Kingdom, across 2019 and 2020, the Labour Party saw a bitter factional dispute between those aligned to its leader Sir

Keir Starmer and Jeremy Corbyn's acolytes (*Economist* 2020c). An ancient source of parochialism, anti-Semitism, seems to be the root cause of this self-destructive argument (EHRC 2020).

There are many more examples across the world, including China's extreme suppression of the Uyghurs (*Economist* 2020d), Thailand's persecution of Rohingya Muslims (UNHRC 2018) and Australia's appalling treatment of refugees (AHRC 2020).

Business Impacts

In business, toxic leadership equates to decreased employee work effort of about 48%, a decrease in work quality of about 38%, and an association with about 73% of employee turnover (Laguda 2020, p. 20). A vibrant metaphor characterises toxic leadership as a poisonous, destructive, virulent, metastasising cancer scarring both those in its path and others seemingly unconnected to the leader concerned. It consumes individuals, groups, and left unchecked, organisations (Laguda 2020, p. 20). Unquestionably, the Global Financial Crisis (GFC) of 2008 was set up by toxic leadership across the US financial services sector (Boddy 2015a; Lewis 2010), at the cost of US$700 billion just to bail out US banks alone, never mind the rest of the world's economy. People lost homes, superannuation and pensions. The cause was banks, hedge funds and other investment funds purposefully developing a collateralised debt obligation market that was bound to fail, given its foundation in so-called 'junk' bonds and bad mortgage debt. In the film *The Big Short*, a fictionalised take on Lewis (2010), the metaphor of a 'Jenga' tower illustrates the debt market that financial leaders developed, with debt bundled with debt over and again. Removing the wrong block means that the tower collapses; it is also an excellent metaphor for toxic leadership.

Drawing on a range of highly credible sources, Laguda (2020, pp. 20-21) noted an extensive list of individual physiological and psychological negative impacts of toxic leadership, which are supported by a range of other authorities (Bhandarker & Rai 2019; Boddy & Taplin 2017; Boddy 2015a). Among these impacts, arguably the most troubling is the number of suicides in the United States military and the nursing profession.

Organisationally, Laguda (2020, pp. 21-22) cited evidence that toxic leadership is negatively associated with group cohesion, job satisfaction, productivity, organisational trust, and organisational commitment. It is further linked to reduced organisational performance, unit cohesion, team spirit, dysfunctional group behaviours, and reduced organisational health and survival. Laguda (2020, pp. 21-22) further found that toxic leadership is associated with high absenteeism rate, reduced personnel efficiency, negative cost-benefit relationship for organisations, and increased personnel transfer and groupthink. If left unchecked, Laguda (2020, p. 22) cited further evidence that toxic leadership impacts organisational growth and output, harming overall profitability.

In a genuine sense, in business, these 'monsters' become hidden 'appreciating liabilities' that resist standard accounting measures but have a considerable cost to the companies who employ them (Michalak & Ashkanasy 2018).

Toxic Leadership is Not the 'Luck of the Draw.'

So, why do so many people have to put up with bad leaders? The challenge is that one person's toxic leader is another's heroic saviour. Toxic leadership is not a one-way street; it is enabled by followers consciously blind to the havoc wreaked by their adored leader, interacting with them to execute the leader's agenda (Hurst et al 2019; Lipman-Blumen 2004; Milosevic et al 2019). The manipulative skills of highly adroit toxic leaders commonly induce in their followers a state of steadily escalating commitment to a cause that defies all contrary evidence and reasonable logic. Followers are metaphorically encouraged to wade through the 'big muddy', be they knee-, waist- or chest-deep in an execrable cause (Drummond 1996; Staw 1976). It is also common for followers of such leaders to succumb to 'groupthink' (Janis 1972).

By now, the reader should have become inured to the present author's citation of former President Trump, but he is a larger-than-life, genuine example for all, and his so-called 'leadership' spans both business and politics. Why did 70+ million people twice vote for a man widely regarded as a buffoon at best and a sexual predator and fascist at worst?

The answer is culturally complicated, founded on the USA's revolutionary republican roots. However, in 2016, rather than the widely accepted hypothesis that it was those suffering economic hardship who voted Trump in, "it was about dominant groups that felt threatened by change and a candidate who took advantage of that trend" (Mutz 2018, p. E4331). Trump worked in concert with hard-right electoral advisors and the connivance of a Republican Party desperate to reassert itself following the Obama Presidency. Together, they constructed and communicated the position that "for the first time since Europeans arrived in this country, white Americans ... will soon be a minority race" (racial status threat). They attributed job losses in America to globalisation, emphasising China's 'theft' of American jobs (global status threat) (Mutz 2018, p. E4331). They singled out America's increasing interdependence on other countries as an enabler of this theft (Mutz 2018, p. E4331).

Mutz (2018 p. E4332) notes that separating racial and global status threats is challenging, although the former seems to have a more significant impact on voting than the latter. In any case, she notes that when members of a historically dominant group feel threatened, many of their members will seek psychological 'safety' by committing to decisions that defy evidence and logic (Drummond 1996; Staw 1976). Such suppression of reality is only surprising if we accept that decision-making is purely objective; *it is not*. In making decisions, ordinary people apply their heuristic models of the world (Gigerenzer 2007; Gigerenzer & Selten 2001), which may or may not be rational (Gigerenzer & Selten 2001). Skilled manipulation by Trump's advisers nudges them along (Thaler & Sunstein 2008). They react positively to cues (Klein 1998) that support their position, dismissing or decrying those that do not. They frequently multiply and deepen their commitment, however illogical it may seem to a reasonable person (Drummond 1996; Staw 1976). When they associate with like-minded people, they become victims of 'groupthink' (Janis 1972), reinforcing commonly held positions.

In political movements such as Trumpism, followers become nostalgic, trying to protect the *status quo*. Alternatively, they may try and reassert a former (often non-existent) dominant position. For example, witness the near-hysterical levels of nostalgia for non-existent British global power of the so-called 'Brexiteers' in the lead up to the referendum that led to 'Brexit' and since (Campanella & Dassù 2019). Followers 'defend' their group ('all lives matter'). They start behaving in ways previously consigned to history (e.g. the use of racist or fascist insignia and symbols). They react negatively toward other groups, often along political or racist lines.

In the four years following his election, Trump 'doubled down' on his 'Make America Great Again' rhetoric (actually a catch cry created by Reagan's speech writers). He reinforced this with legislation, and executive orders, focused intensely on reducing America's commitment to globalisation. Trump belittled and blamed global institutions for America's woes, and singled out China as the target for much invective, especially around Covid-19. In all of this, he was explicitly appealing to a supporter base in fear of losing their status. And then *he* lost.

The virtual and physical assaults on democracy by Trump, his advisors and his supporters are the least edifying processes the author has seen in nearly 50 years of watching politics. The hyperbole, frivolous and vexatious litigation, ignorance of due electoral processes, and the deliberate intimidation of officials (public servants, Republican and Democrat governors, members of Congress, even the Vice President) is on a par with any so-called 'banana' republic. Trump and his followers rapidly waded deeper and more profoundly into a morass, over their heads in a swamp of fantastical conspiracy theories and corruption. At the time of writing (early January 2021), they seem fully immersed and will not go 'quietly into the good night'.

In business, the GFC origins saw thousands of employees in the financial sector worldwide charge blindly into positions advocated by the leaders of stock exchanges and investment funds worldwide. Mortgage brokers in particular over-sold high-risk loans. There are other examples of similar folly further back.

The Case of LTCM

Long-Term Capital Management (LTCM) was an American hedge fund that coupled absolute-return trading strategies with high financial leverage. LTCM was founded in 1994 by John Meriwether, a former senior executive at Salomon Brothers. LTCM's board included Myron Scholes and Robert Merton, who shared the 1997 Nobel Prize for Economics for a "new method to determine the value of derivatives" (Lowenstein 2001; Miller 2001; Prabhu 2001; Smallman 2000; Stein 2003; Stonham 1999).

LTCM enjoyed a successful first year, returning over 21% (after fees), with 43% in the second year and 41% in the third. However, in 1998 it lost US$4.6 billion in less than four months due to a combination of high leverage and exposure to the 1997 Asian financial crisis and the 1998 Russian financial crisis. Its master hedge fund collapsed in the late 1990s, leading to an agreement on September 23, 1998, for a US$3.6 billion recapitalisation under the Federal Reserve's supervision. Fourteen financial institutions bore the brunt: Bankers Trust, Barclays, Chase Manhattan Bank, Crédit Agricole, Credit Suisse First Boston, Deutsche Bank, Goldman Sachs, JP Morgan, Merrill Lynch, Morgan Stanley, Paribas, Salomon Smith Barney, Société Générale, and UBS. Had the fund collapsed, its exposure was over US$1 trillion. The fund liquidated and dissolved in early 2000 (Lowenstein 2001; Miller 2001; Prabhu 2001; Smallman 2000; Stein 2003; Stonham 1999).

What went wrong? LTCM hired the finest PhD graduates of the US's very best economics departments, notably MIT. Scholes and Merton were so convinced that their algorithm could effectively manage risk in the derivatives market, that they just kept trading. The initial returns convinced some of the finest financial institutions in the world. The issue was that, as trading conditions changed, they began to bet against the market, convinced that their algorithm was impregnable. Irrationality was unbounded, enabled by organisational narcissism (Stein 2003). As Leo Melamed, legendary trader and pioneer of financial futures, recalled in the 1999 *BBC Horizon* documentary *The Midas Formula: A Trillion Dollar Bet*, "you gotta be able to get out when the getting' is good". LTCM did not get out, because they both lacked the experience of conventional trading, and also exhibited narcissistic self-belief.

After LTCM's failure, in 2001, the author attended an address given by Merton at Cambridge University's Judge Business School. Merton claimed that had LTCM been allowed to continue trading, his algorithm's strength was such that the fund's performance would have returned to the supernormal levels of its early years. As a risk management researcher, the author was stunned by Merton's claim (Smallman 2000). However, who could doubt a Nobel Prize-winning economist with a PhD from MIT, who is Emeritus Professor of Finance at the Harvard Business School?

Moreover, he had been invited to the School by its Professor of Finance, who once told the author that *all* risk could be predicted mathematically. The audience was many fine, successful financial brains, academics, and practitioners (one could almost 'feel' the money). Merton's narcissism, further indulged by a politically powerful faithful, was palpable.

These examples demonstrate that people often choose to follow toxic leaders on the promise of some form of reward. They are all too often disappointed. To an extent, it is the 'luck of the draw' as to whether a person works for a toxic leader. Choosing to continue to work for one, or follow one in politics, is up to the individual, although sadly, the opportunity to choose is infrequent and not solely in the individual's gift.

A Leadership Typology

There are many leadership typologies, some informed by social science, others not. It is not possible in a work of this length to do justice to the breadth of the scientifically informed typologies, let alone demonstrate the inadequacies of many others. Given this work's focus, to further the discussion, the author now focuses on arguably the definitive work on toxic leadership by Marcia Whicker (1996). She distinguishes between three leadership classes: *trustworthy*, *transitional* and *toxic*.

Trustworthy Leaders

Whicker (1996, pp. 26-31) characterises the trustworthy leader as having:

1. Knowledge of themselves.
2. Knowledge of the external world.
3. Self-motivation and drive.
4. The ability to motivate others.
5. Integrity.
6. An ability to formulate persuasive, uplifting and unifying messages for followers.
7. Cultivation of talent.
8. Vision.

Whicker (1996) further defines trustworthy leaders in aligning them to Burns (1978) transformational leaders, which in turn, he defines in terms of Maslow's (1987) hierarchy of needs. Burns (1978), and by adoption Whicker (1996, pp. 32-33), identifies transformational and trustworthy leaders respectively with levels four and five of Maslow's (1987) hierarchy: esteem and self-actualisation needs.

Whicker (1996, p. 32) contends that in operating 'at' level four, trustworthy leaders have considerable self-respect. Accordingly, they can command the respect of others and work to expand that respect. Their healthy self-image further means that they neither need to put others down nor hold them back to advance their self-image. Trustworthy leaders do not play destructive games or deploy malevolent tactics. As such, they enjoy enhanced esteem from those with whom they work.

Better yet are those leaders who are motivated by self-actualisation (Whicker 1996, pp. 32-33); driven by learning and as a part of their leadership skills, they actively seek to develop others' talents. They are not above making tough, difficult decisions that command the respect of their followers. Although they are empathic, level five leaders are seldom profoundly concerned about what others think of their behaviours. Leaders such as this contribute at least as much to their organisation and society as they take. They are maximisers operating from an ethic of giving from their talents.

Whicker (1996, pp. 37-48) distinguishes between three types of trustworthy leaders:

1. *Commanders* use meetings to communicate information downward to followers, focus on task achievement and distribute rewards based on productivity.
2. *Team leaders* use meetings to exchange information with followers emphasise mentoring, developing followers' skills, and distributing rewards based on impartial, external standards.
3. *Consensus builders* use meetings to gather information and build consensus, emphasise diverse opinions through consultation and distribute rewards to minimise conflict and differences.

Transitional Leaders

Whicker (1996, pp. 32-33, 59-68, 71-111) identifies transitional leaders with level three of Maslow's (1987) hierarchy: social needs. They lack the capacity or reserves to uplift followers that trustworthy leaders hold. Transitional leaders (aligned to Burns' (1978) transactional leaders) are concerned with 'belonging' above all else. They want to be an essential part of the organisation and a member of groups. They seek affection more than respect. Despite seeking organisational status, their personal goals do not align to organisational goals; instead, their objectives enjoy primacy over those of the organisation. Hence, through grandstanding, controlling the transmission of information, hedonism and poor decision-making, they often lead organisations on a downward spiral towards dysfunction and decline, at best existing in a state of persistent failure (Anheier & Romo 1999).

Whicker (1996, pp. 59-68, 71-111) defines three types of transitional leaders:

1. *Controllers* are rigid perfectionists often bound by tradition. They are micromanagers, reflecting their need to control, and lack charisma. Their primary control tool is the restriction of information, effected through elaborate and selective deployment rules. They desire obedience and attention.

2. *Busybodies* crave affection and attention. They are energetic, relentlessly dynamic and fear alienation of themselves and others. They have to be the centre of attention and communication through manipulating opinion and rumourmongering. They rarely resolve conflict among their followers (more accurately subordinates in the busybody leader's eyes), ensuring that complaints flow and attention is further assured.

3. *Absentee leaders* are remote and disengaged, distancing themselves from decision-making. Their focus is on symbolism over substance. Like busybodies, their desire is for affection and approval, and they seek the consensus of followers around these. They are rarely malicious and more mindless, but their disengagement leaves power vacuums that ambitious and often toxic followers seek to fill. Turmoil, chaos, or malaise are symptomatic of absentee leadership.

Toxic Leaders

Whicker's (1996, p. 11) basic definition of toxic leaders is 'malad-justed, malcontent and often malevolent, even malicious'. She then identifies toxic leaders with the lowest levels, one and two of Maslow's (1987) hierarchy: survival needs and security needs (Whicker 1996, pp. 32-33). Like transitional leaders, they lack the capacity or reserves to uplift followers that trustworthy leaders hold (Whicker 1996, pp. 32-33).

Toxic leaders typically are more malevolent that transitional leaders. They are self-obsessed and typically narcissists (American Psychiatric Association 2013). Functional territorialism and emo-tional or psychological stressors targeting non-followers express these characteristics. Toxic leaders are always on the defensive, seek-ing actual or creating imaginary attacks. Their favourite leadership metaphor is commonly 'warfare', with co-workers, subordinates, and superiors identified as 'the enemy'. While their ruthless pursuit of per-sonal gain might incidentally drag an organisation with them, over time, they will stimulate decline, exacerbating and compounding dys-function and disruption (Whicker 1996, pp. 59-68).

As with the other classes of leadership, Whicker (1996, pp. 59-68, 116-172) defines three toxic leader styles:

1. As in the case in broader life, *Bullies* are at odds with every-one and everything, pugnacious and fundamentally angry. Their jealousy of others, particularly those who 'beat' them is unbounded. Their routine mission is to diminish or invalidate others anywhere and anytime. Their malevolence is com-monly grounded in bitterness over past personal failures; denigrating others is a proxy for admitting their shortcom-ings. They are overly emotional, frequently lashing out an-grily and inappropriately with personalised abuse.

2. In their own eyes, *Streetfighters* are the 'king of the castle', and naturally, everyone else is a 'dirty rascal'. If that seems a childish metaphor, it is singularly appropriate for these char-ismatic egotists who look to manipulate and dominate through gang politics. Their leadership 'style' (a misnomer for something so innately unstylish) is about rewards and punishments for their gang based on their visceral

interpretation of events; it is all about winning at any price. They listen to other gang members as suits them but will not hesitate to put down dissent and crush challengers. They are generous to the loyal and viciously merciless to those they view as disloyal.

3. *Enforcers* are often second-in-command and subservient to street fighters, bullies or absentee leaders, adopting or mirroring their leader's style. They are motivated by money and status but are risk-averse. They are adept at reaching consensus with their leaders while enforcing the same on followers. They typically do not rise to peak leadership positions but assure the success of those to whom they report.

Switching Styles

Leaders switch styles, usually within classes and sometimes deliberately in the class of trustworthy leaders, as different circumstances require. Transitional and toxic leaders may switch between classes and certainly between styles. For example, in his business life, Trump was a busybody always on the move between different construction sites and properties (Whicker 1996, pp. 84-85). Negotiating and socialising formed a significant part of his life; he craved attention, exemplified in his television series *The Apprentice*. Coincidentally it was there that his shift across classes began, as first seen in his inclination to be a street fighter and his encouragement of a 'win at whatever cost' mentality.

Thus, it came to pass that Trump the street fighter formed a political gang, which he manipulated all the way into the White House. This style is visible across his Presidential campaigns and his tenure in the White House. On his loss to Biden, the street fighter remained Trump's dominant style. However, he lost court case after court case, and was (in his eyes) obstructed by election officials and his beloved *Fox News*. Not surprisingly, the bully burst through, lashing out with little attachment to facts and in ignorance of due processes and the law.

Genuine business turnarounds require trustworthy leaders. For example, at the time of writing, the author had the privilege of watching a close colleague deliberately and slowly turn round an underperforming business. The organisation was previously under the thumb of a pair of controllers-cum-street fighters. Moving between the team leader and consensus builder styles, this colleague is slowly rebuilding the enterprise.

The Next Step: Positive Leadership

Trustworthiness is essential and progressive, but when organisations and society are recovering from the worst forms of transitional or toxic leadership, the need is for transformational leaders. In business, organisations require lifting, financially and culturally. Where politics has been toxic or transitional, the need is for leaders that enable society to become more civil, pursuing a good and humane agenda (Galbraith 1996), a well-established historical precedent (Guazzo 1574/1925). For the author, the source of transformation lies in his take on the positive leadership paradigm (Cameron et al 2017; Cameron 2012; Pascale et al 2010) grounded in positive psychology (Diener & Seligman 2004; Peterson & Seligman 2004; Seligman 2012; Seligman et al 2005) and positive deviance (Cameron et al 2017; Pascale et al 2010).

Like so many leadership challenges, it is about negotiating order in complicated socio-technical systems (Baiada-Hireche et al 2011; Fine 1984; Mnookin 2004; Schulman 1993; Strauss 1978). Establishing order relies on creative problem-solving (Brown 2009), excellent communication (Carey 2009; Craig & Muller 2007), and evidence-baased decision-making (Klein 1998).

Negotiating Order

Positive leadership is the ability to negotiate order by setting the direction and the 'tone' in business and political conversations between people as they interact socially, negotiating an orderly and ideally civil workplace or society (Fine 1984; Maines 1982; Strauss 1978). Conversations resolve multiple and complicated options and tensions in workplace operations and political dialectics. They are how positive leaders manage power asymmetries, differing interests and complex issues. The central factors required are effective communication, chiefly deep listening (Trimboli 2017), healthy working or political relationships, based on positive culture (Cameron 2012), and the establishment of conversations grounded in principles rather than ideological positions or dogma (Fisher & Brown 1988; Fisher et al 2011; Scott

2004; Zeldin 1998). Ideological and dogmatic positionings are a significant barrier to effective negotiations, conversations, civility, and workplace and societal order (Mnookin 2010).

Negotiations construct social order in workplaces and society. Mnookin (2004; 2010) identifies three critical "tensions" (challenges) to resolve in these negotiations. The first is to resolve the tension between opportunities to create value ('expanding the pie' through growth or creating solutions to the negotiation challenge) and the necessity of distributing value (dividing the pie). At the heart of this negotiating challenge is what and how much information can be disclosed to another party? Limiting disclosure limits the opportunities to create value, and overly generous disclosure leads to the risk of exploitation. The tipping point here is how to best serve underlying interests, that is how can the differing principles of the negotiating parties be aligned?

Mnookin's next challenge is the resolution of the tension between empathy and assertiveness. How to effectively express to the other side one's interests, needs and perspectives?

The third challenge is the tension between principals and agents, a tension that stretches far back in time in the form of capital versus labour. Agents negotiate on behalf of individuals and groups; the most typical example is trade unions. Principals are either the manager or owner of some entity to which the individuals or groups represented by the agents contribute something. This standard tension arises because the principals' positional interests and the agents' positional interests do not align.

Mnookin majors on the second challenge because he finds that it is foundational to resolving the other two. As he put it in a workshop a few years back: "you have to teach people to negotiate".

Creativity

For some artists and others, creativity is a solitary affair. However, in organisations, it is a 'contact sport' (Brown 2009; Ogilvie & Liedtka 2011). The process of creating a solution to a challenge or refining an existing solution to a problem that affects an organisation or community requires contact with communities that consume or build the solution. It requires:

1. *Collecting* information on what people need by asking good questions,
2. Developing *breakthrough* ideas by pushing past incremental or obvious solutions,
3. *Building* prototypes to learn how to improve ideas, and
4. *Communicating* the story to encourage others to act.

Communication

Communication in the second machine age is complex yet vital to effective leadership (Barrett 2006). Its purpose is to successfully share information through interwoven digital, visual, verbal, and non-verbal channels.

Digital communication refers to communication through social media, texting, messaging and email. Digital technologies have transformed communication (Willis 2017), creating a sense of urgency and a need to share. Conventional communication is information transmission and feedback. Telephony aside, it was the case that written communication took a little while to compose and send. Social media now balances the opportunity for instant gratification in sending messages while allowing recipients the opportunity to respond. However, enabling and encouraging rapid and accidental transmission has opened a huge window for error. The physical process of writing letters, and transmitting them via post, telex or fax, would usually cause pause for thought. The immediacy of digital transmission confers no such discipline. In short, what happens in *Facebook, LinkedIn* and on email is on the Internet for life.

Decision-making

There are many models of decision-making presented as a rational process. Frequently, it is irrational. Even decisions based on the fullest information possible rely on someone, somewhere to make a subjective judgment based on expertise or experience, or both.

The naturalistic decision-making paradigm deconstructs decision-making through detailed analyses of discourse, narrative and social action by decision-makers with a strong focus on context (Gore et al 2006). It has been used extensively in the study of real-world decision-makers, particularly in high-risk work environments (Elliott 2005; Gore et al 2006; Gore et al 2015; Klein 1998; Lipshitz et al 2001;

Lipshitz et al., 2006; McDaniel 1993; Shattuck & Miller 2006; Zsambok & Klein 1997). It describes what people do under the pressure of time, ambiguous or absent information, ill-defined goals, and an evolving context (Klein 1997). Further, it describes how people can use their experience (in the form of heuristics) to arrive at sound decisions without the need to compare potential positive and negative outcomes of a course of action. Finally, its tacit acceptance of the discursive mind's role (Edwards & Potter 1992; Harré & Gillett 1994; Moore 2002) in decision-making represents a marked departure from earlier decision-making paradigms (Smallman & Moore 2010, pp. 401-402).

In this paradigm, decision-making is not about rational choice. We all develop heuristics through which we make decisions. These heuristics are the product of lived or simulated experiences, including learning and training; indeed, the word's etymology is the Greek έβρίκά (evrika—"I have found"). We use heuristics to make decisions based on interpreting patterns that we perceive in cues (signals, or evidence) that we perceive in the context in which we work and live. The human senses (taste, sight, touch, smell and sound) yield the cues we use.

Positive Leadership Defined

Like their toxic counterparts, 'positive leaders' have almost certainly existed for as long as *homo sapiens*. Positive leaders are well-adjusted, contented, benevolent and supportive. They engage in constructive, productive behaviours and exhibit highly functional personality characteristics, both to the extent that they bring lasting and enduring benefit to their followers, organisations, society, or the natural environment.

Returning to Whicker's (1996) alignment of trustworthy leaders with Burns' (1978) transformational leaders, and so to Maslow's (1987) hierarchy of needs, trustworthy, positive leaders essentially operate with a growth mindset (Dweck 2016). They encourage employee engagement, productivity, innovation and self-expression. Their position on Maslow's (1987) hierarchy means they have a transcendent sense of self in which they embrace deep listening (Trimboli 2017) so that they might be changed.

Positive leaders' success comes through promoting others and their works. Their mission is to uplift followers, vicariously but humbly sharing their successes. They seek to mentor, relishing consensus and openness. In short, they induce flow in individuals (Csíkszentmihályi 2008, pp. 39-41), organisations (Marer et al 2016) and politics (Mutz 2011). They delight in promoting and encouraging the virtues of wisdom, courage, humanity, justice, temperance and transcendence (Jarvis 2004; Peterson & Seligman 2004). They provide coherent direction and structure, developing their followers' self-efficacy, promoting the ideal conditions for experiential learning (Bandura 1977; 1982; 1986; 2005; Kolb 2015). They support followers and question opponents by offering clear feedback on actions taken at their behest, promoting structured rationality.

Based on one of only two scientifically valid personality tests, a recent university study of 1.5 million people revealed a commonly occurring 'role model' personality type, identified with good leaders who are dependable (a synonym of trustworthy) and open to new ideas. Role models tend to be stable, honest, humble, agreeable and conscientious extraverts (Ashton 2017; Gerlach et al 2018).

In corporations, positive leadership ultimately creates improved performance, productivity and output. Positive leaders are strongly associated with strong economic performance, operational excellence and extraordinary efficiency, high quality, ethical behaviour, strong and enduring positive relationships. Organisations so led flourish, and individuals within such organisations commonly enjoy vitality and flow. Such organisations positively impact society more generally (Cameron et al 2017; Cameron 2005; 2012; Hsieh 2014).

A Corporate Case of Positive Leadership

The late and sorely missed Tony Hsieh, joined Zappos, an online shoe store, as CEO in 2000. Starting with sales of US$1.6m, by 2009 revenues reached US$1bn (Witkin 2012). An online sales pioneer, Hsieh faced the twin challenges of enabling customers to feel comfortable and secure when shopping online. Zappos offered free shipping and returns, sometimes of several pairs. Hsieh radically rethought and restructured Zappos. In 2013, it became for a while an 'holacracy', distributing authority and decision-making throughout the company, defining people by roles rather than hierarchy and titles (Laloux 2014; Robertson 2015). Hsieh's aim was a have a fast, agile but above all, *purposeful* organisation grounded in his belief in Zappos' employees and their ability to self-organise (Hsieh 2014). Not surprisingly, since 2013, Zappos has featured in Fortune's *100 Best Companies to Work For*. In July 2009, Amazon acquired Zappos in a deal valued at approximately US$1.2 billion (Witkin 2012). Hsieh retired as the CEO of Zappos in August 2020 after 21 years. Sadly, he died as a result of a shed fire in November 2020. He was 46 years old. By all accounts, Hsieh exemplified positive leadership and its impacts on followers and consequently, a company.

Political Cases of Good Leadership

The nature of politics means that positive political leaders are either rare, or simply do not rise above the hostile milieu of everyday politics. Also, as this is politics, one person's positive leader may appear to another as a fascist or communist. Moreover, perceptions of political leaders do shift and often quite radically. For example, for all his achievements as British Prime Minister, Tony Blair's record, rightly or wrongly, will always be scarred by his willing embrace of George W. Bush's arguably illegal Iraq war. Hence, it is not easy to provide politically balanced examples. That said, for the author, there are one or two exceptional politicians.

Jacinda Ardern, New Zealand's Prime Minister and leader of the Labour Party, is a widely respected leader internationally. Her open, honest and effective approach to handling day-to-day politics is noteworthy (Ardern 2020). Her authentic, kind, empathic yet strong responses to three major crises: the Christchurch mosque shootings (Royal Commission 2020), the Whakaari (White Island) volcanic eruption and Covid-19, enjoy broad support internationally.

The next example may not be popular with some New Zealanders. However, despite not agreeing with everything he did, the author found John Key, one of Ardern's recent predecessors as New Zealand PM, to be a positive leader. His was a different style and he is from a different wing of politics. However, he had a clear vision of what he wanted for New Zealand. He was courageous, making some unpopular decisions (rather like Ardern in calling an early Covid lockdown), but staying true to his convictions. He focused on his and others' strengths, maintaining his team's focus on achieving significant results. He was also humble (especially considering his substantial personal wealth) and a great communicator (Roughan 2017).

For the author, Barack Obama is also an outstanding leader. Were it not for the brakes placed on his Presidency by an implacably opposed Congress, his tenure would likely have seen a remarkable shift in the fortunes of many Americans. In reading his autobiographies (Obama 2004; 2006; 2020) and the account of his partner of their life together (Obama 2018), his authentic, kind, empathic, progressive nature as a leader is readily apparent. That noted, he did not shirk tough decisions, inheriting the consequences of his predecessor's ill-advised and probably illegal Iraq invasion and a sprawling conflict in Afghanistan.

Taking Action

Working or Living with Toxic Leaders

Unless you are a willing member of their tribe (or even if unwilling), working with a toxic leader or living under their rule can be hell. If they are a politician, you can protest, vote, live with it, or go and live elsewhere. Protesting or voting may impact a toxic leader, but only if most of the rest of the population agrees. The skills required for living with toxic political leadership are similar to those required in the workplace.

Moving to another country appears drastic. Stimulated by a job opportunity, the author and his family's move from the UK to New Zealand nearly 20 years ago was not to get away from Blair and 'New' Labour. However, it was undeniable that Aotearoa promised a markedly better physical and social environment for childhood and adolescence. Other Brits, Canadians and lots of Americans were also resettling, seeking a simpler life and for many a perceived much less toxic political environment. To some, it may seem a drastic step, but the author would make the same choice again in a heartbeat.

What about working with toxic leaders? It is a question of proximity. Toxic leaders' effects can be both proximal and distal. If you are close to such a leader but not in the tribe, life will be difficult. If you are not 'in', it is probably best to be 'out' (entirely). The alternatives are to endure the life of a victim, markedly develop mental toughness (Smallman 2020, pp. 45-57; Strycharczyk & Clough 2015) or find a means of 'blowing the whistle'. The same goes for those who are less close to a toxic leader.

Conclusion—Becoming a Positive Leader

Toxic leaders are characterised by being 'maladjusted, malcontent and often malevolent, even malicious'. They are certainly harmful to many people, often whole classes of people and, in extreme cases, even the majority of a population. This is as true in the political sphere as in the corporate. The principles of 'good' leadership are well-established (Burns 1978; Cameron et al 2017; Cameron 2012; Whicker 1996). The question is, how can these be put into action?

Cameron (2012, pp. 125-130), an acknowledged thought leader in this domain, found that positive leaders enable extraordinary performance by fostering:

- a positive work climate,
- positive relationships among organisational members,
- positive communication, and
- associating work with a positive meaning.

Developing these factors requires engagement in fierce, supportive conversations (Scott 2004) and listening deeply (Trimboli 2017). It requires wise, courageous, humane, judicious, temperate and self-transcendent leaders (Jarvis 2004; Peterson & Seligman 2004). Positive leadership is contrary to the tendencies of many in leadership positions. However, as illustrated above, the pursuit of authenticity, empathy, kindness and progressive thinking should not be beyond any of us. Becoming a positive leader first requires that we *choose* to do so. After that, it is a matter of experiential learning and practice.

References

AHRC. 2020. *Inspections of Australia's Immigration Detention Facilities 2019 Report*. Australian Human Rights Commission. Sydney, NSW: AHRC.

American Psychiatric Association. 2013. *Diagnostic and Statistical Manual of Mental Disorders: DSM-5* (Fifth ed.). Washington DC: American Psychiatric Publishing. https://doi.org/10.1176/appi.books.9780890425596

Anheier, H. K., and Moulton, L. 1999. "Studying Organisational Failures". In *When Things Go Wrong. Organisational Failures and*

Breakdowns, edited by H. K. Anheier, 273-290. London: Sage Publications Ltd.

Anheier, H. K., and Romo, F. P. 1999. "Stalemate: A Structural Analysis of Organisational Failure". In *When Things Go Wrong. Organisational Failures and Breakdowns,* edited by H. K. Anheier, 241-270. London: Sage Publications Ltd.

Ardern, J. 2020. *I Know This To Be True: On Kindness, Empathy and Strength.* Sydney, NSW: Murdoch Books.

Ashcroft, A. 2016. "Donald Trump: Narcissist, Psychopath or Representative of the People?" *Psychotherapy and Politics International, 14*(3), 217-222. https://doi.org/10.1002/ppi.1395.

Ashton, M. C. 2017. *Individual Differences and Personality* (Third ed.). Waltham, MA: Academic Press.

Babiak, P. and Hare, R.D. 2007. *Snakes in Suits: When Psychopaths Go to Work.* London: Harper Collins.

Baiada-Hireche, L., Pasquero, J., and Chanlat, J.-F. 2011. "Managerial Responsibility as Negotiated Order: a Social Construction Perspective". *Journal of Business Ethics, 101*(1), 17-31.

Bandura, A. 1977. *Social Learning Theory.* Englewood Cliffs NJ: General Learning Press/Prentice Hall.

Bandura, A. 1982. "Self-Efficacy Mechanism in Human Agency". *American Psychologist, 37*(2), 122–147. https://doi.org/10.1037 /0003-066X.37.2.122.

Bandura, A. 1986. *Social Foundations of Thought and Action: a Social Cognitive Theory.* Englewood Cliffs NJ: Prentice-Hall.

Bandura, A. 2005. "The Evolution of Social Cognitive Theory". In *Great Minds in Management: The Process of Theory Development,* edited by K. G. Smith & M. A. Hitt, 9-33. Oxford: Oxford University Press.

Barrett, D. J. 2006. *Leadership Communication.* New York: McGraw-Hill Irwin.

Bhandarker, A., and Rai, S. 2019. "Toxic Leadership: Emotional Distress and Coping Strategy". *International Journal of Organization Theory and Behaviour, 22*(1), 65-78. https://doi.org/10.1108/ijotb-03-2018-0027.

Blackhall, M. 2021. "First Thing: Trump Recorded Pressuring Georgia Official to 'Find' Votes". *The Guardian.* January 4, 2021. https:// www.theguardian.com/us-news/2021/jan/04/first-thing-trum p-recorded-pressuring-georgia-official-to-find-votes.

Boddy, C., and Taplin, R. 2017. "A Note on Workplace Psychopathic Bullying—Measuring its Frequency and Severity". *Aggression and Violent Behaviour, 34*, 117-119. https://doi.org/10.1016/j.a vb.2017.02.001.

Boddy, C. R. 2015a. "Organisational Psychopaths: a Ten-Year Update". *Management Decision, 53*(10), 2407-2432. https://doi.org/10. 1108/md-04-2015-0114.

Boddy, C. R. 2015b. "Psychopathic Leadership: a Case Study of a Corporate Psychopath CEO". *Journal of Business Ethics, 145*(1), 141-156. https://doi.org/10.1007/s10551-015-2908-6.

Brooks, N., Fritzon, K. and Croom, S. 2020. "Corporate Psychopathy: Entering the Paradox and Emerging Unscathed". In *Corporate Psychopathy: Investigating Destructive Personalities in the Workplace*, edited by K. Fritzon, N. Brooks, and S. Croom. 327-365. Cham, Switzerland: Palgrave Macmillan.

Brown, T. 2009. *Change By Design*. Glasgow: HarperCollins.

Burns, J. M. 1978. *Leadership*. Glasgow: HarperCollins.

Cameron, K., Quinn, R. E., and Caldwell, C. 2017. "Positive Leadership and Adding Value—a Lifelong Journey". *International Journal of Public Leadership, 13*(2), 59-63.

Cameron, K. S. 2005. "Organisational Effectiveness: Its Demise and Re-emergence Through Positive Organisational Scholarship". In *Great Minds in Management: The Process of Theory Development*, edited by K. G. Smith & M. A. Hitt, 304-330. Oxford: Oxford University Press.

Cameron, K. S. (2012). *Positive Leadership: Strategies for Extraordinary Performance* (Second edn.). San Francisco: Berrett-Koehler.

Campanella, E., and Dassù, M. 2019. "Brexit and Nostalgia". *Survival, 61*(3), 103-111. https://doi.org/10.1080/00396338.2019.1614 781.

Carey, J. 2009. *Communication as Culture*. New York: Routledge.

Cohen, A. 2016. "Are They Among Us? A Conceptual Framework of the Relationship Between the Dark Triad Personality and Counterproductive Work Behaviours (CWBs)". *Human Resource Management Review, 26*(1), 69-85. https://doi.org/10.1016/j.hr mr.2015.07.003.

Craig, R., and Muller, H. 2007. *Theorising Communication: Readings Across Traditions*. London: Sage Publications.

Csíkszentmihályi, M. 2008. *Flow. The Psychology of Optimal Experience.* New York, NY: HarperCollins.

Davis, Q. L. 2016. *A Comprehensive Review of Toxic Leadership.* Thesis. Air War College. Air War University. Maxwell AFB, AL: Air War College.

Diener, E., and Seligman, M. E. P. 2004. "Beyond Money: Toward an Economy of Wellbeing". *Psychological Science in the Public Interest, 5*(1), 1-31.

Drummond, H. 1996. *Escalation in Decision-Making: The Tragedy of Taurus.* Oxford: Oxford University Press.

Dweck, C. S. 2016. *Mindset. The New Psychology of Success.* (Second edn.). New York; Penguin Random House.

Economist. 2020a. "In his Dubious Clemency, Donald Trump Breaches Yet Another Norm". *The Economist.* December 24, 2020. https://www.economist.com/united-states/2020/12/24/in-his-dubious-clemency-donald-trump-breaches-yet-another-norm.

Economist. 2020b. "The Spreading Scourge of Voter Suppression". *The Economist.* October 10, 2020. https://www.economist.com/leaders/2020/10/10/the-spreading-scourge-of-voter-suppression.

Economist. 2020c. "Britain's Labour Party Suspends Jeremy Corbyn Over Antisemitism". *The Economist.* October 29, 2020. https://www.economist.com/britain/2020/10/29/britains-labour-party-suspends-jeremy-corbyn-over-anti-semitism.

Economist. 2020d. "Torment of the Uyghurs and the Global Crisis in Human Rights". *The Economist.* October 17, 2020. https://www.economist.com/weeklyedition/2020-10-17.

Economist. 2021. "For All Donald Trump's Efforts, Joe Biden's Victory Will Stand". *The Economist.* January 3, 2021. https://www.economist.com/united-states/2021/01/03/for-all-donald-trumps-efforts-joe-bidens-victory-will-stand.

Edwards, D., and Potter, J. 1992. *Discursive Psychology.* London: Sage Publications Ltd.

EHRC. 2020. *Investigation into Antisemitism in the Labour Party.* October 29, 2020. Equality and Human Rights Commission. London: EHRC. https://www.equalityhumanrights.com/en/publication-download/investigation-antisemitism-labour-party.

Elliott, T. 2005. *Expert Decision-Making in Naturalistic Environments: A Summary of Research* (DSTO-GD-0429). Australian Department of

Defence. Defence Science and Technology Organisation. Edinburgh, S. Aus: DSTO.

Fennimore, A. 2017. "Natural Born Opportunists". *Management Decision, 55*(8), 1629-1644. https://doi.org/10.1108/MD-11-2016-0786.

Fennimore, A., and Sementelli, A. 2016. "Public Entrepreneurship and Sub-Clinical Psychopaths: a Conceptual Frame and Implications". *International Journal of Public Sector Management, 29*(6), 612-634. https://doi.org/10.1108/IJPSM-01-2016-0011.

Fine, G. A. 1984. "Negotiated Orders and Organisational Cultures". *Annual Review of Sociology, 10*, 239-262.

Fisher, R., and Brown, S. 1988. *Getting Together. Building Relationships as We Negotiate*. Penguin.

Fisher, R., Ury, W., and Patton, B. 2011. *Getting to Yes. Negotiating an Agreement with Giving In* (Third edn. revised). New York: Penguin.

Fritzon, K., Bailey, C., Croom, S. and Brooks, N. 2016. "Problem Personalities in the Workplace: Development of the Corporate Personality Inventory". In *Psychology and Law in Europe: When West Meets East.* Edited by P.A. Granhag, R. Bull, A. Shaboltas, and E. Dozortseva, 139-166. Boca Raton, Fl: Taylor & Francis.

Furnham, A., Richards, S.C. and Paulhus, D.L. 2013. "The Dark Triad of Personality: a 10 Review". *Social and Personality Psychology Compass*, 7(3), 199-216.

Galbraith, J. K. 1996. *The Good Society. The Humane Agenda*. London: Sinclair-Stevenson.

Gerlach, M., Farb, B., Revelle, W., et al. 2018. "A Robust Data-Driven Approach Identifies Four Personality Types Across Four Large Data Sets". *Nature Human Behaviour, 2*, 735-742.

Gigerenzer, G. 2007. *Gut Feelings. The Intelligence of the Unconscious*. London: Penguin Allen Lane.

Gigerenzer, G., and Selten, R. 2001. "Rethinking Rationality". In *Bounded Rationality: The Adaptive Toolbox*, edited by G. Gigerenzer & R. Selten, 1-12. Cambridge MA: MIT Press.

Gigerenzer, G., and Selten, R. (eds). 2001. *Bounded Rationality: The Adaptive Toolbox*. Cambridge MA: MIT Press.

Gore, J., Banks, A., Millward, L., et al. 2006. "Naturalistic Decision-Making and Organisations: Reviewing Pragmatic Science". *Organisation Studies, 27*(7), 925-942.

Gore, J., Flin, R., Stanton, N., et al.. 2015. "Editorial. Applications for Naturalistic Decision-Making". *Journal of Occupational and Organizational Psychology, 88*(2), 223-230.

Guazzo, M. S. 1574/1925. *The Civile Conversation.* Translated by G. Pettie and B. Young. London: Constable and Co. Ltd.

Hare, R.D. 2003. *Manual for the Revised Psychopathy Checklist*, 2nd edition. Toronto, Canada: Multi-Health Systems.

Hare, R.D. 2016. "Psychopathy, the PCL-R, and Criminal Justice: Some New Findings and Current Issues". *Canadian Psychology*, Vol 57(1), Feb 2016, 21-34.

Harré, R., and Gillett, G. 1994. *The Discursive Mind.* London: Sage Publications, Inc.

Hsieh, T. 2014. *Delivering Happiness: A Path to Profits, Passion and Purpose.* New York: Grand Central Publishing.

Hurst, C., Simon, L., Jung, Y., et al. 2019. "Are 'Bad' Employees Happier Under Bad Bosses? Differing Effects of Abusive Supervision on Low and High Primary Psychopathy Employees". *Journal of Business Ethics, 158*(4), 1149-1164. https://doi.org/10.1007/s1 0551-017-3770-5.

Janis, I. L. 1972. *Victims of Groupthink.* Boston MA: Houghton Mifflin.

Jarvis, W. 2004. *Four Quadrant Leadership (Stage One)* (Ninth ed.). Cupertino CA: The Wilfred Jarvis Institute.

Kellerman, B. 2004. *Bad Leadership: What It Is, How It Happens, Why It Matters.* Boston MA: Harvard Business School Press.

Kets De Vries, M.F.R. 1993. *Leaders, Fools, and Impostors: Essays in the Psychology of Leadership.* San Francisco: Jossey-Bass.

Klein, G. A. 1997. "The Recognition Primed Decision (RPD) Model: Looking Back, Looking Forward". In *Naturalistic Decision Making*, edited by C. E. Zsambok & G. Klein, 285-292. Mahwah NJ: Lawrence Erlbaum Associates, Publishers.

Klein, G. A. 1998. *Sources of Power: How People Make Decisions.* Cambridge MA: MIT Press.

Kolb, D. A. 2015. *Experiential Learning: Experience as the Source of Learning and Development* (Second ed.). New York: Pearson Education, Inc.

Kulik, B. W., Alarcon, M., & Salimath, M. S. 2020. "The Manipulative Business and Society", C. E. Zsambok & G. Klein (Eds.),. *Business and Society Review, 125*(1), 89-118. https://doi.org/10.1111/basr.12195.

Laguda, E. 2020. "Toxic Leadership: Managing Its Poisonous Effects on Employees and Organisational Outcomes". In *The Palgrave Handbook of Workplace Well-Being*, edited by S. Dhiman. London: Palgrave MacMillan.

Laloux, F. 2014. *Reinventing Organisations—a Guide to Creating Organisations Inspired by the Next Level of Human Consciousness.* Fownhope, Hereford UK: Nelson Parker.

Lewis, M. 2010. *The Big Short: Inside the Doomsday Machine.* London: W. W. Norton & Company.

Lipman-Blumen, J. 2004. *The Allure of Toxic Leaders: Why We Follow Destructive Bosses and Corrupt Politicians—and How We Can Survive Them.* Oxford: Oxford University Press.

Lipshitz, R., Klein, G., Orasanu, J., et al. 2001. "Taking Stock of Naturalistic Decision Making". *Journal of Behavioural Decision Making, 14,* 331-352.

Lipshitz, R., Klein, G., & Carroll, J. S. 2006. "Introduction to the Special Issue. Naturalistic Decision Making and Organisational Decision-Making: Exploring the Intersections". *Organisation Studies, 27*(7), 917-924.

Lowenstein, R. 2001. *When Genius Failed. The Rise and Fall of Long-Term Capital Management.* London: Fourth Estate.

Maines, D. R. 1982. "In Search of Mesostructure: Studies in the Negotiated Order". *Journal of Contemporary Ethnography, 11*(3), 267-279.

Marer, P., Buzady, Z., and Vecsey, Z. 2016. *Missing Link Discovered: Planting Csikszentmihalyi's Flow Theory into Management and Leadership Practice by using FLIGBY, the official Flow-Leadership Game.* Los Angeles CA: ALEAS Group.

Maslow, A. H. 1987. *Motivation and Personality* (Third ed.). Glasgow: HarperCollins Publishers.

McDaniel, W. C. 1993. "Naturalistic Group Decision-Making: Overview and Summary". In *Individual and Group Decision-Making: Current Issues,* edited by N. J. Castellan, 200-216. Mahwah NJ: Lawrence Erlbaum Associates.

Michalak, R. T., and Ashkanasy, N. M. 2018. "Working with Monsters: Counting the Costs of Workplace Psychopaths and Other Toxic Employees". *Accounting and Finance, 60*(S1), 729-770. https://doi.org/10.1111/acfi.12369.

Miller, E. A. 2001. "Yes! There are Limits to Arbitrage: Lessons From the Collapse of Long-Term Capital Management". *The Journal of Social, Political, and Economic Studies, 26*(1), 321-328.

Milosevic, I., Maric, S., and Loncar, D. 2019. "Defeating the Toxic Boss: the Nature of Toxic Leadership and the Role of Followers". *Journal of Leadership and Organisational Studies, 27*(2), 154805181983337-154805181983137. https://doi.org/10.1177/1548051819833374.

Mnookin, R. H. 2004. *Beyond Winning: Negotiating to Create Value in Deals and Disputes.* Boston MA: Harvard University Press.

Mnookin, R. H. 2010. *Bargaining with the Devil: When to Negotiate, When to Fight.* New York: Simon & Schuster.

Moore, K. 2002. "The Discursive Tourist". In *The Tourist as a Metaphor of the Social World*, edited by G. M. S. Dann, 41-59. Wallingford, Oxon: CABI Publishing.

Mutz, D. C. 2011. "Political Psychology and Choice". In *The Oxford Handbook of Political Science* (Kindle ed.), edited by R. E. Goodin. Oxford: Oxford University Press.

Mutz, D. C. 2018. "Status Threat, Not Economic Hardship, Explains the 2016 Presidential Vote". *Proceedings of the National Academy of Sciences of the United States of America, 115*(19), E4330–E4339.

Nai, A. 2018. "Disagreeable Narcissists, Extroverted Psychopaths, and Elections: a New Dataset to Measure the Personality of Candidates Worldwide". *European Political Science, 18*(2), 309-334. https://doi.org/10.1057/s41304-018-0187-2.

Neo, B., Sellbom, M., Smith, S. F., et al. 2016. "Of Boldness and Badness: Insights into Workplace Malfeasance from a Triarchic Psychopathy Model Perspective". *Journal of Business Ethics, 149*(1), 187-205. https://doi.org/10.1007/s10551-016-3108-8.

Obama, B. 2004. *Dreams From My Father: a Story of Race and Inheritance* (Second ed.). Edinburgh, Scotland: Canongate.

Obama, B. 2006. *The Audacity Of Hope: Thoughts on Reclaiming the American Dream.* Melbourne, Victoria, Aus: The Text Publishing Company.

Obama, B. 2020. *A Promised Land*. New York: Penguin.

Obama, M. 2018. *Becoming*. New York: Penguin.

Ogilvie, T., and Liedtka, J. 2011. *Designing for Growth: A Design Thinking Toolkit for Managers*. New York: Columbia University Press.

Pascale, R., Sternin, J., and Sternin, M. 2010. *The Power of Positive Deviance: How Unlikely Innovators Solve the World's Toughest Problems*. Boston MA: Harvard Business Press.

Peterson, C., and Seligman, M. E. P. 2004. *Character Strengths and Virtues: A Handbook and Classification*. American Psychological Association and Oxford University Press.

Picketty, T. 2014. *Capital in the Twenty-First Century*. London: Belknap Press.

Post, J.M. 2015. *Narcissism and Politics: Dreams of Glory*. Cambridge: Cambridge University Press.

Prabhu, S. 2001. *Long-Term Capital Management: the Dangers of Leverage*. Thesis. Duke University. May 2001. https://sites.duke.edu/djepapers/files/2016/08/prabhu.pdf [accessed January 9, 2021]

Robertson, B. J. 2015. *Holacracy: The New Management System for a Rapidly Changing World*. New York: Henry Holt and Co.

Roughan, J. 2017. *John Key: Portrait of a Prime Minister*. Melbourne, Victoria, Aus: Penguin.

Royal Commission. 2020. *Ko tō tātou kāinga tēnei. Report: Royal Commission of Inquiry into the Terrorist Attack on Christchurch Mosques on 15 March 2019*. New Zealand Government, Department of Internal Affairs. https://christchurchattack.royalcommission.nz/the-report/.

Schulman, P. R. 1993. "The Negotiated Order of Organisational Reliability". *Administration and Society, 25*(3), 353-372.

Scott, S. 2004. *Fierce Conversations: Achieving Success at Work and in Life One Conversation at a Time* (Second ed.). New York: Penguin Random House.

Seligman, M. E. P. 2012. *Flourish. A Visionary New Understanding of Happiness and Wellbeing*. London: William Heineman.

Seligman, M. E. P., Steen, T. A., Park, N., et al. 2005. "Positive Psychology Progress: Empirical Validation of Interventions". *American Psychologist, 60*(5), 410-421.

Shattuck, L. G., and Miller, N. L. 2006. "Extending Naturalistic Decision Making to Complex Organisations: a Dynamic Model Situated Cognition". *Organisation Studies, 27*(7), 989-1010.

Smallman, C. 2000. "What is Operational Risk and Why is it Important?" *Risk Management: An International Journal, 2*(3), 7-14.

Smallman, C., and Moore, K. 2010. "Process Studies of Tourists' Decision-Making: the Riches Beyond Variance Studies". *Annals of Tourism Research, 37*(2), 397-422.

Smith, D. 2020. "Trump's Coup is Failing but American Democracy is Still on the Critical List". *The Guardian*. December 12, 2020. https://www.theguardian.com/us-news/2020/dec/12/donald -trump-coup-american-democracy.

Staw, B. M. 1976. "Knee-Deep in the Big Muddy: A Study of Escalating Commitment to a Chosen Course of Action". *Organisational Behaviour and Human Performance, 16*, 27-44.

Stein, M. 2003. "Unbounded Irrationality: Risk and Organisational Narcissism at Long Term Capital Management". *Human Relations, 56*(5), 523-540.

Stonham, P. 1999. "Too Close to the Hedge: the Case of Long-Term Capital Management LP. Part One: Hedge Fund Analytics". *European Management Journal, 17*(3), 282-289.

Strauss, A. 1978. *Negotiations: Varieties, Contexts, Processes, and Social Order.* Hoboken NJ: Jossey-Bass.

Strycharczyk, D., and Clough, P. 2015. *Developing Mental Toughness. Coaching Strategies to Improve Performance, Resilience and WWellbeing* (Second ed.). London: Kogan Page.

Thaler, R. H., and Sunstein, C. R. 2008. *Nudge: Improving Decisions about Health, Wealth, and Happiness.* New Haven CT: Yale University Press.

Trimboli, O. 2017. *Deep Listening: Impact Beyond Words.* Sydney NSW: Oscar Trimboli.

UNHRC. 2018. *Report of the Independent International Fact-Finding Mission on Myanmar.* Geneva, Switzerland: United Nations Human Rights Council.

Walton, M. 2007a. "Leadership Toxicity—an Inevitable Affliction of Organizations?" *Organizations and People, 14*(1), 19-27.

Walton, M. 2007b. "Toxic Leadership". In *Leadership: The Key Concepts*, edited by J. Gosling and A. Marturano. Oxford: Routledge.

Walton, M. 2020a. "Leadership Toxicity: Our Own Corporate 'Covid-Tox' Pandemic". *Effective Executive*. IUP Publications, Vol XXIII, (2), 7-11.

Walton, M. 2020b. "Tackling Leadership Toxicity: An HRM Priority". *HRM Review*. IUP Publications, Vol XVI (3), June, 25-34.

Walton, M. 2020c. "Identify, Track and Trace Disruptive Workplace Behaviour: Towards Enhancing Organisational Performance". *HRM Review*. IUP Publications, Vol XVI (4), December, 1-7.

Whicker, M. L. 1996. *Toxic Leaders: When Organisations Go Bad*. Westoport CT: Quorum Books.

Willis, A. 2017. "6 Ways Social Media Changed the Way We Communicate". *Higher Ed Marketing Journal*. August 15, 2017.

Witkin, J. 2012. "How Zappos Profits From the Happiness Business". *The Guardian*, June 15, 2012. https://www.theguardian.com/sustainable-business/zappos-shoes-profits-happiness-business.

Zeldin, T. 1998. *Conversation*. Santa Monica, CA: HiddenSpring.

Zsambok, C. E., and Klein, G. A. (eds.). 1997. *Naturalistic Decision Making*. Mahwah NJ: Lawrence Erlbaum Associates

Part 2:

Perspectives on
the Corporate/Radical-Right Axis

Chapter 5:
Corporate Authoritarianism and Its Abusive Impacts in Democratic Societies

By Alan Waring[1]

Abstract

This chapter examines the authoritarian characteristics of some corporations and their leaders, describing how such characteristics are typically harmful to such parties as customers, employees, contractors and to society more broadly, for example corporate abuses of product safety and of Covid-19 protection rules. Case study examples from some industry sectors are described. The chapter includes an analysis of similarities and overlaps between corporate authoritarianism and radical-right authoritarianism. In contrast to pejorative critiques of corporate authoritarianism, elite deviance, and wrongdoing (e.g. Bakan 2004; Birch 2007; Bloom & Rhodes 2016; 2018; Crouch 2014; Kohl & Makary 2016; Simon 2018; Zuboff 2019), the prospective 'new model corporation' (British Academy 2018) is discussed. Risks for various parties, including broader society, as well as for corporate authoritarians and authoritarian corporations, are identified.

Key words: authoritarianism, abuses, corporate, sectors, radical-right, risks

Corporate Authoritarianism

As stated in chapter 1, in this volume as in Volumes 1 and 2, authoritarianism is defined as: (1) A belief in or support for strict obedience to the authority of a particular orthodoxy, dogma, individual, or group, at the expense of personal freedom, (2) The overbearing and intimidating tactics frequently displayed by authoritarians. Authoritarianism has a deeper and more perseverant character than mere bossiness, or unpleasant conduct towards other parties. For relevant psychological factors, see chapter 1 and Waring and Paxton (2018, 55-58; 2019, 63-66). Depending on an individual's personality, beliefs, needs

---

[1]   See contributor affiliations and biography, page 525.

and motives, authoritarianism ranges on a continuum from relatively harmless manifestation through an increasingly pathological character to an extreme expression typical of neo-Nazis. In effect, this continuum reflects the radical-right spectrum. As the 'dark triad' proposition suggests, and more recent studies confirm (Brooks et al 2020; Fritzon et al 2016), concurrent psychological factors, e.g. narcissism, Machiavellianism and psychopathic traits such as manipulation (Brooks 2020), may also apply. Thus, caution is required, so as to avoid misleading assumptions that may, on the one hand, falsely categorize bossy, lazy, or self-centred individuals as being authoritarian and/or suffering from a personality disorder, or that, on the other, conversely may falsely dismiss personality disorders in an individual as merely evidence of a colourful, flamboyant or roguish character.

In this volume, corporate authoritarianism refers either to individual corporate executives and leaders who exhibit the characteristics of authoritarianism (as defined above), and/or to particular organisations whose leaders and executives collectively exhibit such characteristics. Corporate authoritarianism in the locus of high-level political engagement and corrupt influence is an area of major concern (e.g. Bakan 2004; Birch 2007; Bloom & Rhodes 2016; 2018; Crouch 2014; Michaels 2020; Oklobdzija 2019). However, corporate authoritarianism may also operate negatively in other ways, namely in attitudes towards and treatment of customers, employees, contractors, and other stakeholders. For example, Robinson and Murphy (2008) and Simon (2018) explore the concept of elite deviance i.e. improper conduct for the benefit of corporate elites and/or organisation, whereby such conduct (e.g. white collar crime, wilful safety or environmental violations, profit without honour) serves selfish interests at the expense of others. As Bloom and Rhodes (2016) noted, "....elite authority all too often knows no limits, and doesn't take 'no' for an answer", and that "...economic and social elites are all too often granted sovereign privilege without any sense of responsibility or accountability. It is the very definition of an authoritarian culture dressed up as political democracy." Birch (2007, 156) went further: "It is the institutionalisation and naturalisation of corporate agendas in different governance structures that most clearly illustrate what can be seen as totalitarian features of the corporation." Zuboff (2019, 8) referred to the "surveillance capitalism" power abuses of the

Internet and social media giants seeking to control not just information exchange between individuals but also information and information flows *about* individuals and, worse, "ever-more-predictive sources of behavioral surplus", the ultimate goal being to *"automate us"* for commercial gain. While not suggesting that all examples of bad corporate attitudes and conduct reflect conscious and wilful political support for radical-right ideology per se, nevertheless their general tone and character may be remarkably similar to those of radical-right authoritarianism. Indeed, the author argues that radical-right authoritarianism and corporate authoritarianism are essentially the same commensal phenomenon and cooperate for perceived shared interests. The two authoritarian groups—corporate and radical-right—share similar traits, as outlined in Table 5.1.

The rest of this chapter presents, firstly, examples and evidence of corporate authoritarianism (whether by individual corporate leaders, or by corporate entities whose leaders and executives collectively exhibit such characteristics). Presentation of cases and evidence is then followed by overall analysis in relation to existing relevant theories and potential explanation of evidence. The following sections examine how corporate/radical-right authoritarianism has adversely affected a spectrum of parties or interests: customers, employees, and contract-out workers, as well as the general public. Numerous examples in other sectors also warrant exposure but space was limited.

Abuse of Customers

Customer complaints about what amounts essentially to corporate authoritarianism focus primarily on three characteristics: (1) evasion of responsibility, accountability and liability by policy, contractual terms, mendacity, and amoral calculation (Waring 2019a), (2) unwarranted inflation of consumption data, charges and prices, and (3) arrogant and disdainful contempt by some senior executives towards individual customer complaints, examples of which feature in Table 5.1.

The Covid-19 pandemic of 2020, which severely damaged the economies of most nations, as well as the income and financial stability of many sectors, companies and individuals, also provided an opportunity for businesses to demonstrate whether they were adhering to high standards of corporate ethics and integrity regarding this topic. For example, Jones, C. et al (2020), Norfolk and Jones (2020), and Russell (2020) cite virtuous companies in the UK in the Covid-19 context. The corporate chiefs of Microsoft (Bill Gates) and *Twitter* (Jack Dorsey) also pledged donations of US$ billions to the global battle against Covid-19 and its impact. In contrast, Duke and Jones (2020), Jones, C. et al (2020), Kenber (2020c); Norfolk and Jones (2020), Purves (2020), Russell (2020), Walsh (2020), and Walsh and Jones (2020) cite companies judged to be particularly bad.

Table 5.1:   Analogous Authoritarian Traits of Radical-Right Leaders and Some Corporate Leaders

Authoritarian Traits	Radical-Right Leaders	Some Corporate Leaders
Ruthless drive to attain objectives by any and all means necessary, regardless of harm to others.	Ideological and/or political objectives.	Personal and/or corporate objectives.
Organisation 'too big to fail' and more important than 'the little people', despite self-congratulatory public mantras of 'caring' about and championing people.	Political party or group more important than electorate, despite rhetoric embracing 'the people'.	Company more important than customers and employees, despite not observing in practice its mission statements, governance statements, websites, advertisements, and PR.
Accrual of power and vast rewards take absolute precedence over any moral imperatives or genuine concern for others.	Accrual of power, political advancement, financial enlargement, vast rewards packages etc.	Corporate profits, market share, accrual of power, career advancement, financial enlargement, bonuses, vast rewards packages etc.
People seen as either (a) serving the interests of authoritarians and to be used/manipulated for their ends, or (b) an undeserving underclass of 'others' to be	Citizens seen as either (a) ideological support/electoral units (i.e. meeting far-right nationalist/nativist ethno-religious criteria for deserving 'producerist' patriots), or	Customers, employees and contractors seen as economic/consumer units to be manipulated or abused for personal and/or corporate objectives, rather than as human beings with

discriminated against or victimized.	(b) an undeserving underclass of 'others' who warrant discriminatory policies, rather than all citizens seen as equal.	inherent rights and privileges.
Evasion of responsibility, accountability and liability.	Evasion by decree, statute, policy, mendacity, and amoral calculation.	Evasion by policy, contractual terms, mendacity, and amoral calculation.
Arrogant and disdainful behaviour towards those entitled to be treated with respect.	Contempt by leading radical-right politicians for individual citizens requesting assistance who do not fit radical-right ideology e.g. the poor, the chronically ill, immigration cases, ethno-religious harassment, hate crime victims.	Contempt by some senior and lesser executives for individual customer complaints, e.g. refusal to answer letters; deployment of deliberately dysfunctional remote call-centres as the only means for customers to communicate with them*.
Authoritarians regarding people as too stupid to see through their deception and hypocrisy.	In a populist right-wing dominated society, electorate regarded as too stupid to see through the deception and hypocrisy of radical-right political leaders and elite supporters.	In a populist consumer economy, public regarded as too stupid to see through the deception and hypocrisy of some corporations and corporate elites.

*Footnote: Bryan (2020) and *Times* (2020) 'name and shame' a list of large UK companies allegedly guilty of deliberately blocking and frustrating customers' attempts to complain by a combination of removing company e-mail addresses from their websites, ceasing all complaint handling by e-mail, and forcing complaining customers to engage with dysfunctional automated call centres.

Among business sectors that have registered a persistently high level of customer complaint regarding all three primary characteristics cited above, (before, during and since the Covid-19 pandemic), the following are prominent:

- Health Care
- Phone/IT/Internet/Social Media
- Banks and Financial Services
- Energy Providers
- Supermarkets and Large Retailers
- Immovable Property Sector (see e.g. Waring 2013, 133-150)
- Airlines and Travel

The following sub-sections address some of these sectors, limited only by space considerations. Sectors and cases not included present examples as equally bad as those that are included.

Health Care Sector

The health care sector in the US provides graphic examples of how its customers (i.e. patients) have been impacted adversely by long-term authoritarian abuses. Many consider the US health care system to be dysfunctional and catering only for the wealthy and the fortunate (Cutler 2014; Greer 2017; Himmelstein et al 2017; Millenson 2018), and which is dominated by commercial interests of private medicine, pharmaceutical companies, and insurers, as willing primary co-enactors of ultra-conservative political ideology on health care. After President Obama had reduced the number of uninsured (i.e. those denied health care) from 48 million in 2010 to 28.1 million in 2016 (Barnett & Berchick 2017), the uninsured number continued to fall to 25.6 million in 2017 before incoming President Trump's anti-Obamacare policy started to impact the attitudes of insurers. Data for 2018 (Berchick et al 2019) show the number of uninsured rising again for the first time since 2010, to 27.5 million with an upward trend projected so long as Trump remained president.

Those uninsured are in this predicament for a variety of reasons (see e.g. Brill 2013; Kliff 2017; Himmelstein et al 2017; Millenson 2018), such as being too poor to afford premiums, unemployed, being chronically ill and thus rejected by insurers, or being undocumented migrants. Under Trump's anti-socialized medicine policy, the previously declining numbers rose again to around 28 million and experts predicted an inevitable rise again under Trump's proposed American

Health Care. Cutler (2016) noted that Trump's model would be devoid of consumer protection and could only work to the benefit of the insurance companies involved and, moreover, would conveniently advance the positions and mutual interests of not only Trump and his radical-right agenda but also of the insurance, medical and pharmaceutical sectors. See also Falkenbach and Greer (2021).

Case 5.1 Shkreli and Price Gouging

A high-profile example of ruthless exploitation of patients for profit by the pharmaceutical industry is provided by the Shkreli case in the US. Martin Shkreli was a young entrepreneur and former hedge fund manager who in 2014 set up Turing Pharmaceuticals, a company trading in prescription pharmaceuticals. Shkreli's speciality was, in concert with other companies, to create artificial monopoly control of the supply of particular pharmaceuticals and then to inflate the price, sometimes by as much as 55 times (FTC 2020a, b), a process termed 'price gouging'. One of the drugs involved was *Daraprim*, which at the time sold for between US$1 and US$2 per unit globally, although typically $13.50 in the US where drug prices are frequently inflated for profit. However, Shkreli and Vyera Pharmaceuticals (the new name for Turing) acquired the rights to *Daraprim* and proceeded to inflate the price per tablet to US$750. In March 2018, Shkreli was convicted of securities fraud against his former hedge fund investors and sentenced to 7 years imprisonment. Both before and during his fraud trial, he showed no contrition or remorse regarding his *Daraprim* activities or his fraudulent conduct, on the contrary, engaging in issuing numerous personal insults, outbursts and accusations on social media and in court against many parties, including the prosecutor and the judge (Rushe 2018). On the evidence, he presented as an authoritarian predator focussed only on his own narcissistic gratification, and having no concern or regard for the harm caused by his conduct.

In January 2020, the US Federal Trade Commission and the State of New York filed charges against Vyera Pharmaceuticals LLC, Phoenixus AG (a Swiss company), Martin Shkreli (individually, and as an owner and former director of Phoenixus and a former executive of Vyera), and Kevin Mulleady (as an owner and director of

Phoenixus, and as a former executive of Vyera). The charges (FTC 2020a) alleged an "elaborate anticompetitive scheme to preserve a monopoly for the life-saving drug, Daraprim". On April 14, 2020, the case against the defendants was amended to include six additional US states as co-complainants (FTC 2020b).

Case 5.2: Fludrocortisone and Cancer Drug Price Gouging

In the UK, the case of Amit Patel and his companies Auden McKenzie (Pharma Division) and Amilco Ltd, included a monopolistic price-fixing conspiracy with the South African-parented pharmaceutical company Aspen UK and others. The Competition and Markets Authority (CMA) began investigations in 2017 into an anticompetitive conspiracy involving collaborative conduct and agreements between a number of companies (Lexon (UK), Accord-UK, Auden McKenzie, King Pharmaceuticals, and Alissa Healthcare Research Ltd).The focus of that investigation centred on cartel abuses in the control of supply and pricing of nortryptiline tablets. The CMA found against all the companies for breaches of market-sharing and competition law and issued fines ranging from £75,573 to £1,882,238 (CMA 2019a).

In October 2019, the CMA issued a determination that in 2016 Aspen had unlawfully agreed to pay two other firms, Amilco and Triofarma, to stay out of the UK market for fludrocortisone acetate tablets, used to combat the effects of the otherwise lethal Addison's disease (CMA 2019b). This market fixing agreement protected Aspen's monopoly to supply the drug to the National Health Service (NHS) and enabled them to inflate prices for this drug by up to 1,800%. As compensation for its part in the cartel, Aspen agreed to pay the NHS £8m and committed itself to ensure that there will always be at least two independent suppliers of fludrocortisone in the UK. Nevertheless, although Aspen's egregious activities may have been curbed in the UK, in 2017 the European Commission began its own investigation into Aspen's alleged market fixing and price abuses across the EU in relation to such drugs as *Busulfan*, and anti-cancer drugs such as *Leukeran* and *Alkeran* (Forster 2017).

> In June 2020, the CMA announced (CMA 2020; Kenber 2020a) that, following the Auden McKenzie and Amilco price-fixing determinations, Amit Patel had been disqualified from being a director of any UK company for 5 years. For his part, Dr Philip Hallwood, director of King Pharmaceuticals and Praze Consultants Ltd, was also disqualified as a director of any UK company for a period of 7 years from March 2020. It also transpired that Patel had been charged in 2014 by HM Customs and Revenue with arranging for fake invoices totalling some £14m to be paid by Auden McKenzie to companies in Dubai. It is reported that he agreed to pay £14.6m to HMRC (Kenber 2020b).

All the above pharmaceutical market abuse cases demonstrate a fundamental authoritarianism involving wilful free-market 'what can we get away with?' predatory thinking and conduct on the part of the organisers, with no concern for the obvious harm, whether clinical, financial, or mental stress to patients, or harm to public health service finances and taxpayers.

In addition to such market abuses, the 2020 Covid-19 viral pandemic threw into sharp relief the fragility, inequalities, and domination by politico-commercial interests within the US health care system. The historical context of institutionalized discrimination of the health care sector against the BAME (Black, Asian and Minority Ethnic) population in the US was revealed by the disproportionately high infection and death rate among the BAME population compared with the majority white population. In addition to historical discrimination (e.g. BAME comprise a high proportion of those denied health insurance in the US), this demographic is also disproportionately represented in low paid so-called 'frontline' jobs that necessarily entail a high risk of Covid-19 exposure (e.g. paramedics, cleaners, nursing auxiliaries, taxi drivers, bus drivers, care workers). The evidence points, at least in part, to the effects of pre-existing systemic discrimination having been worsened by the radical-right discriminatory policies of the Trump administration and the amoral calculations of a profit-fixated healthcare industry.

Unlike the US, in the UK, government policy and structural discrimination against BAME or minorities generally for health care access, and low concern for minority disempowerment, is traditionally considered much less significant (owing to universal health care and an NHS). Nevertheless, UK studies have shown that BAME also suffer a disproportionately high prevalence of Covid-19 infections and a much higher fatality rate than does the overall population (Campbell & Siddique 2020; PHE 2020a; Smyth 2020). Susceptibility resulting from genetic factors, as well as socioeconomic factors and racial prejudice and discrimination, has been posited e.g. Professor Kevin Fenton's controversial BAME report commissioned by Public Health England but initially not published until pressured by the medical professions, the media and public disquiet (PHE 2020b). Fenton's report stated (page 6): "It is clear from discussions with stakeholders that COVID-19 in their view did not create health inequalities, but rather the pandemic exposed and exacerbated longstanding inequalities affecting BAME groups in the UK". Further, the report stated that "racism and discrimination" was felt by stakeholders to be a significant "root cause affecting health, and exposure risks and disease progression risk" (page 7).

All these issues continue to be investigated in the UK. For example, as in the US, BAME groups are disproportionately represented in low paid 'frontline' jobs that necessarily entail a high risk of Covid-19 exposure. However, unlike the US, BAME representation at all levels in the NHS, especially as physicians and other clinicians, is much higher than is its proportion of the general population. Kattikireddi et al (2020) also showed that within the BAME population wide variations in prevalence occur between different ethnic groups, with black and south Asian groups having significantly higher rates of infection and death.

On Trump's handling of the Covid-19 crisis, Bryant (2020) unfavourably commented "Once again, those who live in developed nations have been left to ponder why the world's richest country does not have a system of universal health care." The persistently extreme reluctance of a majority of the US population to demand universal health care, a position both echoed and encouraged by Trump and the US Alt-Right overall, may well be a reflection of the uniquely American concept of 'freedom' (see chapter 1) and the low social solidarity exhibited within the US compared, for example, with European countries (Hermanus 1999; Waring 2018, 308-316). Such a view encourages a false belief that government-funded universal health care systems prevalent in most other developed nations connote 'communism' and therefore must be rejected for the US as being un-American (see the critique of Allitt 2020). Factually, in the post-2000 EU for example, only one EU country (Cyprus) has had a communist party in power (2008-2013). Neo-liberal capitalism with pragmatic elements of socialism has been the hallmark of most developed nations for many decades and could not accurately be described as communism or, indeed, radical socialism.

Airlines and Travel

In the airlines and travel sector, the following case examples 5.3 and 5.4 are presented as evocative and not as ones that are necessarily representative of the airline industry or from which generalisations may be drawn about this industry. These are also cases that necessarily rely heavily on anecdotal reportage and media commentary rather than from independent academic study and analysis.

Case 5.3: United Airlines and Dr Dao

A particularly graphic example of corporate authoritarianism towards customers was provided by the draconian treatment of a United Express (United Airlines) passenger in April 2017 (Goldstein 2017; Victor & Stevens 2017). The passengers having boarded at Chicago O'Hare airport, the cabin crew announced that as the flight was over-booked four passengers would have to give up their seats and fly on a later flight. Cash compensation was offered, and three passengers opted to give up their seats. However, Dr David Dao Duy Anh, an American physician of Vietnamese-Chinese ancestry, declined as he had important surgery appointments to attend at his destination. The cabin crew persisted in seeking to persuade him to give up his seat, but Dr Dao persisted in declining. Fellow passengers reported that a United employee on board then threatened to call security to have him forcibly removed, to which Dr Dao complained that he was being singled out because he looked Chinese.

When several airport security officials came on board, they forcibly removed him from his seat and dragged him off the plane. During this assault and manhandling, Dr Dao reportedly suffered concussion, a broken nose, loss of two front teeth, and bled profusely. For unexplained reasons, he was then allowed to re-board and sought to retake his old seat. Unsuccessful, and still bleeding, he took a seat near the front but collapsed sideways and was then taken off the plane semi-conscious on a stretcher.

His mistreatment, ostensibly triggered by the overbearing attitude of United personnel on board, was then compounded by United Airlines CEO, Oscar Munoz, issuing a public statement seeking to justify the mistreatment and accusing Dr Dao of "disruptive" and "belligerent" conduct, which was contradicted by passenger eye-witness accounts as well as their video evidence (Goldstein 2017). Munoz also sought to trivialize the overbooking issue by referring to the operational need to "reaccommodate" customers, and apologizing only for the "overbook situation" but not for the specific mistreatment of Dr Dao (Victor & Stevens 2017). Passenger on-board videos of the confrontation and assault on Dr Dao went viral on social media and the Internet, leading to passenger boycotts of United and widespread condemnation of its perceived bullying and arrogance. Public anger increased when evidence emerged that the flight had not been 'overbooked' and that Dr Dao and the other three passengers asked to de-board had been properly boarded and not by mistake. Indeed, it was unclear on what criteria these four were selected, and by whom, to be de-boarded. It transpired that United had decided unilaterally that it needed urgently to fly four of its own employees on this already full flight and that therefore four passengers already boarded had to be sacrificed.

In addition to adverse impacts on United's corporate reputation and consumer trust and confidence, legal experts quickly publicized opinions that legally United was on very weak grounds in both its justification for forcibly de-boarding Dr Dao and its actual mistreatment of him (e.g. Ben-Shahar & Strahilevtiz 2017). For his multiple injuries and other damages, he received a swift out-of-court settlement from United for an undisclosed sum in late April 2017. In the highly competitive domestic airline market of the US, United was forced as a result of this high-profile case to agree to significantly improve its policies, procedures, and training. Other airlines also sought to capitalize on United's bad publicity by emphasizing how superior their passenger-facing policies and procedures were compared to United's. For his part, Mr Munoz's part in the debacle did not result in his dismissal and he did not forfeit his forthcoming planned chairmanship, contrary to widespread speculation. Munoz went on to take up chairmanship of United until stepping down in May 2020. Moreover, Klint (2020) reported that "every United employee who talks to me off-the-record still thinks Dao was belligerent and deserved to get dragged off the plane." Despite being contradicted by video evidence and eyewitness accounts, if accurate that such prejudice is still widespread within United, it suggests that whereas official policies, procedures and training may have changed, the underlying authoritarian culture had not.

Such resistance to change following a disaster (of whatever kind) is not uncommon. For example, according to the account of someone engaged in the investigation of the King's Cross fire on London Underground in 1987 (Waring 2013), refusal to acknowledge and accept that this particular safety disaster had resulted from management failures and a weak safety culture was widespread among London Underground employees, despite the findings of the official government inquiry (Fennell 1988). As Waring (2013, 56) noted, "the herd was in denial" and that "in view of such ingrained denial and false beliefs about cause-and-effect, it would take perhaps ten years to implement a robust safety management system in the company and embed a radically different safety culture." By analogy, a ten-year timeframe may equally be required of United Airlines in relation to eradicating a culture apparently predisposed to wilfully mistreat passengers.

Case 5.4: TUI and Cancellation Refund Refusals

Regarding the German-based airline and travel company TUI, it is reported that their CEO in the UK and their Group CEO in Hannover, refuse to reply to customers' letters of complaint, and similarly their customer service functions fail to respond, prompting such unflattering comments about TUI as *Schwein-Umwissenheit* ('pig-ignorance'). Similar complaints about TUI have been raised across Europe. Moreover, during the early months of the Covid-19 pandemic March-June 2020, despite having made a commercial decision to cease all flights in mid-March, TUI studiously avoided formally cancelling tickets already issued (Paton 2020) until well into April. Instead, even when finally forced to cancel tickets, it did so with a no-refund policy, offering passengers a euro-for-euro or pound-for-pound voucher against future travel valid for 12 months.

Although, at first sight, their offer may seem praiseworthy, in fact under EU regulations any airline that cancels a passenger's ticket is required to reimburse the full price paid within 7 days (or 14 days if combined with accommodation) but may only offer the alternative option of a voucher against future flights provided it is not as an imposed substitute for a cash refund. In reality, in addition to this unlawful conduct, TUI sought to pass all the decision-making responsibility onto the customer to make a judgement as to whether TUI was likely to remain in business long enough, whether any future ticket's cost would not have increased, and whether the customer themselves would be in a position to use such a voucher, e.g. if the Covid-19 pandemic and lockdown remained or returned over the next 12 months. If a pre-paid passenger used common sense and decided, for self-protection, to cancel or just not fly, in the light of strong government instruction not to or even the non-availability of grounded TUI flights, TUI would simply keep the original money without compensation. The passenger's only re-course then would be either a claim against their credit card company under Consumer Credit legislation, or against their own travel insurer.

TUI's apparent artfulness and 'sharp practice' (i.e. amoral cal-culation) in this matter was exposed further by the announcement on March 27, 2020 (Weiss 2020) that TUI had received a German government Covid-19 bailout of US$2 billion (€1.8 billion) i.e. in addition to all the fares and holiday payments already received that it refused to pay back in cash to customers. Customer and media reaction against TUI accelerated throughout April and May 2020 (Byers 2020) and the airlines regulator in the UK, the Civil Aviation Authority, opened an investigation into the alleged unlawful anti-consumer practices of TUI and other airlines in the Covid-19 con-text.

Phone/IT/Internet/Social Media

As an example of the genre in this sector, Virgin Media, a major phone/IT/internet company in the UK, has been heavily criticised for exhibiting characteristic (3) i.e. arrogant and disdainful contempt by some senior executives towards individual customer complaints.

Case 5.5: Virgin Media and Its 'Labyrinth of Hell' Customer Complaints System

It is reported by customers that registering an issue or a complaint with Virgin Media is typically an exhausting battle of wits and stamina against an automated phone menu system with key options missing, and then, an impossible 'conversation' with a call centre operative speaking from a fixed script in a robotic monotone and a heavy foreign accent. See, for example, a customer's online *TrustPilot* negative 1-star review on March 7, 2020, referring to "VM's 'Labyrinth of Hell' customer 'care' system". Names and contact details of key officials are conspicuously absent from the company's website and its call centres are instructed not to divulge this information. If and when the Chief Operating Officer's name and location are tracked down (in 2020, a male), he refuses to reply to letters of complaint. The author has seen documentary evidence that the company's own Customer Services Director and various other members of her 'Customer Resolutions' team engage in repeatedly sending a complainant over several months essentially the same computer-generated letters full of blandishments and a vague impression that remedies will be done but not actually specifying or closing these out, prompting the jibe 'How many Virgin Media employees does it take to change a light bulb?' Despite the company's much vaunted official mantra of "Let's Make Good Things Happen", and without any other plausible explanation, it is difficult not to conclude that this 'system' has been deliberately designed by Virgin Media to deter, exhaust and thwart customers' attempts to register effectively a complaint and to obtain redress.

It is important to restate that not all organisations are authoritarian or demonstrate such egregious characteristics towards customers as Virgin Media, United Airlines, and TUI, appear to have done.

The deciding factors in whether an organisation becomes authoritarian lie in the personal beliefs, character, policy decisions, and operational style of its leaders and senior executives, which in turn frame and mediate the organisation's culture, systems and stance towards both its own personnel and towards customers and others. Of relevance, Brooks et al (2020), Fritzon et al (2016), and Walton (2007a; b; 2010; 2020a; b; c) have conducted studies on the psychopathology of toxic corporate leaders, the dynamics of boardroom, employee and wider relationships, and adverse effects and consequences. The chapters by Antony Vass and Clive Smallman in this volume add further analysis and weight to the crucial necessity to understand both corporate and radical-right authoritarianism and their interactions.

In addition to abuses against customers, some large companies have also adopted an authoritarian stance against their own employees and/or contract suppliers.

UK Contracting-Out Abuses

Globalization and the so-called global economy involve the location of capital, production units, labour sources, and sources of goods from wherever provides the most efficient and cost-effective advantages. There are undoubted benefits from globalization, such as access to markets, cost and price reduction, and corporate efficiency. The model inevitably has resulted in companies searching continuously for the best sources and relationships, and contracting-out significant portions of their operations and work so as to concentrate on their core strengths and reduce overhead costs. This has included large numbers of employee-status jobs (i.e. under a contract *of* service) being transferred to contracted-out status (i.e. under a contract *for* services), whether on an individual basis or through contractor companies. In a contracted-out status, the principal avoids responsibility for such things as employee-status statutory benefits, paid holidays, company pensions, national [social] insurance and income tax. Further contract-out refinements have arisen, such as zero-hours contracts and the so-called 'gig economy', in which individuals' income becomes highly variable and precarious. However, advantages for principal employers are offset by such problems as supply chain risks (Waring 2013), including the need for multiple parallel suppliers and reserve pools of contract-out workers to avoid single-source risks and interruption of supplies, whether materials or labour. In addition, interfaces with multiple contractors raise increased boundary risks in terms of control, communication, work and product quality, and presumption of legal liabilities.

Many principals believe wrongly that contracting-out enables them to transfer all liabilities by contract term. For example, in the UK, liability cannot be transferred in this way to a contractor for such matters as statutory duties that fall on the principal, and then only to limited extent—for example, contributory negligence for common law duties of care, such as health, safety and environmental obligations (Bennett 2013; Ford & Clarke 2016). Nevertheless, many principals seek to impose unfair contracts, while contractors often feel intimidated and vulnerable by virtue of their priority need for income. A particularly egregious example of a large organisation exercising authoritarian abuse against its contractors is provided by how, over at least a 12-year period, the UK national Post Office behaved towards its sub-postmasters, as summarised by *Private Eye* (Brooks & Wallis 2020) in a 6-page report and in numerous earlier stage reports over many years. In their 2020 report, they described (page 27) the Post Office as "an authoritarian body whose bosses were used to getting their own way."

Case 5.6: The UK Post Office's Abuse of Its Contract Sub-Postmasters

In addition to its own larger post offices, for many years the Post Office has contracted with a large number (some 9,000) of small shopkeepers, especially in small towns and villages, to provide Post Office services within their premises. These sub-postmasters are generally not Post Office employees but are remunerated by the Post Office by contracts for services and are subject to various contractual obligations and restrictions, which include being held liable for any accounting shortfall involving "carelessness or error". Between 1996 and 1999, the Post Office ran a major project to modernize its IT system for the payment of state pensions and benefits from Post Office branch counters. However, the Horizon Project turned into a major fiasco for non-delivery, which by 1999 had cost taxpayers some £700 million, and which the House of Commons public accounts committee described as "one of the biggest IT failures in the public sector." Nevertheless, Post Office senior management decided to convert Horizon into a comprehensive electronic system for its full range of services. According to Brooks and Wallis (2020, 24), the project "became the largest non-military IT contract in Europe", even though at that early stage the Post Office board of directors noted in September 1999 that serious doubts existed over the software's reliability.

Horizon went live in 2000 and within two months it was reporting unexplained large accounting variances at individual sub-post offices. The Post Office then invoked the contract clause for liability for shortfall, asserting that "carelessness or error" on the part of the sub-postmaster was the only possible cause. The number of such cases escalated, with alleged shortfalls ranging from £1,000 to typically tens of thousands of pounds and, in one case, over £1 million. Over the next few years, the Post Office racked up over 550 such cases in which sub-postmasters were coerced into covering alleged shortfalls and typically were sacked from their Post Office role. In some cases, criminal prosecutions were launched for such alleged offences as theft, fraud and false accounting, and several sub-postmasters were convicted on the basis of 'fool-proof Horizon' evidence and jailed.

As the number of cases mounted, both the Post Office and its Horizon software provider Fujitsu (which had inherited it from its predecessor ICL) steadfastly maintained that the software was "absolutely accurate and reliable" and that all the actions against sub-postmasters with shortfalls were fully justified. Nevertheless, by 2012, a growing number of MPs concluded that both the technical reliability of Horizon and the honesty and integrity of the Post Office's and Fujitsu's senior managements were in question. By 2015, Post Office Chief Executive Paula Vennells was summoned by the House of Commons business committee to account for why her previous pledge to resolve the Horizon debacle had not been met. Brooks and Wallis (2020, 27) reported that her claim to be running a "caring" business and having "no evidence" of any miscarriages of justice was met by "barely disguised derision" by committee members, one of whom described the Horizon affair as a "shambles".

The Post Office and its Horizon deliverer Fujitsu continued to maintain its 'paragons of virtue' self-assertion, to deny that Horizon was in any way faulty or responsible for false errors in sub-postmasters' accounts, and to deny that they were in any way responsible for false charges, false convictions, and all the damage to the lives of falsely accused sub-postmasters. However, in March 2017, the High Court granted a group litigation order to 555 sub-postmaster litigants to sue the Post Office. Over the next two years, in a series of trials and appeals by the Post Office to overturn judgements against them, the Post Office lost in every instance and came in for excoriating criticism by judges. The Hon Mr Justice Fraser (POGL 2019a) variously described the Post Office as "aggressive", attempting "to put the court *in terrorem*", seeking to "obfuscate matters, and mislead me", "obdurate", and guilty of "oppressive behaviour". The contractual relationship was judged to be unfair in its coercive disadvantage to sub-postmasters. The Post Office then attempted to have Mr Justice Fraser removed for alleged bias and, when this failed, they lodged an appeal. In hearing this appeal, Lord Justice Coulson rejected it outright, describing the appellants' arguments as "misconceived", "fatally flawed", "untenable", "demonstrably wrong", and "without substance". He stated that the appeal had been based "on the idea that the Post Office was entitled to treat [sub-postmasters] in capricious or arbitrary ways which would not be unfamiliar to a mid-Victorian factory-owner...." (Slingo 2019).

Evidence submitted by senior Fujitsu witnesses for the defence was systematically discredited and shown as false, revealing a 'party line' conspiracy over many years to hide evidence of the fundamental flaws of the Horizon product that had led to the false charges and convictions. Mr Justice Fraser noted that two large organisations [Post Office and Fujitsu] had cheated the litigants and lied to them, and that the Post Office's approach amounted to "bare assertions and denials that ignore what actually occurred.....[and] amounts to the 21st century equivalent of maintaining the earth is flat." (POGL 2019b). The Post Office agreed to pay £57.75 million in settlement, plus its own costs, the expected total to exceed £90 million, which was footed by the taxpayer as the Post Office is a public body. Subsequently, an additional 485 victims sought compensation under a scheme operated by the law firm Herbert Smith

Freehills on behalf of the Post Office (Post Office Trial 2020a; b; UKParl 2019).

In addition, sub-postmasters were authorised to pursue the Post Office for malicious prosecution and Mr Justice Fraser sent a file on Fujitsu to the Director of Public Prosecutions. The Criminal Cases Review Commission referred many sub-postmaster convictions to the Courts of Appeal. In February 2020, the UK government committed to an independent official inquiry into the scandal.

While the Post Office case exemplifies the damaging extent to which 'white collar' abuses of contract-out arrangements may develop on a large scale, Boustras and Waring (2020) highlighted a much darker side to free-market abuses in which the health, safety and even lives of subjugated individuals are put at risk. Human trafficking of illegal immigrants into prosperous economies is closely entangled with modern slavery (IASC 2018; UKDoJ 2017). Such enslavement typically centres on illicit employment in prostitution, agricultural work, car washes, and food processing factories. Unscrupulous businesses are supplied by traffickers with victims to be engaged under duress to pay off huge debts to their traffickers, in frequently illegal or unlicensed activities for exceptionally long hours and minimal remuneration. The UK conviction in 2019 of eight slave masters for trafficking over 80 alleged victims and probably more than 400 (*BBC* 2019a; Frazer 2019) exemplifies the phenomenon. Work conditions and procedures are often degrading, unhealthy and unsafe. Trafficked individuals also frequently die *en route* before ever having the 'opportunity' to be enslaved, for example drowning at sea or suffocating in sealed containers. The death of 39 Vietnamese trafficked migrants in a single incident in October 2019 highlighted how goods transport firms are frequently engaged in smuggling illegal immigrants into the UK as part of a supply chain for slave masters (*BBC* 2019b).

Employee Rights Abuses

Neiwert (2017, 364) asserted that, as the most high-profile radical-right national leader, President Trump went to great lengths to exploit feelings of victimization, portraying himself and his supporters as somehow victims of a manifestly intolerable and insidious enemy that had brought America to its knees. This ill-defined enemy comprised (in their minds) a fusion of liberal elites, experts, science, social welfare propositions, environmentalists, immigrants, ethno-religious minorities, foreign-owned corporations, foreign governments, and multi-lateral ideas. Trump, and the radical right generally, are convinced that a coalition of left-wing supporters, liberals, elites, corrupt business leaders, and corrupt politicians have conspired to exaggerate a wide range of problems and issues as a pretext to impose socially liberal ideas that have weakened society and the nation and which must be curtailed or even radically removed. Such radical-right targets include workers' rights in general, occupational safety and health (Hood 1995; Reisman 2003a, b), environmental protection (BHI 2015 a to d; Reisman 2005; 2006; 2007), social welfare, and women's rights. Griffin and Wall (2019) summarised a spectrum of employee rights issues in the US on which it was alleged that bad employers had been enabled and encouraged to abuse those rights as a result of the direct intervention of Trump. Simon (2018) is also relevant. "President Trump ran for office as a champion of American workers and a friend of labor unions, but his administration has systematically favoured employers at the expense of workers" (*NYT* 2019). This contradiction also demonstrates the observation made in chapter 1, namely that whereas in 2016 Trump promised that he would clear out the liberal elites and protect the 'little man', in reality, his radical-right administration, on the contrary, strengthened its ties with big corporations and wealthy oligarchs at the expense of ordinary citizens.

Waring (2019b) argued that the relevance of radical-right/Alt-Right ideology and practice to occupational safety and health in particular, for example, arises as a result of: (a) direct and indirect influence of radical-right ideology on mainstream parties and government policies, (b) radical-right enthusiasm for 'freedom' for producers, a free-market economy, and antipathy towards regulation, (c) a radical-right 'winners and losers' belief in a Darwinian survival-of-the-fittest and most deserving (Neiwert 2017, 359; Paxton 2005), whereby those injured or killed at work are merely collateral damage and are thus of no significance, and (d) a radical-right fear of experts and an enthusiasm for 'alternative facts' and 'alternative science', whereby normal science is denied, inverted, and subverted to support radical-right assertions (Neiwert 2017; Paxton 2018; Waring 2018). As noted in chapter 1, their anti-science characteristic is reflective of a reductionist world-view that artificially posits all problems and issues as being based on over-simplified cause-and-effect relationships, which require equally over-simplified sure-fire solutions (Waring 2020a; b).

While it is yet unclear how far the radical-right alternative science agenda, combined with its free market and deregulation agendas, will impact OSH directly, it is more likely that effects will be adverse. Adverse impacts on OSH arising from the Trump administration's first eighteen months of radical-right policies in the US have been reported by Bernstein and Spielberg (2017), Eilperin and Palette (2017), and NELP (2018). Further decline is reported by Berkowitz (2019; 2020), Michaels (2020), and *NYT* (2019).

Elsewhere, the picture is unclear. However, according to Waring (2019b), the fact that, for example, populist radical-right parties (e.g. Front Rassemblement in France, AfD in Germany, and UKIP in Britain) exhibit antagonism towards environmental concerns and have climate change denial policies, suggests that they are likely to show similar hostility towards OSH. Reduction of workers' rights such as paid leave, favourable working hours, contract-out protections, and anti-discrimination laws, has been a longstanding policy of UKIP in Britain. It is reasonable to infer that any specific policy on OSH is unlikely to be different in tone and stance to their anti-workers' rights policies.

The review by Cumming et al (2020) of human resource management practices in a context of rising right-wing populism suggested that, at workplace level, populist authoritarianism undermines workforce diversity and makes transnational mobility more difficult. Structural pressures, such as overhead costs and commitments, and high domestic wages compared to overseas alternatives, has led not only to contracting-out, part-time contracts, and zero-hours contracts, but also to a diminution of commitment to employees and to their development and well-being. Such a loosening of ties and commitment to employees is likely to contribute to greater job insecurity which, in turn may encourage populist responses and antagonism against immigrants perceived as stealing jobs from native workers or as being otherwise undeserving, a long-standing slur in radical-right propaganda. Nevertheless, such relentless actions against employees by some employers are also likely to engender an intensification of an anti-corporate climate among workers.

Corporate Abuses of Product Safety

Michaels (2020) exposed how 'dark money' has enabled US corporations, in the pursuit of profit, to manipulate science so as to not only design, create and defend dangerous products and processes but also to market them as 'safe'. The well-established methodology for ensuring product safety (and therefore minimizing the likelihood of product liability suits) is based on a life-cycle approach, which systematically applies a rigorous regime of hazard identification, risk assessment, and safety assurance procedures to the product life-cycle phases of research, design, testing and approvals, manufacture, product launch, service life, and final end-of-life and decommission (Waring 2013, 163-167; Waring & Glendon 1998, 420-422; Waring & Tyler 1997). For many products, such life-cycle product safety methodology does ensure the desired outcome. However, in some companies, no matter what the espoused product safety policy may be, a culture of amoral calculation has arisen whereby enacted policy seeks to nullify the impact of the overall safety assurance programme, to whatever extent is deemed necessary to minimize cost, delays and inconvenience, and to maximize market penetration, market share and customer/consumer acceptance and confidence. Such pathological conduct involves a wilful prioritisation of speculative/opportunity risk evaluation at the expense of product safety as a pure risk (see explanation in chapter 10 of differences between pure and speculative risks). Companies engaging in such misapplications argue (if only to convince themselves) that it is defensible to make risk decisions that trade off safety for commercial and financial returns. In doing so, they place themselves in the role of amoral calculators who decide for themselves that it is acceptable to harm, injure or kill people with dangerous products so long as profits increase, and shareholders can be kept happy.

Michaels (2020) provided ample evidence and examples of such amoral calculation within corporations in such industries as car manufacture, food-and-drink, tobacco, and fossil fuel energy. He argued that the anti-science policies of the Trump administration are not new but represent a more strident amplification of long-standing campaigns by some sectors or corporations that are little more than application of the science of deception to promote their products and interests. He also cited the propensity for supposedly independent research reports that are little more than bogus scientific studies full of confirmation bias, which support decisions taken by CEOs and/or boards of particular industries or corporations. For example, on bogus data, he included a chapter dedicated to how the Volkswagen automobile company over the period 2008 to 2015 systematically falsified exhaust emission data on its diesel engine vehicles, in order to make them appear less polluting than they were and so meet federal environmental protection standards. In 2016, the Federal Trade Commission filed an action against the Volkswagen Group of America for advertising falsely that its diesel vehicles were environmentally benign—for example e.g. that its VW Jetta "reduces nitrogen dioxide (NOx) emissions by up to 90 percent" and that such 'clean' vehicles would have strong resale values (Rechtin 2016). VW had fitted to such vehicles during tests a special emissions-defeating device that artificially masked the true NOx levels, and it admitted in 2015 that 11 million of its vehicles worldwide had been fitted with such devices. Multiple legal actions against VW, both by governments and vehicle purchasers, then ensued around the world. By the end of 2019, VW had already paid out over €30billion (£26bn) in fines, civil claims settlements and costs of recalling 9 million vehicles, with much litigation continuing after that date (e.g. *BBC* 2019c; Moody 2020).

Corporate Abuses of Covid-19 Protection Rules

As noted above in relation to the impact on customers and self-employed contractors, the Covid-19 pandemic in 2020 had a similarly bad impact on employees—that is, persons employed under a 'contract of service' as opposed to a 'contract for services'. In the UK, proper employees enjoy full employee rights and protection under the laws of this particular jurisdiction. However, authoritarian abuses by some employers have been reported, especially for failing to provide adequate Covid-19 personal protective equipment, or forcing staff to ignore government Covid-19 'social distancing' and 'work from home' rules for both occupational and public health protection, or for peremptory wage stoppage and/or mass sackings despite a government guarantee to underwrite up to 80 per cent of wages (PHE 2020c).

Of special concern has been the persistent refusal by some of the UK's national supermarket chains to abide by the government's Covid-19 public health regulations introduced in March 2020. In March 2020, as the scale of the growing public health threat from the Covid-

19 pandemic became clear, the British government issued its first national 'lockdown' rules under the Coronavirus Act 2020, a broad enabling act. The essence of these rules was to (a) maintain social distancing with a minimum of 2m separation between any two individuals, and (b) self-isolate by staying at home as far as possible and only to venture out for such essential purposes as medical appointments, essential shopping, and exercise. Specified categories of essential worker, such as hospital workers, emergency services staff, local authority employees, and grocery store employees, were exempt from rule (b), whereas non-essential businesses were required to close temporarily until authorised to reopen after the pandemic had passed.

Subsequently revised and reissued a number of times, by May 2020 the government guidance for how employers and workers should observe the rules was set out in its *Working Safely During Coronavirus (COVID-19)* document. A special section (UK-Covid 2020) was included for shops, and *BBC News* (Jones & Wakefield 2020) summarised the rules so far as they applied to shoppers in supermarkets. Although ministers and other senior officials frequently reiterated at the Prime Minister's daily televised press conferences on Covid-19 the '2m separation, single person, essential shoppers only' rule, it soon became evident that the non-doctrinaire wording of the official rules, which used such words and phrases as "guidance" instead of "instruction", and "should be encouraged to" instead of "are required to", allowed a very wide latitude in interpretation. It emerged that the so-called 'rules' were in fact not enforceable absolute rules but strong advice, which thereby enabled (if not encouraged) supermarket managers and staff to engage in creative interpretation that appeared superficially to comply with the letter of the rules but which in fact did not observe their spirit or intent.

While publicly proclaiming their espoused support for the regulations, and even boasting about how they were implementing them, there is persuasive anecdotal evidence that they were in fact knowingly violating the rules in their stores, in so far as protection of customers was concerned. The author personally witnessed over several months repetitive Covid-19 rule violations by customers that involved staff connivance at Tesco, Lidl and Iceland stores. The case of Tesco Stores Plc is illustrative.

Case 5.7: Tesco Stores Plc and Its Policy on Customer Violations of Covid-19 Rules

Tesco Stores Plc has the largest share of the UK grocery market at 27.5% (Wunsch 2020), nearly double its nearest rivals Sainsbury at 16% and Asda at 15%. It has stores across the UK, ranging from the small local Tesco Express, through mid-range superstores, to large megastores.

The author personally witnessed on at least eight occasions between mid-April and late-June 2020, as a customer at one of Tesco's in-town superstores, numerous manifest violations of the '2m separation, single person, essential shoppers only' rule. Typically, on each visit, approximately 20% of customers were being allowed into and to shop in the store not as single individuals but as units of two, three, and even four individuals shopping together and less than 1m apart within each unit. Of those observed in this mode, all appeared to be able-bodied and shopping together for companionship and not necessity—e.g. friends, partners, parents and teenage children. The government's public health statements had made it quite clear that this mode of shopping was unacceptable, as it manifestly violated the social separation rules and was unjustifiable. For example, disabled or otherwise infirm shoppers were expected to arrange for someone else to do their shopping rather than go to the store themselves accompanied by one or more helpers. There was no justification for teenage children to accompany a parent while shopping. There was no justification for friends to shop together, unless they maintained the 2m separation rule. To do otherwise would amount to irresponsible self-indulgence.

At no time during any of these visits did the author observe any attempt by Tesco employees to challenge these transgressors or to remove anyone unrepentant from the store. Indeed, when he raised the matter with local staff on April 14, 2020 they responded with diffidence and unconcern. The store manager was equally dismissive and asserted that:

- The way the Covid-19 rules were being interpreted and operated in this store was as instructed by senior management of Tesco HQ.

- Tesco's own interpretation and instructions on Covid-19 took absolute precedence over public policy, government regulations and prescribed public health rules.
- The responsibility for obeying the safe distancing and single person rules was entirely that of the shopper and it was not the store management's job to police it inside the store.
- Any attempt by external agencies such as the Police or the media to investigate breaches or enforce the rules inside the store would be prevented by store management.

Anticipating that this apparent defiance of government rules was a local aberration, the author wrote a letter of complaint reporting his experience directly to Mr Dave Lewis, who at that time was the Group Chief Executive of Tesco Stores Plc. However, instead of receiving an apology and a promise to correct the rule violations witnessed, on the contrary by way of reply his delegated spokesperson, in an e-mail dated April 23, 2020, sought to deny that Tesco had in any way done anything wrong, or that the local store manager had been incorrect in his statements. After listing seven practical Covid-19 protection measures that the company (in common with most other supermarkets) had introduced in stores, the spokesperson stated that "We can only ask customers to follow the measures put in place as our colleagues are not in a position to police this" and "we are encouraging our customers to, where possible, shop alone", and further "if customers need to bring someone with them such as a partner, child or carer, they can".

This single short riposte from the Group Chief Executive's office stated Tesco's official national policy position that it had absolutely no responsibility (legal or moral) for controlling what customers did on its premises in relation to Covid-19 compliance and, by inference, any other health, safety, or security matter. It appeared that Tesco believed that customers' legal responsibility for their own compliance (which indeed they do have) was an *exclusive* one that somehow automatically precluded any legal responsibility whatsoever for Tesco. On the contrary, these respective responsibilities are not mutually exclusive but separate and co-existing. One does not cancel the other. The company's bold assertion to the contrary will come as some surprise to those knowledgeable on both criminal and civil law and the long-standing statutory and precedent responsibilities of employers and controllers of premises towards third parties such as visitors, customers, suppliers, neighbours and passers-by (see, for example, Bennett 2013; Ford & Clarke 2016).

Irrespective of specific responsibilities of companies such as Tesco towards customers under Covid-19 rules, all employers and controllers of premises have long-standing pre-existing statutory duties of care for the safety and health of third parties (e.g. customers) under S3 and S4 of the Health & Safety at Work etc Act 1974 and its subordinate regulations, as well as other statutes such as the Public Health (Control of Disease) Act 1984 and the Occupiers Liability Act 1984. No company is allowed to cherry-pick which parts of applicable laws it will comply with (e.g. the commonplace physical precautions for Covid-19 in stores) and which it will ignore (e.g. the requirement to challenge and effectively control non-compliant anti-social customer behaviour towards covid-19 rules).

Tesco's motives, for defying the spirit, if not the letter, of Covid-19 protection rules and a host of pre-existing legal duties of care, are open to speculation. Potential motives may include, for example, laziness and avoidance of managerial inconvenience, and/or not wishing to upset or antagonise customers who disobeyed the rules (e.g. fear of assault on staff or other reprisals), and/or minimizing adverse impact on customer footfall, customer loyalty and revenue resulting from its strict enforcement of the rules, and/or an authoritarian determination to impose the company's own writ and, as far as possible, evade perceived intrusion by government rules. Whatever the motivations, the net effect of the company's cavalier stance was to 'drive a coach-and-horses' through the intent of the Covid-19 protection rules.

An Analysis of Overlaps of Corporate and Radical-Right Authoritarianism

While, in the absence of published academic studies, much of the data presented in this chapter is necessarily anecdotal, and therefore not readily generalizable, nevertheless such evidence is a powerful and evocative indication that corporate authoritarianism (as defined in this volume) is widespread and potentially harmful to many people.

As the sample spectrum of industry sectors, corporations, and cases summarised in this chapter has shown, corporate authoritarianism typically encompasses a range of overbearing, if not dictatorial, stances and bad conduct by some corporate leaders towards customers, employees, contractors, and society in general. Sometimes their motivation appears to be greed and a narcissistic sense of superiority and entitlement at the expense of 'lesser' people, whom they believe they can ignore or dismiss as inconsequential. While some motivations evidently emerge from pathological or anti-social personalities, other motivations may be simply laziness and avoidance of managerial inconvenience, or minimizing adverse impact on revenue (an aspect of greed and/or misplaced competitiveness), or an indignant free-market determination not to recognise rules and limits set by 'big government'. Some corporate leaders may possess all these motivations.

With such a range of potential sources of authoritarian conduct, which may co-exist with other anti-social traits that may or may not be pathological (as summarised at the start of this chapter), any analysis is necessarily cautious and speculative. For example, while it is evident that pathological anti-social traits do exist in some corporate leaders and senior executives, it cannot be safely assumed that the prevalence is high or widespread among such groups. For example, the prevalence of narcissistic personality disorder (Post 2015) in the general population is estimated to be between 0.5 and 1.0% and, for antisocial personality disorder, the prevalence is approximately 3% (NICE 2010). Even if borderline and weaker presentations of these traits are considered, the prevalence in the general population alone could not account for more than a minimal presence in corporate boardrooms—unless, of course, the boardroom lure of power tends to attract such individuals more than do other job functions. For example, the psychological study of 261 senior executives in Australia (Fritzon at al 2016) and subsequent work (Brooks et al 2020) suggest that approximately 20% of CEOs are classifiable as exhibiting clinically elevated psychopathic personality traits. The power attractiveness of boardroom jobs may explain why toxic personalities appear to have a disproportionate presence among corporate leaders (see also Walton 2007a; b; 2020a; b; c).

Moreover, while it is also evident that some corporate leaders and senior executives do consciously share radical-right political ideology, again the prevalence of radical-right world-views in the general population is not as high as their 'noisy' public presence might suggest. Turner-Graham (2019, 143) estimated that in 2018 the total number of UK supporters of the radical right, ranging from the 'softer' populist end of the spectrum to the hard extremist end, to be some 1.82 million or 3.8% of the UK electorate of 47.93 million. Therefore, if the prevalence in the general population holds true, it would not be expected to be much different in boardrooms—unless, as with anti-social and/or psychopathic traits, those with radical-right proclivities are also attracted disproportionately to gain powerful positions.

It is both unsafe and wrong to suppose or suggest that all toxic corporate leaders are automatically supporters of radical-right politics. Those who are, tend to keep their support out of the public eye, individuals such as Arron Banks, Robert Mercer, Robert Shillman and Donald Trump being exceptions. In the author's professional experience, radical-right world-views of individual directors tend to be exhibited in boardroom settings in the form of pejorative prejudicial remarks about ethno-religious groups or others they dislike. The author is not aware of any studies that have cast any light on what the likely proportion of directors might be who are radical-right supporters. However, it is defensible to posit the following, namely that:

(a) A minority of corporate leaders exhibit an authoritarian world-view (potentially co-existing with other anti-social and/or psychopathic traits) and egregious conduct that is potentially harmful to many people, including employees, contractors, customers, and society in general;

(b) Some of those authoritarian corporate leaders will possess personalities and world-views that are predisposed to be supportive of radical-right ideology, and may tacitly or actively engage in radical-right policies and conduct;

(c) Those in category (b) are more likely to acquiesce with, or fall into line with, radical-right government policies or populist pressures (e.g. in such areas as ethno-religious prejudice, discrimination, anti-workers' rights, anti-environmental conduct, and anti-OSH conduct).

(d) An unchecked presence in a corporate organisation of any of categories (a), (b) and (c) in any combination is likely to result in harm for many parties and, ultimately, to undermine the reputation and long-term future of the organisation.

Recognition in both academic and corporate circles that authoritarian corporate organisations and their leaders had become not just an embarrassing anachronism, but also a dysfunctional stumbling block to the survival and continuity of corporations in the 21st century, has arisen relatively recently. This chapter began with some strongly pejorative observations from Bakan (2004), Birch (2007), Bloom and Rhodes (2016; 2018), Kohls and Makary (2016) and Zuboff (2019) about how far corporate authoritarianism had degenerated in its egregious nature and consequences. Robinson and Murphy (2008) and Simon (2018) elaborate on the dark side of elite deviance in corporations. The graphic charts by Swinn (2019) [if validated] also emphasize apparent substantive relationships between corporate oligarch donors, intermediaries, and far-right activists. More generally, in the last quarter of the 20th century, such acknowledged authorities on corporate organisations and strategy as Professors Gerry Johnson (1987; 1992), Henry Mintzberg (1994), Gareth Morgan (1986), Andrew Pettigrew (1987; 1992; 2012), and Jeffrey Pfeffer (1981; 1982) were all independently suggesting that significant gaps were frequently evident between espousal, enactment, and results of corporate strategies, and that unintended and often damaging consequences frequently ensued. By 2010, failures by corporate leaders to recognize, understand, and respond appropriately to such fundamental issues as organisational culture and climate, and power relations and potential abuses of them within their organisation, as well as leadership failures, were already emerging as a recognized major impediment to corporate success and sustainability. See e.g. Pfeffer (2010; 2018).

What is emerging at the beginning of the third decade of the 21st century is an analysis that (a) states emphatically that many corporations have 'lost their way' in terms of properly understanding their purpose and then enacting it, and (b) then proposes a radical new paradigm to replace the present dysfunctional one. As the seminal review by the British Academy (2018, 8) put it, "Corporations were originally established with clear public purposes. It is only over the last half century that corporate purpose has become equated solely with profit. This has been damaging for corporations' role in society, trust in business and the impact that business has had on the environment, inequality and social cohesion. In addition, globalisation and technological advances are exacerbating problems of regulatory lag." An article in the business press by Manyika and Tuin (2020) echoed much of the British Academy's thrust on this matter. In a similar vein, 181 CEOs of major US corporations at the US Business Roundtable (BRT 2019) also issued a statement redefining the purpose of a corporation with a focus on benefitting all stakeholders and not just stock shareholders.

Thirteen papers in British Academy (2018) demonstrated an intensifying need for a substantive reconceptualization of the corporation around purpose. Three key interconnected principles were proposed: (1) well-defined and aligned purposes e.g. Hsieh et al (2018), (2) commitment to trustworthiness, and (3) embedding an enabling culture. Five practical levers to achieve these principles were identified: (1) ownership, (2) corporate governance, (3) regulation, (4) taxation, and (5), investment.

Contemporary world-views, policies, and conduct of corporate authoritarians focus on profit, personal greed, personal gratification, predatory unilateral competition, callous disregard for the classes of people they harm, and a belief that the only stakeholders to be serviced and protected are themselves and corporate shareholders. The "framework for the future of the corporation" is a radical new paradigm that inherently and explicitly rejects all the characteristics of corporate authoritarianism. Nevertheless, as Bakan (2004, 28-59) argued, there are inevitable tensions between the legal duty of corporate directors and officers to always act in the best interests of the corporation and its owners and shareholders [usually taken to mean profits and share values], and support for other stakeholders and moral causes. This tension is examined further in the final chapter (12), including whether corporate authoritarianism can ever be eradicated, or whether containment and marginalisation are the best that can be hoped for.

Conclusions

The 'what can we get away with?' arrogance and egregious conduct of many corporate authoritarians undoubtedly harms a large number of people, and discredits the perpetrators. Some corporate leaders who exhibit such traits appear also predisposed, either pre-consciously or consciously, to sympathise with or support radical-right ideology and causes. Authoritarianism among radical-right politicians and authoritarianism in corporations are essentially the same underlying phenomenon, which projects shared interests and promotes symbiosis.

Those corporate leaders and executives who support radical-right ideology and objectives will not care that their conduct and character are subject to criticism and opprobrium, in whatever context or medium. As proud supporters and true believers, some may even revel in the notoriety and reinforcement of the radical-right cause which their contribution seeks to advance. However, corporate authoritarians who do not consciously espouse radical-right ideology may find themselves nonetheless increasingly likened to, and categorized as fellow travellers of, the radical right by virtue of exhibiting similar rhetoric, ideas and conduct. As Purves (2020) observed in relation to corporate responses to Covid-19, "Companies and individuals should know that the stigma of having behaved badly during this crisis will be long-lasting".

Increasingly, corporations and their directors must ask themselves, and will be challenged by others such as investors, investment analysts, independent governance auditors, and government regulators, with searching interrogatories: What are the corporation's true, stated purposes and whose interests are being pursued and served? Who are the perceived stakeholders? Are the inter-related goals of market share/dominance, profit, share values, and shareholder interests sufficient in a 21st century context of corporate social responsibility, corporate governance, risk management, and a broad stakeholder spectrum? Can the wilful prioritisation by corporations of speculative/opportunity risk evaluation in risk trade-offs at the expense of safety (in all its many categories), or other pure risks such as environment, be tolerated any longer? What are the objectives: long-term sustainability or short-term profit margins? Why are inappropriate attitudes, priorities, and criteria not being reined in?

Clearly, the new model for corporations based on broad-based stakeholder fairness and equity (not necessarily equity in shares or asset rights) is totally at odds with authoritarianism. The kinds of corporate authoritarian attitudes, amoral calculation, and cavalier conduct exemplified in this chapter will have no place or acceptance in the new model corporation.

In summary, identifiable risk exposures include the following, which are assessed further in chapter 10:

Risks Exposures of Various Parties from Corporate Authoritarianism

Risk Exposure 1: Customers

Corporate authoritarianism is likely to expose customers to violation of both their statutory and civil rights in respect of: personal safety and health hazards at company premises; product safety hazards; fraud, obtaining money by false pretences, and failure to deliver goods and services already paid for; market fixing and inflated price fixing; refusal to provide adequate redress for customer complaints.

Risk Exposure 2: Employees

Corporate authoritarianism is likely to expose employees to violation of both their statutory and civil rights in respect of: bullying and coercion; ethno-religious or other prejudices; discrimination; occupational safety and health (OSH) violations; unfair remuneration; unfavourable terms for working hours, paid leave, maternity leave, and pensions; unfair redundancy and dismissal.

Risk Exposure 3: Contractors

Corporate authoritarianism is likely to expose contractors to violation of both their statutory and civil rights in respect of: bullying and coercion; zero hours contracts; unfair remuneration and payment terms; ethno-religious or other prejudices; discrimination; occupational safety and health (OSH) violations; human trafficking and slavery.

Risks Exposures of the Public and Society from Corporate Authoritarianism

Risk Exposure 1: Public and environmental health and safety

Corporate authoritarianism is likely to increase risks to public and environmental health and safety in relation to corporate policies that either defy government regulation and/or seek to avoid cost and inconvenience, resulting in violations of statutory regulations for: pandemics and other infectious diseases; toxic, harmful and general waste disposal; contamination of air, land, water, or effluent.

Risk Exposure 2: Climate change denial

Corporate authoritarianism is likely to involve an anti-science stance, pseudo-scientific beliefs, and a determination to avoid cost and inconvenience, and perceived government interference, which may result in corporate policies that refuse to substitute processes, procedures, materials, and products by those less likely to contribute to climate change that is harmful to humankind and society.

Risk Exposure 3: Democracy and human rights

Corporate authoritarianism, whether explicitly or implicitly, is consistent with radical-right ideology and favours and frequently contributes to radical-right political objectives that may undermine democracy by e.g. maintaining and extending inequalities in society; discrimination against ethno-religious minorities; discrimination against unemployed, benefits claimants and other vulnerable groups; curbs on press freedom and control of the media; advocating reversal or removal of workers' rights; countering representative democracy.

Risks Exposures of Corporate Authoritarians and Authoritarian Corporations

Risk Exposure 1: Personal and corporate reputation damage

Authoritarian attitudes, policies and conduct are likely to engender among many parties adverse evaluations of the individual authoritarians and/or the corporations they inhabit, to the extent that their reputations are damaged.

Risk Exposure 2: Criminal and civil legal liabilities

Excessive authoritarian policies and conduct are likely to attract criminal and/or civil legal liabilities to the individual authoritarian directors or officers and/or the corporations they inhabit, which may result in criminal prosecutions, other regulatory actions, or civil proceedings against them as individuals and/or as corporate bodies.

Risk Exposure 3: Disinvestment

Excessive authoritarian attitudes, policies and conduct by corporations are likely to result in disinvestment by institutional shareholders, pension funds, and ethical investment funds.

Risk Exposure 4: Marginalisation and quarantine

Excessive authoritarian attitudes, policies and conduct by individual authoritarian directors or officers and/or the corporations they inhabit are likely to result in their estrangement from the business and investment community, and ultimately their marginalisation and quarantine as 'untouchables'.

Risk Exposure 5: Decreasing relevance and role in the economy and society

In the medium to long-term, corporate authoritarians and authoritarian corporations are likely to suffer a diminishing role and relevance in the economy and society, as public and regulatory expectations of corporate integrity continue to rise, corporate social responsibility and corporate governance gain traction, and the new model corporation becomes the benchmark.

References

Allitt, P. 2020. "America is Socialist, Dummy". *The Spectator*, US April 2020 edition. March 21, 2020. https://www.spectator.us/amer ica-socialist-dummy.

Bakan, J. 2004. *The Corporation: The Pathological Pursuit of Profit and Power*. London: Constable.

Barnett, J.C. and Berchick, E.R. 2017. *Health Insurance Coverage in the United States: 2016*. Report Number P60-260. September 12, 2017. Washington DC: US Census Bureau.

BBC. 2019a. "UK Slavery Network 'Had 400 Victims'". *BBC News*. https://www.bbc.news.co.uk/news/uk-england-birmingham-48881327.[accessed July 7, 2019].

BBC. 2019b. "Lorry Driver Mo Robinson Admits Plot After 39 Migrant Deaths". *BBC News*. November 25, 2019. https://www.bbc.co.uk /news/uk-england-50545658. [accessed June 7, 2020].

BBC 2019c. "Volkswagen: UK Drivers Fight for 'Dieselgate' Compensation". *BBC News*. December 2, 2019. https://www.bbc.co.uk/ne ws/business-50631823. [accessed June 8, 2020].

Bennett, D. 2013. *Munkman on Employer's Liability*. 16th edition. London: LexisNexis.

Ben-Shahar, O. and Strahilevitz, L.J. 2017. "David Dao Versus United— What Does the Airline Contract Say?" *Forbes*. April 14, 2017. https://www.forbes.com/sites/omribenshahar/2017/04/14/ david-dao-versus-united-what-does-the-airline-contract-say/# 69f741eb18ad.

Berchick, E.R., Barnett, J.C. and Upton, R.D. 2019. *Health Insurance Coverage in the United States: 2018*. Report Number P60-267 (RV). November 8, 2019. Washington DC: US Census Bureau.

Berkowitz, D. 2019. *Workplace Safety Enforcement Continues to Decline in Trump Administration*. Report March 14, 2019. Washington DC: National Employment Law Project. https://www.nelp. org/publication/workplace-safety-enforcement-continues-dec line-trump-administration/. [accessed May 13, 2020].

Berkowitz, D. 2020. *Worker Safety in Crisis: The Cost of a Weakened OSHA*. Report April 28, 2020. Washington DC: National Employment Law Project. https://www.nelp.org/publication/worker-safety-crisis-cost-weakened-osha/. [accessed May 13, 2020]

Bernstein, J. and Spielberg, B. 2017. "The Trump Administration's Ongoing Attack on Workers". *The Washington Post*. August 30, 2017. https://www.washingtonpost.com/. Accessed August 26, 2018.

BHI. 2015a. "Iowa: Obama-Inspired EPA Carbon-Dioxide Regulations May Bankrupt Iowans". *Policy Studies No. 98*. January 2015. Boston MA: Beacon Hill Institute. www.beaconhill.org.

BHI. 2015b. "New Mexico: The Economic Effects of New EPA Rules in the State of New Mexico". *Policy Studies No. 94*. January 2015. Boston MA: Beacon Hill Institute. www.beaconhill.org.

BHI. 2015c. "South Carolina: New EPA Rules Will Cost South Carolina a Fortune". *Policy Studies No. 97.* February 2015. Boston MA: Beacon Hill Institute. www.beaconhill.org.

BHI. 2015d. "Virginia: The Costs of New EPA Rules to Virginia". *Policy Studies No. 100.* March 2015. Boston MA: Beacon Hill Institute. www.beaconhill.org.

Birch, K. 2007. "The Totalitarian Corporation?" *Totalitarian Movements and Political Religions,* Vol 8 No 1, 153-161, March 2007.

Bloom, P. and Rhodes, C. (2016). "Corporate Authoritarianism and the New American Anti-democracy". *Common Dreams.* October 23, 2016.

Bloom, P. and Rhodes. C. 2018. *CEO Society: The Corporate Takeover of Everyday Life.* London: Zed Books.

Brill, S. 2013. "Bitter Pill: Why Medical Bills are Killing Us. How Outrageous Pricing and Egregious Profits are Destroying Our Health Care". *Time Special Report,* March 4, 2013.

Boustras, G. and Waring, A. 2020. "A Review of Safety and Security, their Interactions, and Policy Implications, in a Contemporary Context". Special Issue: The Future of Safety Science. *Safety Science.* 132 (2020), 104942.

British Academy. 2018. *Reforming Business for the 21st Century—A Framework for the Future of the Corporation.* November 2018. London: The British Academy.

Brooks, N. 2020. "The Tangled Web: Psychopathic Personality, Vulnerability and Victim Selection". In *Corporate Psychopathy: Investigating Destructive Personalities in the Workplace,* edited by K. Fritzon, N. Brooks, and S. Croom. 295-325. Cham, Switzerland: Palgrave Macmillan.

Brooks, N., Fritzon, K. and Croom, S. 2020. "Corporate Psychopathy: Entering the Paradox and Emerging Unscathed". In *Corporate Psychopathy: Investigating Destructive Personalities in the Workplace,* edited by K. Fritzon, N. Brooks, and S. Croom. 327-365. Cham, Switzerland: Palgrave Macmillan.

Brooks, R. and Wallis, N. 2020. "Justice Lost in the Post. How the Post Office Wrecked the Lives of its Own Workers". *Private Eye,* No. 1519, April 3-April 23, 2020, 24-29.

BRT. 2019. "Business Roundtable Redefines the Purpose of a Corporation to Promote 'An Economy that Serves All Americans'".

Business Roundtable. August 19, 2019. Washington DC: Business Roundtable. https://www.businessroundtable.org/business-roundtable-redefines-the-purpose-of-a-corporation-to-promote-an-economy-that-serves-all-americans. [accessed September 6, 2020].

Bryan, K. 2020. "Any Complaints? Yes, it's Too Damn Hard to Complain". *The Times.* March 7, 2020. Page 15.

Bryant, N. 2020. "Coronavirus: What This Crisis Reveals about US—and its President". *BBC News.* March 24, 2020. https://www.bbc.co.uk/news/world-us-canada-52012049.

Byers, D. 2020. "If You Want a Trip Refund, You'll Need a Doctor's Note". *The Times.* May 16, 2020. Page 55.

Campbell, D. and Siddique, H. 2020. "Covid-19 Death Rate in England Higher Among BAME People". *The Guardian.* June 2, 2020. https://theguardian.com/world/2020/jun/02/covid-19-death-rate-in-england-higher-among-bame-people.

CMA. 2019a. "Nortryptiline Investigation: Anti-competitive Agreement and Conduct". Press release. June 18, 2019. London: Competition and Markets Authority. https://www.gov.uk/cma-cases/pharmaceutical-sector-suspected-anti-competitive-agreements-and-conduct-50507-2. [accessed June 8, 2020].

CMA. 2019b. "3 Drug Firms Accused of Illegal Market Sharing". Press release. October 3, 2019. London: Competition and Markets Authority. https://www.gov.uk/government/news/3-drug-firms-accused-of-illegal-market-sharing. [accessed June 8, 2020].

CMA. 2020. "Pharma Company Director Disqualified for Competition Law Breaches". Press release. June 4, 2020. London: Competition and Markets Authority. https://www.gov.uk/government/news/pharma-company-director-disqualified-for-competition-law-breaches. [accessed June 8, 2020].

Crouch, C. 2014. "Dealing with Corporate Political Power". *Open Democracy.* February 3, 2014. https://www.opendemocracy.net/en/opendemocracyuk/dealing-with-corporate-political-power/. [accessed April 4, 2020].

Cumming, D.J., Wood, G. and Zahra, S.A. 2020. "Human Resource Management Practices in the Context of Rising Right-wing Populism". *Human Resource Management Journal*, February 3, 2020. https://doi.org/10.1111/1748-8583.12269.

Cutler, D.M. 2014. *The Quality Cure*. Oakland, CA: University of California Press.

Cutler, D.M. 2016. "Here's Why Trump is Already Waffling on Obamacare". *The Washington Post*. November 12, 2016.

Duke, S. and Jones, C. 2020. "Mike Ashley Apologises for Trying to Keep Sports Direct Open". *The Times.* March 27, 2020. https://www.thetimes.co.uk/ashley-eats-humble-pie-after-row-with-staff-public-and-government-P5927k25s.

Eilperin, J. and Palette, D. 2017. "Trump Administration Cancels Hundreds of Obama-era Regulations". *The Washington Post.* July 20, 2017. https://www.washingtonpost.com/. [accessed August 26, 2018].

Falkenbach, M. and Greer, S.L. (eds). 2021. *Populist Radical Right and Health: National Politics and Global Trends*. Springer.

Fennell, D. 1988. *Report of the Official Inquiry into the King's Cross Fire*. Chairman Desmond Fennell QC. London: The Stationery Office.

Ford, M. and Clarke, J. 2016. *Redgraves Health & Safety*. 9th edition. London: LexisNexis.

Forster, K. 2017. "Pharmaceutical Giant 'Plotted to Destroy Cancer Drugs to Drive Prices Up 4,000%". *The Independent.* April 15, 2017. https://www.independent.co.uk/news/health/drug-giant-aspen-plot-destroy-cancer-medicine-big-pharma-times-investigation-a7683521.html. [accessed June 9, 2020].

Frazer, L. 2019. "Solicitor General Welcomes Modern Slavery Conviction". Attorney General and Lucy Frazer QC, MP. Press release. July 5, 2019. https://www.gov.uk/government/news.[accessed July 7, 2019].

Fritzon, K., Bailey, C., Croom, S. and Brooks, N. 2016. "Problem Personalities in the Workplace: Development of the Corporate Personality Inventory". In *Psychology and Law in Europe: When West Meets East.* Edited by P.A. Granhag, R. Bull, A. Shaboltas, and E. Dozortseva, 139-166. Boca Raton, Fl: Taylor & Francis.

FTC. 2020a. "Vyera Pharmaceuticals, LLC". Complaint for injunctive and other equitable relief. Civil action number 20-cv-00706. January 27, 2020. Federal Court of Southern District of New York. Federal Trade Commission. New York

FTC. 2020b. "Six More States Join FTC and NY Attorney General's Case Against Vyera Pharmaceuticals, Martin Shkreli, and Other

Defendants". Press release. April 14, 2020. Federal Trade Commission. New York. https://www.ftc.gov/news-events/press-releases/2020/04/six-more-states-join-ftc-ny-attorney-gener als-case-against-vyera. [accessed June 8, 2020].

Goldstein, M. 2017. "Biggest Travel Story of 2017—the Bumping and Beating of Dr David Dao". *Forbes.* December 20, 2017. https://www.forbes.com/sites/michaelgoldstein/2017/12/20 /biggest-travel-story-of-2017-the-bumping-and-beating-of-doc tor-david-dao/#51e09972f61f.

Greer, S.L. 2017. "Medicine, Public Health and the Populist Radical Right". *Journal of the Royal Society of Medicine,* Vol 110 Issue 8, 305-308, June 1, 2017.

Griffin, S. and Wall, M. 2019. "President Trump's Anti-worker Agenda". *American Progress Action.* August 28, 2019. Center for American Progress Action. https://www.americanprogressaction.org/iss ues/economy/reports/2019/08/28/174893/president-trump s-anti-worker-agenda/. [accessed May 13, 2020].

Hermanus, M.A. 1999. *Trends in Occupational Health and Safety Policy and Regulation—Issues and Challenges for South Africa.* Takemi Program in International Health. Harvard School of Public Health. June 1999.

Himmelstein, D.U., Woolhandler, S., Almberg, M. et al. 2017. "The US Health Care Crisis Continues: a Data Snapshot". *International Journal of Health Services*, Vol 48 (1), 28-41.

Hood, J. 1995. "OSHA's Trivial Pursuit: in Workplace Safety, Business Outperforms the Regulators". *Policy Review*, No 73, Summer 1995.

Hsieh, N., Meyer, M., Rodin, D. and van't Klooster, J. 2018. "The Social Purpose of Corporations: a Literature Review and Research Agenda". *Journal of the British Academy*, 6(s1), 49-73.

IASC. 2018. *Human Trafficking and Modern Slavery Report 2018.* Independent Anti-Slavery Commissioner, sponsored by *London Evening Standard* and *The Independent.* https://www.antislavery commissioner.gov.uk. [accessed June 16, 2019].

Johnson, G. 1987. *Strategic Change and the Management Process.* Oxford: Basil Blackwell.

Johnson, G. 1992. "Managing Strategic Change—Strategy, Culture and Action". *Long Range Planning,* 25(1), 28-36.

Jones, C. 2020. "Emergency 999 Staff 'Are Packed in Like Sardines'". *The Times*. March 27, 2020. Page 14.

Jones, C., Gosden, E. and Ralph, A. 2020. "While Some Fight, Others are Fighting Shy". *The Times*. March 25, 2020. Pages 36-37.

Jones, L. and Wakefield, J. 2020. "Coronavirus: Supermarkets Limit Shoppers as Rules Tighten". *BBC News*. https://www.bbc.co.uk/news/business-52022240.

Kattikireddi, S.V., Niedzwiedz, C.L., O'Donnell, C.A., et al. 2020. "Ethnic and Socioeconomic Differences in SARS-CoV-2 Infection". *BMC Medicine*, 18, article 160, May 29, 2020. https://bmcmedicine.biomedcentral.com/articles/10.1186/s12916-020-01640-8.

Kenber, B. 2020a. "Drug Firm Boss is Banned over NHS Price Fixing". *The Times*. June 5, 2020. Page 6.

Kenber, B. 2020b. "Tories Accepted £50,000 Gift from Tax Fraudster who Ripped off NHS". *The Times*. June 9, 2020. Page 4.

Kenber, B. 2020c. "Green Grabs Furlough Millions While Axing Staff on the Cheap". *The Times*. September 12, 2020. Pages 10-11.

Kliff, S. 2017. "The Problem is the Prices. Opaque and Sky High Bills are Breaking Americans—and Our Health Care System". *Vox*. October 16, 2017.

Klint, M. 2020. "Oscar Munoz's Legacy at United Airlines". *Live and Let's Fly*. May 23, 2020. https://liveandletsfly.com/oscar-munoz-legacy/.

Kohls, G.G. and Makary, M.A. 2014. "The Powers and Abuses of America's Mega-Corporations". *Global Research*. March 4, 2014. https://www.globalresearch.ca/the-powers-and-abuses-of-americas-mega-corporations/5371901. [accessed April 4, 2020].

Manyika, J. and Tuin, M. 2020. "It's Time to Build 21st Century Companies". *Milken Institute Review*. May 4, 2020. https://www.milkenreview.org/articles/its-time-to-build-21st-century-companies. [accessed June 9, 2020].

Michaels, D. 2020. *The Triumph of Doubt—Dark Money and the Science of Deception*. Oxford UK: Oxford University Press.

Millenson, M.L. 2018. "Half a Century of the Health Care Crisis (and Still Going Strong)", *Health Affairs* blog, September 12, 2018. https://www.healthaffairs.org/do/10.1377/hblog20/80904.457305/full/.

Mintzberg, H. 1994. "Rethinking Strategic Planning, Part 1: Pitfalls and Fallacies". *Long Range Planning,* 27(3), 12-21.

Moody, O. 2020. "German Judges Deal Costly Blow to 'Immoral' VW". *The Times.* May 26, 2020. Page 34.

Morgan, G. 1986. *Images of Organization.* (Updated edition, 2006). London: Sage.

Neiwert, D. 2017. *Alt-America: The Rise of the Radical Right in the Age of Trump.* London: Verso.

NELP. 2018. *OSHA Enforcement Activity Declines Under the Trump Administration.* Data Brief. June 2018. New York: National Employment Law Project.

NICE. 2010. *Anti-Social Personality Disorder: NICE Guideline on Treatment, Management and Prevention.* National Clinical Practice Guideline Number 77. Revised 2013, 2018. National Collaborating Centre for Mental Health. London: British Psychological Society and Royal College of Psychiatrists.

Norfolk, A. and Jones, C. 2020. "Poor Excuses of the Profiteers Won't Wash with the Public". *The Times.* April 1, 2020. Page 13.

NYT. 2019. "Trump's War on Worker Rights". *The New York Times*, editorial board. June 3, 2019. https://www.nytimes.com/2019/06/03/opinion/trump-worker-safety-osha.html. [accessed May 13, 2020].

Oklobdzija, S. 2019. "Public Positions, Private Giving: Dark Money and Political Donors in the Digital Age". *Research & Politics.* February 25, 2019. https://doi.org/10.1177/2053168019832475. [accessed May 21, 2020].

Paton, G. 2020. "Airlines Still Selling Tickets for May Despite Global Quarantine". *The Times.* April 4, 2020. Page 2.

Paxton, R.O. 2005. *The Anatomy of Fascism.* London: Penguin Books.

Paxton, R. 2018. "The Alt-Right, Post-truth, Fake News, and the Media". In *The New Authoritarianism Vol 1: A Risk Analysis of the US Alt-Right Phenomenon,* edited by Alan Waring, 337-361. Stuttgart: Ibidem Verlag.

Pettigrew, A. 1987. "Context and Action in the Transformation of the Firm'. *Journal of Management Studies,* 24(6), 649-670.

Pettigrew, A. 2012. "Context and Action in the Transformation of the Firm: a Reprise". *Journal of Management Studies*, 49(7), 1304-1328.

Pettigrew, A., McKee, L. and Ferlie, E. 1992. *Shaping Strategic Change*. London: Sage.

Pfeffer, J. 1981. *Power in Organizations*. London: Pitman.

Pfeffer, J. 1982. *Organizations and Organization Theory*. London: Pitman.

Pfeffer, J. 2010. *Power: Why Some People Have it and Others Don't*. New York: Harper Collins.

Pfeffer, J. 2018. *Dying for a Pay Check*. New York: Harper Business.

PHE. 2020a. *COVID-19: Review of Disparities in Risks and Outcomes*. June 2, 2020. London: Public Health England.

PHE. 2020b. *Beyond the Data: Understanding the Impact of COVID-19 on BAME Groups*. London: Public Health England.

PHE. 2020c. *COVID-19: Guidance for Employees*. April 3, 2020. Public Health England and Department for Business, Energy & Industrial Strategy. https://www.gov.uk/publications/guidance-to-employers-and-businesses-about-covid-19/covid-19-guidance-for-employees.

POGL. 2019a. *The Post Office Group Litigation*. Alan Bates and others and Post Office Limited. Judgement No 3. Common Issues. EWHC 606 (QB), case number HQ16X01238, March 15, 2019. https://www.judiciary.uk/wp-content/uploads/2019/03/bates-v-post-office-judgement-no3-15-mar19.pdf.

POGL. 2019b. *The Post Office Group Litigation*. Alan Bates and others and Post Office Limited. Judgement No 6. Horizon Issues. EWHC 3408 (QB), case number HQ16X01238, HQ17X02637, HQ17X0424 8. December 12, 2019. https://www.judiciary.uk/wp-content/uploads/2019/12/bates-v-post-office-judgement.pdf.

Post Office Trial. 2020a. "One of the Worst Disasters in Public Life". June 12, 2020. https://www.postofficetrial.com/2020/06/one-of-worst-disasters-in-public-life.html.

Post Office Trial. 2020b. "Fujitsu Tries to Dodge the Blame Bus". June 26, 2020. https://www.postofficetrial.com/2020/06/.

Purves, L. 2020. "We'll Remember Covid's Heroes and Villains". *The Times*. September 14, 2020. Page 25.

Rechtin, M. 2016. "FTC Charges Volkswagen with False Advertising". *Consumer Reports*. March 29, 2016. https://www.consumerreports.org/volkswagen/ftc-charges-volkswagen-with-fasle-advertising/. [accessed June 8, 2020].

Reisman, G. 2003a. "The Free Market and Job Safety". *Mises Daily Articles*. Vienna, Austria: Mises Institute. https://mises.org/. [accessed September 13, 2018].

Reisman, G. 2003b. "What is Interventionism?" September 10, 2003. *Mises Daily Articles*. Vienna, Austria: Mises Institute. https://mises.org/. [accessed September 13, 2018].

Reisman, G. 2005. "The Toxicity of Environmentalism". October 3, 2005. *Mises Daily Articles*. Vienna, Austria: Mises Institute. https://mises.org/. [accessed September 13, 2018].

Reisman, G. 2006. "The Environmentalists are Trying to Frighten the Natives". March 25, 2006. Vienna, Austria: Mises Institute. https://mises.org/. [accessed September 13, 2018].

Reisman, G. 2007. "Global Warming is Not a Threat but the Environmentalist Response". March 12, 2007. Vienna, Austria: Mises Institute. https://mises.org/. [accessed September 13, 2018].

Robinson, M. and Murphy, D. 2008. *Greed is Good: Maximisation and Elite Deviance in America*. Lanham, MD: Rowman & Littlefield.

Rushe, D. 2018. "Martin Shkreli Pays Price for Arrogance—and "Egregious Multitude of Lies"'. *The Guardian*. March 9, 2018. https://www.theguardian.com/us-news/2018/mar/09/martin-shkreli-sentence-jail-arrogance-sentencing-fraud. [accessed June 8, 2020].

Russell, J. 2020. "Remember the Heroes and Villains of this Crisis". Comment. *The Times*. March 26, 2020. Page 26.

Simon, D.R. 2018. *Elite Deviance*, 11th edition. Abingdon, Oxon: Routledge/Taylor & Francis.

Slingo, J. 2019. "Post Office Appeal Dismissed by Court as Costs Soar". *Law Gazette*. November 22, 2019. https://www.lawgazette.co.uk/news/post-office-appeal-dismissed-by-court-as-costs-soar/5102286.article.

Smyth, C. 2020. "Ethnic Minorities Face Double the Risk of Death from Virus". *The Times*. June 3, 2020. Page 12.

Swinn, J. 2019. "Shillman/Mercer/Rosenwald Alt-media Network". Alternative Media Infographic. Jon Swinn blogspot. March 8, 2019. https://theworldneedsthisman.blogspot.com/2019/03/bob-shillman-robert-mercer-nina.html. [accessed July 3, 2020].

Times. 2020. "Can I See the Manager? Complaining About Poor Service is Not Only Good Fun, it is Vital". Editorial leader. *The Times.* March 7, 2020.

UK-Covid. 2020. *Working Safely During Coronavirus (COVID-19). Subsection for Shops and Branches.* UK Government. May 11, 2020, revised May 29, 2020. https://www.gov.uk/guidance/working-safely-during-coronavirus-covid-19/shops-and-branches.

UKDoJ. 2017. *UK Annual Report on Modern Slavery.* October 2017. HM Government, Department of Justice: London: DoJ.

UKParl. 2019. *Herbert Smith Freehills and Post Office.* https://www.parliament.uk/business/publications/written-questions-answers-statements/written-question/Commons/2019-07-09/275136/.

Victor, D. and Stevens, M. 2017. "United Airlines Passenger is Dragged From an Overbooked Flight". *New York Times.* April 10, 2017. https://www.nytimes.com/2017/04/10/business/united-flight-passenger-dragged.html.

Walsh, D. 2020. "The Ugly—Martin Blocks Staff Pay After Pub Closures". *The Times.* March 25, 2020. Page 37.

Walsh, D. and Jones, C. 2020. "Boss of Wetherspoons Backs Down on Refusing Staff Pay". *The Times.* March 26, 2020. Page 41.

Walton, M. 2007a. "Leadership Toxicity—an Inevitable Affliction of Organizations?" *Organizations and People,* 14(1), 19-27.

Walton, M. 2007b. "Toxic Leadership". In *Leadership: The Key Concepts,* edited by J. Gosling and A. Marturano. Oxford: Routledge.

Walton, M. 2010. "Senior Executives: Behavioural Dynamics". *HRM Review,* August, 10-18.

Walton, M. 2020a. "Leadership Toxicity: Our Own Corporate 'Covid-Tox' Pandemic". *Effective Executive.* IUP Publications, Vol XXIII, (2), 7-11.

Walton, M. 2020b. "Tackling Leadership Toxicity: An HRM Priority". *HRM Review.* IUP Publications, Vol XVI (3), June, 25-34.

Walton, M. 2020c. "Identify, Track and Trace Disruptive Workplace Behaviour: Towards Enhancing Organisational Performance". *HRM Review.* IUP Publications, Vol XVI (4), December, 1-7.

Waring, A. 2013. *Corporate Risk and Governance: an End to Mismanagement, Tunnel Vision and Quackery.* Farnham, UK: Gower/Taylor & Francis.

Waring, A. (ed). 2018. *The New Authoritarianism Vol 1: A Risk Analysis of the US Alt-Right Phenomenon.* Edited by A. Waring. Stuttgart: Ibidem Verlag.

Waring, A. 2019a. "The New Authoritarianism and the Glorification of Amoral Calculation". *CARR Insight Blog.* October 1, 2019. London: Centre for Analysis of the Radical Right. https://www.radi calrightanalysis.com/2019/10/01/the-new-authoritarianism-and-the-glorification-of-amoral-calculation/.

Waring, A. 2019b. "The Five Pillars of Occupational Safety and Health in a Climate of Authoritarian Socio-political Climates'", Special Issue: The Future of Safety Science. *Safety Science*, 117, 152-163.

Waring, A. 2020a. "Can the Radical Right's Reductionist Narrative Withstand Real World Complexity?" *Fair Observer.* April 24, 2020. https://www.fairobserver.com/region/north_america/ alan-waring-radical-right-reductionism-narratives-donald-tru mp-politics-news-14311/.

Waring, A. 2020b. "Can the Radical Right's Reductionist Narrative Withstand Real World Complexity?" *CARR Insight Blog.* July 3, 2020. London: Centre for Analysis of the Radical Right.

Waring, A. and Glendon, A.I. 1998. *Managing Risk: Critical Issues for Survival and Success into the 21st Century.* Aldershot, UK: Thomson/Cengage.

Waring, A. and Tyler, M. 1997. "Managing Product Risks". *Risk Management Bulletin*, 2(5), 4-8.

Weiss, R. 2020. "TUI Gets 2 Billion Bailout after Pandemic Halts Tour Activities". *Bloomberg News.* March 27, 2020. https://www.bloo mberg.com/news/articles/tui-gets-2-billion-bailout-after-pand emic-halts-tour-activities.

Wunsch, N-G. 2020. *Market Share of Grocery Stores in Great Britain from January 2015 to January 2020.* February 28, 2020. Hamburg, Germany: Statista. https://www.statista.com/statistics/280208/gro cery-market-share-in-the-united-kingdom-uk/.

Zuboff, S. 2019. *The Age of Surveillance Capitalism: the Fight for the Future at the New Frontier of Power.* London: Profile Books.

Chapter 6:
Covid-19 and US Politicisation of Fear

By Vasiliki Tsagkroni[1]

Abstract

This chapter focusses on how the Covid-19 pandemic, and the crisis surrounding it, was used as a populist political instrument in the US to dominate public and political discourse and steer opinion towards supporting President Trump's radical-right agenda. The politicisation of fear as a strategy in pursuit of radical-right agendas, with the objective of retaining political power at all costs, is examined at length. Ruthless exploitation of fear of the unknown by Trump and his close aides and leading supporters led to blaming, demonisation, and scapegoating of 'the other,' whether foreign nations, foreigners, scientists, and medical experts holding evidence-based positions that contradicted radical-right emotional or political opinions, or indeed anyone daring to challenge radical-right assertions or their numerous conspiracy theories. The chapter addresses how, in an attempt to hijack national virtues, radical-right populists sought to strengthen their identity through 'othering,' juxtaposing themselves with 'the other,' and projecting themselves as sole paragons of conservatism, patriotism, and protecting democracy. Risks to various parties are systematically identified.

Keywords: Covid-19, discourse, fear, politicisation,
conspiracy theories, crisis

Introduction

Since early 2020, Covid-19 has been a drawn-out crisis, with daily new infections and death toll still rising in Spring 2021, and a health care system and health policy-making that have been constantly challenged and tested worldwide. At the time of writing, more than 26 million Americans had been infected by Covid-19, resulting in more than 436,000 deaths (CDC 2021). The pandemic health crisis that Covid-19

---

[1]   See contributor affiliations and biography, page 527.

brought to the world became a critical determining factor of new re-alities and backdrop for public life. In countries worldwide, the re-sponses to this pandemic health crisis had been innumerable, from re-strictions on individual liberties in terms of mobility and traveling to restrictions on economic activities in order to control viral spread, something that generated public dissatisfaction, disappointment, and distrust towards governments, authorities, and institutions. In line with these new realities, authoritarian propensities, conspiracy theo-ries, and misinformation have endured and gained ground and ad-versely affected the content of public and political discourse.

In any type of crisis, a moment of uncertainty occurs. During a crisis situation, there is a battle of understanding that emerges, in terms of what caused the crisis, who is responsible for the crisis, but also what will be the potential solutions. Blame attribution, subver-sive, anti-establishment, or even anti-populist narratives are being de-veloped by actors whose main focus is imposing and framing their own perception as the right one to the masses. As Katsambekis and Stavrakakis (2020) note, when addressing the issue of populism and the Covid-19 pandemic, a crisis creates a fertile ground for populist actors and movements to arise. It tends to exaggerate and even in-crease socio-political divisions between institutions and the masses, as it is not just a public health crisis but also affects e.g. the economy, politics, and society. The uncertainty the crisis creates leads to doubts towards society's institutions, which are perceived as disconnected from popular demands, and therefore both unresponsive and unrep-resentative. This gives an opportunity for populists to use 'crisis' as part of their own narrative in an effort for further mobilisation against the institutions, who are perceived as responsible for the crisis (Moffit 2016) and for generating this notion of uncertainty and fear.

This chapter examines Covid-19 from a US domestic perspective and examines the role and prospects of populism in the context of the pandemic in the US. It focuses on how President Trump and the radi-cal right have sought to accentuate the pandemic and its risks to the US population's wealth and the economy and, at the same time, play down its danger and threat to public health. The chapter looks at data produced by President Trump, e.g. White House statements and Covid-19 task force meeting minutes, along with information shared on media platforms that engage in promulgating conspiracy theories regarding the pandemic. The aim is to identify and examine the public discourse surrounding the challenging emotional arguments raised against science-based and evidence-based policy on Covid-19.

The Developing 'Covid Hoax' Discourse and its Orchestration

> "Humanity is imprisoned by a killer pandemic. People are being arrested for surfing in the ocean and meditating in nature. Nations are collapsing. Hungry citizens are rioting for food. The media has generated so much confusion and fear that people are begging for salvation in a syringe. Billionaire patent owners are pushing for globally mandated vaccines. Anyone who refuses to be injected with experimental poisons will be prohibited from travel, education, and work. No, this is not a synopsis for a new horror movie. This is our current reality." *Plandemic* (2020)

This is the picture of our future approaching, as imagined by *Plandemic* (2020), an American film that alludes to Covid-19 disease as being a product of human design, and that behind the pandemic, there is a rogue lobby that aims to make billions, infecting millions of people with a contagious virus and killing them with infected vaccines. The video was uploaded to *Facebook* and *YouTube* on May 4, 2020, and only a week later, it counted millions of views. Among the active supporters of *Plandemic's* argument, one can identify several well-known conspiracy theory platforms, e.g. *Infowars*, which embrace and contribute to the debate. These add further arguments for alternative therapies to combat the virus while making declarations on the value of anti-vaccination, creating a movement against Covid-19 public health policy, and taking their argument to the streets. Examples include demonstrators in London calling for an 'end to medical tyranny,' Berlin protesters against the Covid-19 lockdown, and protests in Paris and Zurich against government response measures to the virus (e.g. making wearing masks mandatory), which argued that such measures are based on lies that result in restraining the individual's freedom and objected to mandatory vaccinations. However, the movement against public policy on Covid-19 does not simply focus on medical aspects but also offers an opportunity for the radical right to strengthen their voices, attract the attention of the public, and grow,

The 2016 election of Donald Trump as President of the United States brought a qualitative change in terms of conspiracy theories mentioned above and in the empowerment of their supporters. Conspiracy theories and misinformation are no longer on the side-lines.

President Trump himself transmitted large amounts of misinformation regarding Covid-19, which, according to (Evanega et al. 2020), constituted 37.9% of the overall misinformation on this topic in 38 million English language media articles, and that few article writers and editors had fact-checked Trump's statements. Accurate information is essential, as it is one of the core tools of framing the credibility that political leaders need to create in crisis times. American followers of conspiracy theories frequently are followers of Donald Trump. A couple of months into the pandemic, he claimed to be taking a hydroxychloroquine pill every day as a form of anti-Covid medication. However, it had no FDA medical approval for such use.

In times of crisis, such as during a pandemic, there is a high expectation of public leadership, which requires their grasping present realities and prioritising their action options. Yet, as Covid-19 started to spread globally, so did the discourse on 'othering' and blaming people from outgroups. Much of this discourse was generated by political and other public leaders. This focus on attacking scapegoats, rather than getting a practical grip on combatting the pandemic, was particularly evident from Trump, his administration, and his radical-right supporters.

By bringing together theories on 'othering' and crisis exploitation, the role of the leader, and the circulation of misinformation, this chapter analyses anti-science theories of President Trump and the radical right on the causes, transmission, treatment, and management of the disease and the pandemic, and their anti-expert narrative. Crisis in this context is seen as the means of nurturing a specific agenda, where governing leadership makes decisions by the operationalising crisis to foster its own doctrine. The aim is to explore the amplification and politicisation of fear about 'the other,' the invisible foreign 'other,' the invasive enemy asserted to be aided and abetted in the US by elites, scientists, experts, socialists, Democrats, liberals, and others. The study argues that the discourse that is created under the Covid-19 health crisis seeks (possibly unwittingly) to undermine and destroy the US in multiple respects. In this context, by identifying the 'other' as the source of danger, the dominant group minimises the notion of helplessness during such circumstances while structuring an identity that stigmatises the 'other,' e.g. 'unhealthy and contagion' (Crawford 1994), something that can be seen in the prevalence of anti-

Asian attitudes and violent attacks in the case of Covid-19 (see Rehy & Barreto 2020).

Reflecting on the bigger question of what is the impact of such discourse on the US, Europe, and the rest of the world, this study focuses on the case of the US by providing compelling evidence of 'othering' discourse and misinformation and highlighting the dangerous effects such attitudes can produce.

Crisis-Exploitation and a Window of Opportunity

A crisis may be defined as a sudden focusing event (Kingdon 1995), or as Boin, 't Hart, Stern & Sundelius put it, crises are defined as "events or developments widely perceived by members of relevant communities to constitute urgent threats to core community values and structures" (Boin et al. 2009, 83). Rather than a static event in time, a crisis can be seen as a process that demands attention at different points in time. This depends not only on the perspective and understanding of the event by the public but also on the various and changing themes and issues that require attention, since a crisis imposes and is formed by the "broader developmental context of the society in which it occurs" (Porfiriev 1996 in Boin and t'Hart 2003, 546). For Rosenthal, a crisis can constitute one focal event among many potential related events over time and throughout the social structure (Quarantelli 1998, 200). Therefore, a crisis may be socially defined.

In times of crisis, there is a level of incrementalism in relation to the remedial process, with decisions rarely being deposed in a rational and comprehensive way. The process involves a variety of competing moralities that government and policymakers have to consider to ensure citizens' safety while still being able to preserve the democratic principles of self-determination. In the case of a health pandemic, this means combining and unifying apparently contradictory principles, such as individual freedom and collective safety. When discussing in terms of policy change in times of a crisis, a defining moment for policy change occurs, known as a "window of opportunity" (Birkland 2005), such that when it is open, it can allow policymakers and governance mechanisms to put forward selective solutions-in-action. However, this chapter puts forward the idea that a window of opportunity can be taken even further and be applied in relation to the policy change and discourse structure in times of a crisis as an additional form of action.

In order for an event to be identified as a crisis, three variables need to be considered: threat, urgency, and uncertainty (Boin et al. 2005). Initially, suppose a crisis in society presents a threat to the public, e.g. public safety. In that case, it induces a sense of urgency for dealing with it quickly. Lastly, it creates uncertainty about both the nature and scale of the threat itself and the potential consequences (Boin et al. 2005), resulting in the disruption of a wide range of socio-political and organisational processes. In a situation where a combination of these variables is presented, a window of opportunity appears, giving the space and opportunities for governance mechanisms and policy-makers to take action and exploit any advantage they may have. Additionally, as Rosenthal (in Quarantelli 1998) highlighted, the modern crisis is not confined by common boundaries since it is an outcome of modern processes, e.g., globalised information flow, technological advances, and related developments. In conjunction with organisational responses, media pressure, and erroneous information flow (Boin and t'Hart 2003), technology makes crisis and crisis exploitation rather complex processes.

With a crisis unfolding, and the challenges that arise from a crisis, political leadership has to deal with the damage that has been inflicted while also addressing the issue of accountability that crisis triggers and to altering perceptions and public emotions the crisis creates in an effort "to minimize the consequences of—and make the most of the opportunities associated with—crisis" (Boin et al. 2016, 12) and ultimately providing a sense of return to normality. For t'Hart (2014), by introducing ambitions and ideas to the public, they will highlight the course of action that will be decided upon. The leadership uses the opportunity to make a crisis malleable so as to foster a specific agenda.

However, a crisis does not mean with certainty that there will be a window of opportunity for political abusers. In order to understand the circumstances that assist in opening such a window of opportunity, one has to emphasise the aspect of crisis exploitation. The latter defines the crisis-type discourse that public leaders use in seeking to exploit the opportunity the crisis has created—in other words, to assemble and offer a 'winning frame' to the public that seeks to strengthen their levels of support (Boin et al. 2009). For these authors, the crisis produced characteristics that include denial, crisis as a threat, and crisis as an opportunity (Boin et al. 2009, 84). For this chapter's purposes, the argument focuses on the Covid-19 crisis as a form of opportunity. There is a political stance focussing on the blame of the 'other' as a victim, which makes conceivable the prospect of a formalisation of a specific agenda.

Looking back at Moffit's argument (2016), a crisis can be a trigger or a precondition for the rise of populism. However, the notion of a crisis, or more accurately the uncertain notion of a crisis, creates recursion problems, as Fischbacher-Smith (2014) discusses. In reference to how a crisis develops and evolves, in terms of, e.g. systemic failure, a crisis can be perceived as highly related to uncertainty regarding the stability and continued existence of a system. It nurtures notions of loss of control, further instability and system failure (Paxton 2018). Reflecting on Moffit (2016) and Fischbacher-Smith (2014), Paxton, referring to a crisis, highlighted the significance of failure (e.g. financial, political, social), which, when it is "widely regarded as salient through its mediation into the political, cultural or ideological spheres, then it is seen as symptomatic of a wider problem" (2018, 344). When examining populist politics in a crisis context, there is thus a considerable variety of heterogeneity and diversity in terms of expressions.

Populism: The 'People' Versus 'The Other' in Times of Pandemic Crisis

Populism has been extensively used as an umbrella label within the political scene, something that has often been compared to a 'chameleon' phenomenon (see Taggart 2000). As most recent definitions of populism make references and appeal to "the people" (Canovan 2004), this provides an indicator of using populism as a tool to understand populist subjects and, therefore, the way in which people comprehend their social existence and themselves, how they fit and interact with others and how they position themselves in relation to others (see Taylor 2002). For instance, in times of a crisis, a specific discourse on the 'other' offers the opportunity for fostering a specific policy agenda, e.g. the migrant crisis and tougher migration policies. Crisis, in this sense, is used to structure the power of discourse and its impact.

The notion of the 'other' constitutes a sense of exclusion, which makes the constituted self possible. Irigaray (1985), when discussing the 'other woman', for example, refers to it as a constituted abjection condition of becoming. Building on Irigaray's concept of abjection, the 'other' is a form of exclusion, and identities are self-dependent on the 'other.' In the case of populism, there is a mutual dependence in relation to the 'otherness,' system, and abjection, with populism becoming a tool for a constitutional and political base. In other words, populism establishes specific constituencies and/or creates identities of a constituency, e.g. believing in conspiracy theories or categorizing 'others' is a form of creating an identity for oneself. An example is provided by the recent mob attack on January 6, 2021, on the US Capitol building in Washington DC. The mob participants, comprising a wide range of radical-right devotees including a number being pursued by the FBI and Department of Homeland Security as domestic terrorists, believed that the November 2020 presidential election results were rigged and that there had been voter fraud. Thus, by weaponizing this motivated reasoning (however remote from the factual evidence), they created an identity for themselves as self-styled protectors of democracy.

Moreover, similar to Reinfeldt's (2000) model, the general understanding of populism divides society into two opposing groups, the 'true people-we/us' and the 'others,' i.e., both internal and external enemies. 'We' therefore 'not them,' in the same sense of opposition to 'them' can be interpreted as 'not us.' 'Them' can refer to multiple actors, e.g. established political parties and the political elite, while 'not us' can refer to foreigners, migrants, or any other distinguishable or marginalised group. These differentiations serve to justify and rationalise the distinction from the 'other' as alien and dissimilar, emphasising the differences between groups (Wistrich 1999). For Wistrich, it is the need and desire to distinguish one's self from the other in order to maintain one's identity, and therefore, draw boundaries between 'us' and 'them.' In relation to conspiracy theories, which by definition are an explanation for events that relies on the assertion that, for example, the 'elite' is dishonestly manipulating society, 'othering' can be mobilised to believe someone's prejudices towards the elite, regardless of whether they are true or not. In the case of Covid-19, for example, a conspiracy theory concerning the rationale behind the alleged creation of the virus in a scientific lab could be that powerful people created the virus in order to establish a new world order. Similar conspiracy theories abound in the febrile milieu of QAnon and other conspiracist groups (see later section).

Taking this forward, populism creates modes of identification that contribute to constructing differences and antagonisms and drawing divisions between 'insiders' and 'outsiders' (Howarth 2000). Therefore, populism may be interpreted as a form of identity politics, essentially 'equivalence' reinforcing the selected discourse. This conceptual reflection of populism strongly articulates a division between exclusion and inclusion of specific groups, e.g. based on class, religion, culture, ethnicity, or political beliefs. For Laclau, the process of creating populist identities forms around certain signifiers whose role is "not to express any positive content but to function as the name of a full identity which is constitutively absent" (2005, 96), and in this way contributing to the marginalisation of different groups. Targeting marginalised groups is the discourse of 'othering' in practice.

As mentioned above, a crisis situation creates a sense of threat, urgency, and uncertainty that affects the way people exist and understand the world around them, while shifting the focus onto dominant discourses and creating additional dynamics as part of the outputs. In this case, it is an urgency that opens the window of opportunity. It is fear of the unknown, uncertainty, and urgency as the driving force behind the argument that *now* is the time to take action that creates the need to blame 'the other.' In a time of a health crisis and cross-border pandemics, new boundaries are set between identity groups, focusing on distancing self from the group that is perceived as responsible for the virus (as an unhealthy group or as carriers of the virus), then to take measures to isolate the groups that allegedly pose a health threat, and finally generating an indictment of the groups that are targeted as the threat (Kam 2019). For Flowers (2001), infectious virus outbreaks usually are accompanied by misinformation or little in-depth medical opinion, something that contributes to a redistribution of blame, followed by prevailing patterns of discrimination against 'the other'. Dionne and Turkmen (2020) historicize and classify pandemic 'othering' and blame by drawing on existing scholarship examining previous pandemics. They conclude that pandemics aggravate the marginalisation and scapegoating of already less powerful and oppressed groups (e.g. migrants), and consequently shape and activate hostile and even violent attitudes towards those groups, and embrace a discourse of stigma and discrimination. Recent anecdotes of 'othering' during a health pandemic crisis can be found in reports on the Black Death and the Jewish community, Spanish flu and Spanish and Portuguese nationals, HIV/AIDS and the LGBTQ+ community, and most recently, the SARS-CoV-2 case and the Chinese (see Dionne and Turkmen 2020).

Finally, leadership has been recognised as a key to populism since the discourse that leaders use is a tool to transform social problems into social demands in an effort to attract the support of the public. Some leaders may also exploit a pandemic health crisis such as Covid-19 and rely on populism to foster a specific political agenda. Thus, populism is signified in a crisis environment and provides opportunities for emergency politics, a marginalisation of the opposition and the media. The role of the media is crucial at this point. The media and social media, e.g. *Twitter*, provide cheap and instantaneous communication, something that instantly expands the audience range and typology, spreading information and misinformation alike on a global scale.

US Domestic Responses to Covid-19: the Evolution of the Asserted Danger of the 'Other'

First reported in December 2019 by the Chinese authorities in Wuhan province in China, this particular coronavirus (Covid-19) has managed to rapidly spread throughout the globe and was declared a pandemic by the World Health Organisation (WHO) in mid-March 2020, with (to date) 218 countries and territories that have reported to be impacted by the virus. While the WHO and the world's scientific community and global health experts are collaborating to accelerate the research and development process, focusing on the containment of virus spread while seeking effective vaccines, the political response to the virus in the US from President Trump and his administration appeared more to emphasise blame rhetoric and alleged Chinese patterns of misconduct.

In a crisis, it appears that the structure of discourse is not the one that actually changes. It is the evolving essence of the perceived danger that actually motivates the shift. It is also essential for the 'otherness' to be identified by politicians seeking scapegoats, as its danger is reframed in a specific context and a crisis environment. By structuring a discourse that is triggered by the urgency aspect of the danger of 'the other' (in a variety of ways throughout the discourse), a new agenda is fostered. In this, the 'other' becomes an evolving metaphor for danger in the discourse, reframing the threat to the current crisis format, in this case, Covid-19. This can also be understood through the concept of intertextuality. As Allen (2000) highlights, dialogue refers to social 'positionings' that characters enact, where the text is the absorption and transformation of another (Kristeva 1986). Thus texts can be seen as being in conversation with the other. This can be applied to understand discourse and the essence of the danger of the 'other' in crisis format, as it constantly changes its structure through this filtering process.

Even during the first months of 2020, it was clear that the coronavirus phenomenon's impact was evolving into a threat to President Trump's career, with the Republican Party worrying about the impact on the forthcoming November presidential election campaign. The main concern at the time was the White House's ineffective and slow reaction and the potential blow to the US economy. For months into the pandemic, President Trump downplayed the situation by avoiding masks, criticising others who wore them, and holding large rallies with supporters who did not wear them in defiance of expert advice, constantly emphasising that the situation was under control and that the virus would 'miraculously' disappear. In addition to Covid-19 evolving into a major threat to public health and the national economy, only a few months after the virus took hold in the US, the demonisation of the Chinese and Asian communities emerged, followed by a reference to the virus as 'Wuhan virus,' 'Chinese virus' or a 'Kung flu,' a choice of language that was adopted by President Trump and that inspired racism and violence against those communities (see Reny and Barreto 2020). This relates not only to pejoratively identifying the 'other' but also to the notion of danger the 'other' is allegedly posing to society. Months into the pandemic, President Trump's discourse continued to escalate on the Chinese government's alleged malfeasance, with a dominant focus on China's accountability and responsibility for allegedly unleashing the plague of Covid-19 (Trump, September 22, 2020).

While the selected discourse clearly demonises foreigners as threatening and dangerous, President Trump continuously defended the use of such language as "not racist" but indeed as "accurate" (Trump, March 18, 2020), while the WHO advised against terms that link the virus to China to avoid any form of stigmatisation and 'othering.' This does not come as a surprise. Refugee and migration issues have been high on the agenda of Trump's presidency, similar to those of radical-right movements across the globe, and the pandemic offered a new opportunity for exploitation of these issues. Taking advantage mainly of the ignorance, fear, and indisputable fatigue of citizens, the agenda may have evolved but has not fundamentally changed. In a health crisis such as Covid-19, the scientific and expert focus may be on wearing masks, scientific facts, or vaccinations. However, the public and political discourse still targets opposing political arguments or embellishment of unscientific theories with 'othering' and exclusion-oriented comments. President Trump and his Administration portrayed themselves as the sole possessors of the truth on Covid-19 (and indeed many other topics) in a year were gaining influence and attracting voters was deemed essential for their electoral campaign. Fear and ignorance, cynically exploited as they were, evolved to become a source of tension and despair that assisted the arguments made by this administration, namely that Trump's re-election would be their only salvation.

Furthermore, mistrust of and suspicion towards governance institutions was deliberately fostered, a tactic seen both among conspiracists and populist actors, which also involved provoking disbelief in science to help fuel further fear and ignorance public. In line with this growing populist mood, President Trump, in May 2020, announced the termination of US funding and the country's relations with the WHO, accusing the organisation of protecting China and highlighting Trump's distrust in the role of the organisation and its alleged misconduct (Trump, May 29, 2020). The argument made by Trump against the WHO was twofold: first, it alleged WHO withheld information and ignored warnings in relation to the danger of Covid-19; second, it alleged that WHO has been 'virtually' controlled by China, and that China had pressured the organisation to strategically mislead the world regarding the virus (Trump, May 29, 2020).

However, targeting China and Chinese and Asian communities as an alleged threat was not confined to Covid-19. They were also targeted as an economic threat. This can be detected in the statements of President Trump, in the name of protecting the integrity of the American financial system and American investors, in which Chinese companies listed on the US financial markets should be investigated and accused of conferring 'undue' and hidden risks (Trump, May 29, 2020). In addition, the argument put forward brought focus on claims regarding continuing efforts by China to obtain intellectual property and technology secrets from American industries illicitly, also raising potential national security risks for the US. Further, the argument highlights transparency and fairness issues that extend beyond China's economic and financial policy and reflects on supplementary indicators of China's longstanding tactics.

Through the spread of the virus, China's stigmatisation took various forms during President Trump's discourse. In an effort to highlight the differences between China and the US, President Trump also challenged their principles, values, and tactics in comparison to the US, e.g. commenting on China's foreign affairs with Hong Kong (Trump, May 29, 2020). The confrontational attitude of the Trump administration towards China, in relation to the economy, right from the beginning of Trump's presidency, was eclectic in its range of topics, e.g. from tariffs to trade agreements, security threats, and human rights, and contributed to his generally unilateral foreign policy agenda (see e.g. Waring 2018).

Conspiracy Theories and Misinformation as Covid-19 Response

Newly formed conspiracy theories appear to appeal differently to various radical-right groups. In contrast, many existing conspiracy theories appear to have been deliberately reframed to serve the purpose of the Covid-19 narrative, building on existing prejudices. Additional conspiracy theories also contribute to broadening the xenophobic and 'othering' exclusion item related to the Covid-19 crisis. Following traditional patterns of the radical-right discourse, during the Covid-19 crisis, there has been a series of conspiracy theories that degenerate into anti-Semitism and target the Jewish community, who are alleged to be responsible for distributing the virus in the first place. The false association of Jews with diseases has a long history and is deeply-rooted within anti-Semitism, e.g. the Black Death plague. In the case of Covid-19, the Jewish conspiracy theory takes different forms, from claims that the virus is a hoax concocted by Jews to its being real but still fabricated by Jews in order to manipulate the global economy, or even the Jewish community being the primary spreader of the virus (see Anti-Defamation League 2020). An example of such discourse can be found on the *TruNews* media, a radical-right Christian channel, alleging that the Jews created the virus in order to kill the Christian population and overthrow President Trump (Weiner 2020).

The rapid spread of conspiracy theories and disinformation raises the prospect of polarisation and further division among the population in an effort to recruit supporters and further inspire additional threatening trends and radicalisation, including impact on terrorism and generating and promoting violence and hate worldwide, e.g. numerous QAnon conspiracy theory devotees, radical-right extremists, and possibly domestic terrorists in the radical-right mob attack on the US Capitol, January 6, 2020. The study by Evanega et al. (2020) highlighted the role of Trump's leadership in the spreading of misinformation by identifying Trump as the single largest driver of misinformation around Covid-19, an "infodemic", something that makes it difficult to separate truth from fiction. The study underlined the role of misinformation in relation to attitudes towards the virus itself, e.g. mistrust of medical experts and beliefs in worthless 'miracle cures,' contributing to a further spread of the virus. For wider examination of radical-right conspiracism, see e.g. CCDH (2020), Douglas et al. (2019), Nagel (2017), van Prooijen (2018), and Waring (2021, chapter 9 in this volume).

The political exploitation of the pandemic by the Trump administration, and radical-right voices within and beyond the US, also liberally employs various conspiracy theories in its mix of misinformation, misdirection, anti-science attitudes, and 'othering' discourse. As one example, the *Plandemic* video alleges an orchestrated attempt by 'Big Pharma' companies, in collaboration with philanthropist Bill Gates as a scapegoat, to sponsor a large-scale Covid-19 vaccination programme knowingly using a harmful vaccine, with the hidden aim of eliminating a significant proportion of the population while generating huge profits or even using the vaccine as a disguise in order to insert digital microchips into people *en masse*. The use of Bill Gates as a scapegoat by anti-vaccine activists and QAnon supporters, for creating the virus and seeking profit out of it in an effort to control the global health system (Wakabayashi, Alba, and Tracy 2020), has led to false information about Bill Gates being spread through online, social and other media.

With the *Plandemic* video, the radical-right found an opportunity to exploit the crisis in order to promote their extremist ideas. Even in early March 2020, anti-vaccine activist Larry Cook raised the discussion on *Facebook,* calling Covid-19 a pandemic being used to "usher in mandatory testing, tracking, and vaccination" #ResistThePlan (Cook 2020). Members of Cook's group on *Facebook* Stop Mandatory Vaccination (with more than 195,000 members), further used the platform to spread other conspiracy theories and false health information (Zadrozny 2020). The group was eventually banned from *Facebook* for "militarised social movements and violence-inducting conspiracy networks, such as QAnon" (Sulleyman 2020). See also Amarasingam and Argentino (2020).

A Pew Research report in April 2020 revealed that a third of the American population believed the virus was created in a laboratory by human scientists (Pew Research 2020) or held ideas that it was even created as a biological weapon at the Wuhan Institute of Virology linked to Beijing's covert bio-weapons programme. As the Pew Research report pointed out, the proportions of Americans who believe or partially believe in the conspiracy that the Covid-19 was planned differ by demographics and partisanship. The results showed that less-educated Americans (around 48%) were more inclined to accept some truth in the conspiracy theory, whereas a third of Republicans or people that identify with the GOP agreed or partially agreed with the theory that the virus was planned, compared with 18% of Democrats and people that leant towards the Democratic party. The denial of the Trump administration, in reference to the danger and state of the virus for many months since its first emergence, appeared to foster further trust in conspiracy theories about the origin of the virus per se, creating further questioning of the validity of official narratives and figures on the pandemic.

In the first months of the Covid-19 pandemic, Trump embraced and enacted a populist approach in the form of daily briefings in the

White House. In many of the press briefings, Trump openly challenged expert and scientific knowledge and suggested instead untested treatments, e.g. hydroxychloroquine, while at the same time refusing to use protocols as suggested by the WHO (e.g. wearing a mask) or also openly opposing lockdown measures being adopted by different states.

Conspiracy theories and disinformation spread rapidly via social media platforms, as Covid-19 also began to spread globally. As a report from ISD (2020) highlights, between January and April 2020, 34 known disinformation-hosting websites gathered 80 million interactions on *Facebook*, whereas, over the same time period, posts linking to the WHO's website or the US Centers for Disease Control received less than 6.5 million. In the same report, ISD researchers highlighted an increased volume of threads within radical-right circles about so-called 'elites,' e.g. Bill Gates, George Soros, and Jeff Bezos, along with also replicating false and misleading information about their alleged role in the creation and spread of the virus.

Conspiracy theories connected to Covid-19 are also connected to radical-right extremism. As discussed above, there is an increase in plots and attacks against Asian communities, but it is not confined to the latter. As Silke (2020) points out, there have been attacks planned against medical and other critical infrastructure, e.g. Timothy's Wilson attack in Kansas City (*BBC* 2020). Moreover, there is also an overall increase in online extremist activity that raises the risk of increasing short-to-medium term radicalisation. For Comerford and Davey (2020), the engagement of extremist groups with Covid-19 emphasises the argument of crisis exploitation and the opportunity to mobilise the masses by promoting conspiracy theories, e.g. that the virus is an opportunity for state authorities to curb civil liberties, target minority communities, and build on existing prejudices to fit the crisis (e.g. accusing minorities of spreading the virus), while also inciting hate and violence.

Reflecting on the points above, the Covid-19 phenomenon has provided a vehicle for blending multiple stands of conspiracy theory thinking, radical-right politics, and populism. The anti-vaccine movement, since the start of the pandemic, took a radical shift, with such groups as Stop Mandatory Vaccination focusing their discourse not only on the danger that vaccines allegedly pose but also on attacking the Democrats for promoting the vaccine agenda, or posting pro-Trump campaign messages, while also making references to QAnon (Butler 2020). However, while conspiracists have become more radical, it seems that the radical right have also become more conspiracist, by publicly questioning vaccine effectiveness, engaging in Jewish collusion theories, or, in the case of Trump, making claims that Joe Biden is controlled by people who are in "the dark shadows" (Buranyi 2020). Such baseless assertions support the argument that populism and the radical right have not been weakened by the Covid-19 situation, but rather have been energised by it and continue to thrive, not only in society but also increasingly within mainstream politics.

Conclusion

Populist leaders tend to challenge commonly accepted facts and data for fear of alienating or antagonising their electoral base. In the case of Covid-19, this is evidenced by why they are reluctant to tell people to observe social distancing, avoid unnecessary social mixing, self-quarantine as necessary, or wear masks in public. Additionally, they tend to create divisions in society, either with nationalist/nativist banners or by demonising those they consider elite or unwilling to accept their populist ideology. They typically embrace a unique personal style that eschews giving wise advice or demonstrating self-restraint (Daniszewski 2020). On the contrary, their rhetoric, advice and cavalier personal conduct frequently rejects out-of-hand authoritative medical advice. In the case of the Trump administration, one tactic was to advocate antidotes or treatments that have not been shown to be effective. Moreover, scientists and health officials were often sidelined by the Trump administration, and instead of developing a consistent anti-virus strategy, state and local leaders were left to their own devices to battle the spread of the virus if at all. As Daniszewski (2020) pointed out, populism in practical politics means promoting policies that are popular with the masses and not the elites or even the experts, and instead adopting a discourse that minimises disruption for a radical-right administration while undermining trust in institutions.

Opponents of government responses to the Covid-19 pandemic have initiated protests across the globe, often including violent attacks. Media platforms have offered a space for highly misleading

Covid-19 content to be spread online, e.g. the QAnon conspiracy theories and the *Plandemic* video that gathered millions of views, but also for attacking and scapegoating vulnerable groups as being responsible for the crisis and spreading radical discourse against the 'other' in a wider audience in order to inspire further conspiracies theories and attacks. Covid-19, in this sense, is capitalised in order to expand propaganda against the allegedly dangerous 'other' while at the same time spreading narratives of mistrust towards institutions and government.

The success of 'anti-Covid-19 protection' movements, from public and political discourse to street protests, lies in the fact that their radicalised message has managed to spread widely and rapidly among a public audience and involves various aspects of populism and self-defining negative attitudes. When looking at the case of the US and its domestic response, the pandemic health crisis has contributed to a radicalised version of reality, having only a weak base of evidence to support it. With Covid-19 still the predominant global health crisis, radical narratives on the danger of the 'other' and misinformation related to the virus continue to find their way to a growing audience, which opens a window of opportunity for different discourses to flourish.

As discussed above, the radical right reframed its long-standing radicalised discourse to fit with the Covid-19 narrative, encouraging the pandemic to amplify ideas on race, class, and welfare and entangle them with that of perceptions of a spreading virus. From anti-migrant, anti-Semitic, anti-Asian, and a broad 'othering' discourse, to discussion on the end of institutions and economic collapse and claims that 5G mobile telephony infrastructure is responsible for the spread of the virus, the pandemic crisis created new opportunities for constructing and disseminating the overall radical-right discourse. What is essential, though, is to explore how radical-right actors respond to the pandemic and explore how the pandemic and the populist narrative are being used, reframed, and co-opted in the new circumstances created by Covid-19. Additionally, the battle against conspiracy theories and an 'infodemic' is challenging, with experts and public actors and institutions emphasising constantly the importance of factual information.

Covid-19 developed into a health crisis and an economic, political, and societal crisis, challenging the structures of social cohesion and democracy itself. With the discourse still in process, xenophobic, anti-institutional, exclusive, and individualistic narratives found their way into the public domain. Scapegoating of the 'other,' in the name of fighting a posited danger, offers a potential emotional escape from the apprehension (if not anxiety) brought on by the health crisis, something that builds on existing and longstanding prejudices and discriminatory attitudes. As argued throughout this chapter, populism and construction of the 'other' changes the urgency of the agenda and inflates the Covid-19 health crisis context. In addition to how the 'other' is mobilised to seize the window of opportunity, the self and the 'other' serve as a domestic response with an altered version of danger from others. In line with this, understanding the opportunities for exploitation in terms of public discourse and leadership offers the prospect of further comprehension of the process of shifting attention and blame in a crisis context.

In summary, identifiable risk exposures include the following, which are assessed further in chapter 10:

Risk Exposures of US Public and Society

Risk Exposure 1: Scapegoating of others and politicisation of fear

US radical-right political leaders and others who amplify and politicise fear among the public by falsely blaming and scapegoating particular nationalities, ethno-religious or other minorities, or those who reject radical-right ideology, as being responsible for the Covid-19 crisis or its economic consequences, are likely to increase harmful division and polarisation of US society.

Risk Exposure 2: Exclusion and violent extremism

'Othering' and marginalisation via the discourse of exclusion create a fertile ground for propagating violence towards communities considered responsible for spreading Covid-19. Expression of prejudice, e.g. racism and ethnocentrism towards the targeted communities, increases as well as the likelihood of violence.

Risk Exposures of US Democratic Governance and Institutions

Risk Exposure 1: Undermining public trust and confidence in democratic order

US radical-right political leaders and others who promulgate baseless conspiracy theories, misinformation, misdirection, manipulation and exploitation of crises, and egregious discourse, are likely to undermine public trust and confidence in US institutions of democratic governance and scientific and medical authorities.

Risk Exposure 2: Denigration of institutions

US radical-right political leaders and others who promulgate baseless conspiracy theories, misinformation, misdirection, manipulation, and exploitation of crises are likely to disregard and disrespect institutions that could challenge them, and project a discrediting animus against their role. This denigration may lead in the US to a more radical and anti-social discourse, an undermining of rational debate, and also provocation of conflict and violence.

Risk Exposures of US Trade and Foreign Policy

Risk Exposure 1: False allegations against other countries as a political tactic

US radical-right political leaders and others who blame and scapegoat particular countries or nationalities with false allegations (e.g. concerning Covid-19, trade violations, cyber-attacks) are likely to engender foreign policy mis-steps, international tensions, and anti-US reactions, which may damage US foreign relations.

Risk Exposure 2: International economic impact

US radical-right political leaders and others who blame and scapegoat particular countries or nationalities with false allegations (e.g. concerning Covid-19, trade violations, cyber-attacks) are likely to engender foreign policy that may damage international trade, create damaging shifts in finance and stock markets, and possibly lead to global economic recession.

References

Allen, G. 2000. *Intertextuality.* London, New York: Routledge.

Amarasingam, A. and Argentino, M-A. 2020. "The QAnon Conspiracy Theory: a Security Threat in the Making?" *CTC Sentinel*, Vol 13, Issue 7, July 2020. Combatting Terrorism Center, at West Point. https://www.ctc.usma.edu/the-qanon-conspiracy-theory-a-se curity-threat-in-the-making/. [accessed August 12, 2020].

Anti-Defamation League. 2020. "Coronavirus Crisis Elevates Antise- mitic, Racist Tropes." https://www.adl.org/blog/coronavirus-cr isis-elevates-antisemitic-racist-tropes.

BBC. 2020. "Coronavirus: Man Planning to Bomb Missouri Hospital Killed, FBI Says". *BBC News.* March 26, 2020. https://www.bbc. co.uk/news/world-us-canada-52045958.

Birkland, T. A. 2005. *An Introduction to the Policy Process: Theories, Concepts, and Models of Public Policy Making.* New York: M.E. Sharpe.

Boin, A., 't Hart, P., and McConnell, A. 2009. "Crisis Exploitation: Polit- ical and Policy Impacts of Framing Contests." *Journal of European Public Policy*, Vol. 16, No. 1, 81–106.

Boin, A., et al. 2005. *The Politics of Crisis Management: Public Leader- ship under Pressure.* Cambridge, England: Cambridge University Press.

Boin, A., 't Hart, P., Stern, E., et al. 2016. *The Politics of Crisis Manage- ment: Public Leadership under Pressure* (2nd ed.). Cambridge, England: Cambridge University Press.

Boin, A., Hart, P.'t. 2003. "Public Leadership in Times of Crisis. Mission Impossible?" *Public Administration Review*, September/October 2003, Vol. 63, No. 5, 544-553.

Buranyi, S. 2020. "How Coronavirus Has Brought Together Conspiracy Theorists and the Far-Right," *The Guardian.* September 4, 2020, https://www.theguardian.com/commentisfree/2020/sep/04/ coronavirus-conspiracy-theorists-far-right-protests.

Butler, K. 2020 "The Anti-Vax Movement's Radical Shift From Crunchy Granola Purists to Far-Right Crusaders," *Mother Jones*, June 18, 2020, https://www.motherjones.com/politics/2020/06/the-an ti-vax-movements-radical-shift-from-crunchy-granola-purists-t o-far-right-crusaders/.

Canovan, M., 2004. "Populism for Political Theorists?" *Journal of Political Ideologies*, 9(3), 241–252.

CCDH. 2020. *Failure to Act–How Tech Giants Continue to Defy Calls to Rein in Vaccine Misinformation.* Report. July 2020. Center for Countering Digital Hate. London: CCDH. https://www.counter hate.co.uk. [accessed October 3, 2020].

CDC. 2021. Covid-19 Infections and Deaths in the US as of January 28, 2021. US Centers for Disease Control. https://www.cdc.gov/covid-data-tracker/index.html#cases. [accessed January 28, 2021].

Comerford, M. and Davey, J. 2020. Comparing Jihadist and Far-Right Extremist Narratives on COVID-19, April 17, 2020, https://gnet-research.org/2020/04/27/comparing-jihadist-and-far-right-ex tremist-narratives-on-covid-19.

Crawford, R. 1994. "The Boundaries of the Self and the Unhealthy Other: Reflections on Health, Culture, and AIDS." *Social Science and Medicine*, Vol. 38, Issue 10, 1347-1365.

Daniszewski, J. 2020. "In Struggle Against Pandemic, Populist Leaders Fare Poorly". *Associated Press.* July 23, 2020, https://apnews.com /article/brazil-u-s-news-ap-top-news-understanding-the-outbre ak-mexico-2a4b5159e9c8b1510973801297243c3d.

Dionne, K.Y. and Turkmen, F.F. 2020. *The Politics of Pandemic Othering: Putting COVID-19 in Global and Historical Context.* International Organisation. Published online by Cambridge University Press: December 15, 2020.

Douglas, K., Uscinski, J.E., Sutton, R.M. et al. (2019). "Understanding Conspiracy Theories." *Advances in Political Psychology.* Vol 40 Suppl 1. Doi: 10.1111/pops.12568. [accessed November 26, 2020].

Fischbacher-Smith, D. 2014. "Organisational Effectiveness: Environmental Shifts and the Transition to Crisis." *Journal of Organisational Effectiveness,* Vol 1 Issue 8, 423-446.

Flowers, Paul. 2001. "Gay Men and HIV/AIDS Risk Management." *Health,* Vol. 5, No. 1, 50–75.

Evanega, S, Lynas, M., Adams, J. et al. 2020. *Coronavirus Misinformation: Quantifying Sources and Themes in the COVID-19 'Infodemic.'* Research Report. Cornell Alliance for Science, Department of Global Development. Ithaca, NY: Cornell University. https://allianceforscience.cornell.edu/wp-content/uploads/

2020/10/Evanega-et-al-Coronavirus-misinformation-submit ted_07_23_20-1.pdf.

Howarth, D. 2000. *Discourse*. Buckingham, UK: Oxford University Press.

ISD. 2020. Far-Right Exploitation of COVID-19. *ISD Global*. May 12, 2020. https://www.isdglobal.org/wp-content/uploads/2020/ 05/20200513-ISDG-Weekly-Briefing-3b.pdf.

Irigaray, L. 1985. *Speculum of the Other Woman*. Ithaca, NY: Cornell University Press.

Kam, Cindy. 2019. 'Infectious Disease, Disgust, and Imagining the Other.' *Journal of Politics* Vol 81 No 4, 1371–1387.

Katsambekis, G. and Stavrakakis, Y. 2020. "Populism and the Pandemic: Introduction and Preliminary Findings". In *Populism and the Pandemic: A Collaborative Report*, edited by Katsambekis, G. and Stavrakakis, Y., 3-9, Populismus Interventions No. 7.

Kingdon, J.W. 1995. *Agendas, Alternatives, and Public Policies*. New York: Longman.

Kristeva, J. 1986. *The Kristeva Reader*. Edited by Toril Moi. New York: Columbia University Press.

Laclau E. 2005. *On Populist Reason*. London: Verso.

Moffitt, B. 2016. *The Global Rise of Populism: Performance, Political Style, and Representation*. California: Stanford University Press.

Nagle, A. 2017. *Kill All Normies: Online Culture Wars from 4chan and Tumblr to Trump and the Alt-Right*. Winchester UK: Zero Books.

Paxton, R. 2018. "The Alt-Right, Post-Truth, Fake News, and the Media." In *The New Authoritarianism Vol 1: A Risk Analysis of the US Alt-Right Phenomenon*, edited by A. Waring, 337-361. Stuttgart: Ibidem Verlag.

Pandemic. 2020. The Documentary. https://www.brighteon.com/edd dd3ce-a71a-4f46-ab27-96bca82350e5. [accessed December 28, 2020].

Quarantelli, E. 1998. *What Is a Disaster? Perspectives on the Question*. London: Routledge

Pew Research. 2020. "Nearly Three-in-Ten Americans Believe Covid-19 Was Made in a Lab". https://www.pewresearch.org/fact-ta nk/2020/04/08/nearly-three-in-ten-americans-believe-covid-19-was-made-in-a-lab/?utm_source=Pew+Research+Center&ut m_campaign=9a8a1fc2a0-

EMAIL_CAMPAIGN_2020_04_09_06_59&utm_medium=email
&utm_term=0_3e953b9b70-9a8a1fc2a0-400906701.

Reny, T.T. and Barreto, M. 2020. "Xenophobia in the Time of Pandemic: Othering, Anti-Asian Attitudes, and COVID-19". *Politics, Groups, and Identities.* https://doi.org/10.1080/21565503.2020.1769693.

Reinfeldt, S. 2000. *Nicht-wir und Die-da. Studien zum Rechten Populismus.* Wien: Braumüller.

Silke, A. 2020, *COVID-19 and Terrorism: Assessing the Short- and Long-Term Impacts.* Pool Re and Cranfield University https://www.poolre.co.uk/wp-content/uploads/2020/05/COVID-19-and-Terrorsim-report-V1.pdf

Sulleyman, A. 2020. "Facebook Bans One of the Anti-Vaccine Movement's Biggest Groups for Violating QAnon Rules," *Newsweek.* November 18, 2020, https://www.newsweek.com/facebook-bans-anti-vaccine-group-violating-qanon-rules-154840.

't Hart, P. 2014. *Understanding Public Leadership.* London: Palgrave.

Taggart, P.A. 2000. *Populism 1.* Buckingham, UK: Open University Press.

Taylor, C. 2002. "Modern Social Imaginaries." *Public Cultures*, 14(1), 91-124.

van Prooijen, J-W. 2018. "The Psychology of Qanon: Why do Seemingly Sane People Believe Bizarre Conspiracy Theories?" *NBC News.* August 13, 2018. https://www.nbcnews.com/think/opinion/psychology-qanon-why-do-seemingly-sane-people-believe-bizarre-conspiracy-ncna900171. [accessed August 10, 2020].

Wakabayashi, D., Alba, D. and Tracy, M. 2020. "Bill Gates, at Odds With Trump on Virus, Becomes a Right-Wing Target". *New York Times.* April 17, 2020, https://www.nytimes.com/2020/04/17/technology/bill-gates-virus-conspiracy-theories.html.

Waring, A. 2018. "The Alt-Right and US Foreign Policy." In *The New Authoritarianism Vol 1: A Risk Analysis of the US Alt-Right Phenomenon*, edited by A. Waring, 169-205. Stuttgart: Ibidem Verlag.

Weiner, A. 2020. 'Global Trends in Conspiracy Theories Linking Jews with Coronavirus.' https://www.ajc.org/news/global-trends-in-conspiracy-theories-linking-jews-with-coronavirus.

Wistrich, R. S. 1999. *Demonizing the Other: Antisemitism, Racism, and Xenophobia.* London: Routledge.

Zadrozny, B. 2020. "On Facebook, Anti-Vaxxers Urged a Mom Not to Give Her Son Tamiflu. He Later Died." *NBC News*. February 6, 2020. https://www.nbcnews.com/tech/social-media/facebook-anti-vaxxers-pushed-mom-not-give-her-son-tamiflu-n1131936.

Chapter 7:
Suppressing the 'Seeker of Truth' in the Covid-19 Pandemic: Medical Populism, Radical Uncertainty, and the Assault on Expertise

By Denis Fischbacher-Smith[1]

Abstract

This chapter explores the issues around the concept of medical populism developed by Lasco and colleagues and does so within the context of the Covid-19 pandemic. It sets out the core elements of populism in the form of a populist triangle in which the elites, the people (composed of both the in-group and those deemed to be outsiders), and the will of the people form the basis of the construct. The chapter considers some of the underlying drivers that operate in the spaces between these three elements and, in particular, the role of expertise, evidence, and the communication of risk as factors that are shaped by populist narratives. The conclusion identifies a number of risk exposures to different parties that arise from radical-right and other responses to contexts of uncertainty and mass harm.

Keywords: medical populism, Covid-19, populist triangle, experts, elites, evidence

Introduction

> "The mindset of the debater is not that of the calm seeker-of-truth. Opposing arguments are to be caricatured, statistics to be twisted, examples to be cherry-picked. The audience is to be entertained or even enraged as much as persuaded. Politics rewards anger and in-group loyalty." (Harford 2020)

There has been a noticeable downturn in public discourse in the early decades of the 21st Century. Simultaneously, there has also been erosion in the trust placed in many of the core institutions within society, and an apparent willingness on the part of many to simply ignore evidence and those with the expertise needed to interpret that evidence. Some have argued that the erosion of trust in science has been a

---

[1]   See contributor affiliations and biography, page 525.

function of post-modernist perspectives that have stated that science is a socially-constructed process, rather than the objective process that had been previously assumed (e.g. Matthews 1998; Rosenau 1992; Taverne 2005). The scepticism about evidence and the notion of objectivity in science that comes with post-modernist views could also be seen to have infiltrated public life, as evidence and truth are under challenge from conspiracy theorists and populist politicians. Harford's opening quote highlights some of the main elements of populist politics that have been evident within a number of countries, and especially in the aftermath of the financial crisis in 2008. In particular, this relates to the undermining of evidence in support of ideologically-driven perspectives, the recounting of conspiracy theories in the face of that evidence, and the reinforcing of the populist base's views at the expense of those outside 'others' who are caricatured, demonised, and ostracised.

It is understandable that health-related issues have been a key area of attention during the Covid-19 pandemic, but there are elements of that discourse that have echoes of a populist narrative around them. In January 2021, *The Washington Post* reported that the US death toll had passed 350,000 (Kornfield & Jacobs 2021), a figure that President Trump disputed via *Twitter* as fake news, criticising his own Government agencies in the process (Trump 2021e). He was later also to comment on the popularity of Dr Fauci, an infectious disease expert, by tweeting that:

> "....he works for me and the Trump Administration, and I am in no way given any credit for my work. Gee, could this just be more Fake News?" (Trump 2021f).

These were a selection of the attacks made by Trump on healthcare officials along with those on the actions around healthcare of previous administrations and, at the same time, he also sought to take credit for the production of the Covid-19 vaccines (The White House 2020; Trump 2020a; e; l).

This process of attacking healthcare professionals has been termed "medical populism" (Lasco & Curato 2019), and the USA was not the only country where such populist approaches towards healthcare were evident, especially in terms of the public health response to Covid-19 (Lasco 2020a; Lasco & Larson 2020; Ortega & Orsini 2020). The influence of such populist approaches can also be traced back through many of the anti-vaccination debates and the emergence of conspiracy theories, perhaps notably those relating to 5G masts and the claimed erosion of people's immune system (Argentino 2020; Jolley & Lamberty 2020). Medical populism has become more apparent within the context of the Covid-19 crisis, which appears to have served as an amplifier of the issues, and the relationship with the crisis is seen as a key factor in the emergence of this form of populism (Lasco & Curato 2019; Ortega & Orsini 2020).

The purpose of this chapter is to consider the nature of medical populism and, in particular, the management and measurement of uncertainty, the role of expertise within that process, and the ways in which such populist perspectives can impact on the generation of a crisis of trust that may well have ramifications beyond the lifetime of the SARS-CoV-2 virus. The discussion here, in keeping with the overall focus of this current volume, considers these issues from the perspective of right-wing populist groups, but it should be noted that extreme views around healthcare and associated issues of trust can be found across the political spectrum. Similarly, the issues of health-related conspiracies, while often associated with right-wing populism, are not always confined to those groups. Populism is, of course, not a new phenomenon and, while some see it as a response to the 2008 financial crisis, its origins go back beyond that crisis (Eatwell & Goodwin 2018). The term itself is often seen to be ambiguous owing to the different definitions and theoretical contexts in which it is used (Mudde & Kaltwasser 2017) and this adds to the challenges associated with addressing its underlying drivers. The purpose here is not to add to those definitional debates per se, but to examine the notion of medical populism within that wider setting. Before setting out the characteristics of medical populism, it is first necessary to provide the wider context in which it is situated.

Populism and the Politics of Rage

> "As 'social issues' came to define the difference between the right and the left, a new breed of 'populists' began to build a political coalition around lower-middle-class resentment. Like the populists of old, they saw themselves as enemies of wealth and privilege, champions of the 'average man on the street'." (Lasch 1991, 505)

A number of populist leaders have been identified within the academic literature, including nationally elected leaders (Trump, Orbán,

Chavez, Erdogan, Berlusconi, Bolsonaro) and others who have led populist movements (Le Pen, Farage, Hofer) (Inglehart & Norris 2016; Norris & Inglehart 2019). Within the populist setting in the USA, trust in the evidence provided by reputable organisations, and even by agencies of the state, has been called into question (Trump 2020j; 2021b). The tweets by the sitting US President, Donald Trump, for example, set out his claims of victory in the 2020 US Presidential election, despite evidence to the contrary from State legislators (Trump 2020h; o; 2021g). Many of these social media posts stated that a fraudulent election had taken place in certain swing states, and that this had robbed Trump of victory (Trump 2020o). This was despite the fact that no evidence, deemed to be credible by the courts, had been presented in the multiple court cases that were brought by Trump's legal team.

Trump was making these claims as late as January 2021 (Trump 2021a; g), despite the Electoral College confirming Joe Biden as duly elected. President Trump was not alone in making such claims and, in early January 2021, a number of Republican senators stated that they would also be challenging the validity of the votes in those swing states, despite the votes being verified by state officials, some of whom were Republican (Bleau 2021; Zhao 2021). While the position changed after Trump supporters stormed the Capitol Building on January 6, after a rally at which Trump spoke, it was not before Trump had accused Vice-President Pence of failing to stand up for the claims of a fraudulent election (Trump 2021c; d). The behaviour of Trump supporters on January 6 marked a low point in US politics and led to severe criticism of his role in encouraging his supporters to march on the Capitol Building (Kim et al 2021), especially in the aftermath of a tweet (Trump 2021g) that some saw as legitimising the actions of the rioters. This tweet, and an associated video, saw Trump banned from *Twitter* as a consequence of his actions (*Twitter Inc* 2021). This ban prompted a series of tweets from Donald Trump Jr in support of free speech and claims of bias from 'BigTech' against conservatives (Trump Jr 2021a; b; c; d). Other Trump supporters who were outspoken critics of the election result have also had their *Twitter* accounts suspended in the wake of the attacks on Capitol Hill (McNamara 2021; Rodrigo 2021).

The process of denial around the election had taken an alarming turn as *The Washington Post* published an account on January 4, 2021, of a telephone conversation between President Trump (and his legal team), the Secretary of State for Georgia (Brad Raffensperger) and his legal counsel which took place on January 2, 2021[2]. Within the course of that conversation, President Trump asked Raffensperger to "find" the additional votes that were needed to overturn the official result of the election within the State because of Trump's view that he had:

> "...won very substantially in Georgia. You even see it by rally size, frankly. We'd be getting 25-30,000 people a rally, and the competition would get less than 100 people. And it never made sense"[1].

Trump went on to make additional claims that the "people of Georgia are angry" and that, by not addressing the claims of fraud made by Trump, Raffensperger was potentially at risk of making a "criminal offense" and that it would be "a big risk" for him and his lawyer (Garner 2021, A4). On several occasions, both Raffensperger and his office's general legal counsel (Ryan Germany) corrected the information that President Trump had presented. This led to some commentators to point to Trump's own attempts to change the outcome of an election— a process that he was accusing his opponents of and which may have violated State and Federal laws (Lipton 2021; Nakamura 2021). There were also concerns, in the aftermath of Trump's encouragement to his base to attend the rally in Washington DC on the January 6, that it could lead to violence as right-wing social media posts were discussing bringing firearms to the event (Timberg & Harwell 2021).

Trump's telephone conversation with Raffensperger could also be seen to meet key elements of Harford's opening comments in terms of the distortion of information and the use of statistics that do not appear to be grounded in official sources. It points to the apparent reluctance of certain groups to consider evidence that contradicts their world-views, along with the selective use of 'evidence' (loosely defined) as a means of reinforcing those world-views. It also illustrated the processes through which a populist leader can use social media to enrage their particular political base. Ironically, when Brad

---

[2]   The transcript of the almost hour-long conversation was posted at https:// www.washingtonpost.com/politics/trump-raffensperger-call-transcript-geor gia-vote/2021/01/03/2768e0cc-4ddd-11eb-83e3-322644d82356_story.html

Raffensperger pointed out that President Trump might have a problem with the social media stating that "people can say anything" in such a forum (implying a lack of evidence), Trump replied:

> "Oh this isn't social media. This is Trump media. It's not social media. It's really not; it's not social media. I don't care about social media. I couldn't care less. Social media is Big Tech. Big Tech is on your side, you know. I don't even know why you have a side because you should want to have an accurate election. And you're a Republican"[1].

It isn't clear what President Trump meant by "Trump media" in this case, but it does imply that the messages sent by the President and his team were carefully managed, as well as highlighting the extent to which Trump was willing to ignore certain forms of evidence. It might also have been a reference to Trump's own social media ambitions to create a platform of his own. After this conversation with Raffensperger, President Trump took to social media to denounce him stating that he "had no clue" (Trump 2021b). Harford also highlights the key tactics used by populist groups in terms of belittling opponents (usually via personal attacks), the diminishing of evidence from experts (who are portrayed as being part of the elite), and the aggressive nature of many of the responses made by the supporters of populist leaders (especially via social media). Many of President Trump's tweets display evidence of such a belittling approach to his opponents (Trump 2020c; f).

Perhaps one of the worst examples of this aggressive stance occurred in an interview with President Trump's former strategist Steve Bannon who stated that:

> "Second term kicks off with firing Wray, firing Fauci.....no I actually want to go a step further but the president is a kind-hearted man and a good man......I'd actually like to go back to the old times of Tudor England. I'd put their heads on pikes, right. I'd put them at the two corners of the White House as a warning to federal bureaucrats, you either get with the programme or you're gone." Steve Bannon (2020) (cited in Beaumont 2020)

Bannon was permanently suspended from *Twitter* as a consequence of these statements (Beaumont 2020; Devine, O'Sullivan, & Scannell 2020). This was not the first time that Dr Fauci had been the subject of verbal attacks, including from President Trump (Peiser 2020), with much of the criticism coming via social media (e.g. Trump 2021f). Against this background, we need to consider the core elements of populism as a construct, in order to provide a platform for exploring the notion of medical populism.

Core Elements of Populism

While there are multiple perspectives that have been put forward to explain the rise in populist movements, there are two main theoretical perspectives that have been used to explain the underlying drivers— these are, the economic insecurity and the cultural backlash perspectives (Inglehart & Norris 2016; Norris & Inglehart 2019). In essence, the two processes could be seen to be self-reinforcing in terms of driving certain groups to follow a particular ideological viewpoint. The economic insecurity perspective accounts for the ways in which certain groups are disenfranchised by the loss of jobs, which is often seen as a function of globalisation, as low-skilled, expensive, or polluting forms of activity are exported to low-cost providers within a global market. This leaves areas that are hollowed out economically with the attendant social problems that such a process brings. This can lead to a sense of alienation and cultural backlash against other groups within society that are held responsible for those changes (especially those perceived elite groups) or where the influx of groups from different cultures are felt to be causing changes to the established culture of a country or region. There is an argument to suggest that both processes were at work in the election of Donald Trump to the US presidency and in the UK's decision to leave the European Union (Brexit).

The emergence of such populist approaches has a much longer history than provided by these recent examples and, whilst populism is something of a contested term, there are seen to be three core elements to it—the people, elite groups, and the notion of the general will (Mudde & Kaltwasser 2017). While the critique of elites within society is common across populist groups, it should not be taken as the defining characteristic of the construct on its own (Müller 2017). A critique of societal elites can, of course, be found in other perspectives on social issues and, particularly, in terms of the role played by expert groups within policy-making. Another key component of a populist perspective is the notion of the 'people', but this is also problematic due to the diverse nature of the public in any one societal setting. As a consequence, any practical definition of populism is also potentially challenging as it can be framed in different ways across the political spectrum. This ambiguity allows influential leaders to frame the constituency associated with 'the people' in ways that suit their worldviews along with those held by those groups that constitute their base of support (Mudde & Kaltwasser 2017). The religious dimension, for example, has proved to be particularly important under the presidency of Donald Trump, who has evoked Christian imagery in an appeal to elements of his evangelical base, sometimes in controversial ways (Bashir 2021; Zurcher 2020).

The focus on specific groups of the population and seeing them as being legitimate representatives of the people (that is, the ingroup) has led to the development of the notion of a "theological conception of politics" (de la Torre 2015) in which:

> "...to evoke the name of 'the people' is to raise the possibility of a theological conception of politics. When the term 'the people' is used to describe those who are to be liberated, alleged enemies of the people—such as 'illegal aliens' or the 'evil oligarchy'—are constructed as external 'Others' who represent a threat to the homogenous body of the people." (de la Torre 2015)

Such a representation of good versus evil is an important dimension of the populist agenda as it allows the 'other' to be demonised, again evoking a theological term. This process of demonisation was in evidence during the Covid-19 pandemic, as certain key individuals—notably, George Soros, Bill Gates, and even public servants such as Dr Anthony Fauci—were singled out for severe and unfounded criticism, especially within some of the more outlandish conspiracy theories (Goodman & Carmichael 2020b). One conspiracy theory, for example, argued that the Covid-19 vaccine was an attempt by the global elite to control the public (Goodman & Carmichael 2020a, b). Others made the link between the spread of Covid-19 and the alleged erosion of people's immunity arising from 5G masts (*BBC News* 2020b; Kelion 2020). For many, such views are seen as bizarre, especially as they are not based on any verifiable forms of evidence. They do, however, form the basis of an anti-establishment and anti-expert world-view that runs through many populist perspectives.

The demonisation of scientific experts, and the associated lack of trust in established organisations, is therefore a key component of populist movements. For example, there is some evidence to suggest that the scepticism that exists around the use of vaccinations and other public health interventions is correlated with the growth in populist parties (Kennedy 2019). A particular example involved the reluctance to accept the views of experts around the use of masks as a means of curtailing the spread of Covid-19. This was an issue that even prompted comment from President Trump, who was critical of mask wearing as an intervention strategy, despite the advice from his own officials on the issue (*BBC News* 2020a). Much of this discussion was set against the economic cost of shutting down cities as a means of arresting the spread of the virus. This was evidenced by his tweets to end lockdowns in certain key cities (Egan 2020) and also holding large-scale rallies as part of his campaign strategy. In this way, one form of 'risk' was set against another, but the significance of the virus was also minimised by populists in the early stages as being akin to the 'flu and this also undermined trust in the expert assessments of the hazard (Brooks 2020). Again, President Trump was a key figure in this process, despite claims that he was briefed early in 2020 about the dangerous nature of the virus (Woodward 2020). The crisis became portrayed more in terms of an economic crisis than a public health one, with many of the protests in some cities being about opposition to lockdown and mask wearing. Kennedy (2019) suggests that such oppositional movements are driven by an underlying mistrust of expertise (which is seen as part of the elite group) combined with the disenfranchisement of those sections of society in which populist views are dominant.

Other definitions of populism add to the importance of the three core elements i.e. the people, the elites, and the general will of the people, by arguing for example that:

> "an ideology that considers society to be ultimately separated into two homogeneous and antagonistic groups, 'the pure people' versus 'the corrupt elite', and which argues that politics should be an expression of the *volonté générale* (general will) of the people." (Mudde 2004, 543)

The notion of an elite group can, of course, be seen as a fluid concept depending on the issues being considered and the nature of those elites could be seen to encompass those with economic, positional, political, as well as expert power that provides them with elite status. Similarly, the notion of 'the people' is also potentially problematic, as it implies a homogenous grouping when the reality is that society is multi-faceted. Populists tend, however, to make the distinction between the in-group and those that are deemed to be the outsiders, with the former being seen in terms of virtuous members of society and the others being perceived as dangerous in some way or another (Norris & Inglehart 2019). Whilst these two elements are challenging to define because of their multi-faceted nature, the notion of the 'general will'—as the third element of the populist approach—is potentially more challenging.

This idea of the general will is, of course, a key aspect of the democratic process, but for many populists the issue concerns the definition of those groups who they believe should be seen to constitute the basis for determining that general will. Within the context of a populist perspective, the group whose 'general will' has validity can often be dynamic but is invariably seen through a nationalistic, or in-group, lens and is often defined by populist leaders (Müller 2017). Thus, the oft-used notions by populist leaders of 'real, hard-working people', who are often described in terms of being 'decent' and 'honest citizens', are those who typically constitute the group whose general will should be enforced (Müller 2017; Norris & Inglehart 2019). President Trump, for example, has referred to his supporters as "great patriots" (Trump 2021g; h) and has been seen to pit them against the elites within US society, and especially in Washington DC (Trump 2020h; k; 2021d). This notion of a core group within society is also evidenced in the post-election rhetoric of President Trump who, in a series of four linked tweets, talked about illegal votes being cast by "dead voters", "illegal immigrant voters" and ballots that had "fake signatures", all of which contributed to his overall narrative around a stolen election[3] (Trump 2020m). The criticism of 'the others' was also extended to the elites, including the US Supreme Court (Trump 2020n), the Justice Department, FBI (Trump 2020h) and a number of Republican Senators and officials (Trump 2020b; g). In a high profile case, President Trump sacked Christopher Krebs, the Director of the Cybersecurity and Infrastructure Security Agency (Collins & LeBlanc 2020), after Krebs had stated that the elections were secure, thereby being deemed to have contradicted the President's claims of a fraudulent election (LeBlanc & Marquardt 2020). The sacking was carried out via *Twitter* (Trump 2020d; j) and served to provide an addition level of humiliation that

---

[3]   These were issues that were also raised in the telephone conversation between President Trump and Brad Raffensperger in January 2021.

would serve as a warning to others not to stand against the populist leader's narrative. Such attacks via social media would continue against those members of the so-called elites who criticised Trump's interpretation of events (Trump 2021b; d; f).

This criticism against elements of the state was also evident in the UK's Brexit process and particularly those with expertise (Gove 2016). When the judiciary determined that Article 50 (which was the official mechanism for leaving the EU) had to be triggered by the UK Parliament, they were subsequently portrayed as 'enemies of the people' by elements of the UK press in that they were deemed to have violated the general will of the people. More recently, social media accounts have been used to actively critique government contingency planning policies on the provision of Covid-19 surge capacity (Tice 2020a; b), whilst also claiming that "Brexit Britain" had saved lives in terms of the vaccine programme (Tice 2021).

While there has been criticism of the use of the term 'populism', it has been seen as a useful construct in bringing together families of issues, in which the combinations of those elements are seen as crucial in categorising the various forms of populist movements (Brubaker 2017). Against that broad background on the nature of populism, Dikötter highlights a number of characteristics associated with cults which can be seen to be intertwined with the personality of the leader and which are relevant to the present discussion. The following are seen as important elements of that relationship:

- There are often ideological or theological overtones associated with the tribe and the role of the leader and which are central to the development and maintenance of the overarching perspective around which the tribe coalesces;
- Ultimately, this coalescing around key issues manifests itself in an overarching loyalty to the leader and which surpasses that of the ideological perspective itself, as it is the leader who sets out the parameters of that ideology and allows it to evolve over time
- The nature of the resultant 'cult' can become typified by a confusion around the factual basis for views and, because of the power of the leader, can undermine the ability of the

members to challenge the orthodoxy of the leader's message (Dikötter 2020).

We cannot, therefore, consider the leaders of the tribe separately from those who follow, as the latter empower the former and, thereby, contribute to the "cult of the individual"[4] that was highlighted by Khrushchev in his critique of Stalin (Dikötter 2020). Within the context of the tribe, or cult, the notion of seeking the truth is overwhelmed by the dominance of the trusted leader. The leader provides the basis for the group's beliefs and plays a role in undermining of other forms of interpretation that contradicts the core message. The result is the seeding of confusion and contradiction in which the tribe's world-view serves to dominate the roles played by evidence and expertise—both of which are downgraded unless they support that world-view. In some contexts, this has also led to established government agencies being undermined and denigrated in support of the dominant views of the tribe.

These three issues—the people, the elites, and the general will—are seen to form a core of the populist approach and have been described as first-order principles by Norris and Inglehart (2019). They argue that populism can be seen as:

> "....a style of rhetoric reflecting first-order principles about who should rule, claiming that legitimate power rests with 'the people' not the elites. It remains silent about second-order principles, concerning what should be done, what policies should be followed, what decisions should be made. The discourse has a chameleon-like quality which can adapt flexibly to a variety of substantive ideological values and principles." (p. 4)

Figure 7.1 illustrates the context in which populism can be framed and represents the first order principles that Norris and Inglehart highlighted. It also highlights some of the underpinning processes that might drive relationships between those first-order elements. Key amongst these is the role played by powerful interests in shaping and sustaining the underpinning processes that are found within the spaces that exist between the in- and out-groups and the elites. These

---

4   This initial description has often been translated as 'personality cult'. Throughout this chapter, the term 'cult of the individual' will be used as no attempt can be made to determine the personality profiles of key individuals within the issues discussed.

are shown in Figure 7.1 as three interacting dimensions which provide a basis for these principles—the economic, cultural, and technocratic dimensions. For example, the economic dimension provides a counterweight to the top-down, technocratic approaches that are typical of public health interventions and which were in evidence within the Covid-19 pandemic. The conflict between these two issues serves to generate a climate in which the cultural dimension is set against the top-down advice of scientific groups, by emphasising the immediate financial impact that is felt by those marginalised sections of society for whom the immediate economic factors are pressing. The boundaries between these issues are likely to be fluid and will change over time.

Figure 7.1—The Populist Triangle

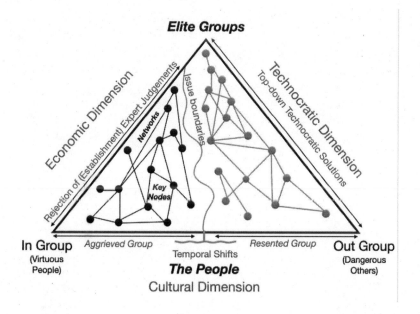

Building upon Norris and Inglehart's notion of second-order principles, some of the key elements that serve to drive the interactions between the people, elites, and the general will can be identified. These can be set out in terms of: the processes around communication, the nature and operation of networks and critical nodes within those networks, and the portrayal of uncertainty within populist discourse (and, by extension, the nature of risk as measurable uncertainty).

Second-Order Drivers of the Populist Triangle

> "In the 'age of information' the American people are notoriously ill in-formed.......Having been effectively excluded from public debate on the grounds of their incompetence, most Americans no longer have any use for the information inflicted on them in such large amounts. They have become almost as incompetent as their critics have always claimed.....In the absence of democratic exchange, most people have no incentive to master the knowledge that would make them capable citizens." (Lasch 1995, 11-12)

A key aspect of the populist triangle, relates to the ways in which the messages from leaders are transmitted to the base supporters. This is shown in Figure 7.1 in terms of the key nodes and networks through which those messages are transmitted and reinforced. Social media have served to enable more direct communication between leaders and their supporters, as indicated by President Trump's reliance on *Twitter* as a communications medium. In parallel, he has also sought to demonise and marginalise the mainstream media by labelling them as "fake news" or "lamestream" media, thereby effectively cutting off his supporters from those communications channels and directing them to those media that support the core message (see, Habgood-Coote 2018; Silverman 2017; Yates 2016). Block and Negrine (2017) provide a useful perspective on this issue as they see populism as:

> "a particular style of political communication because it is primarily an act of speech, as populist actors use words, signs, and images—forms of communi-cation—to connect with *the people* (the disenchanted, disadvantaged, ag-grieved groups...) and demonize the Other, usually the center-ground elite, or *the establishment.*" (p.179)

In that context, the messages around uncertainty need to be framed in a language that the various public groups can relate to rather than the "elaborated code" (Bernstein 1962; 1964) of the expert. Language be-comes, as a consequence of the different 'codes' used by experts, a per-ceived driver in the use of expert power in the communications pro-cess.

The ability to influence the views and behaviours of others has long been an important element associated with the use of power within organised societies. That power has traditionally rested with the state but this has been eroded as a function of the networked nature of society that has been empowered by changes in the communications process (Castells 2007). It has become even more problematic in the context of the so-called "age of anger" (Mishra 2017), in which populists have been able to disseminate the message to a global audience through social media. Castells (2007) argued that this shift in power is a function of the processes of globalisation that serve to diminish the role of the state in generating and maintaining a regulatory framework that can control information flows within an increasingly deregulated operating environment. Whilst state intervention around information flows clearly has a dark side, as evidenced by the use of propaganda during the 20th Century (Lumley 1933; O'Shaughnessy 2004; Stanley 2015), social media have created an almost unfettered mechanism for the dissemination of both misinformation and disinformation and empowered social groups in delivering their message to a wider audience and bypassing the mainstream media in the process. Here, Castells (2004) argued that:

> "Power does not reside in institutions, not even the state or large corporations. It is located in the networks that structure society." (p. 224)

Within a populist context, this power lies in the ability of key influencers to engage directly with their supporting base in order to communicate their message while, at the same time, undermining contradictory messages from other, more mainstream, sources who are labelled as part of the elite, or dismissed pejoratively as 'fake news'.

Within the context of the relationships shown in Figure 7.1, power can take multiple forms which include positional, economic, expert, and political forms among others. The populist context for debates, especially within the context of radical uncertainty, changes the dynamics of these conventional power relationships. This is particularly the case in terms of information flows which have traditionally been mediated through expert groups, largely via a top-down technocratic approach. Such a technocratic approach has not been without its criticism (Collingridge 1992; Collingridge & Reeve 1986a; b), and there has also been extensive debate around the role of expert judgement within the assessment of hazards, and especially in those areas where the burden of proof for safety has been problematic (see, for example, Fischer 1990; 2005; Smith 1990; Wynne 1989; 1996). Whilst there has been valid criticism around the boundaries of expert judgement, and particularly through the role of what has become known as 'citizen science' (Irwin 1995; 2001), there has still been an overarching view that an evidence-based approach to dealing with uncertainty remains a valid basis for assessing hazards in their multiple forms. However, populists can be seen to take a very different approach to the determination of valid evidence and cause-and-effect relationships are not always subjected to the requirements around test-retest validity that is required by a scientific approach. Herein lies a fundamental problem. If the argument that science is driven by ignorance and uncertainty (Firestein 2012) is accepted, then effective risk communication will often be unable to provide the clarity that is required as a response to a crisis. This is especially challenging in a public health crisis, where the uncertainty is high in the initial stages owing to the emergent nature of the problems. The scientific approach is also relatively slow, as it requires research that conforms to the test-retest validity requirements of the scientific method, which are usually achieved through the peer-review process or via clinical trials. Clearly, such constraints do not apply to those who espouse theories that are not grounded in a burden of proof. Within public health debates, the processes around risk communication and the nature of uncertainty are likely to be significant factors in shaping those second-order principles.

These second-order elements are also likely to prove particularly challenging under the conditions of radical uncertainty that invariably prevail within a crisis. Radical uncertainty (Kay & King 2020a; b; Roth 2009) has the potential to create a set of conditions in which the burden of proof required of expert judgements is compromised as it is difficult, if not impossible, to prove cause-and-effect relationships with the predictive validity that is required with a burden of proof. The reason for this can be found in the role played by emergence within complex socio-technical systems which impacts on the calculative practices used within risk analysis (Fischbacher-Smith 2010; Smith 2005). In the case of the Covid-19 pandemic, the interconnected nature of modern societies, combined with the highly infectious nature of the virus, ensured that the spread of Covid-19 was rapid. This was especially problematic in the mutated form of the virus that was identified in the UK in late 2020. The public health response to such an outbreak, in the absence of an effective and widely available vaccine, would normally be driven by a precautionary

approach designed to curtail the spread of infections. This would usually take the form of restrictions on social mixing and unnecessary
travel. Such constraints would impact on the economic performance
of those countries that advocated such restrictions which, in turn,
would impact on those sections of society that were already disenfranchised. This may have served to drive some of them to support a
economically-driven populist agenda. If the expert elites are going to
be ignored, and the will of the (virtuous and legitimate) people is to
prevail, then it raises questions about how that radical uncertainty is
to be managed without the insight provided by those with expertise
in a particular field. For populist leaders, this has the effect of leaving
the policy space open to infiltration by conspiratorial theories (Brown
2021; Ortega & Orsini 2020).

These second-order principles can also be considered to operate
within the context of the process of medical populism (see Lasco &
Curato 2019) and they provides a basis for considering some of the
drivers that underpin the three core elements of the populist triangle.
Of particular importance here are the ways in which uncertainty can
prove to be an important element in the populist narrative in allowing
the emergence of conspiratorial views as a means of addressing that
uncertainty, irrespective of their evidential validity (Argentino 2020;
BBC News 2020b). The relative importance of these second-order
principles is likely to be issues-based and, as a result, the strategies
and practices associated with them will need to be dynamic.

Covid-19 and the Emergence of Medical Populism

The core elements of populist approaches identified earlier also carry
over into the notion of medical populism. These include:

- The perceived importance of the wisdom of the people and
  especially those from within the in-group. This wisdom of the
  people is, however, selectively determined by populist leaders and is essentially drawn from those deemed to be within
  the in-group;
- A rejection of the views of the liberal elites who are deemed
  to be corrupt, highly mobile, and influenced by outside
  groups (often internationally orientated). In the case of

medical populism, these would include healthcare professionals, pharmaceutical companies, and policy makers;

- The importance of strong leaders and opinion shapers for populist groups. This is especially the case when those leaders are operating within an environmental setting that lends itself to a tendency towards authoritarianism. This is often framed as opposition to the established political elites.

- The importance of the majority view (that is, in a democratic context), but one that is often mediated through the notion of what is essentially a mono-cultural and, invariably, nationalistic perspective. This view was much in evidence after the 2020 US elections and the allegations of electoral fraud.

In addition to those elements, Lasco and colleagues (2020a; b; Lasco & Curato 2019; Lasco & Larson 2020) highlight a number of other issues that are important in shaping the nature of medical populism.

The first of these is the simplification of the problem space—in this case the underlying hazards that are associated with the pandemic and the implications that the virus has for healthcare provision. This was certainly self-evident in Trump's early proclamations on the virus as being akin to the 'flu and that it would disappear as the weather improved (Bump 2020; Milbank 2020). This claim was made despite the fact that Trump was allegedly briefed on the severity of the virus in early 2020, along with threat that it posed (Woodward 2020).

The first issue ties into Lasco's second element, which is that claims around knowledge from within the populist perspective may go against the more conventional, evidence-based, scientific views. In the case of the Covid-19 pandemic, this involved Trump's touting of untried and unproven medication hydroxychloroquine (Samuels & Kelly 2020) as a means of addressing the symptoms of the virus. Competing claims around treatment have had the effect of creating what has been described as an "infodemic" (Islam et al 2020).

The third element of medical populism is an extension of the more mainstream approaches to defining populism, namely that of forging division within society. In the case of medical populism, this involved President Trump going so far as to challenging the established government agencies responsible for the production of data when that information did not correspond with his own world-view (Bump 2020; Trump 2021e; f). Again, this can be seen to contribute to the challenges associated with the communication of uncertainty, the associated flows of information, and the validation of any evidence that is presented.

The final element outlined by Lasco and colleagues relates to the portrayal of a public health crisis as a form of drama. Again, this is often done by attacking the 'others' as being responsible while also seeing a process of virtue signalling by leaders in terms of their role in dealing with the crisis (Trump 2020a; e; l). The relationship between a crisis and its dramatic components also has some traction within the academic literature (Elliott, Harris, & Baron 2005; McDowell 2011). For example, Coleman (2013) argued that:

> "For a situation to be recognised in the way that a political leader wants it to be, it must be enacted in a particular way. The scene must be set—for scenes do not arrive with their own flavours or accounts of themselves. Turning a situation into a crisis entails a performative construction of meaning which relies not only upon words spoken, but tonal inflections, images, gestures and appeals to memory." (p. 330)

Clearly, Trump was more than capable of delivering such a performance as evidenced by his set piece speeches and his ability to work the crowd at his many rallies. In the case of Covid-19, much of this "performative construction of meaning" (Coleman 2013) was carried out by President Trump through social media, and especially in terms of the hazards associated with the virus, the potential mechanisms for treating its symptoms, and the production and deployment of the vaccine (Trump 2020a; l; 2021e; f). This notion of crisis-as-drama can also be seen to play out in the rallies that Trump held, and especially the one close to the White House on the January 6, 2021 at the same time that the senate was expected to recognise the electoral college votes (Kanno-Youngs & Rosenberg 2021). However, the notion of crisis is double-edged, as the potential for that crisis can be incubated by those very leaders who seek to dramatise it for personal gain (Turner 1976; 1978; 1994). There is an argument which suggests that Trump has incubated the problems that have come to the fore in the last years of his presidency (Owen 2018; Trump 2020p). The events of the 6th January could be seen as the culmination of that process as hubris began to shape Trump's decision-making.

Discussion

The first of the second-order drivers for populism outlined earlier, re-lates to the role of expertise and the nature of the evidence-base that is used in support of policies and practices. Given that experts are likely to form part of the elite group, then the means by which the evidence that they provide is analysed can lead many within the populist tribe to reject that information if it goes against their world-views. It will then be left to the trusted 'insiders' to provide the findings of their own 'research' and 'insights' to the group through their self-appointed role as "truth seekers" (Hill, Canniford, & Murphy 2020) and these 'citizen accounts' have been found to be influential within social media and particularly in the development of conspiratorial perspectives (Ahmed 2020). Such citizen accounts could be seen to represent the darker side of "citizen science" approaches, but without the rigour (and associated validation of information) that should come with any conventional citizen science approach around the provision of evidence (Irwin 1995; 2001; Wynne 1989). In these cases, it is likely that the networks through which those opinion shapers operate will be important both in terms of disseminating the message, but also countering the challenges made to their underpinning theories. In order to examine the context in which evidence is presented, it is important to consider the different layers in which expert advice is provided into the policy-making process. In order to explore the role of expertise and evidence, their role in the policy process can be contextualised by using a framework developed by Fischer (1980) and shown in a modified version of that framework in Figure 7.2.

Figure 7.2—Fischer's Policy Analysis Framework

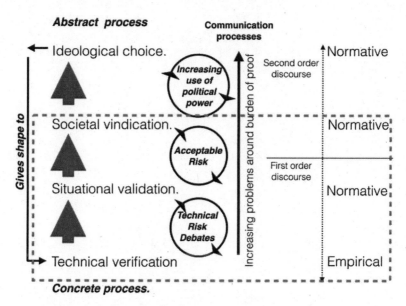

Source: Based on Fischer (1980; 2019)

The challenge of considering discourse within policy issues is that it takes place at multiple levels and between different groups, each of whom bring a different balance of evidence to bear on the problem. In the context of Trump's claims around the election, then it is clear that much of the information provided by his supporters is normative hearsay and seemingly unverifiable, at least in terms of the legal cases that have been brought. Within the context of Covid-19, then the issue becomes one of how the discourse, at the various levels in Figure 7.2, incorporates the expert judgements around the technicalities of the virus and the mitigation strategies that are used to deal with it, relative to the views of more citizen-based narratives. Part of the challenge here is with the nature of risk itself, especially when defined as measurable uncertainty (Knight 1921), and its acceptability by those who might be affected by the consequences of those hazards. Different interpretations of that uncertainty exist at multiple levels, and the balance between the various forms of potential impact becomes an issue at the local level. In terms of the role played by evidence in the policy process, then this discourse will move from the concrete to the more abstract, or ideological. The core question is whether the ideological elements shape the supposed concrete, empirically-grounded activities that are used to calculate risk. As the discourse moves from the concrete, more technocratic level, then the emphasis shifts from the calculative practices used within risk analysis to the more normative-based discussions around the acceptability (and accuracy) of those calculated risks. It is here that questions are often raised about the technical validity of expert judgement, especially under conditions of radical forms of uncertainty.

Part of the problem here is that risk is seen to be a "conceptual pollutant" (Dowie 1999) in that it means different things to different people. Risk can be seen to be composed of two elements—probability and consequence—associated with a particular hazard. Risk analysis, which represents the series of calculative practices that are undertaken to determine risk, works well for those failures that are random in nature and where probabilities can be determined that have a robust degree of predictive validity. As such, risk analysis is effective when used in the analysis of the failure of mechanical components, where those probabilities can be aggregated upwards to calculate an overall sense of the likely failure and its associated consequences. Its predictive capabilities start to break down when those probabilities are not random, or where human actors play a role in shaping the nature of the failure. Given that risk is "measurable uncertainty" (Knight 1921), then the ability to measure those probabilities and associated consequences in an accurate manner is critical. Here, Knight, outlined three forms of measuring uncertainty—*a priori,* statistically-based, and expert-determined—with the latter being seen as the weakest of the three in terms of predictive validity. At the outset, therefore, there is scope for challenging those technical determinations of risk where the assessment is based on the views of experts and the associated failures within those systems are not deemed to be random.

The starting point in Figure 7.2 is with a consideration of the nature of evidence that supports any analysis of risk and this is shown in terms of the technical debates that can take place around hazards such as the Covid-19 virus. At the concrete level, Fischer argues that there is a technical verification process in which debates around the nature and quantification of particular hazards would occur. It is here that expertise would be brought to bear on particular issues that would require an evidential basis in order for those empirical perspectives to be verified. Whilst much of this discourse would be typically carried out by those deemed to have expertise in a particular technical field, it has also been an area where citizen science has been utilised in terms of burden-of-proof debates. The discourse between expert groups has also been subject to debates around the role played by other non-technical interests in shaping the nature of that discourse (Collingridge & Reeve 1986a; b; Fischer; 2005; Smith; 1990; Wynne; 1989; 1996). Within a populist environment, it is likely that such expert judgements will be dismissed if the assessments run counter to the dominant ideology of the group and those key influencers that the group relies upon. Again, this was evident in the pandemic, as Trump often contradicted his technical advisors on some key issues that were important to his base of support. These included, mask wearing and the possible treatments that could be used for Covid-19, as well as the statistics provided on infection and death rates (*BBC News* 2020a; Brooks 2020; Trump 2020i; 2021e).

Under normal policy conditions, the technical calculations of risk would then lead to a process of what Fischer (1980) terms "situational validation". Here, the assessments of hazard would be tested in a local context, often drawing upon the evidence provided by local groups. This would be shaped through the processes by which emergence within systems generates conditions that may not have been considered in the earlier processes of technical verification. Much of the debate around vaccinations takes place in this context, as anecdotal evidence is invariably provided to undermine claims of safety associated with a vaccine. The anti-vaccination movement in the USA was supported by Andrew Wakefield who had been struck off in the UK by the General Medical Council but who was seemingly rehabilitated in the US as a leading member of the anti-vaxxer movement (Bricker & Justice 2019; Deer 2011a; b; 2020; Hussain et al 2018). Whilst many of the anti-vaxxers' claims can be refuted by the provision of evidence, the lack of trust in the scientific elites will impact on that process, especially for those individuals who subscribe to conspiratorial views. Many of these discussions will also take place outside of the empirically-driven processes of risk analysis. Because emergent conditions may not have been considered as part of the analytical process, this allows critics to present a counter-argument about the nature of the hazard. This marks the boundary of the processes around first-order discourse outlined by Fischer (1980) and moves the discussion into the more normative processes around social vindication and ideological choice.

These second-order discussions centre on the acceptable nature of those calculated risks and the trade-offs that are made between the interventions made to manage the hazards and their consequences. Within the Covid-19 example, the issues of mass vaccinations, mask wearing, and the lock-down of cities or, in some cases, whole countries have been subject to considerable debate and disagreement, especially in terms of core ideological differences. It is within this part of the framework that conspiracy theories around the nature of those hazards can also begin to gain traction. Social media that speak directly to sections of the population can ensure that these conspiracies can often go unchecked within their social groups and their acceptance or rejection will be shaped by ideological choice, thereby making the process inherently 'political' in its nature (Argentino 2020; *BBC News* 2020b; Goodman & Carmichael 2020b). In this context, the technical aspects of risk are often discounted, and other interests can shape the role that information can play in the discourse (Adekola, Fischbacher-Smith, & Fischbacher-Smith 2019; Collingridge & Reeve 1986b; Jackson 2012). Within a populist political environment, this relationship between ideological choice and the ways in which expertise is shaped by processes around second-order discourse becomes critical to the framing of medical populism. This is especially important as ideological choice feeds directly into the processes of situational validation to allow the outright rejection of any technical verification process in favour of the more ideologically shaped, and inherently normative, evidence provided by the inside group.

Within the framework set out in Figure 7.2, the issue of communication plays a significant role in shaping the ways in which information is shared within formal and informal networks. It is also a function of the trust that is placed in those individuals and groups who act as information nodes within those populist networks. The language used here is also important and can serve to reinforce the problems associated with the failure to accept the views of scientists.

Bernstein (1962; 1964) argued that the language used to communicate is of critical importance in ensuring the development of understanding. He argued that there were two ways of codifying information—the elaborated code (the language of the expert) and the more restricted code of the general population. Again, this could be seen to play into the criticism of the elites within society as the language that is used to communicate does not always resonate with all sections of the population. Populist leaders will seek to use language that is more easily accessible and do so in a way that undermines the comments made by more elite groups. Fortune and Peters (1995) set out a communications framework which states that for information to be effectively communicated then the encoder of the message should use the same 'rules for systems use' as the decoder of the message. This will minimise the effects of system noise within the communications channel and it will also serve to reinforce the core ideology by providing a degree of immunity to competing messages (particularly those that are codified in a different way, and especially those from within the expert elites and the mainstream media). These rules for systems use can be seen to incorporate the codes that Bernstein outlines, but they also include the channels through which leaders can communicate. One of the factors surrounding Trump's initial popularity was his ability to communicate directly to his supporters. In particular, his use of *Twitter* as a means of by-passing conventional political communication channels was also seen to give him more direct access to his base. The combination of new channels of communication and the synergistic relationships provided by highly focussed news channels has led to claims that a process termed 'disinformatics' is seen to exist:

> "...at the intersection of technology, propaganda, and miscreants. It's the glue that holds together modern faux news outlets, AM talk radio, *Twitter* storms, and sundry other sorts of sociopolitical babble." (Berghel 2018, 89)

The notion of "disinformatics" sits at the core of many of the challenges around the public responses to the pandemic. In many respects the pandemic, which should be a public health issue, has become so politicised that any attempts at the 'seeking of truth' are framed through the political lenses provided by key influencers—many of whom have a strong ideological perspective on the nature of the problems being considered and, in some cases, who make claims without a clear evidential basis. In the process of truth-seeking the burden of proof has been relegated to a subsidiary position.

It is clear from many of the conflicts around both Covid-19 and the outcome of the US Presidential election in 2020 that there is often little in the way of trust between opposing groups and a reluctance on the part of many to accept evidence that contradicts their world-views on the issues. While unwillingness to fact-check or to accept evidence that contradicts a group's world-views can transcend the ideological and theological spectrum, it is clear that those at the extremes of those perspectives are often only willing to accept evidence that meets their interpretation of reality. Berghel (2017) observes that the tribalists have no interest in fact-checking and that it acts as:

> "as a kind of rhetorical tear-gas—something painful and to be avoided at all costs." (p. 113)

Given that populist leaders, as well as their followers, will invariably share the same tribalist mentality, then it will generate a self-reinforcing relationship around the rejection of certain forms of fact and evidence that serves to protect the core views of the tribe from external challenge and reinforces their core views in the process.

Radical uncertainty leaves open the prospect for different groups to lay claims about the nature of risk, and especially around the cause-and-effect relationships in which the burden of proof and the associated predictive validity of those calculative practices are open to debate. In this context, the relatively slow pace of science in terms of providing quick answers to complex problems, leaves open the possibility for alternative theories and narratives to proliferate and for popularist commentators to attack the validity of the scientific approach because of the time needed for the scientific method to function effectively (see, for example, Fischbacher-Smith 2013; Roth 2009). It is within this environment that medical populism generates problems around the communication and acceptability of risk, the nature of evidence within the determination of acceptability, and the role played by expertise in dealing with complex multi-level technical issues.

The final element in the development of the second-order processes in Fig 7.2 concerns the role played by crises in shaping both the nature of, and cohesion within, the in-group by providing a mechanism by which the "people" can be divided into its tribal elements.

While the crisis could be externally generated, as in the case of Covid-19, it can also be generated by populist leaders as a means of enraging and energising their core base. President Trump, for example, continually spoke of Covid-19 as the "China Virus" (Trump 2021e), often weaving the response to the virus into both an attack on his political opponents and the problems associated with the economy (Trump 2020a; i; l). On the warroom.org website, Steve Bannon reportedly claimed that the Covid-19 pandemic was "a biological Chernobyl" and accused the Chinese Government of "premeditated murder" over the virus (*War Room* 2020). This had the effect of moving responsibility for the crisis to a third party, thereby generating a sense of victimhood within the base and unifying them against an external agent. It is also possible for the populist leader to generate a crisis as a means of ensuring that they are also part of the in-group and, therefore, a victim due to the attacks by the external others (Trump 2020c; h; m; n). Lasch (1984), for example, has highlighted the role of the "trivialization of crisis" within a societal setting that sees life as a "succession of crises" (p. 64) and argues that there is a growing sense of victimisation within elements of society that have been seized upon by politicians who act on behalf of those victims, because they believe that they too are subject to victimisation in one form or another. The result has been the development of resentment across many societal groupings that have led to a sense of marginalisation and anger (Mishra 2017). Added to this, is a sense that the elites within society are so far removed from other segments of the population (Lasch 1995) that it is easy to see how this has built a platform for the development of populist movements.

Conclusions

The Covid-19 pandemic has highlighted the darker side of the move towards a post-modernist perspective on the nature of evidence and the role of science within the decision-making process. The erosion of faith in science and expertise can be seen as being in a synergistic relationship with populist political movements and the effects of that toxic combination have been in evidence during the Covid-19 pandemic. The failure to accept validated evidence has allowed for less scientific views to gain traction within elements of public discourse, and this has led to the radicalisation of parts of society who believe the claims of populist leaders over the repeated assurances of public officials. In many respects, the crisis of trust in expertise that has surrounding some of the discourse around the Covid-19 pandemic has been incubating for a considerable period of time. It has occurred as a function of the erosion of trust in empirically-grounded science, and populist politicians have occupied the fractured ground of ambiguity that has been generated as a consequence. The emergence of conspiracy theories has been both a function of this process and also a factor in the generation of that mistrust.

This chapter has sought to provide some insights into the unwillingness of sections of the population to accept medical evidence during the Covid-19 pandemic. This is not simply a function of the nature of that particular crisis but it can be considered as an extension of a wider anti-science movement that has developed in some sections of society over the last twenty years. The failure to address that growing movement has both contributed to the febrile conditions into which the crisis unfolded but has also compounded the problems facing organisations in terms of responding to that crisis. It raises some serious concerns about the extent to which trust in state-based organisations has been eroded and it is difficult to see a simple solution to this problem. Lasch (1995) had warned of the problem of the elites losing touch with society and the impact it could generate. This breakdown has given scope for populist movements to reject many state organisations and their expertise as part of that supposed self-serving elite group. Trump's stated claim of wanting to "drain the swamp" as part of his 2016 election campaign played into that scepticism and has subsequently built on it.

As the conclusions to this chapter were being written in January 2021, a significant number of Trump supporters had breached security at the Capitol building in one of the saddest examples of the dark side of populism. This followed a speech in which Trump was felt to have encouraged his supporters to march on Capitol Hill and make their voices heard, along with a tweet in which he encouraged his Vice-President Mike Pence to "decertify" the election result (Trump 2021c). This was despite the fact that, constitutionally, VP Pence had no authority to overturn the election results.

The eventual response from Trump to the violence, in a video that was inevitably tweeted, asked for calm, but reiterated his claims of a stolen election as he told his supporters to go home. There was no condemnation of the violence in the video. By reinforcing the message of electoral fraud, Trump was seen to continue to undermine the trust that some of his supporters have in government institutions. In response to that tweet, *Twitter* blocked Trump's account for 12 hours before suspending his account indefinitely (*Twitter Inc* 2021).

The events of January 6 marked a low point in the populist culture in the USA, and followed the events on Capitol Hill followed on from over four years of unsubstantiated claims and conspiracy theories. At the same time, the US Centers for Disease Control was reporting 1,526,460 new cases of Covid-19 in the 7 days preceding the 6th January.

The total deaths, reported on the same date, were 356,005 across the USA. The pandemic had taken a back seat in the narrative of the final stages of the Trump presidency to make way for the fraudulent claims of election theft.

The initial aim for this concluding section was to explore possible points of intervention into the dislocation that clearly exists between populists and other sections of society, and especially with the scientific and expert communities. The events of the 6th January incursion in Washington DC have highlighted the challenges that elected officials face in addressing the challenges presented by those extremist views that have flourished within some groups. To echo President Biden's comments, in the aftermath of the riot, the USA had clearly entered a "dark moment", but that transition into darkness had taken place over a period of time. The inflammatory comments of Trump were the trigger that exposed the underlying malaise that had fermented in a populist environment. Moving away from that darkness will not be a simple or a rapid process. It will involve a major change in the discourse that takes place in public life as well as in the worldviews of significant numbers of people. The starting point has to be an attempt to repair the damage caused by the erosion of trust in science, the nature of evidence, and its validation. This requires people to recognise that whilst science is driven by uncertainty, it does not mean that it is a flawed process but that it adheres to the principles of test-retest validity in an attempt to understand the complex problems that society faces. This not only requires a shift in the ways that we teach the principles of science, but also that we move away from the disdain that some people have about the agencies of government. While we need to encourage open debate around issues, rather than constrain them or cancel the people who engage in those discussions, that discourse has to recognise the importance of the verification of evidence in terms of a burden of proof. This will require that the rhetoric of fake news and alternative facts comes to an end.

As a final comment, and to illustrate the extent of the challenge facing those who oppose populist cultures, it is worth highlighting the tweet made by Trump after the Senate building was finally secured by law enforcement. Trump tweeted[5] that:

> "These are the things and events that happen when a sacred landslide election victory is so unceremoniously & viciously stripped away from great patriots who have been badly & unfairly treated for so long. Go home with love & in peace. Remember this day forever!" (Trump 2021g)

The protesters who were earlier described by Trump as being "special" after they stormed the Senate were now being referred to as "great patriots" who have been "badly & unfairly treated" by unnamed others. More than anything, this captures the essence of a populist culture and the challenge that exists for all to overcome its toxic nature.

There are a number of vulnerabilities that are generated within a populist environment, especially during a period of great uncertainty, and which have the potential to generate significant harm unless they are addressed. In essence, these issues relate to how humans collectively may incubate the potential for crisis by dismissing evidence that does not fit within their individual or group world-views. These identifiable vulnerabilities may be summarised as potential threats or risk exposures as follows, and which are assessed further in chapter 10:

Societal Risk Exposures

Risk Exposure 1: Loss of Trust in Science Leading to Bad Policy and Mass Harm

Continued promulgation of conspiratorial views may further undermine trust in agencies of government, especially under conditions of great uncertainty. Evidence-based policies may be marginalised or

---

5   This tweet was subsequently removed by *Twitter*.

abandoned in such threat areas as climate change and pandemics, where denial of scientific evidence and failure to act promptly may result in catastrophe for the planet and humankind.

Risk Exposure 2: Harmful Impact of Early Warnings Denial

Denial of global risk exposures, and the belittling of those who raise valid concerns about scientific evidence, will prevent society from dealing with the early warnings of catastrophe. Ironically, many of those who would deny the existence of such threats as climate change or Covid-19 are willing to accept conspiracy theories that have a much weaker evidential base.

Risk Exposure 3: Populist Fantasies Dominating Political Agendas and Decisions

Continued populist attacks on the validity of established scientific expertise, combined with a readiness to accept non-experts who claim superior knowledge, are likely to generate a toxic culture in which populist manipulators can shape and dominate the nature of public discourse e.g. on Covid-19, climate change. The history of 1930s fascist dictatorships should have provided sufficient contemporary insight to stop populist imaginations dominating political agendas and decision-making. History tells us that hegemonic 'personality cults' invariably end badly.

Organisational Risk Exposures

Risk Exposure 1: Inadequate Public Accountability of Digital Platforms for Disseminating Harmful Information and Fake Conspiracy Theories

Short-term gains for some organisations can have longer-term detriment for society. This requires greater public accountability of those organisations that propagate lies, hate, and discord generated by some populist leaders. Freedom of speech is vital but does not extend to the freedom to disseminate harmful assertions, incitement to violence, or claims that cannot be supported. Social media, Internet and traditional media outlets therefore have a particular responsibility to ensure that they meet the highest standards of probity. Both self-regulation and public accountability of such organisations are thus far inadequate.

Risk Exposure 2: Inadequate Self-Regulation by Privileged Elites on Claims to Expertise

Privileged opinion-shaping elites need to be held to a high governance and probity standard. In making statements on risk exposures (e.g. Covid-19, climate change), such individuals should not be claiming expertise for which they have inadequate verifiable qualifications or experience. Universities also need to hold academic staff accountable if they fail to conform to such self-regulation and the standards of research integrity. Both self-regulation and institutional accountability of such elites are thus far inadequate.

Risk Exposure 3: Inadequate Systems for Coping with Uncertainty and Risk

Tutored knowledge on uncertainties and risks is not universal or even widespread. This weakness is exploited by those seeking to spread extreme ideology via conspiracy theories, misinformation, lies and hate-filled propaganda, together with incitement to insurrection and violence. Therefore, in order to evaluate uncertainty and threats alleged by radical-right sources, organisations and their key personnel need to acquire relevant knowledge and skills, including evaluation of evidence and burden of proof. Thus far, few organisations possess a robust methodology and systems for coping with such uncertainty and risk.

References

Adekola, J., Fischbacher-Smith, D., and Fischbacher-Smith, M. 2019. "Light Me Up: Power and Expertise in Risk Communication and Policy-Making in the e-Cigarette Health Debates". *Journal of Risk Research*, 22(10): 1294-1308.

Ahmed, W. 2020. "'Film Your Hospital'—the Anatomy of a COVID-19 Conspiracy Theory". *The Conversation*. October 15, 2020. [accessed January 5, 2021].

Argentino, M.-A. 2020. "QAnon Conspiracy Theories About the Coronavirus Pandemic are a Public Health Threat". *The Conversation*. April 8, 2020. https://theconversation.com/qano

n-conspiracy-theories-about-the-coronavirus-pandemic-are-a-public-health-threat-135515.

Bashir, M. 2021. "George Floyd Death: Trump's Church Visit Shocks Religious Leaders". *BBC News*. https://www.bbc.co.uk/news/world-us-canada-52890650. [accessed January 10, 2021).

BBC News. 2020a. "Coronavirus: 'I'm All For Masks,' Says Trump in Change of Tone". *BBC News*. July 2, 2020. https://www.bbc.co.uk/news/world-us-canada-53258792 [accessed January 10, 2021].

BBC News. 2020b. "Ofcom: Covid-19 5G Theories are 'Most Common' Misinformation". *BBC News (Technology)*. April 21, 2020. https://www.bbc.co.uk/news/technology-52370616) [accessed January 10, 2021).

Beaumont, P. 2020. "Steve Bannon Banned by Twitter for Calling for Fauci Beheading". *The Guardian*. November 6, 2020. https://www.theguardian.com/us-news/2020/nov/06/steve-bannon-banned-by-twitter-for-calling-for-fauci-beheading. [accessed December 5, 2020].

Berghel, H. 2017. "Alt-News and Post-Truths in the "Fake News" Era". *Computer*, 50(4): 110-114.

Berghel, H. 2018. "Disinformatics: The Discipline Behind Grand Deceptions". *Computer*, 51(1): 89-93.

Bernstein, B. 1962. "Social Class, Linguistic Codes and Grammatical Elements". *Language and Speech*, 5(4): 221-240.

Bernstein, B. 1964. "Elaborated and Restricted Codes: Their Social Origins and Some Consequences". *American Anthropologist*, 66(6_PART2): 55-69.

Bleau, H. 2021. "GOP Senators Including Cruz, Blackburn to 'Reject the Electors from Disputed States' January 6". *Breitbart*. January 2, 2021. https://www.breitbart.com/politics/2021/01/02/gop-senators-including-cruz-blackburn-to-reject-the-electors-from-disputed-states-january-6/. [accessed January 3, 2021].

Block, E. and Negrine, R. 2017. "The Populist Communication Style: Toward a Critical Framework". *International Journal of Communication*, 11: 178-197.

Bricker, B. and Justice, J. 2019. "The Postmodern Medical Paradigm: A Case Study of Anti-MMR Vaccine Arguments". *Western Journal of Communication*, 83(2): 172-189.

Brooks, B. 2020. "Like the Flu? Trump's Coronavirus Messaging Confuses Public, Pandemic Researchers Say". *Reuters*. March 13, 2020. https://www.reuters.com/article/us-health-coronavirus-mixed-messages/like-the-flu-trumps-coronavirus-messaging-confuses-public-pandemic-researchers-say-idUSKBN2102GY. [accessed January 10, 2021].

Brown, E. 2021. "Voting Machine Company Sues Pro-Trump Lawyer Powell". *The Washington Post*. January 9, 2021: A3.

Brubaker, R. 2017. "Why Populism?" *Theory and Society*, 46(5): 357-385.

Bump, P. 2020. "210,000 Deaths Later, Trump Reverts to Comparing the Coronavirus to the Flu". *The Washington Post*. October 6, 2020. https://www.washingtonpost.com/politics/2020/10/06/210000-deaths-later-trump-reverts-comparing-coronavirus-flu/. [accessed January 5, 2021].

Castells, M. 2004. "Afterword: Why Networks Matter". In *Network Logic: Who governs in an interconnected world?* edited by H. McCarthy, P. Miller, and P. Skidmore, 221-225. London: DEMOS.

Castells, M. 2007. "Communication, Power and Counter-Power in the Network Society". *International Journal of Communication*, 1: 238-266.

Coleman, S. 2013. "How to Make a Drama Out of a Crisis". *Political Studies Review*, 11(3): 328-335.

Collingridge, D. 1992. *The Management of Scale: Big Organizations, Big Decisions, Big Mistakes*. London: Routledge.

Collingridge, D., and Reeve, C. 1986a. "Science and Policy–Why the Marriage Is So Unhappy". *Bulletin of Science, Technology & Society*, 6(4): 356-372.

Collingridge, D., and Reeve, C. 1986b. *Science Speaks to Power: the Role of Experts in Policy-Making*. London: Francis Pinter.

Collins, K., and LeBlanc, P. 2020. "Trump Fires Director of Homeland Security Agency who had Rejected President's Election Consiracy Theories". *CNN Politics*. https://edition.cnn.com/2020/11/17/politics/chris-krebs-fired-by-trump/index.html. [accessed January 1, 2020].

de la Torre, C. 2015. "Introduction: Power to the People? Populism, Insurrections, Democratization". In *The Promise and Perils of*

Populism. Global Perspectives, (Kindle Edition), edited by C. de la Torre. Lexington, Kentucky: The University Press of Kentucky.

Deer, B. 2011a. "How the Case Against the MMR Vaccine was Fixed". *BMJ*, 342: c5347.

Deer, B. 2011b. "How the Vaccine Crisis was Meant to Make Money". *BMJ*, 342: 136-142.

Deer, B. 2020. *The Doctor who Fooled the World. Andrew Wakesfield's War on Vaccines*. London: Scribe.

Devine, C., O'Sullivan, D., and Scannell, K. 2020. "Twitter Permanently Suspends Steve Bannon Account After Talk of Beheading". *CNN*. https://edition.cnn.com/2020/11/05/tech/steve-bannon-twitter-permanent-suspension/index.html. [accessed January 4, 2021].

Dikötter, F. 2020. *How to Be a Dictator: The Cult of Personality in the Twentieth Century*. London: Bloomsbury Publishing.

Dowie, J. 1999. "Communication for Better Decisions: Not About 'Risk'". *Health, Risk & Society*, 1(1): 41-53.

Eatwell, R., and Goodwin, M. 2018. *National Populism. The Revolt Against Liberal Democracy*. London: Pelican.

Egan, L. 2020. "Trump Says Some State Orders are 'Too Tough', Stands by 'LIBERATE' Tweets Encouraging Anti-Lockdown Groups". *NBCNews*. April 17, 2020. https://www.nbcnews.com/politics/donald-trump/trump-encourages-anti-lockdown-group-oppose d-stay-home-order-minnesota-n1186331. [accessed January 10, 2021].

Elliott, D., Harris, K., and Baron, S. 2005. "Crisis Management and Services Marketing". *Journal of Services Marketing*, 19(5): 336-345.

Firestein, S. 2012. *Ignorance. How it Drives Science*. Oxford: Oxford University Press.

Fischbacher-Smith, D. 2010. "Beyond the Worse Case Scenario. 'Managing' the Risks of Extreme Events". *Risk Management: An International Journal*, 12(1): 1-8.

Fischbacher-Smith, D. 2015. "Through a Glass Darkly: Expertise, Evidence, and the Management of Uncertainty". *Risk Management*, 17(4): 352-372.

Fischer, F. 1980. *Politics, Values, and Public Policy: The Problem of Methodology*. Boulder, CO: Westview Press.

Fischer, F. 1990. *Technocracy and the Politics of Expertise*. Newbury Park, CA: Sage.

Fischer, F. 2005. "Are Scientists Irrational? Risk Assessment in Practical Reason". In *Science and Citizens. Globalization and the Challenge of Engagement*, edited by M. Leach, I. Scoones, and B. Wynne, 54-65. London: Zed Books.

Fischer, F. 2019. Private communication.

Fortune, J., and Peters, G. 1995. *Learning from Failure—The Systems Approach*. Chichester, UK: John Wiley and Sons.

Garner, A. 2021. "Trump Pressures GOP Official in Ga. to 'Find' Votes". *The Washington Post*. January 4, 2021. A1 and A4.

Goodman, J., and Carmichael, F. 2020a. "The Coronavirus Pandemic 'Great Reset' Theory and a False Vaccine Claim Bebunked". *BBC News—Reality Check*. November 22, 2020. https://www.bbc.co.uk/news/55017002. [accessed January 10, 2021].

Goodman, J., and Carmichael, F. 2020b. "Coronavirus: Bill Gates 'Microchip' Conspiracy Theory and Other Vaccine Claims Fact-Checked". *BBC News*. May 29, 2020.

Gove, M. 2016. "'Experts' Like Carney Must Curb their Arrogance". *The Times*. October 21, 2016. Page 27.

Habgood-Coote, J. 2018. "The Term 'Fake News' is Doing Great Harm". *The Conversation*. July 27, 2018. https://theconversation.com/the-term-fake-news-is-doing-great-harm-100406.   [accessed January 5, 2021].

Harford, T. 2020. "We Will Not Understand Covid Until We Give Up Debating It". *Prospect Magazine*. October 2, 2020. https://www.prospectmagazine.co.uk/magazine/coronavirus-covid-debate-culture-war-boris-johnson. [accessed December 5, 2020].

Hill, T., Canniford, R., and Murphy, S. 2020. "Why 5G Conspiracy Theories Prosper During the Coronavirus Pandemic". *The Conversation*. April 9, 2020. https://theconversation.com/why-5g-conspiracy-theories-prosper-during-the-coronavirus-pandemic-136019 [accessed January 5, 2021].

Hussain, A., Ali, S., Ahmed, M., et al. 2018. "The Anti-Vaccination Movement: A Regression in Modern Medicine". *Cureus*, 10(7): e2919-e2919.

Inglehart, R., and Norris, P. 2016. *Trump, Brexit, and the Rise of Populism: Economic Have-Nots and Cultural Backlash*. HKS

Faculty Research Working Paper (RWP16-026). Boston, MA: Harvard Kennedy School.

Irwin, A. 1995. *Citizen Science. A Study of People, Expertise and Sustainable Development*. London: Routledge.

Irwin, A. 2001. "Constructing the Scientific Citizen: Science and Democracy in the Biosciences". *Public Understanding of Science*, 10(1): 1-18.

Islam, M. S., Sarkar, T., Khan, S. H., et al. 2020. "COVID-19–Related Infodemic and Its Impact on Public Health: A Global Social Media Analysis". *The American Journal of Tropical Medicine and Hygiene*, 103(4): 1621.

Jackson, S. 2012. "Black Box Arguments and Accountability of Experts to the Public". In *Between Scientists and Citizens: Proceedings of a Conference at Iowa State University, June 1-2, 2012*, edited by J. Goodwin. Ames, IA: Great Plains Society for the Study of Argumentation.

Jolley, D., and Lamberty, P. 2020. "Coronavirus is a Breeding Ground for Conspiracy Theories—Here's Why That's a Serious Problem". *The Conversation*. February 28, 2020. https://theconversation. com/coronavirus-is-a-breeding-ground-for-conspiracy-theorie s-heres-why-thats-a-serious-problem-132489. [accessed July 22, 2020].

Kanno-Youngs, Z., and Rosenberg, M. 2021. "Washington Gearing up for Pro-Trump Protesters". *New York Times*. January 6, 2021. Page A13. https://www.nytimes.com/2021/2001/2005/us/po litics/dc-protests.html?action=click&module=Spotlight&pgtype =Homepage. [accessed January 6, 2021].

Kay, J., and King, M. 2020a. "The Radical Uncertainties of Coronavirus". *Prospect*, May 2020(277). https://www.prospect magazine.co.uk/magazine/coronavirus-model-uncertainty-kay-king. [accessed July 28, 2020].

Kay, J., and King, M. 2020b. *Radical Uncertainty. Decision-Making for an Unknowable Future*. London: The Bridge Street Press.

Kelion, L. 2020. "Coronacirus: Tech Firms Summoned Over 'Crackpot' 5G Conspiracies". *BBC News (Technology)*. April 5, 2020. https:// www.bbc.co.uk/news/technology-52172570. [accessed January 10, 2021].

Kennedy, J. 2019. "Populist Politics and Vaccine Hesitancy in Western Europe: An Analysis of National-Level Data". *European Journal of Public Health*, 29(3): 512-516.

Kim, S. M., Dawsey, J., DeBonis, M., et al. 2021. "Increasing Chorus Pushes to Impeach. President Faces Possible Criminal Liability in Riot". *The Washington Post*. January 9, 2021. A1, A7.

Knight, F. H. 1921. *Risk, Uncertainty and Profit* (2006 reprint). Mineola, NY: Dover Publications Inc.

Kornfield, M., and Jacobs, S. 2021. "As U.S. Death Toll Surpasses 350,000, Trump Calls Count 'Far Exaggerated'". *The Washington Post*. January 4, 2021. A8.

Lasch, C. 1984. *The Minimal Self. Psychic Survival in Troubled Times*. New York: W.W. Norton & Company.

Lasch, C. 1991. *The True and Only Heaven. Progress and Its Critics*. New York: W.W. Norton & Company.

Lasch, C. 1995. *The Revolt of the Elites and the Betrayal of Democracy*. New York: W.W. Norton & Company.

Lasco, G. 2020a. "Challenging World Leaders Amid Medical Populism". *The Lancet*, 396(10265): 1802-1803.

Lasco, G. 2020b. "Medical Populism and the COVID-19 Pandemic". *Global Public Health*, 15(10): 1417-1429.

Lasco, G., and Curato, N. 2019. "Medical Populism". *Social Science & Medicine*, 221: 1-8.

Lasco, G., and Larson, H. J. 2020. "Medical Populism and Immunisation Programmes: Illustrative Examples and Consequences for Public Health". *Global Public Health*, 15(3): 334-344.

LeBlanc, P., and Marquardt, A. 2020. "Election Officials, Including Federal Government, Contradict Trump's Voter-Fraud Conspiracy Theories". *CNN Politics*. November 13, 2020. https://edition.cnn.com/2020/11/12/politics/2020-election-trump-voter-conspiracies/index.html. [accessed January 1, 2021].

Lipton, E. 2021. "Trump Call to Georgia Might Violate State and Federal Law". *New York Times*. January 4, 2021. A16. [accessed January 16, 2021].

Lumley, F. E. 1933. *The Propaganda Menace*. London, England: Century/Random House UK.

Matthews, W. J. 1998. "Let's Get Real: The Fallacy of Post-Modernism". *Journal of Theoretical and Philosophical Psychology*, 18(1): 16-32.

McDowell, L. 2011. "Making a Drama Out of a Crisis: Representing Financial Failure, or a Tragedy in Five Acts". *Transactions of the Institute of British Geographers*, 36(2): 193-205.

McNamara, A. 2021. "Twitter Suspends Trump Allies Michael Flynn and Syndey Powell for Sharing QAnon Content". *CBS News*. January 8, 2021. https://www.cbsnews.com/news/twitter-sus pends-trump-allies-michael-flynn-and-sidney-powell-qanon-content/. [accessed January 10, 2021].

Milbank, D. 2020. "The New Season of Trump's Pandemic Reality Show is Headed for Early Cancellation". *The Washington Post*. July 22, 2020. https://www.washingtonpost.com/opinions/20 20/07/21/new-season-trumps-pandemic-reality-show-is-head ed-early-cancellation/. [accessed January 5, 2021].

Mishra, P. 2017. *Age of Anger. A History of the Present* (2018 ed.). London: Penguin Books.

Mudde, C. 2004. "The Populist Zeitgeist". *Government and Opposition*, 39(4): 541-563.

Mudde, C., and Kaltwasser, C. R. 2017. *Populism. A Very Short Introduction*. Oxford: Oxford University Press.

Müller, J.-W. 2017. *What is Populism?* London: Penguin Books.

Nakamura, D. 2021. "Amid Brazen Election Assault, Trump Critics Warn of a Coup". *The Washington Post*, Wednesday 6th January 2021. A8.

Norris, P., and Inglehart, R. 2019. *Cultural Backlash: Trump, Brexit, and Authoritarian Populism*. Cambridge: Cambridge University Press

O'Shaughnessy, N. J. 2004. *Politics and Propaganda: Weapons of Mass Seduction*. Manchester: Manchester University Press.

Ortega, F., and Orsini, M. 2020. "Governing COVID-19 Without Government in Brazil: Ignorance, Neoliberal Authoritarianism, and the Collapse of Public Health Leadership". *Global Public Health*, 15(9): 1257-1277.

Owen, D. 2018. *Hubris: The Road to Donald Trump. Power, Populism, Narcissism*. York, England: Methuen.

Peiser, J. 2020. "Twitter Bans Steve Bannon for Video Suggesting Violence Against Fauci, FBI Director Wray". *The Washington Post*. https://www.washingtonpost.com/nation/2020/11/06/

twitter-bannon-beheaded-fauci-wray/. [accessed January 4, 2021].

Rodrigo, C. M. 2021. "Twitter Permanently Suspends Michael Flynn, Sidney Powell and Others". *The Hill*. January 8, 2021. https://thehill.com/policy/technology/533424-twitter-permanently-suspends-michael-flynn-sidney-powell-and-others. [accessed January 10, 2021].

Rosenau, P. 1992. "Modern and Post-Modern Science: Some Contrasts". *Review (Fernand Braudel Center)*, 15(1): 49-89.

Roth, W.-M. 2009. "Radical Uncertainty in Scientific Discovery Work". *Science, Technology, & Human Values*, 34(3): 313-336.

Samuels, E., and Kelly, M. 2020. "How False Hope Spread About Hydroxychloroquine to Treat COVID-19-and the Consequences that Followed". *The Washington Post*. April 13, 2020. https://www.washingtonpost.com/politics/2020/04/13/how-false-hope-spread-about-hydroxychloroquine-its-consequences/. [accessed January 5, 2021].

Silverman, C. 2017. "I Helped Popularize the Term 'Fake News' and Now I Cringe Every Time I Hear It". *BuzzFeed News*. December 31, 2017. https://www.buzzfeednews.com/article/craigsilverman/i-helped-popularize-the-term-fake-news-and-now-i-cringe#.yaKaGpd9V. [accessed January 5, 2021].

Smith, D. 1990. "Corporate Power and the Politics of Uncertainty: Risk Management at the Canvey Island Complex". *Industrial Crisis Quarterly*, 4(1): 1-26.

Smith, D. 2005. "Dancing With the Mysterious Forces of Chaos: Issues Around Complexity, Knowledge and the Management of Uncertainty". *Clinician in Management*, 13(3/4): 115-123.

Smith, K. E. 2013. "Understanding the Influence of Evidence in Public Health Policy: What Can We Learn From the 'Tobacco Wars'"? *Social Policy & Administration*, 47(4): 382-398.

Stanley, J. 2015. *How Propaganda Works*. Princeton NJ: Princeton University Press.

Taverne, D. 2005. *The March of Unreason. Science, Democracy, and the New Fundamentalism*. Oxford: Oxford University Press.

The White House. 2020. "The Trump Administration Initiated the Single Greatest Mobilization in U.S. History—Pioneering, Developing, and Manufacturing COVID-19 Therapies and

Vaccines in Record Time!" Press Briefing. December 8, 2020. https://www.whitehouse.gov/briefings-statements/president-donald-j-trumps-effort-provide-americans-safe-effective-vaccine-delivering-results/.

Tice, R. 2020a. "I did go to one...3,000 bedder ...& none of NHS, DHSC, PHE, GLA, knew that it had disappeared under their very eyes....been dismantled yet 30,000 retired nurses and doctors waiting since March for call up. Management of NHS shambolic, wasted some £200 million + on these". In @TiceRichard (Ed.), 0905 hours December 29, 2020. ed: *Twitter*.

Tice, R. 2020b. "NHS Nightingale decommissioned! Did @MattHancock deliberately mislead MPs & on media yesterday? It's not on standby, nor being readied. NHS media now confirmed its been dispersed. Why did he let it go, given his 2nd wave worries? Shocking waste taxpayers cash". In @TiceRichard (Ed.), 1415 hours December 31, 2020. ed: *Twitter*.

Tice, R. 2021. Brexit Britain is saving lives.... thank heavens we are not stuck in EU vaccine programme.... In @TiceRichard (Ed.), 0913 hours January 3, 2021. ed: *Twitter*.

Timberg, C., and Harwell, D. 2021. "Pro-Trump Forums Erupt with Violent Threats Ahead of Protests in D.C.". *The Washington Post*. January 6, 2021. A18.

Trump, D. 2020a. "Another Vaccine just announced. This time by Moderna, 95% effective. For those great "historians", please remember that these great discoveries, which will end the China Plague, all took place on my watch!" In @realDonaldTrump (Ed.), 1419 hours November 16, 2020. ed: *Twitter*.

Trump, D. 2020b. "At a meeting in Florida today, everyone was asking why aren't the Republicans up in arms & fighting over the fact that the Democrats stole the rigged presidential election? Especially in the Senate, they said, where you helped 8 Senators win their races. How quickly they forget!" In @realDonaldTrump (Ed.), 2043 hours December 24, 2020. ed: *Twitter*.

Trump, D. 2020c. "@BrianKempGA, his puppet Lt. Governor @GeoffDuncanGA, and Secretary of State, are disasters for Georgia. Won't let professionals get anywhere near Fulton County for signature verifications, or anything else. They are virtually controlled by @staceyabrams & the Democrats. Fools!"

In @realDonaldTrump (Ed.), 0938 hours December 30, 2020. ed: *Twitter*.

Trump, D. 2020d. "Chris Krebs was totally excoriated and proven wrong at the Senate Hearing on the Fraudulent 2020 Election. Massive FRAUD took place with machines, people voting from out of state, illegals, dead people, no signatures—and so much more!" In @realDonaldTrump (Ed.), 1851 hours December 16, 2020. ed: *Twitter*.

Trump, D. 2020e. "Distribution of both vaccines is going very smoothly. Amazing how many people are being vaccinated, record numbers. Our Country, and indeed the World, will soon see the great miracle of what the Trump Administration has accomplished. They said it couldn't be done!!!" In @realDonaldTrump (Ed.), 1426 hours December 22, 2020. ed: *Twitter*.

Trump, D. 2020f. "Hearings from Atlanta on the Georgia Election overturn now being broadcast. Check it out. @OANN @newsmax and many more. @BrianKempGA should resign from office. He is an obstructionist who refuses to admit that we won Georgia, BIG! Also won the other Swing States". In @realDonaldTrump (Ed.), 1426 hours December 30, 2020. ed: *Twitter*.

Trump, D. 2020g. "I saved at least 8 Republican Senators, including Mitch, from losing in the last Rigged (for President) Election. Now they (almost all) sit back and watch me fight against a crooked and vicious foe, the Radical Left Democrats. I will NEVER FORGET!" In @realDonaldTrump (Ed.), 1106 hours December 24, 2020. ed: *Twitter*.

Trump, D. 2020h. "The "Justice" Department and the FBI have done nothing about the 2020 Presidential Election Voter Fraud, the biggest SCAM in our nation's history, despite overwhelming evidence. They should be ashamed. History will remember. Never give up. See everyone in D.C. on January 6th." In @realDonaldTrump (Ed.), 1314 hours Decembver 26, 2020. ed: *Twitter*.

Trump, D. 2020i. "The lockdowns in Democrat run states are absolutely ruining the lives of so many people—Far more than the damage that would be caused by the China Virus. Cases in California have risen despite the lockdown, yet Florida & others

are open & doing well. Common sense please!" In
@realDonaldTrump (Ed.), 1902 hours December 26, 2020. ed:
Twitter.

Trump, D. 2020j. "The recent statement by Chris Krebs on the security
of the 2020 Election was highly inaccurate, in that there were
massive improprieties and fraud—including dead people voting,
Poll Watchers not allowed into polling locations, "glitches" in the
voting machines which changed....votes from Trump to Biden,
late voting, and many more. Therefore, effective immediately,
Chris Krebs has been terminated as Director of the Cybersecurity
and Infrastructure Security Agency". In @realDonaldTrump
(Ed.), 1207 hours December 18, 2020. ed: *Twitter*.

Trump, D. 2020k. "The Supreme Court really let us down. No Wisdom,
No Courage!" In @realDonaldTrump (Ed.), 0450 hours
December 12, 2020. ed: *Twitter*.

Trump, D. 2020l. "The Swine Flu (H1N1), and the attempt for a vaccine
by the Obama Administration, with Joe Biden in charge, was a
complete and total disaster. Now they want to come in and take
over one of the "greatest and fastest medical miracles in modern
day history." I don't think so!" In @realDonaldTrump (Ed.), 1222
hours December 11, 2020. ed: *Twitter*.

Trump, D. 2020m. "Time for Republican Senators to step up and fight
for the Presidency, like the Democrats would do if they had
actually won. The proof is irrefutable! Massive late night mail-in
ballot drops in swing states, stuffing the ballot boxes (on video),
double voters, dead voters." In @realDonaldTrump (Ed.), 1123
hours December 26, 2020. ed: *Twitter*.

Trump, D. 2020n. "The U.S. Supreme Court has been totally
incompetent and weak on the massive Election Fraud that took
place in the 2020 Presidential Election. We have absolute
PROOF, but they don't want to see it—No "standing", they say. If
we have corrupt elections, we have no country!" In
@realDonaldTrump (Ed.), 1351 hours December 26, 2020. ed:
Twitter.

Trump, D. 2020o. "We now have far more votes than needed to flip
Georgia in the Presidential race. Massive VOTER FRAUD took
place. Thank you to the Georgia Legislature for today's revealing

meeting!" In @realDonaldTrump (Ed.), December, 30 2020: ed: *Twitter.*

Trump, D. 2021a. "How can you certify an election when the numbers being certified are verifiably WRONG. You will see the real numbers tonight during my speech, but especially on JANUARY 6th. @SenTomCotton Republicans have pluses & minuses, but one thing is sure, THEY NEVER FORGET!" In @realDonaldTrump (Ed.), 1507 hours January 4, 2021. ed: *Twitter.*

Trump, D. 2021b. "I spoke to Secretary of State Brad Raffensperger yesterday about Fulton County and voter fraud in Georgia. He was unwilling, or unable, to answer questions such as the "ballots under table" scam, ballot destruction, out of state "voters", dead voters, and more. He has no clue!" In @realDonaldTrump (Ed.), 1357 hours January 3, 2021. ed: *Twitter.*

Trump, D. 2021c. "If Vice President @Mike_Pence comes through for us, we will win the Presidency. Many States want to decertify the mistake they made in certifying incorrect & even fraudulent numbers in a process NOT approved by their State Legislatures (which it must be). Mike can send it back!" In @realDonaldTrump (Ed.), 0600 hours January 6, 2021. ed: *Twitter.*

Trump, D. 2021d. "Mike Pence didn't have the courage to do what should have been done to protect our Country and our Constitution, giving States a chance to certify a corrected set of facts, not the fraudulent or inaccurate ones which they were asked to previously certify. USA demands the truth!" In @realDonaldTrump (Ed.), 1924 hours January 6, 2021. ed: *Twitter.*

Trump, D. 2021e. "The number of cases and deaths of the China Virus is far exaggerated in the United States because of @CDCgov's ridiculous method of determination compared to other countries, many of whom report, purposely, very inaccurately and low. "When in doubt, call it Covid." Fake News!" In @realDonaldTrump (Ed.), 1314 hours January 3, 2021. ed: *Twitter.*

Trump, D. 2021f. "Something how Dr. Fauci is revered by the LameStream Media as such a great professional, having done, they say, such an incredible job, yet he works for me and the Trump Administration, and I am in no way given any credit for my work. Gee, could this just be more Fake News?". In @realDonaldTrump (Ed.), 1511 hours January 3, 2021. ed: *Twitter.*

Trump, D. 2021g. "These are the things and events that happen when a sacred landslide election victory is so unceremoniously & viciously stripped away from great patriots who have been badly & unfairly treated for so long. Go home with love & in peace. Remember this day forever!" In @realDonaldTrump (Ed.), 2301 hours January 6, 2021. ed: *Twitter.*

Trump Jr, D. 2021a. "Free Speech Is Under Attack! Censorship is happening like NEVER before! Don't let them silence us. Sign up at http://DONJR.COM to stay connected! If I get thrown off my social platforms I'll let you know my thoughts and where I end up". In @DonaldJTrumpJr (Ed.), 0157 hours January 9, 2021. ed: *Twitter.*

Trump Jr, D. 2021b. "Get this! If you want to follow Iran's Ayatollah, he's now got MULTIPLE Twitter feeds. In multiple languages. Italian has just been launched, so the message of hate can be fully understood! To stay in touch case I'm next connect @ http://donjr.com." In @DonaldJTrumpJr (Ed.), 1906 hours January 9, 2021. ed: *Twitter.*

Trump Jr, D. 2021c. "It continues... Big tech has totally eliminated the notion of free speech in America". In @DonaldJTrumpJr (Ed.), 2041 hours January 9, 2021. ed: *Twitter.*

Trump Jr, D. 2021d. "My thoughts this morning on the flagrant assault on free speech that's happening in America today. Check it out and let me know your thoughts". In @DonaldJTrumpJr (Ed.), 1623 hours January 9, 2021. ed: *Twitter.*

Trump, M. L. 2020p. *Too Much and Never Enough. How My Family Created the World's Most Dangerous Man.* London: Simon & Schuster.

Turner, B. A. 1976. "The Organizational and Interorganizational Development of Disasters". *Administrative Science Quarterly*, 21: 378-397.

Turner, B. A. 1978. *Man-Made Disasters.* London: Wykeham.

Turner, B. A. 1994. "The Causes of Disaster: Sloppy Management". *British Journal of Management*, 5: 215-219.

Twitter Inc. 2021. Permanent suspension of @realDonaldTrump. *Twitter Inc Blog.* https://blog.twitter.com/en_us/topics/company/2020/suspension.html.

War Room. 2020. "Bannon: CCP Guilty of 'Premeditated Murder' for Concealing Threat of Coronavirus Outbreak". *War Room 2020.* May 3, 2020. https://warroom.org/bannon-on-sinclair/. [accessed December 5, 2020].

Woodward, B. 2020. *Rage*. London: Simon & Schuster.

Wynne, B. 1989. "Sheepfarming After Chernobyl: A Case Study in Communicating Scientific Information". *Environment: Science and Policy for Sustainable Development*, 31(2): 10-39.

Wynne, B. 1996. "May the Sheep Safely Graze? A Reflexive View of the Expert-Lay Knowledge Divide". In *Risk, Envi}ment and Modernity. Towards a New Ecology,* edited by S. Lash, B. Szerszynski, and B. Wynne, 44-83. London: Sage.

Yates, S. 2016. "'Fake News'—Why People Believe It and What Can Be Done to Counter It". *The Conversation.* December 13, 2016. https://theconversation.com/fake-news-why-people-believe-it-and-what-can-be-done-to-counter-it-70013. [accessed January 5, 2021].

Zhao, C. 2021. "'Embarrassing': Ted Cruz-Led Plan to Challenge Electoral Votes Draws Bipartisan Scorn". *Newsweek.com.* January 2, 2021.

Zurcher, A. 2020. "Trump's Unlikely Christian Covenant". *BBC News.* October 16, 2017. https://www.bbc.co.uk/news/world-us-canada-41617793. [accessed January 10, 2021].

Chapter 8:
Lockdowns, Riots, and a Contested Election– Could the 2020 Crises Reinvigorate the US Far Right?

By George Michael[1]

Abstract

This chapter examines how three parallel and interacting crises that befell the United States during 2020 impacted both the far right and public responses towards them and towards radical conservatism as personified by President Trump, during and since his term of office. These crises were: the Covid-19 pandemic, the apparent epidemic of killings of black people by police, and the unsubstantiated allegations that Trump lost the 2020 US presidential election owing to electoral fraud. Evidence is presented that the far right, and alt-right overall, seek to capitalize on the likely political, social, and economic chaos in the long-tail aftermath of Covid-19, a growing anxiety among whites that their traditional dominance of US society may be diminishing permanently, and the Trump legacy of undermined public trust and confidence in US representative democracy and governance. Corporate opportunists have also sought to capitalize on mass dissemination of far-right ideology. The chapter concludes that the American far right appears to be well-poised for regeneration. Risks to various parties are systematically identified.

Key words: crisis, far-right, Covid-19, racial killings, white dominance, democracy

Introduction

The far-right sub-culture has long predicted the collapse of the American nation. Prognosticators in the movement are keen on extrapolating trends in demographics, crime, economics, and culture to foretell a dismal future in which the United States implodes under the weight of racial strife. To date, these prophecies have not been realized, but a

---

[1]   See contributor affiliations and biography, page 526.

concatenation of events in 2020—Covid-19 and the ensuing lock-down, the death of George Floyd and urban unrest, and a very contentious presidential election—have made them seem much more plausible.

This chapter examines these recent crises through the lens of the American far-right sub-culture. First, the movement's reaction to Covid-19 is examined. Next, the controversial killing of yet another black man in police custody, and the urban unrest it precipitated, is explored. Reactions to the 2020 presidential election are then analyzed. Finally, the conclusion speculates on how these crises might impact the far right in the future. Will the far right come out more energized and potentially snowball into a mass movement? Or, will these crises impel the movement into a more nihilistic direction, thereby predisposing it toward violence?

Covid-19 and the Lockdown

The coronavirus pandemic of 2020 (Covid-19) originated in late 2019 and involved a highly contagious disease that causes severe acute respiratory syndrome (SARS), similar to the SARS epidemics of 2003 and 2009 which involved another coronavirus. Common symptoms of the disease include cough, fever, fatigue, diarrhoea, and breathing difficulties. Although most people afflicted with Covid-19 experience only minor symptoms, others develop acute respiratory distress syndrome. Certain demographic groups, including the elderly, the obese, and people with cardiovascular disease, seem to be most susceptible to the disease. As of March 11, 2021, a reported 527,726 people in the United States and 2.62 million world-wide had died as a result of Covid-19. US infections had already exceeded 29 million (CDC 2021) and continued to rise.

Coronavirus infections are believed to have first broken out in Wuhan in November of 2019. On December 31, 2019, Chinese officials announced the discovery of a cluster of pneumonia cases around the city. On January 6, 2020, the US Department of Health and Human Services offered to send a team of experts from the Centers for Disease Control (CDC) to China to help contain the outbreak, but the Chinese government did not take up the offer. The next day, the CDC issued an official health advisory. The lack of transparency on the part of the Chinese authorities perhaps contributed to the slowness of the initial federal response to the coronavirus in the United States, such as preparing the healthcare system for this eventuality and restricting travel and testing for the virus.

The first recorded case in the United States involved a Chinese man who returned to the country on or about January 14, 2020, after he visited his family in Wuhan (Robinson et al 2020). Initially, President Trump downplayed the threat posed by Covid-19. However, on March 6, he signed the Coronavirus Preparedness and Response Supplemental Appropriations Act, which provided US$8.3 billion in emergency funding for federal agencies to respond to the outbreak (Hirsch & Brueninger 2020) By mid-April, cases had been confirmed in all fifty US states and the District of Columbia, and the federal government had approved emergency declarations in all fifty states.

The opaqueness surrounding Covid-19 gave rise to much speculation as to the nature and origins of the novel virus. Inasmuch as anti-Semitism looms large in the world-view of the far right, it is not surprising that Jews were initially implicated in the pandemic. The fact that an American-Jewish scientist, Charles Lieber, a renowned scientist (the Mark Hyman Jr. Professor of Chemistry at Harvard), was arrested in January of 2020, for lying about his connections to a research laboratory in Wuhan, added credence to this theory. According to a press release on the Department of Justice website, Dr. Lieber failed to inform authorities about possible foreign financial conflicts of interest. In this case, Lieber failed to disclose that he was a "strategic scientist" at Wuhan University of Technology and was a participant in China's "Thousand Talents Plan", a programme designed to recruit high-talent to further China's scientific development, economic prosperity, and national security (USDoJ 2020). Reportedly, he was involved in various types of research and development within the fields of neurobiology and nanotechnology. Previously, Lieber had been awarded the prestigious Wolf Prize in Israel. The fact that a number of high-ranking officials in Iran—one of Israel's chief geo-political adversaries—were among the first people in the world reported to be infected with the disease, suggested to David Duke that the coronavirus had been weaponized by the Mossad to kill off its rivals (Duke 2020; Schrader 2020; USIP 2020).

Another conspiracy theory which gained much more currency alleged that Chinese had engineered the virus in a lab. The main evidence adduced to support this claim was the fact that one of only two of China's Biosafety Level 4 labs (BSL-4, the maximum safety level used to deal with highly dangerous pathogens) just so happened to be located in Wuhan (ISD 2020a). To add more grist to the mill, was the fact that the Chinese government restricted air travel within China, but allowed it overseas. For this reason, Trump's National Security Adviser Robert O'Brien suggested that the Chinese had repurposed Covid-19 into a bio-weapon (Woodward 2020). Officials had halted all internal domestic travel in China by the end of January 2020, but permitted foreign travel till the end of March. According to this line of reasoning, Chinese leaders deliberately infected the world so that their economy would not be the only one to suffer from the fallout of the pandemic (Carlson 2020).

The 'blame China' theory gained traction in some quarters of the mainstream media. For example, the popular *Fox News* host, Tucker Carlson, interviewed a Chinese scientist, Dr. Li-Meng Yan, who claimed that she could "present solid scientific evidence" that Covid-19 did not emerge from nature. Instead, she claimed that it was "a man-made virus created in the lab." The segment was widely viewed, as Carlson's show is reported to be the most-watched programme on cable network television. The consensus from the scientific community and international public health organisations, though, is that Covid-19 originated from bats and later jumped to humans (Funke 2020).

The Trump administration also promoted the theory at times. President Trump frequently referred to Covid-19 as the "China virus", thereby underscoring the provenance of the disease. When pressed to explain what evidence he had seen to indicate that the virus had emerged in a Chinese lab, Trump answered "I can't tell you that. I'm not allowed to tell you that." The president sought to make Beijing's handling of the outbreak a major issue for his re-election campaign. His Secretary of State, Mike Pompeo, placed blame on an institute operated by the Chinese Academy of Sciences, which had conducted groundbreaking research tracing the likely origins of the SARS virus. Pompeo exclaimed, "We know that there is the Wuhan Institute of Virology just a handful of miles away from where the wet market was." The institute is reported to be located eight miles away from the market. The radical-right activist Steve Bannon [President Trump's first chief strategist until his departure in August 2017] also supported the theory. The Chinese government rejected such theories, calling them "unfounded and purely fabricated out of nothing" (Singh et al 2020).

Writing on the right-wing website, *Taki's Magazine*, David Cole criticized Trump's conspiracy theory, characterizing it as a form of "MAGA[2] glue-sniffing." Instead of blaming the outbreak on an arcane theory that it was concocted in a Chinese lab, Cole counselled that Trump would have been better off pressuring China to shut down the wet markets from which Covid-19 most likely originated. As far back as 2017, Western researchers determined that the Wuhan wet market was a hot spot for zoonotic diseases. Cole lambasted the "Franken-Covid" obsession on the right as wrong-headed. As he pointed out, it took the focus off the actual things the Chinese did that caused the pandemic. By doing so, it had effectively absolved them of their real crimes while accusing them of invented ones. As a result, the Chinese could depict themselves as victims of Trump's lurid fantasies. Cole suggested that Trump should stick to the facts, because they did not favour China. After all, there was much evidence to suggest that China was well aware of the perils of deadly zoonotic diseases stemming from its wet markets, yet did next to nothing about them (Cole 2020a) Instead of holding China accountable for its wet markets, the far right promoted a dubious conspiracy theory that Chinese officials were sure to debunk, thus exonerating them of culpability for the pandemic. This strategy, according to Cole, was emblematic of the MAGA right's obsession with tactics and skirmishes rather than achieving clearly defined goals (Cole 2020b).

Seeking to deflect blame, the Chinese government attempted to convince the world that the coronavirus did not originate in the Chinese city of Wuhan, but was brought to China from elsewhere. First, Chinese officials implied that the virus might have originated with the US military or perhaps from an American lab (Carlson 2020). Next, a story was floated that the coronavirus travelled to China by way of frozen food imports, an unlikely scenario according to epidemiologists (Moran 2020). Chinese CDC experts claim that the coronavirus may remain latent in contaminated food during cold-chain processing, storage, and transportation from one country to another at standard

---

[2]   MAGA—acronym of Trump's 'Make America Great Again' slogan.

temperatures of -18 °C or lower (Chen 2020). For his part, Ryan Clarke, a senior research fellow at the National University of Singapore's East Asian Institute, is sceptical about the Chinese claims. As he pointed out, evidence so far indicates that Covid-19 originates from a unique bat species found in Yunnan and other nearby areas of southwest China and northeast India (Chen 2020).

Other representatives of the far right eschewed conspiracy theories and instead framed their analysis of the Covid-19 crisis within a standard far-right narrative. For instance, writing for the *National Vanguard*, Richard Houck blamed liberal open borders immigration policies for the spread of Covid-19 in the West. He also decried the practice of the Wuhan market's sale of live animals—including dogs, cats, foxes, koalas, bats, and other meats that are uncommon to Europeans—as barbaric and indicative of a "radically alien people." Globalism and neo-liberalism, he asserted, with their commitment to open borders and the free movement of people, ultimately prepared the way for the catastrophe that followed. The US government's hesitancy to act, was all the more evidence to suggest that it did not prioritize the health of its people above its ideological commitment to diversity (Houck 2020).

In a similar vein, David Sims pointed out that the pandemic illustrated the vulnerability of the modern capitalist system of the West, which includes such features as economic interdependence, and just-in-time supply practices. Moreover, he argued that wealthy Jews used this system to their advantage as evidenced by the "too big to fail" doctrine in which the government bailed out big banks and firms on the premise that their survival was necessary for the economy to function. According to Sims, the system amounted to a ticking time-bomb. The free market, he argued, had been transformed into a state-sponsored corporate system favouring the Jewish elite without the virtue of a genuine laissez-faire system (Sims 2020).

Some representatives of the far right acknowledged the seriousness of the Covid-19 pandemic, but believed that the government had overreacted with widespread lockdowns. For example, Dr. Anthony Fauci, a well-respected immunologist who has served as the director of the National Institute of Allergy and Infectious Diseases (NIAID) since 1984 and also one of the lead members of the Trump administration's White House Coronavirus Task Force, was often depicted as a 'deep state' stooge who exploited the crisis to undermine Trump's chances of re-election (Nguyen 2020). The fact that President Trump recovered so quickly was seen as more evidence that the severity of the pandemic had been overblown. Writing on the *Daily Stormer*, Andrew Anglin heralded the recovery of Donald Trump after he fell ill from the coronavirus. Inasmuch as Trump was 74 years old, obese, and did not exercise, suggested to Anglin that the CDC had exaggerated the lethality of Covid-19 (Anglin 2020).

As the lockdowns persisted, people's nerves became frayed and the prospect of violence seemed more and more likely. On March 27, 2020, the FBI shot and killed Timothy R. Wilson in Belton, Missouri, who was suspected of plotting an attack on a hospital that was treating Covid-19 patients (ISD 2020a). In October 2020, police in Michigan arrested thirteen men having far-right connections and charged them with plotting to kidnap Governor Gretchen Whitmer [who promoted social distancing and other covid protective measures, and is a Democrat] and seize the capital in a plot to foment a civil war (Winter et al 2020).

Hungry for information, more and more, Americans reached out to alternative media for information, bypassing the mainstream media. Far-right media outlets seem to be increasingly popular, as people became more distrustful of established sources of information. There is concern in some quarters that people are susceptible to disinformation on the Internet. According to a joint study conducted by the Institute for Strategic Dialogue and *BBC News 'Click'*, thirty-four known disinformation-hosting websites gathered a staggeringly high volume of 80 million interactions concerning Covid-19 on *Facebook* between January and April 2020. By contrast, the WHO's (World Health Organization) website during this same period received only 6.2 million interactions through posts on *Facebook* (ISD 2020b).

The economic impact of the pandemic has been substantial. Millions of people have lost their jobs (Wheelock 2020)[3]. Secondary

---

[3]   According to David C. Wheelock, the deputy director of research for Federal Reserve Bank of St. Louis, "the cumulative decline in economic activity during the first two quarters of the 2020 recession was somewhat larger than the GNP [Gross National Product—an annual measure of national economic activity] decline during the first two quarters of the Great Depression. Moreover, the fall in real GDP during the second quarter of 2020 exceeded the largest one-quarter real GNP

effects have rippled throughout the fabric of American society (Campion et al 2020). A perfect storm was forming and finally triggered by a catalyzing event.

The Death of George Floyd and Urban Mayhem

On May 25, 2020, a black man named George Floyd was arrested by police in Minneapolis, for passing a counterfeit $20 bill. While being detained, Floyd stopped breathing and eventually died. A video of police officer Derek Chauvin kneeling on Floyd's neck to restrain him went viral on the Internet and social media. The coroner who performed the original autopsy concluded that Floyd died because of a combination of intoxication, damage to his organs due to cocaine addiction, and excessive roughness by the police (Donaghue 2020).

Not long thereafter, the Floyd family hired a celebrity forensic pathologist Dr. Michael Baden, and Dr. Alicia Wilson from the University of Michigan, to conduct an independent autopsy. Disagreeing with the original report, they found that Floyd had died of asphyxiation, which would support a homicide charge against Chauvin. Afterwards, the county amended its report by acknowledging that the knee on the neck restraint combined with fentanyl intoxication and recent methamphetamine use, along with Floyd's existing heart disease, caused his death (Perira 2020). Consequently, Chauvin was charged with second-degree unintentional murder and second-degree manslaughter. Three other officers involved in the incident were charged with aiding and abetting second degree murder (Higgins 2020).

Less than a week after his death, widespread urban mayhem convulsed cities all over America, and rivalled the intensity of the Black Lives Matter (BLM) protests in 2014-2015. The mainstream media were generally quite sympathetic to the protestors, often characterizing them as "peaceful." Likewise, corporate America and the entertainment industry were also very supportive, and millions of dollars were donated to BLM and related organisations (Stern 2020).

For this series of riots, BLM and related activists were joined by those who identified with the Antifa movement, a decentralized left-wing anti-fascist pressure group seeking enforced radical change in

---

contraction during the Depression." Moreover, the unemployment rate climbed to nearly 15 percent in April, but fell back to 11.1 percent in June.

US governance rather than policy reform. Reports emerged of stacks of bricks being left in front of buildings, seemingly for the convenience of rioters to use for vandalizing purposes. Some observers suspected that these had been strategically planted by Antifa activists. Antifa is not a formal organisation with members; rather, it could be more aptly described as a movement whose followers act largely on their own volition. Working in tandem, BLM and Antifa have attained a synergy that has proven to be quite destructive in cities throughout the United States (Kingson 2020; Polumbo 2020).

Inasmuch as most Antifa protestors seem to be white, this has led some people to speculate that perhaps white nationalists had infiltrated the protests. The theory was that white nationalists were blending into the protests, encouraging lawlessness, thus accelerating the crisis (Devereaux 2020). In particular, people associated with the so-called Boogaloo Bois were thought to be involved. The term boogaloo was first used on *4chan* in 2012, where the meme was often associated with references to "Civil War 2: Electric Boogaloo", "race war", and "dotr" (day of the rope) (Zadrozny 2020)[4]. According to the etymology of the term, boogaloo is believed to stem from obscure jokes about the 1984 breakdancing film *"Breakin' 2: Electric Boogaloo".* The word sometimes gets mutated in to "Big Igloo." Hence, the igloo patches that are sometimes adorned by members of the movement (ADL 2019). The lockdowns which were implemented to slow down the spread of Covid-19 increased the popularity of the meme.

A variety of ideologies organized under the Boogaloo umbrella, including libertarian anarchists, pro-gun, anti-government groups, as well as white nationalists and neo-Nazis. At the present time, they remain a movement and not a membership organisation. Their values and goals remain vague and flexible enough to appeal to a broad assortment of those on the radical right. Public knowledge of the movement increased after an incident that occurred on March 12, 2020, when police shot and killed Duncan Lemp, a Boogaloo *Facebook* group

---

[4]   The "day of the rope" meme can be traced back to William L. Pierce's 1978 underground novel—*The Turner Diaries*—which tells the story of a race war that convulses America in the late 1990s. In one episode in the novel, so-called "race traitors" are hanged from lampposts in California. Andrew Macdonald, (pseudonym for William Pierce), *The Turner Diaries* (Hillsboro, WV: National Vanguard Books 1978).

leader during a no-knock raid on his home in Potomac, Maryland. Some of his sympathizers theorized that he had been killed because of his anti-government world-view and his position in the Boogaloo movement (Sommer 2020).

Some people who identify with Boogaloo saw the instability of 2020 as an opportunity to strike a blow against a tyrannical government, while others saw it primarily as a racial conflict and an opportunity to launch a second civil war. Some of the more radically-inclined in the movement adhere to the idea of accelerationism, that is, any action that speeds up the impending race war is to be desired. According to Brian Levin, the director of the Center for Study of Hate and Extremism at California State University, the movement is characteristic of the post-Charlottesville right which follows more of a lone-wolf model (Ellis 2020). Emblematic of this trend, is the case of Steve Carrillo, an Air Force sergeant, who was charged with killing two law enforcement officers in the Bay area. Carrillo was accused of killing a Federal Protective Service officer in Oakland on May 29 and the murder of a Santa Cruz County deputy on June 6, 2020. Cruz served in an elite Air Force unit that guarded military personnel at unsecure foreign airfields (Mendoza & Dazio 2020).

As America's domestic front became increasingly chaotic, federal authorities weighed in and planned a response. Testifying before the House Homeland Security Committee, FBI Director Christopher Wray expressed concern that both ends of the political spectrum were inciting violence, which added "to the combustibility and danger of the situation." Wray claimed that white supremacists were responsible for most of the lethal terrorist attacks inside the United States in recent years (*Daily Sabah* 2020). On June 26, 2020, US Attorney General William Barr announced that the Justice Department had created a task force to investigate anti-government extremists who had disrupted protests and attacked members of law enforcement. In the memo, both the Boogaloo and Antifa movements were identified (Benner 2020). In May 2020, President Donald Trump announced by way of a tweet that the US government would designate both Antifa and the Ku Klux Klan as terrorist organisations. However, under current law, only foreign entities can receive that designation by the US State Department. Therefore, it is unclear on what legal authority the president could make that determination for domestic extremist groups (MacFarquhar 2020). US Attorney General Barr also referred to the violent protestors as domestic terrorists (MacFarquhar 2020).

Despite allegations of complicity in the riots, there is not compelling evidence that far-right platforms have exhorted their followers to violence. Even Howard Graves, a research analyst at the Southern Poverty Law Center, conceded that there was no clear substantiation adduced that suggested that white supremacists or militiamen were "masking up and going out to burn and loot" (MacFarquhar 2020). After the debacle three years earlier in Charlottesville, representatives of the far right counselled caution for no other reason than the forces arrayed against them are formidable. Law enforcement agencies, monitoring groups (such as the Southern Poverty Law Center and the Anti-Defamation League), and street protestors fighting under the rubric of Antifa, collectively are far more powerful than the far right. To date, no viable revolutionary infrastructure exists across the far-right sub-culture.

Nevertheless, far-right commentators occasionally saw a silver lining amidst all the mayhem. Writing on the *Affirmative Right* blog, Daniel Barge wryly proclaimed that through the havoc it was wreaking, the Black Lives Matter was effectively "red-pilling the normies"[5] to the white nationalist cause. Not unlike a Marxian analysis, he said that the white nationalist movement could "simply do nothing and wait for the inherent contradictions of Western society to make the Blacks kids angry and assertive." In that sense, Black Lives Matter were allies because they were "tearing apart the fake society of the West." Black protestors were doing much of the work of white nationalists, who could now just "sit back and look on." To make his point, at the bottom of the article was an old picture of Black slaves working in a cotton field, carrying bales of red pills (Barge 2020).

---

5   In essence, to take the red pill, means to see reality the way it appears to be. The meme has gained currency in both the alt-right and the manosphere sub-cultures. Thus, in these contexts, someone who is red-pilled has a more right-leaning and patriarchal worldview. The origin of the meme can be traced back to *The Matrix* film series in which the main character Neo offers a choice to the rebel leader Morpheus. By taking the blue pill, Morpheus will remain in blissful ignorance. By taking the red pill, an unpleasant truth will be revealed—i.e. how the world really operates.

To be expected, Jews were often blamed for having an outsized role in the urban unrest. For instance, Hadding Scott blamed Israeli influence over US police departments for the death of George Floyd. According to this argument, the knee-to-the-neck technique employed by Officer Derek Chauvin on George Floyd was a common tactic used by Israeli security personnel against Palestinians. As he pointed out, a number of US police personnel have received training in Israel (Scott 2020).

Culpability for the urban unrest continues to be debated. Generally speaking, the political left blamed systemic racism in American policing as the root cause which occasioned the protests that were often characterized as "peaceful" despite overwhelming evidence for the contrary. The political right blamed Antifa along with George Soros, a billionaire investor and philanthropist who is Jewish and has donated billions of dollars to liberal causes, most notably, his Open Society Foundations (*Reuters* 2020)[6]. When pressed during the September 29th presidential debate by moderator Chris Wallace if he would condemn white supremacist and militia groups, Trump deflected blame on the right, responding, "Proud Boys, stand back and stand by. But I'll tell you what. Somebody has to do something about Antifa and the left. This is not a right-wing problem. This is a left-wing problem" (*Axios* 2020). Although characterized by its critics as "white supremacist" and "neo-fascist," the Proud Boys is an exclusively male group whose membership is multi-racial and multi-ethnic in composition (though mostly white), that could be more aptly described as "western chauvinist" and "civic nationalist" (Sales 2020). Soon after Trump made his comments, the Proud Boys expressed delight for a seeming endorsement on their social media channels (Subramanian & Culver 2020). Just a few days later, however, Trump explicitly condemned the Proud Boys by name and "all white supremacists" in an interview with *Fox News* host Sean Hannity (Knutson 2020). As Trump prepared for the upcoming election, rhetoric became even more shrill among both his supporters and detractors.

---

[6]   Rumours persist that Soros-funded enterprises fund protest groups such as Antifa and Black Lives Matter. To date, however, solid evidence for this claim has not been forthcoming.

The 2020 Presidential Election

Scepticism over the November 2020 presidential election only added more fuel to the fire. Even before the election, Donald Trump cast doubt on the integrity of the process. In particular, he attacked the propriety of mail-in voting, claiming that it would invite widespread fraud thus enabling the Democrats to steal the election (Kiely & Reider 2020).

The fact that Trump had a comfortable lead in key battleground states into the early hours of the morning of November 4, led many of his supporters to believe that he would win the election. A sharp reversal which favoured Joe Biden after vote-counting resumed later in the day, raised suspicion that the Democrats had stuffed bogus ballots after the polls had officially closed. A markedly sharp rise in votes for Biden, when vote-counting recommenced on the morning of November 4, added credence to these assertions (*Trad News* 2020).

Post-election analysis carried out by some sceptics claimed that it was well-nigh impossible for Joe Biden to have won fair and square. A statistical analysis carried out by the American economist Charles Ciccheti claimed that the probability of Joe Biden winning the popular vote in four states—Georgia, Michigan, Pennsylvania, and Wisconsin—given Trump's early lead in those states as of 3 a.m. on November 4, was less than one in a quadrillion (Litke 2020). This claim served as the basis for an unprecedented lawsuit filed by the attorney general of Texas to overturn the election in the aforementioned four battleground states. White House Press secretary Kayleigh McEnany repeated this claim at press briefings and interviews with the media. For its part, the US Supreme Court declined to hear the case, effectively ending Trump's legal remedies for victory (Totenberg & Sprunt 2020).

In some quarters of the far right, the Leninist dictum "worse is better" resonated. Writing on *Counter-Currents*, Jef Costello argued that the suspicion surrounding the election would serve to alienate more whites making them more susceptible to the white nationalist message. He noted that Trump enjoyed enormous grassroots support. His rallies were packed. He also received at least 70 million votes—more than any Republican candidate in history—in a race that pollsters projected that he would soundly lose. By losing faith in the electoral system, white Americans could become more amenable to radical politics. The assertion that 'big tech' censored news damaging to Joe Biden, such as alleged scandals involving his son Hunter, seemed to reveal more bias against Trump and, by extension, the 57 percent of whites who voted for him. Costello argued that the first step in arriving at the day whereby whites could openly stand up for themselves is self-awareness. Second, it would require anger as many whites feel that they are "pushed to a point that they must speak and behave imprudently, damning the consequences." As Donald Trump Jr. tweeted, "70 million pissed off Republicans and not one city burned to the ground." But, as Costello pointed out, this situation might not last, as the alleged rigged election could serve as "the proverbial last straw." "The camel may be about to metamorphose into the lion." Despite all of the doom and gloom over 2020, he believed that "[w]hite nationalism [had] taken a giant step forward" (Costello 2020).

The controversy surrounding the presidential election is indicative of a broader crisis in American democracy. As the political scientist Francis Fukuyama opined, liberal democracy is currently under attack both by the progressive left and the populist right. As he noted, classical liberalism can best be understood as an institutional solution to the problem of governing over diversity. Fukuyama is concerned that if diverse societies move away from liberal principles and instead try to base national identity on race, ethnicity, or religion, they could be inviting a return to violent conflict (Fukuyama 2020)[7]. The American far right seems well positioned to leverage the growing discontent in the mainstream conservative movement. In recent months, Nick Fuentes has emerged as perhaps the most mediagenic figure in the American far right. Only twenty-three years of age, he has established a sizeable online following for his organisation, America First. In 2019, Fuentes garnered a considerable amount of publicity as the leader of the so-called Groyper Army, a movement of rightists who are critical of mainstream conservatism. The Groyper Army trolled speaking events of mainstream conservatives, such as Charlie Kirk, the leader of Turning Point USA, and even Donald Trump Jr. During Q & A

---

[7]   As Fukuyama noted, the religious wars that had ravaged Europe gave rise to a new political creed in which different Christian sects could live side-by-side. Liberalism sought to resolve conflicts in diverse societies by lowering the temperature of politics and removing questions of final ends and moving them into the sphere of private life.

sessions, the members of the Groyper Army would press conservatives on sensitive topics, such as US support for Israel and the racial demographic impact of immigration, thus pressuring them to support the Groyper positions or cave in and "cuck" (Coaston 2020). As the controversy surrounding the result of the election escalated, conservatives conducted a number of protests in various American cities including Phoenix, Harrisburg, and Washington, DC. Fuentes and Alex Jones were in the forefront of these protests. In Washington, DC, members of the Proud Boys clashed with representatives of Antifa. The post-election protests were significant because they were the first rallies since the debacle at Charlottesville where the far right demonstrated that they could hold their own in street confrontations (Hayden 2020).

Reflections and Future Projections

The 2016 presidential campaign of Donald Trump had a galvanizing effect on the American far right, which some observers believed could propel it to become a viable mass movement. Some far-rightists were so optimistic that they waxed excitely that they "are the establishment now" and that they "deserved a seat at the table" for their support of candidate Trump. After all, members of the alt-right were among Trump's most loyal and enthusiastic supporters. Furthermore, there is anecdotal evidence suggesting that they were among his most avid foot soldiers in getting out the vote in both the primaries and general election (Michael 2017).

However, such high hopes were quickly dashed and the movement that had come to be known as the alt-right quickly imploded. Much of the damage was self-inflicted. First, there was Hailgate. In late November 2016, Richard Spencer, who did much to popularize the alt-right brand, held a conference for his National Policy Institute's conference in Washington, DC. The mood at the meeting was very positive. Near the end of the event, he made a toast and in an unguarded moment of exuberance, exclaimed to his audience: "Hail Trump! Hail our people! Hail Victory!" At this point, several of the attendees gave a celebratory Roman salute reminiscent of Hitler's Third Reich. The event was covered by *Atlantic* magazine. At the time, the mainstream media were looking for any opportunity to cast the alt-right as a neo-Nazi movement. Spencer gave them that opportunity on a silver platter. This incident was captured by the media and reinforced the image that the alt-right was a Nazi-style movement. In retrospect, this proved to be a notorious case of what is known in the vernacular of the alt-right as "bad optics." Up to that point, some relatively mainstream conservatives were comfortable with the alt-right label. This incident, however, split the alt-right between moderates and hardliners. More and more, the alt-right movement came to be associated with the caricature of neo-Nazis, as already labelled by its detractors.

Second, in February of 2017 Milo Yiannopoulos, a charismatic rising star in the conservative movement, who was regarded as a sort of fellow traveller of the alt-right, suffered a near career-ending scandal after it transpired that he had given an interview on a 2015 Joe Rogan podcast which was construed by some listeners as a defence of pederasty. As a consequence, much of the respectable conservative movement ostracized him. CPAC (Conservative Political Action Conference) quickly rescinded its invitation to serve as the organisation's keynote speaker at its 2017 annual convention. To make matters worse, Simon & Shuster cancelled the publication of his book, for which it had given a US$250,000 advance to him just a month before. In what seemed to have been a manoeuvre to spare a revolt at *Breitbart News*, Milo gracefully resigned from his position as technology editor with his employer. Still, Yiannopoulos managed to self-publish his book—*Dangerous*—which rocketed to number one on *Amazon's* bestsellers list even before its release. Nevertheless, he lost momentum and was forced on the defensive for several months (Yiannopoulos 2017).

Third, there was the debacle at a Unite-the-Right Rally in Charlottesville, Virginia. Ostensibly organized to protest the removal of a statue of Robert E. Lee from the city square, the event attracted an assortment of rightists including neo-Nazis and Klansmen. Furthermore, Antifa counter-protesters also showed up in force. During the fracas, a young woman, Heather Heyer was killed when James Fields drove his Dodge Challenger into a crowd of protestors. Although Donald Trump averred that there was "blame on both sides," the alt-right in particular was held largely responsible and vehemently condemned, not only by the mainstream media, but also by some Republicans, including Arnold Schwarzenegger and Mitt Romney. The alt-right was delegitimized and there followed a new wave of suppression. This included "de-platforming," which made it more difficult for alt-right organs to get their message out. Still another consequence of Charlottesville was an increase in 'doxxing'. A number of participants at the rally were 'outed' and, as a result, suffered ostracism in their communities. Some even lost their jobs. For this reason, there came to be a real chilling effect on public expressions associated with the alt-right.

Finally, one of the most charismatic and capable leaders of the alt-right—Matt Heimbach—was sidelined. By his mid-twenties, Heimbach had become an accomplished orator and was seen my many observers as the youthful face of white nationalism. An indefatigable organizer, he led Traditionalist Youth Network and espoused a leftish white nationalist ideology that resonated with many disaffected young people. He was not one to flinch from street activism, despite the violent opposition he often faced from various Antifa counter-protestors. He seemed poised to become perhaps the most promising leader of the American far right since David Duke (Heim 2016; Tenold 2015). However, in March of 2018, Heimbach was arrested for domestic battery after a bizarre incident in a trailer park in Indiana. Allegedly, he was involved in a tryst with the wife of his father-in-law, Matthew Parrott (Eltagouri & Selk 2018). In early 2020, Heimbach returned to politics, but announced that he had left white nationalism. He now works for the Light Upon Light organisation and dedicates his efforts to helping people leave the white nationalist movement (Heimbach 2020).

TV, Online and Social Media Involvement

Despite the setbacks outlined above, the American far right endures. Over the years, the movement has demonstrated a remarkable capacity to keep reinventing itself. The far right has become an integral part of the meme and trolling culture in cyberspace. Through the use of memes, the far right has established a notable presence in the virtual world. As a result of de-platforming, far-right figures have been migrating to alternative sites such as *Twitch, DLive,* and *TikTok.* As Megan Squire, a computer scientist at Elon University who tracks online extremism noted, "[t]hese people build their brand on *You-Tube*, and when they get demonetized or feel under threat, they'll set up backup channels on *DLive* or *BitChute*" (Bergengruen 2020). Even Donald

Trump recently moved over to *Gad*, a free-speech platform that includes a number of dissidents and extremists. It is worth mentioning that stories that resonate with the alt-right and white nationalist movements—for example, racially-charged news items—seem to get a lot of clicks from readers. As a consequence, platforms now have a strong economic incentive to carry these stories (Wilson 2016)[8]. What is more, in the United States cable television has steadily chipped away at the dominance of the so-called 'big three' television networks—*ABC, NBC*, and *CBS*—which has led to greater market segmentation resulting in a more fragmented media landscape. Right-wing cable news and internet have sites that have occasioned a polarizing shift in America's political culture. As noted above, some major US corporate organisations in the online and media sector that facilitate dissemination of radical-right publicity, propaganda, and conspiracy theories are clearly doing so out of commercial opportunism. However, others are motivated by ideological support e.g. funding support from corporate and family foundations and trusts, for such radical-right vehicles as *Breitbart, Infowars, Front Page, Rebel Media* and *Project Veritas*. See sections and Table 1.1 in chapter 1.

Fears of a Declining White Dominance

Perhaps more important, key issues that have fuelled the alt-right—to wit—massive immigration concomitant with fears of white demographic displacement, remain salient issues, not only to the alt-right but also to many white Americans. Far-right commentators often cite changing demographics which they believe portend the end of the whites as a distinct racial group. Those with a more conspiratorial bent, believe that this is no accident, but has been deliberately orchestrated. Popularized by the French writer Renaud Camus, the "Great Replacement" posits that European Union elites carry out a systematic plan to erase the autochthonous people of Europe. Similar forces are argued by some to also be at work in North America. There is certainly an element of truth to the Great Replacement narrative in the sense

---

[8]   For instance, although *Breitbart News* is not a white nationalist site—in fact Jews and ethnic minorities have always played a leading role in the organisation—over the past few years, the platform has carried many stories that resonated with white nationalists. So in a sense, they have become fellow travelers with *Breitbart*.

that white ethnic demographic groups have been declining numerically vis-à-vis non-whites in the West. Moreover, there is some similarity in rhetoric that can be discerned between the Great Replacement narrative and the pronouncements of Donald Trump. There are, however, important differences. Whereas proponents of the Great Replacement couch their rhetoric in the verbiage of race and ethnicity, Donald Trump, to date, has couched his opposition in the language of state interests, including alleged connections with terrorism, crime, and welfare dependency.

Concomitant with these developments is the shrill rhetoric from the political far left, some of which castigates white people as morally inferior and inherently evil, for example, the popularity of a "white privilege" discourse in academia. For the far right, these are ominous indications that the future for white people in 21st century America is precarious. Increasingly, these anxieties are finding expression among mainstream media and observers. For instance, back in 2018, the popular *Fox News* commentator Laura Ingraham sparked controversy when she opined on her television segment that the "America we know and love doesn't exist anymore" because of "massive demographic changes that have been foisted upon the American people" (*BBC News* 2018). This is a sentiment that seems to be gaining traction. In his 2019 book *White Shift: Populism, Immigration, and the Future of White Majorities*, Eric Kaufmann predicted that as whites decline as a proportion of the population in the West, the confidence that incubated political liberalism was likely to wane; hence, he sees a growing unwillingness on the part of the white masses to indulge in the anti-white ideology of the cultural far left (Kaufmann 2019).

For years, the far right has predicted that American society would someday in the not too far distant future face a crisis that would usher in a collapse of the system. Their only chance for success, they assert, would be to take advantage of this situation to bring about their revolutionary goals. As Guillaume Faye, the late writer and leading intellectual of the French New Right, predicted in his influential book, *Convergence of Catastrophes*, a concatenation of unfortunate events could precipitate the downfall of the West (Faye 2012).

The events of 2020 would seem to give credence to Faye's prognostications. The incoming Biden administration will have its hands full guiding the nation to a post-Covid-19 recovery. His advanced age and potential mental decline might even occasion a succession crisis in which Vice President Kamala Harris assumes the reins of power. In the light of Biden's narrow victory and Harris' only modest support in the Democratic primaries, there may be no strong mandate for her administration. The economic impact of Covid-19 has been devastating. Even before the onset of the crisis, the federal government was in a precarious fiscal predicament, as gargantuan budget deficits had been the norm since the global war on terror commenced after the 9-11 terrorists attacks. With many people out of work, there will be tremendous public pressure for the federal government to do something to alleviate the economic crisis. Eventually, something will have to give and the federal government will be forced to limit spending.

Perhaps most troubling is the return of urban unrest on a scope and scale that the nation has never experienced before. Indeed, it does not seem unreasonable to say that the nation might soon be on the cusp of a "1989" moment not unlike Eastern Europe witnessed in the last days of the Soviet bloc. When faced with widespread rioting and lawlessness during the summer of 2020, authorities at the federal, state, and local levels seemed to have lost their nerve. A remarkable scene took place on the evening of May 30, when protestors gathered in front of the White House and threw rocks at police barricades. The situation was so tenuous that Secret Service agents rushed President Trump to the White House bunker (Lemire & Miller 2020). Had the crowd acted more boldly and impudently, President Trump might have suffered a humiliating *sauve qui peut* flight from the White House, or even *in extremis* shared a similar fate to that of the Romanian leader Nicolae Ceaușescu thirty-one years earlier.

On the flip side, on January 6, 2021, supporters of Donald Trump stormed the US Capitol building after he gave a speech exhorting them to march there and "peacefully and patriotically make your voices heard." The stridency of the response was unexpected; after all, the last time the US Capitol Building was stormed was in 1814 by British troops, during the War of 1812. Although Trump is often excoriated in the mainstream media, he still has enormous grassroots support among significant portions of the American population. In the weeks running up to the elections, his rallies were packed. The fact that he received at least 74 million votes—more than any Republican candidate in history in a race that pollsters projected that he would soundly lose—demonstrated the depth of his support. Ominously, the president's son—Donald Trump Jr.—tweeted on November 7: "70 million pissed off Republicans and not one city burned to the ground." The fallout of the Capitol episode could further radicalize the far right after the FBI announced that it had arrested a number of activists involved in the melee which left five people dead.

Conclusion

In Spring 2021, the American far right remains a marginalized and stigmatized movement. There continues to be a significant chasm between the far right and mainstream conservatism. However, with the emergence of Trumpism, that gap appears to be narrowing. Although losing the 2020 Presidential election, his narrow defeat illustrates the acute dissatisfaction that many American conservatives have with the establishment wing of the Republican Party. Many voters feel as though the surrounding culture has abandoned them.

Changing demographics in the United States, which project that over half of the population will be non-white by mid-century, make a racial exclusionist party not feasible at the national level. For these and other reasons, some elements of the far right have decided that a strategy of revolution and terrorism is the only viable alternative in order to attain their political and social goals. Sensationalist stories of clandestine right-wing groups such as Atomwaffen and the Base have raised concerns in recent years (De Simone et al 2020; SPLC 2020). However, to date, their violence seems quite isolated and haphazard and certainly presents no existential threat to the American system.

The political radical right seems to be more effective as an oppositional movement rather than one in power. Not long after Barack Obama assumed the presidency in 2009, the Tea Party emerged as a broad-based, grassroots movement that reinvigorated American conservatism. In 2016, candidate Donald Trump managed to tap into a vein of populism which catapulted him to the White House and radically transformed the conservative movement that had been dominated by neo-conservatives during the Bush administration. However, during his presidency, Trump and his allies were continuously on the defensive, fighting off charges of Russian collusion and later impeachment. Consequently, Trump's agenda languished. His signature campaign promise—"build the wall"—met with only moderate success

(Rodgers & Bailey 2020). As 2020 drew to a close, it was right-wing activists who took to the streets to protest what they believed was a rigged election. Now Trump is out of power, expect to see the far right once again to go on the offensive. Because Joe Biden's victory was narrow, his administration does not have an unequivocally strong mandate, and to date his calls for national unity may seem more wishful thinking than achievable. Although the events of 2020 may have ultimately doomed Donald Trump's re-election aspirations, then and possibly for 2024, the American far right appears well-poised for regeneration as it seeks to capitalize on the chaos in the aftermath of Covid-19.

In summary, identifiable risk exposures include the following, which are assessed further in chapter 10:

Risk Exposures of Representative Democracy, Governance and Institutions

Risk Exposure 1: Far-Right Infiltration of Republican Party

A determined and emboldened far right may seek to gain indirect power and influence by further infiltration of the Republican Party (GOP) at multiple levels, thereby potentially converting the GoP from a 'one nation' party into a de facto nationalist/nativist far-right party, and a consequent further polarization of US governance and a harshening of policies.

Risk Exposure 2: Far-Right Sympathizers in Armed Forces

A continued infiltration of US armed forces by far-right sympathizers may result in a continuing threat of support by such individuals (however small in number) for insurrectionist ideas and activities, thereby potentially undermining national security. [see evaluation and discussion in chapter 10].

Risk Exposure 3: Far-Right Sympathizers in Police Forces

A continued infiltration of US armed police forces by far-right sympathizers may result in the current epidemic of killings of BAME individuals by police officers continuing, thereby undermining public trust and confidence in the institutions of law and order. [see evaluation and discussion in chapter 10].

Risks Exposures to Public and US Society

Risk Exposure 1: White Victimhood Aggravating Racial Resentment

Continued dissemination by the far right and their sympathizers, of such unsubstantiated conspiracy theories as the Great White Replacement Theory, is likely to cement a popular belief and consequent anxiety among white people that their historical racial dominance is inexorably waning and that they will be compelled to reassert that dominance as a means of self-protection. This victimhood attitude is likely to result in increased inter-racial tensions and resentment.

Risk Exposure 2: Far-Right Intimidation and Violence Against Minorities

More extreme sections of a determined and emboldened far right may increasingly resort to intimidation and violence towards such targets of hate as ethnic and religious minorities and other vulnerable sections of society.

Risk Exposure 3: Discrimination of Minorities by Far-Right Sympathizers

Far-right sympathizers in positions of authority, such as public servants, officials, police and law enforcement officers, justice officials, and administrators of institutions, may discriminate against minorities and vulnerable sections of society by exercising their prejudices. [see evaluation and discussion in chapter 10].

Risk Exposure 4: Far-Right Intimidation and Violence Against Political Adversaries

More extreme sections of a determined and emboldened far right may increasingly resort to intimidation and violence towards actual or perceived political enemies of the radical right, such as liberal/centrist Republican politicians, Democrats (e.g. the Gretchen Whitmer kidnap plot; the violent mob attack on the Capitol, January 6, 2021), symbols of liberal elitism (e.g. the excoriation of George Soros), and Antifa and BLM (e.g. street battles in various cities).

Risk Exposures for the US Far Right

Risk Exposure 1: Demographics

The changing demographics of the US, with an increasing shift away from a historical white racial predominance, may result in the medium-to-long term in an electorate less willing to vote for radical-right candidates, or for a Republican Party perceived as sympathizing with white supremacy. This fact may weaken the prospects of far-right Presidents and related policies and governance being realized.

Risk Exposure 2: Marginalisation

With no identifiable far-right or radical-right Republican candidates in the foreseeable future who are of comparable electoral magnetism to Donald Trump, it is unlikely that the far right will be able to secure as great an influence on US politics and governance as it achieved during the 2016-2020 Trump presidency. This significant change is likely to marginalise the far right to the role of noisy protestors and polemicists, online hatemongers, and occasional street thugs, albeit that, like Trump, Republican politicians will continue to curry their favour when deemed convenient.

Risk Exposure 3: Hubris

The radical right are vulnerable to the adverse consequences of egregious gaffes and actions e.g. the 'Hailgate' Nazi salute video at Richard Spencer's NPI meeting, the arrest of far-right activists plotting to kidnap and possibly murder the Democrat Governor of Michigan, and the universal condemnation of Trump for praising far-right violence in Charlottesville in 2017. The insurrectionist mob attack on the Capitol in Washington DC (January 6, 2021) epitomized the genre. Such incidents are likely to alienate mainstream voters, media and opinion-formers, and Republican politicians concerned with their public image and future prospects.

References

ADL. 2019. "The Boogaloo: Extremists' New Slang Term for A Coming Civil War". Anti-Defamation League. November 26, 2019, https://www.adl.org/blog/the-boogaloo-extremists-new-slang-term-for-a-coming-civil-war.

Anglin, A. 2020. "Epic Return to Glory! President Posts Video Proving That Coronavirus Is A Bitch Disease! Nothing!" *The Daily Stormer*. October 6, 2020, https://dailystormer.su/trump-leave s-hospital-posts-video-implying-he-had-to-get-the-virus-to-pro ve-a-point/.

Axios. 2020. "Trump to Far-right Proud Boys: "Stand Back and Stand By". *Axios*. September 30, 2020, https://www.axios.com/trump-biden-proud-boys-condemn-97fc56d8-9041-4bae-9ec1-b0c54 d863d30.html.

Barge, D. 2020. "The Outsourcing of White Nationalism to 'Black Lives Matter'". *Affirmative Right*, June 29, 2020, https://affirmativeri ght.blogspot.com/2020/06/the-outsourcing-of-white-nationali sm-to.html.

BBC News. 2018. "Laura Ingraham: Demographic Changes 'National Emergency'". *BBC News*. August 10, 2018, https://www.bbc.com /news/world-us-canada-45146811.

Benner, K. 2020. "Justice Dept. to Take Aim at Antigovernment Extremists". *The New York Times*, June 28, 2020, https://www.ny-times.com/2020/06/26/us/politics/justice-department-protes ts-violence.html.

Bergengruen, V. 2020. "How Far-Right Personalities and Conspiracy Theorists are Cashing in on the Pandemic Online". *Time*. August 20, 2020, https://time.com/5881595/right-wing-conspiracy-theorists-coronavirus/.

Campion, J., Javed, A., Sartorius, N., and Marmot, M. 2020. "Addressing the Public Mental Health Challenge of COVID-19". *The Lancet*. Volume 7, Issue 8, August 2020. Pages 657-659, https://www. ncbi.nlm.nih.gov/pmc/articles/PMC7282758/.

Carlson, T. 2020. "For China, the Coronavirus Pandemic has been a Blessing as it Plans to Rule the World". *Fox News*. May 5, 2020, https://www.foxnews.com/opinion/tucker-carlson-for-china-the-coronavirus-pandemic-has-been-a-blessing-as-it-plans-to-rule-the-world.

CDC. 2021. CDC COVID Data Tracker. March 11, 2021. US Centers for Disease Control. https://covid.cdc.gov/covid-data-tracker/#cas es_casesper100klast7days.

Chen, F. 2020. "China Seeks to Flip the Script on Covid Blame Game". *Asia Times*. November 4, 2020, https://asiatimes.com/2020/11/china-seeks-to-flip-the-script-on-Covid-blame-game/.

Coaston, J. 2020. "Why Alt-right Trolls Shouted Down Donald Trump Jr.". *Vox*. November 11, 2020, https://www.vox.com/policy-and-politics/2019/11/11/20948317/alt-right-donald-trump-jr-conservative-tpusa-yaf-racism-antisemitism

Cole, D. 2020a. "No Recount Needed: China Won". *Taki's Magazine*. December 1, 2020, https://www.takimag.com/article/no-recount-needed-china-won/

Cole, D. 2020b. "Trump's Wuhan WMDs (This'll End Well)". *Taki's Magazine*. May 12, 2020, https://www.takimag.com/article/trumps-wuhan-wmds-thisll-end-well/.

Costello, J. 2020. "The Stolen Election Will Red-Pill 70 Million Americans". *The Unz Review*. November 9, 2020, https://www.unz.com/article/the-stolen-election-will-red-pill-70-million-americans/.

Daily Sabah. 2020. "Concern Grows Over Extremist Clashes in US Before November Election," *Daily Sabah*. September 18, 2020, https://www.dailysabah.com/world/americas/concern-grows-over-extremist-clashes-in-us-before-november-election.

De Simone, D., Soshnikov, A. and Winston, A. 2020. "Neo-Nazi Rinaldo Nazzaro Running US Militant Group The Base from Russia". *BBC News*. January 24, 2020, https://www.bbc.com/news/world-51236915.

Devereaux, R. 2020. "Leaked Documents Show Police Knew Far-Right Extremists were the Real Threat at Protests, Not 'Antifa'". *The Intercept*. July 15, 2020, https://theintercept.com/2020/07/15/george-floyd-protests-police-far-right-antifa/.

Donaghue, E. 2020. "Two Autopsies Both Find George Floyd Died by Homicide, but Differ on Some Key Details". *CBS News*. June 4, 2020, https://www.cbsnews.com/news/george-floyd-death-autopsies-homicide-axphyxiation-details/.

Duke, D. 2020. "Does President Donald Trump Have Coronavirus? Are Israel and the Global Zionist Elite up to their Old Tricks?". *DavidDuke.com*. March 12, 2020, http://renseradioarchives.com/archives/dduke/031220.mp3.

Ellis, E.G. 2020. "The Meme-Fueled Rise of a Dangerous, Far-Right Militia". *Wired*. June 18, 2020, https://www.wired.com/story/boogaloo-movement-protests/.

Eltagouri, M. and Selk, A. 2018. "How a White Nationalist's Family Came to Blows over a Trailer Tryst". *The Washington Post*. March 14, 2018, https://www.washingtonpost.com/news/post-nation/wp/2018/03/13/white-nationalist-leader-matthew-heimbach-arrested-for-domestic-battery/?utm_term=.1b6c6465aeea.

Faye, G. 2012. *Convergence of Catastrophes*. Berwick-on-Tweed, UK: Arktos Media Ltd.

Fukuyama, F. 2020. "Liberalism and Its Discontents". *American Purpose*. October 5, 2020, https://www.americanpurpose.com/articles/liberalism-and-its-discontent/.

Funke, D. 2020. "Tucker Carlson Guest Airs Debunked Conspiracy Theory that COVID-19 was Created in a Lab". *Politifact*. September 16, 2020, https://www.politifact.com/factchecks/2020/sep/16/li-meng-yan/tucker-carlson-guest-airs-debunked-conspiracy-theo/.

Hayden, M.E. 2020. "Far-Right Extremists Heading to Washington Amid Talk of Trump 'Coup'". *Hatewatch*. November 12, 2020, https://www.splcenter.org/hatewatch/2020/11/12/far-right-extremists-heading-washington-amid-talk-trump-coup.

Heim, J. 2016. "This White Nationalist who Shoved a Trump Protestor May Be the Next David Duke". *The Washington Post*. April 12, 2016, https://www.washingtonpost.com/local/this-white-nationalist-who-shoved-a-trump-protester-may-be-the-next-david-duke/2016/04/12/7e71f750-f2cf-11e5-89c3-a647fcce95e0_story.html?utm_term=.7d0ac58f17ab.

Heimbach, M. 2020. "In From the Cold: Why I Left White Nationalism". *Light Upon Light*. https://www.lightuponlight.online/in-from-the-cold-why-i-left-white-nationalism/. [accessed December 14, 2020].

Higgins, T. 2020. "3 More Cops Charged in George Floyd Death, Other Officer's Murder Charge Upgraded". *CNBC*. June 3, 2020, https://www.cnbc.com/2020/06/03/3-more-cops-charged-in-george-floyd-death-other-officers-murder-charge-upgraded.html.

Hirsch, L. and Breuninger, K. 2020. "Trump Signs $8.3 Billion Emergency Coronavirus Spending Package". *CNBC*. March 6, 2020,

https://www.cnbc.com/2020/03/06/trump-signs-8point3-bil
lion-emergency-coronavirus-spending-package.html.

Houck, R. 2020. "Open Borders Caused the COVID-19 Pandemic". *National Vanguard*, May 5, 2020, https://nationalvanguard.org/20
20/05/open-borders-caused-the-Covid-19-pandemic/.

ISD. 2020a. "Far-right Mobilisation". *ISD.* April 9, 2020, https://www.isd
global.org/wp-content/uploads/2020/04/Covid-Briefing-2.pdf.

ISD. 2020b. *BBC Click Investigation and ISD*. May 12, 2020, https://
www.isdglobal.org/wp-content/uploads/2020/05/20200513-
ISDG-Weekly-Briefing-3b.pdf.

Kaufmann, E. 2019. *Whiteshift: Populism, Immigration, and the Future
of White Majorities*. New York: Abrams Press.

Kiely, E. and Reider, S. 2020. "Trump's Repeated False Attacks on Mail-
In Ballots". *FactCheck*. September 25, 2020, https://www.factch
eck.org/2020/09/trumps-repeated-false-attacks-on-mail-in-ba
llots/.

Kingson, J.A. 2020. "Exclusive: $1 Billion-plus Riot Damage is Most Ex-
pensive in Insurance History". *Axios.* September 16, 2020,
https://www.axios.com/riots-cost-property-damage-276c9bcc
-a455-4067-b06a-66f9db4cea9c.html.

Knutson, J. 2020. "Trump Condemns White Supremacists and the
Proud Boys Militia Group". *Axios.* October 2, 2020, https://www.
axios.com/trump-condemn-proud-boys-fox-417ad2b1-6579-4
551-b2e6-bd9aaf51c735.html.

Lemire, J. and Miller, Z. 2020. "Trump Took Shelter in White House
Bunker as Protests Raged". *Associated Press*. May 31, 2020,
https://apnews.com/article/a2326518da6b25b4509bef1ec85
f5d7f.

Litke, E. 2020. "Lawsuit Claim that Statistics Prove Fraud in Wisconsin, Elsewhere is Wildly Illogical". *Politifact.* December 9, 2020,
https://www.politifact.com/factchecks/2020/dec/10/faceboo
k-posts/texas-lawsuit-statistics-fraud-wisconsin-michigan/.

MacFarquhar, N. 2020. "Many Claim Extremists are Sparking Protest
Violence. But Which Extremists?". *The New York Times*. June 22,
2020, https://www.nytimes.com/2020/05/31/us/george-floy
d-protests-white-supremacists-antifa.html.

Mendoza, M. and Dazio, S. 2020. "California Sheriff: Gunman 'Very Intent' on Killing Police". *Associated Press.* June 9, 2020, https://ap news.com/article/9186215f571341b8e344a17402fa73e9.

Michael, G. 2017. "The Rise of the Alt-Right and the Politics of Polarization in America". *Skeptic.* Vol. 22, No. 2. (2017), p. 15.

Moran, R. 2020. "Chinese Government Stepping Up Propaganda to Change COVID Origin Story". *PJ Media.* November 29, 2020, https://pjmedia.com/news-and-politics/rick-moran/2020/11/29/chinese-government-stepping-up-propaganda-to-change-Covid-origin-story-n1179966.

Nguyen, T. 2020. "Anthony Fauci Becomes a Fringe MAGA Target". *Politico.* March 24, 2020, https://www.politico.com/news/2020/03/24/anthony-fauci-fringe-maga-target-147401.

Perira, I. 2020. "Independent Autopsy Finds George Floyd Died of Homicide by Asphyxia". *ABC News.* June 1, 2020, https://abcnew s.go.com/US/independent-autopsy-george-floyd-findings-anno unced/story?id=70994827.

Polumbo, B. 2020. "George Floyd Riots Caused Record-Setting $2 Billion in Damage, New Report Says. Here's Why the True Cost Is Even Higher". *Foundation for Economic Education.* September 16, 2020, https://fee.org/articles/george-floyd-riots-caused-re cord-setting-2-billion-in-damage-new-report-says-here-s-why-the-true-cost-is-even-higher/.

Reuters. 2020. "Fact Check: False Claims about George Soros". *Reuters.* September 29, 2020, https://www.reuters.com/article/uk-fact check-false-george-soros-claims/fact-checkfalseclaims-about-g eorge-soros-idUSKBN23P2XJ.

Robinson, P., Bass, D., and Langreth, R. 2020. "Seattle's Patient Zero Spread Coronavirus Despite Ebola-Style Lockdown". *Bloomberg Businessweek.* March 9, 2020, https://www.bloomberg.com/news/features/2020-03-09/how-coronavirus-spread-from-pa tient-zero-in-seattle.

Sales, B. 2020. "A Proud Boys Leader is Trying to Rebrand the Group as Explicitly White Supremacist and Anti-Semitic". *Sun Sentinel.* November 11, 2020, https://www.sun-sentinel.com/florida-je wish-journal/fl-jj-proud-boys-rebrand-20201111-kp4cr7l5pbd nxguwyb3xq4m63e-story.html.

Schrader, E. 2020. "The Virus Spreading Faster than Coronavirus: Anti-Semitism". *The Jerusalem Post*. March 24, 2020, https://www.jpost.com/opinion/the-virus-spreading-faster-than-coronavirus-antisemitism-622206.

Scott, H. 2020. "Jewish Influence Caused the Death of George Floyd as Well as the Violent Reaction That Followed". *National Vanguard*. June 2, 2020, https://nationalvanguard.org/2020/06/jewish-influence-caused-the-death-of-george-floyd-as-well-as-the-violent-reaction-that-followed/.

Sims, D. 2020. "Will the Capitalist West Learn the Lessons of COVID-19". *National Vanguard*. April 5, 2020, https://nationalvanguard.org/2020/04/will-the-capitalist-west-learn-the-lessons-of-Covid-19/.

Singh, M., Davidson, H., and Borger, J. 2020. "Trump Claims to Have Evidence Coronavirus Started in Chinese Lab but Offers No Details". *The Guardian*. April 30, 2020, https://www.theguardian.com/us-news/2020/apr/30/donald-trump-coronavirus-chinese-lab-claim.

Sommer, W. 2020. "Anti-Lockdown Protesters Now Have a 21-Year-Old Martyr". *Daily Beast*. May 11, 2020, https://www.thedailybeast.com/anti-lockdown-boogaloo-protesters-now-have-a-21-year-old-martyr-in-duncan-lemp.

SPLC. 2020. "Atomwaffen Division". Southern Poverty Law Center. https://www.splcenter.org/fighting-hate/extremist-files/group/atomwaffen-division. [accessed December 16, 2020].

Stern, K. 2020. "'This Does Feel Like a Different Moment': As Public Support for Black Lives Matter Drops Off, Will Corporate America Stay the Course?". *Vanity Fair*. September 24, 2020, https://www.vanityfair.com/news/2020/09/will-corporate-america-stay-the-course-with-black-lives-matter.

Subramanian, C. and Culver, J. 2020. "Donald Trump Sidesteps Call to Condemn White Supremacists—and the Proud Boys were 'Extremely Excited' About It". *USA Today*. September 29, 2020, https://www.usatoday.com/story/news/politics/elections/2020/09/29/trump-debate-white-supremacists-stand-back-stand-by/3583339001/.

Tenold, V. 2015. "The Little Führer". *Al Jazeera in America*. July 26, 2015, http://projects.aljazeera.com/2015/07/hate-groups/.

Totenberg, N. and Sprunt, B. 2020. "Supreme Court Shuts Door On Texas Suit Seeking To Overturn Election". *NPR*. December 11, 2020, https://www.npr.org/2020/12/11/945617913/suprem e-court-shuts-door-on-trump-election-prospects.

Trad News. 2020. "Clear Evidence of Vote Rigging Emerges". *Trad News*. November 4, 2020, https://affirmativeright.blogspot.com /2020/11/clear-evidence-of-vote-rigging-emerges.html.

USDoJ. 2020 ."Harvard University Professor and Two Chinese Nationals Charged in Three Separate China Related Cases". The United States Department of Justice. January 28, 2020, https://www. justice.gov/opa/pr/harvard-university-professor-and-two-chi nese-nationals-charged-three-separate-china-related.

Wheelock, D.C. 2020. "Comparing the COVID-19 Recession with the Great Depression". Economic Research Federal Reserve Bank of St. Louis. August 8, 2020, https://research.stlouisfed.org/publi cations/economic-synopses/2020/08/12/comparing-the-Cov id-19-recession-with-the-great-depression.

Wilson, J. 2016. "Clickbait Scoops and an Engaged 'Alt-right': Everything to Know about Breitbart News". *The Guardian*. November 15, 2016, https://www.theguardian.com/media/2016/nov/15/brei tbart-news-alt-right-stephen-bannon-trump-administration.

Winter, T., Kosnar, M. and Li., D.K. 2020. "13 Men Charged in Alleged Plot to Kidnap Michigan Gov. Gretchen Whitmer". *NBC News*. October 9, 2020, https://www.nbcnews.com/news/us-news/six-men-charged-alleged-plot-kidnap-michigan-gov-gretchen-whit mer-n1242622.

Woodward, B. 2020. *Rage*. Page 333. New York: Simon & Schuster.

Yiannopoulos, M. 2017. *Dangerous*. Tampa, Florida: MILO Worldwide LLC.

Zadrozny, B. 2020. "What is the 'Boogaloo'? How Online Calls for a Violent Uprising are Hitting the Mainstream". *NBC News*. February 19, 2020, https://www.nbcnews.com/tech/social-media/what-boogaloo-how-online-calls-violent-uprising-are-getting-organi zed-n1138461.

Chapter 9:
Radical-Right Conspiracy Theories and Corporate Collusion

By Alan Waring[1]

Abstract

This chapter examines the phenomenon of conspiracy theories disseminated by radical-right sources and agents and, further, the role of corporations in such dissemination. Account is taken of the comprehensive review of the conspiracy theories phenomenon by Douglas et al (2019), along with studies such as Amarasingam and Argentino (2020) on the QAnon radical-right conspiracy cult. The parsimony test and the causation test are discussed in relation to evaluating the validity of a conspiracy theory. Various kinds of potential harm caused by conspiracy theories are considered. In addition to radical-right conspiracy theorists, the motives and activities of two categories of corporate colluder are examined: ideological supporters and commercial opportunists. Among the latter are major online platform operators, most of which have been very reluctant to self-regulate and thereby control, curb or ban extremist content emanating from the radical right, including harmful fake conspiracy allegations. Methods for neutralising fake conspiracy theories are summarised. Risks to various parties are systematically identified.

Key Words: radical-right, conspiracy theories, QAnon, corporations, collusion, risks

The Conspiracy Theories Phenomenon

Throughout these three volumes, a working assumption has been that radical-right ideology and conduct arise more or less spontaneously among leaders, adherents and supporters, albeit that there is persuasive evidence (e.g. Douglas et al 2019) of a mix of precursors, such as psychological and personality predispositions, genetic predisposition in radical-right psychopaths (e.g. Brooks 2020; Brooks et al 2020),

---

[1]   See contributor affiliations and biography, page 525.

societal and sociological factors, embedded cultural prejudices, economic anxieties, and phobias about 'others'. The thesis assumes that right-wing authoritarianism in all its manifestations, whether politically orientated and/or entangled with corporatism, is self-generated and self-directed. In systems terms, applying the Formal System Paradigm (Checkland 1999), radical-right leaders and authoritarian corporate leaders together comprise the autopoietic self-legitimizing system that provides their operational sub-systems with policy, resources, and authority to act. Also, as has been amply demonstrated in earlier chapters, in the outer context or beyond the wider system boundary, exist patrons, donors, funding bodies, intermediaries, and enablers whose agency provides financial resources, and either implicitly endorses or even actively influences the thinking and direction of its servants.

The fusion of interests and dark money illustrated and discussed throughout the book might lead one to believe that the whole phenomenon of radical-right and corporate symbiosis is what it appears to be, namely a self-bounded authoritarian autopoiesis directing itself to secure permanent radical-right control of nations and societies and impose radical-right ideology on their populations and economies. However, a deeper question raised by some is whether radical-right leaders and ideologues are really self-directed or rather are being manipulated by more malign interests beyond the known financiers and benefactors—so-called 'longarming'. Are there even greater 'dark forces' pulling their strings'?

As the 21st century has progressed, a populist feeling that 'dark forces' are manipulating and directing what people are allowed to see, read and know and what they should think, has taken hold, actively encouraged by conspiracy theorists on the Internet and social media. While a majority of these conspiracists are associated with the radical right (Waring 2018, 283-285), some are on the radical left (e.g. Piers Corbyn) or members of radical anti-capitalist and anti-science groups which at times even collaborate with radical-right conspiracists (see examples in Kennedy & Ellis 2020). One of the more notable on the radical right is David Icke who, over some years, has put forward a number of 'alternative science' conspiracy theories to debunk such phenomena as climate change (Icke 2017) and the Covid-19 pandemic (Icke 2020a, b), as well as promoting conspiracy theories regarding the motives of liberal elites. His publicly released videos in March 2014 and July 2017 rejected the idea that global warning was human-created and dismissed it as a "scam" (Icke 2017). He has made anti-Semitic speeches that include conspiracy allegations (Lawrence 2018; Solomon 2017). In his *The Lion Sleeps No More* seminars, he articulates the theory that many world leaders share alien reptilian DNA, which predisposes them to conspire to control the world's human population. Having been blocked by *Facebook* and other social media platforms for posting unacceptable material, he courted further controversy by switching to the far-right platform *BitChute* (Dearden 2020). According to Ellery (2020), by 2020 Icke had also entrained his two sons, Gareth and Jaymie, into his Covid-19 conspiracy theory campaign, thereby creating an Icke cult dynasty. A report (CCDH 2020) on online promulgation of anti-vaccine conspiracy theories, together with the report by Ellery (2020), highlights the public health concerns about the Icke cult and similar conspiracy theory activists.

Conspiracy theories disseminated by the radical right and their associates range from the obviously far-fetched and bizarre, such as Icke's alien DNA assertions, to dangerously false assertions, such as those (e.g. by Wakefield) alleging that MMR vaccinations cause autism in infants (Deer 2020), or that the Covid-19 pandemic is a hoax by liberal-left conspirators and is no more harmful than seasonal influenza (Betz 2021) (a "little flu" according to Presidents Trump and Bolsonaro), or the dangerous notion that drinking hypochlorite bleach will ward off the 'hoax' Covid-19 infection (Trump), or that climate change does not exist and therefore requires no human intervention, e.g. Icke, and by Trump as embedded by deliberate omission from US policy (White House 2017). All such conspiracy theories share in common a paranoid delusional quality, in which typically the alleged conspirators against 'the people', 'society', 'God-fearing people', 'hard-working patriots', 'the white underclass', 'freedom lovers' and so on, are either not identified explicitly (e.g. referred to as 'they' and 'them'[2]), or are identified as amorphous entities such as 'the government', 'the elites',

---

[2]   The 'they' and 'them' identifiers are also observed frequently in individuals suffering from clinical paranoid delusions. When pressed to identify 'they' and 'them', or why these parties would wish to spy on them or harm them, the individuals often avoid answering, implying that they may not have a clear articulation of the perceived threat.

'the liberals', 'the Washington swamp', 'the unpatriotic', 'commies', and so on.

QAnon and the Deep State Conspiracy Theory

Numerous on-line networks of conspiracy websites serve the radical-right—see e.g. Nagle (2017). One of the most successful in terms of growth and widespread support is QAnon, which alleges a 'deep state' conspiracy run by political elites, business leaders, intellectuals, Hollywood and pop music celebrities, Democrat supporters, former Democrat US Presidents, and the Black Lives Matter movement (Betz 2020). In other words, the so-called 'deep state' conspiracy appears to be little more than a shorthand label used by the radical right for all those who oppose, or who are presumed to oppose, the radical right. President Trump has been a leading user of the 'deep state' conspiracy notion and publicly praised QAnon supporters as being "patriotic".

According to the study by Amarasingam and Argentino (2020), QAnon is a "bizarre assemblage of far-right conspiracy theories that holds that US President Donald Trump (during and after his presidency) has been waging a secret war against an international cabal of satanic pedophiles", but which itself "represents a public security threat" with a potential to evolve into a "domestic terror threat". Aaronovitch (2020a) agreed that, with QAnon using the angry language of soldiers and warriors fighting battles against evil, it would not take much for followers to resort to violence, as in cases analysed in Amarasingam and Argentino (2020). Indeed, in August 2020, some Internet and social media platforms including *Facebook* and *Google* blocked QAnon (*BBC* 2020), and *Twitter* removed 7,000 offending QAnon accounts. Further blocking of much larger swathes of QAnon accounts occurred in January 2021, following the radical-right mob attack on the Capitol in Washington DC on January 6, in which QAnon devotees prominently participated and used social media as a means of communication and apparent coordination.

QAnon allegations include the following (Waring 2020a): the US Democrats created the breakaway Confederacy of US southern states in 1861 (despite contrary evidence that it was a Republican initiative); they also created the Ku Klux Klan (KKK) and Covid-19; the Democrats along with elites in business, politics, science and medicine are part of a world-wide cabal of Satanists determined to control the world.

However, QAnon adherents believe that a day of populist reckoning will come, which they call 'The Storm', when this alleged conspiracy will be crushed. QAnon followers are recognisable by the *Twitter* hashtag #WWG1WGA i.e. Where We Go One, We Go All, referring to the QAnon 'Take the Oath'. Aaronovitch (2020a) noted that in July 2020 General Michael Flynn, the former US Defense Intelligence Agency and national security adviser to President Trump, took this oath of loyalty publicly with his family and friends. In August 2020, it became clear that several Republican congressional members or candidates had also taken the QAnon oath (Stracqualursi 2020) and later reports put the number at a minimum of 24. For example, Republican Representative for Georgia, Marjorie Taylor Greene, has openly supported QAnon. Videos and her *Facebook* postings have enthusiastically supported a conspiracy theory that Hillary Clinton murdered a child in a satanic ritual. They also approved violence (including murder) against Democrat politicians, Barack Obama and Hillary Clinton (Foran et al 2021; Hoyle 2021).

Among the more bizarre, if not absurd, allegations that spawned QAnon is the so-called 'Pizzagate' conspiracy theory (Amarasingam & Argentino 2020; van Prooijen 2018), which suggested that a cabal of powerful elites, including leading Democrats, controls the world and uses its power for covert child abuse. Allegedly, prominent Democrats, including presidential candidate Hillary Clinton (sic), were running a child-sex ring using a pizzeria in Washington DC popular with children.

Both Aaronovitch (2020a) and Betz (2020) argued that QAnon is not simply a 'deep state' conspiracy theory network but also one that has evolved into an online cult, albeit a self-perpetuating leaderless one. The evidence for this lies not just in the Where We Go One, We Go All oath but also the fixated relentlessness with which comment posters and respondents engage in a narrative of enraged victimhood and a total belief that the coming QAnon 'Storm' will save them and humankind (Waring 2020a). Such a victim-salvation thesis was noted by Neiwert (2017) as one of the key characteristics of the far right, and Woods (2020) considered the influence of authoritarian personalities in the phenomenon. Ultimately, the QAnon 'Storm' is promoted as the crucial event that will sweep away all the alleged liberal decay, corruption and evil and replace it with a new and pure 'people's order' based on the movement's notions of right and wrong, good and bad, and strong (radical-right) government to protect the nation against enemies, foreign and domestic. In other words, QAnon is a beacon of hope for those seeking a palingenetic rebirth of a nation cleansed of all liberal 'weaknesses', and is thus redolent of fascism, proto-fascism and the far right (Neiwert 2017, 357-366; Paxton 2005).

Van Prooijen (2018) noted that, although wildly far-fetched conspiracy theories of a paranoid delusional nature are disseminated by QAnon, it does not necessarily mean that all QAnon devotees are mentally ill. People who feel psychically lost, abandoned, powerless and fearful also frequently feel victims of systematic wrongdoing by others, rather than as a result of bad luck or their own failings. They may then in desperation resort to ascribing their misfortunes to evil forces conspiring to harm good people like themselves. He also observed that studies have shown (e.g. Goertzel 1994; 2010) that "accepting one conspiracy theory as true makes it much easier to believe in other [such] theories". This observation tallies with confirmation bias, whereby an individual becomes predisposed to seek out alleged incidents, events, stories, writings and utterances that appear to confirm and reinforce their prejudices, while systematically rejecting any that appear to disconfirm them (Dror & Fraser-MacKenzie 2008; Kahan et al 2017; Nickerson 1998; Zimmerman 2011). A comprehensive review of the conspiracy theory phenomenon by Douglas et al (2019) also observed that "....although both extreme left-wing and right-wing ideologies foster conspiracy convictions, right-wingers are more predisposed to believe in conspiracy theories because they are also more likely to exhibit the personality predispositions that foster conspiracy thinking, such as the need to manage uncertainty". Key predispositions are: low political trust, feelings of powerlessness, uncertainty, and unpredictability, coupled with an authoritarian outlook—see Waring and Paxton in chapter 2: Psychological Aspects of the Alt-Right Phenomenon of Vol 1 (2018) and Vol 2 (2019). See also Betz (2021) and Charron et al (2020) on common characteristics of conspiracy theory adherents in relation to Covid-19.

An obvious irony of the radical right's allegations of massive conspiracies by liberal-elites and all others who appear to them as their enemies is that such allegations themselves are actually part of a radical-right conspiracy seeking to (a) damage and diminish potential opposition and resistance to the radical-right cause, and (b) encourage radical-right supporters and attract potential new recruits. Moreover, the shrieking yah-boo hyperbole of the radical right's promulgation of online fake stories and allegations of their enemies' conspiracies often has a self-parodying character, almost tongue-in-cheek akin to the tendency of some titles of the British tabloid press to shamelessly print fake news stories in full expectation that readers are likely to spot them as obvious spoofs and hopefully would be amused (e.g. Hughes 2019). However, while many may laugh at the ludicrousness of QAnon, devotees are utterly convinced they are right.

Other Grand Conspiracy Theories Used by the Radical Right

Beyond the apocryphal, the bizarre, the comical, the authoritarian, and the hate-mongering, some conspiracy theories assert that we are but pawns in a much bigger game. For example, Zia-Ebrahimi (2018) on conspiratorial racialization argued that the fake conspiracy embedded in the notorious *Protocols of [......] the Elders of Zion* forgery (i.e. that the alleged conspiracy to dominate nations and the world is the essence of Jewishness that goes beyond biology, culture and religion) has close similarities to the Eurabia Islamic conspiracy thesis promoted by Bat Ye'or (2005) (i.e. that Islam is fundamentally and irredeemably violent and that its essence is to seek to conquer Europe through a devious alliance with European institutions). Both demonize their targets, alleging hegemonic conspiracies. Other hegemons refer to such alleged mega conspiracies as part of their own arguments e.g. Alexander Dugin's combatting Eurabia justification for aggressive Russian expansionism southwards to annexe vast predominantly Muslim territories, and westwards to reabsorb former Russian or Soviet bloc territories corrupted by the lure of a weakened liberal EU (Dugin 2012).

As Waring (2020b) observed, far from being two separate, distinct and independent phenomena, contemporary Islamophobia and anti-Semitism are closely analogous and linked products of a single, artful far-right narrative (see also e.g. Hoffman & Moe 2020). Far-right disparaging stereotyping has gone further than alleged *different* conspiracies by Jews and Muslims, by promulgation of theories that allege a high-level conspiracy *between* prominent Jews and Muslims to harm the native populations of Europe. The leading US far-right activist

David Duke (2012), for example, asserted that Jews are prominent among global elites orchestrating the mass immigration of Muslims into Europe, with the aim of destroying Europe's white Christian culture and its various national economies. In this regard, the international investor and philanthropist George Soros, (who is Jewish), became the far right's *bête noire* by being characterized as the instigator of a combined and terrifying Jewish-Islamic threat. In a resurrection of the longstanding alleged Jewish financial conspiracy to control countries and regions, Soros is portrayed by Hungary's Premier Viktor Orbán as a financial and economic abuser who, in addition, is undermining Europe through orchestrating Muslim migration as David Duke asserted (Boffey 2018; Miller 2017). In a further example of the alleged Jewish-Islamic common conspiratorial purpose, far-right anti-Semitic conspiracy promulgators have repeatedly alleged since 2001 that Jews were closely engaged in facilitating the Al Qaeda '9/11' terrorist attacks on the US (Tobias & Foxman 2003). Dyrendal (2020) found that in Norway conspiracy stereotypes of Jews and Muslims were closely linked to general xenophobia and measures of social distance, and that belief in such conspiracy theories was more frequently found among far-right adherents.

Prominent among other mega conspiracy theories which play, either directly or indirectly, to a radical-right audience are those which require a belief in diabolical hegemonic forces that are alleged to have been controlling and manipulating the world for decades, if not centuries. QAnon is currently at the forefront of promoting such 'longarming' theories, but they have been around in various forms for up to a century or more e.g. Carr (1958; 1959), Cherep-Spiridovich (1926), de Poncins (1928). Those entities supposedly being controlled include political parties, governments, national economies, financial institutions, industrial corporations, the military, scientific research, education, and public health. Political and corporate leaders who are not actively and willingly engaged in the conspiracy allegedly become, unwittingly or not, pawns and puppets of the conspirators. The alleged control and manipulation is by 'dark forces' who believe they have the right to wield such power outside and beyond the system of normal democratic structures and processes, while appearing nonetheless to abide by its rules. The alleged 'dark forces' goal is to protect and enhance their selfish interests at the expense of the masses and anyone opposing their interests, without regard to the scale of harm this may cause. The supposedly selfish interests include, for example, not only national and institutional policy decisions favouring their ideology and interests but also vast amounts of money to be made by speculation on stock markets, securing monopoly of supplies, stock-piling of commodities, arms dealing, trafficking, currency speculation, and immovable property speculation. Examples of such mega conspiracy theories are those put forward by Docherty and MacGregor (2013; 2018), in which they asserted that the First World War was not only instigated by a cabal of oligarchs, international speculators, bankers, and self-appointed elites (e.g. the Illuminati), but was also extended by the cabal for three-and-a-half years so as to maximize their financial gain and secure the long-term debt of Germany and other nations which the conspirators could also manipulate for further gain.

Barkun (2004; 2016) noted that grand conspiracy theories that have been prominent since the 18th century include those alleging that the Illuminati, or the Jews, or both in cahoots, plotted relentlessly to take over the world. Other similar conspiracy theories (e.g. Carr 1958; de Poncins 1928) also cited Freemasonry among the 'dark forces' having a similar mission. The Illuminati was founded as the Bavarian Illuminati in 1776 as a private group of like-minded individuals who believed that they were 'the enlightened' who possessed a superior intellect and special knowledge and insight, which privileged status compelled them to apply it all to the betterment of humankind. However, such an espoused benign intent did not save it from opposition and dysfunctionality, and by the turn of the 19th century it was in marked decline. Nevertheless, what the 18th century Illuminati failed to achieve as a purported force for good has been outstripped since by the increasing notoriety of its name throughout the 20th century as an alleged malevolent grand conspiracy organ (*not* a benevolent one), which has been magnified in the 21st century by its exponential dissemination by the radical right online and by social media. Moreover, a number of contemporary entities with the word Illuminati in their names claim to be the inherited continuing embodiment of the original Illuminati e.g. Illuminati (2020). Such claims have not been verified and no official address or headquarters is cited [at least 15 have been suggested]. Nonetheless, these claims provide conspiracy theorists with an opportunity, albeit unconvincing, to assert that the alleged Illuminati conspiracy continues in the modern world e.g. QAnon assertions.

Barkun (2004) also noted that, in the second half of the 20th century, grand conspiracists fell into two main distinct groups—the "politically disaffected" such as the far right, and the "culturally suspicious" such as those believing in hegemonic conspiracies involving any combinations selected from UFOs, Rockwell, aliens, human-reptilian chimeras (e.g. one of Icke's theories), the Kennedy assassination, and a Jewish conspiracy behind the 9/11 attacks. By the 21st century, he argued that not only were these two groups already barely distinguishable but were also joining forces with occultists and those committed to alternative science (e.g. climate change denial) and alternative medicine (e.g. SARS, and currently Covid-19, as hoax threats; MMR as a cause of child autism—see Deer 2020). This merging was described by Kelly (1995) as "fusion paranoia". It not only gave a new lease of life to such conspiracy theories as malevolent world leaders having reptilian DNA and Illuminati devils with hegemonic plots, but it also provided through the rapidly spreading Internet and social media a mass self-certifying 'real facts' network of fake facts and fake news that demand the inversion of logic. Barkun (2016) argued that, in the world-view of the conspiracists, taken-for-granted facts are *necessarily* false, with the corollary that theories disproved by evidence or normal science *must* be true—because 'the Establishment' and all its instruments are part of the alleged corrupt conspiracy that keeps the population compliant with fake science, fake facts and fake news. As a result, conspiracism and its "stigmatized knowledge", however apocryphal, absurd and delusional, "has the potential to leap into public discourse" as a mainstream normality that encourages a generalisation of disbelief in information and advice from any authoritative source, as echoed by Varis (2019).

As grand conspiracy theories go, the treatise of William Guy Carr (1958; 1959) is among the most all-embracing. Like many others, he reiterated (1958, chapter 6) the well-worn saga of a conspiracy to control the world involving the Illuminati, international freemasonry, international Zionism, international bankers, and monetary manipulation. However, he went further by suggesting (chapter 1, pages 4-6) that the Illuminati were prominent in this conspiracy by sponsoring not only Karl Marx and Friedrich Engels as far-left proto-communists, *but also at the same time* those antithetical to communism, such as the imperial nationalism of von Treitschke and Karl Ritter (and later Nietzsche). Carr's polemic argued that the alleged conspirators did this deliberately so as to set the two contrasting ideologies at loggerheads and sow the seeds of division, enmity, and conflict in society as a means to weaken democratic governance and social accord and thereby conquer and control nations and populations, a process he called "the despotism of Satan". This alleged process was akin to 'hedging their bets' to ensure that, whichever would win, the conspirators' interests would be secured. Carr's thesis also sought to explain, in considerable detail, every significant historical event (e.g. the French Revolution, Russian Revolution, World War I, World War II, and the Spanish Civil War) as a product of an alleged universal all-consuming satanic plot orchestrated by the Illuminati, freemasons, Zionists, international bankers, and money manipulators. His final polemical work (Carr 1959) elaborated on his 1958 thesis, referring to an over-arching "Synagogue of Satan". His chapter on 'Secret Societies and Subversive Movements' (pages 42-49) reiterates his assertions about the Illuminati, freemasons, Jews and so on, and a later chapter (pages 61-64) claims to provide proof of the conspiracy.

Other grand conspiracy theories include those alleging that since WWII the US Federal Government has operated a massive covert surveillance programme on the US population, coupled with an equally massive programme of mind control, all of which has been greatly expanded and facilitated by advances in the power and sophistication of computers, telecommunications, and IT in the present century. Such alleged programmes are intended to apply social and economic engineering techniques, together with mass psychological manipulation, to produce social order, peace and tranquillity for the ruling elites. For example, the polemic *Operation Mind Control* (Bowart 1994) described what is alleged to have already been perpetrated, whereas *Silent Weapons for Quiet Wars* (*Silent Weapons* 1979) provided a purportedly factual US government 'operational research' blueprint for such programmes.

Nevertheless, Noam Chomsky (1999, 8) posited a purposive, almost preconscious, conspiracy of a sort in his assertion that in modern democratic societies "ideological institutions" channel public thoughts and attitudes within "acceptable" bounds, while tacitly "deflecting substantive challenge to established privilege and authority" before it can crystallize and gather strength. In essence, this is an example of unobtrusive power (Hardy 1985). Chomsky also referred to much of this 'thought control' power being in the hands of private entities and specifically national media and "related elements of intellectual culture." Although written at the end of the 20th century, it resonates with the major criticisms of some contemporary corporate controllers of Internet and social media platforms twenty years later, who have been extremely reluctant to remove extremist material and messages.

Corporations and Conspiracy Theories

Corporations have become entrained in the conspiracy theories phenomenon into two distinct ways. On the one hand, some corporations (category A) either share radical-right predilections and/or seek to gain financially or from political advantages that endorsing such theories may confer. On the other hand, other corporations (category B) may find themselves being cast as villains in conspiracy theories of an anti-corporate nature. Although category A are clearly the focus in this volume, for completeness category B is also addressed but to a more limited extent.

A: Ideological and Opportunist Corporations Promulgating Conspiracy Theories

As discussed in chapters 1 and 5, a number of corporate entities and their leaders are engaged in support for radical-right ideology (either as ideological supporters or unwittingly), and this includes promulgation of conspiracy theories that seek to advance the radical-right cause. Prominent among those consciously supporting the ideology is a highly reticulated web of corporations, foundations, activist campaigns, and media companies, sponsored and funded by such protagonists as Robert Shillman, CEO of Cognex, Robert Mercer, CEO of Renaissance Technologies, and Nina Rosenwald, heiress to Sears, Roebuck & Co. Propaganda channels which this group, either directly or indirectly, funds or supports include The *Rebel Media* group (www.rebelnews.com) funded by Mercer, *Infowars* (www.infowars.com) led by the high-profile Alex Jones, and *Stop Islamization of America (SIOA)* (www.sioaonline.com) led by Pamela Geller, all of which promulgate radical-right conspiracy theories. Other 'fellow travellers' include Julie Jenkins Fancelli, the Publix heiress (Rama-chandran et al 2021) and the ubiquitous radical-right conspiracist Alex Jones. Their implied, if not stated, conspiracy theme overall, as publicised on their websites, social media, and *YouTube*, is that politi-cians and authorities at national, state and city levels have engaged—and continue to engage—in a range of conspiracies, including hege-monic control of the population and denial of freedom by way of an exaggerated Covid-19 threat and unnecessary protective measures, and 2020 election fraud seeking to deny Trump's allegedly rightful re-election. In addition, *SIOA* alleges a conspiracy to promote Islamic re-ligion, culture and influence which allegedly threatens US culture, na-tional security, and public safety. *Infowars* also publicises David Icke's various conspiracy theories and lauds the activities and opinions of Tommy Robinson (Stephen Yaxley-Lennon), the British far-right anti-Muslim activist.

While major hosting platforms such as *Facebook, Twitter, YouTube* and *Instagram* have taken action (so far, modest) to ban ex-treme material, fake news and fake conspiracy theory propagators, a number of smaller but rising platform companies such as *Grab, Pat-reon* and *Pinterest* have welcomed such material and enthusiasts. The ethos and policy of such platforms are radical-right orientated. For ex-ample, *Grab.com* has reportedly become a prime hosting platform for QAnon (Jasser 2020). *BitChute* platform (www.bitchute.com) has also established itself as an unfettered dedicated radical-right alternative to mainstream platforms. In addition to anti-immigrant, white su-premacist, and ethno-religious hate material, all manner of radical-right conspiracists and conspiracy theories are aired on the *BitChute* host e.g. Alex Jones, David Icke, and output from *Breitbart News, In-fowars*, and *Rebel News*.

The close involvement of prominent radical-right activists across the individual groups and media emphasizes the network's complex integration. Typically, key individuals have worked for more than one organisation in the network and regularly write articles for several different media in it. For example, both Laura Loomer and Tommy Robinson are connected to *Infowars* and have worked for *Re-bel Media*, as has Pamella Geller of *SIOA* and Jack Posobiec. Both Geller and Robert Spencer of *SIOA* are also writers for *Breitbart News*, another Mercer-funded promulgator of radical-right propaganda and conspiracy theories.

Another ideological source of radical-right conspiracism is the VDare Foundation and its platform www.vdare.com, on which such writers as Ann Coulter, Peter Brimelow, and Michelle Malkin advance a variety of anti-immigrant and white supremacist arguments as part of a mass immigration conspiracy theory, in addition to Covid-19 hegemony assertions such as Malkin's 'covidgate' conspiracy theory.

In addition to ideologically-committed corporate leaders who aid and abet radical-right conspiracism out of conviction, a much more powerful group do so for commercial opportunism, or what Robinson and Murphy (2008) and Simon (2018) referred to as elite deviance and others refer to as the inherently egregious character of corporate authoritarianism, greed, and malfeasance (Bakan 2004; Barkun 2004; 2016; Birch 2007; Bloom & Rhodes 2016; 2018; Crouch 2014; Kohl & Makary 2016; Michaels 2020; Oklobdzija 2019; Simon 2018). By far the largest identifiable category of commercial opportunists is that comprising the major Internet and social media platform companies. Of the six primary categories of abuse alleged against such companies detailed in chapter 11, one (dissemination of fake facts and fake news) implicitly covers fake conspiracy theory promulgation, and at least two others also entrain culpability for spreading aspects of harmful conspiracy theory material.

Donovan (2020) quoted a former *Facebook* monetization director who, in testimony to Congress, had likened the present state of social media platforms to that of the tobacco industry in the 20th century, in which "both focussed on increasing the capacity for addiction by slowly modifying their products over time". This observation implied that the actions of online platform companies were being driven by a need to create an ever-expanding population of 'addicted' users whose patronage could be monetized. Zuboff (2019, 8) went further to accuse such companies of "surveillance capitalism" seeking ultimately to control information about individual users and "ever-more-predictive sources of behavioral surplus", the ultimate goal being to subliminally determine user responses for commercial gain.

B: Corporations Accused by Anti-Corporate Activists of Engaging in Conspiracies

Corporations whose products, activities, or technologies may be deemed unacceptable by some sectors of society may find themselves accused of engaging in harmful conspiracies. Of course, such observations on conspiracy theories as those in Donovan (2020) and by Zuboff (2019) are in themselves conspiracy theories. The plausibility of suggested motivations behind such alleged conspiracies notwithstanding, Gray (2011) downplays corporate conspiracy theories on experiential grounds: "Large organizations seem incapable of two critical elements for any successful conspiracy: impeccable organization and impenetrable secrecy". Nevertheless, conspiracies involving companies having imperfect organisation, inadequate competence, and 'hiding in plain sight' execution, do get away with conspiracies for long periods before getting exposed or stopped (e.g. in chapter 5, price gouging conspiracies, cases 5.1 and 5.2, and defrauding contractors *en masse*, case 5.6).

Some of the wilder allegations of corporate conspiracies, if rather dated, appear on the *Illuminatirex* website (https://www.illumi natirex.com/corporate-conspiracies/). Examples of more up-to-date corporate conspiracy theories include:

- Allegations that oil & gas exploration companies deliberately downplay seismic risks to neighbouring populations from their land-based fracking activities, so as to not impede production monetisation, and that relevant authorities collude in the risk denial. Such allegations appear to be an issue in particular jurisdictions e.g. UK rather, than pan-global.
- Allegations that industrial companies wilfully or negligently contaminate water supplies in pursuit of profit, thereby irreparably harming public health, and then cover up and deny their wrongful acts. While there is no real evidence of widespread systematic abuses of this kind, the well-documented Erin Brockovich case on behalf of hundreds of plaintiffs against Pacific Gas & Electric, alleging toxic contamination of water supplies at Hinckley, resulted in a record settlement of US$333m (Justia 2020) in 1996 and US$335m in 2006 for similar contamination at Kettleman Hills.

- Allegations that banks and the finance sector cause and exploit financial crises, not just in relation to the 2008-9 global financial crisis but as an on-going feature of their alleged exploitative world-view and 'what can we get away with?' methods. There is some evidence of particular abuses by UK banks, such as mass mis-selling of poor value endowment mortgages (Peachey 2013) and mass mis-selling of poor value mortgage payment protection insurance (PPI) (Treanor 2016). In addition, Lloyds Bank and its HBOS subsidiary were found liable in 2017 for £100m in compensation for operating a systematic fraud against hundreds of small business customers (Chapman 2017; O'Dwyer 2020). Two senior managers, described by the judge as "utterly corrupt", were jailed, one for 11 years and the other for 4½ years.

Anti-corporatism conspiracy theories are typically tacitly accepted, if not advanced, by campaigning bodies whose motivation and justification are claimed to be to protect the planet and human existence in the inter-related areas of sustainability, environment, and climate change, for example the Post Carbon Institute. Lent (2020) gave a clear indication of the present anti-corporatism conspiracy theories in circulation in this subject area.

Evaluating Conspiracy Theories

In evaluating radical-right grand conspiracy theories, the author declares his position as a sceptic, not to disbelieve the possibility of conspiracies (which, of course, may exist) but on four grounds (Waring 2020a). First, the sheer number and frequency of conspiracy theories disseminated by radical-right interests defies credibility—it is almost as if they are coming off a production line. Second, each theory individually has poor 'face validity' i.e. it lacks common-sense plausibility. Third, they all seem so far-fetched and clearly intended to damage their targets and stir up mistrust and even hatred, rather than serve a public good, that the motives of their originators and disseminators must be suspect as egregious.

Fourth, in addition, such conspiracy theories are also suspect on scientific grounds. For acceptability, explanations and theories require substantive testable evidence as well as a capacity to pass the parsimony test and causation test. In essence, the parsimony test is a rule-of-thumb heuristic often referred to as Ockham's Razor (Wardrop 2008). William of Ockham was a 14th century English monk who observed that the simplest and most unifying explanation for a phenomenon is the most likely to be correct. Thus, the greater the number of elements and links (i.e. complexity) of a conspiracy theory, the greater is its vulnerability to anomalies, breakdown, implausibility, and poor prediction. Such poor prediction and control of outcome of over-elaborate systems is well known in systems science, for example, the more so where large numbers of people are involved—or as Vickers (1983) put it "human systems are different". The fact that complex human or 'soft' systems, whether designed or evolutionary (such as populations), are often wickedly contrary and resistant to manipulation and control (Checkland 1999), renders grand conspiracy theories automatically improbable. Such posited conspiracy theories as those of Icke, QAnon, and Bowart (1994), Carr (1958; 1959), and *Silent Weapons* (1979), for example, contain a surfeit of *necessary* collaborating elements that would *necessarily have to work accurately and reliably in perfect harmony on a long-term basis*, thereby defying normal rational expectation. They fail the parsimony test conclusively.

As Waring (2020a) observed, in addition to the parsimony test, a robust theory needs to be able to pass the causation test. In other words, does the theory prove (as a result of no disproof) that variable A causes variable B? Whereas this may seem a simple test, in reality many if not most relationships between two variables demonstrate not causation but association or correlation, a much weaker relationship and one that may be wholly misleading. As a simple example, a person's weight is associated with their height, but height does not cause weight. Also, associations are often spurious and coincidental, however plausible they may seem (for graphic examples, see Burlando 2014; Evans et al 2008). Where complex human systems are involved, such as those featuring so prominently in grand conspiracy theories, the most that may be confidently demonstrated will be *associations* between variables. However, such theories are typically articulated with a narrative constructed from a mix of some relevant facts to convey authenticity and a preponderance of fiction and conjecture, but all intended to imply that the theory demonstrates *causality*. For example, Fact A, it is true that George Soros is an international financial guru, is Jewish, and promotes neo-liberal economics, liberal multi-lateralism, and liberal migration policies. It is also true, Fact B, that some European countries, including Hungary, have suffered both economic difficulties and coping with mass transit of migrants escaping from wars and hardship and on their way to Germany and northern Europe. But, Fact B is only weakly (i.e. incidentally) associated with Fact A—and the latter certainly did not cause the former. To suggest otherwise, as do contemporary radical-right conspiracy theories, is wishful thinking and an artful lie.

Overall, grand conspiracy theories, on which the radical right and its supporters and collaborators depend for so much of their self-justification, have a flavour of dramatic plots in popular fictional novels and Hollywood movies and very little real-world credibility. Those who believe such theories to be literally true probably represent a mixture of such characteristics as: gullibility; a need for the excitement and drama that conspiracy theories may bring to otherwise drab and jaded outlooks; a morbid vicarious fascination in dreadful events involving human tragedy, terror, and potential harm, well known in psychology (Oosterwijk 2017); prejudices and radical ideological commitments which such theories support; anti-rational anti-science world-view; paranoid delusional feelings of being a victim of 'dark forces'; beliefs based on faith not fact; and compulsive belief in palingenetic salvation typically offered as a corollary to such theories e.g. The QAnon Storm.

Despite the dismissal and discrediting of such theories, the radical right and its fellow travellers, including those in positions of corporate power and media influence, continue to repeat and disseminate them, aided and abetted by the Internet and social media. For example, in 2020 the radical right's arch-revolutionary Steve Bannon[3], a one-time Strategy Adviser to President Trump, repeatedly publicized

---

[3]   In August 2020, Bannon was charged on federal indictment, ironically with "conspiracy to defraud" via concealed payments, hundreds of thousands of campaign donors in connection with an online crowdfunding campaign, from which he was accused of personally receiving more than US$1 million (USDC 2020; Zeffman 2020a, b). He was also permanently suspended from *Twitter* in November 2020 for urging that White House chief medical adviser Dr Anthony Fauci and FBI director Christopher Wray should be beheaded (Devine & O'Sullivan 2020). Bannon was pardoned before going to trial, by Trump on his last day in office (January 19, 2021).

one of the conspiracy theories about the Covid-19 virus, alleging that the virus had been leaked (implying deliberately) from a covert bio-weapons facility in Wuhan, China (Beltz 2020), an allegation flatly and consistently refuted by authorities internationally. As the Nazi propaganda minister, Joseph Goebbels, is reported to have said "If you repeat a lie often enough, people will believe it, and you will even believe it yourself", and "A lie told once remains a lie but told a thousand times becomes the truth". It is therefore to be anticipated that dissemination of grand conspiracy theories will be expanded and intensified by the radical right and their supporters, whether in corporate organisations, or as enablers, or among the public at large. Effective strategies to curb and control the egregious impact of such propaganda, and the conspiracy theories embedded in it, therefore become all the more urgent, as indicated in the sections above.

Yet, there remains a crucially important aspect of this whole conspiracy theories phenomenon that may be easily overlooked. It is clear that not all among the radical right and fellow travellers believe these grand conspiracy theories to be literally true, but they nonetheless continue their campaign on an end-justifies-the-means basis in the Goebbels tradition. Their aim is not to get all recipients to believe the lies, although if some do that is a bonus. If the majority only half believe the allegations on a 'no smoke without fire basis', that will be a major success for them. Their primary aims include sowing the seeds of doubt, uncertainty, confusion, anxiety, disturbance, and chaos in society, in such a way and to such a degree that the radical right and their policies are then seen as the only logical saviours from such calumny.

In such amoral calculation, some of the radical right and their followers will undoubtedly believe their grand conspiracy theories with absolute conviction, no matter how absurd or how cogently discredited. In this, they may well delude themselves into believing they are saviours of their nation, if not human existence. However, it could be argued that, by their actions, they are not only being naïve but are also unwitting pawns in a very real grand conspiracy—albeit not one that features in their own list of theories. The following section explains.

Active Measures and *Maskirovka*

It is well established that for at least 70 years, both during the Cold War and Soviet era and in the post-Soviet Russian nationalist era up to present, the Russian state has been engaged in a continuous strategy of "active measures" of psycho-political warfare to undermine and weaken the West in order to protect its own interests (as it perceives them) (Radin et al 2020). It operationalizes the subversion strategy in a variety of ways, a prominent one being at the human level whereby its *maskirovka* programme seeks by deception and lies to undermine both the emotional tranquillity and the beliefs-and-values systems of Western citizens (Cipher Brief 2018). Russian strategy, especially during the Putin era, has been to foster in Western populations doubt, uncertainty, discord, anxiety, dissatisfaction, mistrust and distrust (especially in their governments, politicians, the Establishment, organs of state, democratic institutions, the economy, and policy areas such as foreign policy, immigration, defence, and race relations). One high profile example is the 2015-2016 operation by Russian government agents to interfere with, and bring undue influence to bear on, voters' decision-making in the US presidential election (*BBC* 2019; NIC 2017), including placement of false and/or inflammatory advertisements, blog articles, reader comments to online publications, and social media comments (US Senate 2019), all of which were from covert Russian *agents provocateurs* pretending to be ordinary members of the public. Another example of 'longarm' subversion is Russian attempts to undermine public trust and confidence in official public information on the Covid-19 pandemic from European governments (Dudik 2020).

In all this, for the Russians, the conspiracy theories from the radical right are a welcome additional ingredient to the toxic brew they themselves feed to Western populations via their covert online and social media programme. QAnon and other radical-right conspiracists are regarded by the Russians [as in Lenin's phrase] "useful idiots" in this regard (Radin et al 2020). For example, Sylvester (2020) provides graphic evidence that, in their attempts to appeal to populism, right-wing nationalist elements within the British Conservative Party have mimicked conspiracy assertions of Trump and QAnon. One local constituency party, whose MP is a prominent Conservative on the radical-right, issued a newsletter in late 2020 praising Trump, advocating using fake news as a political weapon, and referring to a "deep state" conspiracy of liberal and left-wing subversives in the UK, citing as an example anti-discrimination legislation as a product of their alleged activities. However, whereas such political manipulators may imagine that their 'conspiracy theory machine' is greatly helping them reach their goal of a permanent radical-right stamp and grip on national governance, culture and social norms, in reality while this may or may not happen, they are unwittingly being manipulated and encouraged in their task by the much more powerful longarm subversive 'dark forces' of the Russian state. If a conspiratorial threat exists, it is not so much an imaginary 'deep state' within the US or UK, as more plausibly a very real 'deep exo-state' of Russian neo-imperialist interests engaged in psycho-political warfare.

Neutralising Fake Conspiracy Theories

Combatting harmful conspiracy theories based on unsubstantiated assertions and fiction may appear relatively straightforward, in view of the wide range of methods available that could be used in combination, such as all those cited above and in chapter 12. However, in reality it is extremely difficult. For example, most of these theories, along with other fake news and fake facts, are disseminated via online platforms which, as discussed above, thus far have failed to self-regulate to any meaningful extent. To effectively prevent the large number of radical-right interests and individuals using Internet and social media platforms to disseminate such harmful material would require a radical change of attitude and conduct by platform owners and a no-nonsense approach to rapid blocking and removal of offenders.

However, even if some of the major platforms do become enlightened and act responsibly, there are always likely to be others that do not. Moreover, a more fundamental problem centres on the very nature of conspiracy theories and fake news and their role in society. People in general are attracted to scandal, outrage, and the thrill of fear, which typically feature in such material. If nothing else, such stories and reports provide a welcome relief to boredom as well as a rich source of vicarious experience, confirmation bias, and conversation fodder. Expecting to eliminate or control the dissemination of such material [i.e. expunging gossip] by whatever means is akin to expecting to herd cats successfully. For example, the Cornell study by

Evanega et al (2020) revealed how misinformation on Covid-19, including conspiracy theories, issued by President Trump accounted for some 38% of the misinformation on this topic in 38 million English language media articles, and that most such article writers and editors had not fact-checked Trump's statements.

Attempts to control or mitigate such apocryphal information by logical argument and unassailable facts are hampered by four factors (Waring 2020a): (1) the time and sustained effort required to repeatedly demolish absurd conspiracy theories—once a theory is released it is extraordinarily difficult to expunge; (2) counter-actions are nearly always reactive and too late to prevent or reverse any harmful impact; (3) legal constraints on governments seeking to prevent dissemination of such material, and (4) the unrestrained availability of the Internet and social media for dissemination purposes. Thus, overall, much more work needs to be done to find effective ways to interdict, block, dissipate, and ridicule conspiracy theories and other fake stories. The late James Randi (1928-2020), for example, spent decades debunking and ridiculing such material (Aaronovitch 2020b), with his *'Orac Knows' Science Blogs* on 'respectful insolence', 'doubtful news', 'pseudoscience', and 'quack medicine' (https://web.randi.org).

So far, such online platform companies as *Facebook, Twitter* and *Google* have been very reluctant to self-regulate to the degree necessary to prevent public harm resulting from fake conspiracy theories (and other fake information) which their platforms distribute. There are some signs, as in chapter 11, that commercial pressures from advertisers have some persuasive effect, as well as government actions to limit the current unfettered power of platform companies e.g. the US congressional investigation of such companies, the added factor of the January 6, 2021 mob attack on the Capitol (in which the mobsters extensively used social media to communicate and coordinate), the forthcoming Online Harms Act in the UK (DCMS 2019), and the UK's use of cyberwarfare expertise to disrupt online dissemination of anti-vax conspiracy theories (Fisher & Smith 2020).

One promising line (Waring 2020c) might be to expose publicly the personality, character, background, ideology, political connections, public statements, extremist connections, personal scandals and other profile characteristics of individual conspiracy theorists and prominent believers. It is notable that such people like to propagate an illusion that they are righteous paragons of virtue, almost saints, with special superior perception and insight, and are only interested in saving humankind (or at least those they deem deserving). Such inflated egos of conspiracy theory cults need to be set against their 'feet of clay' reality.

Conclusion

The phenomenon of conspiracy theories and their spread has existed for a long time, certainly centuries. Many such theories come and go, while a few are persistent, especially those that tap into deeply held fears and prejudices of a racial and/or religious nature. Despite most conspiracy theories remaining unconvincing, even preposterous, and abjectly failing simple validation tests, nonetheless they typically enjoy widespread popularity, acceptance of their truth, and a willingness of devotees to disseminate them as widely as possible. Those conspiracy theories invented by radical-right sources, and disseminated on an epidemic scale by devoted followers using online channels, are typically of an egregious nature intended to damage the standing and credibility of those hated by the radical right, especially centrist and liberal mainstream political enemies, vulnerable minorities, and anyone in society who refuses to accept radical-right ideology and policies. The overall objective of radical-right conspiracism is to undermine public trust and confidence in mainstream representative democracy and governance, so that radical-right virtue-and-salvation policies may appear an attractive alternative.

Different kinds of corporate collusion with radical-right conspiracism are evident, ranging from committed ideological support for conspiracy theories among some organisations to tacit laissez-faire acceptance in others. Commercial monetizing opportunism as a corporate motive to facilitate dissemination of such conspiracy theories looms large among the major online platform providers. Such amoral calculation by such corporate leaders underscores their organisations' contribution to the undermining of public trust and confidence in democracy. A shift towards the 'new model corporation' approach, based on an anti-authoritarian world-view and multi-stakeholder engagement, provides an escape route for those organisations wishing to disengage from collusion with radical-right conspiracism. Whether companies, such as online platform operators for example, will take this option voluntarily out of a sense of enlightened self-interest, remains to be seen. Those that do not may face increasing pressure from corporate advertisers, regulators, enforcement action, and penalties, as well as marketplace displeasure.

In summary, identifiable risk exposures include the following, which are assessed further in chapter 10:

Risk Exposures of Public and Society

Risk Exposure 1: Public Health

Dissemination of unsubstantiated conspiracy theories about health issues may adversely affect large numbers of people, both in terms of their mental health by engendering fear and anxiety and by dissuading them from following authoritative medical advice (e.g. Covid-19 protection, vaccinations) in favour of 'quack alternatives' or threat denial.

Risk Exposure 2: Climate Change Impacts

Dissemination of unsubstantiated conspiracy theories seeking to deny or trivialise climate change may adversely affect large numbers of people, even whole populations, both in terms of their personal safety by engendering a false sense of security in relation to extreme weather events, forest fires, and other human-influenced phenomena, and in terms of potential asset losses, loss of livelihood, and loss of food supplies.

Risk Exposure 3: Democratic Governance

Dissemination of unsubstantiated conspiracy theories seeking to denigrate the character, honesty, integrity and motives of duly elected public representatives or public officials, may undermine public trust and confidence in (a) the character, traditions and norms of democratic institutions (e.g. the legislature, the judiciary), (b) the probity of democratic processes and standards (e.g. electoral regulations), and (c) the authority, independence and impartiality of expert advice to government and the public (e.g. CDC, WHO etc).

Risk Exposures of Corporations

Risk Exposure 1: Reputation and Standing

Corporations that participate in, or facilitate dissemination of, unsubstantiated conspiracy theories may invite not only ridicule but may also damage their public and market reputation, credibility, and standing, if they become perceived as acting against either the public interest and/or the interests of individuals who may be harmed as a result of actions which such theories may provoke.

Risk Exposure 2: Free-Market Restrictions and Advertiser Actions

Media and online platform corporations that fail to self-regulate, and fail either to curb or cease dissemination of unsubstantiated conspiracy theories, run the risk of (a) increasingly stringent controls and penalties imposed by regulatory authorities, and (b) withdrawal of advertising by major brands seeking to abide by their own internal rules of corporate governance and risk management policies.

Risk Exposure 3: Marginalisation and Market Value Impacts

Corporations that participate in, or facilitate dissemination of, unsubstantiated conspiracy theories run the risk of their estrangement from the business and investment community, and ultimately their marginalisation and quarantine as 'untouchables', which will adversely impact their market value.

Risk Exposures of the Radical Right

Risk Exposure 1: Conspiracy Theory Fatigue and Loss of Credibility and Relevance

The contemporary popularity of radical-right conspiracy theories may wane as people tire of their increasingly bizarre content and unsubstantiated assertions, few of which result in radical-right objectives being reached. Such exposure fatigue is more likely to occur among mainstream conservatives and other persuadable sympathisers than among the hard-core committed radical right whose belief in conspiracy theories is likely to be unswerving.

References

Aaronovitch, D. 2020a. "This Online Cult is a Danger in the Real World". *The Times.* July 30, 2020. Page 27.

Aaronovitch, D. 2020b. "We've Lost a Hero in the War on Stupidity". *The Times.* October 29, 2020. Page 27.

Amarasingam, A. and Argentino, M-A. 2020. "The QAnon Conspiracy Theory: a Security Threat in the Making?" *CTC Sentinel*, Vol 13, Issue 7, July 2020. Combatting Terrorism Center, at West Point. https://www.ctc.usma.edu/the-qanon-conspiracy-theory-a-security-threat-in-the-making/. [accessed August 12, 2020].

Bakan, J. 2004. *The Corporation: The Pathological Pursuit of Profit and Power.* London: Constable.

Barkun, M. 2004. *A Culture of Conspiracy: Apocalyptic Visions in Contemporary America.* Revised edition 2013. Oakland, CA: University of California Press.

Barkun, M. 2016. "Conspiracy theories as stigmatized knowledge". *Diogenes.* October 25, 2016. https://doi.org/10.1177/0392192116669288. [accessed August 15, 2020].

BBC. 2019. "Russian Trolls' Chief Target was 'Black US Voters' in 2016". *BBC News.* October 10, 2019. https://www.bbc.co.uk/news/technology-49987657.

BBC. 2020. "Facebook Removes QAnon Conspiracy Group with 200,000 Members". Technology. *BBC News.* August 7, 2020. https://www.bbc.co.uk/news/technology-53692545.

Beltz, M. 2020. "Bannon Spreads Conspiracy Theories About Origins of Coronavirus". *The National Memo.* July 2, 2020. https://www.nationalmemo.com/bannon-spreads-conspiracy-theories-about-origin-of-coronavirus. [accessed August 23, 2020].

Betz, H-G. 2020. "QAnon: A Conspiracy Theory for Our Time". *CARR Insight Blog.* October 5, 2020. Centre for Analysis of the Radical Right. https://www.radicalrightanalysis.com/2020/10/05/qanon-a-conspiracy-for-our-time/. [accessed October 5, 2020].

Betz, H-G. 2021. "Beware! Populism in Conjunction with Conspiracy Theories Might Be Bad For Your Health". Parts 1 to 3. *CARR Insight Blog.* February 1, 2 and 3, 2021. https://www.radicalrightanalysis.com. [accessed February 4, 2021].

Birch, K. 2007. "The Totalitarian Corporation?" *Totalitarian Movements and Political Religions*, Vol 8 No 1, 153-161, March 2007.

Bloom, P. and Rhodes, C. 2016. "Corporate Authoritarianism and the New American Anti-democracy". *Common Dreams*. October 23, 2016.

Bloom, P. and Rhodes. C. 2018. *CEO Society: The Corporate Takeover of Everyday Life.* London: Zed Books.

Boffey, D. 2018. "Orbán Claims Hungary is Last Bastion Against 'Islamization' of Europe'". *The Guardian*. https://theguardian.com/world/2018/feb/18/orban-claims-hungary-last-bastion-against-islamization-europe [accessed December 28, 2019].

Bowart, W.H. 1994. *Operation Mind Control.* Revised and expanded researcher's edition. Fort Bragg, Ca: Flatland Editions.

Brooks, N. 2020. "The Tangled Web: Psychopathic Personality, Vulnerability and Victim Selection". In *Corporate Psychopathy: Investigating Destructive Personalities in the Workplace*, edited by K. Fritzon, N. Brooks, and S. Croom. 295-325. Cham, Switzerland: Palgrave Macmillan.

Brooks, N., Fritzon, K. and Croom, S. 2020. "Corporate Psychopathy: Entering the Paradox and Emerging Unscathed". In *Corporate Psychopathy: Investigating Destructive Personalities in the Workplace*, edited by K. Fritzon, N. Brooks, and S. Croom. 327-365. Cham, Switzerland: Palgrave Macmillan.

Burlando, A. 2014. "Power Outages, Power Externalities, and Baby Booms". *Demography,* August 2014, 51(4), 1477-1500. doi:10.1007/s.13524-014-0136-7. https://pubmed.ncbi.nlm.nih.gov/25007970/. [accessed August 27, 2020].

Carr, W.G. 1958. *Pawns in the Game.* Willowdale, Ontario: Federation of Christian Laymen. https://brunner-architekt.ch/wp-content/uploads/Carr_Pawns_in_the_Game.pdf. [accessed July 28, 2020].

Carr, W.G. 1959. *Satan, Prince of This World.* Released post-mortem in 1966. https://www.threeworldwars.com Satan: Prince of this World : William Guy Carr : Free Download, Borrow, and Streaming : Internet Archive. [accessed November 29, 2020].

CCDH. 2020. *Failure to Act—How Tech Giants Continue to Defy Calls to Rein in Vaccine Misinformation.* Report. July 2020. Center for Countering Digital Hate. London: CCDH. https://www.counterhate.co.uk. [accessed October 3, 2020].

Chapman, B. 2017. "Lloyds Bank to Pay Out £100m Compensation to HBOS Fraud Victims". *The Independent.* April 7, 2017. https://www.independent.co.uk/news/business/news/lloyds-bank-hbos-fraud-pay-out-compensation-ps100-million-small-business-customers-a7671646.html. [accessed November 27, 2020].

Charron, N., Lapuente, V., and Rodriguez-Pose, A. 2020. *Uncooperative Society, Uncooperative Politics or Both? Polarization and Populism Explain Excess Mortality for COVID-19 Across European Regions.* Working Paper Series 2020:12. The Quality of Government Institute. Gothenburg, Sweden: University of Gothenburg.

Checkland, P. 1999. *Systems Thinking, Systems Practice—Includes a 30-year Retrospective.* Chichester UK: John Wiley & Sons.

Cherep-Spiridovich, A. 1926. *The Secret World Government: or the Hidden Hand—the Unrevealed in History, 100 Historical Mysteries Explained.* Originally published by the Anti-Bolshevist Association, NY. Republished in 2000. San Diego, Calif: Book Tree.

Chomsky, N. 1999. *Necessary Illusions: Thought Control in Democratic Societies.* London: Pluto Press.

Cipher Brief. 2018. "Threat Report 2018: Russia's Military Doctrine of Deception and Deniability". In *The Cipher Brief Annual Threat Report.* May 31, 2018. Atlanta, GA: Cipher Brief. https://www.thecipherbrief.com/article/asia/threat-report-2018-russias-military-doctrine-of-deception-and-deniability. [accessed August 27, 2020].

Crouch, C. 2014. "Dealing with Corporate Political Power". *Open Democracy.* February 3, 2014. https://www.opendemocracy.net/en/opendemocracyuk/dealing-with-corporate-political-power/. [accessed April 4, 2020].

DCMS. 2019. *The Online Harms White Paper: Government Response to the Committee's Twelfth Report.* Received July 23, 2019. Published September 9, 2019. Commons Select Committee. London: UK Parliament. https://www.gov.uk/government/consultations/online-harms-white-paper.

Dearden, L. 2020. "Inside the UK-based Site that has Become the Far-right's YouTube". *The Independent.* July 22, 2020. https://www.independent.co.uk/news/uk/home-news/bitchute-far-right-youtube-neo-nazi-terrorism-videos-a9632981.html. [accessed August 8, 2020].

Deer, B. 2020. *The Doctor Who Fooled the World: Andrew Wakefield's War on Vaccines.* London: Scribe.

Devine, C. and O'Sullivan, D. 2020. "Twitter Permanently Suspends Steve Bannon Account After Talk of Beheading". *CNN Business.* November 6, 2020. https://edition.cnn.com/2020/11/05/tech /steve-bannon-twitter-permanent-suspension/index.html. [accessed Nov 6, 2020].

de Poncins, L. 1928. *Les Forces Secrètes de la Révolution: Franc-Maçons, Judaisme.* Paris: Editions Bossard.

Docherty, G. and MacGregor, J. 2013. *Hidden History: The Secret Origins of the First World War.* Edinburgh: Mainstream Publishing.

Docherty, G. and MacGregor, J. 2018. *Prolonging the Agony: How International Bankers and their Political Partners Deliberately Extended World War 1 by Three-and-a-Half Years.* Waterville, Oregon: Trine Day.

Donovan, J. 2020. Testimony statement. Hearing on "Misinformation, Conspiracy Theories, and Infodemics: Challenges and Opportunities for Stopping the Spread Online". October 15, 2020. Dr J. Donovan, Research Director, Harvard Kennedy School's Shorenstein Center on Media, Politics and Public Policy. House Permanent Select Committee on Intelligence. Washington DC: HIC. https://docs.house.gov/meetings/IG/IG00/20201015/111087 /HHRG-116-IG00-Wstate-DonovanJ-20201015.pdf.   [accessed November 27, 2020].

Douglas, K., Uscinski, J.E., Sutton, R.M. et al. 2019. "Understanding Conspiracy Theories". *Advances in Political Psychology.* Vol 40 Suppl 1. Doi: 10.1111/pops.12568. [accessed November 26, 2020].

Dror, I.E. and Fraser-Mackenzie, P.A.F. 2008. "Cognitive Biases in Human Perception, Judgement and Decision Making: Bridging Theory and the Real World". In *Criminal Investigative Failures*, edited by Kim Rossmo. 53-67. Abingdon, Oxon UK: Taylor & Francis.

Dudik, A. 2020. "Russia Aims to Stir Distrust in Europe on Virus Disinformation". *Bloomberg News.* March 19, 2020. https://www.bl oomberg.com/news/articles/2020-03-19/russia-aims-to-stir-distrust-in-europe-on-virus-disinformation. [accessed August 23, 2020].

Dugin, A. 2012. *The Fourth Political Theory.* London: Arktos Media.

Duke, D. 2012. "Rabbi Wants an Islamic Europe as Jewish Revenge!—with Dr Duke Commentary". November 12, 2012. https://david duke.com/the-unending-hatred-israeli-settler-rabbi-praises-islamic-takeover-of-europe [accessed December 28, 2019].

Dyrendal, A. 2020. "Conspiracy Beliefs About Jews and Muslims in Norway". In *Shifting Boundaries of Prejudice: Anti-Semitism and Islamophobia in Norway,* edited by C. Hoffmann and V. Moe, 187-210. Oslo: Universitetsforlaget AS. https://www.universitetsforlaget.no/en/the-shifting-boundaries-of-prejudice.

Ellery, B. 2020. "Sons of David Icke Take Centre Stage in Covid Conspiracy Movement". *The Times.* October 3, 2020. Pages 8-9.

Evanega, S, Lynas, M., Adams, J. et al. 2020. *Coronavirus Misinformation: Quantifying Sources and Themes in the COVID-19 'Infodemic'.* Research Report. Cornell Alliance for Science, Department of Global Development. Ithaca, NY: Cornell University.

Evans, R.W., Hu, Y. and Zhao, Z. 2008. "The Fertility Effect of Catastrophies: U.S. Hurricane Births". *Journal of Population Economics,* doi:10.1007/s.00148-008-0219-2. http://www.econ2.jhu.edu/people/hu/fertility_jpope2010.pdf. [accessed August 27, 2020].

Fisher, L. and Smith, C. 2020. "GCHQ in Cyberwar on Antivax Propaganda". *The Times.* November 9, 2020. Pages 1-2. https://www.thetimes.co.uk/edition/news/gchq-in-cyberwar-on-anti-vaccine-propaganda-mcjgjhmb2.

Foran, C., Diaz, D., Grayer, A. et al. 2021. "Most House Republicans Silent Over Violent Marjorie Taylor Greene Comments as Democrats Condemn Them". *CNN Politics.* January 28, 2021. https://edition.cnn.com/2021/01/27/politics/marjorie-taylor-greene-comments-reaction/index.html.

Goertzel, T. 1994. "Belief in Conspiracy Theories". *Political Psychology,* 15(4), 731-742. https://doi.org/10.2307/3791630.

Goertzel, T. 2010. "Conspiracy Theories in Science". *EMBO Reports,* 11(7), 493-499. European Molecular Biology Organization. https://doi.org/10.1038/embor.2010.84.

Gray, P. 2011. "Conspiracy Theories and Large Corporations". *Tech Republic Blog.* August 30, 2011. https://www.techrepublic.com/blog/tech-decision-maker/conspiracy-theories-and-large-corporations/.

Hardy, C. 1985. "The Nature of Unobtrusive Power". *Journal of Management Studies*, 22 (4), 384-399.

Hoffmann, C. and Moe, V. (eds). 2020. "Introduction". *Shifting Boundaries of Prejudices: Anti-Semitism and Islamophobia in Contemporary Norway.* Oslo: Universitetsforlaget AS. https://www.universitetsforlaget.no/en/the-shifting-boundaries-of-prejudice.

Hoyle, B. 2021. "QAnon Congresswoman Embraced Online Violence". *The Times.* January 28, 2021. Page 28.

Hughes, D. 2019. "'Freddie Starr Ate My Hamster': What This Bizarre Tabloid Story Was All About—and If it was True". *iNews.* May 12, 2019. https://inews.co.uk/news/uk/freddie-starr-ate-my-hamster-true-story-max-clifford-the-sun-explained-289955. [accessed August 11, 2020].

Icke, D. 2017. "Global Warming Scam". A video by Andrew Cheetham. July 4, 2017. https://davidicke.com/article/418249/global-warming-scam-david-icke/.

Icke, D. 2020a. "COVID-19—The Real Truth". March 29, 2020. https://davidicke.com/2020/03/09/covid-19-real-truth/. [accessed August 8, 2020].

Icke, D. 2020b. "My Investigation of COVID-19". July 9, 2020. https://davidicke.com/2020/07/09/my-investigation-of-covid-19/. [accessed August 8, 2020].

Illuminati. 2020. "The Illuminati—a Brief Introduction. Our Core Beliefs". The Official Illuminati Organization. https://www.illuminatiofficial.org. [accessed August 15, 2020].

Jasser, G. 2020. "The Social Media Platform that Welcomes QAnon with Open Arms". *CARR Insight Blog.* November 28, 2020. https://www.radicalrightanalysis.com/2020/11/27/the-social-media-platform-that-welcomes-qanon-with-open-arms/. [accessed November 28, 2020].

Justia. 2020. *Anderson v. Pacific Gas & Electric Company (1993).* https://law.justia.com/cases/california/court-of-appeal/4th/14/254.html. [accessed November 27, 2020].

Kahan, D.M., Jamieson, K.H., Landrum, A.R. et al. 2017. "Culturally Antagonistic Memes and the Zika Virus: an Experimental Test". *Journal of Risk Research*, 20(1), 1-40.

Kelly, M. 1995. "The Road to Paranoia". *The New Yorker.* June 12, 1995. https://www.newyorker.com/magazine/1995/06/19/the-roa d-to-paranoia. [accessed August 15, 2020].

Kennedy, D. and Ellis, R. 2020. "Antivax Leader is Banned Nurse who Fears 5G Networks". *The Times.* September 12, 2020. Page 12.

Lawrence, D. 2018. "Inside David Icke's Watford Talk". *Hope Note Hate.* November 26, 2018. https://www.hopenothate.org.uk/20 18/11/26/inside-david-ickes-watford-talk/. [accessed August 8, 2020].

Lent, J. 2020. "The Five Real Conspiracies You Need to Know About". *Patterns of Meaning.* October 1, 2020. https://patternsofmean ing.com/2020/10/01/the-five-real-conspiracies-you-need-to-know-about/. [accessed November 27, 2020].

Michaels, D. 2020. *The Triumph of Doubt—Dark Money and the Science of Deception.* Oxford UK: Oxford University Press.

Miller, S. 2017. "Hungary Accuses EU and Billionaire George Soros of Trying to Muslimize Europe". July 23, 2017. *Mail Online.* https://www.dailymail.co.uk/.../Hungary-accuses-EU-Soros-M uslimization-Europe.html [accessed December 28, 2019].

Nagle, A. 2017. *Kill All Normies: Online Culture Wars from 4chan and tumblr to Trump and the Alt-Right.* Winchester UK: Zero Books.

Neiwert, D. 2017. *Alt-America—The Rise of the Radical Right in the Age of Trump.* London: Verso.

NIC. 2017. *Background to "Assessing Russian Activities and Intentions in Recent US Elections": The Analytic Process and Cyber Incident Attribution.* Intelligence Community Assessment Report ICA 2017-01D. January 6, 2017. Office of the Director of National In- telligence. National Intelligence Council. Washington DC.

Nickerson, R.S. 1998. "Confirmation Bias: a Ubiquitous Phenomenon in Many Guises". *Review of General Psychology*, 2, 175-220.

O'Dwyer, M. 2020. "Lloyds Bank: Anatomy of a Scandal". *The Daily Tel- egraph.* March 8, 2020. https://www.telegraph.co.uk/business /2020/03/08/lloyds-bank-anatomy-scandal/

Oklobdzija, S. 2019. "Public Positions, Private Giving: Dark Money and Political Donors in the Digital Age". *Research & Politics.* February 25, 2019. https://doi.org/10.1177/2053168019832475. [ac- cessed May 21, 2020].

Oosterwijk, S. 2017. "Choosing the Negative: a Behavioural Demonstration of Morbid Curiosity". *PLoS One.* 12(7):e0178399. https://doi.org/10.1371/journal.pone.0178399. [accessed October 29, 2020].

Paxton, R.O. 2005. *The Anatomy of Fascism.* London: Penguin Books.

Peachey, K. 2013. "Endowment Mortgages: Legacy of a Scandal". *BBC News.* January 4, 2013. https://www.bbc.co.uk/news/business-20858236. [accessed November 27, 2020].

Radin, A., Demus, A. and Marcinek, K. 2020. *Understanding Russian Subversion—Patterns, Threats, and Responses.* Perspectives Paper. RAND Army Research Division. DOI: 10.7249/PE331. Santa Monica, CA: RAND Organization. https://www.rand.org/pubs/perspectives/PE331.html. [accessed February 02, 2021].

Ramachandran, S., Berzon, A. and Ballhaus, R. 2021. "Jan. 6 Rally Funded by Top Trump Donor, Helped by Alex Jones, Organizers Say". *Wall Street Journal.* January 30, 2021. https://www.wsj.com/articles/jan-6-rally-funded-by-top-trump-donor-helped-by-alex-jones-organizers-say-11612012063?st=yckxwlyitkb0ozr&reflink=share_mobilewebshare. [accessed February 1, 2021].

Robinson, M. and Murphy, D. 2008. *Greed is Good: Maximisation and Elite Deviance in America.* Lanham, MD: Rowman & Littlefield.

Silent Weapons. 1979. *Silent Weapons for Quiet Wars. An Introductory Programming Manual.* Operations Research Technical Manual TM-SW7905.1. May 1979. Clackamas, Oregon: Emissary Publications. https://www.lawfulpath.com/ref/sw4qw/index.shtml. [accessed August 17, 2020].

Simon, D.R. 2018. *Elite Deviance*, 11th edition. Abingdon, Oxon: Routledge/Taylor & Francis.

Solomon, M. 2017. "Is David Icke Britain's Leading Anti-Semite?" *Hope Not Hate.* November 10, 2017. https://www.hopenothate.org.uk/2018/11/26/inside-david-ickes-watford-talk/. [accessed August 8, 2020].

Stracqualursi, V. 2020. "The Congressional Candidates Who have Embraced the Baseless QAnon Conspiracy Theory". *CNN Politics.* August 12, 2020. https://edition.cnn.com/2020/08/12/politics/qanon-congressional-candidates/index.html. [accessed August 23, 2020].

Sylvester, R. 2020. "Tories Take a Leaf Out of Trump's Playbook". *The Times.* December 15, 2020. Page 29.

Tobias, G. A. and Foxman, A. H. 2003. *Unraveling Anti-Semitic 9/11 Conspiracy Theories.* New York: Anti-Defamation League, 2003. https://www.adl.org/sites/default/files/documents/assets/pd f/combating-hate/anti-semitic-9-11-conspiracy-theories.pdf.

Treanor, J. 2016. "PPI Claims—All You Need to Know About the Mis-Selling Scandal". *The Guardian.* August 2, 2016. https://www. theguardian.com/business/2016/aug/02/ppi-claims-all-you-need-to-know-about-the-mis-selling-scandal. [accessed November 27, 2020].

USDC. 2020. Federal indictments for wire fraud and money laundering. US vs. Brian Kolfage, Stephen Bannon, Andrew Badalato, and Timothy Shea. 20 Cr 412. 18 USC §§ 1349 and 1956(h). US District Court, Southern District of New York.

US Senate. 2019. *Russian Active Measures Campaigns and Interference in the 2016 U.S. Election. Vol 2: Russia's Use of Social Media with Additional Views.* 116th Congress, Senate Report 116-XX. Select Committee on Intelligence. Washington DC: US Senate.

van Prooijen, J-W. 2018. "The Psychology of Qanon: Why do Seemingly Sane People Believe Bizarre Conspiracy Theories?" *NBC News.* August 13, 2018. https://www.nbcnews.com/think/opinion/p sychology-qanon-why-do-seemingly-sane-people-believe-bizar re-conspiracy-ncna900171. [accessed August 10, 2020].

Varis, P. 2019. *Conspiracy Theorising Online: Memes as a Conspiracy Theory Genre.* Paper 238. Tilburg Papers in Culture Studies. December 2019. Tilburg, NL: Tilburg University.

Vickers, G. 1983. *Human Systems are Different.* London: Harper & Row.

Wardrop, D. 2008. "Ockham's Razor: Sharpen or Resheathe?" *J. Royal Soc. of Medicine*, Feb 101(2), 50-51.

Waring, A. (ed). 2018. *The New Authoritarianism Vol 1: A Risk Analysis of the US Alt-Right Phenomenon,* edited by A. Waring. Stuttgart: Ibidem Verlag.

Waring, A. 2020a. "Infamy! Infamy! They've All Got it Infamy! The Paranoid Delusions of Radical Right Conspiracism". *CARR Insight Blog.* November 19, 2020. https://www.radicalrightanalysis. com/2020/11/19/infamy-infamy-theyve-all-got-it-infamy-the-paranoid-delusions-of-radical-right-conspiracism/.

Waring, A. 2020b. "Impacts of Islamophobia on Some Muslims in Two European Countries". *CARR Insight Blog.* May 21, 2020. https://www.radicalrightanalysis.com/2020/05/21/impacts-of-islamophobia-on-some-muslims-in-two-western-countries/.

Waring, A. 2020c. "Radical Right Conspiracy Theories are a Threat to Democracy". *Rantt Media.* November 18, 2020. https://rantt.com/radical-right-conspiracy-theories-2020-election.

White House. 2017. *National Security Strategy of the United States of America.* President Donald J. Trump. December 2017. Washington DC: The White House.

Woods, A. 2020. "Revisiting the Authoritarian Personality: Pseudo Conservatism and QAnon". *CARR Insight Blog.* September 23, 2020. https://www.radicalrightanalysis.com/2020/09/23/revisiting-the-authoritarian-personality-pseudoconservatism-and-qanon/. [accessed September 27, 2020].

Ye'or, B. 2005. *The Euro-Arab Axis.* Madison and Teaneck, NJ: Farleigh Dickinson University Press.

Zia-Ebrahimi, R. 2018. "When the Elders of Zion Relocated to Eurabia: Conspiratorial Racialization in Antisemitism and Islamophobia". *Patterns of Prejudice.* July 13, 2018. DOI: 10.1080/0031322X.2018.1493876.

Zeffman, H. 2020a. "Steve Bannon Charged Over Mexico Wall Fraud Claim". *The Times.* August 21, 2020. Pages 1-2.

Zeffman, H. 2020b. "Trump Junior Builds a Wall Between Himself and Bannon". *The Times.* August 22, 2020. Page 44.

Zimmerman, M. 2011. "Confirmatory Bias". In *Encyclopaedia of Clinical Neuropsychology.* Page 661. New York: Springer.

Zuboff, S. 2019. *The Age of Surveillance Capitalism: the Fight for the Future at the New Frontier of Power.* London: Profile Books.

PART 3:

CONCLUSION

Chapter 10:
A Risk Analysis and Assessment of the Corporate/Radical-Right Axis

By Alan Waring[1]

Abstract

The risk evidence and interpretations from preceding chapters are subjected to a systematic analysis and assessment using a modified Delphi technique. Such relevant factors as objective and subjective risk, pure and speculative risk, assessment methodology, and psychological factors affecting risk analysis and assessment are discussed. Nine common themes are identified among systematically tabulated risk exposures of various parties. From the collated assessments, overwhelmingly negative evaluations reinforce the view that the corporate/radical-right axis presents a multi-dimensional threat to society, human rights, and liberal democracy, as well as to itself. This evaluation should be a signal neither for alarm nor complacency, but for timely actions appropriate to eliminate, reduce, or control the threats and risk levels.

Key words: radical-right, corporate, risk assessment, Delphi technique, heuristic, themes.

A Collated Risk Analysis and Assessment

The preceding chapters provided a detailed description and analysis of a wide range of topics and risk issues on which radical-right worldviews, agendas, and actions have significant impacts. In one direction, the radical right presents threats and risk exposures to a range of individuals, groups, entities, populations, and nations. In another direction, the radical right attracts threats and risk exposures to itself. Both sets of exposures warrant attention.

This chapter provides a risk analysis based on the evidence and interpretations provided in Part 2. However, before addressing the particular risk exposures revealed in those chapters, it is worthwhile

---

[1]   See contributor affiliations and biography, page 525.

reconsidering a number of matters of relevance to any risk analysis of this kind. In particular, how each individual conceives risk, and risks of different kinds in different contexts, is not uniform across a population or across humanity. There are wide variations. Even individuals may be inconsistent in their beliefs and attitudes e.g. an individual may be a heavy cigarette smoker or engage in highly dangerous sports, yet avoid vaccination against dangerous diseases.

Risk as a Cognitive Phenomenon: Objective and Subjective Risk

The integrated multi-level conceptual framework for exploring risk (Waring & Paxton 2018, 58) incorporates cognitive perception of risk (thinking, awareness, appraisal etc including threat perception) as in Table 10.1.

Table 10.1:   A Multi-Level Psychological Framework for Exploring Risk

Psychological Level	Illustrative Variables
Socio-cultural	Peer/family influences, socialization, social environment, political/economic circumstances, organisational memberships/policies/values.
Individual differences	Age, gender, personality, habits, motivation, attitudes, experience, disposition (e.g. risk-taking tendencies, anti-social tendencies, narcissism, socio-pathic/psychopathic disorders).
Risk-related behaviours	Task difficulty/complexity, skills, abilities, training, moderating controls—in a range of situations (e.g. drug-taking, drinking excess alcohol, engaging in anti-social activity, promoting ethnic hatred), workload, fatigue, distractions.
Cognitions and affect	Memory, learning, risk perception, decision-making,

	judgement, mood, biases, stress, awareness, understanding, emotions (e.g. fear, anger, hate).
Neural correlates	Developmental stage, processing efficiency, attentional capacity, integrated reward/affect circuitry, decision-making circuits, response/behavioural inhibition.

Source: adapted from Fig 1.1 of Glendon and Clarke (2016, 2).

However, problems arise from the notion of risk as a cognitive phenomenon. First, the terms used to describe and communicate risk are fluid and variable. The recursive and interchangeable nature in everyday speech of such terms as 'hazard', 'danger', and 'risk, as well as 'assessment', 'analysis', 'appraisal', 'estimation', and 'evaluation', even among risk specialists, creates fertile ground for ambiguity and confusion (Boustras & Waring 2020). Second, since its character, form, qualities, and scale are the product of a cerebral judgement, a particular risk is always subjective. Analogous to such concepts as love and power, a risk has no ontological, reified existence as a tangible object. Whereas many people may agree that a particular risk exists, and concur about its description and likely impact, that consensus cannot objectify the risk. Further, any individual who analyses or assesses a risk, whether risk specialist or lay person, comes to the task bearing the baggage of their individual life experiences, world-views, cognitive biases (Douglas 1992; 1994), and pre-conscious biasing (Dixon 1981). Such a statement counters the claims of some (e.g. Chicken 1996) that objective risks are those determined by experts, whereas subjective risks are determined by non-experts, one challengeable implication of such claims being that expert risk assessment is inherently more accurate, reliable, valuable and trustworthy than that of a non-expert. As Waring and Glendon (1998, 37) pointed out, "Because of its essentially judgemental nature, risk assessment cannot be neutral or value-free, whoever carries it out and however impartial they seek to be". Risk assessment techniques may be objective in the sense that they use validated methodologies consistently. However, the risk assessment process itself is always subjective, because the choice of which particular methodology to use involves personal judgement, even if this is expert judgement. Similarly, most individual determinations about probabilities, frequencies, projected outcomes and other aspects of risk assessment, although they may be based on good or even best available evidence, are nonetheless judgemental. For further discussion of the subjective/objective issues surrounding risk, uncertainty and the so-called 'risk paradox', see Durodié (2017), Fischbacher-Smith et al (2009), and Shrader-Frechette (1991).

A further broad and related area of psychology is also relevant to this chapter, as discussed in detail in Vol 1 (373-381) and Vol 2 (321-328) Appendix 12.1: Factors Affecting Risk Perception and Therefore Risk Analysis, and in Waring (2015), to which readers are referred. Ten sets of key factors are: failure of hindsight, foresight and learning; ignorance and bounded rationality; groupthink, authority and conformity; risk perception and risk attitudes; risk appetite; risk tolerability; motivation and expectancy; risk decision-making; cultural effects; and socially constructed emergence. See also References and Further Reading.

Pure Risk and Speculative/Opportunity Risk

Two classes of risk are generally recognized (IRM 2010)—pure risks (sometimes referred to as 'downside risks') and speculative or opportunity risks (which may be either 'upside', 'downside' or more usually a combination of the two). The distinction is significant to risk analysis, since the two classes warrant different approaches.

A pure risk relates only to negative or undesirable events and impacts and is one that is characterized by (a) the probability or likelihood that the undesirable event will occur, and (b) the scale of the potential or likely undesirable event or impact. In common parlance, a pure risk is one where the best that can happen is that nothing bad happens. Thus, management of pure risks prioritizes the elimination and prevention of threats and hazards (i.e. sources of pure risk exposures) as well as risk reduction and control methods. Typical examples of pure risk sources are: hazards to environment, health and safety; product liability; disaster/crisis preparedness; natural hazards; IT systems failures; information and cyber security threats; piracy; fraud; intellectual property theft; trafficking (people, weapons, drugs); tax evasion; terrorism.

In terms of computation or estimation, a pure risk is measured as the product of the likely scale of impact/severity of the undesired event and the probability of occurrence:

Pure Risk = (Scale of Negative Impact/Severity) x (Probability of Occurrence).

An opportunity or speculative risk may result in either a desirable outcome (benefit, gain, advantage), or an undesirable outcome (detriment, loss, disadvantage), or a combination of desirable impacts in some aspects and undesirable impacts in others. Usually, opportunity risks involve a mixture of good and bad effects, although efforts may be made to maximize desirable outcomes and minimize undesirable ones. Typical examples of opportunity risk sources are: market credibility; bargaining power; strategic alliances; sales growth; brand enhancement; mergers and acquisitions; political risks; economic risks; foreign policy; new technology; investments.

In terms of computation or estimation, an opportunity risk is measured as the product of the likely scale of impact (positive, neutral or negative) and the probability of occurrence:

Opportunity Risk = (Scale of Impact) x (Probability of Occurrence).

It should be noted that some risks may appear to be both pure and opportunity risks or exhibit ambiguous characteristics. In such cases, an analysis should enable sufficient deconstruction to clarify matters. For example, at first glance it may appear that environmental issues and global warming, addressed in chapter 9 of Vol 1, would be classified exclusively as pure risks. However, whereas environmental risks and global warming risk per se are best classified as pure risks, associated political, economic and social risks are really opportunity risks.

In this chapter, the author has chosen to approach all the identified risks for estimation as opportunity risks, as these overwhelmingly predominate in this book's context. Pure risk elements, such as environmental damage, are encompassed for this chapter's purposes as negative impacts within the opportunity risk estimation formula applied.

Risk Analysis and Assessment Methodology

Risk assessment may be defined (Waring & Glendon 1998, 45) as: "the process of estimating and evaluating a defined risk in order to determine whether current risk strategies are appropriate and adequate".

The ultimate purpose of risk assessment, therefore, is to inform decision-making about whether the current level of a particular risk is acceptable, and whether further action is required to manage the risk more effectively. That principle applies regardless of whether the assessment is being done by a risk expert or non-expert. Clearly, processes of identification and analysis of any relevant hazard, threat or opportunity would need to precede any estimation or evaluation.

There is no single, 'standard' method for risk assessment and, for example, methodological differences exist between assessment of pure and speculative risks respectively. IRM (2010; 2018) has recognized the eclectic range of potential techniques in risk assessment methodology. However, the basis of all risk assessment comprises this sequence of linked processes (Royal Society 1992):

- Identification of hazard/threat/opportunity
- Analysis of hazard/threat/opportunity
- Establishing risk acceptability/tolerability criteria
- Risk computation/estimation
- Evaluation of risk estimates against acceptability/tolerability criteria

As noted in Waring and Glendon (1998), two broad approaches to risk assessment technique have arisen—heuristic and scientific. A heuristic approach is primarily qualitative and relies on the judgement (mediated by knowledge and experience) either of the individual conducting the assessment, or of a number of individuals collectively. A heuristic approach is essentially 'rule-of-thumb', usable both by experts and non- experts, and may involve modest quantification, typically in the form of risk scores and ratings e.g. the Delphi technique—see later. Although some individuals may find the scoring and rating processes challenging, since they require the cerebral collapsing and merging (consciously and pre-consciously) of many ill-defined sub-component variables into a single measure, in fact this process approximates systematically the 'how big?/how small?/how likely?' judgements that humans make naturally, and often informally, in their daily lives when addressing the multitude of risk exposures they face. See Shrader-Frechette (1991) for further discussion on scientific and other approaches to risk assessment.

Glendon and Clarke (2016, 364) pointed out that increasingly the complexity of risk issues has been reflected in the plethora of sophisticated risk assessment methodologies, models, and statistical procedures that continue to emerge, and that a "considerable diversity, almost a profusion, of conceptual frameworks and methodologies is available for the study of risk. This reflects the complexity and multidimensional nature of risk concepts", as discussed further by Durodié (2017).

Some risk experts believe that a scientific approach, employing quantitative modelling and probabilistic computation, is inherently superior to that of heuristics. However, such an assertion suggests a structural/functionalist world-view (Burrell & Morgan 1979), which has been challenged in the risk assessment context by such authors as Burgess (2015); Douglas (1992; 1994); Durodié (2017); Mudu and Beck (2012); Toft (1996); Waring and Glendon (1998); and Waring (2013). As Glendon and Clarke (2016) noted, current trends in risk research involve increased adoption of multi-disciplinary approaches, as well as socially constructed and multi-scalar definitions of key risk terms across a range of dimensions. This book follows such trends.

Appendix 10.1 provides a reference utility which adopts a relatively simple risk-rating heuristic approach, based loosely on the well-known Delphi technique originated in the 1950s by the Rand Corporation (Linstone & Turoff 1975; 2002). Appendix 10.2 summarises the rating and scoring heuristics used in Appendix 10.1.

Findings and Conclusion

This Volume's sub-title, 'A Risk Analysis of the Corporate/Radical-Right Axis', clearly states its primary focus. This chapter has provided a risk evaluation in relation to the array of risks identified and analysed in chapters 5 to 9. A number of points that require comment emerge from this analysis and evaluation.

1. All the evaluated risk exposures in Appendix 10.1 indicate negative impacts. The overwhelmingly negative evaluations reinforce the view that the corporate/radical-right axis presents a multi-dimensional threat to society, human rights, and liberal democracy, as well as to itself.

2. A majority of the evaluated risk levels in Appendix 10.1 fall within the high negative range, although the potential impact scores of a number of them point to exceptional detriment. As for any high impact/low likelihood risk exposure, those with expected exceptional detriment should be given priority attention along with all high impact/high likelihood exposures. This evaluation should be a signal neither for alarm nor complacency, but for timely actions appropriate to eliminate, reduce, or control the threats and risk levels.

3. Common themes among risk exposures identified in this volume are (1) violation of statutory and civil rights of employees, contractors, customers and other sectors of society; (2) discrimination, bullying, coercion, unfair treatment, and exposure of such categories to health and safety risks and fraud; (3) discriminatory denial of health care, denial of Covid-19 public health crisis, removal of environmental health protections, and climate change denial; (4) loss of public trust in science, leading to bad public policy and potential and actual mass harm; (5) conspiracy theories and populist fantasies dominating political and public discourse to the detriment of both representative democracy and public safety and health; (6) promoting, maintaining and extending inequalities in society to favour corporate/radical-right interests; (7) poor self-regulation and public accountability, both of claims to expertise and of platforms for dissemination of harmful communications on risk-related matters; (8) curbs by radical-right administrations on, and interference with, press/media freedom and other human rights; (9) in organisations, poorly tutored knowledge and weak systems for coping adequately with uncertainties and risk exposures.

4. In relation to the US, an unanswered question arising from chapter 8 is whether the epidemic of police killings of black people implicitly reflects racism, or whether it suggests only that US police officers are excessively authoritarian and primed to 'shoot first' to subdue suspects regardless of their race, or whether black people as a group commit a disproportionately high amount of crime which brings them into

potential confrontation with armed police, or indeed whether ubiquitous gun possession in the US coupled with a fear-induced self-protection motive precipitates a 'shoot first' reflex in police officers. The study by Johnson et al (2019) suggested that there is not compelling evidence of a racial animus by US police in such killings. Nevertheless, it is possible that all the above factors are involved. Studies have shown that the US homicide-by-firearm rate of 3.6 per 100,000 population is seven times the next highest (Canada) and that sixteen of the other twenty-one developed countries had gun homicide rates at least 18 times lower than the US (Grinshteyn and Hemenway 2010; GVA 2017; HICRC 2017; Quealy and Sanger-Katz 2016; Swedler et al 2015; Waring 2018, 317-322; Webster and Vernick 2013).

5. A related question to point 4 concerns how much US police forces have been infiltrated by far-right sympathisers. An FBI Policy Guide from April 2015, and a report from 2006 eventually released un-redacted for a Congressional committee hearing on September 29, 2020, suggested that the far right had been conducting "strategic infiltration and recruitment campaigns" among police forces. (German 2020; Speri 2017; 2020). The radical-right insurrectionist mob attack on the Capitol on January 6, 2021, with allegations of police collusion being investigated by the FBI, brought this issue into sharp relief (Johnson 2021). Certainly, in view of well-documented similar infiltration of police forces in Europe, for example, it would be surprising if US police forces were not also contaminated.

6. Putting to one side potential infiltration of armed forces and police by radical-right supporters and extremists as an exception, there is also the potential for such infiltration of other public offices resulting in prejudicial conduct towards colleagues, employees, contractors, and the public, whether as individuals, as categories, or *en masse*. In countries that are longstanding representative democracies (e.g. US, UK, Western democracies), the likelihood (while conceivable) is not supported by evidence of wide-scale instances, and this is attributed primarily to robust anti-discrimination policies

and systems. Hence, this potential risk exposure identified in chapter 8 (in relation to the US) is given a probability score of 3 (conceivable). However, in other self-styled democracies run by authoritarian radical-right or nationalist/nativist regimes (e.g. Brazil, Hungary, Poland, Russia), where the judicial system, public authorities, and civil service are filled with regime supporters, harmful prejudice and discrimination is more likely (i.e. probability score of either 4 or even 5).

7. Common themes among risk exposures of corporate authoritarians and the corporations they lead are (1) criminal and civil legal liabilities; (2) reputation damage, disinvestment, share value losses, and marginalisation and marketplace quarantine; (3) diminishing relevance to the economy and society.

8. Some of the identified risk exposures are strategic in nature, while others are more operational. Some may respond to relatively quick controls whereas others will require longer-term action. Some will require multiple, different interventions by different agencies or parties, possibly in parallel or perhaps at different times. There is no 'quick fix' or 'single solution' to most of the risk exposures identified, a message taken up in the final chapter.

9. Whereas the risk exposures are those identified by the individual authors, the risk evaluations are those of this chapter's author (the editor) in collaboration with them. They are not the absolute declarations of a 'Risk Oracle' applying universal laws of risk, since no such laws or certitudes exist. Others may disagree with some of the identified risks or the extent of them, and others may disagree with some of the risk evaluations or even many of them. Indeed, such differences of opinion are almost inevitable. As Durodié (2017) noted, "All risk assessments then—despite any objective seeming representation—are inevitably contestable as well as being contingent". However, hopefully the evaluations provide both a basis for discussion and debate i.e. a reference utility for development and pointers to the furtherance

of attenuating harm associated with the corporate/radical-right axis.

The following chapter 11 considers, on the basis of the preceding analysis and risk evaluations, how the corporate/radical-right axis may develop in the short-to-medium term and various scenarios that might unfold.

Appendix 10.1: Risk Assessment Summary Table

This risk assessment summary is necessarily that of this chapter's author (the editor), although steps were taken to validate it with the other relevant authors and to highlight if and where significantly divergent opinions exist. The author takes into account all the caveats and cautions raised in the preceding sections of this chapter and requests that the reader does likewise.

Table 10.2:   Risk Exposures Relating to the Corporate/Radical-Right Axis

The risk scores may be interpreted by reference to Table 10.5 in Appendix 10.2

Risk Exposure (as listed in individual chapters)	Desirable/ Undesirable Score (+5 to -5)	Desirable/ Undesirable Rating	Probability Score (1 to 5)	Probability Rating	Risk Score (-25 to +25)
Corporate Authoritarianism and Its Abusive Impacts [Ch. 5]					
Risk Exposures of Customers, Employees, Contractors from Corporate Authoritarianism					
Risk Exposure 1	-4	Major detriment	4	Likely/high	-16
Risk Exposure 2	-4	Major detriment	4	Likely/high	-16
Risk Exposure 3	-4	Major detriment	4	Likely/high	-16
Risk Exposures of Public & Society from Corporate Authoritarianism					
Risk Exposure 1	-4	Major detriment	4	Likely/high	-16
Risk Exposure 2	-5	Exceptional detriment	4	Likely/high	-20
Risk Exposure 3	-5	Exceptional detriment	4	Likely/high	-20

Risk Exposures of Corporate Authoritarians and Authoritarian Corporations

Risk Exposure 1	-5	Exceptional detriment	4	Likely/high	-20
Risk Exposure 2	-4	Major detriment	4	Likely/high	-16
Risk Exposure 3	-4	Major detriment	4	Likely/high	-16
Risk Exposure 4	-5	Exceptional detriment	4	Likely/high	-20
Risk Exposure 5	-5	Exceptional detriment	4	Likely/high	-20

Covid-19 and US Politicisation of Fear (Ch. 6)

Risk Exposures of US Public and Society

Risk Exposure 1	-4	Major detriment	5	Very likely	-20
Risk Exposure 2	-4	Major detriment	5	Very likely	-20

Risk Exposures of US Democratic Governance and Institutions

Risk Exposure 1	-4	Major detriment	5	Very likely	-20
Risk Exposure 2	-4	Major detriment	5	Very likely	-20

Risk Exposures of US Trade and Foreign Policy

Risk Exposure 1	-4	Major detriment	5	Very likely	-20
Risk Exposure 2	-4	Major detriment	5	Very likely	-20

Suppressing the 'Seeker of Truth' in Covid-19 Pandemic (Ch. 7)

Societal Risk Exposures

Risk Exposure 1	-5	Exceptional detriment	4	Likely/high	-20
Risk Exposure 2	-5	Exceptional detriment	4	Likely/high	-20
Risk Exposure 3	-5	Exceptional detriment	4	Likely/high	-20

Organisational Risk Exposures

Risk Exposure 1	-4	Major detriment	4	Likely/high	-16

Risk Exposure 2	-4	Major detriment	4	Likely/high	-16
Risk Exposure 3	-4	Major detriment	4	Likely/high	-16

Lockdown, Riots and a Contested Election (Ch. 8)

Risk Exposures of Representative Democracy, Governance and Institutions

Risk Exposure 1	-5	Exceptional detriment	4	Likely/high	-20
Risk Exposure 2	-5	Exceptional detriment	4	Likely/high	-20
Risk Exposure 3	-5	Exceptional detriment	3	Conceivable	-15

Risk Exposures of Public and US Society

Risk Exposure 1	-4	Major detriment	4	Likely/high	-16
Risk Exposure 2	-4	Major detriment	4	Likely/high	-16
Risk Exposure 3	-4	Major detriment	2	Unlikely/low	-8
Risk Exposure 4	-4	Major detriment	4	Likely/high	-16

Risk Exposures of the US Far Right

Risk Exposure 1	-3	Moderate detriment	-4	Likely/high	-12
Risk Exposure 2	-4	Major detriment	-4	Likely/high	-16
Risk Exposure 3	-4	Major detriment	-4	Likely/high	-16

Radical-Right Conspiracy Theories and Corporate Collusion (Ch. 9)

Risk Exposures of Public & Society

Risk Exposure 1	-4	Major detriment	5	Very likely	-20
Risk Exposure 2	-4	Major detriment	5	Very likely	-20
Risk Exposure 3	-4	Major detriment	4	Likely/high	-16

Risk Exposures of Corporations

Risk Exposure 1	-4	Major detriment	4	Likely/high	-16
Risk Exposure 2	-4	Major detriment	4	Likely/high	-16
Risk Exposure 3	-4	Major detriment	3	Conceivable	-12

Risk Exposures of the Radical Right

Risk Exposure 1	-3	Moderate detriment	4	Likely/high	-12

Appendix 10.2: Rating and Scoring Heuristics Used in this Chapter

The risks evaluated in this book are predominantly opportunity risks or may be viewed as such. For example, the pure risks of global warming may be viewed as negative opportunity risks. For opportunity risks, the rating and scoring schema in Table 10.3 reflects the fact that impacts may be positive, negative, or neutral, and that in some instances a combination of both positive and negative impacts.

Table 10.3:   Rating and Scoring Heuristic for Estimation of Opportunity Risks

Desirable/Undesirable Rating	Desirable/Undesirable Score
Exceptional benefit	+5
Major benefit	+4
Moderate benefit	+3
Minor benefit	+2
Negligible benefit	+1
Neither benefit nor detriment	0
Negligible detriment	-1
Minor detriment	-2
Moderate detriment	-3
Major detriment	-4
Exceptional detriment	-5

Source: based on Waring and Glendon (1998)

Application of the scores from Table 10.3 in the formula Opportunity Risk = (Scale of Benefit/Detriment) x (Probability of Occurrence) will produce a risk level score in the range -25 to +25.

Table 10.4:   Probability Heuristic for Estimation of Risks

Probability Rating*	Probability Score
Very unlikely	1
Unlikely/low	2
Conceivable	3
Likely/high	4
Very likely	5

*as presently controlled, unless a particular risk is a future or theoretical possibility.

Source: based on Waring and Glendon (1998).

Table 10.5:   Rating Heuristic for Estimation of Risk Levels

Risk Level Scores	Risk Level Rating
- (20 to 25)	Exceptional negative
- (12 to 20)	High negative
- (8 to12)	Medium negative
- (4 to 8)	Low negative
- (1 to 4)	Insignificant negative
+ (1 to 4)	Insignificant positive
+ (4 to 8)	Low positive
+(8 to 12)	Medium positive
+ (12 to 20)	High positive
+ (20 to 25)	Exceptional positive

Source: based on Waring and Glendon (1998).

References and Further Reading

Arai, T., Yamamoto, S. and Makino, K. et al (eds). 2005. *Systems and Human Science, for Safety, Security and Dependability.* Selected papers of the 1st International Symposium SSR 2003, Osaka, Japan, November. Amsterdam: Elsevier.

Aven, T. 2012. "On the Meaning and Use of the Risk Appetite Concept". *Risk Analysis*, Vol 33 Issue 3, 462-468.

Bacharach, S.B. and Lawler, E.J. 1980. *Power and Politics in Organizations: the Social Psychology of Conflict, Coalitions and Bargaining.* San Francisco: Jossey-Bass Inc.

Barberis, N.C. 2013. "Thirty Years of Prospect Theory in Economics: a Review and Assessment". *Journal of Economic Perspectives*, 27(1), 173-196.

Baybutt, P. 2013. "Allocation of Risk Tolerability Criteria". *Process Safety Progress*, Vol 33 Issue 3, 227-230.

Beck, U. 1992. *Risk Society—Towards a New Modernity*. London: Sage Publications.

Beer, M., Eisenstat, R. A. and Spector, B. 1990. "Why Change Programs Don't Produce Change". *Harvard Business Review*, 68(6): 158-166.

Berger, P. and Luckmann, T. 1967. *The Social Construction of Reality*. Garden City, NY: First Anchor Books.

Birks, M. and Mills, J. 2015. *Grounded Theory: a Practical Guide*, 2nd edition. London: Sage.

BoBS. 1995. *Report of the Inquiry into the Circumstances of the Collapse of Barings*. Chairman E.H. George. July 18, 1995. Board of Banking Supervision. London: The Stationery Office.

Boustras, G. and Waring, A. 2020. 'A Review of Safety and Security, their Interactions, and Policy Implications, in a Contemporary Context'. Special Issue: The Future of Safety Science. *Safety Science*, 132 (2020), 104942.

Burgess, A. 2015. "The Social Construction of Risk". In *Sage Handbook of Risk Communication*, edited by H. Cho, T. Reimer and K. McComas, 121-139. London: Sage.

Burrell, G. and Morgan, G. 1979. *Sociological Paradigms and Organisational Analysis*. London: Heinemann.

Campbell, J.P. and Pritchard, R.D. 1976. "Motivation Theory in Industrial and Organizational Psychology". In *Handbook of Industrial and Organizational Psychology*, edited by M.D. Dunnette, 66-130. Chicago, Ill: Rand McNally.

Chicken, J. 1996. *Risk Handbook*. London: Thomson/Cengage.

Davies, L.J. 1988. "Understanding Organizational Culture: a Soft Systems Perspective". *Systems Practice*, Vol 1No 1,1-30.

Deal, T.E. and Kennedy, A.A. 1986. *Corporate Cultures: Rites and Rituals of Corporate Life*. Reading, MA: Addison-Wesley.

Deepwater Commission 2011. *Deepwater—the Gulf Oil Disaster and the Future of Offshore Drilling*. Report to the President. National Commission on the BP Deepwater Horizon Oil Spill and Offshore Drilling, Washington DC.

Dekker, S.W.A. 2011. *Drift into Failure—from Hunting Broken Components to Understanding Complex Systems.* Farnham, Surrey UK: Ashgate/Taylor & Francis.

Dekker, S.W.A. and Nyce, J.M. 2014. "There is Safety in Power, or Power in Safety". *Safety Science,* 67, 44-49.

Dekker, S.W.A. and Pruchnicki, S. 2014. "Drifting into Failure: Theorizing the Dynamics of Disaster Incubation". *Theoretical Issues in Ergonomics Science,* 14(6), 534-544.

Dixon, N.F. 1981. *Preconscious Processing.* Chichester: John Wiley & Sons.

Douglas, M. 1992. *Risk and Blame: Essays in Cultural Theory.* London: Routledge.

Douglas, M. 1994. "Who is the Public?" Pages 48-66, symposium proceedings. *Risks to the Public: The Rules, The Rulers and the Ruled.* December 14, 1994. London: The Hazards Forum.

Douglas, M. and Wildavsky, A. 1982. *Risk and Culture: an Essay on the Selection of Technological and Environmental Dangers.* London: University of California Press.

Dror, I.E. and Fraser-Mackenzie, P.A.F. 2008. "Cognitive Biases in Human Perception, Judgment, and Decision Making: Bridging Theory and the Real World". In *Criminal Investigative Failures,* edited by Kim Rossmo, 53-67. Abingdon Oxon UK: Taylor & Francis.

Durodié, B. 2002. "Trust Comes from Expertise". In *Science: Can We Trust the Experts?* edited by T. Gilland, 17-38. Abingdon, UK: Hodder & Stoughton.

Durodié, B. 2005a. *The Concept of Risk. Risk Case Studies.* Nuffield Trust Global Programme on Health, Foreign Policy and Security. London: Nuffield Trust.

Durodié, B. 2005b. "Limitations of Public Dialogue in Science and the Rise of 'New' Experts". In *The Changing Role of the Public Intellectual,* edited by D. Cummings, 82-92. Oxford: Routledge.

Durodié, B. 2017. "Theory Informed by Practice. Application Informed by Purpose. Why to Understand and Manage Risk, Cultural Context is the Key". *Safety Science,* 99 Part B, 244-254.

Ferraris, C. and Corveth, R. 2003. "NASA and the Columbia Disaster: Decision-Making by Groupthink?" *Proceedings of the 2003 Association for Business Communication Annual Convention.* Blacksburg, Va, USA: Association for Business Communication.

Fincham, R. 1992. "Perspectives on Power: Processual, Institutional and 'Internal' Forms of Organizational Power". *Journal of Management Studies*, Vol 29 No 6, 741-759.

Fischbacher-Smith, D., Irwin, A. and Fischbacher-Smith, M. 2009. "Bringing Light to the Shadows and Shadows to the Light, and Risk Communication". In *Risk Communication and Public Health*, edited by P. Bennett et al, chapter 2, 23-38. Oxford Scholarship. DOI. 10.1093/acprof:oso/9780199562848.001.0001.

Fischhoff, B. 1975. "Hindsight Does Not Equal Foresight: the Effect of Outcome Knowledge on Judgement in Uncertainty". *Journal of Experimental Psychology, Human Perception and Performance*, 1, 288-299.

FSA. 2011. *Report on the Failure of the Royal Bank of Scotland (RBS)*. December 2011. FSA Board, chairman Adair Turner. London: Financial Services Authority.

Gai, P. and Vause, N. 2006. "Measuring Investors' Risk Appetite". *International Journal of Central Banking*, Vol 2 No 6, March, 167-188.

German, M. 2020. "The FBI Warned for Years that Police are Cozy with the Far Right. Is No One Listening?" *The Guardian*. August 28, 2020. https://www.theguardian.com/commentisfree/2020/aug/28/fbi-far-right-white-supremacists-police. [accessed September 7, 2020].

Glaser, B.G. and Strauss, A.L. 1967. *The Discovery of Grounded Theory: Strategies for Qualitative Research*. Chicago: Aldine.

Glendon, A.I. 1987. "Risk Cognition". In *Risk and Decisions*, edited by W.T. Singleton and J. Hovden, 87-107. Chichester: John Wiley & Sons.

Glendon, A.I. 2008. "Safety Culture and Safety Climate: How Far Have We Come and Where Could We Be Heading?" *Journal of Occupational Safety & Health Australia and New Zealand*, 24(3): 249-271.

Glendon, A.I. and Clarke, S.G. 2016. *Human Safety and Risk Management: a Psychological Perspective*. 3rd edition. Boca Raton, Florida: CRC Press/Taylor & Francis.

Glendon, A.I., Clarke, S. and McKenna, E. 2006. *Health & Safety Risk Management*, 2nd edition. Boca Raton FL: CRC Press/Taylor & Francis.

Glendon, A.I. and Stanton, N. 2000. "Perspectives on Safety Culture". *Safety Science*, 34, 193-214.

Glendon, A.I. and Waring, A.E. 1997. *Barings: A Case of Human Resource Mismanagement?* Pages 31-40, in conference proceedings of ANZAM 97 Conference, Management Theory and Practice—Moving into a New Era. Monash University and Macmillan Australia.

Grinshteyn, E. and Hemenway, D. 2010. "Violent Death Rates: the US compared with Other High-Income OECD Countries". *The American Journal of Medicine*, Vol 129 Issue 3, 266-273.

GVA. 2017. "Gun-Related Deaths and Injuries". www.gunviolencearchive.org. [accessed December 3, 2017].

Hardy, C. 1985. "The Nature of Unobtrusive Power". *Journal of Management Studies*, Vol 22 No 4, 384-399.

HICRC. 2017. *Homicide.* Harvard Injury Control Research Center. Harvard T.H. Chan School of Public Health, Harvard School of Public Health. https://www.hps.harvard.edu/hicrc/firearms-research/gunsanddeath/. [accessed December 6, 2017].

Hillson, D. and Murray-Webster, R. 2012. "Using Risk Appetite and Risk Attitudes to Support Appropriate Risk-Taking: a New Taxonomy and Model". *Journal of Project, Program and Portfolio Management*, Vol 2 No 1, 29-46.

HOCTC. 2009. *Banking Crisis: Dealing with the Failure of UK Banks.* Report HC416, May 1, 2009. 7th report of session 2008-9. House of Commons Treasury Committee. London: The Stationery Office.

HSE. 1988. *Out of Control—Why Control Systems Go Wrong and How to Prevent Failure.* Sudbury, Suffolk UK: HSE Books.

HSE. 1989. *The Fires and Explosion at BP Oil (Grangemouth) Refinery Ltd, Report of the Investigation.* Health & Safety Executive. Sudbury, Suffolk UK: HSE Books.

HSE. 2003. *Major Investigation Report: BP Grangemouth, Scotland, 29 May to 10 June 2000*, a public report prepared by the HSE on behalf of the Competent Authority 18 August 2003, Health & Safety Executive and the Scottish Environmental Protection Agency. Sudbury, Suffolk UK: HSE Books.

HSE et al. 2011. *Buncefield: Why Did it Happen? The Underlying Causes of the Explosion and Fire at the Buncefield Oil Storage Depot, Hemel Hempstead, Hertfordshire, 11 December 2005.* The Competent COMAH Authority (Health & Safety Executive, Environment

Agency and Scottish Environmental Protection Agency). Sudbury, Suffolk UK: HSE Books.

IAEA. 1992. *Chernobyl Accident: Updating of INSAG-1 Report.* Safety Series No 75—INSAG 7 Report. Vienna: International Atomic Energy Agency.

IRM. 2010. *A Structured Approach to Enterprise Risk Management (ERM) and the Requirements of ISO 31000.* London: Institute of Risk Management.

IRM. 2011. *Risk Appetite and Tolerance.* Guidance Paper. London: Institute of Risk Management.

IRM. 2018. *Standard Deviations: A Risk Practitioner's Guide to ISO 31000.* London: Institute of Risk Management.

Janis, I.L. 1972. *Victims of Groupthink.* New York: Houghton Mifflin.

Janis, I.L. 1982. *Groupthink: Psychological Studies of Policy Decisions and Fiascos.* 2nd edition. New York: Houghton Mifflin.

Johnson, B.B. and Covello, V.T. (eds). 1987. *The Social and Cultural Construction of Risk: Essays on Risk Selection and Perception.* New York: Springer.

Johnson, D.J., Tress, T., Burkel, N. et al. (2019). "Officer Characteristics and Racial Disparities in Fatal Officer-Involved Shootings". *Proceedings of the National Academy of Sciences PNAS* August 6, 2019, 116 (32), 15877-15882.

Johnson, G. 1987. *Strategic Change and the Management Process.* Oxford: Basil Blackwell.

Johnson, V. 2020. "Capitol Siege Raises Questions Over Extent of White Supremacist Infiltration of Police". *The Conversation.* January 14, 2021. https://theconversation.com/capitol-siege-raises-questions-over-extent-of-white-supremacist-infiltration-of-us-police-153145. [accessed January 17, 2021].

Jongejan, R.B. and Vrijling, J.K. 2009. "The Optimization of System Safety: Rationality, Insurance and Optimal Protection". In *Safety. Reliability and Risk Analysis: Theory, Methods and Applications,* edited by Martorelli et al, 1259-1266. London: Taylor & Francis.

Jonkman, S.N. , van Gelder, P.H.A.J.M. and Vrijling, J.K. 2003. "An Overview of Quantitative Risk Measures for Loss of Life and Economic Damage". *Journal of Hazardous Materials*, A99, 1-30.

Kahneman, D. 2003. "Maps of Bounded Rationality: Psychology for Behavioural Economics". *American Economics Review,* 93(5), 1449-1475.

Kahneman, D. and Tversky, A. 1979. "Prospect Theory: an Analysis of Decision Under Risk". *Econometrica,* Vol 47 No 2, March, 263-292.

Kasperson, R.E. and Pijawka, K.D. 1985. "Societal Response to Hazard and Major Hazard Events: Comparing Natural and Technological Hazards". *Public Administration Review,* 45, 7-18.

Kasperson, R.E., Renn, O., Slovic, P. et al. 1988. "The Social Amplification of Risk: a Conceptual Framework". *Risk Analysis,* Vol 8 No 2, 177-187.

Kirtzman, A. 2010. *Betrayal: The Life and Lies of Bernie Madoff.* London: Harper Perennial.

Lawler, E.E. and Porter, L.W. 1967. "Antecedent Attitudes of Effective Managerial Performance". *Organizational Behaviour and Human Performance,* Vol 2 No 2, 122-142.

Le Coze, J-C. 2005. "Are Organizations Too Complex to be Integrated in Technical Risk Assessment and Current Safety Auditing?" *Safety Science,* Vol 43 No 8, 613-638.

Le Coze, J-C. and Dechy, N. 2005. "The Common System and Organizational Issues of Security and Safety: the 9/11 Case". *Proceedings of the ESRDA 29th Seminar,* October 25-26, 2005. JRC, IPSC, Ispra, Italy.

Leeb, S. 2006. *The Coming Economic Collapse—how you can thrive when oil costs $200 a barrel.* New York: Warner Business Books/Grand Central Publishing.

Leeson, N. 1996. *Rogue Trader.* London: Little Brown.

Linstone, H.A. and Turoff, M. (eds). 1975. *The Delphi Method: Techniques and Applications.* Reading Mass: Addison-Wesley Publishing Co.

Linstone, H.A. and Turoff, M. (eds). 2002. *The Delphi Method: Techniques and Applications.* New Jersey Institute of Technology. Newark, NJ: NJIT.

Lunenburg, F.C. 2010. "Group Decision-Making: the Potential for Groupthink". *International Journal of Management, Business and Administration,* Vol 13 No 1, 1-6.

Maclean, B. and Elkind, P. 2004. *The Smartest Guys in the Room: The Amazing Rise and Scandalous Fall of Enron*. New York: Portfolio Trade, Penguin Group (USA) Inc.

March, J.G. and Simon, H. 1958. *Organizations*. New York: John Wiley.

Morgan, G. 1986. *Images of Organization*. London: Sage.

Mosher, G.A. 2013. "Trust, Safety and Employee Decision-Making. A Review of Research and Discussion of Future Directions". *Journal of Technology, Management and Applied Engineering*, 29(1), 1-11.

Mudu, P. and Beck, E. 2012. "Navigating Scientific Routes to Risk Assessment: a Tortuous Path". *Journal of Risk Research*, 15(10), 1217-1222.

NAIIC. 2012. *The Official Report of the Fukushima Nuclear Accident Independent Investigation Committee*. Chairman Kiyoshi Kurokawa. National Diet of Japan. Tokyo.

Nickerson, R.S. 1998. "Confirmation Bias: a Ubiquitous Phenomenon in Many Guises". *Review of General Psychology*, 2, 175-220.

Perrow, C. 1984. *Normal Accidents: Living with High-Risk Technologies*. New York: Basic Books.

Perrow, C. 2011. "Fukushima and the Inevitability of Accidents". *Bulletin of Atomic Scientists*, 67(6), 44-52.

Perrow, C. 2013. "Nuclear Denial: from Hiroshima to Fukushima". *Bulletin of Atomic Scientists*, 69(5), 56-67.

Pettigrew, A. 1973. *The Politics of Organizational Decision-Making*. London: Tavistock.

Pfeffer, J. 1981. *Power in Organizations*. London: Pitman.

Pidgeon, N.F. 2012. "Complex Organizational Factors: Culture, High Reliability, and Lessons from Fukushima". *The Bridge*. National Academy of Engineering, 42(3), 17-22.

Pidgeon, N., Slovic, P. and Kasperson, R.E. (eds). 2003. *The Social Amplification of Risk*. Cambridge, UK: CUP.

Quealy, K. and Sanger-Katz, M. 2016. "Comparing Gun Deaths by Country: the US is in a Different World". *The New York Times*. The Upshot. June 13, 2016. https://www.nytimes.com/.

Rabin, M. 2000. "Risk Aversion and Expected Utility Theory". *Econometrica*, Vol 68 No 5, September, 1281-1292.

Royal Society 1992. *Risk: Analysis, Perception, Management*. Report of a Royal Society Study Group. London: The Royal Society.

Schein, E.H. 1985. *Organizational Culture and Leadership*. San Francisco: Jossey-Bass Inc.

Shrader-Frechette, K.S. 1991. *Risk and Rationality: Philosophical Foundations for Populist Reforms*. Berkeley: University of California Press.

Simon, H.A. 1972. "Theories of bounded rationality". In *Decisions and Organization*, edited by C.B. MaGuire and R. Radner, 161-176. Amsterdam: North Holland Publishing Co.

Slovic, P., Fischhoff, B. and Lichtenstein, S. 1982. "Why Study Risk Perception?" *Risk Analysis*, Vol 2 No 2, 83-93.

Smircich, L. 1983. "Concepts of Culture and Organizational Analysis". *Administrative Science Quarterly*, 28(3), 339-358.

Speri, A. 2017. "The FBI has Quietly Investigated White Supremacist Infiltration of Law Enforcement". *The Intercept*. January 31, 2017. https://theintercept.com/2017/01/31/the-fbi-has-quietl y-investigated-white-supremacist-infiltration-of-law-enforcem ent/. [accessed September 7, 2020].

Speri, A. 2020. "Unredacted FBI Document Sheds New Light on White Supremacist Infiltration of Law Enforcement". *The Intercept*. September 29, 2020. https://theintercept.com/2020/09/29/po lice-white-supremacist-infiltration-fbi/. [accessed January 17, 2021].

Swedler, D.I., Simmons, M.M., Dominici, F. and Hemenway, D. 2015. "Firearm Prevalence and Homicides of Law Enforcement Officers in the United States". *American Journal of Public Health*, 105, 2042-2048.

Toft, B. 1990. *The Failure of Hindsight*. PhD Thesis. Department of Sociology, University of Exeter, UK.

Toft, B. 1996. "Limits to the Mathematical Modelling of Disasters". In *Accident and Design: Contemporary Debates in Risk Management*, edited by C. Hood and D. Jones, 99-110. London: UCL Press.

Toft, B. and Reynolds, S. 1997. *Learning from Disasters: a Management Approach*, 2nd edition. Leicester: Perpetuity Press.

Turner, B. A. 1988. "Connoisseurship in the Study of Organizational Cultures". In *Doing Research in Organizations*, edited by A. Bryman, 108-122. London: Routledge.

Turner, B. A. 1992. *Organizational Learning and the Management of Risk*. Paper presented at the British Academy of Management 6th

Annual Conference; 14-16 September, Bradford University, England.

Turner, B.A. 1994. "Causes of Disaster: Sloppy Management". *British Journal of Management*, 5, 215-219.

Turner, B.A. and Pidgeon, N. 1997. *Man-Made Disaster: the Failure of Foresight*. 2nd edition. London: Butterworth Heinmann.

Tversky, A. and Wakker, P. 1995. "Risk Attitudes and Decision Weights". *Econometrica*, Vol 63 No 6, November, 1255-1280.

USCSHIB. 2007. *Refinery Explosion and Fire, BP Texas City 23 March 2005*. Investigation Report No. 2005-04-I-TX, March 2007. Washington DC: US Chemical Safety & Hazard Investigation Board.

US Department of Justice. 2012. *Statement on Criminal Conviction and Sentencing of Allen Stanford of Stanford International Bank*. 14 June 2012. Washington DC: US Department of Justice.

Vaughan, D. 1996. *The Challenger Launch Decision: Risk, Technology, Culture and Deviance at NASA*. Chicago, Ill: University of Chicago Press.

Vaughan, D. 1999. "The Dark Side of Organizations: Mistake, Misconduct and Disaster". *Annual Review of Sociology*, 25, 271-305.

Vaughan, D. 2004. "Theorizing Disaster: Analogy, Historical Ethnography, and the Challenger Accident". *Ethnography*, 5(3), 315-347.

Vaughan, D. 2006. "NASA Revisited: Theory, Analogy and Public Sociology". *American Journal of Sociology*, 112(2), 353-393.

Vaughan, D. 2014. "Analogy, Cases, and Comparative Social Organization". In *Theorizing in Social Science: The Context of Discovery*, edited by R. Swedberg, 61-84. Redwood City CA: Stanford University Press.

Vickers, J. 1983. *The Art of Judgement—a Study of Policy Making*. London: Harper & Row.

von Neumann, J. and Morgernstern, O. 1944. *Theory of Games and Economic Behaviour*. Princeton New Jersey: Princeton University Press.

Vroom, V.H. 1964. *Work and Motivation*. Chichester: John Wiley & Sons.

Walton, M. 2007. "Toxic leadership". In *Leadership: The Key Concepts*, edited by J. Gosling and A. Marturano. Oxford: Routledge.

Waring, A.E. 2013. *Corporate Risk and Governance: an End to Misman-agement, Tunnel Vision, and Quackery*. Farnham UK: Gower/ Routledge.

Waring, A.E. 2015. "Managerial and Non-Technical Factors in the Development of Human-Created Disasters: a Review and Research Agenda". *Safety Science*, 79, 254-267.

Waring, A. (ed). 2018. *The New Authoritarianism Vol 1: A Risk Analysis of the US Alt-Right Phenomenon*, edited by A. Waring. Stuttgart: Ibidem Verlag.

Waring, A.E. and Glendon, A.I. 1998. *Managing Risk: Critical Issues for Survival and Success into the 21st Century*. Aldershot, UK: Thompson/Cengage.

Waring, A. and Paxton, R. 2018. "Psychological Aspects of the Alt-Right Phenomenon". In *The New Authoritarianism Vol 1: A Risk Analysis of the US Alt-Right Phenomenon*, edited by A. Waring, 53-82. Stuttgart: Ibidem Verlag.

Webster, D.W. and Vernick, J.S. (eds). 2013. *Reducing Gun Violence in America*. Baltimore MD: John Hopkins University Press.

Westley, F. R. 1990. "The Eye of the Needle: Cultural and Personal Transformations in a Traditional Organization". *Human Relations* 43(3): 273-293.

Westrum, R. 2004. "A Typology of Organizational Cultures". *Quality and Safety in Health Care*, 13, ii22-ii27. DOI: 10.1136/qshc.2003. 009522.

Wilkins, A.L. and Dyer, W.G. 1988. "Towards Culturally Sensitive Theories of Culture Change". *Academy of Management Review*, Vol 13 No 4, 522-533.

Wodak, R. 2015. *The Politics of Fear: What Right-Wing Populist Discourses Mean*. London: Sage.

Wodak, R. and Rheindorf, M. 2019. "The Austrian Freedom Party". In *The New Authoritarianism Vol 2: A Risk Analysis of the European Alt-Right Phenomenon*, edited by A. Waring, 171-197. Stuttgart: Ibidem Verlag.

Wodak, R., Mral, B. and KhosraviNik, M. (eds). 2013. *Right-Wing Populism in Europe: Politics and Discourse*. London: Bloomsbury Academic.

Zimmerman, M. 2011. "Confirmatory Bias". Page 661. *Encyclopaedia of Clinical Neuropsychology*. New York: Springer.

Chapter 11:
A Prognosis for the Corporate/Radical-Right Axis

By Alan Waring[1]

Abstract

This chapter draws together all the preceding content to consider potential scenarios for how the new corporate/radical-right symbiosis may unfold, and makes a prognosis for the most likely outcomes. In proceeding towards a prognosis, authoritarian attitudes and behaviour of some corporate leaders and of collective managements within some corporations need to be examined with caution in order to avoid inadvertently conflating distinct categories. Contexts affecting a prognosis include historical factors as well as those of a more recent and current character, such as the Covid-19 pandemic, laissez-faire policies of Internet and social media platform companies towards radical-right hate mongering and fake propaganda by users, and radical-right reactivity towards weakened US exceptionalism and Trump's re-election defeat. Of four major potential scenarios, the author concludes that (on present data) the most likely in the short- to medium-term is either a gradual or a crisis-driven rapid harshening of the present authoritarian climate in national governance and corporate conduct.

Key words: authoritarianism, corporate, radical-right, symbiosis, contexts, prognosis

Towards a Prognosis for the Corporate/Radical-Right Axis

The first two parts of this volume examined a number of topics and issues relating to the new authoritarianism arising in connection with a fusion of shared characteristics, mutual interests, and 'dark money' funding whereby influences pass in both directions between radical-right political ideologues and 'fellow travellers' in the corporate world. Aberrant representatives of the corporate world who are not consciously radical-right supporters may also nonetheless share many authoritarian behavioural characteristics with them. The

---

[1] See contributor affiliations and biography, page 525.

preceding chapter also provided a summary of risk analyses and evaluations derived from the chapters in Part 2 that cover selected strands of corporate/radical-right authoritarianism. This chapter draws together all the preceding content to consider potential scenarios for how this new authoritarianism may unfold.

Authoritarian attitudes and behaviour of some corporate leaders and of collective managements within some corporations need to be examined with caution. As numerous examples in previous chapters as well as Crouch (2014), Mayer (2016), Michaels (2020), and Oklobdzija (2019) among others show, some corporations and their leaders may indeed consciously support radical-right ideology and objectives, and some may go further in a more activist capacity. However, others again may unwittingly share many similar characteristics with those of radical-right political leaders, while not in fact being ideological or active followers of the radical right. Exhibiting similar attitudes, rhetoric, or conduct to the radical right does not automatically affirm that such corporate leaders and executives are ideological followers of the radical right or that they are necessarily conscious of the similarity. Mindful of the caveats of Brooks et al (2020), Fritzon et al (2016), and Post (2015) on the allied subject of personality disorders among leaders, in order to avoid inadvertently conflating such distinct categories, the four listed observations in chapter 5 require revisiting (see pages 256–257).

Bearing in mind these caveats, what may be deduced about how the symbiosis between the corporate and radical-right worlds, including intermediaries and enablers, may develop in the short- to medium-term? It is fairly certain that the categories of authoritarian corporate leader identified above will continue to exist, along with the potential harm that they may cause. There is no plausible reason to suppose that the well-established pattern of, on the one hand, corporate and intermediary funding of radical-right political interests, organisations, and activities and, on the other, radical-right political support for corporate 'fellow travellers', will diminish in either scope or scale. The on-going financial commitment worth hundreds of millions of US$ from corporate and foundation donors is indicative of the facilitating power available to the radical right. Given the authoritarian nature of the two collaborating entities, and their joint determination to impose a permanent radical-right stamp on national governance and society, and a neo-liberal free-market dominance of the economy with minimal taxation and controls on corporate conduct, the availability of 'dark money' for such purposes is likely to wax rather than wane.

Contexts Affecting Prognosis

Historical Context 2000-2020

A number of major factors will affect any prognosis for the corporate/radical-right axis. In the first decade of the 21st century, headline risk contexts taxing developed nations were the economy, wars and conflicts in the Middle East, international terrorism, demographics, mass migration, pandemics, and climate change. The 2008-9 global financial crisis had passed, albeit with lingering long-term effects on economies. The Second Gulf War ended with the defeat of Saddam Hussein's Iraqi regime and his capture (2003) and execution (2006), but with lingering hangover insurgency problems for the US-led coalition forces that even by 2020 had not been fully eliminated. A similar picture emerged in Afghanistan, following the ousting by US-led coalition forces of the Taleban regime in 2001. The standoff between the US and Iran since 1979 continued, with further sanctions against Iran, a situation that has worsened considerably since 2016. Israel continued to receive full backing from the US. The UN two-state solution for the peaceful coexistence of Israelis and Palestinians, as firmed up in the Camp David agreement of 1978 and the Oslo Accord of 1993, was already fading as a viable proposition given Israeli opposition, and a Second Palestinian Intifada ran from 2001 to 2005. Islamist terrorist groups such as Al Qaeda continued their bombing and other attacks globally throughout the first decade and into the second. Refugees from wars in the Middle East and economic migrants from many countries headed for Europe in increasing numbers. The SARS, avian and swine influenza epidemics raged at various times in the first decade in the Far East and SE Asia and remained a threat more globally into the second decade. Climate change and global warming threats were on the political radar and the Kyoto Protocol of 2005 augured an action programme, but little happened and the whole unresolved issue worsened as it entered the second decade (Waring 2018a).

In the second decade, many of these elements from the first decade carried forward and are still evident and remain unresolved into the third decade. For example, North Korea remains defiant and hostile. The Syrian civil war starting in 2011, and the birth of the Islamic State terrorist regime (and its ISIS derivative in Iraq and Syria), added to the pre-existing complexities of the Middle East conflicts (e.g. Waring 2018b), international rivalries and tensions, and IS-related terrorist attacks in Europe and elsewhere. Russian expansionist objectives saw its invasion of Crimea in 2014 and subsequent annexation, followed by aiding and abetting separatists in Eastern Ukraine, and then 'cyber warfare' interference in US and British voting in 2016 onwards (NIC 2017; USDoJ 2018a, b). Climate change remains an on-going challenge (Waring 2018a), in relation to which radical-right regimes and leaders continue to be the most disengaged and negative, for example, Trump's effective withdrawal in June 2017 from the Paris Climate Accord and making environmental protection subordinate to industry and corporate priorities (White House 2017). Similarly, radical-right regimes continue to respond negatively and typically with hostility towards mass migration, refugees, and immigration in general (e.g. Verney 2018 on the US).

In addition, the second decade saw a resurgence of the radical-right (e.g. Bevelander & Wodak 2019), with a range of new parties and groups across the spectrum, from the populist but usually non-violent end to extremist groups determined to use violence to intimidate, hurt and even murder those they hate in the name of political justification. Older far-right organisations from the 20th century became eclipsed by newer groups that knew how to use the Internet and social media to disseminate propaganda and hate messages with great effect among mass online audiences, for example, UKIP, Brexit Party, EDL, Britain First, Generation Identity (Turner-Graham 2019) and the Alt-Right movement in the US (Nagle 2017; Paxton 2018).

New Contexts and Factors

However, some new additional factors and contexts arose in the second decade, which do not augur well for the short- to medium-term future of national governance, stability and prosperity. Arguably the biggest single 'wild card' political event of the second decade was the 2016 election of Donald Trump as US President. Going against both the consensus of political observers and poll predictions, the radical-right Republican renegade Trump won and embarked on an authoritarian programme of discriminatory nationalist and nativist policies inside America, as well as in foreign policy and foreign relations. Throughout his four-year term, Trump boasted in hyperbolic self-adulatory terms that he was the most competent president in US history. For example, he claimed to have been personally responsible for an exceptionally strong economy, keeping jobs in America, "making America great again", keeping Muslims, Mexicans, asylum seekers and other perceived 'undesirable' threats out of the US, being tough with America's enemies (notably Iran, North Korea), and tough-but-fair with its rivals (Russia, China). Following the arrival of the Covid-19 pandemic in North America in late February 2020, by July 2020 he was boasting (contrary to the evidence) that he had personally masterminded the purported defeat of Covid-19 in the US by emphasizing his personal intellect, his expertise on the Covid-19 pandemic, and his insistence on supremacy of economic activity and individual freedom of choice of citizens to flout science-based public health rules that emphasize self-isolation, social distancing and wearing face masks. Cillizza (2020) examined some of Trump's 'unpresidential' statements on the Covid-19 crisis and other topics made in a *Fox News* interview on July 23, 2020. Then, on September 30, 2020, and with some irony, Trump contracted Covid-19 and, fortunately once hospitalized, recovered relatively quickly. A large number of White House officials, most of whom like Trump forsook social distancing and wearing masks, were also struck down.

In reality, US economic strength in his first three years as president was owed largely to a long-wave trend that transcended the Obama and Bush administrations, plus Trump's additional stimulus policies based on tax cuts and major infrastructure projects, including the infamous 'Mexican Wall' project seeking to prevent illegal immigrants from entering the US across its southern border (Verney 2018, 248-252). Trump's attempts at keeping jobs in America and gaining an upper hand with US trade policies with other countries, notably China and the EU, were only partly successful and resulted in countermeasures and unintended adverse consequences, including heavy impact on the US agriculture sector as a result of China imposing massive retaliatory tariffs on US produce. Trump's rhetoric threatening trade wars with both China and the EU translated only as far as limited skirmishes, but the potential for unbridled economic warfare and devastating consequences for many parties remains a substantial socio-economic threat. The new Biden Democratic administration of 2021 is likely to take a less confrontational, but nonetheless firm, stance on such matters.

The Covid-19 Context

The Covid-19 pandemic, which to all intents and purposes began in February 2020 but probably initiated some weeks earlier in late 2019, proved to be a focussing lens through which to perceive a whole array of inter-related issues and risks affecting, in particular, democratic processes, national governance, public health, economies, corporate viability, employment practices, livelihoods, lifestyles, social welfare, and environment. Governments and populations of all nations were challenged and tested on all these risk issues. Some governments fared better than others in controlling the pandemic and coping with the ramifications. However, it became apparent that some regimes [almost exclusively radical-right[2]] chose to politicise the pandemic. They asserted, for example, that the Covid-19 risks had been deliberately exaggerated for political purposes by a coalition, if not conspiracy, of liberal politicians, liberals, socialists, anarchists, anti-corporatists, and scientists and medical specialists who are either 'quacks' or politically-motivated. They also asserted that, as a relatively harmless nuisance, [Trump and Bolsonaro both referred to it as "a little flu"], Covid-19 would soon succumb to the sheer will of the leader's political authority and that social distancing and face masks were irrelevant to controlling the spread. Chief among such regimes were the Trump administration and the Bolsonaro government in Brazil. Trump went even further by repeatedly accusing the Chinese government of deliberately failing to act swiftly enough to control the original viral spread in Wuhan, and referring to Covid-19 as 'the Chinese virus'.

Despite overwhelming factual evidence as early as March 2020 that Covid-19 was anything but a trivial health threat, and the subsequent daily data on the relentless spread of infections and death as

---

2   A socialist exception was the Belarus presidency of autocrat Alexander Lukashenko, who dismissed Covid-19 as "mass psychosis" (Boyes 2020) and recommended drinking vodka and/or driving a tractor to prevent infection.

published by inter alia the WHO and the US Centers for Disease Control (CDC), both Trump and Bolsonaro continued to deny the scale of the pandemic. Both leaders refused to advocate, and to personally wear, face masks in public settings and to strictly observe social distancing. Levitz (2020) and Spencer (2020) were among many observers highly critical of Trump's obstinacy and manifest resistance to prioritizing public health in which, in effect, he sought to project himself as the nation's true expert on pandemics while dismissing and ridiculing the analyses and recommendations of real pandemic experts.

Eventually, on July 22, 2020, Trump did acknowledge that the Covid-19 epidemic in the US was not beaten (thus contradicting his many previous statements) and that it was likely to get worse before getting better (*France24* 2020). By July 26, the number of US infections had exceeded 4 million, with over 145,000 deaths (CDC 2020a), and by September 1 infections had risen to over 6 million and deaths to nearly 184,000 (CDC 2020b). By the time this chapter was finalised in February 2021, the US numbers had risen to over 27 million infections and almost 500,000 deaths (CDC 2021). The economic impact of the pandemic on countries was extremely serious and immediate, reflecting the consequences of some four months of lockdown on travel, business activity, and employment. Business closures, receiverships, and bankruptcies rose sharply, as did job losses, unemployment benefits, temporary furlough payments to suspended employees, and business bailouts.

More generally, as noted above, the Covid-19 crisis also provided a catalyst for radical-right authoritarian opportunism (Christou 2020a, b; Volk 2020; Weinberg 2020a, b). For example, the far-right "illiberal democracy" regime of Viktor Orbán in Hungary used the crisis as an opportunity to extend his presidential powers into effectively running an elected dictatorship having an indefinite term to be decided solely by himself as president. The Council of Europe's Secretary General sent Orbán a stern reminder that emergency measures taken in the exceptional Covid-19 circumstances (Burić 2020) had to be temporary and also not an opportunity for repression.

Szijarto (2020) reported that, far from heeding Burić's warning, on the contrary Orbán and his acolytes such as the far-right Mi Hazánk Mozgalom party (a derivative of the far-right Jobbik party) used the state of emergency as a cover to increase repression of minorities such as the Roma, trans-sexuals, independent journalists, and those dissenting from far-right policies or far-right political movements. Police intimidation against minorities, as well as violence by far-right activists, has been reportedly used.

It should be born in mind that the Covid-19 pandemic of 2020 is unlikely to be a unique occurrence. Other potential pandemics, whether involving known pathogens or new ones, are possible and should be considered likely, certainly in the medium- to long-term. Any such major threat to public health, livelihoods, normal life, and assumed personal freedoms, is likely to attract radical-right opportunism as it did in Brazil, Hungary, US and elsewhere during the Covid-19 pandemic.

US Exceptionalism under Threat

According to Restad (2014; 2016) and discussed in Waring (2018b, 170-180), the concept of US exceptionalism that has existed since WWII encompasses three essential elements:

- The United States is both different to and better than the rest of the world in total, not just Europe and the 'Old World'.
- The United States enjoys a unique role in world history as the prime leader of nations.
- The United States is the only nation in history that has thwarted, and will continue to thwart, the laws of history in its rise to power, a power that will never decline.

These elements underscore a belief that US superiority and superpower status are warranted and inevitable in every respect. The US exceptionalism thesis does not allow the US to accept a *primus inter pares role* in relation to Russia and China, for example. Trump's version of US exceptionalism (Mead 2017; Payne 2017; White House 2017) involved such rhetorical shorthand devices as "America First" and "Make America Great Again", rejection of such diverse and allegedly un-American ideas as multilateralism and universal health care, repudiation of ethno-religious equality in favour of white Christian nationalism, and unilateral actions against other countries (e.g. military action against Iran and Syria; sanctions against Iran, Syria, Russia, and China; ethno-religious discrimination against citizens of primarily Muslim countries).

Perhaps the most salient element of the US exceptionalism doctrine, as projected by the Trump administration, is that of infinite, undiminished, dominant US power literally 'for ever'. However, such a doctrine defies the laws of history, which assume a population ecology model of nation states (Lowery & Gray 2015) in which nations grow, mature, and eventually decline. As Waring (2018b, 177-180) pointed out, the life-cycle concept is implicit in this model and therefore the inevitability of eventual decline. Strauss and Howe (1997) applied the concept in their study of US history and its likely future into the 21st century. Nevertheless, Trump and the US radical-right in general believe absolutely that the US will always be the dominant global power and that no other nation (specifically China or Russia) will ever overtake and replace it. Increasingly, this faith-based belief is being challenged by China on all main parameters—economic, military capability, political, and science and technology. In particular, Trump's anti-China rhetoric, and various attempts to challenge an expansionist China, demonstrate clearly US anxiety that its perceived exceptional mantle is not guaranteed (e.g. in 2020, the barring of advanced Huawei 5G technology as a perceived national security threat; sending US naval forces to the Far East to challenge China's claim to large tracts of the South China Sea, including islands under sovereignty of Brunei, Indonesia, Malaysia, Philippines, Taiwan, and Vietnam—Widener (2020)).

Both the veracity and validity of US exceptionalism have also been challenged by military and diplomatic failures. For example, despite the aggressive bombast of Trump and his various courtiers, the exceptionally stringent additional sanctions on Iran orchestrated by Trump, his withdrawal from the JCPOA nuclear treaty in May 2018 (Cullis & Parsi 2020; White House 2018), the targeted assassination of Iranian Major General Qasem Soleimani in February 2020 by a US drone strike (Waring 2020), and bellicose statements implying an impending war against Iran (Parsi 2020a), the inevitable collapse of the Iranian regime and/or its compliance with US demands [much bragged about by Trump] never materialized. For reasons why Iran did not capitulate, see Ansari (2006; 2019, Part VI), Cullis and Parsi (2020), Parsi (2018; 2020a, b), Parsi and Costello (2018), and Waring (2018c, 238-239).

US failures in foreign policy towards the Middle East are encapsulated in a report by Pillar et al (2020) for the Quincy Institute for Responsible Statecraft. They argued that US assumptions about its exceptional status and entitlement to dictate a 'New World Order', which includes its domination of the Middle East, are both misguided and not fit for purpose. "Preventing hostile hegemony in the Middle East does not mean the United States must play the role of hegemon itself..." (page 3). The report advocated a new holistic paradigm based on regional security and multilateral relations, in which the US's bilateral relations with individual countries in the region are determined by regional security instead of the latter being a constant casualty of individual bilateral interests. The fact that, (a) diplomatically and militarily, the US was pushed out of Syria and marginalised by Russian and Iranian alliances with Assad, as well as by their military presence, (b) the US totally failed to force Iran to capitulate to its nuclear and other demands, together with (c) the US-backed Saudi military offensive against the Houthis in Yemen failed after several years, and (d) a US attempt to introduce an imposed solution to the longstanding Israeli-Palestinian territorial and governance dispute that would negate UN Resolutions on Palestinian nationhood failed, collectively indicate the extent to which US foreign policy on the Middle East is not fit for purpose. See also Parsi (2020c).

These collective US failures also indicate that its supremacy and purported exceptionalism are in decline. Those countries that have relied heavily on US supremacy for support and protection, whether diplomatic, military, economic or psychological, against enemies or predatory regimes, may have to consider new security-and-defence policies and arrangements in the medium- to long-term (Parsi 2020d). This applies not just in relation to the Middle East but also generally (e.g. China's expansionism in South East Asia; a potential weakening of defence of European NATO members, as foreshadowed by Trump's repeated threats to cut US funds to NATO or even withdraw altogether[3]).

---

[3]   Although with the departure of Trump and a new Biden presidency in January 2021, any anti-NATO action by the US government is much less likely unless another Trump-like administration is elected in the future.

Internet and Social Media Platform Providers

The financial might, as well as technological scale and sophistication, both of their products and their corporate organisations, places media/communication platform companies such as *Facebook, Google,* and *Twitter,* as well as IT companies such as *Microsoft,* in an elite category of mega powerful corporations. *Microsoft* has been included here since, although it is primarily a software provider, its products are increasingly crucial to the functioning and use of Internet and social media products and service provision. Comparative global earnings data for these companies are in Table 11.1.

Table 11.1:   **Comparative Revenues of Four Major Internet-Related and Social Media Corporations**

Corpora-tion	Year	Gross Revenue (US$ billions)	Year	Gross Revenue (US$ billions)
Microsoft	2013	77.85	2020	143.02
Google	2013	51.07	2019	134.81
Facebook	2013	7.87	2018	70.7
Twitter	2013	Not available	2019	3.46

Source: www.statista.com

The ubiquitous products and services provided by such companies have brought undoubted benefits to most sectors of society. However, there are also dis-benefits. Some of the latter have been acknowledged by such companies, and some attempts have been made by them to tackle widespread criticisms, but nevertheless there has been a measure of reluctance and resistance that has set such high-tech companies in conflict with governments, regulators, the courts, elected representatives, and civil society organisations.

Allegations against such companies include:

(1) **Use of market dominance to stifle competition** (e.g. *Microsoft, Google, Facebook*). (*BBC* 2020b, c; CMA 2020; Moore 2020). *Microsoft* in particular has a long history of anti-trust actions against it by governments. For example, in 2004 it was fined €497.2m (US$611m) by the EU and again in 2013 the EU fined it €561m (US$731) for abuse of its near monopoly status in the operating systems software market (Chee 2013). Similarly, *Google* has a history of massive fines, for example in 2018 the EU fined *Google* US$5.1bn for

anti-competition conduct regarding *Android* smartphone technology (Satariano & Nicas 2018). In 2020, the CEOs of *Facebook, Google, Apple*, and *Amazon* were required to give evidence to the US Congress examination of whether such corporations had become too big and too powerful against the public interest (*BBC* 2020c; Hoyle 2020a). *Google's* dominance in online advertising was further examined by the Senate Judiciary Committee's anti-trust panel.

(2) ***Abuse of account holders' data for political and commercial purposes***, often unbeknown to account holders. The most high-profile example has been the Cambridge Analytica/*Facebook* data abuse scandal in 2018 (Paxton 2018, 353-354) reported in chapter 1. One outcome was the Online Harms White Paper (DCMS 2019; 2020) aiming for effective regulatory control of Internet and social media platforms against multiple potential harms as well as data abuse. As if to accentuate the need for such regulation, in the final weeks of the 2020 US presidential election campaigning, an extensive *C4News* investigation in the US revealed (*C4News* 2020a) that in 2016 *Facebook* had worked with the Republican Party to facilitate not only political advertisement targeting of individual account holders but also a specific 'deterrence' campaign seeking to dissuade black voters from voting at all. *C4News* also alleged (*C4News* 2020b) that the Republic Party and *Facebook* were conducting in 2020 a similar mass screening and targeting programme for the Trump re-election campaign, but this time targeting white voters with law-and-order fear messaging against the Biden challenger. A survey of individual voters on the Trump Campaign/*Facebook* database revealed that none was aware that they were being targeted or that the database held covertly such an enormous amount of personal data about them, their beliefs, their personality, their activities, their likely political preferences and so on—not only in 2016 but continuously up to 2020.

(3) ***Providing extremists, terrorists, sexual predators and other criminals with unfettered facilities to promote their beliefs and activities***, and to spread hatred against ethno-religious and other minorities and those holding contrary beliefs. Defensive claims to be merely free-speech information channels and not publishers, put forward by such platform providers as *Twitter* and *Facebook,* have been dismissed as sophistry (*The Times* 2020). In July 2020, Britain's Chief Rabbi, Ephraim Mirvis, wrote an identical official letter of complaint

(Mirvis 2020) to Jack Dorsey, Chief Executive of *Twitter*, and Mark Zuckerberg, Chief Executive of *Facebook*, in which he accused them of a "woeful lack of responsible leadership" in providing "a safe space for those who peddle hatred and prejudice" that "currently thrives on your platform". He added that "Your inaction amounts to complicity".

An example of the reluctance of *Facebook* and *Twitter* to block and remove ethno-religious hate content from their platforms is provided by the blatantly anti-Semitic postings in July 2020 by popular rap star Wiley (real name Richard Cowie), which he defended and refused to recant or apologize. Only after sustained pressure from the public, the media, the Campaign Against Anti-Semitism, and the Board of Deputies of British Jews, did both *Twitter* and *Instagram* (a *Facebook* business) suspend Cowie's account for seven days. When Cowie responded by switching his postings to *Facebook*, the latter banned him from both *Facebook* and *Instagram* (Burgess 2020). However, *Facebook* did eventually ban all Holocaust denial postings (FB 2020). The policy of such companies only reacting to public pressure and adverse publicity, instead of proactively and quickly banning such material and account holders, remains a target of the UK Online Harms Act scheduled for 2021 (DCMS 2019; 2020). Following the instrumental use by Trump of social media to personally orchestrate and encourage the extremist insurrectionist mob to attack the Capitol building in Washington DC on January 6, 2021, and the use of such media by the mobsters *in situ* to video and disseminate their actions, within days and out-of-character, social media companies acted. *Facebook, Instagram, Snapchat* and *Twitch* all suspended Trump's accounts. *Twitter* banned Trump permanently and, when his supporters transferred to the no-limits *Parler* platform, the latter was first removed by *Apple* and *Google* app stores and then removed from *Amazon's* web-hosting service, thus obliterating communication and frustrating any further orchestration of insurrection. *Twitter* also banned account holders promulgating inflammatory extremist material such as QAnon false conspiracy theories, including Trump's former National Security Adviser, Michael Flynn (Charter 2021a). Perhaps such companies foresaw a likely *tsunami* of tough government regulation of Internet and social media platforms in the aftermath of the January 6 attempted coup, not just in the US but globally.

Meanwhile, a boycott of Internet platforms, threatened in 2018 by major corporate advertisers unless they cleaned up their policies, supervision and control of extremist content and hate messaging, had begun in 2020 as a result of insufficient improvement. One of the high-profile clients threatening a boycott in 2018 was Unilever (Gibbons 2018), which annually spends over US$3billion in digital advertising. By July 2020, Unilever, and other corporate clients exasperated by continuing perceived obduracy by *Facebook* in particular, undertook a 1-month advertising boycott of *Facebook* (and in some cases, other platforms) (Hern 2020a). In a WFA survey of companies controlling some US$100billion in advertising (WFA 2020), 31% of them had already joined the boycott or were likely to, with a further 41% considering it. By end of July 2020, Hern (2020b) reported that the boycott continued to grow. Such mass action may provide a pointer to one potential strategy for combatting online racism and hate messaging.

BitChute is another example of hosting platforms used by far-right hate and terror groups, which include such terrorist groups prohibited under UK law as Feuerkrieg Division (Ball 2020). This platform also promulgates radical-right conspiracy theories, such as those from QAnon, concerning the 2020 US presidential election, Covid -19, and vaccines. As the major platforms, under pressure, began slowly to curb far-right excesses on their sites, far-right groups have increasingly switched to the *BitChute* site (Dearden 2020) and the *Parler* social media platform (but see above). In January 2021, *BitChute* (a UK-based company) was referred for investigation to the UK's Ofcom regulator for allegedly hosting hateful, violent, and anti-Semitic content (Hamilton 2021).

(4) ***Facilitating dissemination of false facts and fake news***, which are harmful to many parties and which also may undermine public confidence in democracy and institutions of governance, law and order, and public health (CMA 2020; DCMS 2018; 2019; 2020; HoC 2018; Hoyle 2020b). Prominent among the false facts and fake news in question are grand conspiracy theories, almost exclusively radical-right in origin, alleging an egregious 'deep state' conspiracy against the population by a broad spectrum of liberals, elites, Democrats, Black Lives Matter supporters, Hollywood stars, journalists, academics and celebrities, in short anyone who opposes the radical right and Donald Trump. Other false facts include those of the anti-vax

movement (e.g. alleging that vaccines such as MMR are highly danger-ous) closely allied to the radical right (e.g. David Icke) and the QAnon conspiracist movement.

(5) *Refusal to acknowledge or accept accountability and ex-hibiting arrogance and disrespect* towards both customers and democratic institutions seeking to protect them (e.g. elected repre-sentatives, executive government, regulators, the judiciary, laws and regulations). For example, when *Facebook* CEO Mark Zuckerberg was summoned in March 2018 by the UK Parliamentary DCMS Committee investigating the *Facebook*/Cambridge Analytica data abuse scandal, the committee chairman's letter to him stated "The committee has re-peatedly asked *Facebook* about how companies acquire and hold on to user data from their site, and in particular whether data had been taken without their consent. Your officials' answers have consistently understated this risk, and have been misleading to the committee", adding that *Facebook's* risk management controls had been "a cata-strophic failure of process" (Buchan 2018). Zuckerberg refused to at-tend, sending instead a senior executive (*The Week* 2018; *The Times* 2018). He further snubbed a requested attendance at an international joint hearing in London on disinformation and 'fake news' by the par-liamentary committee chairs of five nations (Argentina, Australia, Canada, Ireland, and UK), prompting a highly critical response from the DCMS chairman hosting the joint hearing (DCMS 2018).

(6) *Conducting, in effect, psychological warfare* against cus-tomers as exploitable revenue targets as well as against organs of state that might thwart their unfettered free-market monetizing pro-grammes. For example, see Zuboff (2019, 8) on the "surveillance cap-italism" power abuses of the Internet and social media giants seeking to control not just information exchange between individuals but also information about them and, worse, "predictive sources of behavioral surplus", the ultimate goal being mass control of populations for com-mercial gain.

Overall, the lasting image that such platform organisations pro-ject is one in which their leaders believe that they are untouchable, above the law, and too big for governments or the courts to challenge. They also appear slippery and devious, and willing to participate in mass data protection breaches, as well as conniving in spread of ha-tred against ethno-religious and other minorities by extremists, terrorists, sexual predators and other criminals. While insisting that they want to abide by the law and a moral and ethical code, and that in reality they do so, their conduct does not match their espoused commitment. Therefore, the speed with which such platforms as *Twitter*, *Facebook* and others shut down the accounts of President Trump and his extremist supporters, and the App technology enabler *Amazon* disabled *Parler* in its entirety, after their incitement to insurrection and violence at the Capitol building in Washington DC on January 6, 2021, was remarkable. Whether such action signals an acceptance, finally, that they have a primary editorial and governance duty to ensure public safety and national security, remains to be seen.

US Presidential Election 2020

The 2020 US Presidential Election was probably the fiercest and ugliest political battle in living memory fought between Democrat and Republican contenders. In principle, the Republican candidate in the form of Donald J. Trump, had an advantage as the incumbent—historically, first-term Presidents nearly always get re-elected. However, over his four-year term, President Trump had been highly controversial in many aspects of his policies, conduct and attitudes, which are summed up as 'negative', 'divisive' and 'polarising'. He projected his radical-right ideas and values as essentially a model of Republican 'winners/predators' (like himself) versus the rest of the population as not only 'losers/victims' but also unpatriotic, "socialist" (i.e. crypto-communist) agitators, and extremists. His shameless narcissism, bombastic bullying style, baseless false allegations, and relentless vicious commentary on anyone perceived as disagreeing with him, won him adulation from radical-right supporters. Although a relatively small proportion of the population, such hard-core supporters were joined by a much larger polity of sympathisers [approximately 50% of voters] who were mainly traditional Republicans and who were persuaded by Trump's egregious characterisation of the Democratic Party and his trivialisation of the Covid-19 threat.

The 2020 election offered voters a stark choice. In the event, Trump's incompetence on a wide range of issues (most notably the Covid-19 crisis), his frequently displayed lack of empathy and lack of humanity, and his perceived recklessness, all stacked against him. With 81.3 million votes, Biden won the overall popular vote by some

7-8 million, but still only marginally at 52.2%, emphasizing the strikingly polarised electorate.

Initially, many hoped that the failure of President Donald Trump to get re-elected in November 2020 would bring an end to the self-indulgent destructiveness of his authoritarian administration and herald a new era in which radical-right excesses would be reversed and radical-right political ideologues would be put firmly 'back in their box'. However, this is highly unlikely for the following reasons: (1) Although the Trump administration has ended, his repeated unsubstantiated claims that Biden's victory was won via voting fraud and conspiracy [he included the phrase "stole the election"], and widespread support for this stance from his supporters, despite all evidence to the contrary (CISA 2020) and the failure of his court actions alleging fraud, suggests the US radical right overall is in denial; (2) QAnon [Trump is a devotee] and other conspiracy theorists of the radical right are likely to continue with wild unsubstantiated allegations seeking to damage and undermine Biden's Democrat administration; (3) A narcissistic Trump, enraged by his public failure to be re-elected, embarked on something of a non-cooperation and 'scorched earth' strategy towards transition and handover to the incoming Biden administration; (4) Trump's public endorsement of the KKK and far-right violence in Charlottesville in 2017 (Verney 2018, 256), and his 2020 election call for the Proud Boys [an armed militia of loosely organized US far-right street protesters and intimidating ruffians] to "stand back, and stand by" was taken by such groups in general as a 'dog whistle' authorisation to prepare for possible armed action against Trump's array of political enemies and even insurrection against the state; (5) On December 3, 2020, Trump appointed Darren J. Beattie, who has publicly expounded racist and neo-Nazi ideas and has extensive far-right connections, to the US Commission for the Preservation of America's Heritage Abroad (Fox 2020); (6) On December 27, 2020, Trump pardoned two high-profile supporters (Paul Manafort and Roger Stone) convicted and jailed for various crimes (some federal), including actions that favoured Trump; (7) In Congress, while the Democrats retained control of the House of Representatives, up to January 6, 2021 the Senate was under Republican control. If Republican Senators had retained control, a number made it clear that they intended to block many, and perhaps all, of Biden's policies and bills, thereby severely hampering his administration's effectiveness. However, the Democrat win of both senatorial seats in Georgia put the Democrats in control of the Senate, thus removing that Republican threat (Zeffman 2021a), and (8) Trump and senior Republican Party supporters suggested a strong likelihood that he would embark early on a high-profile campaign for his re-election in 2024, which almost certainly would be a re-invigorated and more strident version of his 2020 campaign and appealing to his core base and the 74 million who voted for him in 2020. However, if a GOP damaged by Trump's encouragement of the January 6, 2021, mob insurrection at the Washington DC Capitol rejects him, he may decide (as he hinted) to establish a new Patriot Party. This looks less likely, as his second impeachment on February 13, 2021 found him not guilty, and therefore he is not barred from any future public office.

However, above all, after failing to force an election result reversal in his favour and also losing both Georgia senatorial seats, Trump gambled that he could still enforce his will by other means, namely inciting his faithful supporters to insurrection. On January 6, 2021, a violent mob of Trump supporters stormed the US Capitol building in Washington DC while the Senate was formally confirming the election result and Biden as the new President. Over many hours, the mob defied law enforcement officers, smashed doors and windows, ransacked and intimidated congressional members and staff. Video and social media evidence emerged that some of the mob had 'hit lists' of senior political figures, whom they intended to murder. Many were injured in the attack, and five died. Trump personally was blamed for both instigating the attack and then inflaming the mob via his "take back the country" *Twitter* messages rather than appealing for them to disband (Charter 2021b; Zeffman 2021b). A Republican lawmaker, Derrick Evans from West Virginia, was arrested and federally charged, while at least 11 other GOP lawmakers, including two state senators, were also involved as identified by social media videos (Singer 2021). A number came under federal investigation for sedition and conspiracy. A leading radical-right conspiracist Ali Alexander, under investigation for planning the attack, reported that GOP lawmakers Representatives Paul Gosar, Andy Biggs and Mo Brooks actively collaborated with him. Further, it was alleged that GOP lawmakers had taken mob organisers on a drive-through reconnaissance tour of the Capitol the day before the insurrection (Cohen 2021). At least 28 law enforcement officers from 12 states (Goddard 2021), and a number of active and retired military officers, were also among the Capitol attackers. It was also reported that the FBI had evidence that some of the mob went ready with lists and restraints to "capture and assassinate" particular Congressional officials (Polatntz 2021). The FBI also reported that "armed protests" were being planned for all 50 state legislatures and Washington DC as Biden's inauguration on January 20 approached (Cohen & Wild 2021).

As for the Republican Party, the Trump administration brought it to a crossroads. For four years, most Republican congressmen basked in his populist limelight while voicing their fulsome support for his more egregious statements and policies, rather than challenge him and face his notorious wrath and spite towards constructive critics, especially those in his own party or administration. Even after it was clear that Biden had won the 2020 election, many of them continued up to the January 20, 2021 inauguration day to parrot Trump's unsubstantiated allegations that somehow Biden's election was not just unfair but was "stolen" by electoral fraud. Having nailed their colours to the mast of Trump's ship, even if more as a result of feeling intimidated by him than by conviction, they now faced the biggest gamble of their political lives: either continue backing Trump's divisive and polarising radical-right policies, on the basis that in 2024 he was destined to be re-elected and therefore so would they, or recognize the fact that US demography would continue to change in favour of support for Democrat policies rather than regressive or otherwise harmful Republican ones dominated by Trumpian ideology. Responsibility for the disastrous ideology-driven incompetence of the Trump administration on the Covid-19 crisis, climate change, police brutality against ethnic minorities, and his shameful orchestration of the mob attack on the Capitol, for example, cannot be escaped by Republican politicians who so enthusiastically backed Trump's policies and attitudes. Some of them even took part in the Capitol insurrection (Singer 2021). However, they were gambling that by continuing to back Trump, they could rely on populist support sufficient to win their day in 2024. As Parsi observed:

> "Trump reflects the part of the American psyche that believes it must win—that it is entitled to win—by any means necessary. Rules are for others; the

losers. Proudly breaking them doesn't mean that you are wrong or bad. It means that you are a winner." Parsi (2020d)

This arguably amoral mantra of 'win by hook or by crook', in essence, describes the radical-right authoritarian character which is demonstrably backed by 50% of the US population and which many Republican politicians believed would ensure their own electoral longevity. In effect, at a crossroads, by February 2021 a majority of Republican politicians still declared a preference for Trumpism not 'One-Nation Republicanism', and for evolving rapidly into an unconditionally radical-right party rather than remaining merely conservative (Collinson 2021). Of course, by adapting so as to make themselves more hardline, more authoritarian, more callous, and more impervious to facts and environments unfavourable to them and their beliefs, politically they ran the risk of eventually dying away as unelectable GOP dinosaurs. On the other hand, that may take quite a long time and will be subject to many uncertainties and contingencies. The other half of Republican politicians wanted to cleanse themselves of any Trump taint and for the GOP to return to mainstream conservatism. The GOP was now deeply, and possibly irrevocably, divided and may even see a break-up into two separate parties: hard-line Trumpists who quit (potentially the mooted Patriot Party) and moderate conservatives within a smaller GOP, or a smaller radical-right GOP dominated by Trump versus moderates who quit to form a different anti-radical party.

Corporate America is also at a similar crossroads: whether to (a) regard corporations as market predators in a Darwinian competitive struggle where there are only predators and victims, winners and losers i.e. akin to the Trump world-view, or to (b) re-orientate towards the 'new model corporation' (British Academy 2018; BRT 2019), which balances traditional success metrics such as growth, acquisitions, mergers, market share, share values, and shareholder value with duties towards a broad-based inclusive set of stakeholders, corporate governance, corporate social responsibility, and tackling major risk issues such as climate change, environment, and mass migration. In the longer term, those adopting a more global world-view and *realpolitik* are likely to follow path (b) and are more likely to survive than those following path (a) and retaining any kind of allegiance to Trump and radical-right ideas and practices.

Projected Scenarios for Corporate/Radical-Right Interaction

The author posits four potential primary scenarios for future development of the corporate/radical-right axis:

Scenario 1: Status Quo Maintained

Despite some electoral successes, the inability of the radical right in many countries to retain seats and expand its elected representation results in it to remaining a fragmented, minority movement memorable only for noisy protests and controversial rhetoric, albeit harbouring hate mongers and violent elements (Turner-Graham 2019; Waring 2019).

The current characteristics of, and level and extent of interactions between, on the one hand, corporations and their leaders and, on the other, radical-right political interests (including agencies and intermediaries) would continue. A minority of corporate leaders predisposed, either ideologically and/or psychologically, to adopt an authoritarian style and/or radical-right ideas would continue to do so. Corporate donations to radical-right organisations, causes, and activities would remain at their current levels.

A majority of corporations, and especially those of high integrity and ethics, would continue to reject such authoritarianism in the business environment and probably also in the political sphere and public policy. They would also be disinclined to make voluntary financial donations or give other support to radical-right political entities (or indeed to any radical political entity) and would reject overtures seeking to induce such donations or support. Polarization of society would continue.

Scenario 2: Gradual Incrementalism in Authoritarian Control

A slow rightward societal drift may occur and entrenchment into an illiberal democracy in some countries, relying on determined radical-right candidates, entry-ist infiltration of mainstream parties (for example, radical-right infiltration of the UK Conservative Party by UKIP, Brexit Party and other far-right supporters), weak mainstream candidates, and populist radical-right voters. In line with this general and almost imperceptible solidification and normalisation of a radical-right tenor to civil and political governance (i.e. illiberal democracy and elected dictatorships, as in Brazil and Hungary), a similar drift may occur towards a wider prevalence of authoritarianism in corporations whose managements may be encouraged and emboldened by a radical-right climate. This assumes (a) a predisposition among a minority of managements to adopt an authoritarian style and/or radical-right ideas, and (b) increasing willingness among other managements to be persuaded of benefits accruing from adoption of such a position. If Trump had been re-elected as US President in November 2020, this scenario would be likely to be more evident than if the Democrat (Joe Biden) had been elected. Trump's re-election would have encouraged and emboldened like-minded radical-right political and corporate interests in such countries as Brazil, Britain, Germany, Hungary, Italy, and Poland, whose extant governments are either radical-right or increasingly influenced by radical-right ideology (see Bevelander & Wodak 2019 on European trends).

In contrast, high integrity ethical corporations would continue to reject such a drift towards authoritarianism in the business environment, and probably also in the political sphere and public policy. They would also be disinclined to make voluntary financial donations or give other support to radical-right political entities (or indeed to any radical political entity) and would reject overtures seeking to induce such donations or support.

Scenario 3: Crisis-Driven Rapid Harshening of Authoritarian Climate

A major crisis, or multiple major crises, affecting for example society, economy, trade, national security, public order, or public health, may result in both corporate and radical-right interests rallying to each other's protection and also using crisis as an opportunistic pretext to engage in ever more draconian authoritarianism. As noted above, examples of such crises include: pandemics, economic recession, trade wars, international or regional conflicts, and even attempted far-right coups. A number of writers have noted such opportunism in relation to the Covid-19 pandemic, for example, not only authors in this volume but also Christou (2020a; b), Volk (2020), and Weinberg (2020a, b).

In extreme circumstances, a crisis could lead to rapid collapse of current democratic order and opportunistic takeover of some provincial or even national governments by radical-right elements, possibly involving armed force, and leading to pseudo-democracy or dictator-ship. This possibility became glaringly evident when Trump refused to concede defeat in the 2020 US presidential election and made con-certed efforts in November and December 2020 and into January 2021 to stay in power regardless of the election result. The angry his-trionics and intimidating tactics by frequently armed radical-right pro-Trump protestors across the US during the election campaigning, including the far-right Proud Boys whom Trump exhorted to "stand by", amounted to a thinly veiled threat of potential insurrection unless Trump were re-elected. His orchestration of the mob attack on the Capitol on January 6, 2021 speaks for itself, and his impeachment by Congress in February 2021 for inciting insurrection, were almost a logical progression for whom many regard as a megalomaniacal des-pot. Indeed, before this, he is reported to have seriously contemplated during an Oval Office strategy meeting on December 18, 2020 a decla-ration of martial law to impose a second term as president, as urged by former national security adviser, retired General Michael Flynn (Zeffman 2020). Flynn, a highly controversial advocate of radical-right ideology and a QAnon conspiracy theory devotee, also aired the sug-gestion publicly on TV (Reyner 2020).

This unprecedented 'banana republic' conduct overall by a US President and his radical-right caucus within the GOP, including his sustained baseless attacks on the integrity of the electoral system, se-verely damaged not only his own credibility and legitimacy but also the reputation and standing of US democracy, at home and abroad. No longer would the US be entitled to lecture foreign regimes about their lack of democratic credentials. The 'land of the free and the brave' looked increasingly like the 'land of the right-wing bully and the cowed', and no longer the world's leading democracy.

Although Trump and his supporters were eventually defeated in their attempted coup in January 2021, they and fellow travellers have not disappeared. Such far-right militias as the Proud Boys, the Oath Keepers, the Three Percenters, the Boogaloo Bois/Boys, Gun Owners for Trump, and many more, continue to flourish. Without robust coun-ter-action, their threat may well resurface and such developments in the US might even result eventually in secession (Blest 2017) in the form of two different confederacies, styled here as the Confederation of Liberal Progressive States and the Confederation of Nationalist Conservative States (Waring 2018, 420-421).

In the corporate context, a crisis scenario assumes (a) a predisposition among a minority of managements to adopt an authoritarian style and/or radical-right ideas, and (b) an increasing willingness among managements in general to be persuaded of benefits accruing from adoption of such a position. Had Trump been re-elected as President in 2020, or a future radical-right US President arises, this crisis scenario would more likely to be realised. A similar projection is likely for other countries that already have a radical-right government, or one heavily influenced by radical-right parties or ideology, for example Brazil, Britain, Germany, Hungary, Italy, Poland.

Accentuated by pressures arising from crises that affect most or all sectors, populations in particular countries may become increasingly polarised. On the one hand, authoritarian power wielders in government, the Establishment, and some corporations, will be backed both by other companies fearful of being penalised for not accepting authoritarian policies, and by a cowed and increasingly compliant populace fearing uncertainty, unemployment, and reduced living standards more than curbs on democratic rights and freedoms. Such competing fears have been clearly evident in an era of sudden exceptionally high unemployment and severe economic recession resulting from the Covid-19 pandemic. In such a context, short-term perceived self-interest may eclipse moral imperatives among citizens and corporations and, as noted above, the radical right are likely to seize on the political opportunity such vulnerability presents, for example, such inducements as increases to pensions and benefits, coupled with openly pro-government propaganda issued via public broadcast channels by the ruling radical-right PiS [Law and Justice] Party in Poland (see e.g. Balcer 2019 on PiS) during the deeply polarised 2020 presidential election campaigns (Wilczek & Moody 2020). On the other hand, high integrity ethical corporations prepared to continue to reject authoritarianism would become a diminishing beleaguered minority.

Scenario 4: Corporate/Radical-Right Axis in Decline

Of course, although unlikely, it is possible that radical-right ideology may reach a point beyond which it ceases to become strengthened, plateaus, and then suffers substantive decline. Although there is always likely to be a hard core of radical-right supporters in a population, electoral support is volatile and unpredictable, especially for populist radical-right parties. As noted in chapter 1, populist sympathisers and supporters typically enthuse over parties that pander to their prejudices and offer (or appear to offer) 'quick-fix salvation' solutions to their contemporary fears and anxieties. However, as soon as they fail to deliver such salvation, or if their policies begin to appear a liability in other ways, they are likely to be quickly deserted by erstwhile supporters. Examples include: the rapid post-2016 demise of UKIP (Waring 2019, 112) and its derivative Brexit Party in the 2019 general election, the rapid demise of the Austrian FPÖ following the 2019 collapse of the FPÖ-ÖVP coalition [triggered by the Strache bribery scandal, Groendahl (2019)], the further decline of the FPÖ in 2020 relating to its Covid-19 policy and "the fact that the corona virus has exposed the poverty of the FPÖ's program" (Betz 2020), and the diminution of the Italian radical-right Lega party's power following the collapse of its coalition government with the 5 Star MSP populist party (*BBC* 2020a; Tondo 2019).

For other radical-right rulers or their parties, it is too early to predict how they will fare in the short-term. For example: Will Trump continue to be a 'wunderkind' figurehead for the Republican Party? Will Boris Johnson's radical-right Conservative government in the UK survive the economic consequences of the 'double whammy' of the Covid-19 recession and the consequences of Brexit? Will Bolsonaro's radical-right government in Brazil remain popular following the uncontrolled Covid-19 impact on public health and the economy, made worse by his sustained cavalier dismissal of the virus as a serious health threat?

However, substantive and perseverant electoral setbacks for the radical right do not necessarily mean that their political parties or entities will disappear. Hard core members and supporters are likely to remain intact, waiting for new opportunities to gain political traction and power. See, for example, the observations of Mammone (2019) on Salvini's likely fight back following the setbacks of Italy's radical-right Lega party in 2019. Nevertheless, if a marked decline in popular support for radical-right political parties does occur, it is likely to reduce their potential attraction to corporate or foundation donors.

Moreover, high integrity ethical corporations are likely to be even more resistant to corrupt influence by radical-right political interests (or indeed any extreme political interests). In addition, these organisations may increasingly seek to marginalise radical-right influences on them, even to the extent of quarantining and boycotting suspect corporations and their leaders with whom they may have a trading relationship.

Conclusion

The various categories of authoritarian corporate leader identified will continue to exist, as will the potential harm that they may cause. Substantial corporate and intermediary funding of radical-right political interests, organisations, and activities, and radical-right political support for like-minded corporate leaders, is unlikely to diminish. Any prognosis for how the current corporate/radical-right symbiosis will proceed needs to consider both relevant historical contexts and new contexts and factors that will continue to influence the phenomenon (for example, Covid-19; dissemination via uncontrolled Internet and social media platforms of radical-right hate material, fake news, fake facts and fake conspiracy theories; threats to US exceptionalism sparking radical-right reaction).

Reflecting on the four posited scenarios, the author concludes that, in the present and short-term context of multiple crises, the most likely development overall is not clear-cut but one of Scenario 2 (Gradual Incrementalism in Authoritarian Control) progressing to Scenario 3 (Crisis-Driven Rapid Harshening of Authoritarian Climate). A lot will depend on which country is being considered and whether both current and unknown future crises are effectively dealt with by mainstream governments (thereby denying the radical-right opportunities for offering salvation and threatening disruption, if not violence or even insurrection). In particular, in the US President Biden will try to follow Scenario 1 and roll back, if possible, the authoritarian excesses of the Trump administration, but if he fails to obliterate the Covid-19 crisis inherited from Trump, rejuvenate the economy, and enact a Democrat agenda, then Trump or a similar radical-right Republican could well regain the Presidency in 2024 and possibly 2028. In such a development, Scenario 2 would immediately follow Biden's departure and may accelerate to Scenario 3, depending on any future crises that an authoritarian US administration could exploit. Scenario 4 (Corporate/Radical-Right Axis in Decline) is the least likely. However, such a conclusion is speculative, and new developments may intervene that may significantly alter this conclusion.

References

Ansari, A.M. 2006. *Confronting Iran: The Failure of American Foreign Policy and the Next Great Conflict in the Middle East.* New York: Basic Books/Perseus Books Group.

Ansari, A.M. 2019. *Iran, Islam and Democracy: The Politics of Managing Change.* 3rd revised edition. London: Ginko Library and RIIA Chatham House.

Balcer, A. 2019. 'Islamophobia Without Muslims as a Social and Political Phenomenon: the Case of Poland'. In *Europe at the Crossroads: Confronting Populist, Nationalist and Global Challenges*, edited by P. Bevelander and R. Wodak, 207-228. Lund, Sweden: Nordic Academic Press.

Ball, T. 2020. "Free Speech Website Criticised as Recruiting Ground for neo-Nazis". *The Times.* July 27, 2020. Page 17.

BBC. 2020a. "Italy's Far-right Salvini Fails to Gain Foothold in Key Regional Election". *BBC News.* January 27, 2020. https://www.bbc.co.uk/news/world-europe-51259290. [accessed July 12, 2020].

BBC. 2020b. "Slack Makes EU Antitrust Claim Against Microsoft over Teams". *BBC News.* July 22, 2020. https://www.bbc.co.uk/news/technology-53503710. [accessed July 28, 2020].

BBC. 2020c. "Tech Giants Facebook, Google, Apple and Amazon to Face Congress". *BBC News.* July 29, 2020. https://www.bbc.co.uk/news/technology-53571562. [accessed July 29, 2020].

Betz, H-G. 2020."How Covid-19 Deflated the Austrian Populist Radical Right". *CARR Insight Blog.* June 29, 2020. https://www.radicalrightanalysis.com/2020/06/29/how-covid-19-deflated-the-austrian-populist-radical-right/. [accessed July 12, 2020].

Bevelander, P. and Wodak, R. (eds). 2019. *Europe at the Crossroads: Confronting Populist, Nationalist and Global Challenges.* Lund, Sweden: Nordic Academic Press.

Blest, P. 2017. "Blue-state Secession is Dumb and Cruel: All States Matter". *The Nation.* March 13, 207.

Boyes, R. 2020. "Europe's Last Tyrant is Fighting for Survival". Comment. *The Times.* July 29, 2020. Page 26.

BRT. 2019. 'Business Roundtable Redefines the Purpose of a Corporation to Promote "an Economy that Serves All Americans"'. *Business Roundtable.* August 19, 2019. Washington DC: Business Roundtable. https://www.businessroundtable.org/business-ro undtable-redefines-the-purpose-of-a-corporation-to-promote-an-economy-that-serves-all-americans.[accessed September 6, 2020].

British Academy. 2018. *Reforming Business for the 21st Century—A Framework for the Future of the Corporation.* November 2018. London: The British Academy.

Brooks, N., Fritzon, K. and Croom, S. 2020. "Corporate Psychopathy: Entering the Paradox and Emerging Unscathed". In *Corporate Psychopathy: Investigating Destructive Personalities in the Workplace*, edited by K. Fritson, N. Brooks, and S. Croom. 327-365. Cham, Switzerland: Palgrave Macmillan.

Buchan, L. 2018. "UK Parliament Summons Facebook's Mark Zuckerberg to be Questioned Over Cambridge Analytica Scandal". *The Independent.* March 20, 2018. https://www.independent.co.uk/ news/uk/politics/mark-zuckerberg-facebook-mps-evidence-ca mbridge-analytica-data-breach-latest-updates-a8264906.html. [accessed July 29, 2020].

Burgess, K. 2020. "Rapper is Banned from Facebook after Defending Antisemitic Rant". *The Times.* July 29, 2020. Page 25.

Burić, P. 2020. "Secretary General Writes to Viktor Orbán Regarding COVID-19 State of Emergency in Hungary". Council of Europe Newsroom. March 24, 2020. Strasbourg: Council of Europe. https://www.coe.int/en/web/portal/-/secretary-general-writ es-to-victor-orban-regarding-covid-19-state-of-emergency-in-hungary. [accessed July 24, 2020].

CDC. 2020a. Covid-19 Infections and Deaths in the US as at July 26, 2020. US Centers for Disease Control. https://www.cdc.gov/covi d-data-tracker/index.html#cases. [accessed July 26, 2020].

CDC. 2020b. Covid-19 Infections and Deaths in the US as at September 1, 2020. US Centers for Disease Control. https://www.cdc.gov/ covid-data-tracker/index.html#cases. [accessed September 2, 2020].

CDC. 2021. Covid-19 Infections and Deaths in the US as at February 12, 2021. US Centers for Disease Control. https://www.cdc.gov/covid-data-tracker/index.html#cases. [accessed February 13, 2021].

Charter, D. 2021a. "US Capitol Under Siege". *The Times*. January 7, 2021. Page 1.

Charter, D. 2021b. "Pro-Trump Social Network Banned". *The Times*. January 11, 2021. Page 33.

Chee, F.Y. 2013. "EU Fines Microsoft $731m for Broken Promise, Warns Others". https://www.reuters.com/article/us-eu-microsoft-idUSBRE92500520130307. [accessed July 28, 2020].

Christou, M. 2020a. "Is the Radical Right Spreading the Coronavirus?" *CARR Insight Blog*, July 2, 2020. https://www.radicalrightanalysis.com/2020/06/02/is-the-radical-right-spreading-the-coronavirus/. [accessed July 11, 2020].

Christou, M. 2020b. "Nihilism and Hypocrisy is the GOP's Covid-19 Response". *CARR Insight Blog*, June 15, 2020. https://www.radicalrightanalysis.com/2020/06/15/nihilism-and-hypocrisy-is-the-gops-covid-19-response/. [accessed July 11, 2020].

Cillizza, C. 2020. "The 32 Most Bizarre Lines from Donald Trump's Latest Interview with Sean Hannity". *CNN Politics*. July 24, 2020. https://edition.cnn.com/2020/07/24/politics/sean-hannity-donald-trump/index.html. [accessed July 24, 2020].

CISA. 2020. "Joint Statement from the Election Infrastructure Government Coordinating Council & the Election Infrastructure Sector Coordinating Executive Committee". Cybersecurity & Infrastructure Security Agency. November 12, 2020. Washington DC: CISA. https://www.cisa.gov/news/2020/11/12/joint-statement-elections-infrastructure-government-coordinating-council-election. [accessed November 13, 2020].

CMA. 2020. *Online Platforms and Digital Advertising. Final Report*. July 1, 2020. Competition and Markets Authority. London: CMA. https://assets.publishing.service.gov.uk/media/5efc57ed3a6f4023d242ed56/Final_report_1_July_2020.pdf. [accessed July 28, 2020].

Cohen, M. 2021. "Questions Swirl Around Possible 'Insider' Help for Capitol Attack". *CNN Politics*. January 14, 2021. https://edition.

cnn.com/2021/01/13/politics/capitol-insurrection-insider-hel
p/index.html.

Cohen, Z. and Wild, W. 2021. "FBI Warns 'Armed Protests' Being
Planned at All 50 State Capitols and in Washington DC". *CNN Politics.* January 11, 2021. https://edition.cnn.com/2021/01/11/pol
itics/fbi-bulletin-armed-protests-state-us-capitol/index.html.

Collinson, S. 2021. "In the Republican Party, the Post-Trump Era
Lasted a Week". *CNN Politics.* January 28, 2021. https://edition.
cnn.com/2021/01/28/politics/donald-trump-republican-party
/index.html. [accessed January 28, 2021].

Crouch, C. 2014. "Dealing with Corporate Political Power". *Open Democracy.* February 3, 2014. https://www.opendemocracy.net/en/
opendemocracyuk/dealing-with-corporate-political-power/. [accessed April 4, 2020].

Cullis, T. and Parsi, T. 2020. "In Tortured Logic, Trump Begs for a Do-over on the Iran Nuclear Deal". US Foreign Policy. *Responsible
Statecraft.* May 1, 2020. Washington DC: Quincy Institute for Responsible Statecraft. https://responsiblestatecraft.org/2020/05
/01/in-tortured-logic-trump-do-over-iran-nuclear-deal/.   [accessed May 2, 2020].

C4News. 2020a. "Revealed: Trump Campaign Strategy to Deter Millions of Black Americans from Voting in 2020". *Channel 4 News
Investigation.* September 28, 2020. https://www.channel4.com
/news/revealed-trump-campaign-strategy-to-deter-millions-of
-black-americans-from-voting-in-2016. [accessed September
29, 2020].

C4News. 2020b. "How Trump Campaign Targets Millions of White Voters—and Activates Fears over Rioting". *Channel 4 News Investigation.* September 29, 2020. https://www.channel4.com/news
/how-trump-campaign-targets-millions-of-white-voters-and-ac
tivates-fears-over-rioting. [accessed September 29, 2020].

DCMS. 2018. "Mark Zuckerberg "Not Able" to Attend Unprecedented
International Joint Hearing in London". News article. November
14, 2018. https://committees.parliament.uk/committee/378/
digital-culture-media-and-sport-committee/news/135932/ma
rk-zuckerberg-not-able-to-attend-unprecedented-international
-joint-hearing-in-london/. [accessed July 29, 2020].

DCMS. 2019. *The Online Harms White Paper: Government Response to the Committee's Twelfth Report.* Received July 23, 2019. Published September 9, 2019. Commons Select Committee. London: UK Parliament. https://www.gov.uk/government/organisations/department-for-digital-culture-media-sport.

DCMS. 2020. "Government Minded to Appoint Ofcom as Online Harms Regulator". Department for Digital, Culture, Media and Sport. February 12, 2020. London: DCMS. https://www.gov.uk/government/organisations/department-for-digital-culture-media-sport.

Dearden, L. 2020. "Inside the UK-based Site that has Become the Far-right's YouTube". *The Independent.* July 22, 2020. https://www.independent.co.uk/news/uk/home-news/bitchute-far-right-youtube-neo-nazi-terrorism-videos-a9632981.html. [accessed August 8, 2020].

FB. 2020. "Removing Holocaust Denial Content". News release. Monica Bikert, VP of Content Policy. *Facebook.* October 12, 2020. https://about.fb.com/news/2020/10/removing-holocaust-denial-content/. [accessed October 12, 2020].

Fox, M. 2020. "The Trump Appointee Biden Needs to Get Rid Of on Day One". *CNN Opinion.* December 23, 2020. https://www.edition.cnn.com/2020/12/23/opinions/beattie-trump-appointee-biden-should-fire-fox/index.html. [accessed December 27, 2020].

France24. 2020. "Trump Concedes US Covid-19 Crisis to Get Worse Before it Gets Better". *France 24.* July 22, 2020. https://www.france24.com/en/20200722-trump-concedes-us-covid-19-crisis-to-get-worse-before-it-gets-better. [accessed July 23, 2020].

Fritzon, K., Bailey, C., Croom, S. and Brooks, N. 2016. "Problem Personalities in the Workplace: Development of the Corporate Personality Inventory". In *Psychology and Law in Europe: When West Meets East.* Edited by P.A. Granhag, R. Bull, A. Shaboltas, and E. Dozortseva, 139-166. Boca Raton, Fl: Taylor & Francis.

Gibbons, K. 2018. "Drain the Swamp or Lose Advertising, Tech Giants Warned". *The Times.* February 13, 2018. Page 10.

Goddard, J. 2021. "Police Under Investigation for Their Part in Riot". *The Times.* January 15, 2021. Page 31.

Groendahl, B. 2019. "Austria's Nationalist Vice Chancellor Quits Over Video Scandal". *Bloomberg.* May 18, 2019. https://www.bloomberg.com/news/articles/2019-05-18/austria-s-fpoe-offers-to-replace-strache-with-hofer-apa-reports. [accessed July 12, 2020].

Hamilton, F. 2021. "'Hateful' Video Site is First Test for Ofcom". *The Times.* January 28, 2021. Page 15.

Hern, A. 2020a. "Third of Advertisers May Boycott Facebook in Hate Speech Revolt". *The Guardian.* June 30, 2020. https://www.the guardian.com/technology/2020/jun/30/third-of-advertisers-may-boycott-facebook-in-hate-speech-revolt. [accessed July 29, 2020].

Hern, A. 2020b. "Facebook Boycott Grows as US Activists Urge European Firms to Act". *The Guardian.* July 28, 2020. https://www. theguardian.com/technology/2020/jul/28/facebook-boycott-g rows-as-us-campaigners-urge-european-firms-to-act. [accessed July 29, 2020].

HoC. 2018. *Disinformation and 'Fake News': Interim Report.* Digital, Culture, Media and Sports Committee. Report HC 363. July 29, 2018. London: House of Commons.

Hoyle, B. 2020a. "Tech Titans 'Have Too Much Power'". *The Times.* July 30, 2020. Pages 37, 40.

Hoyle, B. 2020b. "Tech Giants Spend Billions to Block Poll Interference". *The Times.* March 31, 2020. Page 30.

Levitz, E. 2020. "Trump's COVID-19 Policy: I, Alone, Can Ignore It". *New York Magazine.* July 16, 2020. https://nymag.com/intellig encer/2020/07/trump-coronavirus-boaters-larry-hogan.html. [accessed July 24, 2020].

Lowery, D. and Gray, V. 2015. "An Introduction to the Population Ecology Approach". In *The Organizational Ecology of Interest Communities,* edited by D. Halpin, D. Lowery, and V. Gray, 1-15. Basingstoke UK: Palgrave Macmillan.

Mammone, A. 2019. "Italy is Braced for a Fascist-style Fightback from a Humiliated Salvini". *The Independent.* September 17, 2019. https://www.independent.co.uk/voices/italy-salvini-coalition-5-star-fascist-far-right-immigration-a9109056.html. [accessed July 12, 2020].

Mayer, J. 2016. *Dark Money: The Hidden History of the Billionaires Behind the Rise of the Radical Right.* New York: Penguin Books.

Mead, W.R. 2017. "The Jacksonian Revolt". *Foreign Affairs.* January 20,2017.

Michaels, D. 2020. *The Triumph of Doubt—Dark Money and the Science of Deception.* Oxford UK: Oxford University Press.

Mirvis, E. 2020. Letters from the Chief Rabbi of Britain, Ephraim Mirvis, to Jack Dorsey of *Twitter* and Mark Zuckerberg of *Facebook.* July 26, 2020. https://www.facebook.com/ChiefRabbiMirvis/. [accessed July 28, 2020].

Moore, M. 2020. "Minister Fears for Democracy as Tech Giants Take Ad Money". *The Times.* July 15, 2020. Page 9.

NIC. 2017. *Background to "Assessing Russian Activities and Intentions in Recent US Elections": The Analytic Process and Cyber Incident Attribution.* Intelligence Community Assessment Report ICA 2017-01D. January 6, 2017. Office of the Director of National Intelligence. National Intelligence Council. Washington DC.

Oklobdzija, S. 2019. "Public Positions, Private Giving: Dark Money and Political Donors in the Digital Age". *Research & Politics.* February 25, 2019. https://doi.org/10.11777/2053168019832475. [accessed May 21, 2020].

Parsi, T. 2018. "Why Trump's Strategy for Iran is Likely to Lead to War". *The Nation.* May 23, 2018. https://www.thenation.com/artyicle/why-abandoning-the-iran-nuke-deal-is-likely-to-lead-to-war/.

Parsi, T. 2020a. "Trump Can Either Leave the Middle East or Have War with Iran. He Can't Have Both". *Real Clear Defense.* April 30, 2020. https://www.realcleardefense.com/articles/2020/04/30/trump_can_either_leave_the_middle_east_or_have_war_with_iran_115236.html?mc_cid=b9313901bb&mc_eid=39438fbd6f. [accessed May 1, 2020].

Parsi, T. 2020b. "Trump Thinks Iran is On Its Knees. But Covid-19 May Have Given It an Unprecedented Path to the Bomb". *Responsible Statecraft.* March 22, 2020. https://responsiblestatecraft.org/2020/03/22/trump-thinks-iran-is-on-its-knees-but-covid-19-may-have-given-it-an-unprecedented-path-to-the-bomb/. [accessed August 9, 2020].

Parsi, T. 2020c. "The Israel-U.A.E. Deal Puts the 'Forever' into Forever War". *New Republic.* August 20, 2020. https://newrepublic.com/article/159010/trump-israel-iran-mideast-forever-war?mc_cid=6b46a5b180&mc_eid=39438fbd6f. [accessed August 21, 2020].

Parsi, T. 2020d. "Trump is No Aberration, Assume it At Your Peril". *Middle East Eye.* November 9, 2020. https://www.middleeast-eye.net/users/trita-parsi?mc_cid=9a34c7ffe9&mc_eid=39438 fbd6f. [accessed November 10, 2020].

Parsi, T. and Costello, R. 2018. "Trump Vindicates Iranian Hardliners and Victimizes Ordinary Citizens". *Huffington Post.* May 9, 2018. https://www.huffingtonpost.com/.

Payne, R.A. 2017. Trump and American Foreign Policy: a Threat to Peace and Prosperity? International Studies Association Annual Meeting, February 22-25, 2017. Baltimore, MD: ISSA.

Paxton, R. 2018. "The Alt-Right, Post-truth, Fake News and the Media". In *The New Authoritarianism Vol 1: A Risk Analysis of the US Alt-Right Phenomenon,* edited by A. Waring, 337-361. Stuttgart: Ibidem Verlag.

Pillar, P.R., Bacevich, A., Sheline, A. and Parsi, T. 2020. *A New U.S. Paradigm for the Middle East: Ending America's Misguided Policy of Domination.* July 17, 2020. The Quincy Institute for Responsible Statecraft. Washington DC: QIRS.

Polantz, K. 2021. "US Says Capitol Rioters Intended to 'Capture and Assassinate' Elected Officials". *CNN Politics.* January 15, 2012. https://edition.cnn.com/2021/01/15/politics/capitol-capture-assassinate-elected-officials/index.html.

Post, J.M. 2015. *Narcissism and Politics: Dreams of Glory.* Cambridge: Cambridge University Press.

Restad, H.E. 2014. *American Exceptionalism: An Idea that Made a Nation and Remade the World.* Abingdon, Oxon UK: Routledge.

Restad, H.E. 2016. "Donald Trump's Calls to "Make America Great Again" Show that American Exceptionalism is Still a Powerful Idea". *LSE Blogs.* London School of Economics. http://blogs.lse.ac.uk/usappblog/2016/03/04.

Reyner, S. 2020. "Michael Flynn to Newsmax TV: Trump Has Options to Secure Integrity of 2020 Election". *Newsmax TV.* December 17, 2020. https://www.newsmax.com/t/newsmax/article/10021 39/1.

Satariano, A. and Nicas, J. 2018. "E.U. Fines Google $5.1bn in Android Anti-trust Case". *New York Times.* July 18, 2018. https://www.nytimes.com/2018/07/18/technology/google-eu-android-fine.html. [accessed July 28, 2020].

Singer, E. 2021. "First GOP Lawmaker Charged for Role in Violent Insurrection at the Capitol". *The American Independent.* January 8, 2021. https://americanindependent.com/derrick-evans-west-virginia-trump-mob-capitol-insurrection-gop-lawmaker-charged/.

Spencer, C. 2020. "I'm an ER Doctor Fighting COVID-19. Trump's Medical Opinion Means Nothing". *Newsweek.* July 16, 2020. https://www.newsweek.com/im-er-doctor-fighting-covid-19-trumps-medical-opinion-means-nothing-opinion-1518156.   [accessed July 24, 2020].

Strauss, W. and Howe. N. 1997. *The Fourth Turning: an American Prophecy.* New York: Broadway Books.

Szijarto, I. 2020. "The Decline of Democracy in Hungary is a Troubling Vision of the Future". *Jacobin Magazine.* June 14, 2020. https://www.jacobinmag.com/2020/06/viktor-orban-hungary-democracy-covid-19. [accessed July 24, 2020].

The Week. 2018. "Cambridge Analytica Scandal: Mark Zuckerberg Refuses to Appear Before MPs". *The Week.* March 27. 2018. https://www.theweek.co.uk/92413/cambridge-analytica-facebook-zuckerberg. [accessed July 29, 2020].

The Times. 2020. "Publish and be Damned. Social Media Firms Should Act to Eliminate Hate Speech Before they are Compelled To". Editorial leader. *The Times.* July 28, 2020. Page 27.

Tondo, L. 2019. "Italy's New Coalition Sworn in as Doubts Cast Over Longevity". *The Guardian.* September 5, 2019. https://www.theguardian.com/world/2019/sep/05/italys-coalition-enemies-open-way-matteo-salvini-return. [accessed July 12, 2020].

Turner-Graham, E. 2019. "The Politics of Cultural Despair: Britain's Extreme-right". In *The New Authoritarianism Vol 2: A Risk Analysis of the European Alt-Right Phenomenon*, edited by A. Waring, 121-147. Stuttgart: Ibidem Verlag.

USDoJ. 2018a. *Indictment: US v. Internet Research Agency LLC et al.* Case 1:18-cr-00032-DLF. 16 February 2018. US Department of Justice. District of Columbia. Washington DC: USDoJ.

USDoJ. 2018b. "Grand Jury Indicts 12 Russian Intelligence Officers for Hacking Offenses Related to the 2016 Election". *Justice News.* July 13, 2018. Office of Public Affairs, US Department of Justice. District of Columbia. Washington DC: USDoJ.

Verney, K. 2018. "The Alt-Right, Immigration, Mass Migration, and Refugees". In *The New Authoritarianism Vol 1: A Risk Analysis of the US Alt-Right Phenomenon,* edited by A. Waring, 247-271. Stuttgart: Ibidem Verlag.

Volk, S. 2020. "Under Lockdown, Germany's PEGIDA Goes to Youtube". *CARR Insight Blog*, June 7, 2020. https://www.radicalrightanaly sis.com/2020/06/07/under-lockdown-germanys-pegida-goes-to-youtube/. [accessed July 7, 2020].

Waring, A. (ed). 2018. *The New Authoritarianism Vol 1: A Risk Analysis of the US Alt-Right Phenomenon,* edited by A. Waring. Stuttgart: Ibidem Verlag.

Waring, A. 2018a. "The Alt-Right, Environmental Issues and Global Warming". In *The New Authoritarianism Vol 1: A Risk Analysis of the US Alt-Right Phenomenon,* edited by A. Waring, 273-301. Stuttgart: Ibidem Verlag.

Waring, A. 2018b. "The Alt-Right and US Foreign Policy". In *The New Authoritarianism Vol 1: A Risk Analysis of the US Alt-Right Phenomenon,* edited by A. Waring, 169-205. Stuttgart: Ibidem Verlag.

Waring, A. 2018c. "The Alt-Right Anti-Iran Project". In *The New Authoritarianism Vol 1: A Risk Analysis of the US Alt-Right Phenomenon,* edited by A. Waring, 273-301. Stuttgart: Ibidem Verlag.

Waring, A. 2019. "Brexit and the Alt-Right Agenda in the UK". In *The New Authoritarianism Vol 2: A Risk Analysis of the European Alt-Right Phenomenon,* edited by A. Waring, 95-120. Stuttgart: Ibidem Verlag.

Waring, A. 2020. 'Radical-right Demonization of Soleimani and Iran: Islamophobic Weaponry in the Public Sphere". *CARR Insight Blog.* February 11, 2020. https://www.radicalrightanalysis.com /2020/02/11/radical-right-demonization-of-soleimani-and-ira n-islamophobic-weaponry-in-the-public-sphere/. [accessed February 12, 2020].

Weinberg, L. 2020a. "Right Wing Push for Premature Reopenings Will Prolong Pandemic". *CARR Insight Blog,* June 13, 2020. https:// www.radicalrightanalysis.com/2020/06/13/right-wing-push-for-premature-reopenings-will-prolong-pandemic/. [accessed July 11, 2020].

Weinberg, L. 2020b. "Will Covid-19 be Another Pearl Harbor Moment for America?" *CARR Insight Blog,* June 16, 2020. https://www.

radicalrightanalysis.com/2020/06/16/will-covid-19-be-anothe
r-pearl-harbor-moment-for-america/. [accessed July 11, 2020].

WFA. 2020. "Nearly a Third of Advertisers Pull Back or Consider Pulling Back from Platforms". News. July 1, 2020. World Federation
of Advertisers. https://wfanet.org/knowledge/item/2020/07/
01/Nearly-a-third-of-advertisers-pull-back-or-consider-pullin
g-back-from-platforms. [accessed July 29, 2020].

White House. 2017. *National Security Strategy of the United States of
America.* President Donald J. Trump. December 2017. Washington DC: The White House.

White House. 2018. *President Donald J. Trump is Ending United States
Participation in an Unacceptable Iran Deal.* Foreign Policy Fact
Sheet. May 8, 2018. Washington DC: The White House.

Widener, L. 2020. "For the First Time Ever, US Officially Rejects
China's 'Unlawful' South China Sea Claims". *American Military
News.* July 13, 2020. https://americanmilitarynews.com/2020/
/for-first-time-ever-us-officially-rejects-chinas-unlawful-south-
china-sea-claims/.[accessed July 28, 2020].

Wilczek, M. and Moody, O. 2020. "Anti-EU President Holds Slender
Lead in Polish Election". *The Times.* July 13, 2020. Page 28.

Zeffman, H. 2020. "Trump 'Considered Martial Law' to Keep Biden Out
of the White House". *The Times.* December 21, 2020. Page 30.

Zeffman, H. 2021a. "Georgia Senate Win Allows Democrats to Set
Their Own Agenda". *The Times.* January 7, 2021. Page 5.

Zeffman, H. 2021b. "Smashing Glass and Gunfire as Mob Shames US
Democracy". *The Times.* January 7, 2012. Pages 2-3.

Zuboff, S. 2019. *The Age of Surveillance Capitalism: the Fight for the
Future at the New Frontier of Power.* London: Profile Books.

Chapter 12:
Potential Strategies to Limit the Corporate/ Radical-Right Threat

By Alan Waring[1]

Abstract

This final chapter identifies and evaluates five principal categories of potential strategies for combatting the threat from corporate/radical-right authoritarianism and from the fusion of mutual interests and 'dark money': legislative, regulatory and judicial; Internet, social media and related; organisational, professional and peer-group; political and economic; and grassroots action. Education as a strategy is subsumed within the 'organisational, professional and peer-group' and 'grassroots' categories. The five categories are not mutually-exclusive and, applied in combination, offer a more credible response to the overall threat than any one of them in isolation. The protective role of altruism is also discussed. Reference is made to the phenomenon of conspiracy theories, as used by radical-right interests as a weapon and discussed in depth in chapter 9. As with Volumes 1 and 2, this final chapter concludes that the essence of the overall approach recommended to combat authoritarianism is one of 'muscular moderation', so as to supplement the quiet laissez-faire tolerance of the moderate majority.

Key words: authoritarianism, radical-right, corporate, threats, strategies, muscular moderation

Combatting Corporate/Radical-Right Authoritarianism

As remarked in chapter 5, while not suggesting that all examples of bad corporate attitudes and conduct reflect conscious and wilful political support for radical-right ideology per se, this volume does observe, with copious evidence, that their general authoritarian tone and character are remarkably similar. Further, this volume argues that radical-right authoritarianism and corporate authoritarianism

---

[1]   See contributor affiliations and biography, page 525.

are essentially the same commensal phenomenon that relies on cooperation for perceived shared interests, albeit that not all corporate authoritarians are necessarily radical-right ideologues. Those corporate
leaders and executives who do consciously support radical-right ideology and objectives may even delight in their notoriety. However,
those corporate authoritarians who do not consciously espouse radical-right ideology may, nonetheless, be condemned as fellow travellers of the radical right by virtue of exhibiting similar rhetoric, ideas
and conduct.

For combatting the radical right per se, appropriate strategies
are those proposed in the final chapters of Vol 1 (pages 425-459) and
Vol 2 (pages 375-411), and are not repeated here. However, for combatting *corporate* authoritarianism and its radical-right entangle-
ments, similar strategic categories may be put forward:

- Legislative, regulatory and judicial
- Internet, social media and related
- Organisational, professional and peer-group
- Political and economic
- Grassroots action

The following sections address each of these categories in turn.

Legislative, Regulatory and Judicial Strategies

Is it possible in a democratic society to legislate against beliefs, ideologies, policies, and practices that are either inherently, or likely to be,
dangerous to the safety, well-being, freedoms, and other human rights
of the population and to democratic institutions and processes? It is
not only possible but arguably essential. However, since democracy
requires inclusion of different views and opinions (even selfish and
illiberal ones), and freedom of speech, there is an inherent tension between democratic principles and an obligation to prevent harm by illiberal vested interests [in this instance, the radical right and corporate authoritarians who support or mimic them]. Nevertheless, as
Waring and Paxton (2019, 405) noted, exercise of such an obligation
in a liberal democracy "must not be allowed to descend into a blanket
oppressive or repressive intolerance no better than that of the Alt-
Right". As has been clearly shown over recent years, the radical right

and their supporters are adept at portraying themselves as victims of allegedly corrupt mainstream governments and a liberal Establishment (e.g. Neiwert 2017, 364, echoing Paxton 2005). They claim an entitlement to express their assertions and opinions and to impose extremist hate-filled judgements and solutions to remove alleged ethno-religious threats to white Christian supremacy and perceived threats to themselves and their interests. Despite the fact that, for at least 70 years, it has been held in democracies that there are specific instances where an absolute freedom of speech is not upheld in law e.g. threats involving harassment, or incitement to crime, or libel and slander; prevention of disorder or crime; public safety; reputation or rights of others; hate crimes (e.g. ECHR 1953; UK Human Rights Act 1998; UK Malicious Communications Act 1988; UK Communications Act 2003; US Hate Crimes Prevention Act 2009), the radical-right typically do not accept such restrictions for themselves.

Given such tensions, and the over-arching need to protect society overall, and especially vulnerable sections of it, what reasonably practical course can be set to neutralize radical-right threats? Ultimately, all strategies for combatting radical-right threats are based on varying degrees of persuasion—to persuade potential or actual wrongdoers to do certain things or not do others. Systems and methods need to be appropriate to the particular persuasion task. These may range from the softer 'contain, absorb, modify, attenuate, convert as far as possible' approaches for lesser offenders, to the tougher 'deter, disrupt, dismantle, isolate, contain, proscribe and punish' approaches applicable to more hard-core offenders. Strategies of persuasion that fall into the legislative, regulatory and judicial area rely to a great extent on a mixture of deterrence, containment, proscription, and punishment. For the dimension of corporate supporters and the spectrum of agencies, enablers and facilitators, a number of operational strands are potentially available in the legislative, regulatory and judicial area, as exemplified in the following sub-sections:

Statutory Legislation

A number of relevant laws to combat extremism (whether right-wing or left-wing, or any other form), and protect national security and human rights, exists in most democracies. There are at least nineteen enabling Acts in the UK alone, which to varying degrees address corporate and individual duties of care relating to harmful conduct and which could be relevant to a corporate/radical-right symbiosis. In addition, there is legislation specifically addressing misuse of public funds or expenses by politicians or their officials—for case examples involving the radical-right party UKIP, see Mostrous and Kenber (2014), Rankin (2019), and Stevens (2015) and allegations made by *C4News* (2019) in relation to corporate largesse towards the former UKIP leader and MEP Nigel Farage and potential breaches of EU declaration requirements.

Most jurisdictions have an array of similar legislation. For example, in the US, there is the Federal Hate Crimes Statute 1968, the Patriot Act 2001, and the Hate Crimes Prevention Act 2009 [the so-called Shepard and Byrne Act] (USDoJ 2018). In France, there is the French press freedom law of 1881 (FPL 1881), as updated in 1990, which proscribes incitement to racial discrimination, hatred, or violence on the basis of origin, membership (or non-membership) of an ethnic, national, racial, or religious group. EU member states are subject to common legislation criminalizing hate speech and hate crime motivated by racism and xenophobia (ECHR 1953; EU 2008). The UN International Convention applies generally (UN 1965).

Regulatory Frameworks to Protect Authorities and Infrastructure from Radical Infiltration

State organisations and national infrastructure organisations, such as the police, armed forces, education, public health, energy supply, telecommunications, and nuclear establishments, normally have in place protective systems designed to ensure that extremists, of whatever persuasion, cannot misuse, disrupt or damage the organisation's functions. See e.g. Cabinet Office (2017), CPNI (2017), ENISA (2017).This would include protection not only against overt actions by extremists, such as blockading the organisation's sites, physical attacks against assets or personnel, and remote cyber-attacks [albeit minor compared to state-based cyber-attacks] against data, communications, or technical process control, but also more covert actions, such as infiltration by joining the organisation without divulging their extremist identity or motives. Covert infiltration would enable the perpetrator not only to engage in acts of sabotage and disruption but also to disseminate propaganda and subvert other personnel to the extremist's cause, as in the following examples relating to the radical right.

An essential part of recruitment, selection, internal promotions, and sensitive postings in state and national infrastructure organisations is so-called 'due diligence' vetting (Waring 2013, 88-98). Such vetting is designed to identify evidence in the individual's background of dishonesty, criminal activity, substance abuse, heavy gambling, reckless conduct, mental instability, or support for anti-social or extremist ideologies, any of which is likely to present undue risk for the organisation. While due diligence vetting is necessary and admirable in its intent, history shows that it is not always successful in preventing employment of those with a predisposition to extremist views and actions. Examples in the UK police include an officer arrested and charged as a member of the proscribed far-right terrorist group National Action (Simpson 2020; Wylie 2020) and four other offences including child sex offences. Another police officer was sacked for supporting the far-right Britain First on *Facebook* and expressing racist and homophobic views (Nsubuga 2020). In the US, infiltration of police forces by white supremacists and other far-right groups is reportedly a longstanding problem (e.g. German 2020; Purdue 2020; Speri 2017; 2020), and one thrown into sharp relief in 2020 by the killing of George Floyd and a series of other black people by officers in different police forces across America (see below).

A number of countries have experienced infiltration of their armed forces by far-right individuals (Ariza 2020). For example, in the US a soldier plotted with neo-Nazis to attack his own unit (Pavia, 2020), while in Germany both the army and the police force have been infiltrated (Ariza 2020; Crossland 2020; *DW News* 2017; Hoff 2020; Sahinkaya 2020; Walsh 2017). In the UK, one of the major cases so far against members of the proscribed far-right terrorist group National Action involved several men serving in the British Army. While two soldiers underwent military disciplinary procedures, including one who was dismissed, a third, Corporal Mikko Vehvilainen, was convicted in 2018 and sentenced to 8 years in jail (Home Office 2018).

In the US, the Trump administration included a large number of cabinet members, senior officials and advisers who were either devotees or supporters of radical-right ideology. Even after the departure of such controversial radical-right figures as Steve Bannon, Sebastian

Gorka, Michael Flynn, and John Bolton, other senior exemplars remained e.g. Mike Pompeio, Betsy DeVos, and Steve Mnuchin. During
Trump's term, he also favoured other examples, such as Darren J.
Beattie who eventually (December 3, 2020) was appointed by Trump
to the US Commission for the Preservation of America's Heritage
Abroad. This Commission, among other things, had responsibilities
for maintaining strong links with Nazi Holocaust survivor bodies
abroad. Yet, for several years, Beattie had reportedly openly expounded racist and neo-Nazi views and had not hidden his far-right
connections. This extraordinary 'fox in the henhouse' appointment by
Trump caused much incredulity and anger (Fox 2020).

A number of individuals having controversial radical-right views
were appointed to posts where they formally advised ministers in the
UK Conservative government of Prime Minister Boris Johnson formed
in 2019. Instances arose where some of these advisers expressed their
radical-right opinions and prejudices in a way that challenged public
perceptions of acceptable conduct from unelected public officials in
positions of significant political influence. The most prominent example is Dominic Cummings, the Prime Minister's personal adviser on
strategy (see profile in chapter 1). Others include the Prime Minister's
social media adviser, Chloe Westley, who expressed anti-Muslim prejudices and described as a "hero" Anne Marie Waters, former leader of
far-right activists Pegida UK (Wright 2019). In 2020, Cabinet Office
policy adviser Andrew Sabisky was forced to resign for alleged racist
policy comments arguing [on Dominic Cummings' website] that enforced contraception should be applied to certain classes of women so
as to avoid over-burdening the economy and the state with an underclass of unwanted births, and [on various other website blogs] arguing
that policies based on eugenics were defensible since black Americans
[he asserted] have a lower IQ than whites and blacks have an "intellectual disability" (BBC 2020a; Proctor 2020). In July 2020, Will
O'Shea, a Cabinet Office adviser on digital services, was sacked after it
was revealed that he had posted *Twitter* comments suggesting that
police should use live rounds and that Black Lives Matter activists
should be shot (Grylls 2020). Despite widespread demands, the Prime
Minister declined to issue any comment or apology on any of these
cases, thereby cementing a perception of connivance and that he apparently supported their views i.e. giving rise to the suspicion that,

like those in the Trump administration, these extreme individuals were welcome invitees rather than unwanted covert infiltrators.

However, it is not just state organisations that are vulnerable to infiltration but also corporate organisations engaged in supporting the state e.g. specialist contractors and suppliers, often employing highly qualified individuals in work requiring high-level security clearance. For some radical-right supporters and extremists, covert infiltration into organisations connected with state functions (whether government departments or their contractors) is regarded as an important contribution to their cause.

With vetting procedures under the Official Secrets Act applying to many UK government departments (and their contractors), why have due diligence procedures apparently sometimes failed as in the examples cited above? One possible reason is that there are two classes of vetting—negative and positive. Most individuals subject to security screening are those whose work will not entail access to any security-classified information, activities, personnel, or locations. This group is deemed to present a lesser security risk and therefore to warrant 'negative vetting', that is the screening criteria focus on identification of anything manifestly wrong, for example criminal convictions, falsification of qualifications or work history, records of anti-social conduct, records of racist or extremist public statements in the press, social media or online. Negative vetting will rely heavily on searches of both public and restricted online databases. Such searches are essential but not necessarily sufficient to identify anyone determined to hide evidence that might thwart their security clearance. While such evasion might be expected of spies working for foreign governments, it is also characteristic of fanatics in general whose mission is to impose their ideology on governance and society e.g. Islamic State, anti-abortion extremists, animal rights extremists, white supremacists, radical-left extremists, radical-right extremists. To identify individuals who are really determined to infiltrate state organs and functions unchallenged requires positive vetting, an altogether more rigorous and time-consuming process that examines in depth all aspects of an individual's life history, ancestry, education, qualifications, career, employment record, finances, references, criminal record, civil judgements, activities, travel history, publishing history, lifestyle, social media and online history, personality profile including mental health history, beliefs, attitudes, proclivities, addictions, deviances, friends, associates, and contacts with radical groups or individuals. Positive vetting procedures will include not only online searches but also personal interviews with the individual, and with third parties such as educators, employers, former employers, neighbours, associates, banks, local shopkeepers, local bars and restaurants. Discreet surveillance may also be warranted in some instances.

Of particular importance for individuals applying for positions or promotions within the police, security services, and armed forces, (and, it could be argued, Cabinet Office advisers) is the need for psychological profiling and, as necessary, psychiatric evaluation. This is to ensure that individuals with psychopathic or sociopathic personality traits, or extreme propensity (whether ideological or personal) for violence or harm to others, are prevented from gaining entry or positions of authority within the service. The need for such preventive action is accentuated, for example, by the number of video-recorded homicides and assaults by police officers, especially but not exclusively in the US, against unarmed members of the BAME community (see below).

In the above examples of radical-right infiltration, it would appear that the individuals involved were not subject to positive vetting, otherwise their sympathies and violent tendencies would have been discovered and their initial appointment or continued posting probably stopped. Whether the criteria for deciding when positive vetting is necessary, and how rigorously it is applied, require review and possible revision, is beyond further examination here.

Regulatory Frameworks to Protect Customers, Employees, Contractors and the Public from Corporate Authoritarianism

If due diligence screening is not always effective in state-controlled organisations, in public and private corporations it is much less so, primarily because (in the author's professional experience) such screening is either perfunctory or non-existent. While there is also an obvious need to weed out from corporate ranks, or deny access to, those with pathological disorders and predisposition to extremist views, mechanisms to achieve this are typically woefully inadequate. As case studies on corporate due diligence in Waring (2013, 87-98) laid bare, at best, to date due diligence screening in non-state organisations has been typically a much-diluted version of negative vetting that would be applicable in state-controlled organisations. If crooks, fraudsters, sexual deviants, substance abusers and others with serious character defects or personality disorders can so easily get jobs—and even promotions—at all levels in major corporations with-out being identified, there is little prospect that ideological extremists or their supporters will be caught. See, for example, the study reports on corporate psychopathy by Brooks (2020), Brooks et al (2020), and Fritzon et al (2016).

In-company protective systems that ought to be in place are ex-amined below under Organisational, Professional and Peer-Group Strategies. Thus far, regulatory frameworks that could assist corpora-tions in this regard are wide-ranging but discreet and not inte-grated—for example, anti-money laundering legislation and systems; Stock Exchange Listing Rules requiring robust corporate governance and risk management, and statements on these in the corporation's annual report and statement of accounts; occupational health and safety legislation; environmental legislation; employment and human rights legislation.

Enforcement

Despite all the above legislation and regulatory frameworks, enforce-ment may sometimes encounter difficulties in relation to offences by the radical-right spectrum, from the populist to the extremist end. For example, as EHRC (2015) and Walters et al (2017) discussed in detail, the UK faces perennial problems associated with definition of of-fences, policing procedures, obtaining evidence, quality of evidence, witness intimidation, and so on. Victims may also be reluctant to re-port such crimes, fearing retribution.

Police resources may also be inadequate in some jurisdictions, while there are deep concerns that in some countries some local po-lice forces harbour officers who are either ideological supporters of the far right or possess personality or mental disorders that present as extreme authoritarianism predisposing them to assault and even kill unarmed suspects. In the first decade of the 21st century, studies showed that black people and other ethnic minorities had a far higher incidence per head of population than whites of being arrested and of being assaulted or killed by police e.g. Brunson and Miller (2006) and

Sharp and Atherton (2007). A decade later, the situation had deterio-rated, with a large number of high-profile police-related deaths of black people reported in the US (*CBC News* 2017). In the US, over the period 2015 to August 2020, Statista (2020) reported that blacks were nearly 2.5 times more likely than whites to be fatally shot by po-lice. Purdue (2020) affirmed that longstanding far-right infiltration of police forces in the US remained a contemporary threat, exacerbated by non-existent or weak 'due diligence' screening of job applicants, as FBI reports laid bare (Speri 2017; 2020).

In 2017, a former police officer in South Carolina, Michael Slager, was sentenced to 20 years in prison for the unlawful shooting and kill-ing of an unarmed black motorist, Walter Scott, in 2015 (*CBC News* 2017). Scott was shot five times in the back by Officer Slager, all of which was captured on video by a bystander's mobile phone. The Scott killing is credited with accelerating the Black Lives Matter (BLM) movement. By 2020, BLM had developed both a national and interna-tional momentum, fuelled by a seemingly endless succession of other killings of black people by police officers, many of which were cap-tured on mobile videos thereby making it much harder for the police to plead innocence.

In May 2020, an unarmed black motorist George Floyd was killed by a police officer in Minneapolis, USA, during an arrest, all of which was captured on police bodycams and mobile phone videos of onlook-ers (*Guardian* 2020; Hill et al 2020). The video evidence showed Of-ficer Derek Chauvin pinning Mr Floyd to the ground and restraining him by pressing his knee on his neck for more than eight minutes, dur-ing which time Mr Floyd can be clearly heard gasping for breath and exclaiming several times "I can't breathe". After Mr Floyd lost con-sciousness, Officer Chauvin maintained his knee on his neck for over a minute after paramedics had arrived on the scene.

Initially, Chauvin and three other officers at the scene were sus-pended and then dismissed from the force. Eventually, Chauvin was charged with 2nd and 3rd degree murder and three other former offic-ers were charged with aiding and abetting 2nd degree murder. Mass public protests, some violent, against the Floyd killing raged for months, not only in Minneapolis but also in urban centres across the US and abroad, with "I can't breathe" becoming a symbolic BLM chant for freedom from perceived police oppression. In general, the protestors were pan-ethnic, multi-class, and all ages, an indication that increasingly the American population was prepared to disavow such police conduct as being un-American and not in their name.

On August 23, 2020, in Kenosha, Wisconsin, another black man, Jacob Blake, was shot in the back seven times by a police officer, while attempting to get into his car containing his young children (*BBC* 2020b). Once again, the incident was video-recorded on the mobile phones of bystanders. Miraculously, he survived and, at the time of writing, was still in hospital and expected to be permanently crippled. The officer identified as carrying out the shooting, Rusten Sheskey, was put on administrative leave but at the time of writing he had not been charged. Civic and political leaders across the US called for formal charges against the officer, but these are likely to be deferred until the formal FBI investigation is concluded. The attack on Blake added to the sustained BLM mass protests across America.

Cohen (2020) summarised the on-going scandal of alleged police brutality against blacks in the US, naming over 160 reported killings by US police in 2020 up to September. One of these, Breonna Taylor a respected medical technician aged 26, was shot eight times in her own home in Louisville, Kentucky, during a bungled police raid where apparently officers seeking a drugs suspect entered the wrong address without warning and opened fire when the occupants resisted what to them looked like a violent home invasion by criminals. A civil action by the deceased's family against the city authorities for wrongful killing, battery, excessive force, and gross negligence was settled in September 2020 for US$12 million (*BBC* 2020c). Only one of the officers (not the one who fired the fatal shots) was eventually arrested in September 2020 and charged with a firearms offence, which enraged many people and sparked off further public protests across the US. The complex and so far inconclusively answered question as to why such an exceptionally high number of black people are killed by US police is addressed in the Findings and Conclusion section of chapter 10.

The gulf of mistrust in the police by the BAME community became widened by a strong suspicion that some police forces had become corrupted by far-right sympathizers and institutionalized racism. President Trump went out of his way to vocally support authoritarian police actions and armed far-right white vigilante counter-demonstrations against BLM protesters in such places as Minneapolis, Kenosha and Portland, Oregon, while accusing such protesters of being anarchists and criminals supported by liberals and Democrats. The radical-right mob attack on the Capitol on January 6, 2021, fomented and apparently encouraged openly by Trump, saw an uncharacteristically weak response by police to contain and repel it [they were overwhelmed, despite weeks of prior alert by Trump to a planned angry march], in stark contrast to their draconian clampdown on peaceful BLM protests in Washington in 2020 (Charter 2021a; Zeffman 2021). Moreover, it emerged that at least a dozen police officers were under investigation on suspicion of aiding and abetting the Capitol mob (Cohen 2021; Goddard 2021; Johnson 2021).

A similar accusation about far-right sympathizers infiltrating police forces has been made in other countries e.g. in the UK over the nearly 30 years since the random murder by stabbing of black teenager Stephen Lawrence by a racist gang in London in April 1993. The casual and incompetent way police handled the investigation in the early years led to compromised evidence, collapsed trials, and the five prime suspects evading justice for nearly 20 years. Under public and media pressure, in 1997 the government established an independent inquiry under Sir William MacPherson, whose damning 350-page report (Home Office 1999) found that police conduct had been "marred by a combination of professional incompetence, institutional racism and a failure of leadership" (para 46.1, page 365). The MacPherson report and recommendations led to wide-ranging changes in official police practice and also to law, most notably the removal of the 'double jeopardy' defence in 2005 whereby previously a defendant could not be tried twice on the same murder charge. In 2011, new forensic evidence led to a new trial of two prime suspects (Gary Dobson and David Norris), who were found guilty in 2012 of Lawrence's murder and sentenced to life imprisonment.

Shaw (2019) commented on how far UK policing had been changed by the Lawrence case and the MacPherson report. The general consensus was that there had been wide-ranging and far-reaching changes in *official* policing procedures and protocols relating to eliminating racial prejudice from them. While the number of deaths of BAME individuals at the hands of UK police officers is small compared to those at the hands of US police officers, nonetheless there is a similar troubling pattern. Moreover, in 2020 the Metropolitan Police Chief Commissioner Cressida Dick admitted (Dick 2020) that it remained a constant battle to eliminate *unofficial* institutional racism from the force [author's emphasis], whether in its internal operations or in its external public-facing law enforcement activities. In 2020 alone, there were numerous instances of BAME members of the public being stopped while driving in London, searched, and in some cases arrested, on suspicion of drug offences. Officers reportedly sought to justify their actions by reference to vehicle occupants behaving and driving suspiciously and being in possession of expensive high-range vehicles normally associated by police with drug dealers. In one case, officers refused to believe that a black husband and wife, both successful business people with impeccable credentials, could possibly own an expensive home in an affluent suburb and afford to own two expensive cars parked in the drive unless they were obtaining their funds illegally. Envy is recognized as a source of antipathy, hatred and anger in racial and religious prejudice (Duarte 2015; Waring 2020; Wodak 2018) and would appear to operate in this context. So far as is known, all those stopped and detained were released without charge. Unbeknown to the officers involved, a number of BAME citizens subjected to such prejudicial conduct were high-profile persons, such as national sports champions, media celebrities, a Metropolitan Police Inspector (Dodd 2020), and even a Member of Parliament (Walker 2020), and clearly they were in a position to ensure a very robust and public condemnation using media interviews, press statements, social media and political connections. Ordinary BAME citizens subject to such abuse may not have such opportunities. Disciplinary proceedings and investigation by the Independent Office for Police Conduct against the officers involved occurred in some instances (Hamilton 2020) but the outcomes are not yet known.

With such a backdrop to contemporary policing, and exacting evidence criteria applied by nervous public prosecutors, it is unlikely that enforcement of all relevant legislation against some kinds of radical-right crimes will be pursued effectively, efficiently, or at all. Those involving extremism, especially terrorism, violence, and national security, are likely to be the most vigorously pursued owing to prioritisation and resource limitations. However, for the rest, enforcement is likely to be patchy, variable, and possibly unenthusiastic and misdirected. The MacPherson conclusion from 1999 of professional incompetence, institutional racism and a failure of leadership in the Metropolitan Police regrettably remains a curse on policing generally and therefore on effective enforcement of legal protections against radical-right crimes. Unless more rigorous vetting procedures are applied to prevent radical-right sympathizers infiltrating police forces, it is likely that law enforcement in the prevention and prosecution of radical-right crimes will be ineffective.

In addition, much of the relevant legislation is enforced not by the police but by an array of other authorities, some national and some local. For example, in the UK environmental legislation is enforced by local authorities and the Environment Agency, whereas occupational safety & health is enforced by the Health & Safety Executive for industry and local authorities for retail, commercial and office-based activities. Consumer legislation is largely enforced by local authorities, whereas discrimination cases are typically adjudicated by statutory tribunals. The Serious Fraud Office investigates and prosecutes serious corporate fraud, sometimes in conjunction with the Financial Conduct Authority, National Crime Agency and the police. The fragmentary and multi-authority reality of law enforcement militates against a consistent and coherent approach to the array of potential offences by radical-right perpetrators.

Penalties

In principle, both the range and level of penalties available to courts for breaches of relevant legislation seem adequate. Whether in any particular case the penalty applied is appropriate is, of course, subject to opinion. For example, some believe that jail sentences handed down in the UK to convicted National Action members, former members, and other far-right extremists should more reflect the gravity of the murderous crimes they were plotting and advocating rather than the fact that they were thwarted in carrying them out. Jail terms of between typically 5 and 8 years received by such extremists since 2018 e.g. Home Office (2018) seem to many to be disproportionately low when convicted terrorists ordinarily might expect at least double that, or even a whole-life sentence, especially if people were killed and injured. Of those convicted for National Action offences (see Turner-Graham 2019, 136-140), only Jack Renshaw finally received a life sentence in 2018 for preparing acts of terrorism (including a plot to kill an MP) and threatening to kill a police officer who was investigating him. His previous sentences were a 3-year jail term for inciting racial hatred (2016) and a 16-month jail term for child sex offences (2018).

Paradoxically, it is right-wing and radical-right politicians, reflecting a populist clamouring, who are typically at the forefront of demanding tougher sentencing generally. The radical right portray themselves as, and probably sincerely if naively believe themselves to be, arch-defenders of law-and-order. However, their salvationist law-and-order prospectus does not admit of the range of offences that their own ilk may (and do) engage in as a consequence of their radical-right world-view. To the radical right, law-and-order should focus not only on violent crime and terrorism but also on lawful categories which they abhor and consider (ideologically and emotionally) to be 'outlawed', such as Muslims, Jews, BAME citizens, immigrants, welfare claimants, and asylum seekers, as well as employment rights, environmental protection, and climate change protection.

Radical-right governments seeking to project an image of being tough on law-and-order are likely to introduce harsher penalties for convicted offenders, but there is no guarantee that such jail sentences will have any deterrent effect on potential terrorists. There is also uncertainty over whether contain-and-convert strategies, involving attendance at compulsory de-radicalization programmes while in jail, are sufficiently effective (Hall 2021). For example, there have been high-profile instances of supposedly de-radicalized Islamist terrorists re-offending. Following the London Bridge terrorist attack in 2019 by Usman Khan, it was revealed that he had attended a Healthy Identity Intervention Programme and a Desistance and Disengagement Programme, both during and after a previous 8-year jail term for a terrorist attack (*BBC* 2019). There is no reason to suppose that such de-radicalization programmes would be any more effective against fanatical far-right terrorists, such as those currently imprisoned in the UK.

For 'lesser' radical-right offenders, who are the majority, while there is some prospect of educational strategies (e.g. Prevent 2015) working at school and community level, this is likely to be less effective at tertiary level and wider society (see observations by Johnson 2017). Contain-and-convert de-radicalization programmes for the far right, such as Small Steps (https://smallstepsconsultants.com/) and Exit UK (https://exituk.org/), may also be effective but operate on a small scale. As Waring and Paxton (2019, 392) pessimistically noted, "While necessary and to be encouraged, such educational efforts are unlikely to persuade the majority of hard-core far-right activists to recant, de-radicalize, and convert to moderate attitudes and behaviour. For these, perhaps realistically only a combination of containment and punishment is possible." This would also include all those corporate supporters of, and sympathisers for, radical-right causes, as much as committed members of the public across the radical-right spectrum, who break the law in pursuit of their objectives.

Internet, Social Media and Related Strategies

Radical-right groups are very active in using the Internet and social media to air their grievances and disseminate their racist and ethno-religious prejudices and invective in relation to all those they hate (e.g. Knowles et al 2020; Tönberg & Wahlström (2018). Whatever the utility and merits of the Internet and social media (and there are many), the all-pervasive presence of these services and their impact on the lives of citizens, governments, and regulators demand an extremely high degree of honesty, integrity, probity, and social responsibility on the part of services and platform providers. The combination of phenomenal wealth and control of account holders' data and usage places a special responsibility on their corporate leaders and owners. It may be reasonably expected, therefore, that Internet and social media platform providers would recognize, out of enlightened self-interest if nothing else, the commercial imperative for them to be responsible and accountable. Regrettably, thus far the history of such companies shows that they have persistently fallen far short of the standards demanded by governments and regulators, including aspects relevant to radical-right abuses. For example, for years Internet and social media companies have needed to act decisively and urgently to combat apocryphal conspiracy theories and other material fomenting hatred against multiple targets and disseminated by radical-right interests via their platforms. However, thus far, they have made merely superficial gestures to eliminate such toxic material. Whether the belated decision in October 2020 by *Facebook*, to ban all Holocaust denial postings (FB 2020), and the actions by *Amazon, Apple, Facebook,*

Google, Instagram, Twitter and other companies against radical-right abusers of their services (Charter 2021b), following the Trump-orchestrated insurrection in January 2021, heralds a change of attitude in their case remains to be seen. Of course, the so-called 'dark web' currently remains beyond regulatory control and increasingly may become the favoured resort for radical-right networking and dissemination of extreme material.

As analysed in chapter 11, the alleged egregious conduct of platform companies spans six primary categories of abuse: market dominance to stifle competition; abuse of account holders' data for political and/or commercial gain; aiding and abetting extremists, terrorists, sex predators and other criminals; dissemination of fake facts and fake news; disrespect for government and refusing accountability; conducting psychological warfare against users.

As platform owners have reacted defensively to criticism and been largely in denial, showing only a grudging reluctance to self-reform, increasingly governments have been moving towards imposing regulation on them, especially in the areas of abuse itemised above (see e.g. Gibbs 2017; Griffin 2017). A leading example is the UK's forthcoming Online Harms Act 2021 (DCMS 2019; 2020). While many are hopeful that this Act will achieve the desired result in so far as cutting off the oxygen of publicity and promulgation for abusers across the radical-right spectrum are concerned, doubts have been raised about whether enforcement resources will be sufficient and whether penalties against offenders will be tough enough. For example, as Waring and Paxton (2018, 436-437; 2019, 387-388) and Table 11.1 in chapter 11 pointed out, with the gross combined annual revenues of *Google* and *Facebook* alone being in excess of US$200 billion, any financial penalties (whether for corporations or executives) that are less than commensurate with such enormous revenues would be unlikely to either punish or to change the behaviour of such companies. Therefore, the effectiveness of the Online Harms Act may be compromised if corporate fines are less than, say, 10% of annual revenue. Whether penalties will also include jail terms is as yet unclear. However, again, to be effective, jail sentences would have to be commensurate with the harm caused by the offender, and for the most serious offences and for repeat offenders this is likely to warrant many years. Potential penalties might also include interlocutory judgements, compensation orders, 'name and shame' publicity orders, director disqualification orders, and cancellation of professional registration and practice licences.

In addition to legislation, regulation and official penalties, methods to contain and punish offenders in online and social media contexts include commercial boycotts by advertisers. As detailed in chapter 11, there have already been short-term mass boycotts in mid-2020 of *Facebook* and other platforms by advertisers in relation to their failure to control egregious content (WFA 2020a). In response to growing dissatisfaction with online platforms among advertisers, the Global Alliance for Responsible Media (GARM) created by the World Federation of Advertisers announced in September 2020 (WFA 2020b) that an agreement had been reached with *Facebook, YouTube* and *Twitter* for a common set of definitions for hate speech and other harmful content. Key areas of agreement were: (a) adoption of GARM common definitions for harmful content; (b) development of GARM reporting standards on harmful content; (c) commitment to independent oversight on brand safety operations, integrations and reporting, and (d) commitment to develop and deploy tools to better manage advertising adjacency [unsolicited commensal advertising by other parties that appears alongside the primary advertiser]. However, while such streamlining is likely to be helpful, it does not address the fundamental requirement of platform companies to remove egregious content decisively and with utmost speed, and to bar offenders permanently from access to and use of their platforms. Espoused policies and commitments, however high-minded, are not always enacted. Actions speak louder than policies, agreements, commitments, and rhetoric.

Other potential online, digital, and media activities combatting radical-right ideology include the overall CARR (Centre for Analysis of the Radical Right) doctoral and post-doctoral research project (https://www.radicalrightanalysis.com/) and the Center for Countering Digital Hate (https://www.counterhate.co.uk/), a campaigning body established to "disrupt the architecture of online hate and disinformation"—the so-called "ecosystem of hate". At a more grassroots level (see below) is the Hope Not Hate (https://www.hopenothate.org.uk/) website and, in the US, the Project Censored tertiary educational initiative seeking to provide students with critical skills in online and media literacy that enable them to combat fake news (https://www.

projectcensored.org/united-states-of-distraction-fighting-the-fake-news-invasion/).

Organisational, Professional and Peer Group Strategies

At an organisational level, a number of strategies are available to counter radical-right insurgency, interference or manipulation. For corporations, these include formal anti-extremist (including anti-radical right) policies as part of corporate governance and risk management. These policies would include such routine protections as:

> (a) Separation of CEO and Chairman/President functions as two separate individuals, so as to prevent a joint Chairman-CEO becoming too powerful, self-serving and beyond effective control if indulging in decisions and conduct damaging to the corporation;
>
> (b) Appointment of fully independent non-executive directors (NEDs) to help steer executive directors away from potentially egregious or damaging decisions and conduct;
>
> (c) Establishing an effective Board Risk Committee (separate from a Board Audit Committee) tasked with ensuring that the Board addresses 'all significant risks' to the business, which would include any potential threats arising from ideological sources of whatever kind;
>
> (d) Requiring effective due-diligence background checks (negative or positive vetting, as appropriate) on all staff appointments, staff promotions, contractor appointments, agent appointments, partnering and joint venture contracts, licensing agreements, and proposed mergers or acquisitions;
>
> (e) As an integral part of due-diligence, requiring psychological evaluation for all individuals subject to positive vetting, and possibly negative vetting.

The essential requirements of corporate governance and risk management within an organisation have been outlined in IRM (2014; 2018), Waring (2013) and, for the UK, in FRC (2014; 2018). Whereas the formal framework for corporate governance and risk management should work to prevent harmful radical ideologies and authoritarianism operating in corporations, and does appear to in general, as chapter 5 amply illustrated there are numerous instances of failure. The reasons for such failures lie in a combination in the particular organi-sation of defective formal frameworks and weak and/or toxic leader-ship. As argued in chapter 4, the characteristics of positive leadership are clear and well known. Ensuring that only positive leaders are ap-pointed is another crucial aspect of due-diligence, and emphasizes the necessity for psychometric and psychological evaluation as well as searching for tell-tale signs of offensive attitudes and conduct.

The importance of competent and positive leadership also re-lates to the 'new model corporation' described in chapter 5, which is implicitly anti-authoritarian. The new organisational purpose model described in British Academy (2018), and also implicitly supported by the US Business Roundtable of major national and global corporations (BRT 2019), is a promising development that potentially heralds a de-cline in corporate authoritarian excesses, whether emanating either consciously or pre-consciously from some corporate leaders' radical-right world-views. Whether the new model corporation gains traction is likely to hinge on a combination of factors, including enlightened self-interest of corporate leaders. This is especially so in the context of the fragile global economy of the Covid-19 and post-Covid era, the policy positions and codes of ethics of professional and sector/trade bodies, and how rapidly the overall management education and train-ing syllabuses of business schools, universities and other centres are able to be re-orientated to reflect the new model.

For those corporations and corporate leaders that do not re-en-gineer themselves around the new model, or for whatever reason ex-hibit authoritarianism, racism or other unacceptable character, they may encounter increasing difficulties. For example, they may face both potential sanctions of a legislative, regulatory or judicial nature, and increasingly peer-group pressure at both the personal and pro-fessional levels as well as the corporate and trading levels. They may find themselves being quarantined or confined to an out-group of os-tracised 'untouchables'. An example of how large corporations are be-ginning to act ethically according to the new model is provided by how in October 2020 Legal & General (L&G), one of Britain's largest insti-tutional investors managing more than £1.2 trillion of assets for pen-sion funds and other funds, advised more than thirty of the FTSE 100 companies with all-white boards of directors that henceforth it would vote against their nominations for key positions, unless they appointed at least one ethnic minority director within the next fifteen months. L&G similarly informed the other FTSE 100 companies and all S&P 500 companies of its policy, giving those not in compliance a deadline of January 1, 2022. The effect of L&G's threat was to put at risk the re-election of the chairmen of offending companies' nomination committees. In turn, this would prevent such committees from making board appointments. According to a report by Hosking (2020), L&G's unprecedented action by such a major corporation was taken on the basis of independent research, the government's Parker Review (Parker 2020), and the BLM protests, following what an L&G communiqué referred to as "the horrifying killing of George Floyd and so many others [which] has led to many institutional investors to think much more seriously about structural racism and inequality."

Another example was Mr Urs Rohner, chairman of Credit Suisse bank and a non-executive director of the pharmaceutical giant GlaxoSmithKline (GSK), reportedly being forced to apologize to GSK over an alleged racist incident at his 60th birthday party in November 2019 (Ralph and Griffiths 2020). Credit Suisse also reportedly made its own corporate apology to GSK. At the party, those at the table of Thiam Tidjane, who was then Chief Executive of Credit Suisse, and included Emma Walmsley, GSK Chief Executive, all reportedly walked out during a cabaret act themed on racial mockery.

Despite such moves against corporate racism and the backdrop of the 'new model' corporation heralding permanent anti-authoritarian change, such a development is primarily viable for publicly listed corporations subject to compulsory corporate governance and risk management requirements under stock exchange Listing Rules. There is no such compulsion on privately owned companies, where in some cases laissez-faire leadership, inferior managerial quality, and authoritarian, prejudicial and discriminatory values may prevail, and where de facto radical-right infiltration may already have occurred. As with listed corporations and their leaders who fail to behave ethically and responsibly, increasingly these 'rogues' too may find themselves being quarantined to an out-group of 'untouchables' whose business no one wants. Of course, the potential to adopt the 'new model' is open to all organisations, whether listed or private, and even those 'rogue corporations' described in chapter 5.

While recognizing the prevailing mood change favouring 'the new model', it is important to acknowledge that, legally, directors and officers of any corporation must always act 'in the best interests of the corporation' and its owners and shareholders as primary beneficiaries. Historically, therefore, this legal reality has placed maximization of profits and share values at the centre of an organisation's raison d'être and world-view. Notions of corporate social responsibility, anti-extremism, anti-racism and diversity policies, charitable acts, and climate change obligations, for example, may seem to some to be contrary to that primary legal duty, a point made strongly by Bakan (2004) throughout his polemical study of corporate excesses. See also Sales (2019). Whereas some corporate leaders and executives may use the 'profits at all costs' mantra to argue that they have no responsibility for, or indeed legitimacy in supporting, noble social and humanitarian causes, Bakan (pages 28-59) argued that others cynically and hypocritically adopt them as a visible cloak of respectability and integrity, while having little or no actual belief in such causes. The author argues, however, that such causes are not automatically at odds with directors' and officers' legal duty. If they choose to view support for such causes as being in the corporation's best interests e.g. by boosting corporate image, customer attraction and ultimately product penetration and market share, then such enlightened corporate self-interest would also meet their legal duty. The question of sincerity or otherwise is beyond further discussion here.

Political and Economic Strategies

Some authors argue that political and economic strategies need to tackle the causes of radical-right expansion and popularity: economic inequalities (Wilkinson & Pickett 2010), immigration (including fear of and envy towards immigrants and ethno-religious minorities, fear of cultural swamping), sympathies for WASP/racist/white supremacist beliefs, and enthusiasm for a radical-right salvationist prospectus. According to e.g. Picketty (2014) and Stiglitz (2013), key strategies would need to be on investment, stimulation and growth, in order to create jobs and raise living standards. In turn, the latter would counter dissatisfaction and disgruntlement on which radical-right ideology can feed in a restless and anxious population beset by social problems, economic problems, and relative decline in living standards coupled with relative decline of national status on the world stage. It was no accident that, for example, President Trump's radical-right prospectus was encapsulated in the slogan 'Make America Great Again', or that in the UK the radical right were so fanatically committed to Brexit as a salvationist offering.

Political efforts to engender trust, social cohesion, and political stability (Kaltwasser 2017) are required on a large number of issues (Wilkinson & Pickett 2010), including Covid-19 pandemic, NHS/health care, social welfare, care homes, Brexit, law and order, immigration, employment, housing, and education. Mainstream politicians need to listen, and be seen to listen, and to act—but not pander to populism for the sake of votes. Such politicians need to avoid amoral calculation and manifest or apparent cynicism, for example by recognizing the moral limits of neo-liberalism and unfettered free market economics (Sandel 2013). Unfettered economic 'freedom' for corporations is unfortunately a key characteristic of radical-right ideology and its corporate supporters, and so it is unlikely to be abandoned by them. However, mainstream politicians have a choice: whether to serve narrow ideological and corporate interests, or whether to serve a broader good.

Countering subversion and manipulation of representative democracy by radical interests (of whatever kind) must be a priority of mainstream politicians. Centrist parties and mainstream conservative parties need to recognize and resist attempts by radical-right interests seeking to subvert them and shift their centre of political gravity further rightwards in harmony with their own position. Such parties need to make more public statements and observable actions in support of liberal values and against authoritarianism. This will include avoidance of such PR disasters as appointment to senior posts of radical-right individuals, especially any who express controversial or offensive far-right opinions in public, as occurred in several cases during the radical-right Conservative administration of UK Prime Minister Boris Johnson.

Grassroots Strategies

Radical-right authoritarianism depends for its success on persuading, duping and, as necessary intimidating and coercing, the mass population into accepting, agreeing with, and even better conniving with, the assertions and policies of radical-right ideology. Corporate authoritarianism, whether explicitly radical-right or not, follows a similar logic in so far as customers, employees, contractors, and the public are concerned. To all intents and purposes, such authoritarianism is often a demonstration of unobtrusive power (Hardy 1985), that is, an ability to secure preferred outcomes by preventing conflict arising between those exercising that power and those subject to it, who are unaware that they are acquiescing to their own domination (Waring & Glendon 1998, 93-94)

For many on the receiving end of authoritarianism, even if they are aware of it, there may appear to be no way out, and so it may be easier to comply and go along with it. However, as Waring and Paxton (2019, 402) observed, if nothing is done, and the radical-right threat "continues to grow, public life will become much more constrained and so, if opposition is delayed, it will require much more courage later, or will become simply impossible." Therefore, implicitly, grassroots actions, whether individually or in concert, are as necessary as others in seeking to blunt radical-right hegemony. Sennett (2013) and Stephan & Snyder (2017) point to the potential effectiveness of grassroots approaches by citizens, as individuals or with others.

The following categories, in no particular order, are indicative of grassroots actions, some of which are applicable to both radical-right and corporate authoritarianism while others are better suited to one or the other.

Boycotts

In addition to boycotts by corporations [for example, withdrawing Internet and social media platform advertising, and institutional investor boycotts of particular funds on ethical grounds relating to radical-right ideology (as exemplified above)], grassroots activists and members of the public may also engage in business, brand and product boycotts. For example, the Blackout Day economic protest in July 2020 against structural discrimination in the US involved blacks shopping only at black-owned businesses and therefore boycotting others, predominantly white-owned (Brown & Tylko 2020). Other boycotts against specific businesses have included one against Goya Foods Inc (McClay 2020; Nguyen 2020), a leading brand of Latin American foodstuffs in the US and Central & South America, following Goya's CEO publicly praising President Trump and Trump's daughter Ivanka publicly endorsing Goya products. The apparent justification for the boycott was Trump's widely publicised statements denigrating Mexicans, including accusing them of being criminals and rapists and stirring up ethnic hatred against Latin American immigrants in general. There is some debate about the effectiveness and sustainability of such boycotts but, judging from the noisy reaction from counter-boycott sources, they appear at least to damage targeted brands and corporate images and possibly revenues. Whether they are likely to achieve permanent changes *both* in enacted corporate policy and conduct *and* corporate culture and attitudes is less certain, as the case of United Airlines (case 5.3 in chapter 5) reported.

Public Media Channels

A variety of media options are available to register or publicise complaints relating to radical-right or corporate authoritarianism. For corporations, these include complaints about specific companies on such review websites as *Tripadvisor* and *Trustpilot*, and various others e.g. focussed on airlines. In addition to review websites, there are social media groups, while newspapers and periodicals offer letters pages, with some offering opportunities to submit blog or feature articles.

Despite media exposure of their alleged wrongdoing, it is not always clear that corporations take any notice of adverse publicity. As discussed in chapter 5, authoritarian corporate regimes often fail to reply to complaints or only provide deflecting PR blandishments, or deliberately obstruct the communication of complaints. Also, media exposure of alleged wrongdoing is less likely to be effective against private companies answerable only to themselves than it is against publicly listed corporations that are subject to a variety of corporate governance and risk management requirements and external monitoring as well as potential sanctions by a number of authorities.

A more activist online media possibility is described by McCleary (2020), who reports on the campaign by her and a loose collection of like-minded anti-racism activists dedicated to exposing individuals who post racist messages, posts, and memes on social media. Such online vigilantes aim to expose "everyday racists" and ultimately to get them sacked from their jobs, arguing that by virtue of their publicly expressed hatred on *Facebook*, where their profile often lists their employer, they present an existential threat to public safety that implicitly entrains their employer. Apparently, disciplinary actions do occur and sackings are not unusual. Whether such extra-judicial 'doxxing' by vigilantes is ethical or commendable involves a debate beyond the scope of this volume.

Complaints and Protests to Authorities

In a democracy, citizens are entitled to raise complaints about alleged amoral or unlawful conduct by political groups, companies, and their individual representatives. Clearly, this would include allegations about radical-right groups and authoritarian corporations or their leaders. An aggrieved person could, for example, contact their elected representative such as a Congressman or MP, who may take up the issue with an appropriate government minister or pass the information to a relevant congressional or parliamentary committee, depending on the seriousness of the complaint. Alternatively or additionally, the person may contact relevant enforcing authorities if potential breaches of criminal law are indicated. This could involve the police or other enforcing or regulatory authority. For example, at any one time, in the UK there are multiple formal investigations under way obtaining evidence and reporting to Parliament, the government, or public prosecutors on a wide range of topics relevant to public health, public safety, racism, discrimination, extremism, terrorism, justice, public order, corporate fraud, and money laundering. The Competition and Markets Authority, for example, has investigated and reported on authoritarian anti-client practices of funeral directors nationally, while also conducting long-term investigations into anti-consumer monopoly price gouging by suppliers of life-critical pharmaceuticals (as exemplified in cases 5.1 and 5.2 in chapter 5).

Expression of concern, anger or complaint to authorities may also be channelled via traditional mechanisms of protest gatherings, demonstrations, or marches. There is a long history of such events, for example the US black civil rights marches of the 1960s across the southern states and to the Lincoln Memorial in Washington, and more recently the Black Lives Matter Commitment March of August 2020, also to the Lincoln Memorial in Washington. The ACLED conflict monitoring project in conjunction with Princeton University reported

(ACLED 2020) that, in the two-and-a-half months from late May to early August 2020, there were 7,750 demonstrations linked to the BLM movement in 2,000 locations across the US. While fewer in number, there were also BLM solidarity marches and demonstrations in other countries, e.g. in Europe and Australia. In the UK in June 2020, there were a number of BLM events in major cities as well as smaller towns, as well as anti-racist demonstrations not linked to BLM.

Marches and demonstrations are sometimes evocative and memorable. They signal depth of feeling, concern, and anger, and may turn the spotlight on as well as potentially embarrass and humiliate targets and constrain what they can say credibly in defence. Typically, such events target both alleged wrongdoers and whichever authorities the demonstrators believe have a responsibility to act to stop or curtail the alleged wrongdoing. However, while undoubtedly powerful communication instruments, such events alone are unlikely to change the thinking, attitudes and conduct of a committed opposition. The adversarial and often provocative nature of such events may provoke counter-events, often at the same location, and a battle of histrionics, rhetoric and slogans, often generating more heat than light on the subject, may ensue. Large demonstrations in cities may also create problems of crowd control, blocking of thoroughfares, and public safety and therefore extra demands on policing. Moreover, there is also an opportunity for more radical and extreme elements or infiltrators to engage in disorder and violence, thereby vitiating the legitimacy of the demonstrators and casting attention away from their cause and argument (Bennett 2020). Indeed, President Trump issued multiple statements denigrating the BLM protests and accusing the demonstrators of being a mixture of violent anarchists, left-wing extremists and criminals.

Education and Constructive Dialogue

Grassroots educational initiatives against radical extremism typically involve local community colleges working in collaboration with a variety of local groups, civic leaders, councillors, schools, police, and others. In the UK, such initiatives form part of the national Prevent anti-radicalisation and anti-extremism strategy which is devolved to local authorities (*BBC* 2017). Prevent targets all forms of radicalisation and extremism, whether right-wing or left or originating in other ideology.

The Project Censored project is a US example of what might be termed a 'strategic grassroots initiative' that seeks to identify and challenge media manipulation and fake news, especially in the context of contemporary dominance of online information, opinion and discourse by platform mega-corporations and radical-right user interests. Project Censored (e.g. see Huff & Higdon (2019) on *Media Manipulation in Post-Truth America*) seeks to provide students with critical skills in online and media literacy that enable them to combat fake news, through critical media literacy learning, curriculum development, student centred publications, a radio show, and documentary films such as the 2020 video *United States of Distraction* (https://www.projectcensored.org/united-states-of-distraction-fighting-the-fake-news-invasion/).

Voting and Candidate Support

Casting one's vote in public elections for a liberal, centrist or other non-radical right political candidate is the essence of grassroots action, as is campaigning for such a candidate or contributing in some way to their campaign. Nevertheless, it should be noted that different electoral systems may be more or less responsive to numbers of votes, for example the significant differences between 'first past the post', proportional representation, and 'electoral college' systems. In the corporate sphere, just as institutional investors such as L&G (see above) are able to exercise ethical voting decisions in favour of chairmen of funds whose boards include BAME directors and against those that do not, individual shareholders (alone or in concert with like-minded shareholders) may also vote disruptively at corporate AGMs against proposals and appointments of authoritarian boards.

Further Potential Strategies

This chapter would not be complete without reference to an intellectual/moral strategy that rarely features in mainstream analyses of radical-right topics. This strategy has no generally agreed label or definition, but in this volume the author gives it a working title of 'innate altruism', which may be defined as 'the collective desire of humans to act for the common good'. The biosocial philosopher Trigant Burrow is credited with expounding the theoretical basis of innate altruism (Burrow 1964) and related aspects of it (Burrow 1953). The theory

counterpoints the timeless and innate biological and social imperatives to protect the human species (e.g. motherhood) with the increasingly relentless cult of individuality, self-centredness, and self-gratifi-
cation at the expense of others (Halmos 1998). MacAskill (2016) offered a conceptual and pragmatic examination of effective altruism in
a 21st century context. The radical-right ideological imperative to acquire freedoms, rights and benefits for themselves and their supporters, but deny these to others whom they hate or despise (on the basis
of race, religion, sexual orientation, political views, unemployment,
poverty, ill-health, or immigration status), is an extreme version of the
antithesis of innate altruism.

In its purest form, innate altruism is reported by adherents to be
spiritual, an almost transcendental, psychic experience. At this level,
altruistic individuals are likely to be few in number. Indeed, although
most individuals may strive to be model citizens and observe a moral
code, and especially those who do altruistic things, they nonetheless
are prone to human foibles, defects and fallibility. For all but a minority, therefore, pure altruism may be too impracticable to cope with reality and human nature, the strategic pragmatism of MacAskill notwithstanding. Nevertheless, pure altruists may argue that not only are
all individuals capable of transcending to pure altruism but, if they did
so, then the world would be transformed for the better, with many of
its ills disappearing as a result.

For the majority, however, a pragmatic approach to altruism is
probably as far as they will develop or realistically could be expected
to. In the context of this volume, examples of those who strive to do
the right thing include all the non-profit organisations, campaigning,
and self-help groups tackling such issues as racism, religious hatred,
and other forms of hatred, authoritarianism and victimisation. In the
corporate sphere, it may be argued that companies that adopt liberal
anti-authoritarian policies for corporate purpose, corporate social responsibility, anti-discrimination, climate change, diversity in employment, stakeholder diversity, and so on, in line with the 'new model
corporation' (British Academy 2018), are implicitly recognizing the
need for, and the role of, a more altruistic set of corporate ethics. Such
corporate strategy may also arise out of enlightened self-interest, but
it would be churlish to imply that such motivation is automatically
bad.

Conclusion

Some corporate interests share authoritarian world-views, attitudes, opinions, judgements and conduct with the radical right. Frequently, such shared world-views and interests involve amoral thinking and calculation. 'Dark money' and corrupt influence in both directions lubricates the fusion of mutual interests—corporate financing of radical-right politics, and radical-right political support for corporate interests, much of which may harm society by undermining democratic order, processes and institutions. Both groups may also be emboldened to cross the line between amoral conduct and into illegal activity. As part of their weaponry, wild allegations against political targets and rivals and a litany of absurd grand conspiracy theories have become a signature characteristic of the radical right.

Strategies to combat the authoritarian threat of the corporate/radical-right axis require multiple integrated approaches rather than an expectation of success with only one or a limited selection. These may be categorized as: legislative, regulatory and judicial; Internet, social media and related; organisational, professional and peer-group; political and economic; and grassroots action. Each category includes a variety of options. Implicitly, many of these strategies rely on the altruism of anti-authoritarian protagonists pursuing the greater public good, the very antithesis of the innate selfishness of radical-right and corporate authoritarian ideology and practice. Where clear pursuit of personal privilege, aggregation of material benefits, and sectoral monopoly of power, infringes the innate rights of the individual, something is manifestly wrong and demands correction.

As proposed in Volumes 1 and 2 (Waring and Paxton 2018; 2019), robust 'muscular moderation' in many forms is the essence of the overall approach recommended to combat authoritarianism, so as to supplement the quiet laissez-faire tolerance of the moderate majority.

References

ACLED. 2020. *Demonstrations and Political Violence in America: New Data for Summer 2020.* US Crisis Monitor report. September 3, 2020. Armed Conflict Location and Event Data (ACLED) in conjunction with Princeton University Bridging Divides Initiative.

Ariza, C. 2020. "Militaries Around the World have a neo-Nazi Problem", *CARR Insight Blog*. August 7, 2020. https://www.radical rightanalysis.com/2020/08/07/militaries-around-the-world-have-a-neo-nazi-problem/. [accessed August 7, 2020].

Bakan, J. 2004. *The Corporation: The Pathological Pursuit of Profit and Power*. London: Constable.

BBC. 2017. "Reality Check: What is the Prevent Strategy?" *BBC News*. June 4, 2017. https://www.bbc.co.uk/news/election-2017-401 51991. [accessed October 8, 2020].

BBC. 2019. "London Bridge: Usman Khan Completed Untested Rehabilitation Scheme". *BBC News*. December 4, 2019. https://www. bbc.co.uk/news/uk-50653191. [accessed September 19, 2020].

BBC. 2020a. "Andrew Sabisky: No 10 Adviser Resigns Over Alleged Race Comments". *BBC News*. February 18, 2020. https://www. bbc.co.uk/news/uk-politics-51538493. [accessed September 8, 2020].

BBC. 2020b. "Jacob Blake: Police Officer in Kenosha Shooting Named". *BBC News*. August 27, 2020. https://www.bbc.co.uk/news/wor ld-us-canada-53927756. [accessed September 14, 2020].

BBC. 2020c. "Breonna Taylor's Family 'Agree Financial Settlement' Over Death". *BBC News*. September 15, 2020. https://www.bbc. co.uk/news/world-us-canada-54165646. [accessed September 15, 2020].

BBC. 2020d. "Teenagers Convicted of Terrorism Could be Jailed for Life". *BBC News*. September 13, 2020. https://www.bbc.co.uk/ news/uk-54135575. [accessed September 13, 2020]

Beckett, L. 2020. "Nearly All Black Lives Matter Protests are Peaceful Despite Trump Narrative, Report Finds". *The Guardian*. September 5, 2020. https://www.theguardian.com/world/2020/sep/ 05/nearly-all-black-lives-matter-protests-are-peaceful-despite-trump-narrative-report-finds. [accessed October 7, 2020].

British Academy. 2018. *Reforming Business for the 21st Century—A Framework for the Future of the Corporation*. November 2018. London: The British Academy.

Brooks, N. 2020. "The Tangled Web: Psychopathic Personality, Vulnerability and Victim Selection". In *Corporate Psychopathy: Investigating Destructive Personalities in the Workplace*, edited by

K. Fritzon, N. Brooks, and S. Croom. 295-325. Cham, Switzerland: Palgrave Macmillan.

Brooks, N., Fritzon, K. and Croom, S. 2020. "Corporate Psychopathy: Entering the Paradox and Emerging Unscathed". In *Corporate Psychopathy: Investigating Destructive Personalities in the Workplace*, edited by K. Fritzon, N. Brooks, and S. Croom. 327-365. Cham, Switzerland: Palgrave Macmillan.

Brown, D. and Tylko, K. 2020. "Blackout Day Economic Protest Encourages Shoppers to Buy Only from Black-owned Businesses Tuesday, Boycott Others". *MSN News.* July 7, 2020. https://www.msn.com/en-us/news/us/blackout-day-economic-protest-enco urages-shoppers-to-buy-only-from-black-owned-businesses-tu esday-boycott-others/ar-BB16p1YU. [accessed October 6, 2020].

BRT. 2019. "Business Roundtable Redefines the Purpose of a Corporation to Promote 'An Economy that Serves All Americans'". *Business Roundtable.* August 19, 2019. Washington DC: Business Roundtable. https://www.businessroundtable.org/business-ro undtable-redefines-the-purpose-of-a-corporation-to-promote-an-economy-that-serves-all-americans. [accessed September 6, 2020].

Brunson, R.K. and Miller, J. 2006. "Young Black Men and Urban Policing in the US". *British Journal of Criminology,* Vol 46 Issue 4, 613-640.

Burrow, T. 1953. *Science and Man's Behavior: The Contribution of Phylobiology.* New York: Philosophical Library.

Burrow, T. 1964. *Preconscious Foundations of Human Experience*, edited by W.E. Galt. London/New York: Basic Books.

Cabinet Office. 2017. *Public Summary of Sector Security and Resilience Plans.* December 2017. London: Cabinet Office.

Charter, D. 2021a. "US Capitol Under Siege". *The Times.* January 7, 2021. Page 1.

Charter, D. 2021b. "Pro-Trump Social Network Banned". *The Times.* January 11, 2021. Page 33.

Cohen, L. 2020. "It's Been Over 3 Months Since George Floyd was Killed by Police. Police are Still Killing Blacks at Disproportionate Rates". *CBS News.* September 10, 2020. https://www.cbsnews.com/news

/george-floyd-killing-police-black-people-killed-164/. [accessed September 13, 2020].

Cohen, M. 2021. "Questions Swirl Around Possible 'Insider' Help for Capitol Attack". *CNN Politics.* January 14, 2021. https://edition.cnn.com/2021/01/13/politics/capitol-insurrection-insider-help/index.html.

CPNI. 2017. *Embedding Security Behaviours: Using the 5 Es.* Centre for the Protection of National Infrastructure. London: CPNI.

Crossland, D. 2020. "German Police Shared Hitler Images". *The Times.* September 18, 2020. Page 33.

C4 News. 2019. "Nigel Farage's Funding Secrets Revealed". *Channel 4 News.* May 16, 2019. https://www.channel4.com/news/nigel-farages-funding-secrets-revealed. [accessed September 5, 2020].

DCMS. 2019. *The Online Harms White Paper: Government Response to the Committee's Twelfth Report.* Received July 23, 2019. Published September 9, 2019. Commons Select Committee. London: UK Parliament. https://www.gov.uk/government/consultations/online-harms-white-paper.

DCMS. 2020. "Government Minded to Appoint Ofcom as Online Harms Regulator". Department for Digital, Culture, Media and Sport. February 12, 2020. London: DCMS. https://www.gov.uk/government/organisations/department-for-digital-culture-media-sport.

Dick, C. 2020. "Met Police Commissioner Cressida Dick Responds to Institutional Racism Claims". Interview by Krishnan Guru-Murthy. *C4 News.* August 13, 2020. https://www.channel4.com/news/met-police-commissioner-cressida-dick-responds-to-institutional-racism-claims. [accessed September 18, 2020].

Dodd, V. 2020. "Black Met Inspector Stopped by Police While Driving Home from Work". *The Guardian.* August 18, 2020. https://www.theguardian.com/uk-news/2020/aug/18/black-met-police-inspector-stopped-by-officers-while-driving-home-from-work. [accessed September 16, 2020].

Duarte, J.L. 2015. *The Role of Envy in Anti-Semitism.* PhD dissertation. Phoenix, Az: Arizona State University.

DW News. 2017. "Far-right Extremism Probe into Elite German Army Unit Opens". *DW News.* August 17, 2017. https://www.dw.com/

en/far-right-extremism-probe-into-elite-german-army-unit-op ens/a-40138355. [accessed September 3, 2020].

ECHR. 1953. *European Convention on Human Rights.* Strasbourg: Council of Europe.

ENISA 2017. *Cyber Security Culture in Organisations.* November 2017. European Union Agency for Network and Information Security. www.enisa.europa.eu [accessed June 15, 2019].

EU. 2008. *EU Framework Decision on Combating Forms and Expressions of Racism and Xenophobia by Means of Criminal Law.* Council of the EU. 2008/913/JHA. November 28, 2008. Brussels: EU.

FB. 2020. "Removing Holocaust Denial Content". News release. Monica Bikert, VP for Content Policy. *Facebook.* October 12, 2020. https://about.fb.com/news/2020/10/removing-holocaust-de nial-content/. [accessed October 16, 2020].

Fox, M. 2020. "The Trump Appointee Biden Needs to Get Rid Of on Day One". *CNN Opinion.* December 23, 2020. https://www.edition. cnn.com/beattie-trump-appointee-biden-should-fire-fox/index. html.

FPL. 1881. *Loi sur la Liberté de la Presse.* July 29, 1881. Subsumed within 1990 law of same title. Paris: Legifrance. https://www. legifrance.gouv.fr/. [accessed January 23, 2018].

FRC. 2014. *Guidance on Risk Management, Internal Control and Related Financial and Business Reporting.* September 2014. London: Financial Reporting Council.

FRC. 2018. *The UK Corporate Governance Code.* July 2018. London: Financial Reporting Council.

Fritzon, K., Bailey, C., Croom, S. and Brooks, N. 2016. "Problem Personalities in the Workplace: Development of the Corporate Personality Inventory". In *Psychology and Law in Europe: When West Meets East.* Edited by P.A. Granhag, R. Bull, A. Shaboltas, and E. Dozortseva, 139-166. Boca Raton, Fl: Taylor & Francis.

German, M. 2020. "The FBI Warned for Years that Police are Cozy with the Far Right. Is No One Listening?" *The Guardian.* August 28, 2020. https://www.theguardian.com/commentisfree/2020/ aug/28/fbi-far-right-white-supremacists-police. [accessed September 7, 2020].

Gibbs, S. 2017. "EU Warns Tech Firms: Remove Extremist Content Faster or be Regulated". *The Guardian.* December 7, 2017. https://www.theguardian.com/.

Goddard, J. 2021. "Police Under Investigation for Their Part in Riot". *The Times.* January 15, 2021. Page 31.

Griffin, A. 2017. "Teresa May to Create New Internet that Would be Controlled and Regulated by Government". *The Independent.* May 19, 2017. https://www.theindependent.co.uk.

Grylls, G. 2020. "Cummings 'Weirdo' Called for Activists to be Shot". *The Times.* September 3, 2020. Page 15.

Guardian. 2020. "Officers Charged in George Floyd Killing Seek to Place Blame on Each Other". *The Guardian.* September 11, 2020. https://www.theguardian.com/us-news/2020/sep/11/george -floyd-killing-death-officers. [accessed September 14, 2020].

Hall, J. 2021. *Report of the Independent Review of Terrorism Legislation for 2019.* Jonathan Hall QC. 23 March 2021. London.

Halmos, P. 1998. *Solitude and Privacy: A Study of Social Isolation, its Causes and Therapy.* London: Routledge/Taylor & Francis.

Hamilton, F. 2020. "Police Investigated for Stopping Athlete". *The Times.* October 9, 2020. Page 5.

Hardy, C. 1985. "The Nature of Unobtrusive Power". *Journal of Management Studies*, 22 (4), 384-399.

Hate Crime. 2016. *Hate Crime.* October 2016. UK Crown Prosecution Service. London: CPS. https://www.cps.gov.uk/sites/default/ files/documents/publications/Hate-Crime-what-it-is-and-how- to-support-victims-and-witnesses.pdf. [accessed September 13, 2020].

Hill, E., Tiefenthäler, A., Triebert, C. et al. 2020. "How George Floyd Was Killed in Police Custody". *The New York Times.* May 31, 2020. https://www.nytimes.com/2020/05/31/us/george-floyd-inve stigation.html. [accessed September 14, 2020].

Hoff, T. 2020. "'Press the Reset Button': Right Wing Extremism in Germany's Military". *CARR Insight Blog.* September 24, 2020. https://www.radicalrightanalysis.com/2020/09/24/press-the- reset-button-right-wing-extremism-in-germanys-military/. [accessed September 27, 2020].

Home Office. 1999. *The Stephen Lawrence Inquiry.* Independent Report by Sir William MacPherson. February 24, 1999. Cm 4262.

London: Home Office. https://www.gov.uk/government/publi cations/the-stephen-lawrence-inquiry. [accessed September 15, 2020].

Home Office. 2018. *National Action Cases—Statement and Factsheet.* Home Office News Team. November 12, 2018. London: Home Office. https://homeofficemedia.blog.gov.uk/2018/11/12/nation al-action-cases-statement-and-factsheet/.

Hosking, P. 2020. "Businesses 'Must Bring Minorities on Board'". *The Times.* October 5, 2020. Page 35.

Huff, M. and Higdon, N. 2019. *Media Manipulation in Post Truth America (and What We Can Do About It).* San Francisco, USA: City Limits Books.

IRM. 2010. *A Structured Approach to Enterprise Risk Management (ERM) and the Requirements of ISO 31000.* London: Institute of Risk Management.

IRM. 2018. *Standard Deviations: A Risk Practitioner's Guide to ISO 31000.* London: Institute of Risk Management.

Johnson, T. 2017. "Fighting the Right Through Education". In *Strategies Against the Far Right. Reporting Back and Moving Forward.* Conference June 15-18, 2017. Conference proceedings, edited by S. Ehmsen and A. Scharenberg, 14-15. New York: Rosa Luxemburg Stiftung.

Johnson, V. 2020. "Capitol Siege Raises Questions Over Extent of White Supremacist Infiltration of Police". *The Conversation.* January 14, 2021. https://theconversation.com/capitol-siege-raises-questi ons-over-extent-of-white-supremacist-infiltration-of-us-police-153145. [accessed January 17, 2021].

Kaltwasser, C.R. 2017. "Populism and the Question of How to Respond to It". In *The Oxford Handbook of Populism,* edited by C.R. Kaltwasser, P. Taggart, P.O. Espejo and P.Ostiguy. Oxford: Oxford University Press.

Knowles, T., Hamilton, F. and Simpson, J. 2020. "Far Right Recruits Children on YouTube". *The Times.* October 6, 2020. Page 15.

MacAskill, W. 2016. *Doing Good Better: Effective Altruism and a Radical New Way to Make a Difference.* July 2016. London: Faber Guardian.

McClay, C. 2020. "Goya Foods: Hispanic Brand Faces Boycott for Praising Trump". *BBC News.* July 10, 2020. https://www.bbc.co.uk/news/world-us-canada-53371392. [accessed October 6, 2020].

McLearly, S. 2020. "Confessions of an Online Anti-racist Vigilante". *Digital Trends.* July 23, 2020. https://www.digitaltrends.com/opinion/anti-racism-vigilante-fired-activists/. [accessed September 29, 2020].

Montague, Z. 2020. " 'They Stand on the Shoulders of Giants': the Next Generation March on Washington". *New York Times.* September 2, 2020. https://www.nytimes.com/2020/09/02/us/politics/blm-march-on-washington.html. [accessed September 14, 2020].

Mostrous, A. and Kenber, B. 2014. "Farage Faces Investigation into 'Missing' EU Expenses". *The Times.* April 15, 2014. https://www.thetimes.co.uk/article/farage-faces-investigation-into-missing-eu-expenses-0qzfvpmbmpf. [accessed September 5, 2020].

Mudde, K. and Kaltwasser, C.R. 2017. *Populism: A Very Short Introduction.* Oxford: Oxford University Press.

Neiwert, D. 2017. *Alt-America—The Rise of the Radical Right in the Age of Trump.* London: Verso.

Nguyen, T. 2020. "Boycotts Show Us What Matters to Americans". *MSN News.* Vox. July 16, 2020. https://www.msn.com/en-us/money/news/boycotts-show-us-what-matters-to-americans/ar-BB16OOLv. [accessed October 6, 2020].

Nsubuga, J. 2020. "Met Police Officer Dismissed After 'Liking' Facebook Group". *Yahoo News UK.* August 8, 2020. https://nz.news.yahoo.com/met-police-officer-britain-firstfacebook-group-far-right-145308850.html. [accessed September 7, 2020].

Parker, J. 2020. *Ethnic Diversity Enriching Business Leadership: 2020 Update Report from the Parker Review.* Independent report by Sir John Parker. February 5, 2020. Department for Business, Energy & Industrial Strategy. London: UK Government. https://assets.ey.com/content/dam/ey-sites/ey-com/en_uk/news/2020/02/ey-parker-review-2020-report-final.pdf. [accessed October 5, 2020].

Pavia, W. 2020. "US Soldier, 22, 'Plotted with neo-Nazis to Attack His Unit'". *The Times.* June 24, 2020. Page 34.

Paxton, R.O. 2005. *The Anatomy of Fascism.* London: Penguin Books.

Paxton, R. 2018. "The Alt-Right, Post-truth, Fake News and the Media". In *The New Authoritarianism Vol 1: A Risk Analysis of the US Alt-Right Phenomenon,* edited by A. Waring, 337-361. Stuttgart: Ibidem Verlag.

Picketty, T. 2014. *Capital in the Twenty-First Century.* Cambridge MA: Belknap Press.

Prevent. 2015. *The Prevent Duty. Departmental advice for schools and childcare providers.* June 2015. London: Department of Education.

Proctor, K. 2020. "Calls for Tory Aide to be Sacked Over 'Enforced Contraception' Remarks". *The Guardian.* February 16, 2020. https://www.theguardian.com/politics/2020/feb/16/tory-aide-wants-enforced-contraception-to-curb-pregnancies. [accessed September 8, 2020].

Purdue, S. 2020. "The Infiltration of Law Enforcement by Racist Extremists". *CARR Insight Blog.* September 7, 2020. https://www.radicalrightanalysis.com/2020/09/07/the-infiltration-of-law-enforcement-by-racist-extremists/. [accessed September 21, 2020].

Ralph, A. and Griffiths, K. 2020. "Credit Suisse Chairman Apologises in 'Racism' Row Over Birthday Party". *The Times.* October 9, 2020. Page 36.

Rankin, J. 2019. "EU Recovers £200,000 from Ukip MEPs Accused of Misusing Funds". *The Guardian.* May 3, 2019. https://www.theguardian.com/politics/2019/may/03/eu-recovers-200000-from-ukip-meps-accused-of-misusing-funds. [accessed September 5, 2020].

Sahinkaya, E. 2020. "Germany Dissolves Elite Army Unit Over Far-right Activity". *VOA News.* August 1, 2020. https://www.voanews.com/extremism-watch/germany-dissolves-elite-army-unit-over-far-right-activity. [accessed September 3, 2020].

Sales, P.J. 2019. *Directors' Duties and Climate Change: Keeping Pace with Environmental Challenges.* Lecture to Anglo-Australian Law Society, Sydney, August 27, 2019. Lord Justice Sales. London: UK Supreme Court. https://www.supremecourt.uk/docs/speech-190827.pdf. [accessed September 5, 2020].

Sandel, M. 2013. *What Money Can't Buy: The Moral Limits of Markets.* London: Penguin.

Sennett, R. 2013. *Together: The Rituals, Pleasures and Politics of Cooperation.* London: Penguin.

Sharp, D. and Atherton, S. 2007. "To Serve and Protect? The Experience of Policing in the Community of Young People from Black and Other Ethnic Minority Groups". *British Journal of Criminology,* Vol 47 Issue 5, 746-763.

Shaw, D. 2019. "Stephen Lawrence: How has his Murder Changed Policing?" *BBC News.* February 2, 2019. https://www.bbc.co.uk/news/uk-47161480. [accessed September 15, 2020].

Simpson, J. 2020. "Police Officer Suspected of Belonging to neo-Nazi Cell". *The Times.* March 6, 2020. Page 7.

Small Steps. 2018. *The Small Steps Story.* London: Small Steps Consultants. https://smallstepsconsultants.com.

Speri, A. 2017. "The FBI has Quietly Investigated White Supremacist Infiltration of Law Enforcement". *The Intercept.* January 31, 2017. https://theintercept.com/2017/01/31/the-fbi-has-quietly-investigated-white-supremacist-infiltration-of-law-enforcement/. [accessed September 7, 2020].

Speri, A. 2020. "Unredacted FBI Document Sheds New Light on White Supremacist Infiltration of Law Enforcement". *The Intercept.* September 29, 2020. https://theintercept.com/2020/09/29/police-white-supremacist-infiltration-fbi/. [accessed January 17, 2021].

Statista. 2020. *Rate of Fatal Police Shootings in the United States from 2015 to August 2020, by Ethnicity.* Statista Report. https://www.statista.com/statistics/1123070/police-shootings-rate-ethnicity-us/. [accessed September 13, 2020].

Stephan, M.J. and Snyder, T. 2017. "Authoritarianism is Making a Comeback. Here's the Time-tested Way to Defeat It". *The Guardian.* June 20, 2017. https://www.theguardian.com/commentisfree/2017/jun/20/authoritarianism-trump-resistance-defeat.

Stevens, J. 2015. "UKIP Official Faces Allegation he Tampered with Election Process". *Daily Mail.* May 26, 2015. https://www.dailymail.co.uk/news/article-3098057/Ukip-official-faces-allegations-tampered-selection-process.html. [accessed September 5, 2020].

Stiglitz, J.E. 2013. *The Price of Inequality.* London: Penguin.

Tönberg, A. and Wahlström, M. 2018. "Unveiling the Radical Right Online: Exploring Framing and Identity in an Online Anti-immigrant Discussion Group". *Sociologisk Forskning*, Vol 55 No 2-3, 267-292. http://www.diva-portal.org/smash/get/diva2:1230 181/FULLTEXT01.pdf. [accessed September 29, 2020].

Turner-Graham, E. 2019. "The Politics of Cultural Despair: Britain's Extreme-right". In *The New Authoritarianism Vol 2: A Risk Analysis of the European Alt-Right,* edited by A. Waring, 121-147. Stuttgart: Ibidem Verlag.

UN. 1965. *UN International Convention on Elimination of All Forms of Racial Discrimination.* Office of Legal Affairs. New York: UN.

USDC. 2020. Federal indictments for wire fraud and money laundering. US vs. Brian Kolfage, Stephen Bannon, Andrew Badalato, and Timothy Shea. 20 Cr 412. 18 USC §§ 1349 and 1956(h). US District Court, Southern District of New York.

USDoJ. 2018. *Hate Crime Laws.* US Department of Justice. Washington DC. https://www.justice.gov/. [accessed January 23, 2018].

Walker, P. 2020. "Labour MP Dawn Butler Stopped by Police in London". *The Guardian.* August 9, 2020. https://www.theguardian. com/uk-news/2020/aug/09/labour-mp-dawn-butler-stopped-by-police-in-london. [accessed September 16, 2020].

Walsh, A. 2018. "German State Probes Frankfurt Police Extremist Network: Report". *DW Deutsche Welle.* December 17, 2018. https:// www.dw.com/en/german-state-probes-frankfurt-police-extre mist-network-report/a-46765959. [accessed September 7, 2020].

Walters, M., Wiedlitzka, S., Owusu-Bempah, A. et al. 2017. *Hate Crime and the Legal Process: Options for Law Reform.* October 2017. Brighton UK: University of Sussex.

Waring, A. 2013. *Corporate Risk and Governance: an End to Mismanagement, Tunnel Vision and Quackery.* Farnham, UK: Gower/Taylor & Francis.

Waring, A. 2019. "The Five Pillars of Occupational Safety and Health in a Climate of Authoritarian Socio-political Climates", Special Issue: The Future of Safety Science. *Safety Science*, 117, 152-163.

Waring, A. 2020. "Impacts of Islamophobia on Some Muslims in Two European Countries". *CARR Insight Blog.* May 21, 2020. https://

www.radicalrightanalysis.com/2020/05/21/impacts-of-islam ophobia-on-some-muslims-in-two-western-countries/.

Waring, A. and Glendon, A.I. 1998. *Managing Risk: Critical Issues for Survival and Success into the 21st Century.* Aldershot, UK: Thomson/Cengage.

Waring, A. and Paxton, R. 2018. "Potential Strategies to Limit the Alt-Right Threat". In *The New Authoritarianism Vol 1: A Risk Analysis of the US Alt-Right Phenomenon,* edited by A. Waring, 425-459. Stuttgart: Ibidem Verlag.

Waring, A. and Paxton, R. 2019. "Potential Strategies to Limit the Alt-Right Threat". In *The New Authoritarianism Vol 2: A Risk Analysis of the European Alt-Right Phenomenon,* edited by A. Waring, 375-411. Stuttgart: Ibidem Verlag.

WFA. 2020a. "Nearly a Third of Advertisers Pull Back or Consider Pulling Back from Platforms". News. July 1, 2020. World Federation of Advertisers. London: WFA. https://wfanet.org/knowledge/item/2020/07/01/Nearly-a-third-of-advertisers-pull-back-or-consider-pulling-back-from-platforms. [accessed July 29, 2020].

WFA. 2020b. "WFA and Platforms Make Major Progress to Address Harmful Content". Press release. September 23, 2020. World Federation of Avertisers. London: WFA. https://wfanet.org/knowledge/item/2020/09/23/WFA-and-platforms-make-major-progress-to-address-harmful-content. [accessed September 28, 2020].

Wilkinson, R. and Pickett, K. 2010. *The Spirit Level: Why Equality is Better for Everyone,* edited by P.H. Merkl and L. Weinberg. London: Penguin.

Wodak, R. 2018. "The Radical Right and Anti-Semitism". In *The Oxford Handbook of the Radical Right,* edited by Jens Rydgren. DOI: 10.1093/oxfordhb/9780190274559.013.4.

Wright, O. 2019. "Social Media Chief Called Far-right Activist a Hero". *The Times.* July 26, 2019. Page 8.

Wylie, C. 2020. "Met Police Officer Charged with Being Member of Far-right Terrorist Group". *The Mirror.* July 9, 2020. https://www.mirror.co.uk/news/uk-news/met-police-officer-charged-being-22331878. [accessed September 7, 2020].

Zeffman, H. 2021. "Smashing Glass and Gunfire as Mob Shames US Democracy". *The Times.* January 7, 2021. Pages 2-3.

About the Editor and Authors

Editor and Primary Author:

Dr Alan Waring: Risk analyst and author, UK. International risk management consultant to government departments, institutions and large corporations 1986-2016. Books include *The New Authoritarianism* Vol 1 (2018) and Vol 2 (2019), *Corporate Risk and Governance* (2013), Gower/Routledge, and *Managing Risk: Critical Issues for Survival and Success into the 21ˢᵗ Century* (1998), Thomson/Cengage, co-authored with Ian Glendon. Articles in peer-reviewed journals, the business and popular press, blog articles, as well as radio and TV interviews. Policy & Practitioner Fellow, CARR (Centre for Analysis of the Radical Right), Visiting and Adjunct Professor roles at CERIDES (Centre for Risk and Decision Sciences), European University Cyprus, since 2014. Adjunct Professor at Hong Kong Baptist University and International Risk Consultant, Tsinghua University, Beijing (2006-2008). Special interest in countering authoritarianism and risks associated with the populist- and far right.

Contributing Authors:

Professor Denis Fischbacher-Smith: Research Chair in Risk and Resilience and Visiting Professor in Risk Management within the Adam Smith Business School, University of Glasgow. Holds a PhD, DLitt and six Masters degrees. For over 25 years, adviser and consultant to UK and foreign governments, local and national authorities, and large corporations, on risk and crisis management, including emergency and contingency planning in urban and corporate contexts. Beforehand, from 2002-2006 he was Professor of Management at the University of Liverpool, including founding director of the University of Liverpool Management School. Previous professorships at Sheffield, Durham and John Moores Universities. Also visiting professor at several British universities as well as Kobe (Japan), San Diego State (USA) and Innsbruck (Austria).

Dr A. Ian Glendon: Adjunct role at the School of Applied Psychology, Griffith University Gold Coast Campus, Queensland, and contributor of the Foreword. From 1996 to 2020, he was Associate Professor at the Griffith's School of Applied Psychology, and was involved in a number of major projects including government Inquiries. After gaining his PhD at the LSE, London, he was a Lecturer in the Applied Psychology Department within Aston University's Business School, where he undertook major research projects for the UK's Department of Employment among others, including field studies relating to the King's Cross Fire major accident Inquiry 1988. For nine years, he was a founder director of Health and Safety Technology and Management Ltd. His books include three editions of *Human Safety and Risk Management*, the latest in 2016 co-authored with Professor Sharon Clarke sub-titled *A Psychological Perspective*. He also co-authored with Dr Alan Waring in 1998 *Managing Risk: Critical Issues for Survival and Success into the 21st Century*, which examined corporate malfeasance and related risk exposures.

Professor George Michael: PhD from George Mason University's School of Public Policy, USA. Currently Professor of Criminal Justice at Westfield State University, Massachusetts, lecturing on terrorism, homeland security, and organized crime. Previously, an Associate Professor of Nuclear Counter-Proliferation and Deterrence Theory at the Air War College in Montgomery, Alabama. In addition, to numerous articles published in academic journals, his books include: *Confronting Right-Wing Extremism and Terrorism in the USA* (Routledge, 2003), *The Enemy of my Enemy: The Alarming Convergence of Militant Islam and the Extreme Right* (University Press of Kansas, 2006), *Willis Carto and the American Far Right* (University Press of Florida, 2006-2008), *Theology of Hate: A History of the World Church of the Creator* (University Press of Florida, 2009), *Lone Wolf Terror and the Rise of Leaderless Resistance* (Vanderbilt University Press, 2012), and *Extremism in America* (editor) (University Press of Florida, 2014).

Professor Clive Smallman: Vice President (Academic), International Institute for MBA Studies and Dean, Higher Education Leadership Institute. Expertise in leadership and team development, specialising in risk and crisis leadership and innovative business modelling. From 2010 to 2016, Professor of Management and Dean of the Business School, University of Western Sydney (Aus), including a period as Assistant Vice-Chancellor. Originally gaining an MBA and PhD at the University of Bradford (UK), he became a Senior Research Associate at the Cambridge University Judge Management School, before becoming Professor of Management at Lincoln University (UK) (2003-2010). Clive trained with the Harvard Program on Negotiation and is a Chartered Fellow of the British Computer Society. He has been consulted by numerous institutions and bodies as well as global corporations.

Dr Vasiliki Tsagkroni: As Assistant Professor in Comparative Politics, Institute of Political Science, Leiden University, Dr Tsagkroni specialises in research into the radical right, especially ideology, political parties, populism, extreme-right movements, counter-narratives, and communication strategies. This work includes best EU practices to counter populism, a cross-European policy analysis on climate change at party level, and a cross-European comparative analysis of political discourse between governments, political parties and citizens. Holding a PhD from Queen Mary University London (2015), Dr Tsagkroni is a Senior Fellow at CARR (Centre for Analysis of the Radical Right). Widely published e.g. chapters in edited books and articles in *Journal of Common Market Studies, Party Politics,* and *British Journal of Politics and International Relations;* Editorial Board member of *Studies in Ethnicity and Nationalism* (SEN) and of *Media and Communication.* Co-convenor of the Greek Politics Specialist Group (GPSG) of the Political Studies Association (PSA).

Emeritus Professor Antony A. Vass PhD: Former Head of School and Senior Academic/Manager of the Faculty of Criminology & Sociology at Middlesex University, London, where he led research, teaching, undergraduate and post-graduate courses and course development in the social sciences, humanities and health sciences. Syllabuses included psychology of health, sociology, law, criminology, social work, probation, nursing, herbal medicine and life sciences. Educated at the London School of Economics and Political Science (LSE) and Middlesex University, he holds a number of postgraduate degrees and professional qualifications. His tutors and mentors included such eminent scholars as A.N. (Bram) Oppenheim, Michael Zander, Terence Morris, Robert (Bob) T. McKenzie, Michael Burrage, Robert (Bob) Pinker, Keith Thurley, David Downes, Paul Rock, Earl Hopper, Jock Young, and Ken Plummer. Professor Vass has authored and co-authored books and articles on criminology, prisons and alternatives to prison, mental health, HIV/AIDS, social problems and social policy, social work and probation, interpersonal relations and social interaction, dementia and Alzheimer's, ethical considerations in research, drugs and the formal economy, as well as politics and governance. Throughout, his core guiding principle has been the promotion of social justice and a humanistic approach to personal and societal issues.

Index